Cross Game

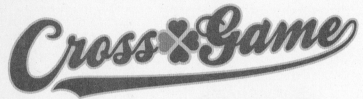

Volume 8

Mitsuru Adachi

Contents Volume 8

Cross Game

16

Story & Art by
Mitsuru Adachi

Story Wrap-Up

Story Wrap-Up
Ko Kitamura, the only son of the family that runs the neighborhood sporting goods store, is in his final year of high school at Seishu Gakuen and happens to be the ace pitcher of the baseball team. He's childhood friends with the four Tsukishima daughters that run the batting center and café in the neighborhood. In the summer of fifth grade, the second daughter, Wakaba, who was born on the same day as Ko, tragically drowned. On the eve of her death, Wakaba dreamt of Seeing Ko pitch in front of a packed crowd at Koshien. This is the last summer that Ko has to fulfill that dream, and thanks to his amazing performance in their first game of the North Tokyo tournament, Seishu advances to the next round. But amidst all the excitement, Akane Takigawa, who happens to be the spitting image of Wakaba, falls ill and is scheduled to have surgery on the day of the regional finals. Now is the time that these two battles are about to quietly begin...

CHAPTER 141
PROBABLY...

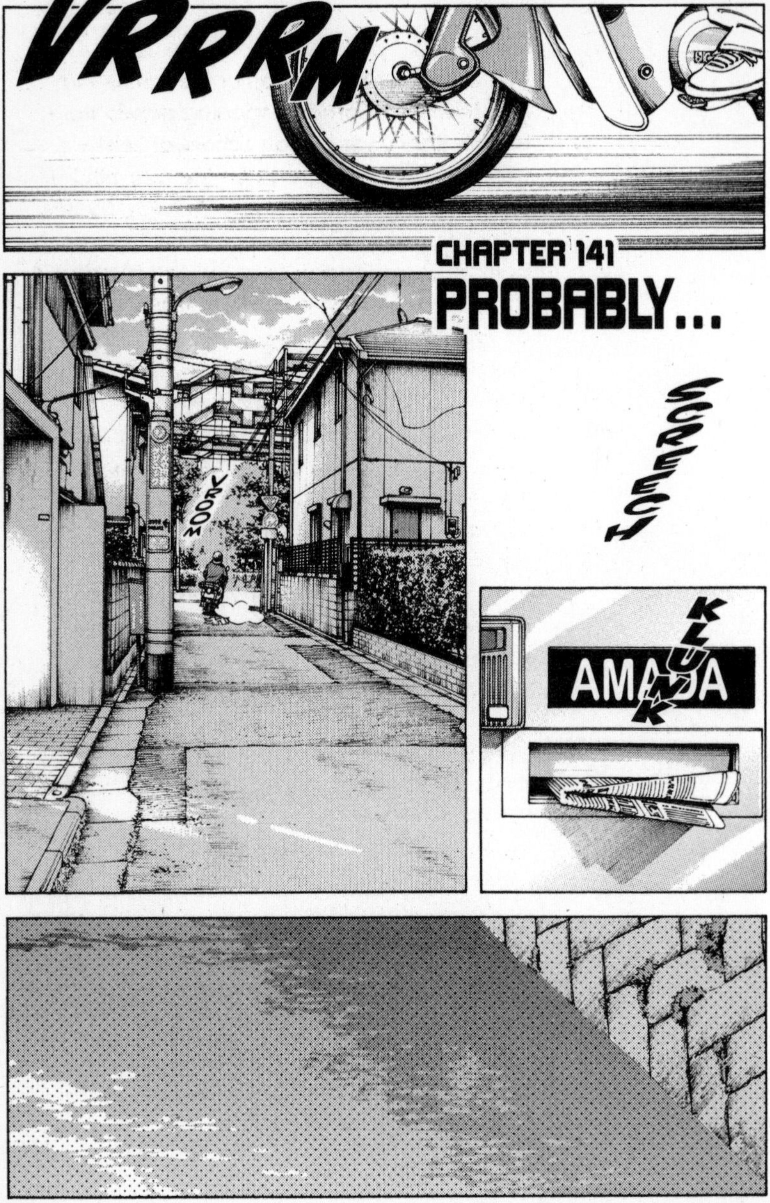
VRRRM
SCREECH
KLUNK
AMANDA
VROOM

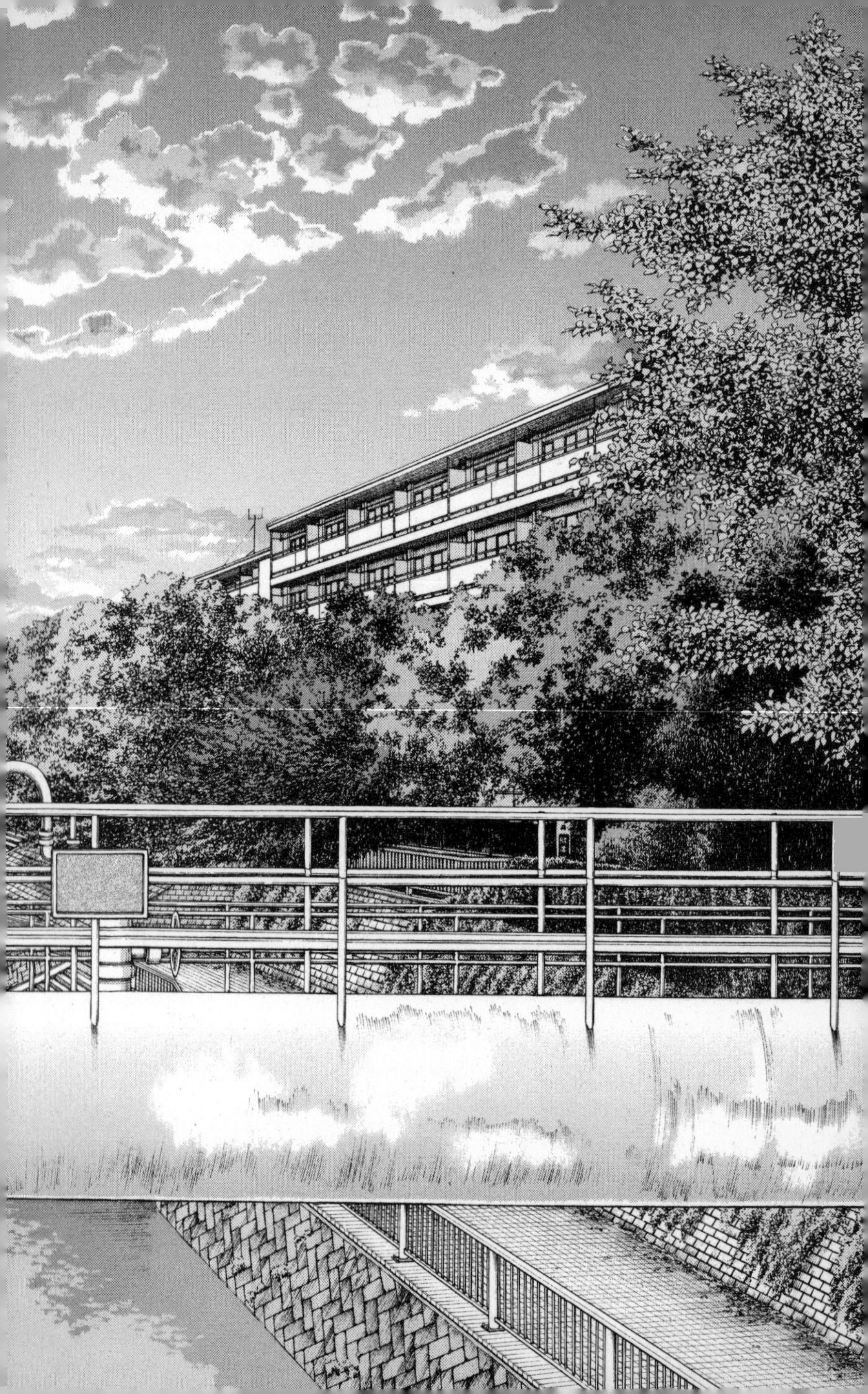

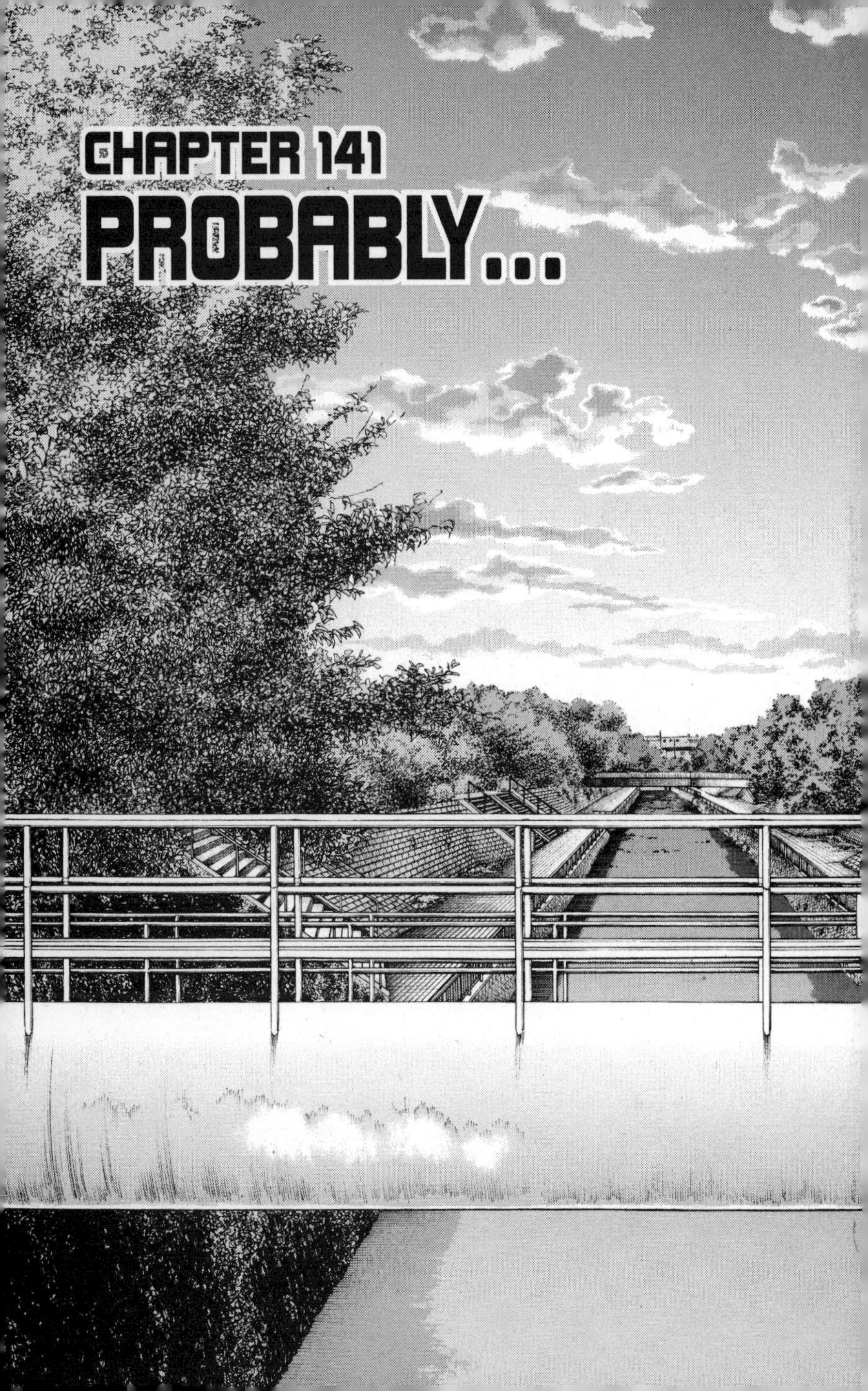
CHAPTER 141
PROBABLY...

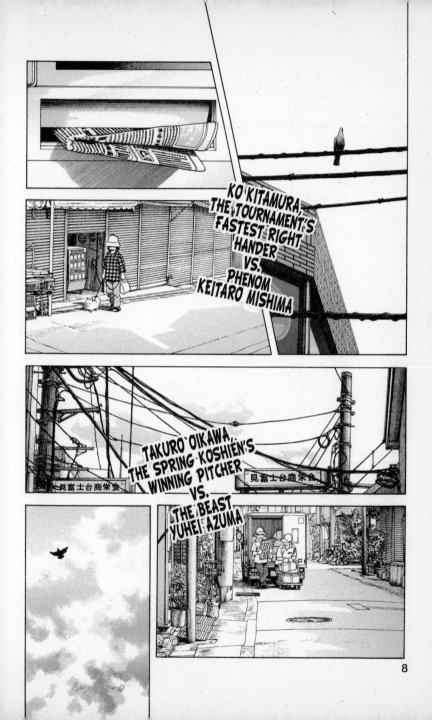

KO KITAMURA, THE TOURNAMENT'S FASTEST RIGHT HANDER VS. PHENOM KEITARO MISHIMA

TAKURO OIKAWA, THE SPRING KOSHIEN'S WINNING PITCHER VS. THE BEAST YUHEI AZUMA

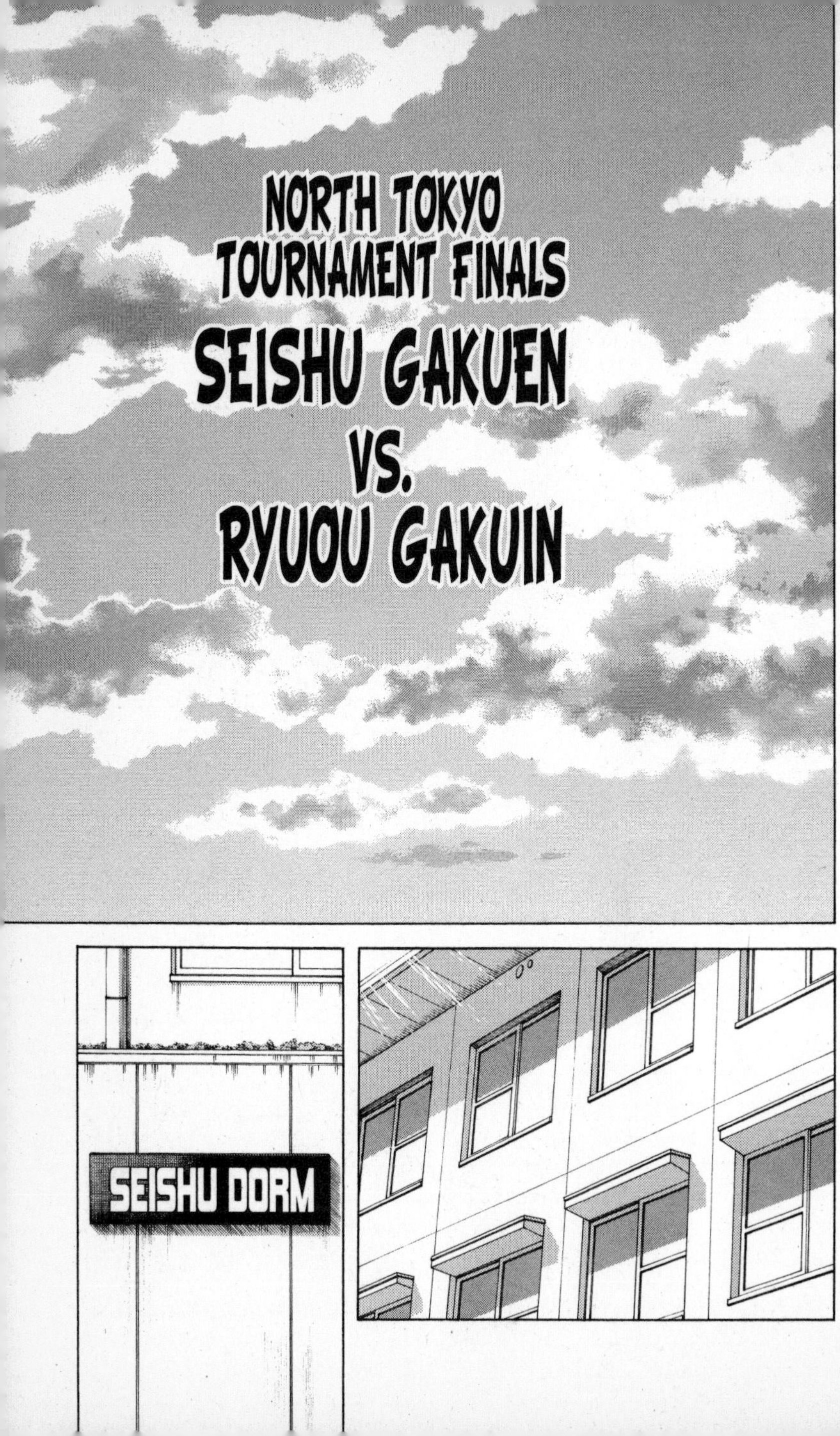
NORTH TOKYO
TOURNAMENT FINALS
SEISHU GAKUEN
VS.
RYUOU GAKUIN
SEISHU DORM

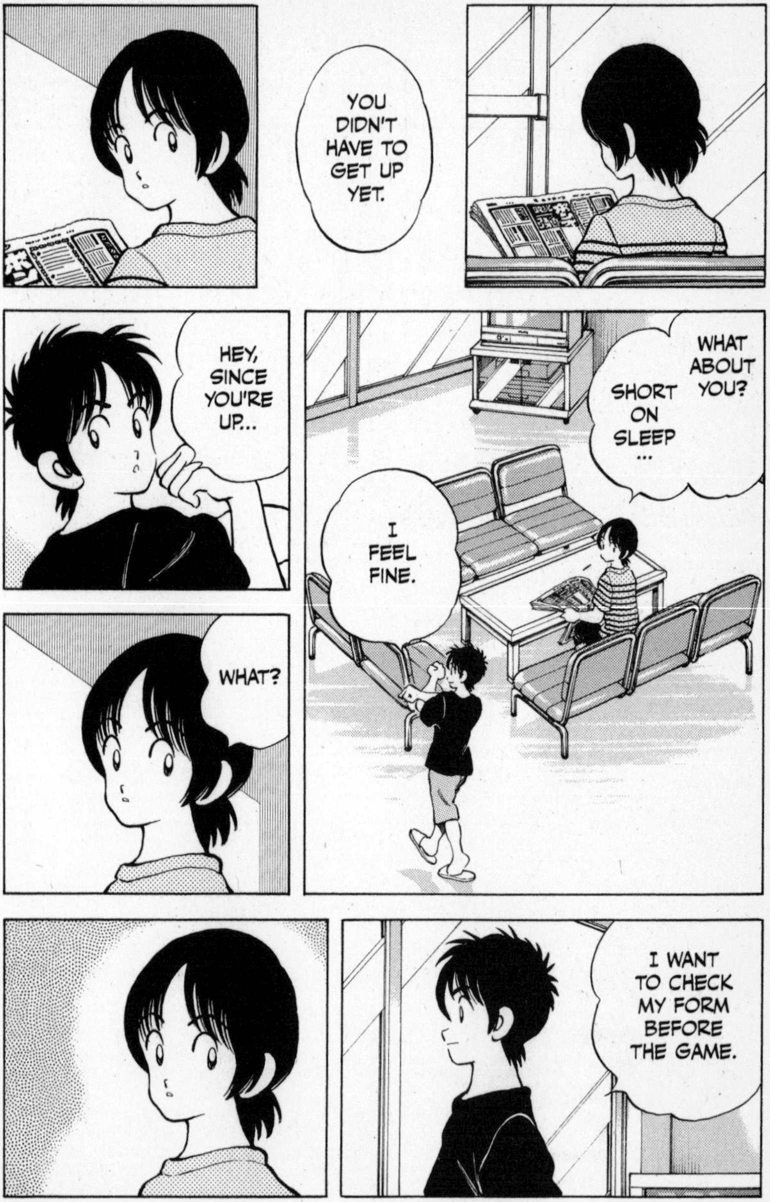
YOU DIDN'T HAVE TO GET UP YET.
SHORT ON SLEEP ... WHAT ABOUT YOU?
I FEEL FINE.
HEY, SINCE YOU'RE UP...
WHAT?
I WANT TO CHECK MY FORM BEFORE THE GAME.

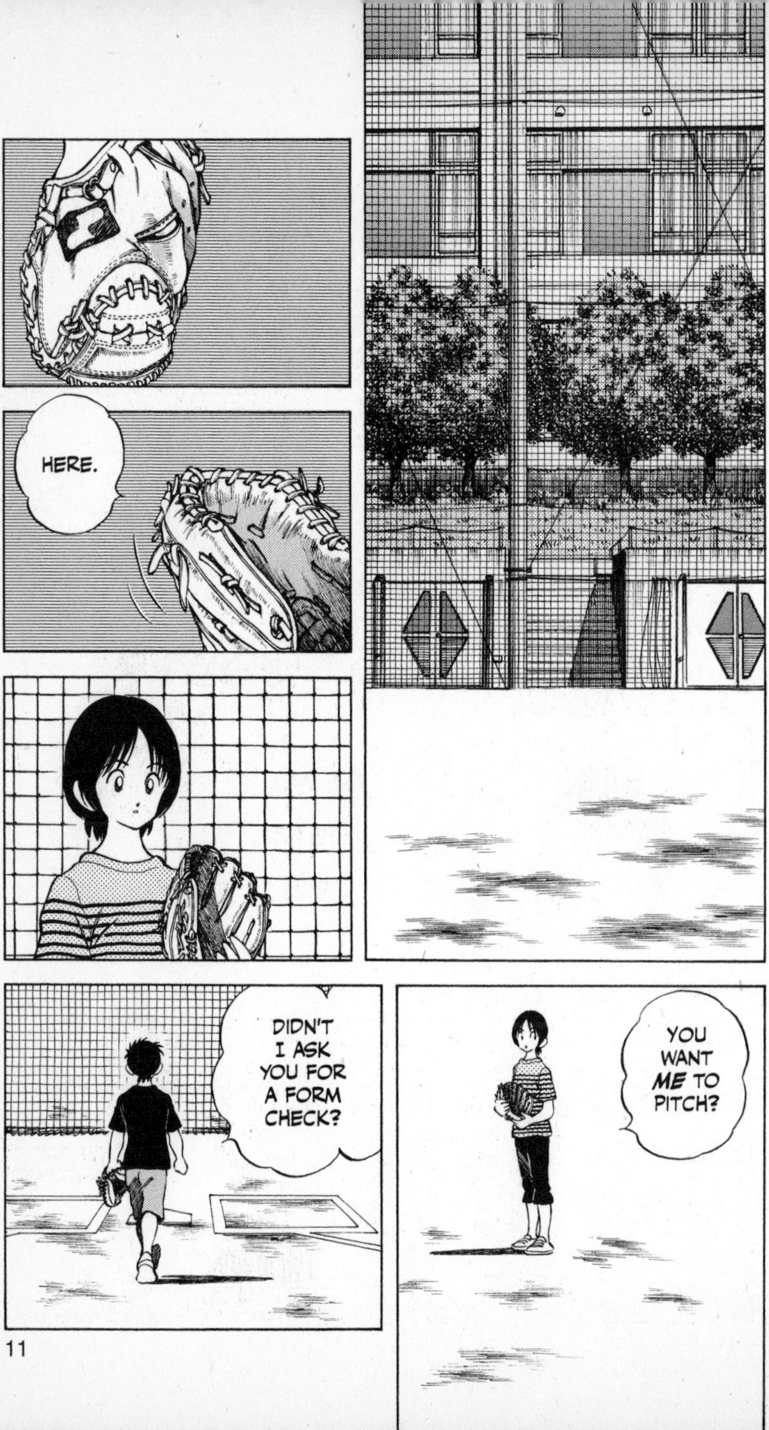
HERE.
YOU WANT *ME* TO PITCH?
DIDN'T I ASK YOU FOR A FORM CHECK?

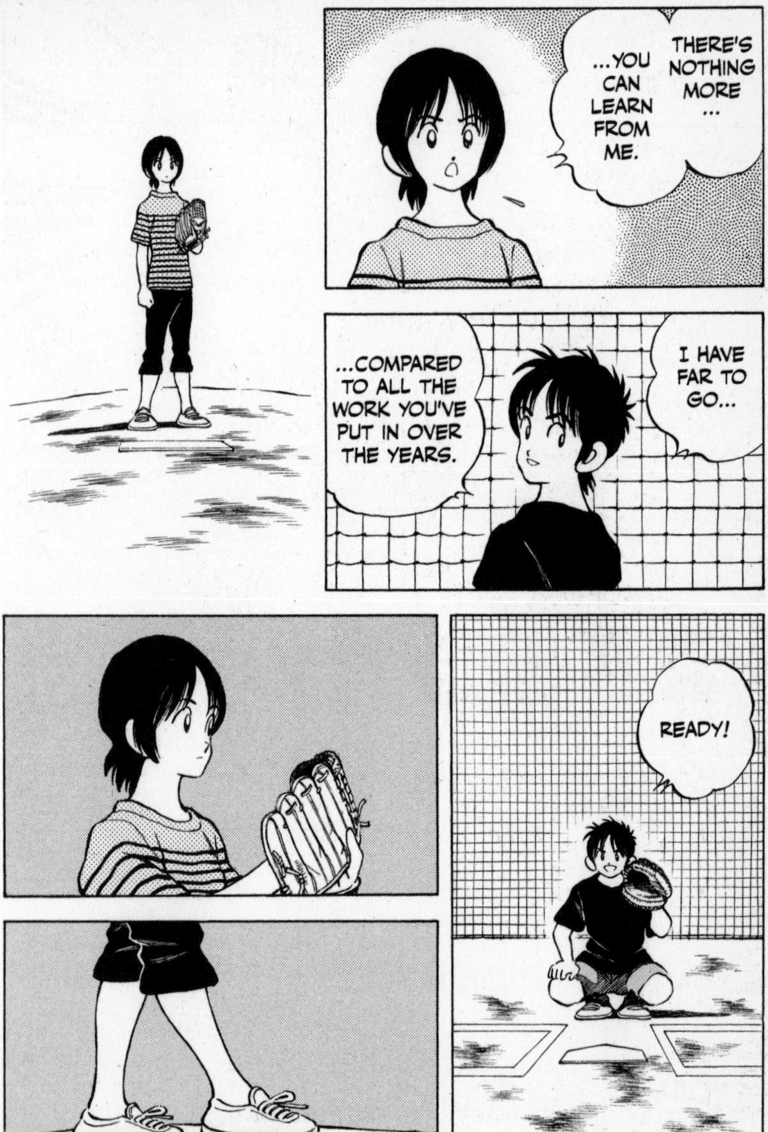
THERE'S NOTHING MORE ...
...YOU CAN LEARN FROM ME.
I HAVE FAR TO GO...
...COMPARED TO ALL THE WORK YOU'VE PUT IN OVER THE YEARS.
READY!

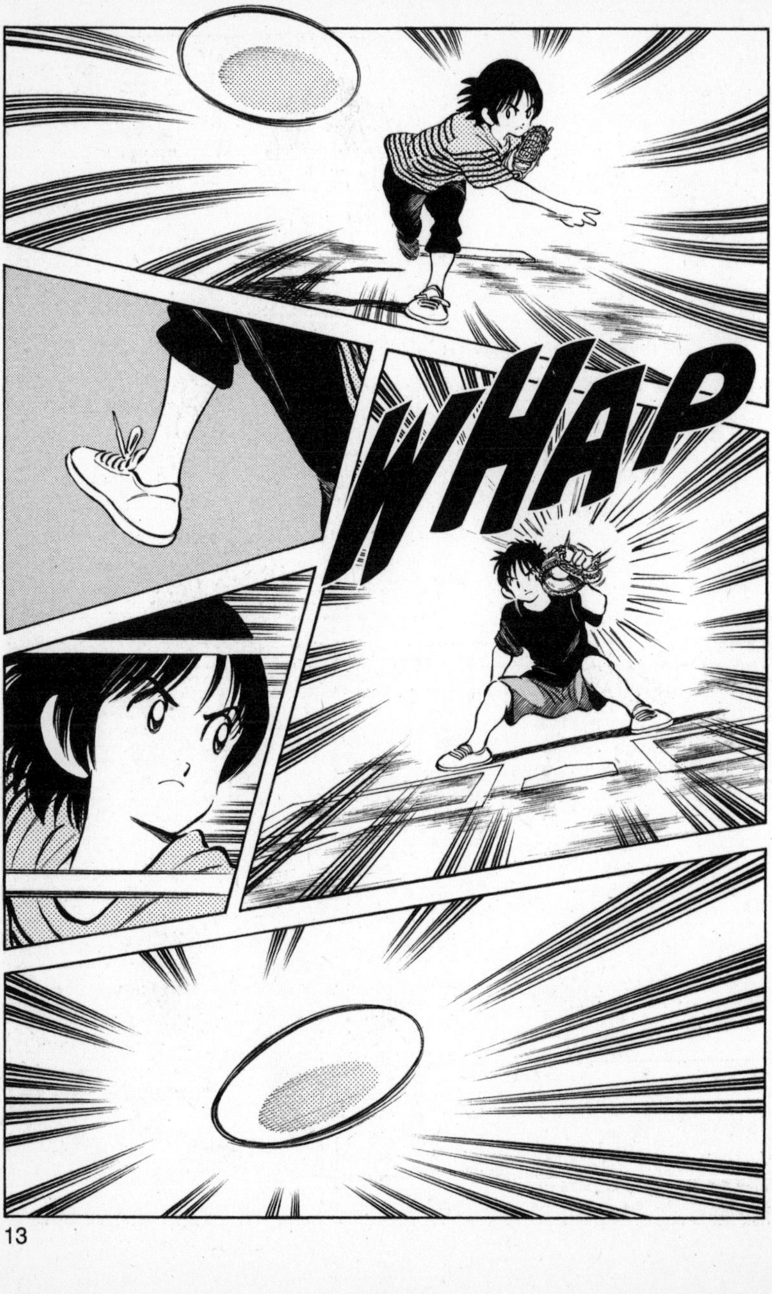
WHAP

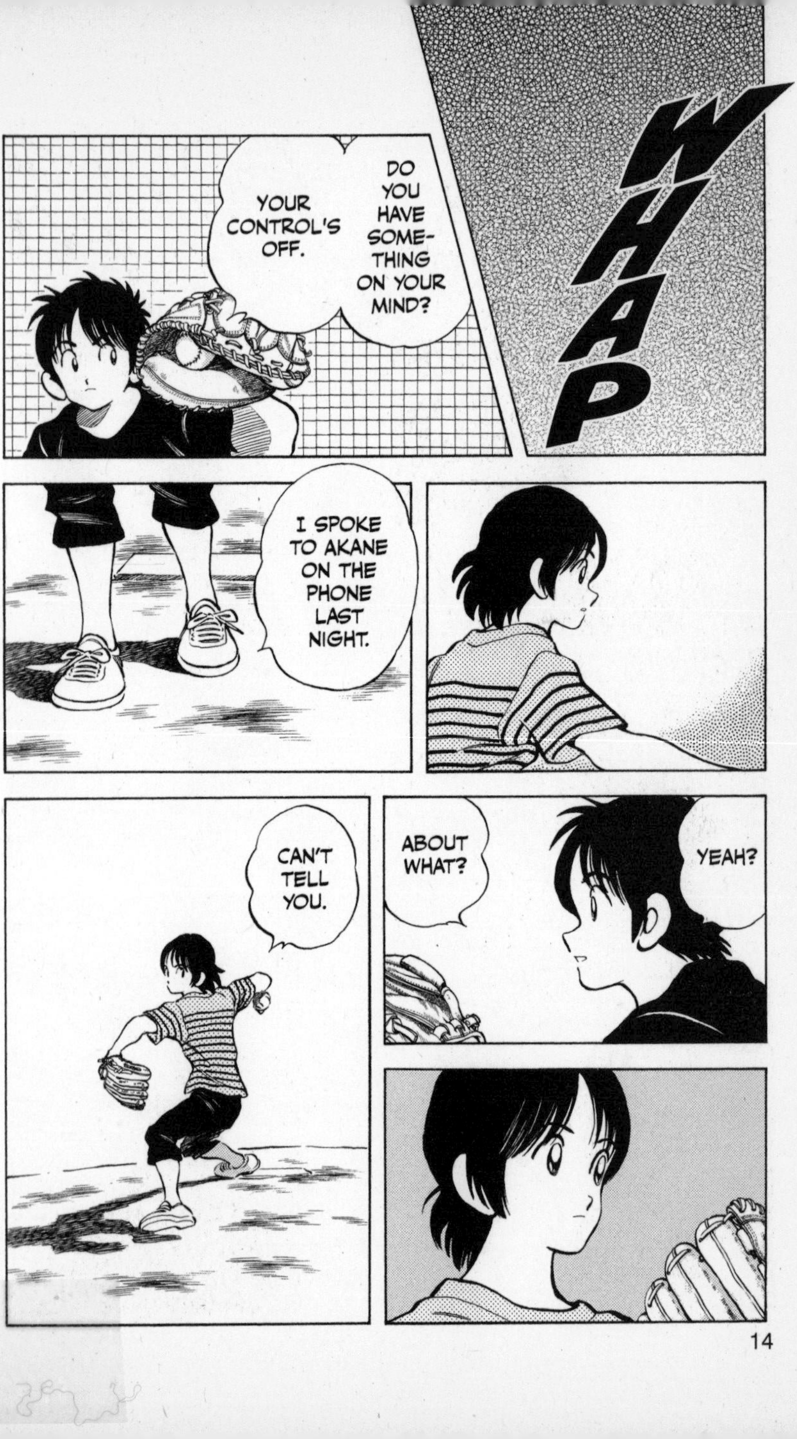
WHAP
YOUR CONTROL'S OFF.
DO YOU HAVE SOME-THING ON YOUR MIND?
I SPOKE TO AKANE ON THE PHONE LAST NIGHT.
YEAH?
ABOUT WHAT?
CAN'T TELL YOU.

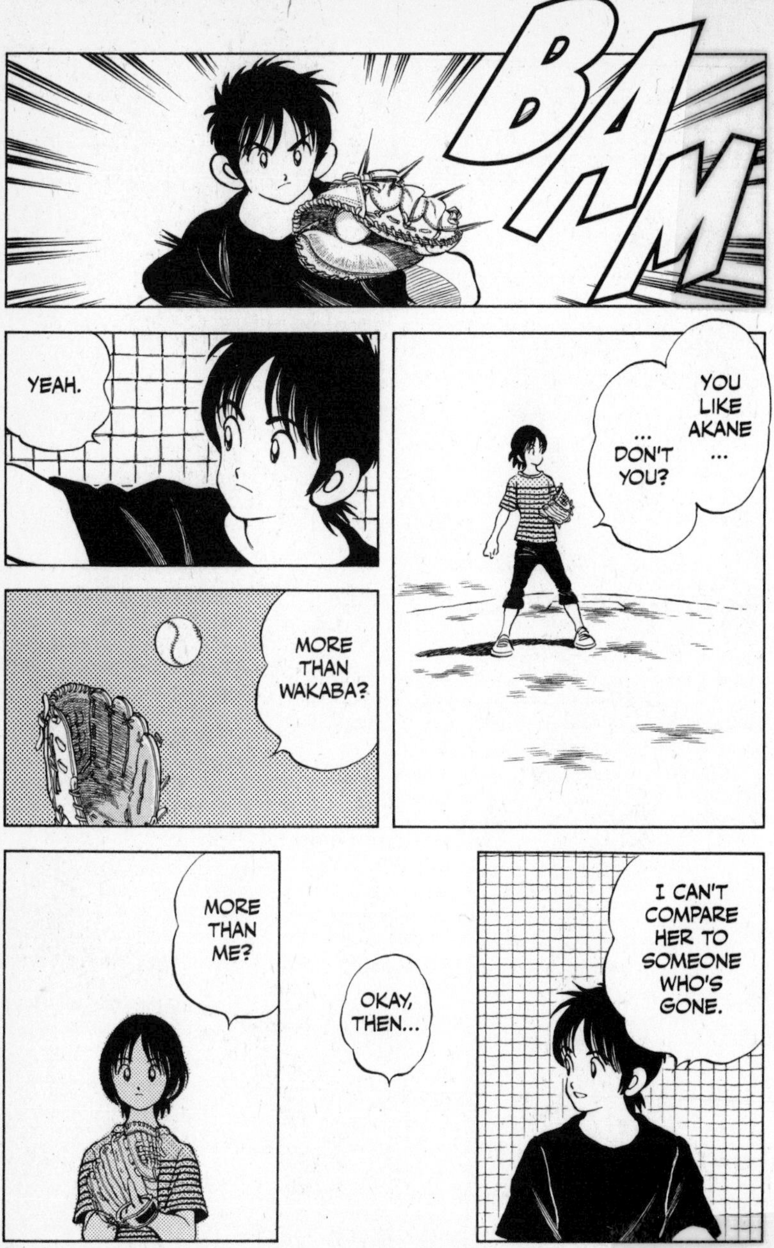
BAM
YOU LIKE AKANE ... ... DON'T YOU?
YEAH.
MORE THAN WAKABA?
I CAN'T COMPARE HER TO SOMEONE WHO'S GONE.
OKAY, THEN...
MORE THAN ME?

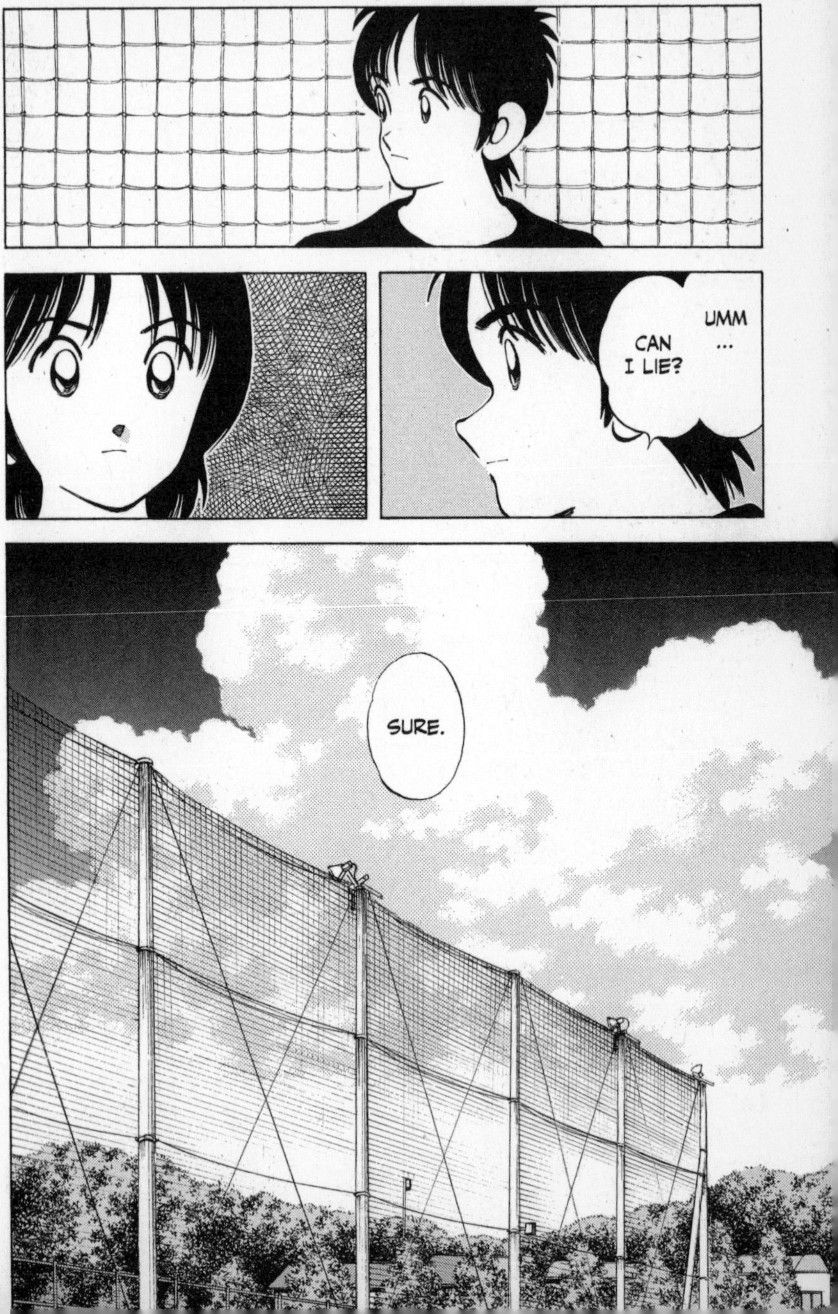
UMM ...
CAN I LIE?
SURE.

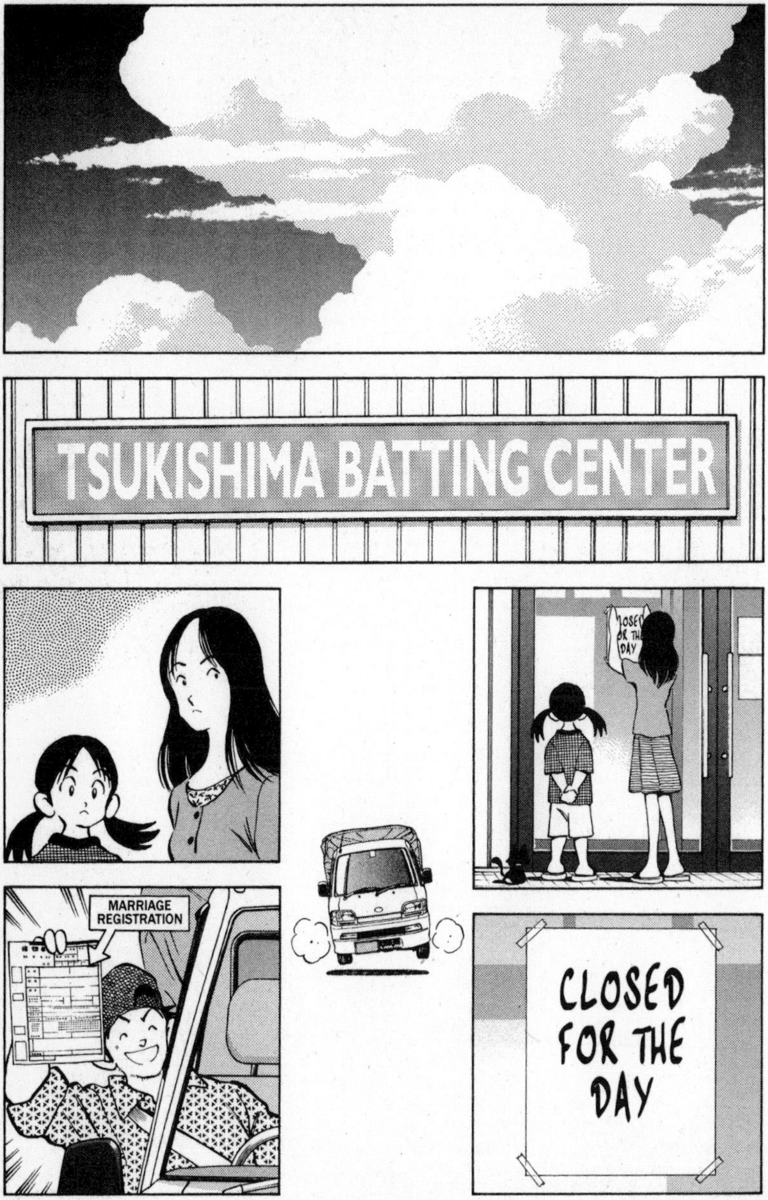
TSUKISHIMA BATTING CENTER
CLOSED FOR THE DAY
MARRIAGE REGISTRATION

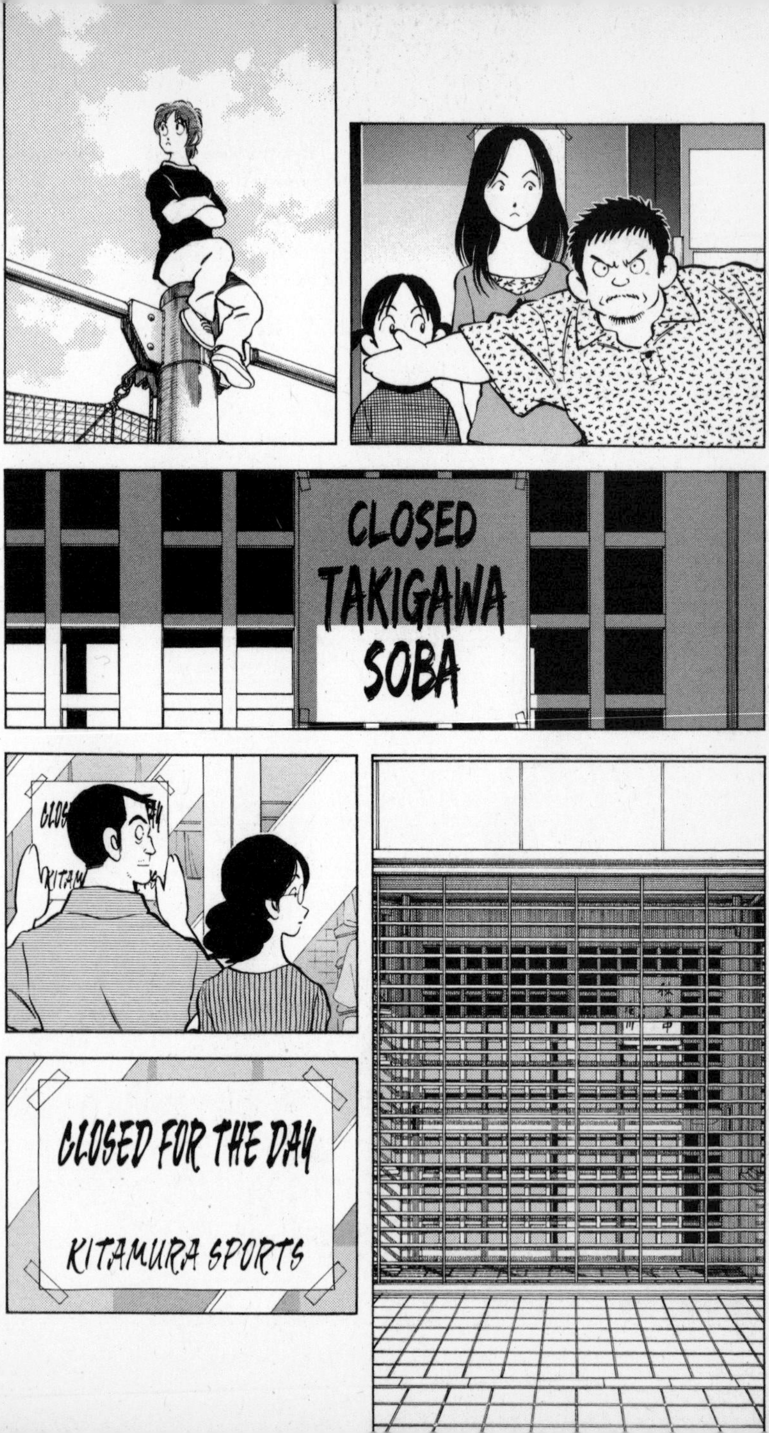
CLOSED
TAKIGAWA
SOBA
CLOSED FOR THE DAY
KITAMURA SPORTS

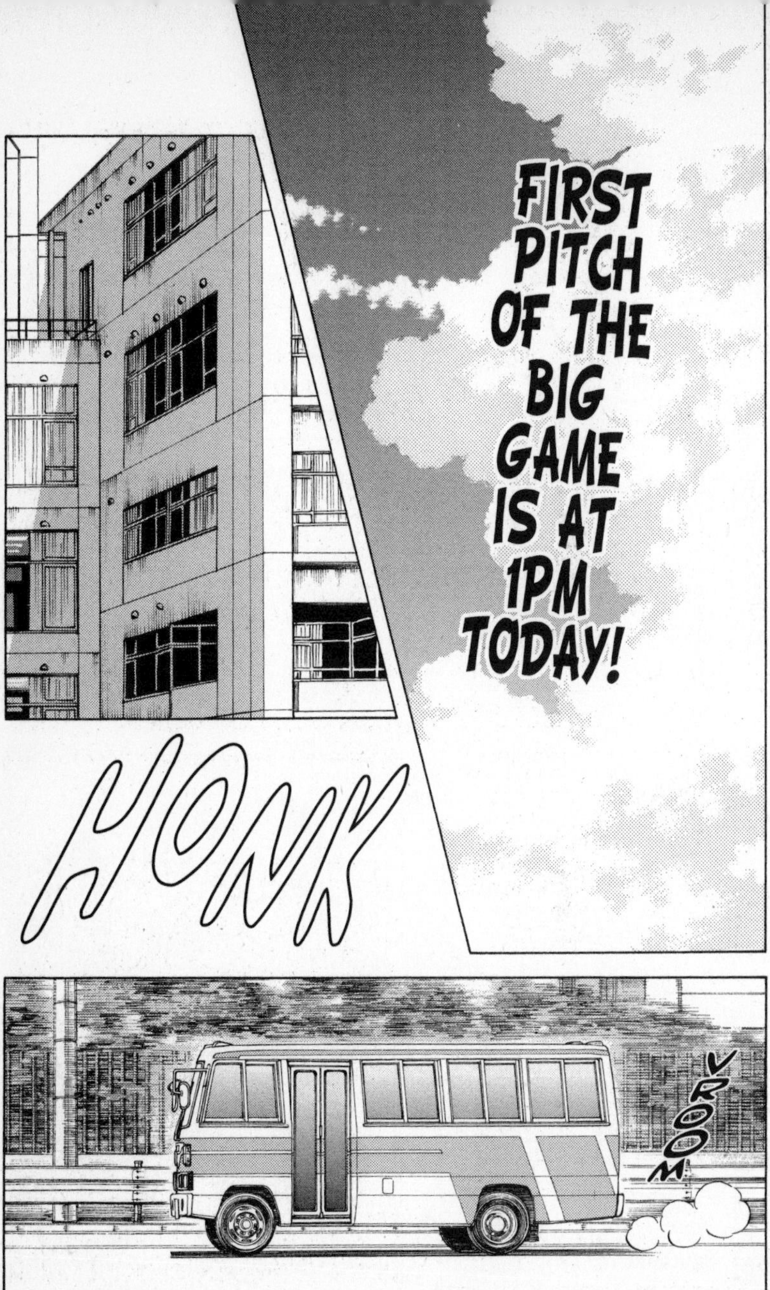
FIRST PITCH OF THE BIG GAME IS AT 1PM TODAY!
HONK
VROOM

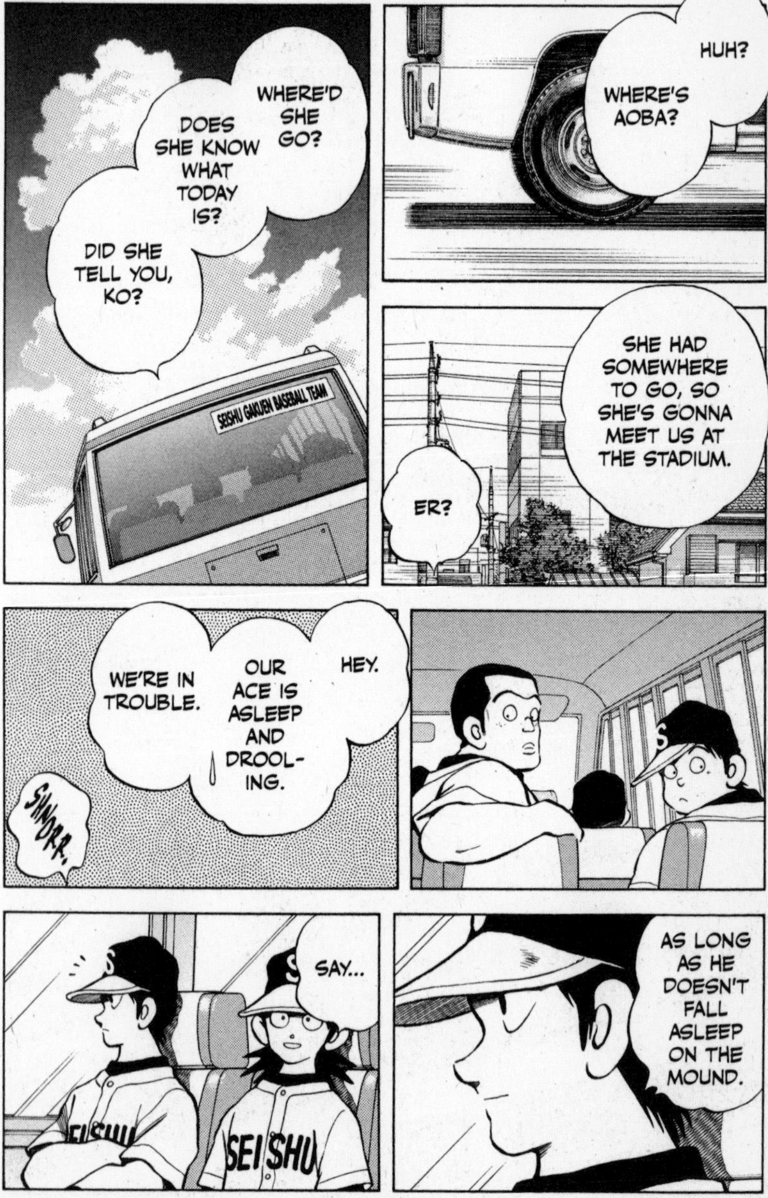
HUH?
WHERE'S AOBA?
SHE HAD SOMEWHERE TO GO, SO SHE'S GONNA MEET US AT THE STADIUM.
ER?
WHERE'D SHE GO?
DOES SHE KNOW WHAT TODAY IS?
DID SHE TELL YOU, KO?
SEISHU GAKUEN BASEBALL TEAM
HEY.
OUR ACE IS ASLEEP AND DROOL-ING.
WE'RE IN TROUBLE.
SHNORR.
AS LONG AS HE DOESN'T FALL ASLEEP ON THE MOUND.
SAY...
SEISHU
SEISHU

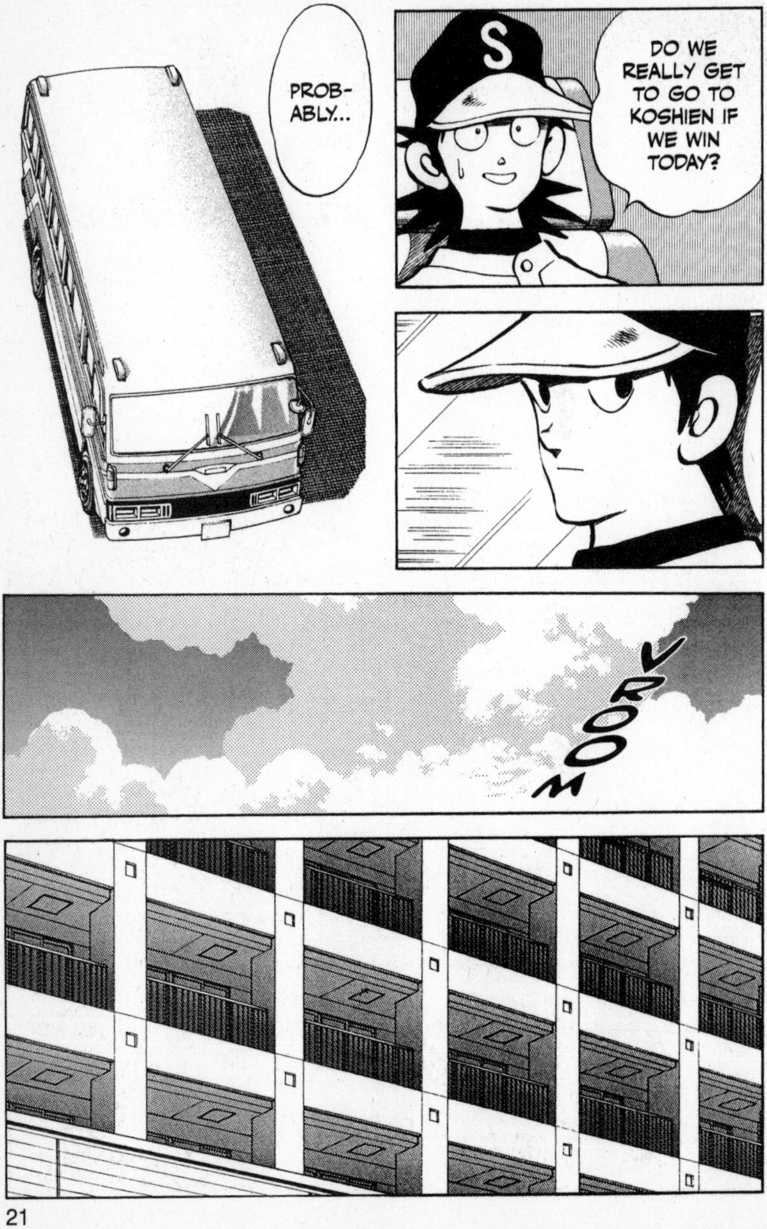
DO WE REALLY GET TO GO TO KOSHIEN IF WE WIN TODAY?
PROB-ABLY...
VROOM

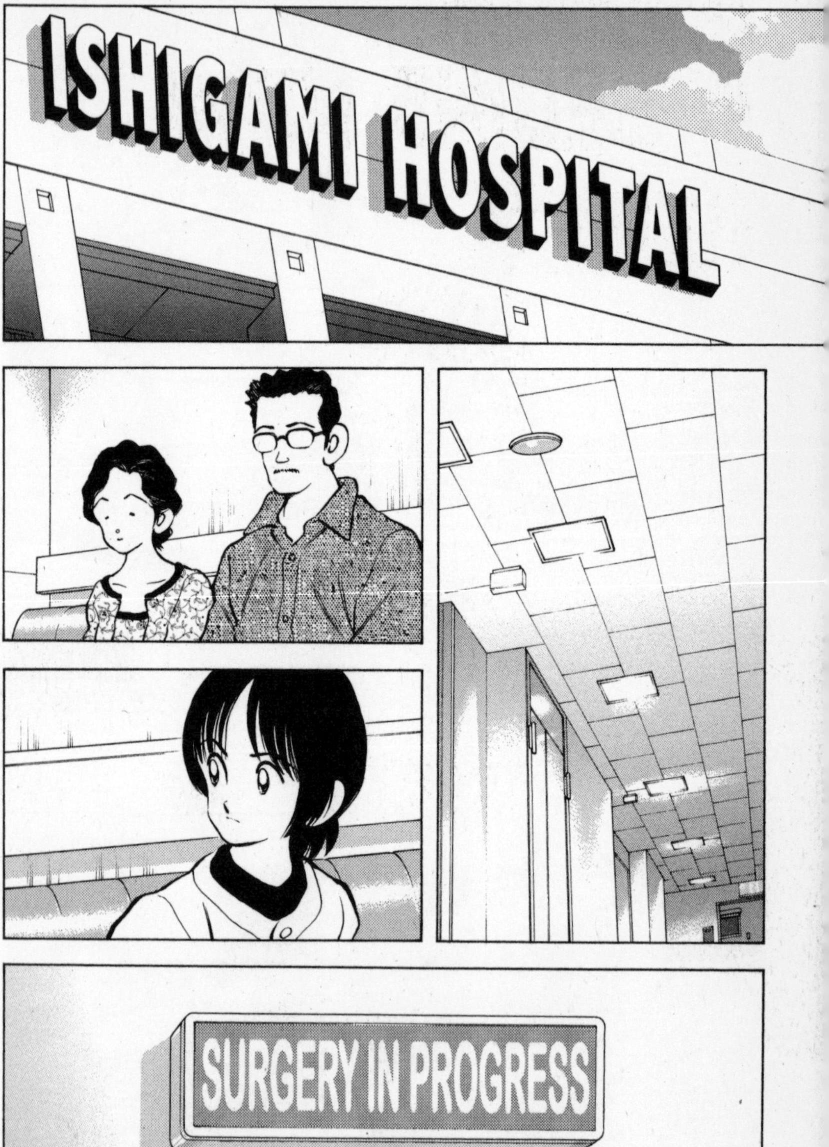
ISHIGAMI HOSPITAL
SURGERY IN PROGRESS

CHAPTER 142
IT BEGINS NOW, RIGHT?

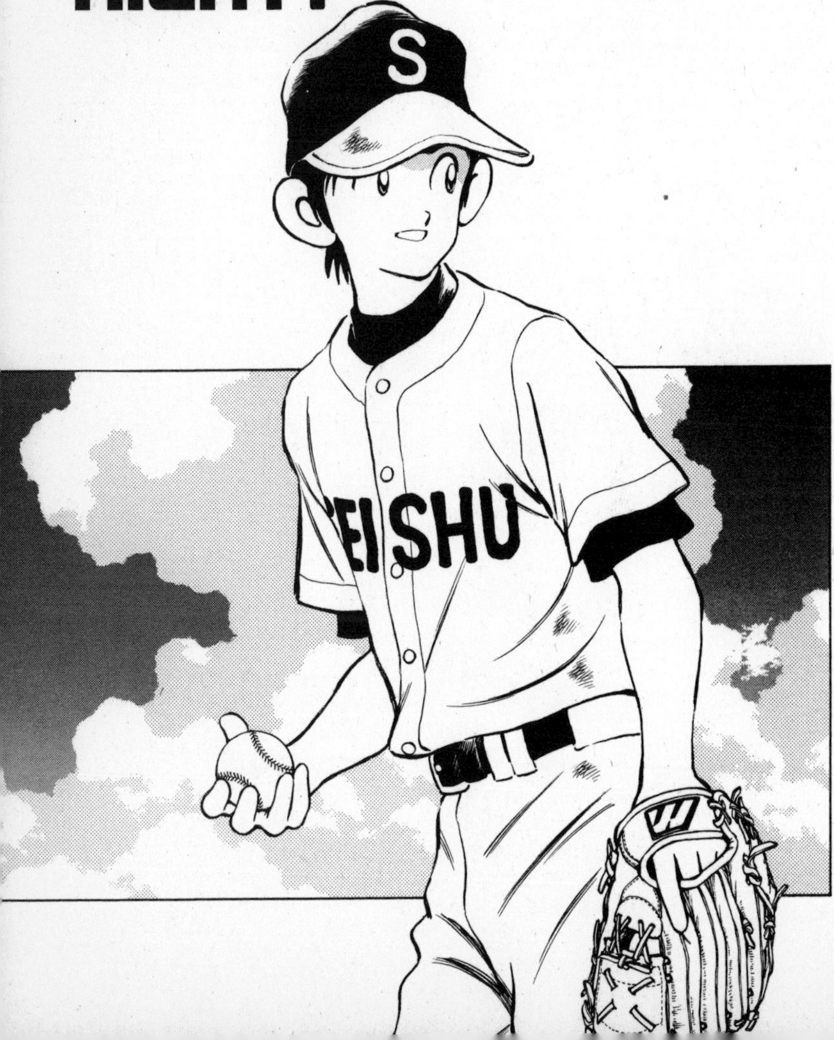

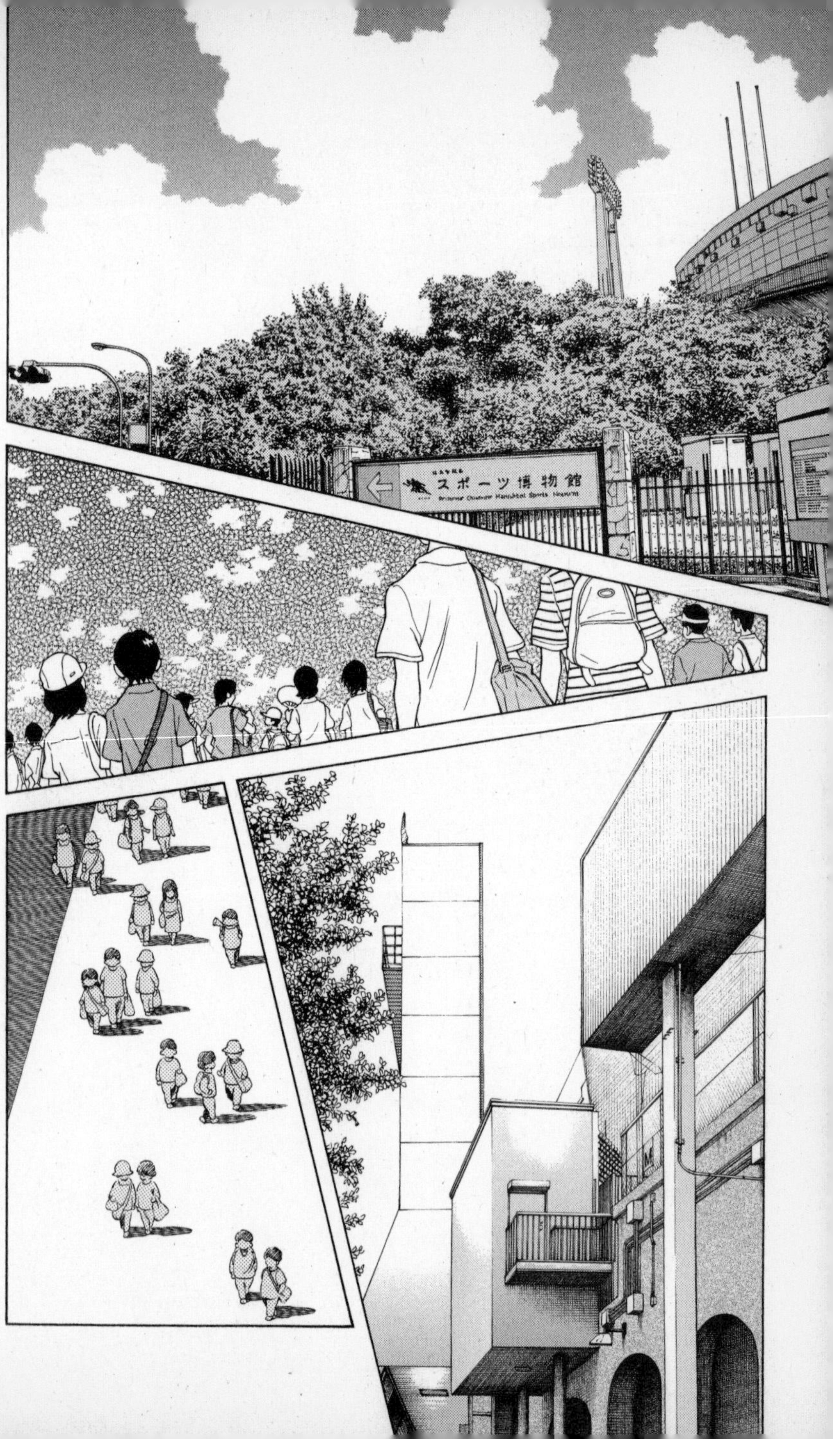
スポーツ博物館

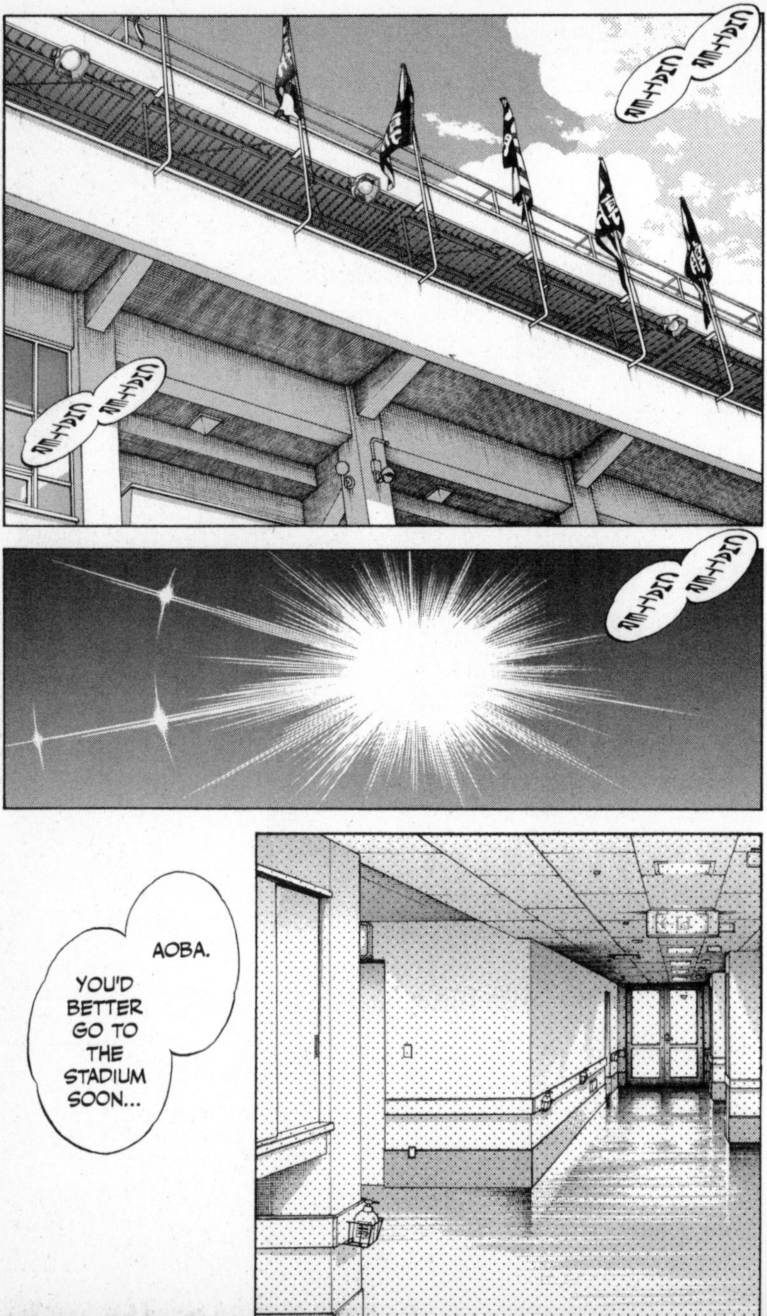
CHATTER CHATTER
CHATTER CHATTER
CHATTER CHATTER
AOBA. YOU'D BETTER GO TO THE STADIUM SOON...

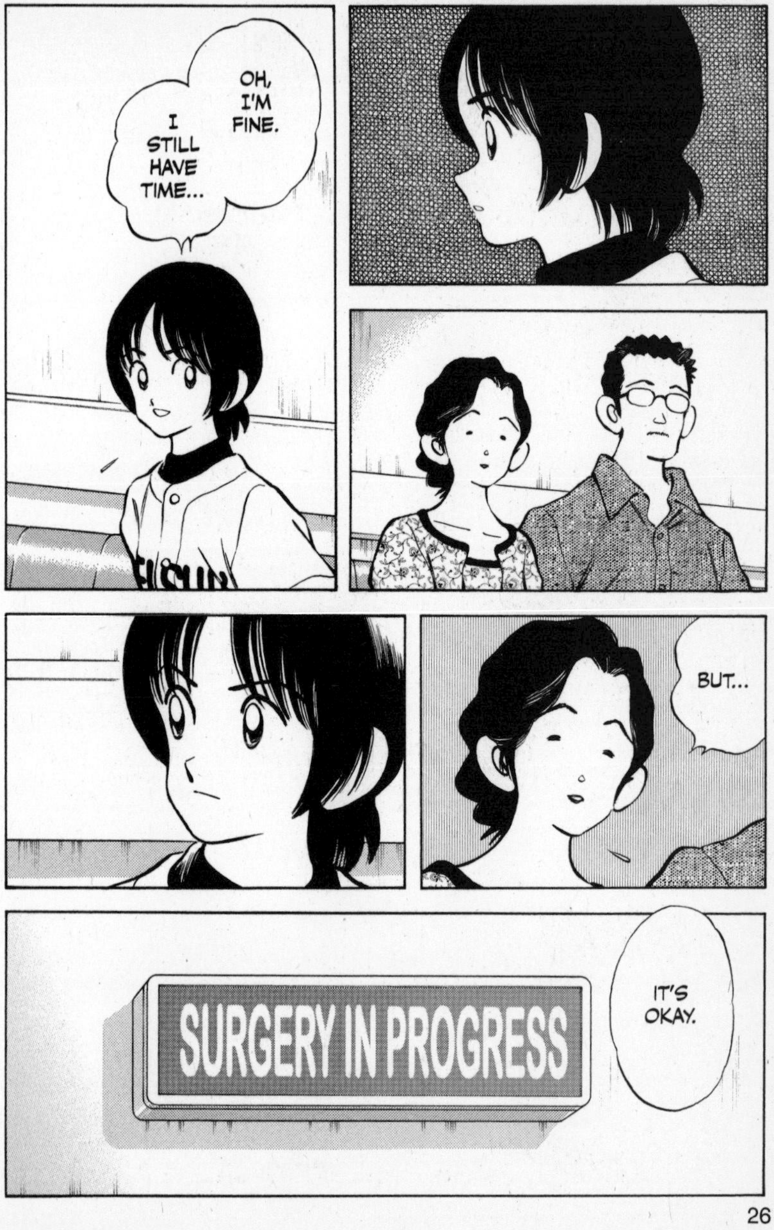
OH, I'M FINE. I STILL HAVE TIME...
BUT...
IT'S OKAY.
SURGERY IN PROGRESS

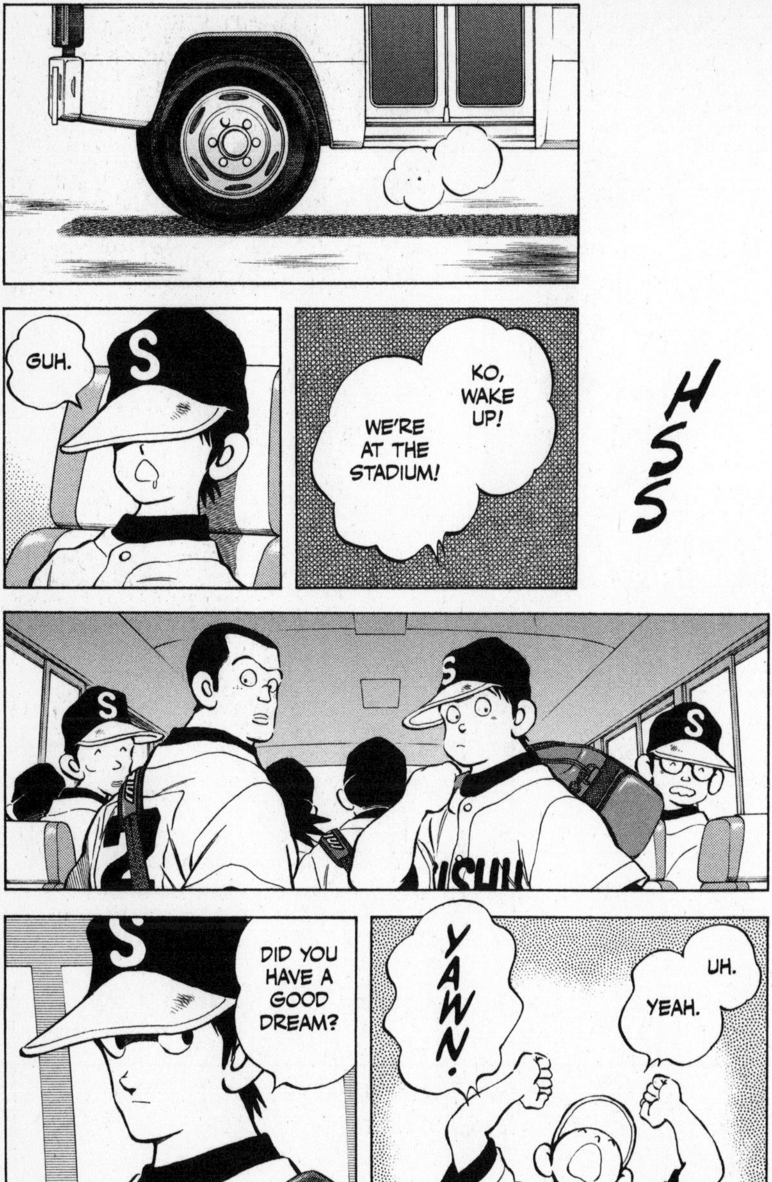
HSS
KO, WAKE UP!
WE'RE AT THE STADIUM!
GUH.
UH.
YEAH.
YAWN!
DID YOU HAVE A GOOD DREAM?

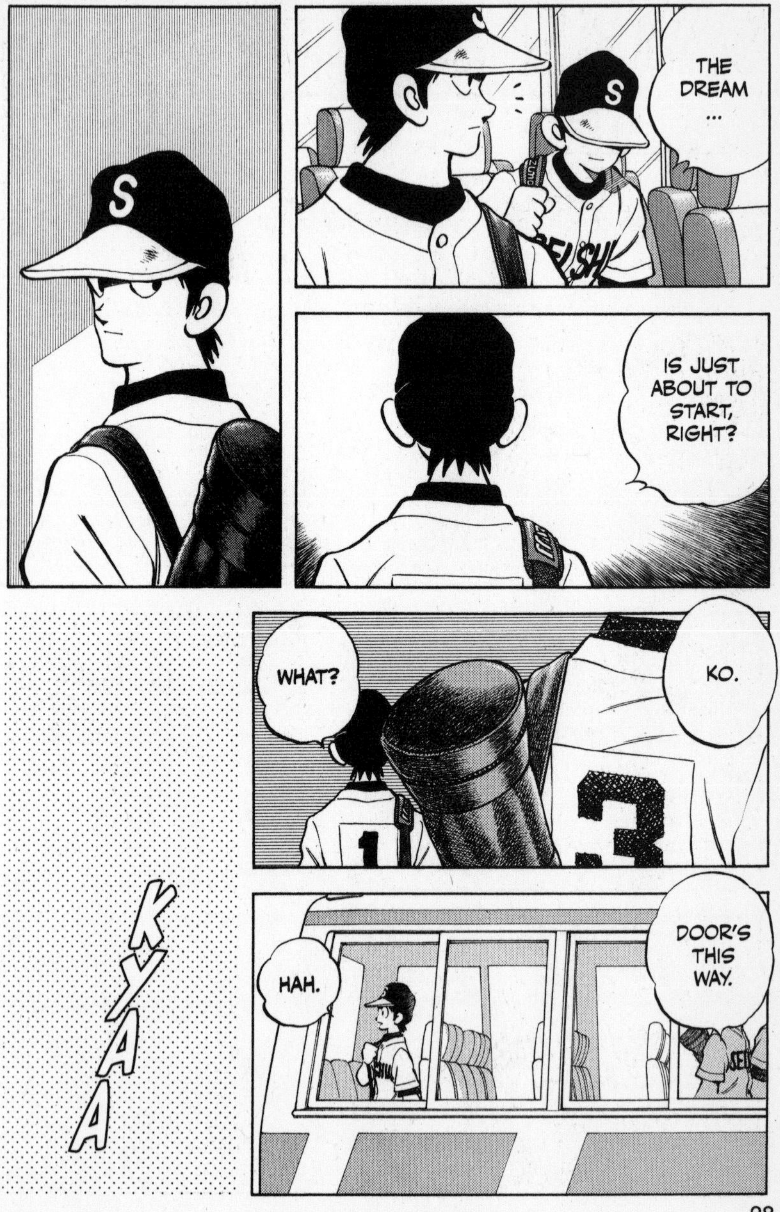
THE DREAM ...
IS JUST ABOUT TO START, RIGHT?
KO.
WHAT?
DOOR'S THIS WAY.
HAH.
KYAAA

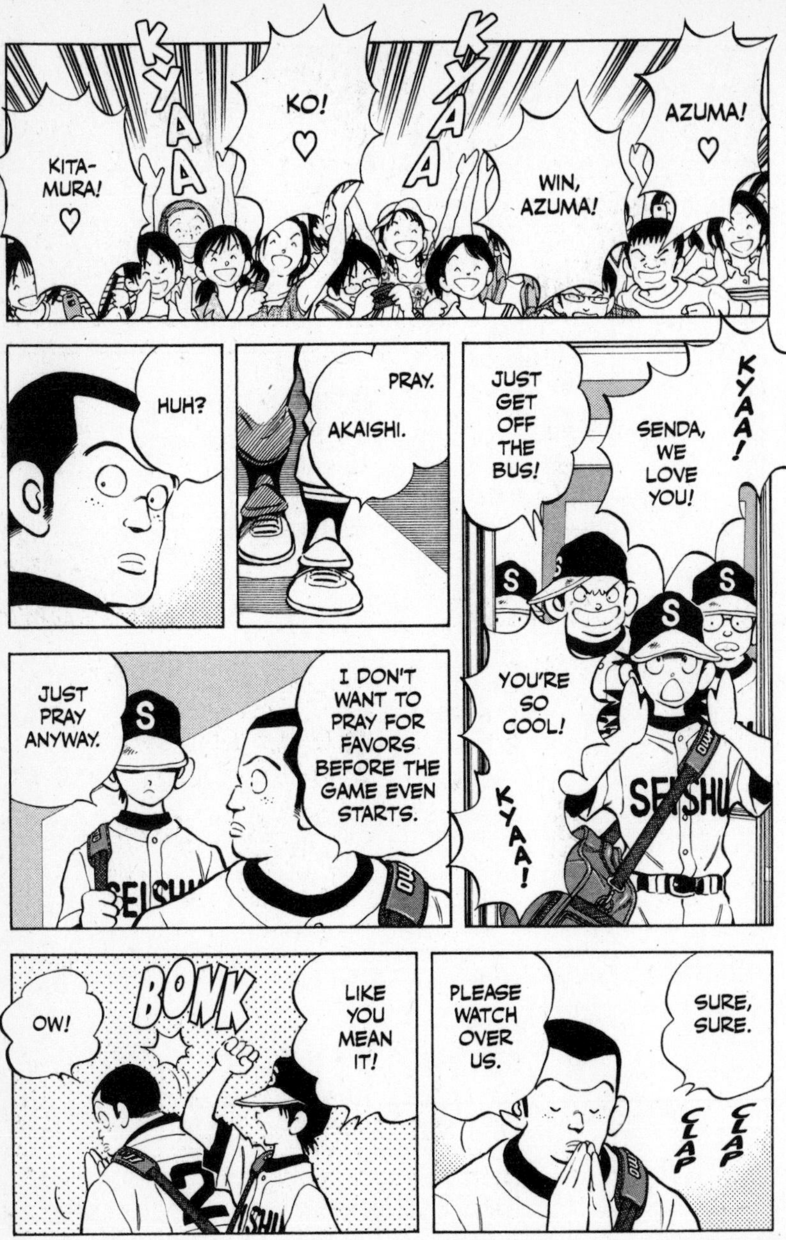
AZUMA! ♡
WIN, AZUMA!
KYAA
KO! ♡
KYAA
KITA-MURA! ♡
KYAA!
SENDA, WE LOVE YOU!
JUST GET OFF THE BUS!
YOU'RE SO COOL!
KYAA!
PRAY.
AKAISHI.
HUH?
I DON'T WANT TO PRAY FOR FAVORS BEFORE THE GAME EVEN STARTS.
JUST PRAY ANYWAY.
SURE, SURE.
CLAP
CLAP
PLEASE WATCH OVER US.
LIKE YOU MEAN IT!
BONK
OW!

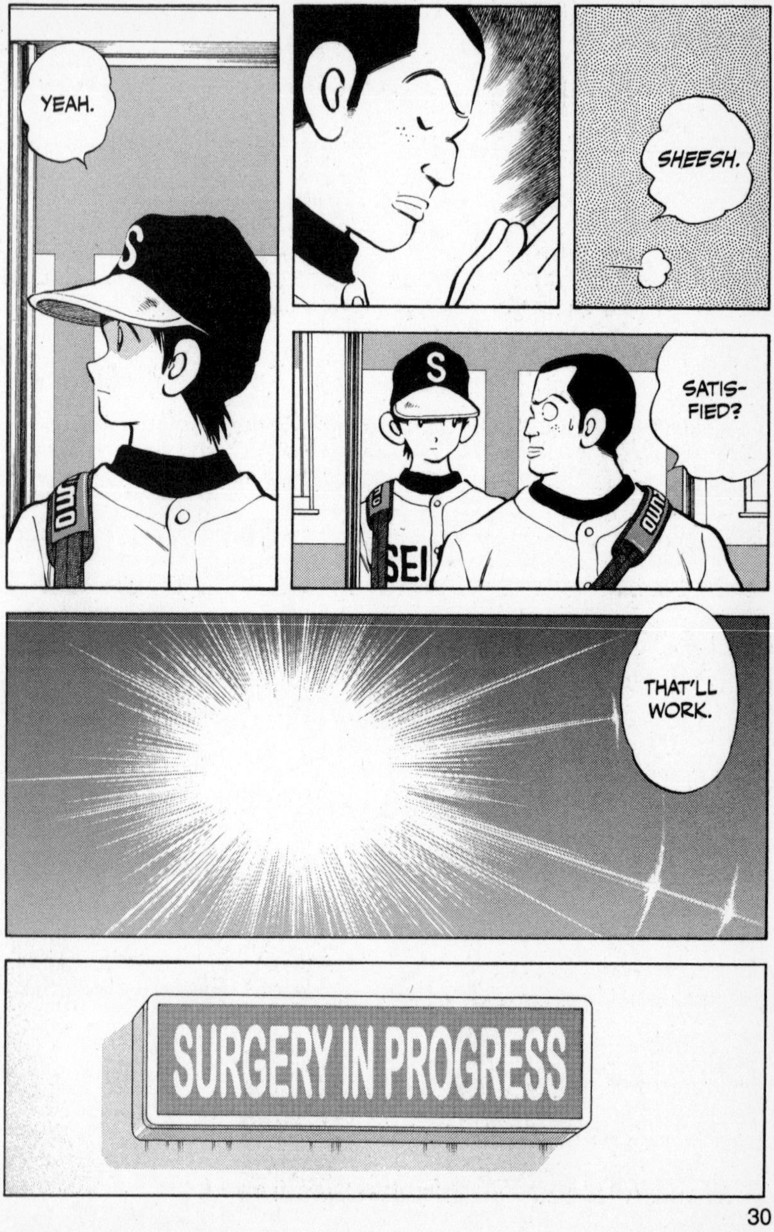
SHEESH.
SATIS-FIED?
YEAH.
THAT'LL WORK.
SURGERY IN PROGRESS

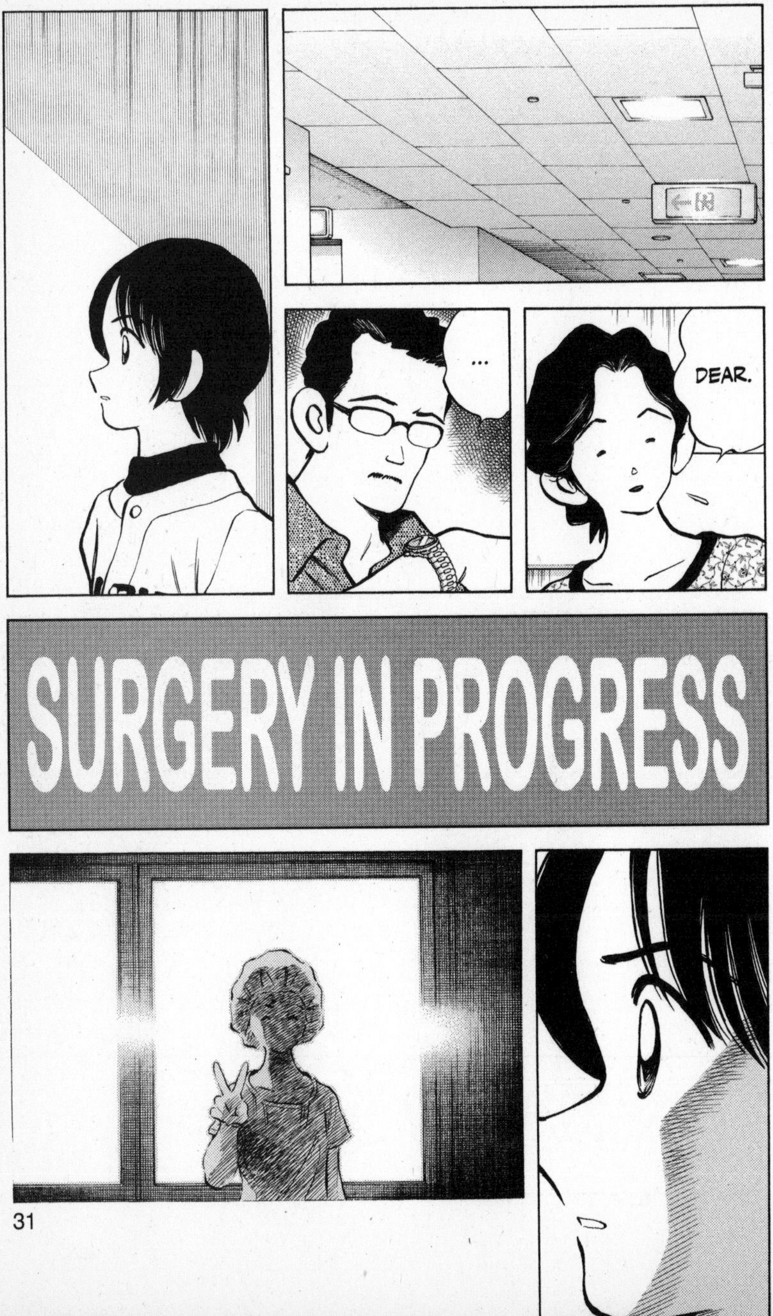
DEAR.
...
SURGERY IN PROGRESS

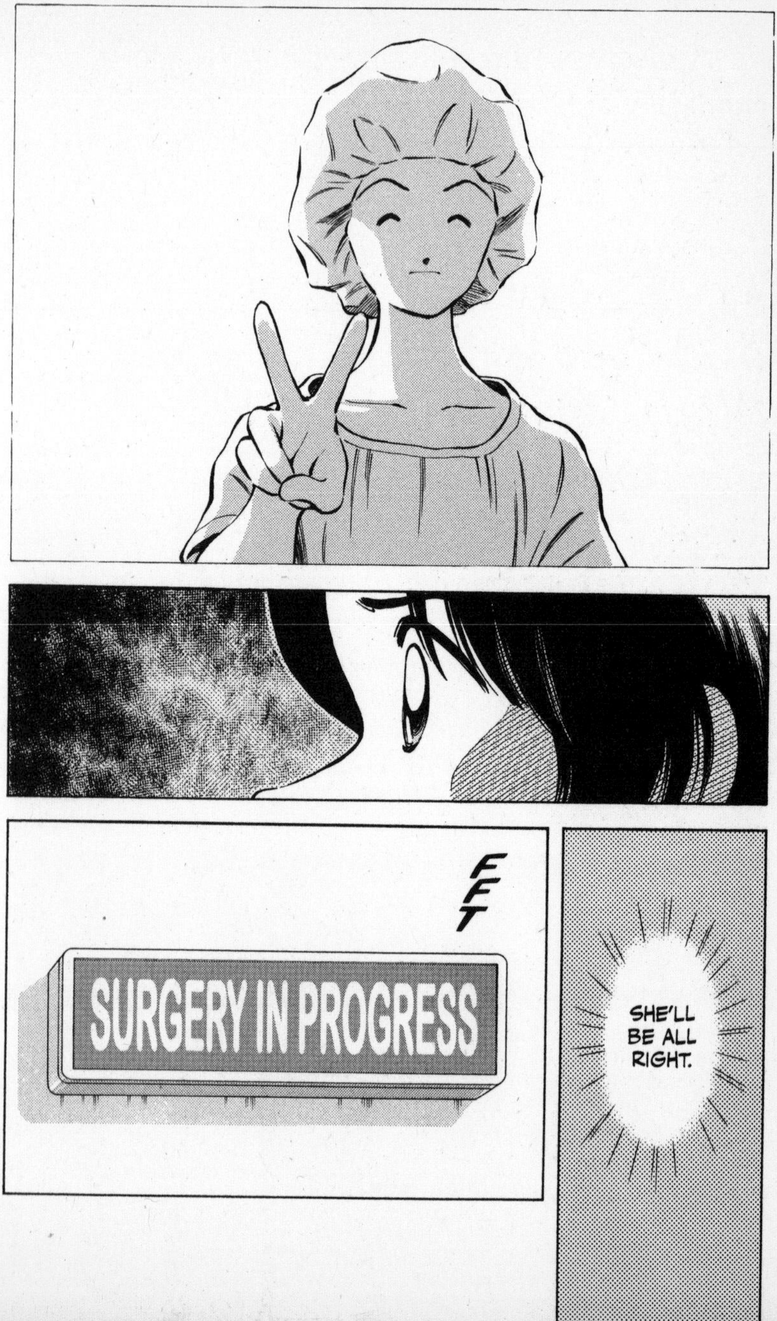
SHE'LL BE ALL RIGHT.
FFT
SURGERY IN PROGRESS

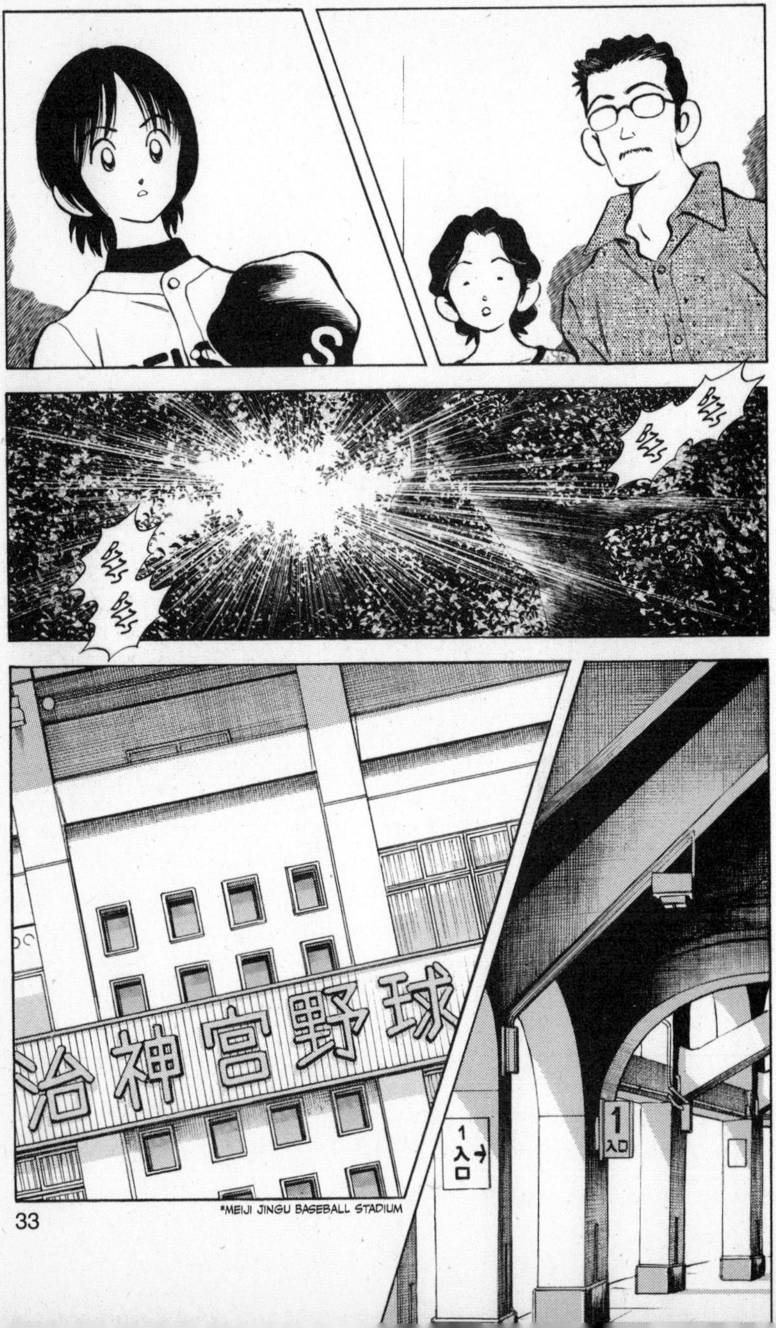
BZZS BZZS
BZZS BZZS
1 入口
1 入口 →
治神宮野球

*MEIJI JINGU BASEBALL STADIUM

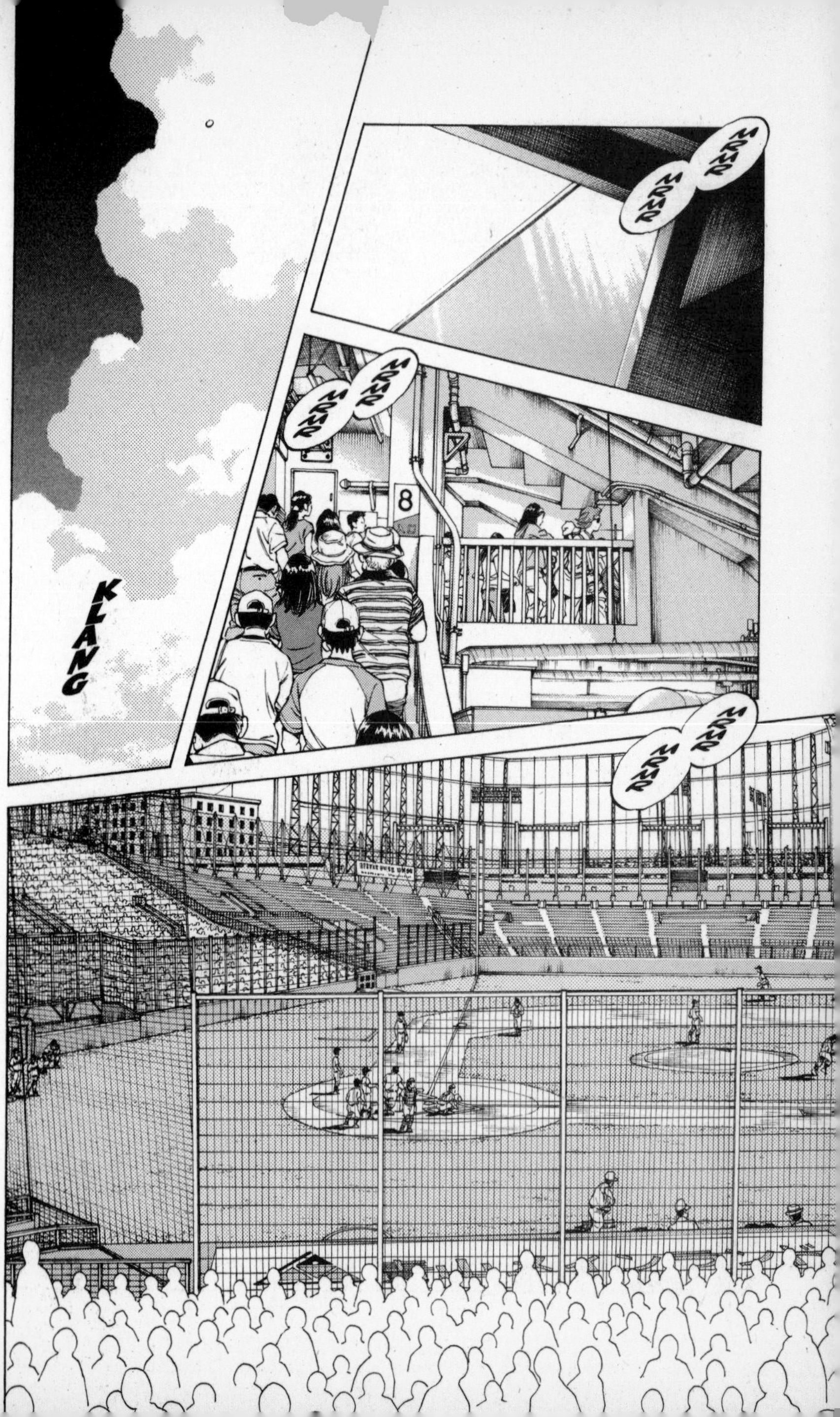
MRMR
MRMR
MRMR
MRMR
KLANG
MRMR
MRMR

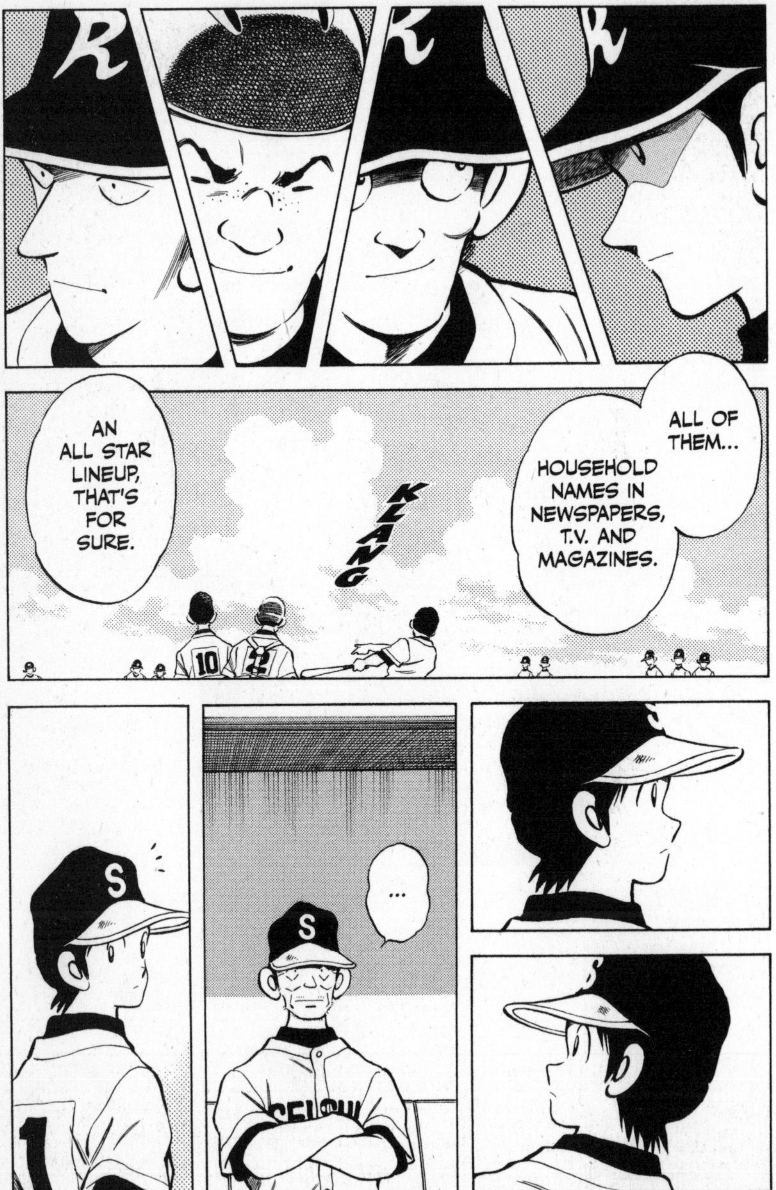
ALL OF THEM...
HOUSEHOLD NAMES IN NEWSPAPERS, T.V. AND MAGAZINES.
KLANG
AN ALL STAR LINEUP, THAT'S FOR SURE.
...

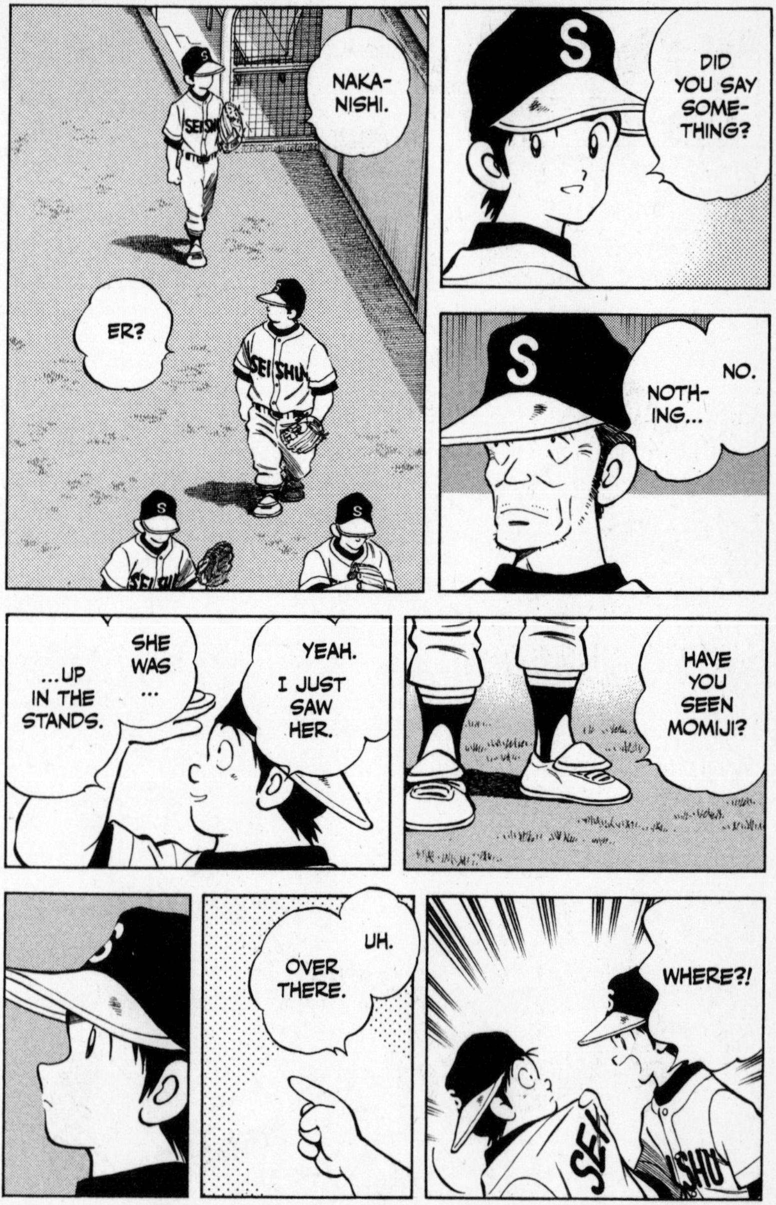
DID YOU SAY SOME-THING?
NO. NOTH-ING...
NAKA-NISHI.
ER?
HAVE YOU SEEN MOMIJI?
YEAH. I JUST SAW HER.
SHE WAS ... ...UP IN THE STANDS.
WHERE?!
UH. OVER THERE.

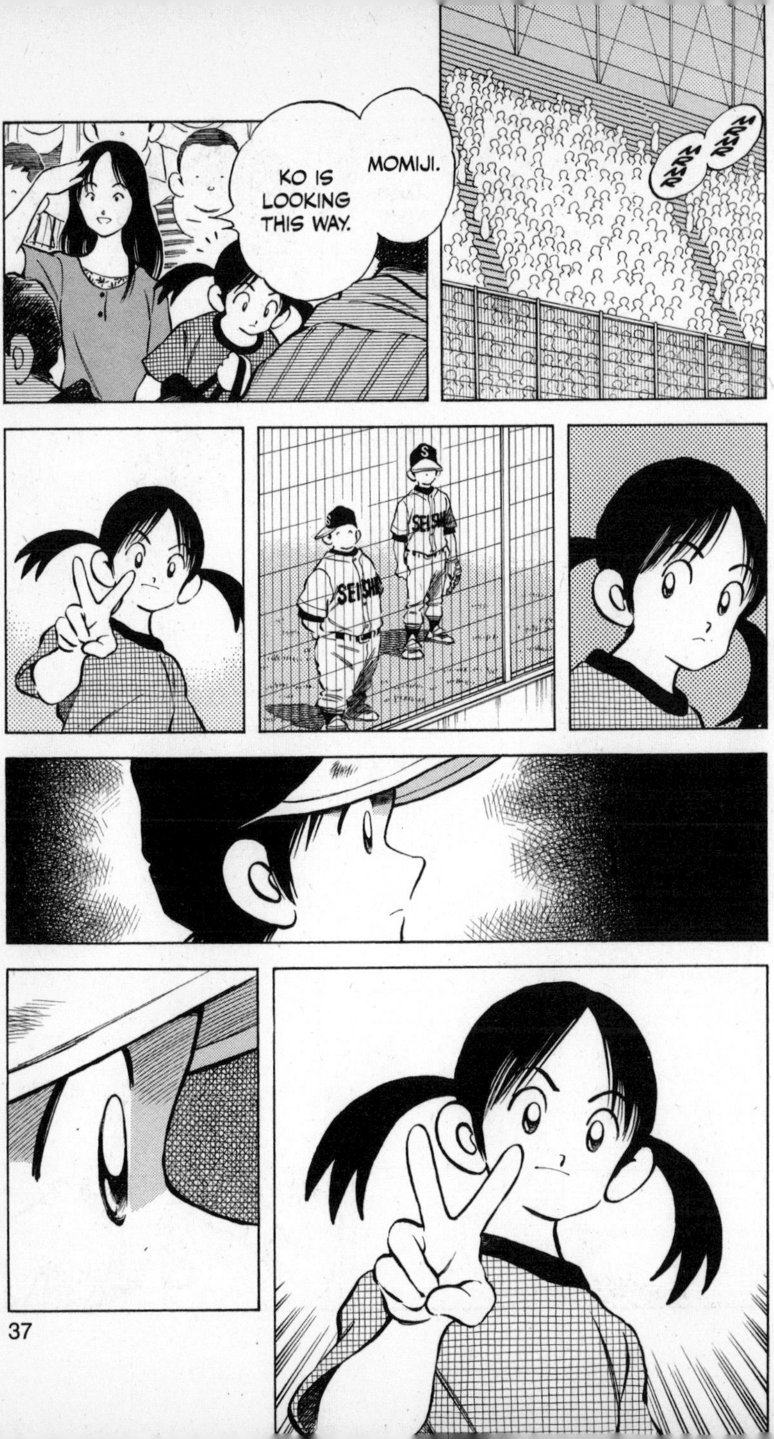
MRMR
MRMR
MOMIJI.
KO IS LOOKING THIS WAY.

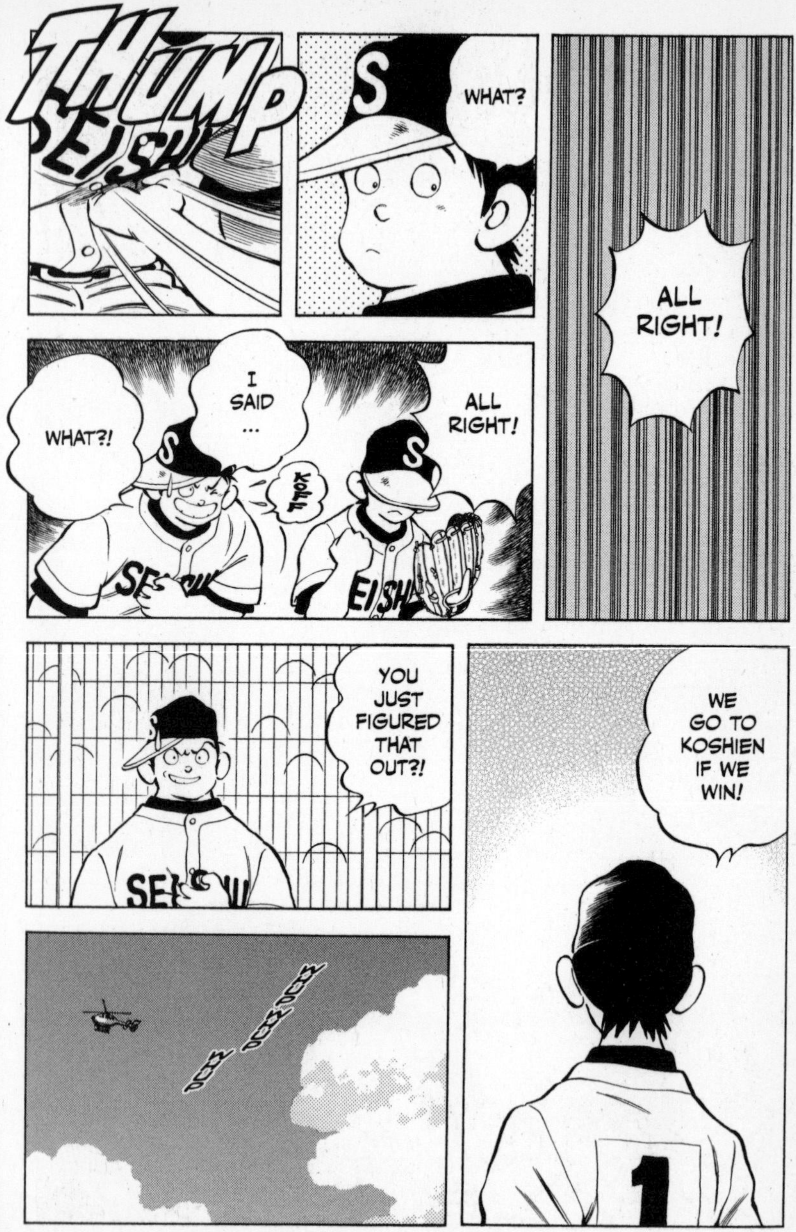
ALL RIGHT!
WHAT?
THUMP
ALL RIGHT!
I SAID ...
KOFF
WHAT?!
WE GO TO KOSHIEN IF WE WIN!
YOU JUST FIGURED THAT OUT?!

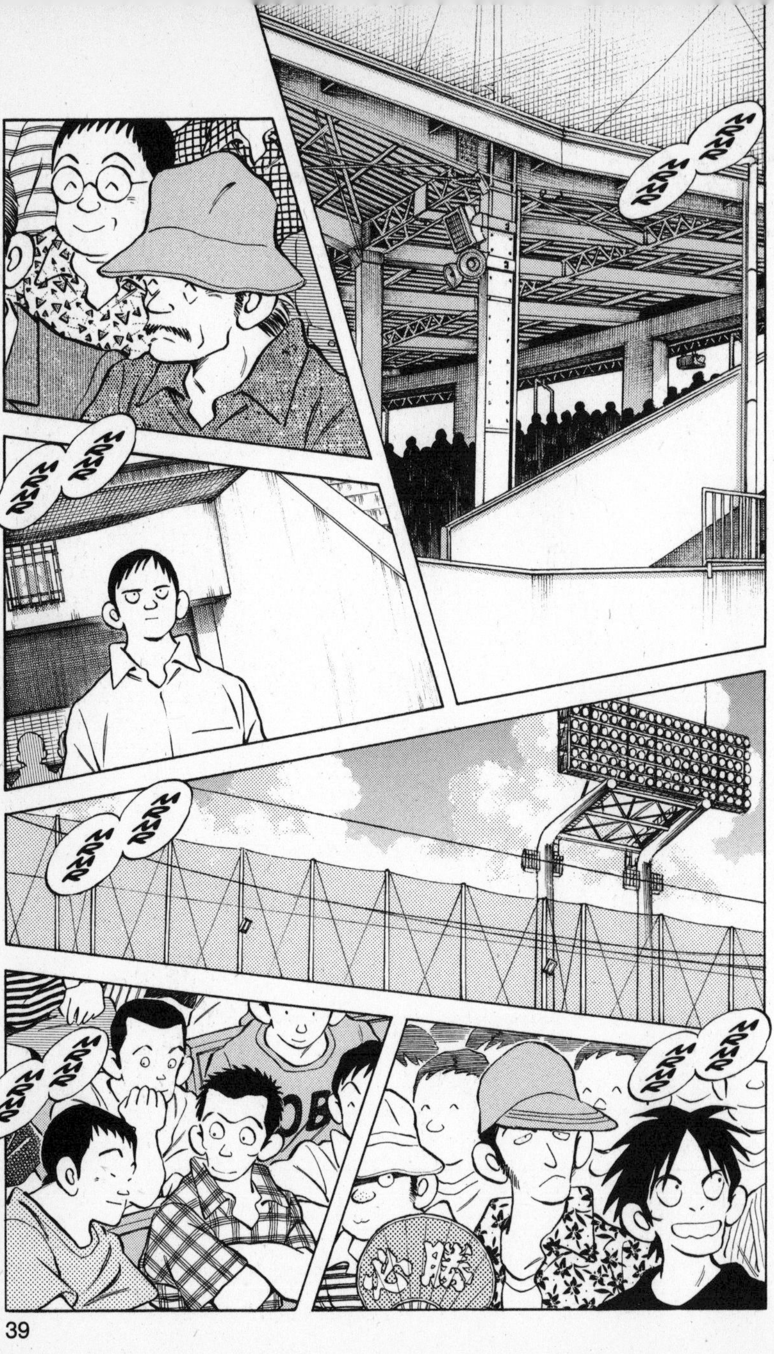
MRMR
MRMR
MRMR
MRMR
MRMR
MRMR
MRMR
MRMR
MRMR
MRMR

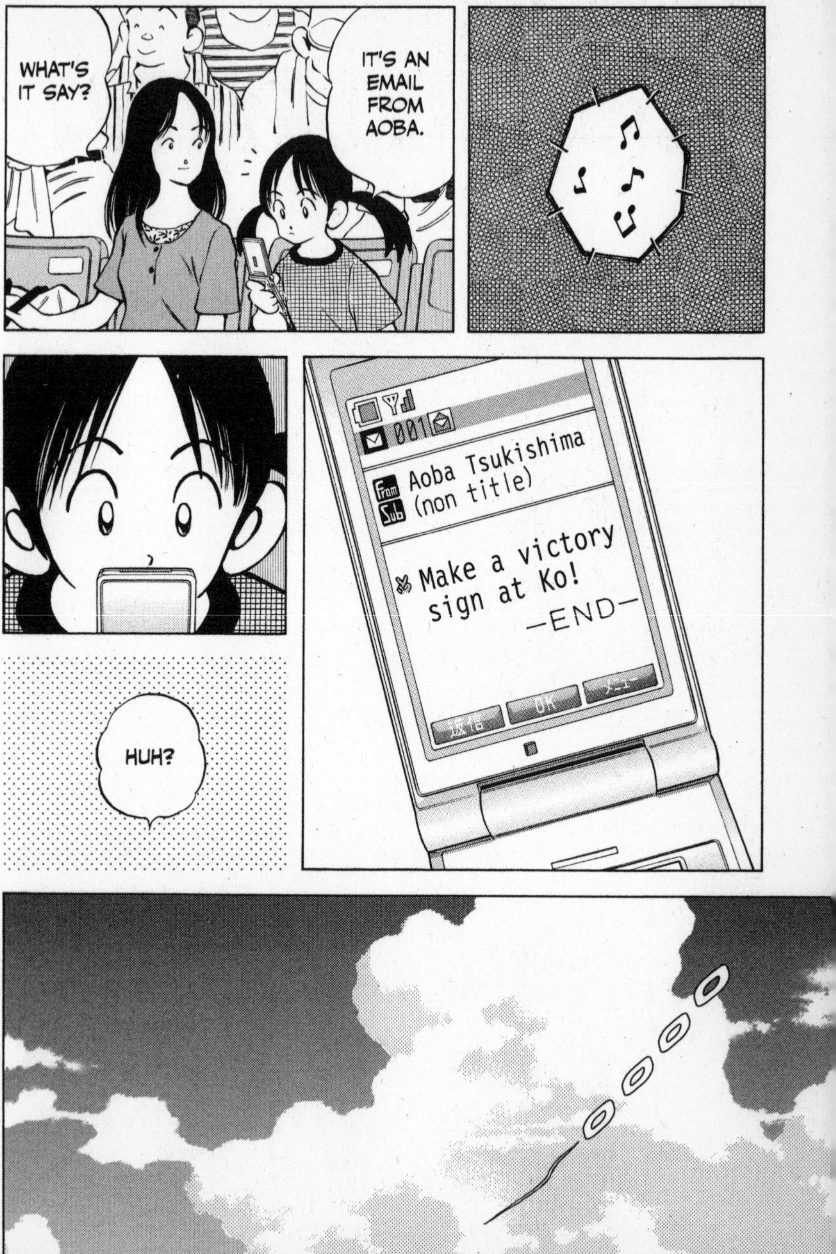
IT'S AN EMAIL FROM AOBA.
WHAT'S IT SAY?
001
From Aoba Tsukishima
Sub (non title)
Make a victory sign at Ko!
—END—
返信
OK
メニュー
HUH?

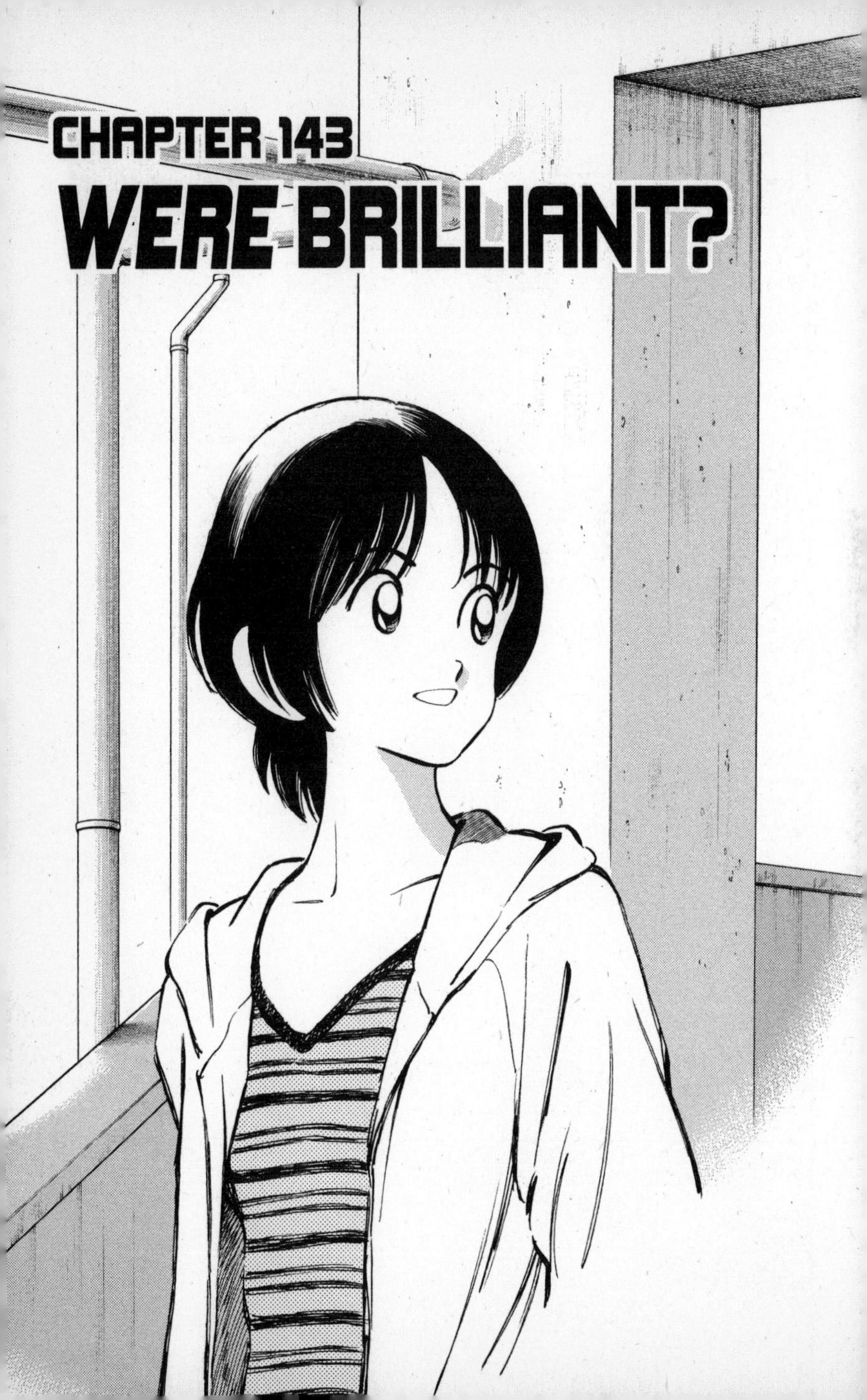
CHAPTER 143
WERE BRILLIANT?

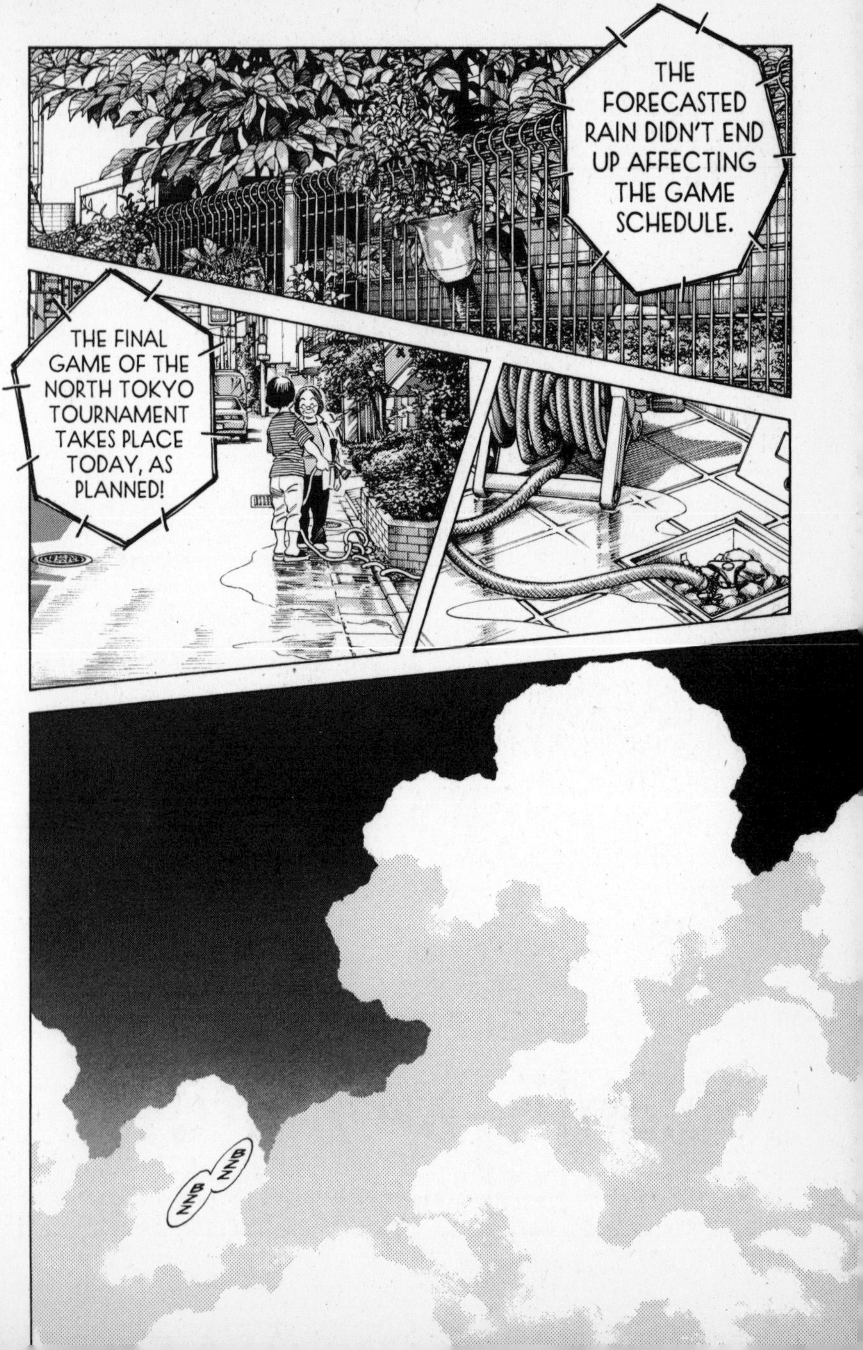
THE FORECASTED RAIN DIDN'T END UP AFFECTING THE GAME SCHEDULE.
THE FINAL GAME OF THE NORTH TOKYO TOURNAMENT TAKES PLACE TODAY, AS PLANNED!
BZZ BZZ

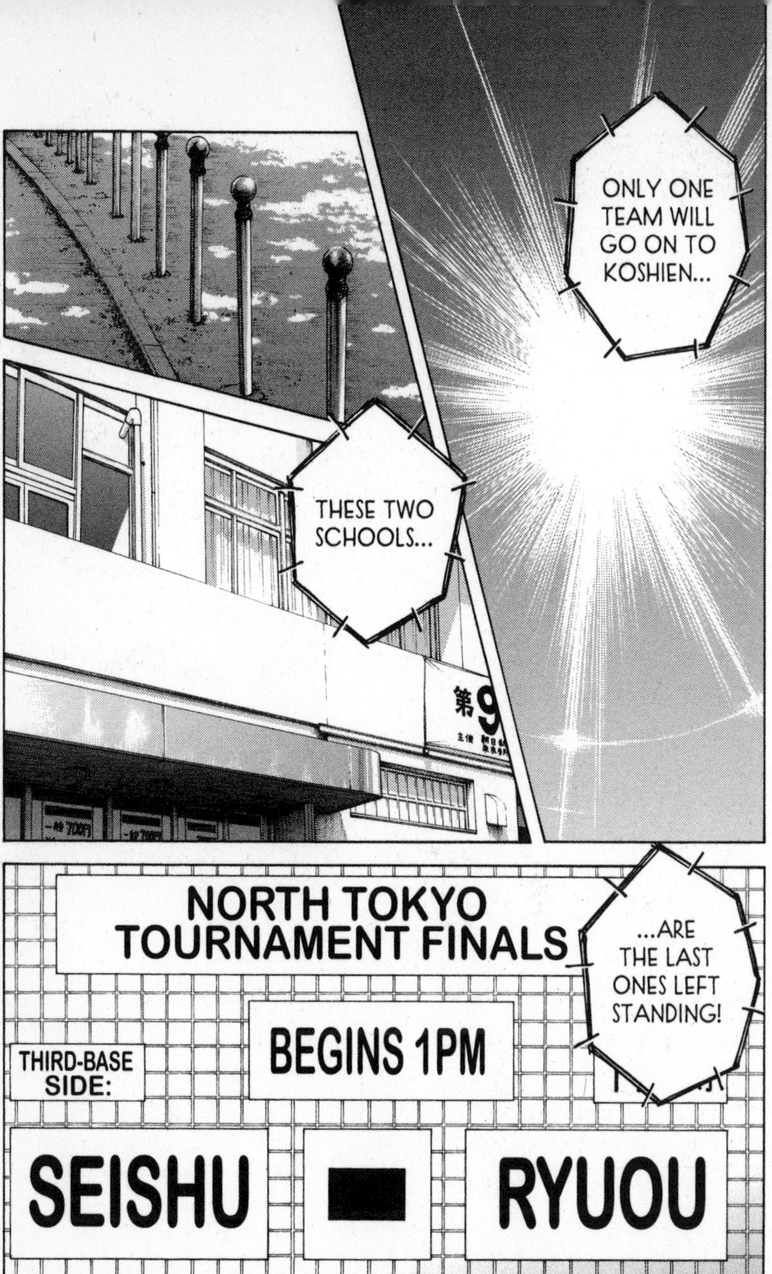
ONLY ONE TEAM WILL GO ON TO KOSHIEN...
THESE TWO SCHOOLS...
第9
...ARE THE LAST ONES LEFT STANDING!
NORTH TOKYO TOURNAMENT FINALS
BEGINS 1PM
THIRD-BASE SIDE:
SEISHU
RYUOU

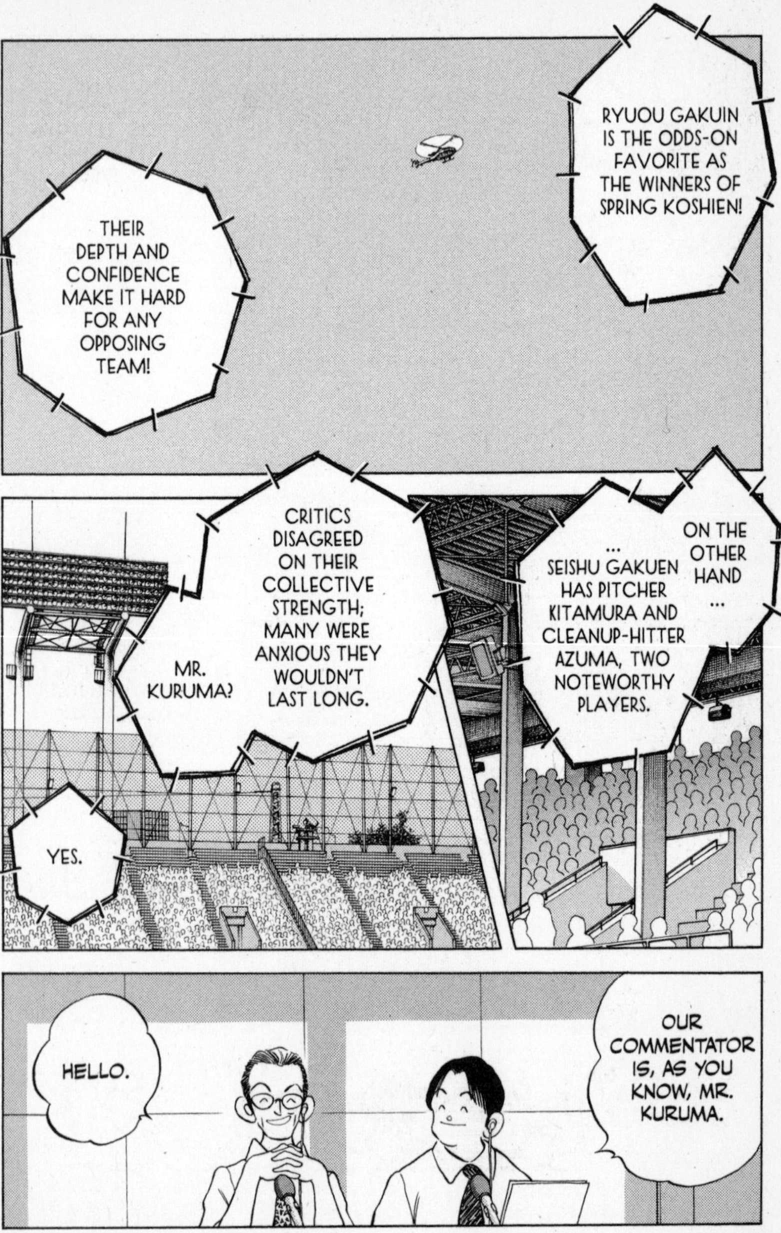
RYUOU GAKUIN IS THE ODDS-ON FAVORITE AS THE WINNERS OF SPRING KOSHIEN!
THEIR DEPTH AND CONFIDENCE MAKE IT HARD FOR ANY OPPOSING TEAM!
ON THE OTHER HAND ...
... SEISHU GAKUEN HAS PITCHER KITAMURA AND CLEANUP-HITTER AZUMA, TWO NOTEWORTHY PLAYERS.
CRITICS DISAGREED ON THEIR COLLECTIVE STRENGTH; MANY WERE ANXIOUS THEY WOULDN'T LAST LONG.
MR. KURUMA?
YES.
OUR COMMENTATOR IS, AS YOU KNOW, MR. KURUMA.
HELLO.

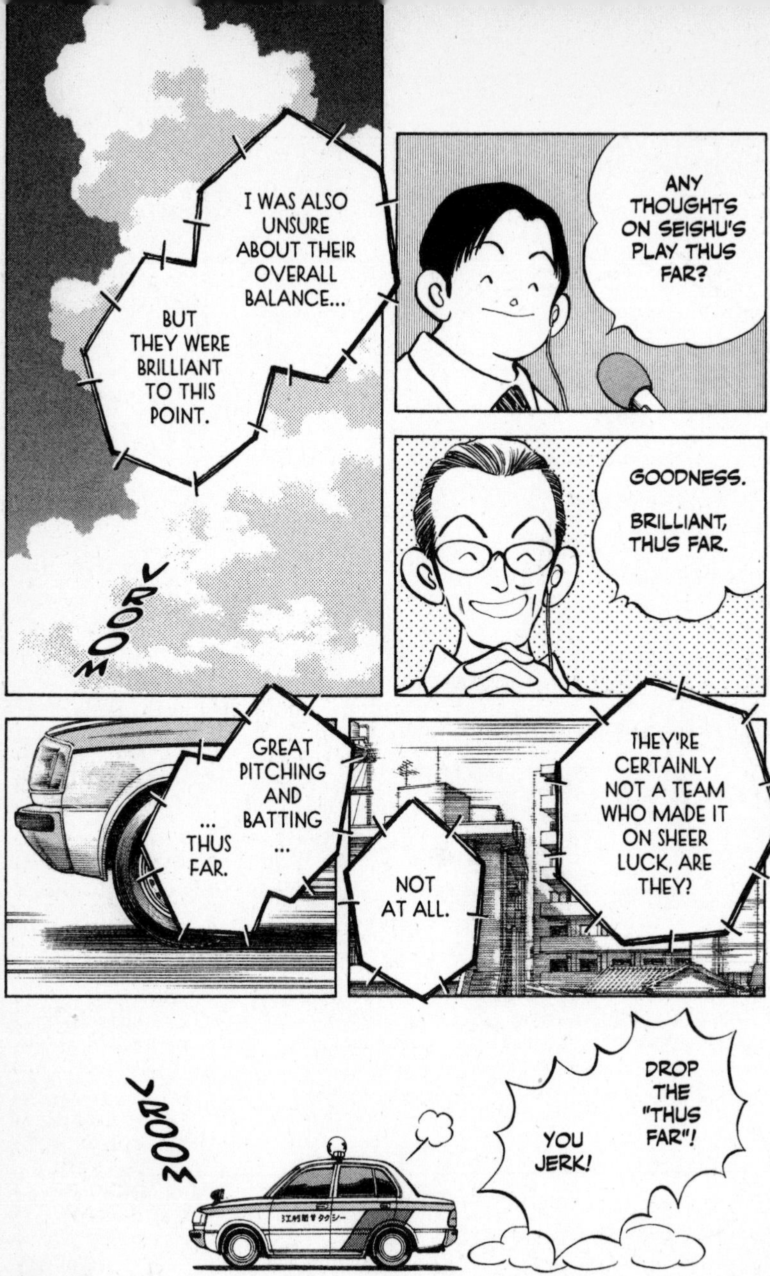
ANY THOUGHTS ON SEISHU'S PLAY THUS FAR?
GOODNESS.
BRILLIANT, THUS FAR.
I WAS ALSO UNSURE ABOUT THEIR OVERALL BALANCE...
BUT THEY WERE BRILLIANT TO THIS POINT.
VROOM
THEY'RE CERTAINLY NOT A TEAM WHO MADE IT ON SHEER LUCK, ARE THEY?
NOT AT ALL.
GREAT PITCHING AND BATTING...
...THUS FAR.
DROP THE "THUS FAR"!
YOU JERK!
VROOM

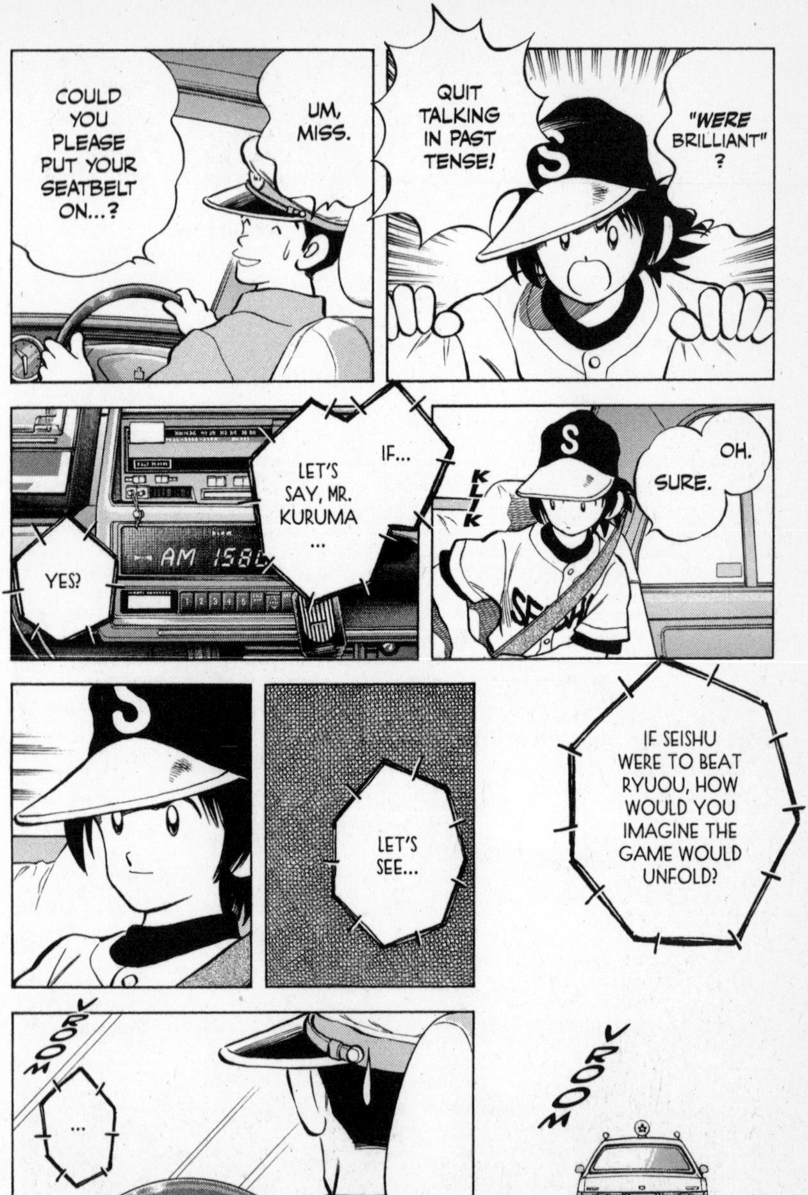
"WERE BRILLIANT"?
QUIT TALKING IN PAST TENSE!
UM, MISS.
COULD YOU PLEASE PUT YOUR SEATBELT ON...?
OH. SURE.
KLIK
IF...
LET'S SAY, MR. KURUMA ...
YES?
IF SEISHU WERE TO BEAT RYUOU, HOW WOULD YOU IMAGINE THE GAME WOULD UNFOLD?
LET'S SEE...
VROOM
VROOM
...

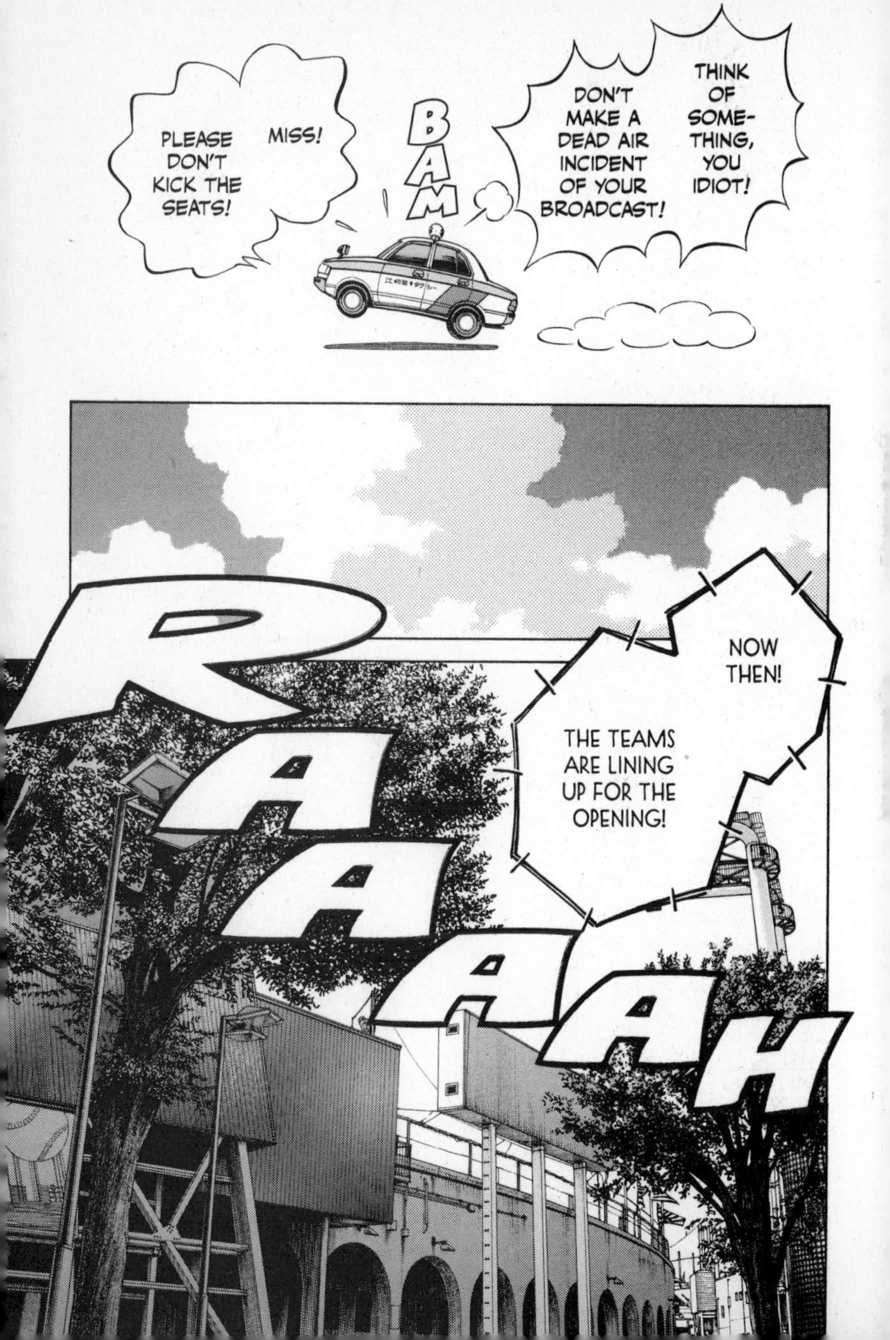
THINK OF SOME-THING, YOU IDIOT!
DON'T MAKE A DEAD AIR INCIDENT OF YOUR BROADCAST!
BAM
MISS!
PLEASE DON'T KICK THE SEATS!
NOW THEN!
THE TEAMS ARE LINING UP FOR THE OPENING!
RAAAAAH

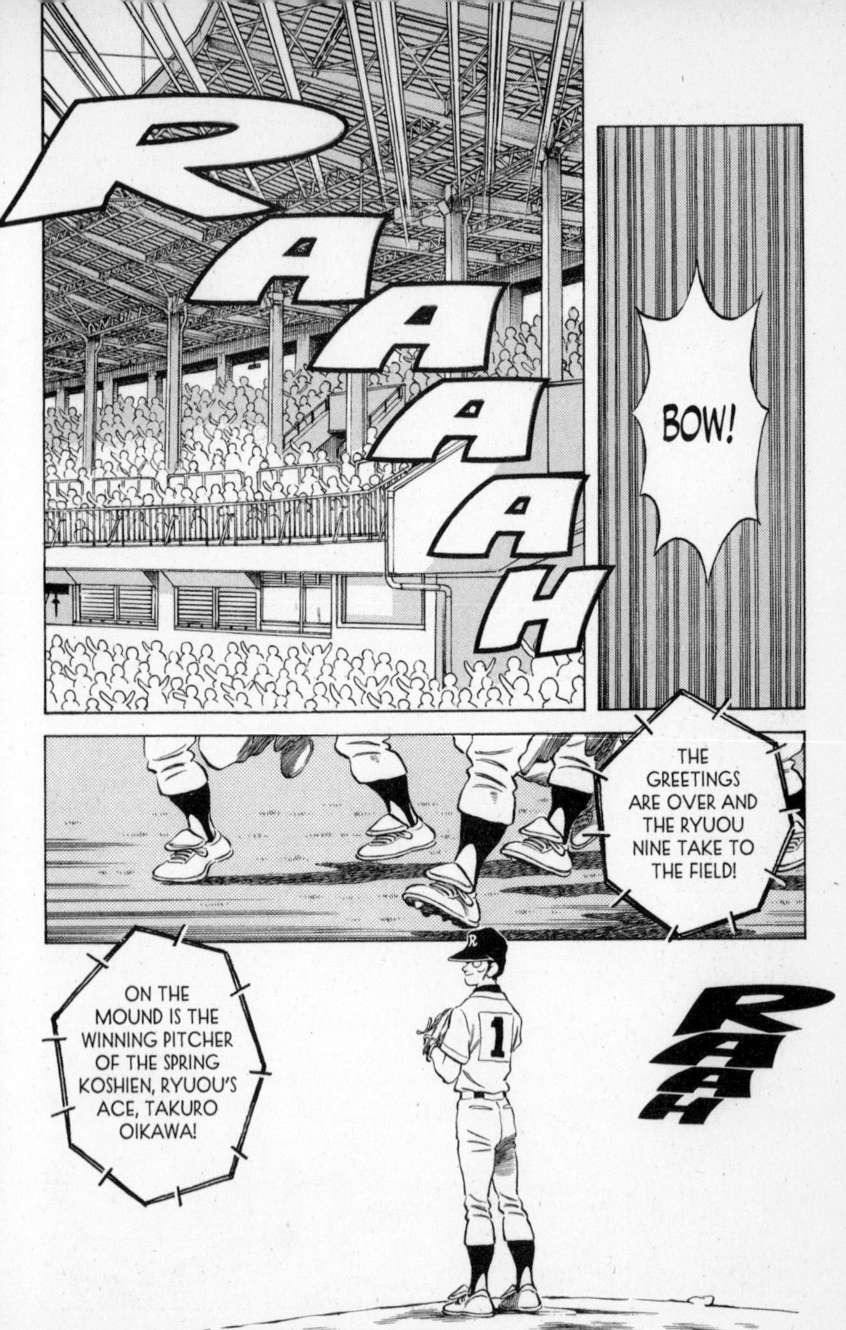
BOW!
RAAAAH
THE GREETINGS ARE OVER AND THE RYUOU NINE TAKE TO THE FIELD!
RAAH
ON THE MOUND IS THE WINNING PITCHER OF THE SPRING KOSHIEN, RYUOU'S ACE, TAKURO OIKAWA!
1

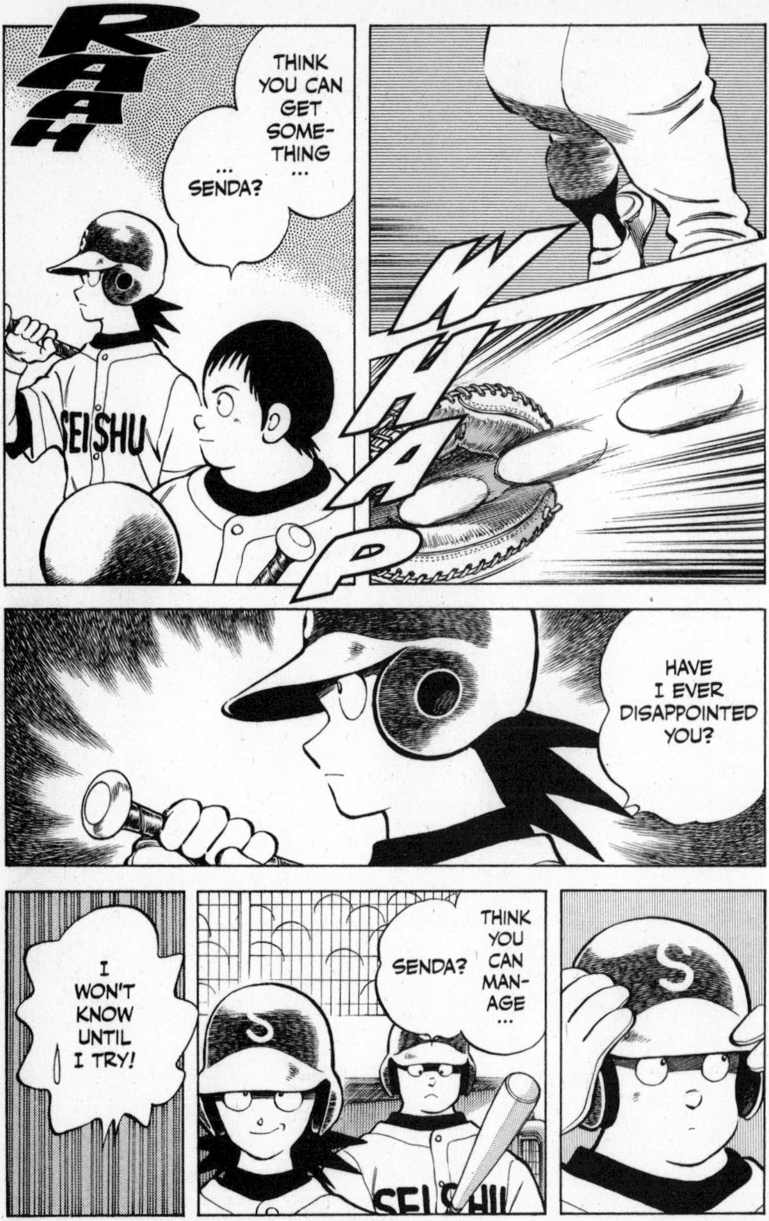
WHAP
RAAH
THINK YOU CAN GET SOME-THING ... SENDA?
HAVE I EVER DISAPPOINTED YOU?
THINK YOU CAN MAN-AGE ... SENDA?
I WON'T KNOW UNTIL I TRY!

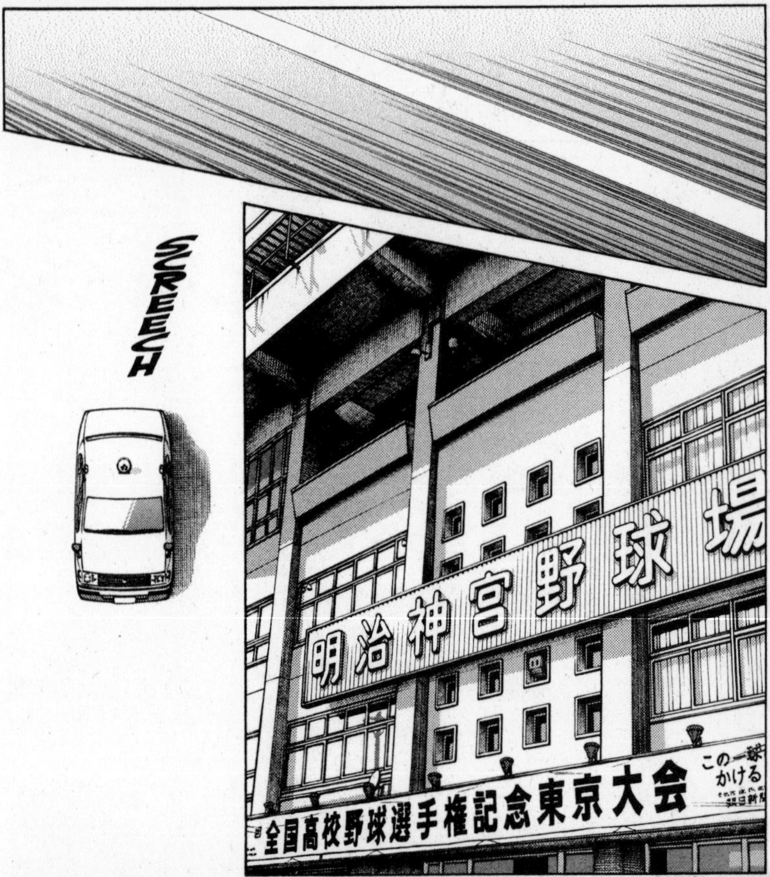
SCREECH
明治神宮野球場
全国高校野球選手権記念東京大会

*MEIJI JINGU BASEBALL STADIUM: NATIONAL HIGH SCHOOL BASEBALL TOKYO CHAMPIONSHIPS

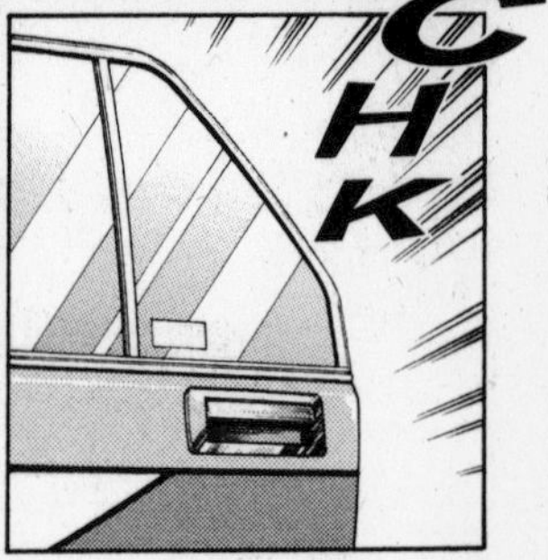
CHK

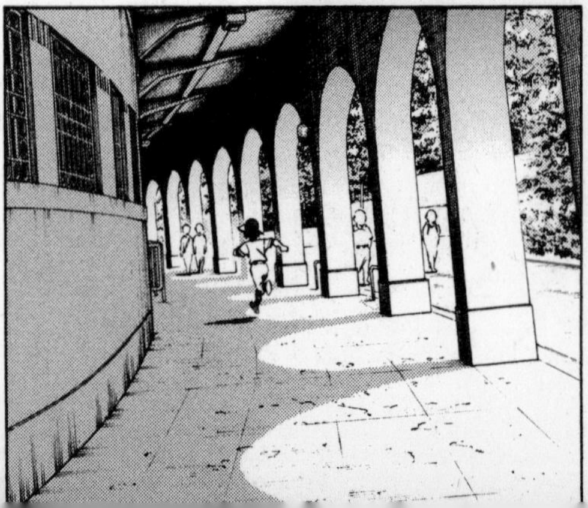

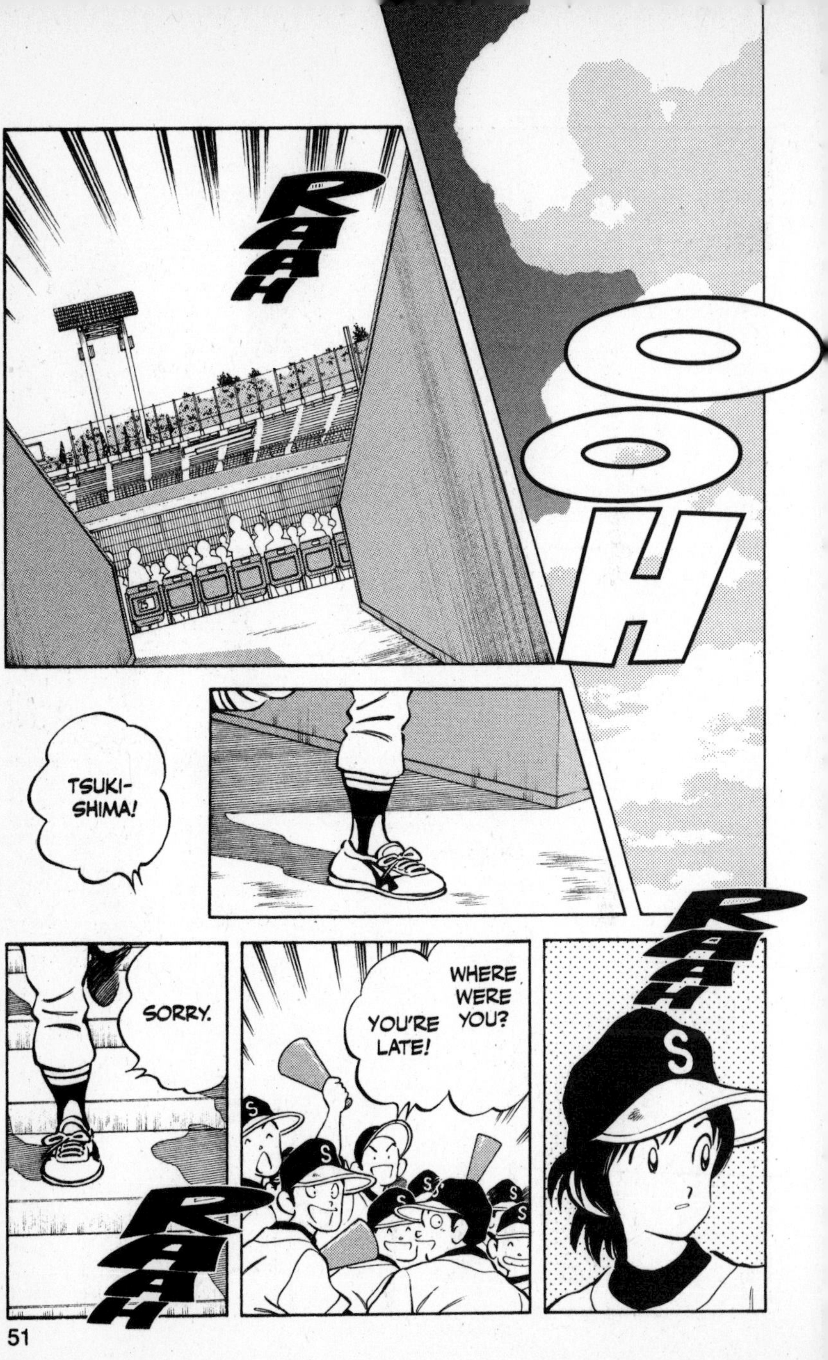
OOOH
RAAH
TSUKI-SHIMA!
RAAH
WHERE WERE YOU?
YOU'RE LATE!
SORRY.
RAAH

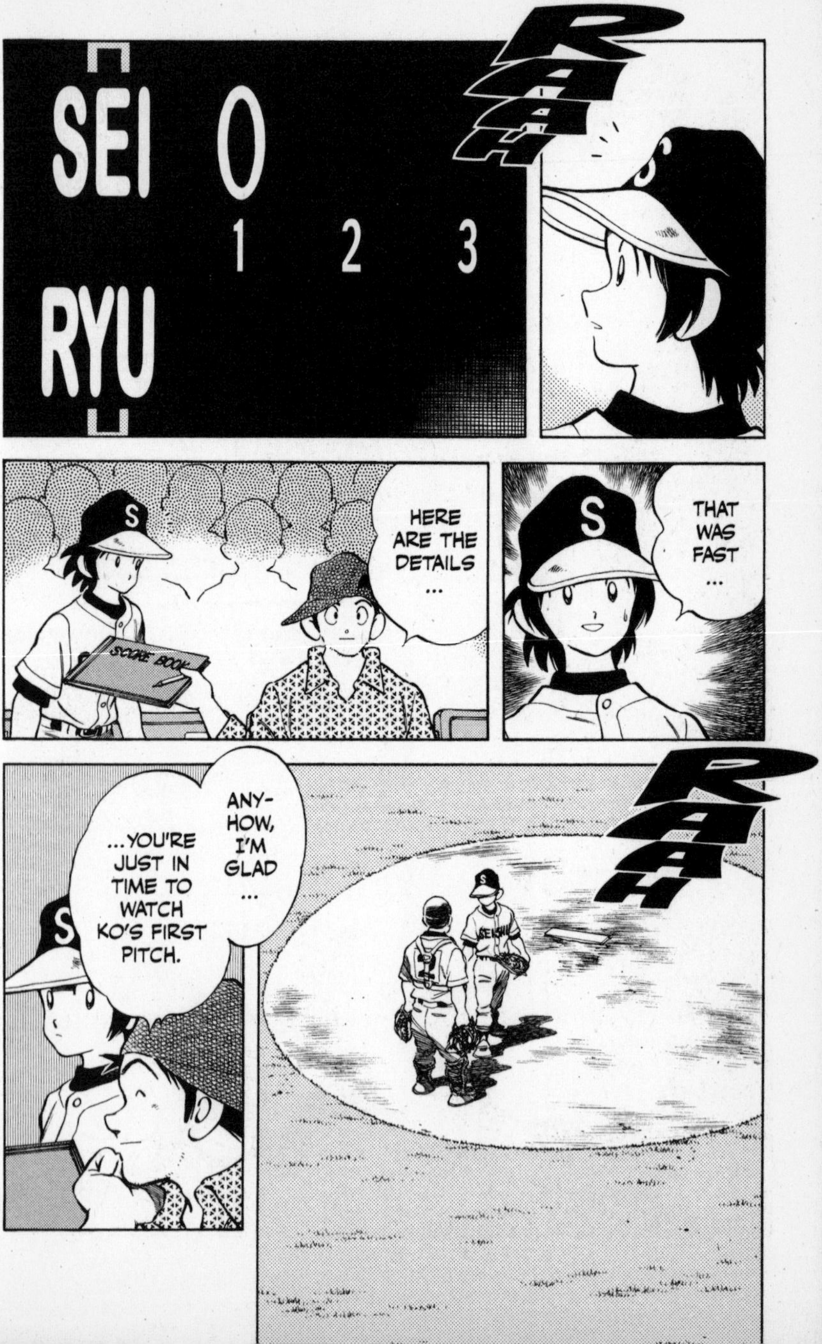
RAAAH
SEI 0
1 2 3
RYU
THAT WAS FAST ...
HERE ARE THE DETAILS ...
SCORE BOOK
RAAAH
ANY-HOW, I'M GLAD ...
...YOU'RE JUST IN TIME TO WATCH KO'S FIRST PITCH.

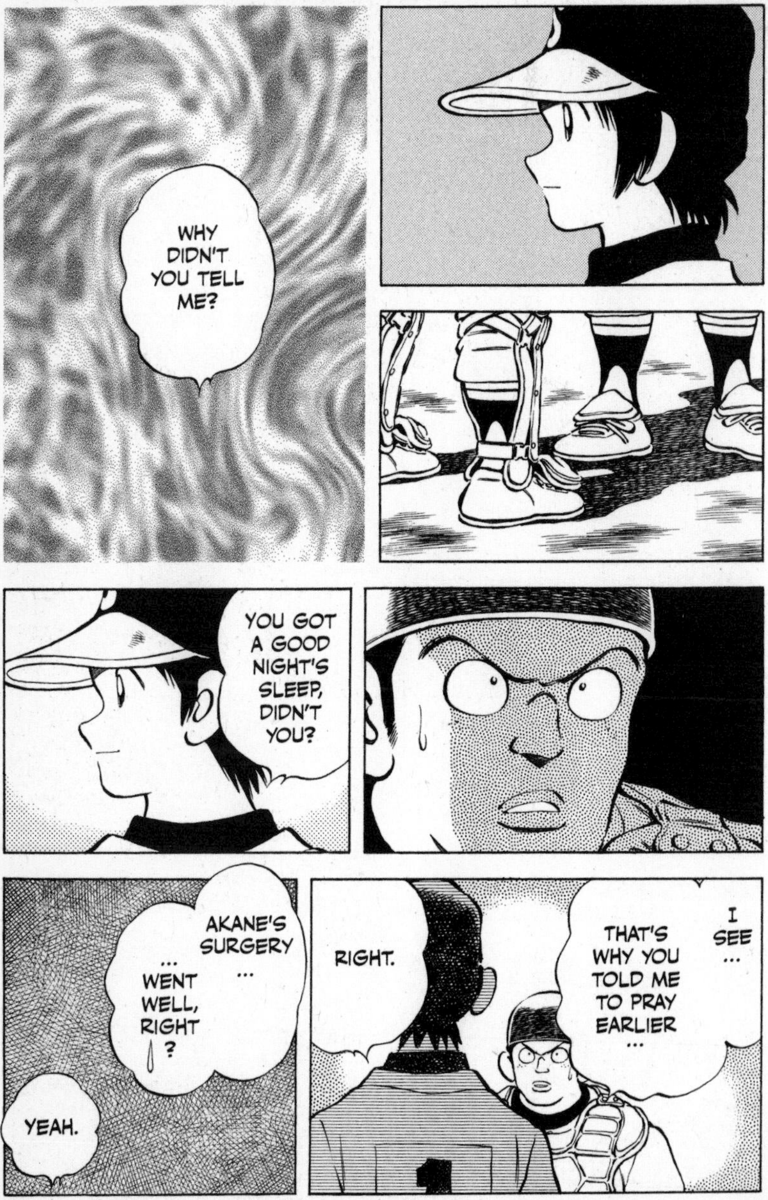
WHY DIDN'T YOU TELL ME?
YOU GOT A GOOD NIGHT'S SLEEP, DIDN'T YOU?
I SEE ...
THAT'S WHY YOU TOLD ME TO PRAY EARLIER ...
RIGHT.
AKANE'S SURGERY ...
... WENT WELL, RIGHT?
YEAH.

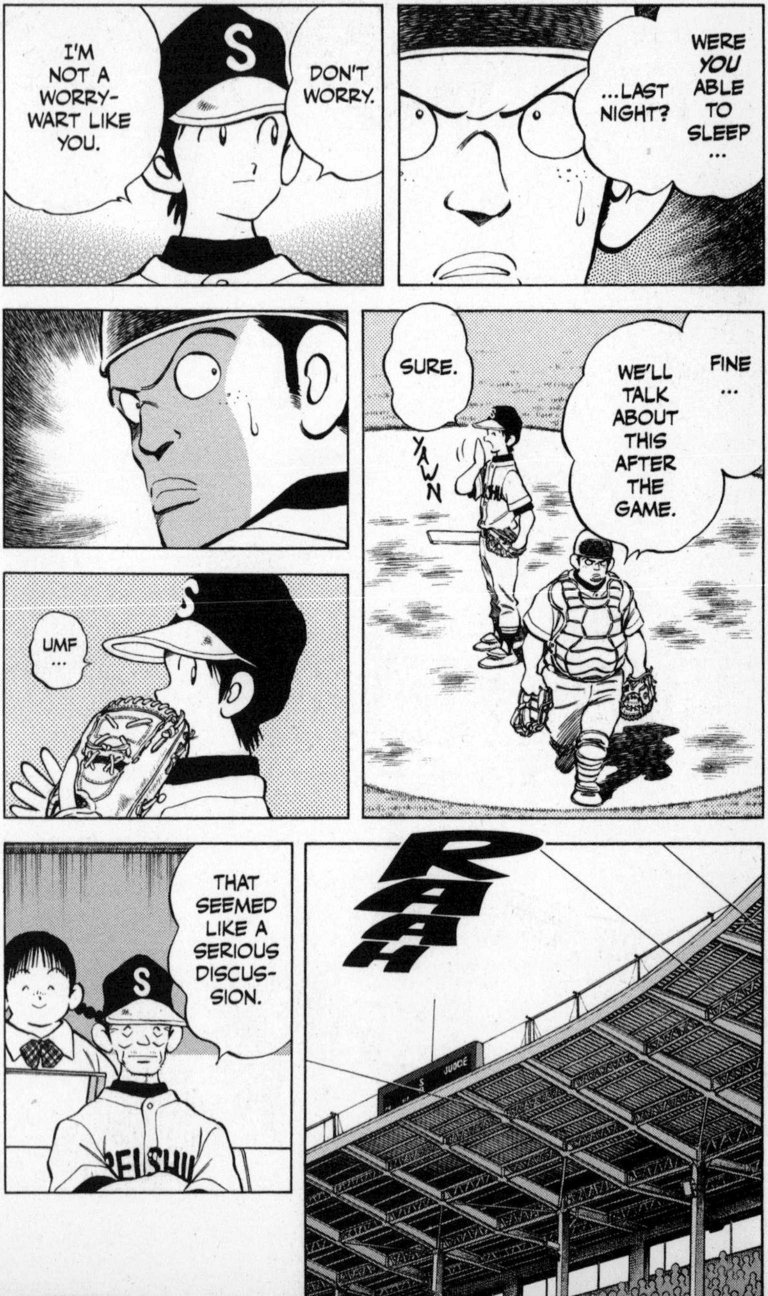
WERE YOU ABLE TO SLEEP ...
...LAST NIGHT?
DON'T WORRY.
I'M NOT A WORRY-WART LIKE YOU.
FINE ...
WE'LL TALK ABOUT THIS AFTER THE GAME.
SURE.
YAWN
UMF ...
RAAAH
THAT SEEMED LIKE A SERIOUS DISCUS-SION.

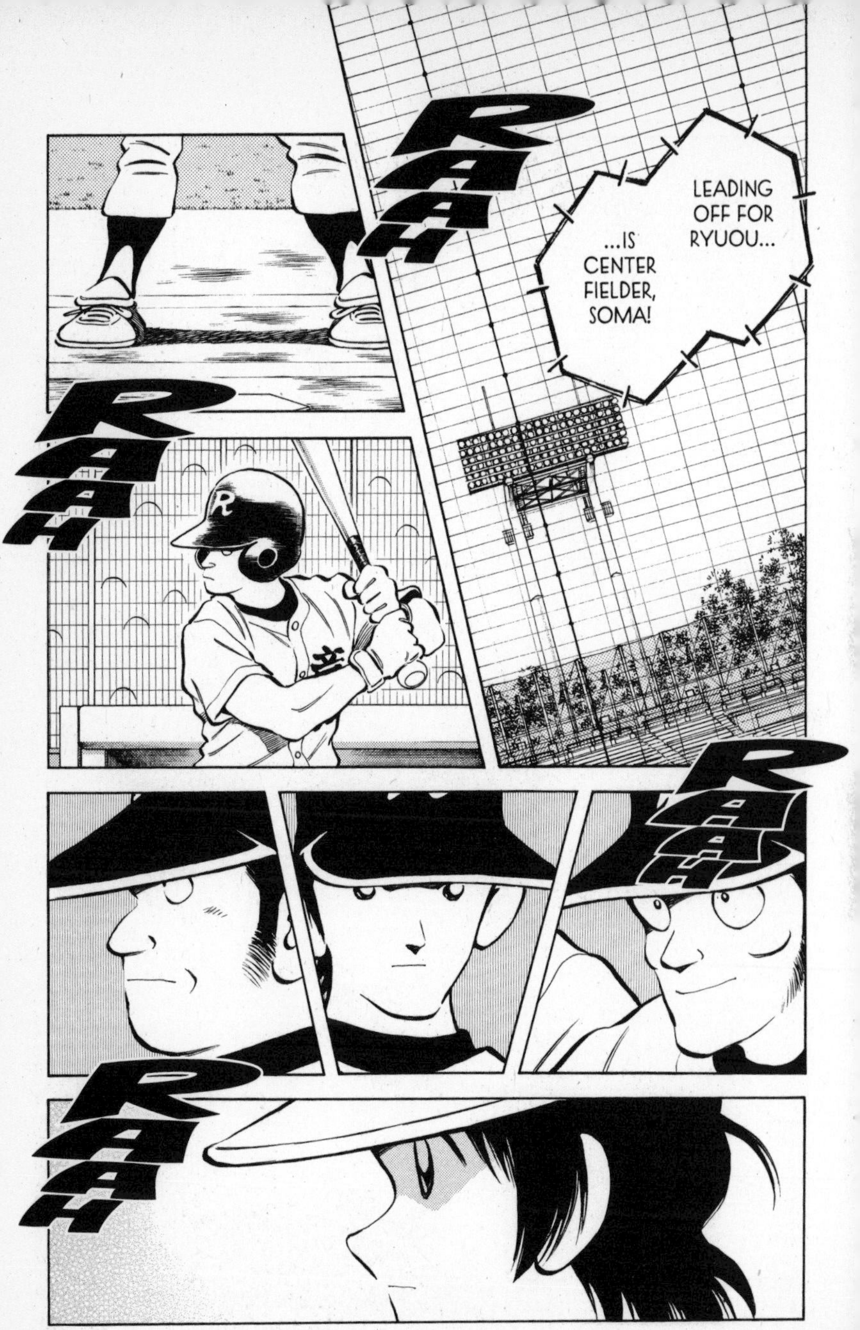
RAAAH
LEADING OFF FOR RYUOU...
...IS CENTER FIELDER, SOMA!
RAAAH
RAAAH
RAAAH

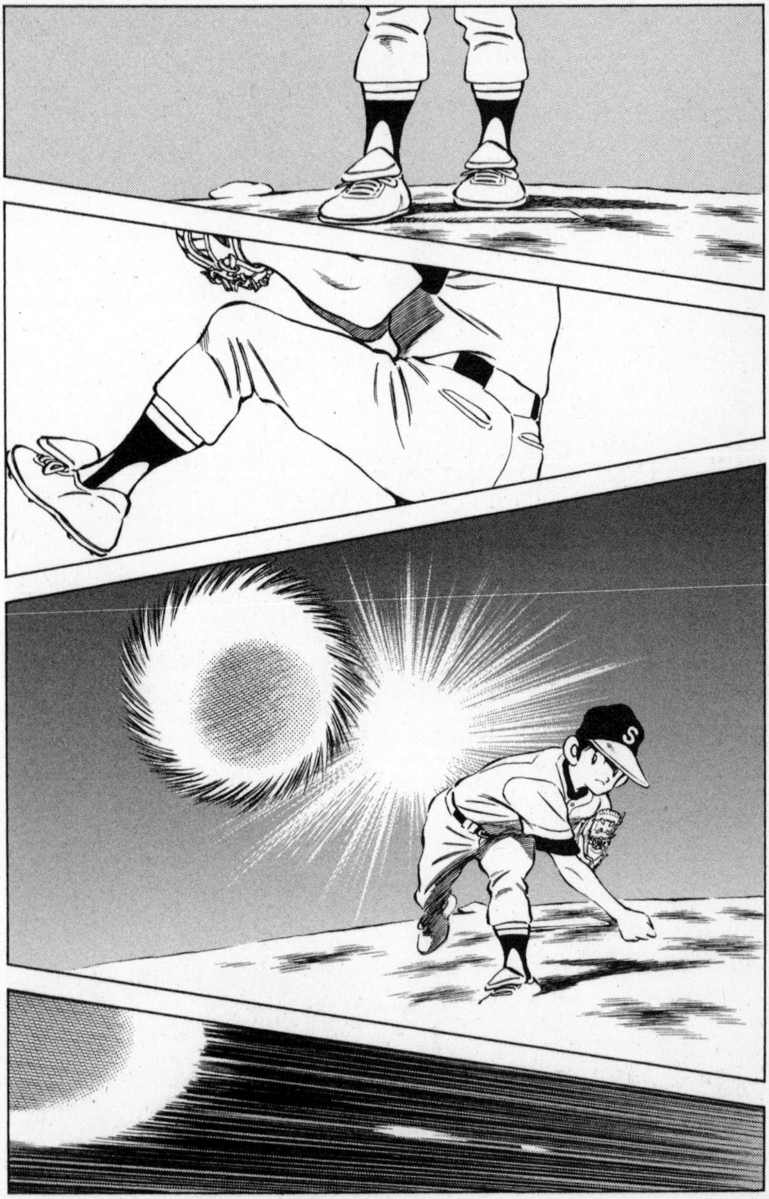

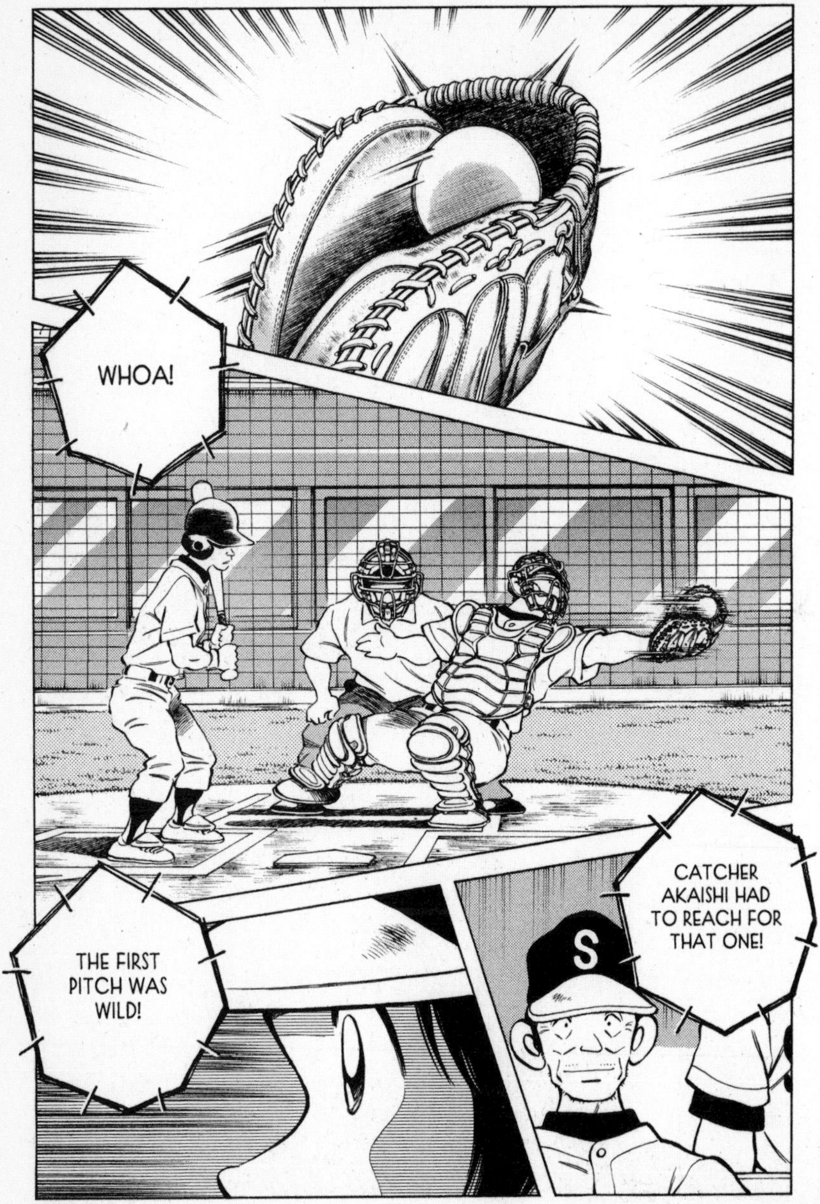
WHOA!
CATCHER AKAISHI HAD TO REACH FOR THAT ONE!
THE FIRST PITCH WAS WILD!

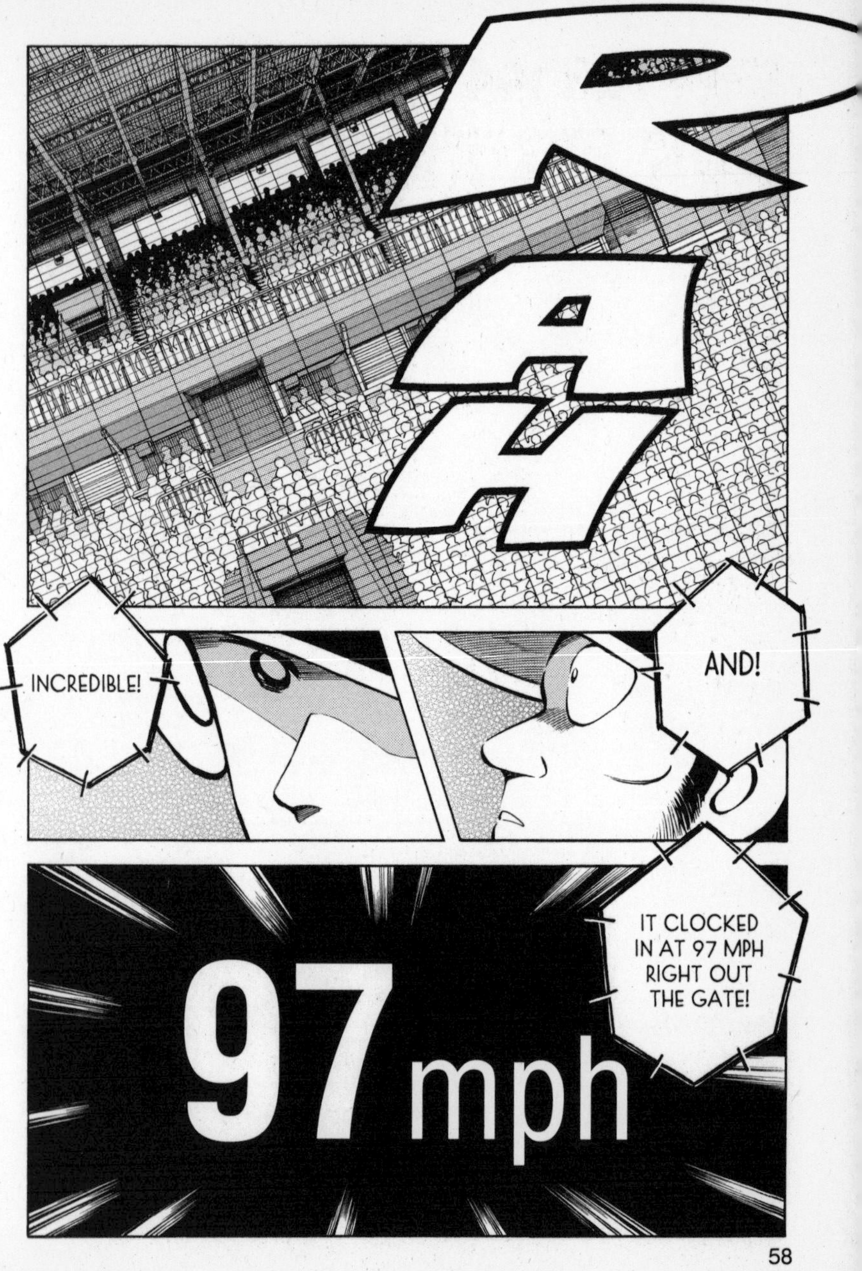
RAH
AND!
INCREDIBLE!
IT CLOCKED IN AT 97 MPH RIGHT OUT THE GATE!
97 mph

CHAPTER 144
I'VE GIVEN UP

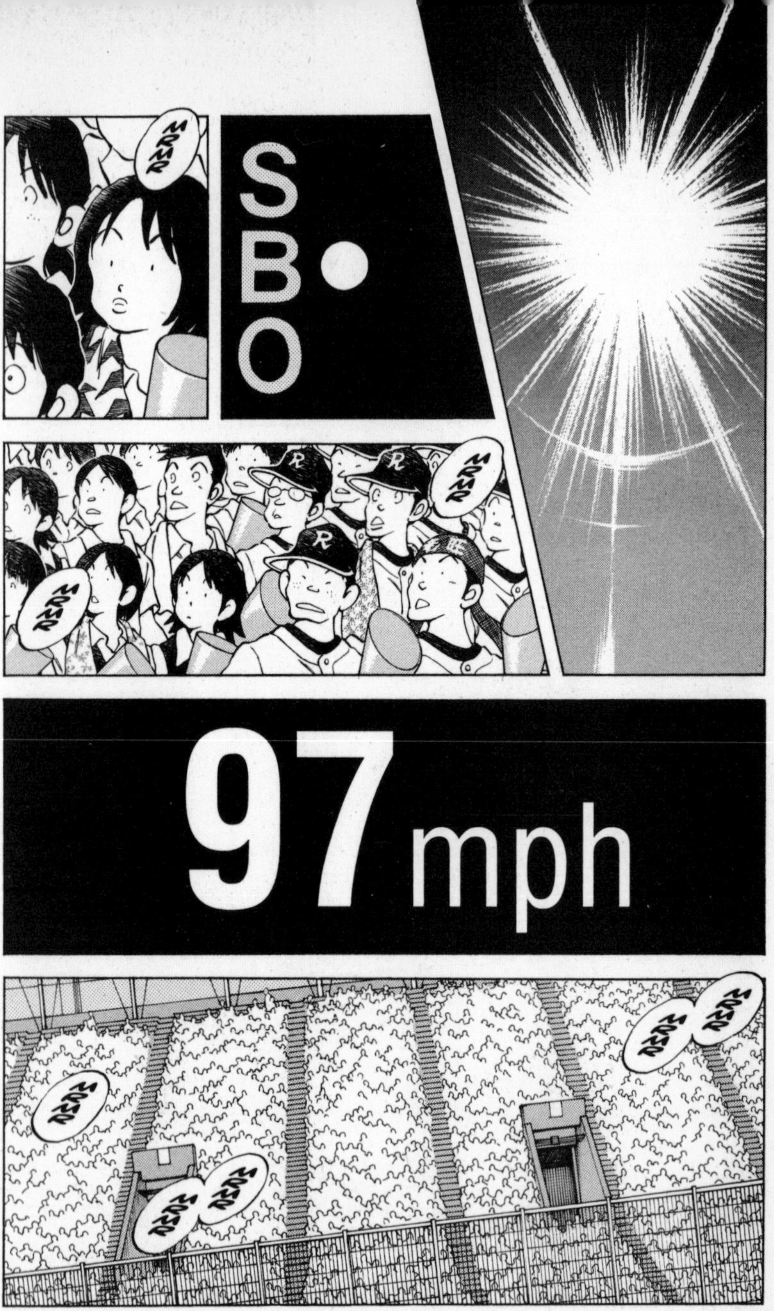

SBO
MRMR
MRMR
MRMR
97 mph
MRMR
MRMR
MRMR
MRMR
MRMR

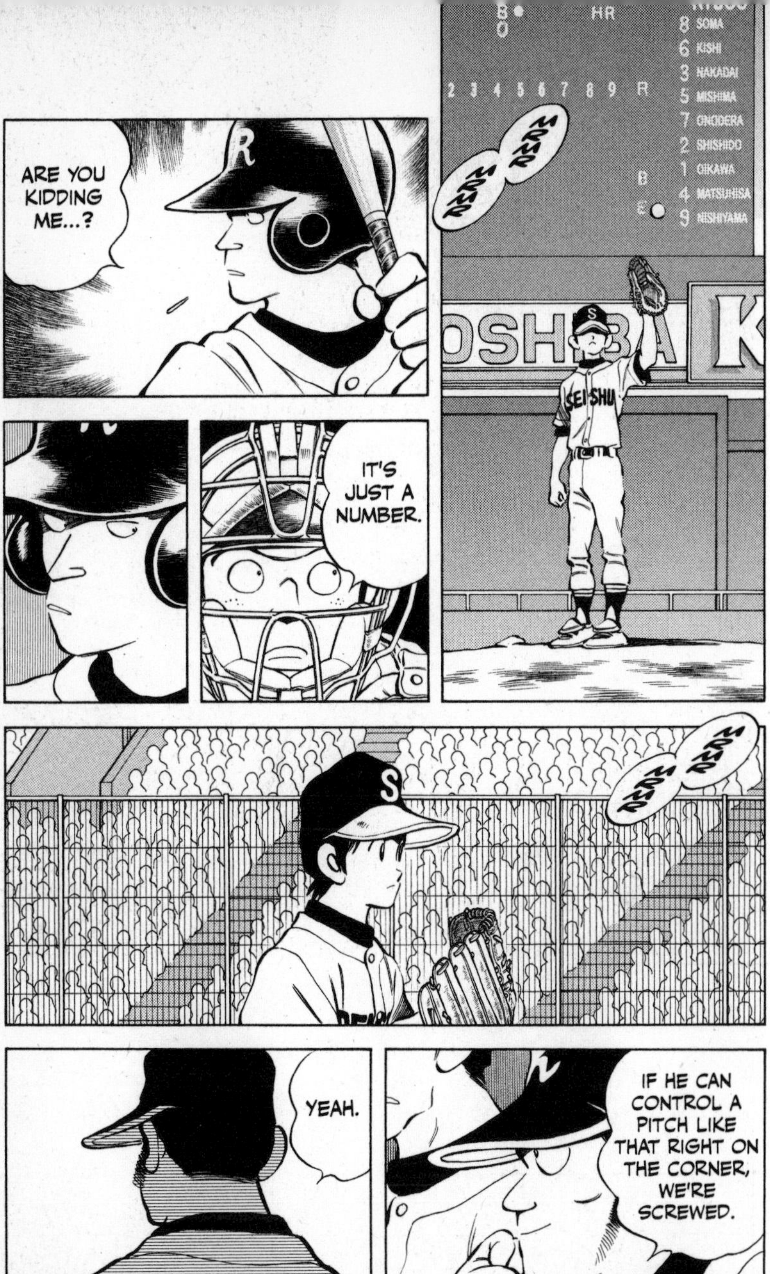
8 SOMA
6 KISHI
3 NAKADAI
5 MISHIMA
7 ONODERA
2 SHISHIDO
1 OIKAWA
4 MATSUHISA
9 NISHIYAMA
MRMR
MRMR
SEISHU
ARE YOU KIDDING ME...?
IT'S JUST A NUMBER.
MRMR
MRMR
IF HE CAN CONTROL A PITCH LIKE THAT RIGHT ON THE CORNER, WE'RE SCREWED.
YEAH.

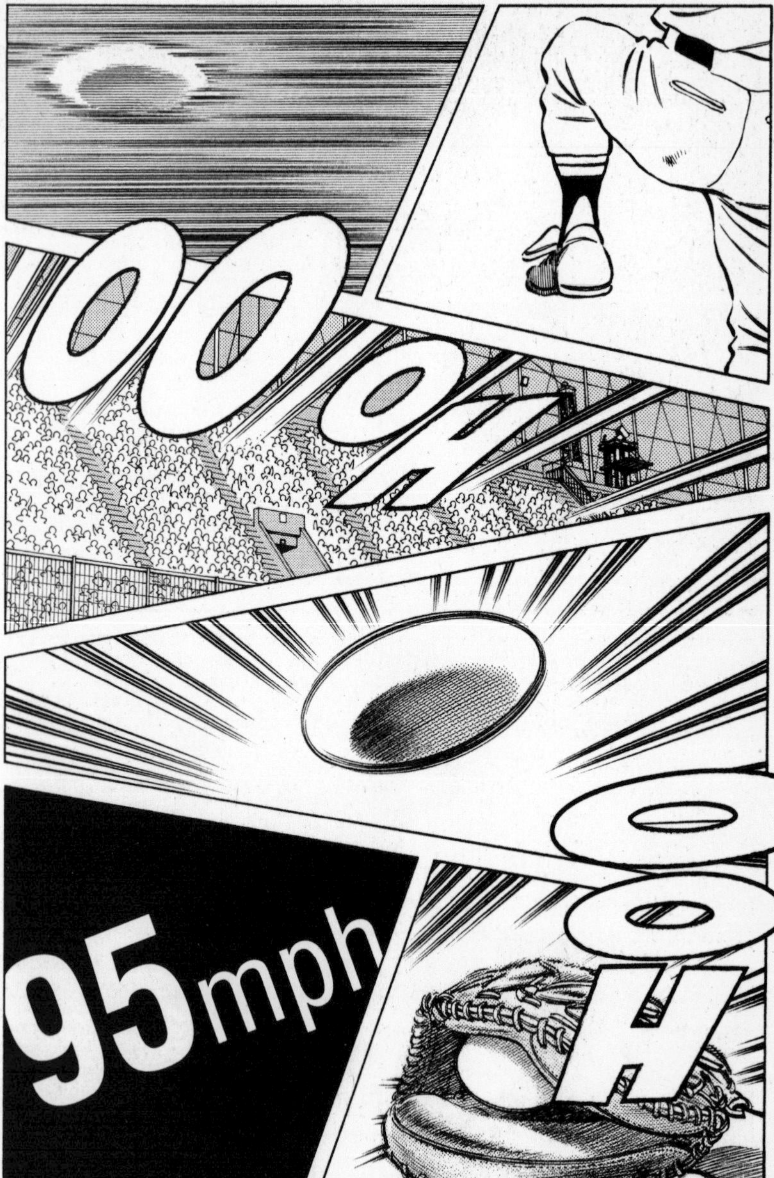
OOOH
OOH
95mph

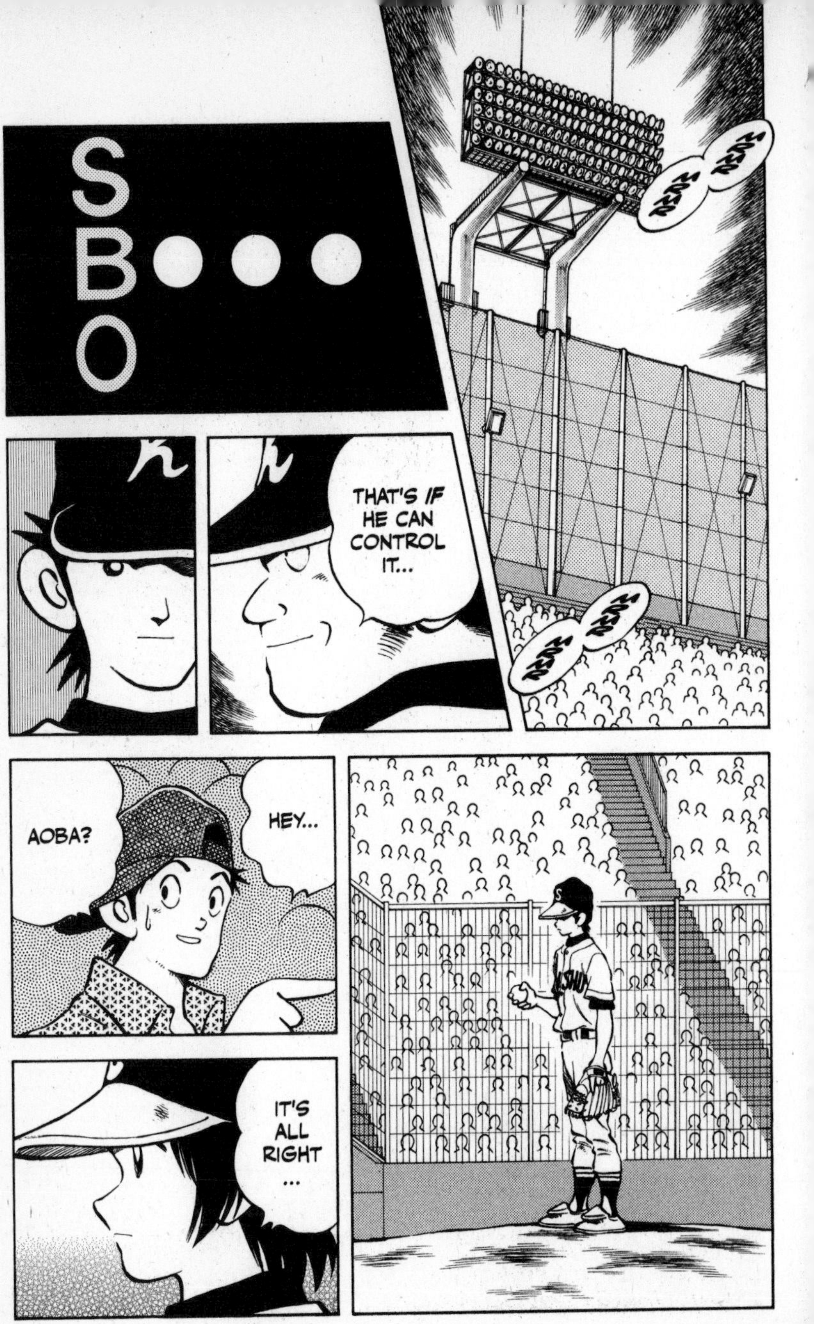
S
B
O
THAT'S *IF* HE CAN CONTROL IT...
HEY...
AOBA?
IT'S ALL RIGHT...

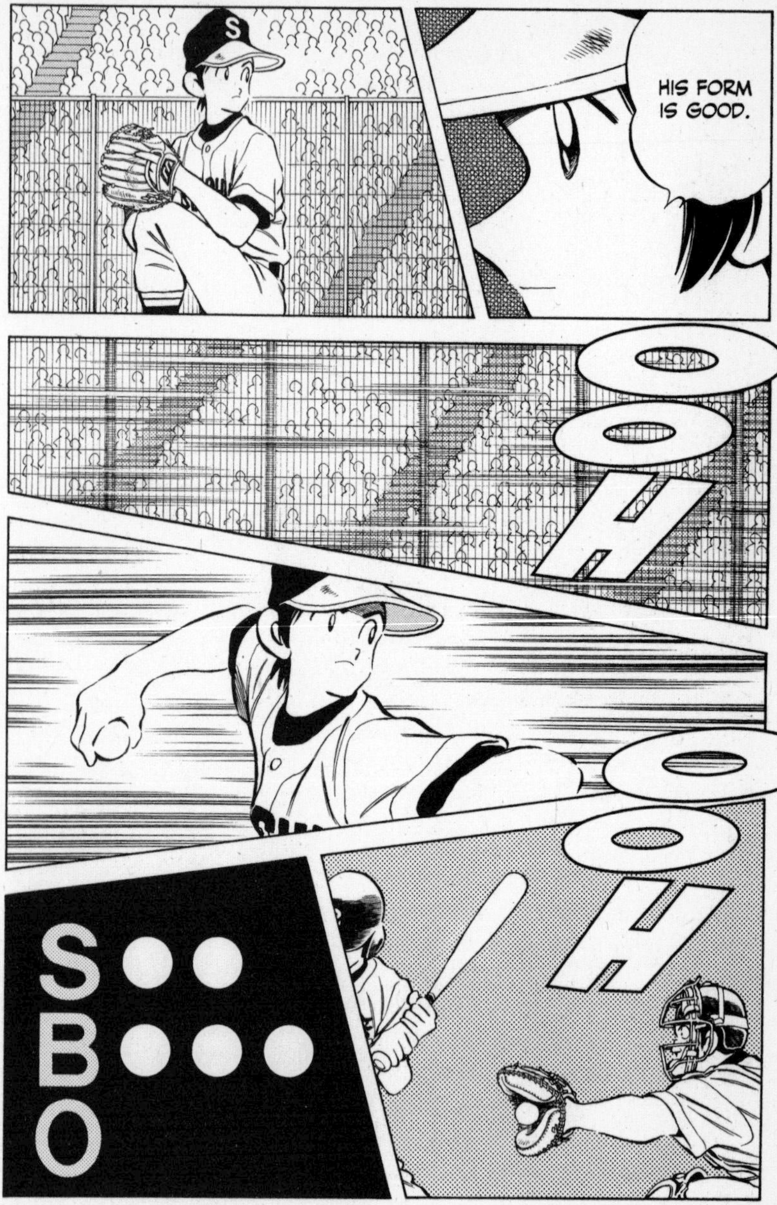
HIS FORM IS GOOD.
OOH
OOH
S
B
O

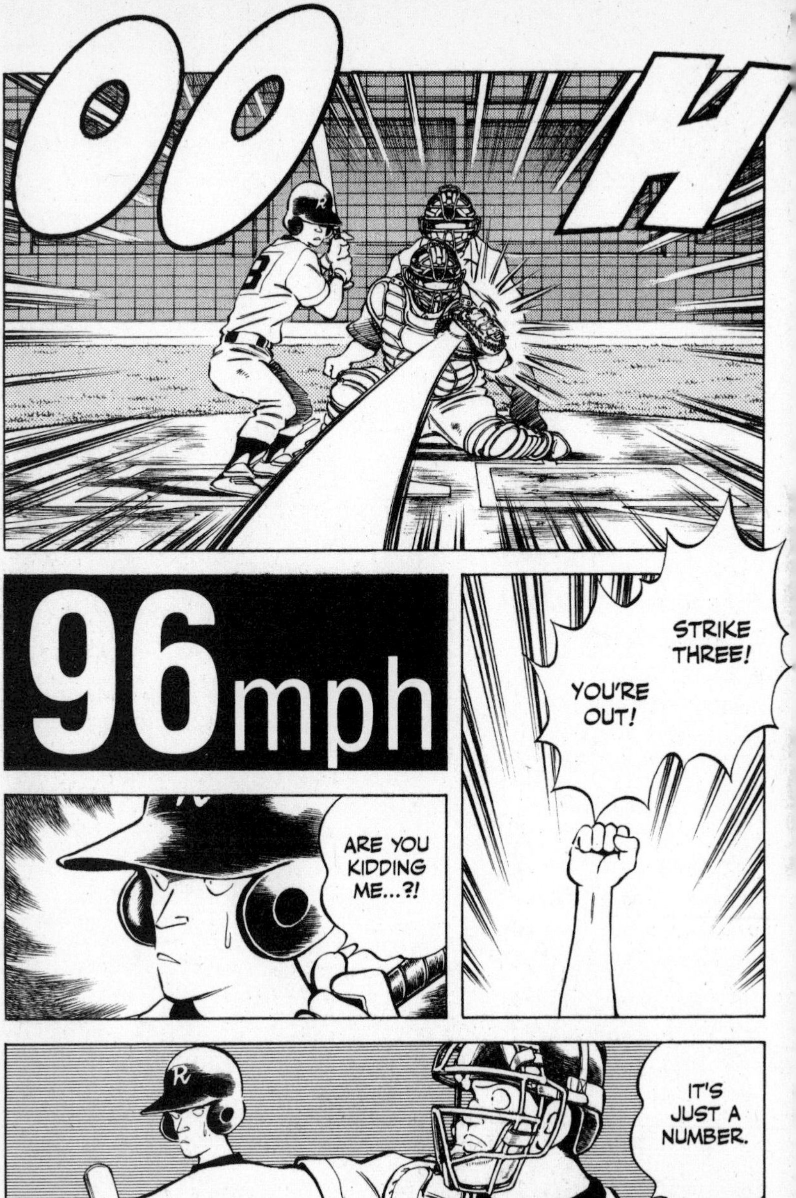
OOH
STRIKE THREE!
YOU'RE OUT!
96mph
ARE YOU KIDDING ME...?!
IT'S JUST A NUMBER.

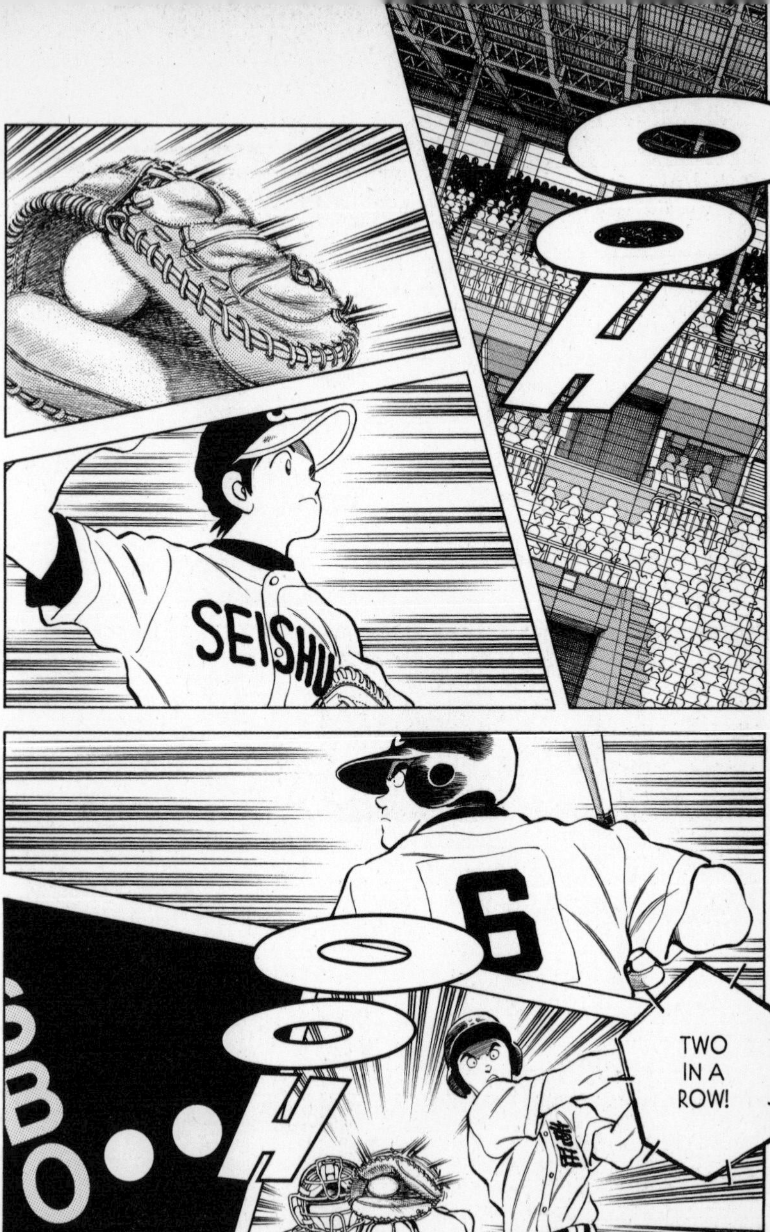
OOH
SEISHU
6
OOH
TWO IN A ROW!
BOO•••

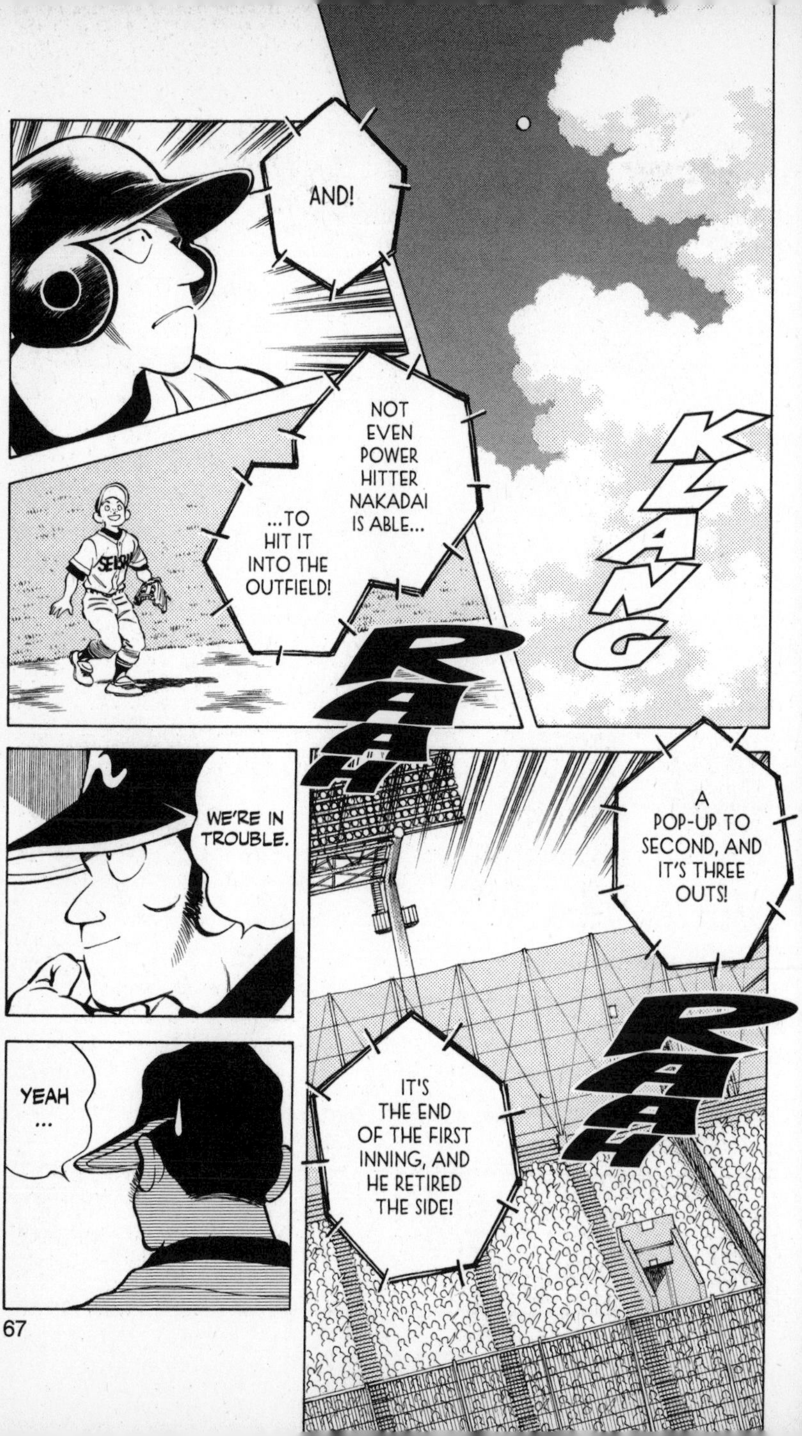
KLANG
AND!
NOT EVEN POWER HITTER NAKADAI IS ABLE...
...TO HIT IT INTO THE OUTFIELD!
RAAAH
A POP-UP TO SECOND, AND IT'S THREE OUTS!
RAAAH
IT'S THE END OF THE FIRST INNING, AND HE RETIRED THE SIDE!
WE'RE IN TROUBLE.
YEAH ...

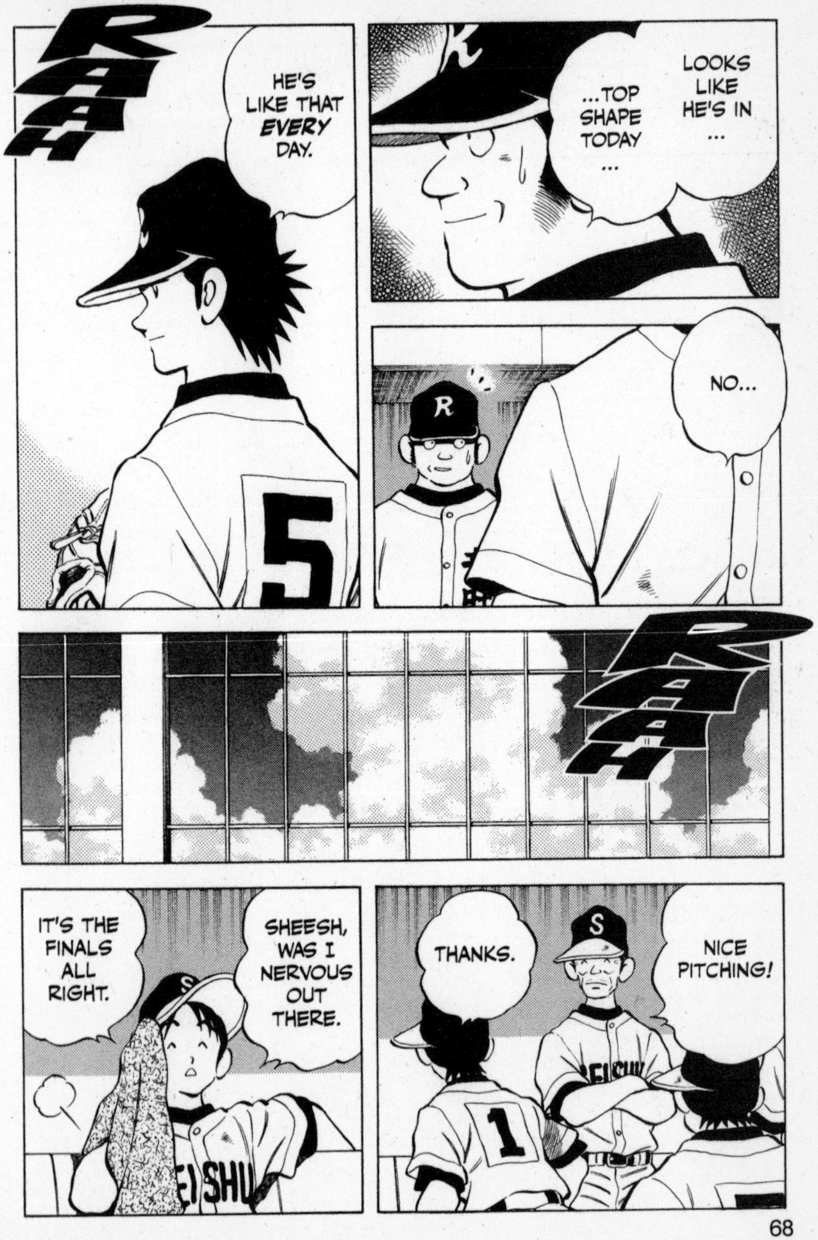
LOOKS LIKE HE'S IN ...
...TOP SHAPE TODAY ...
NO...
HE'S LIKE THAT *EVERY* DAY.
RAAAH
RAAAH
NICE PITCHING!
THANKS.
SHEESH, WAS I NERVOUS OUT THERE.
IT'S THE FINALS ALL RIGHT.

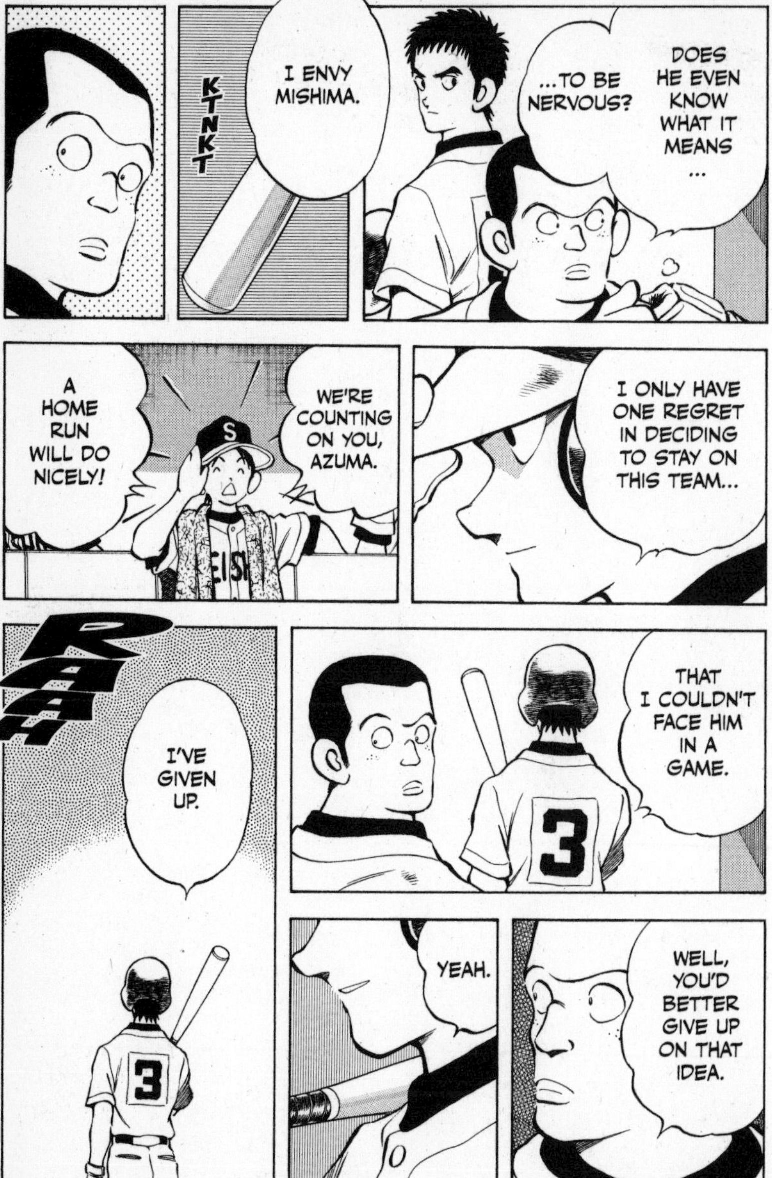
DOES HE EVEN KNOW WHAT IT MEANS ...
...TO BE NERVOUS?
KTNKT
I ENVY MISHIMA.
I ONLY HAVE ONE REGRET IN DECIDING TO STAY ON THIS TEAM...
WE'RE COUNTING ON YOU, AZUMA.
A HOME RUN WILL DO NICELY!
THAT I COULDN'T FACE HIM IN A GAME.
WELL, YOU'D BETTER GIVE UP ON THAT IDEA.
YEAH.
RAAAH
I'VE GIVEN UP.

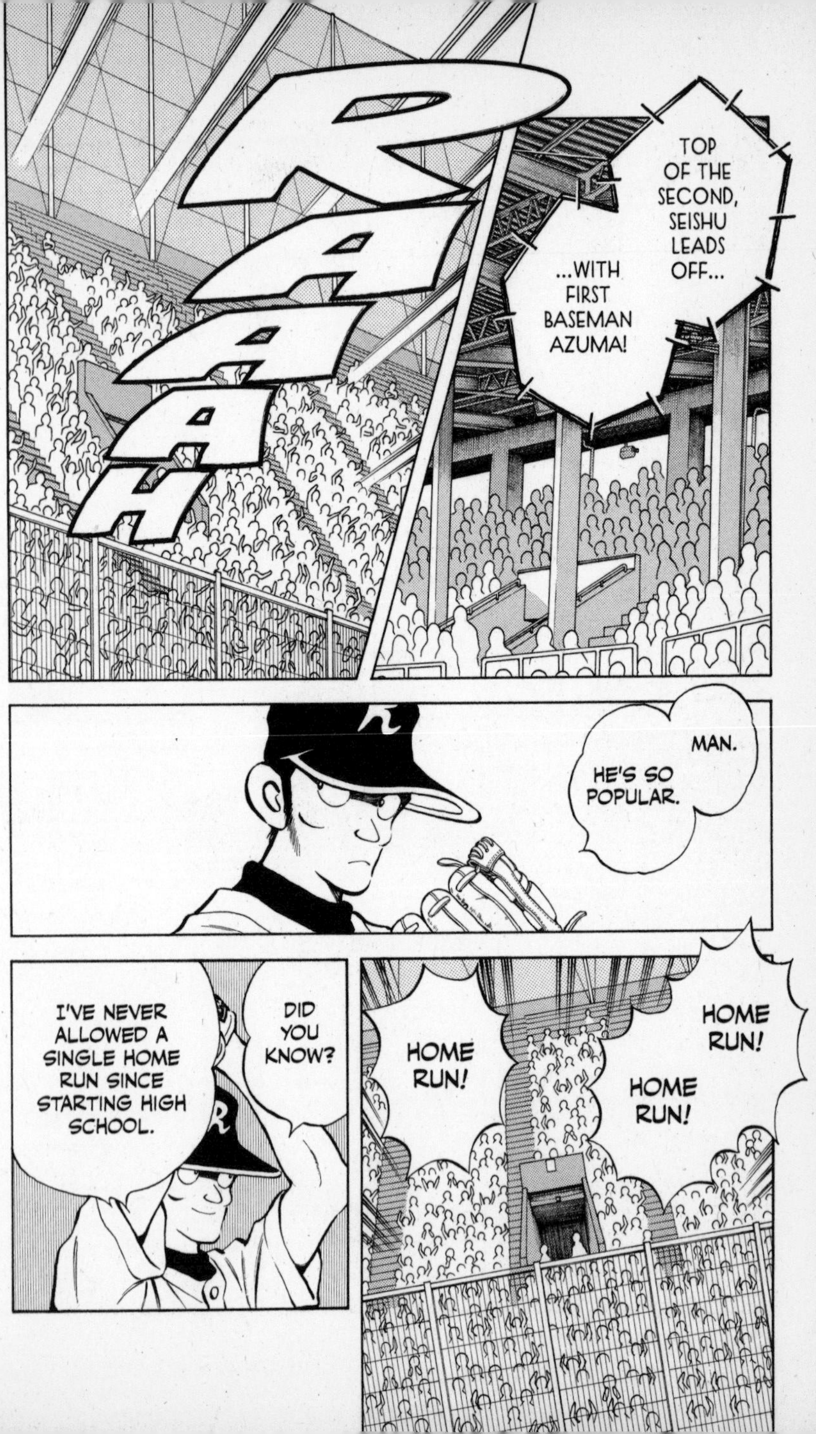
RAAAH
TOP OF THE SECOND, SEISHU LEADS OFF...
...WITH FIRST BASEMAN AZUMA!
MAN.
HE'S SO POPULAR.
HOME RUN!
HOME RUN!
HOME RUN!
DID YOU KNOW?
I'VE NEVER ALLOWED A SINGLE HOME RUN SINCE STARTING HIGH SCHOOL.

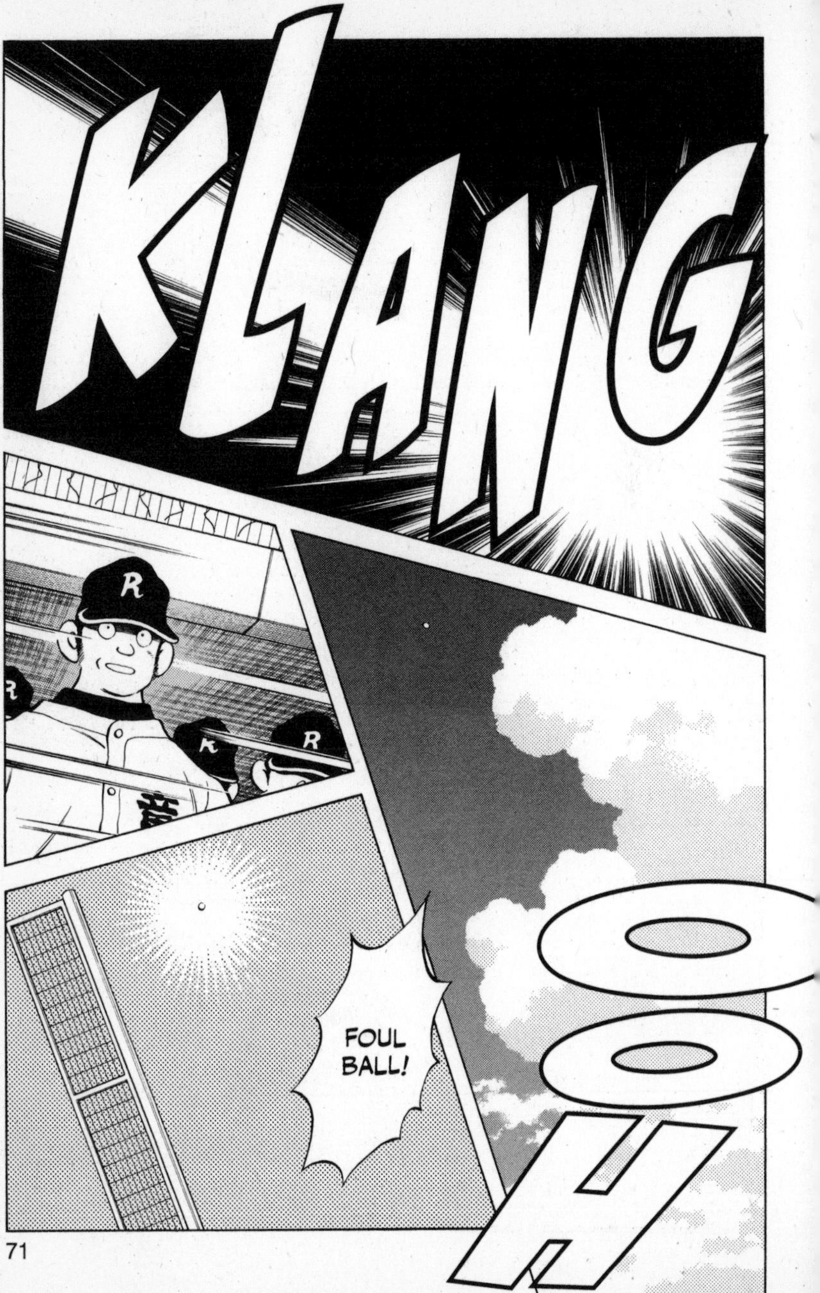
KLANG
OOH
FOUL BALL!

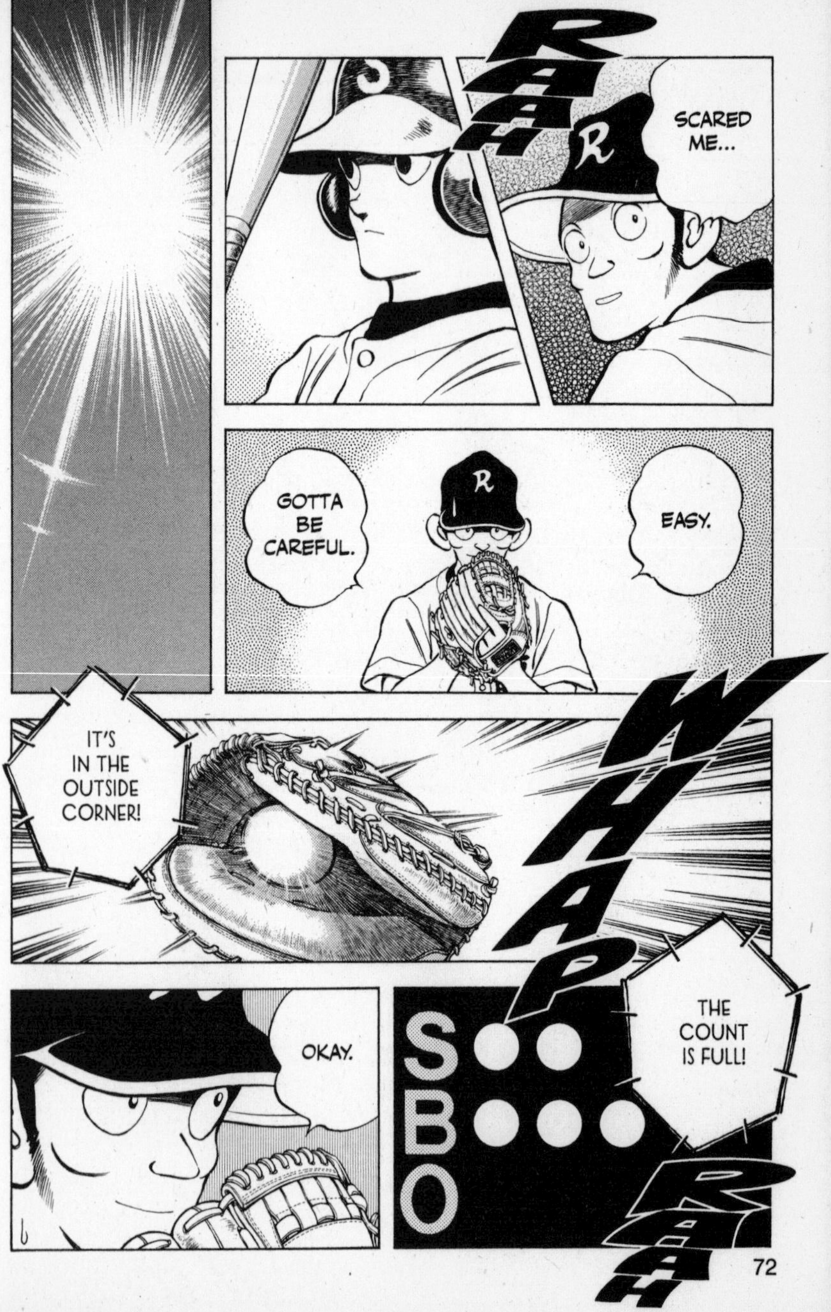
RAAAH
SCARED ME...
EASY.
GOTTA BE CAREFUL.
WHAP
IT'S IN THE OUTSIDE CORNER!
THE COUNT IS FULL!
S
B
O
RAAAH
OKAY.

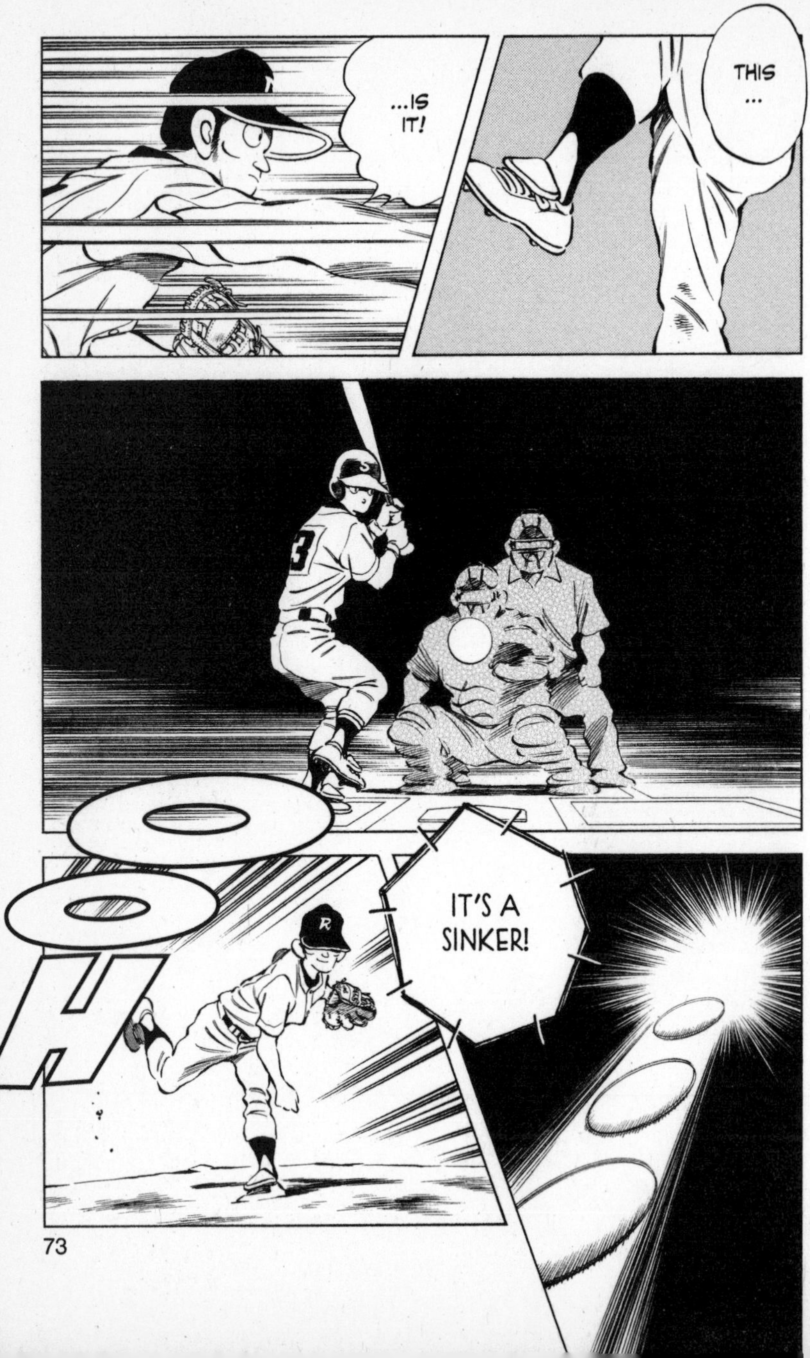
THIS ...
...IS IT!
IT'S A SINKER!
OOH

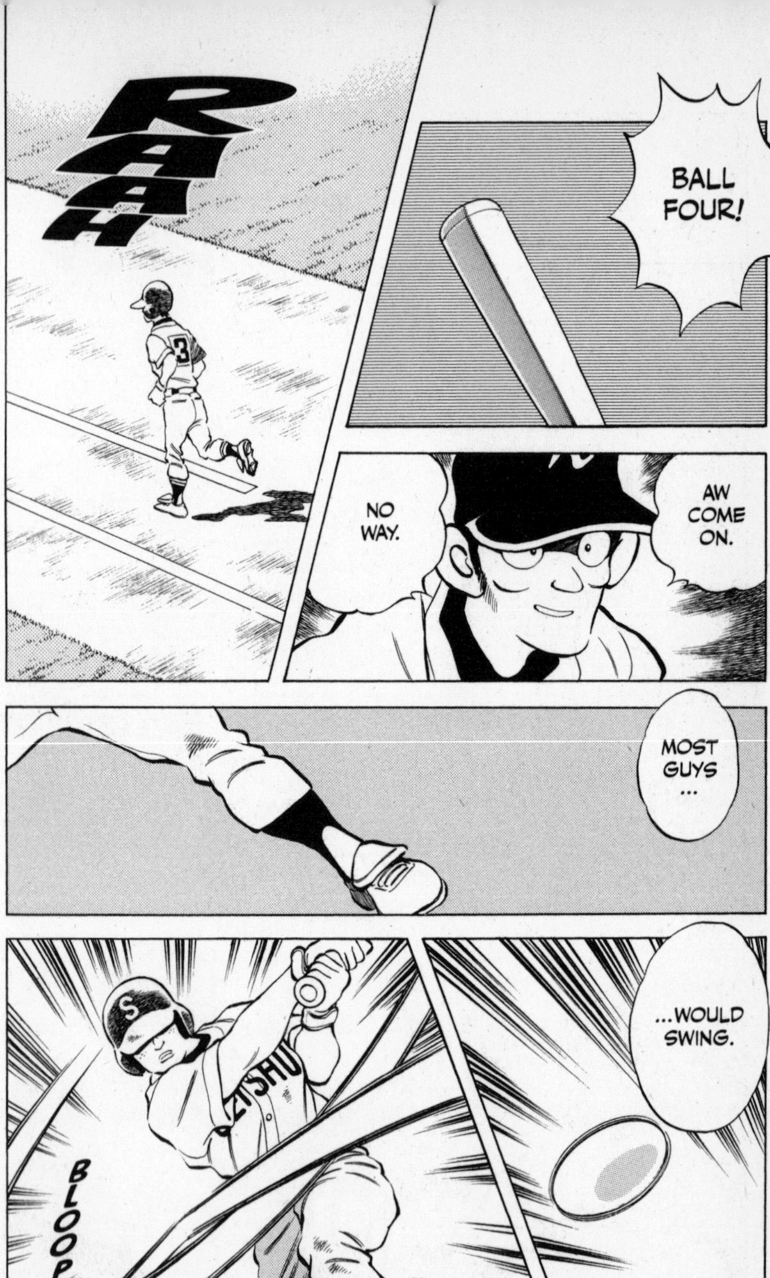
BALL FOUR!
AW COME ON.
NO WAY.
RAAAH
MOST GUYS ...
...WOULD SWING.
BLOOP

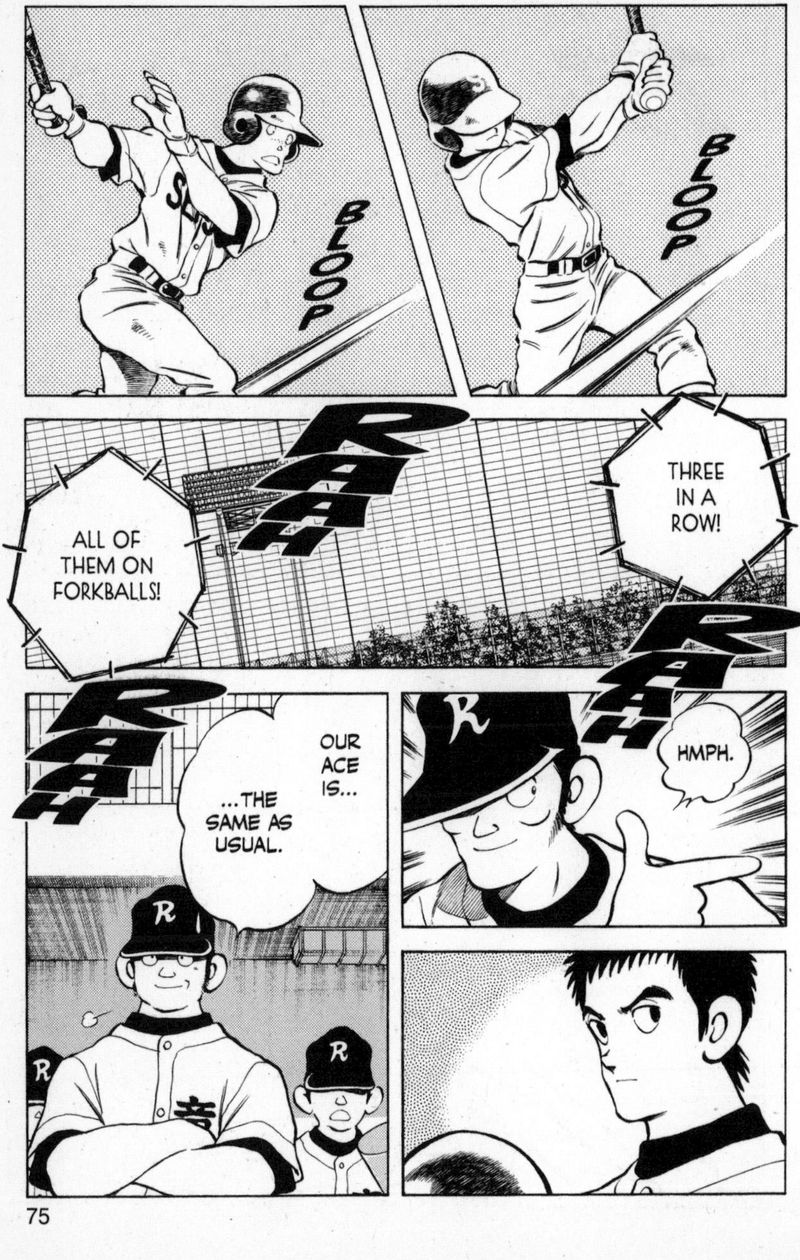
BLOOP
BLOOP
THREE IN A ROW!
RAAAH
ALL OF THEM ON FORKBALLS!
RAAAH
HMPH.
RAAAH
OUR ACE IS...
...THE SAME AS USUAL.

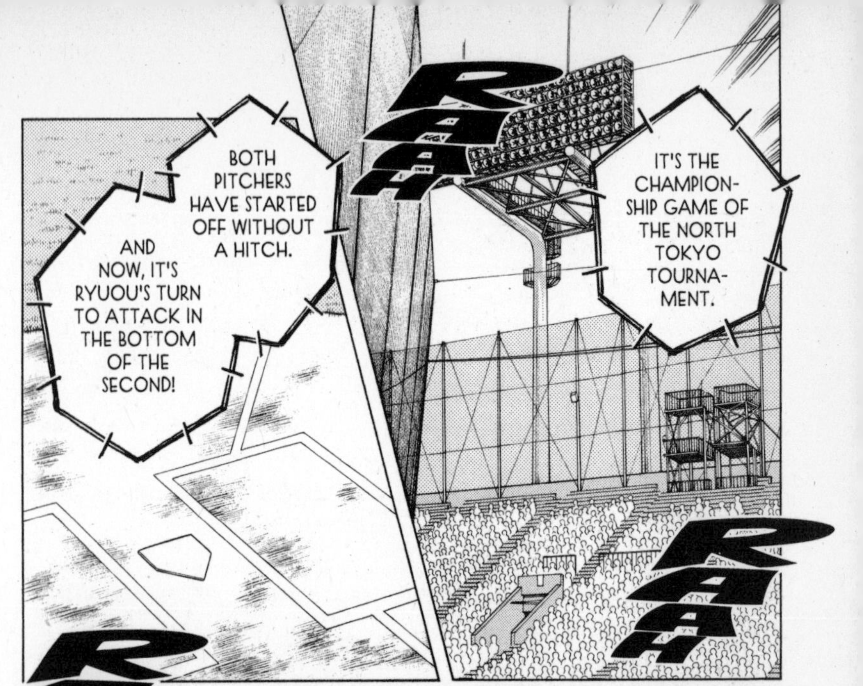
IT'S THE CHAMPIONSHIP GAME OF THE NORTH TOKYO TOURNAMENT.
BOTH PITCHERS HAVE STARTED OFF WITHOUT A HITCH.
AND NOW, IT'S RYUOU'S TURN TO ATTACK IN THE BOTTOM OF THE SECOND!

15 MISHIMA

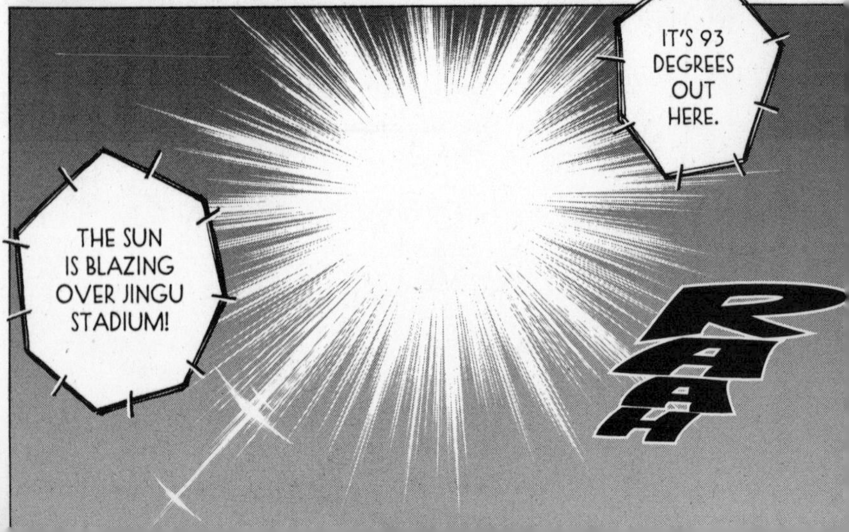
IT'S 93 DEGREES OUT HERE.
THE SUN IS BLAZING OVER JINGU STADIUM!

CHAPTER 145
GO BY IN A FLASH

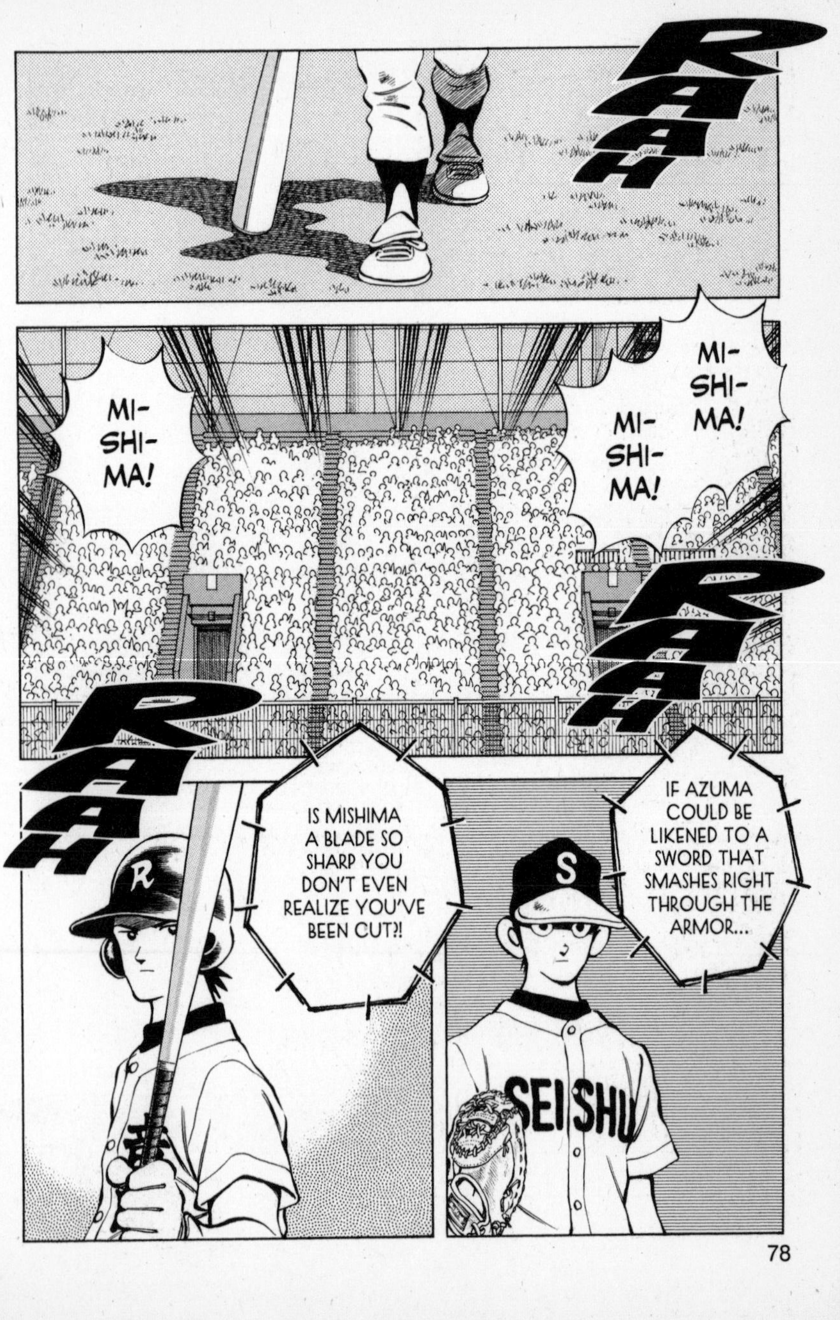
RAAH
MI-SHI-MA!
MI-SHI-MA!
MI-SHI-MA!
RAAH
IF AZUMA COULD BE LIKENED TO A SWORD THAT SMASHES RIGHT THROUGH THE ARMOR...
SEISHU
IS MISHIMA A BLADE SO SHARP YOU DON'T EVEN REALIZE YOU'VE BEEN CUT?!
RAAH

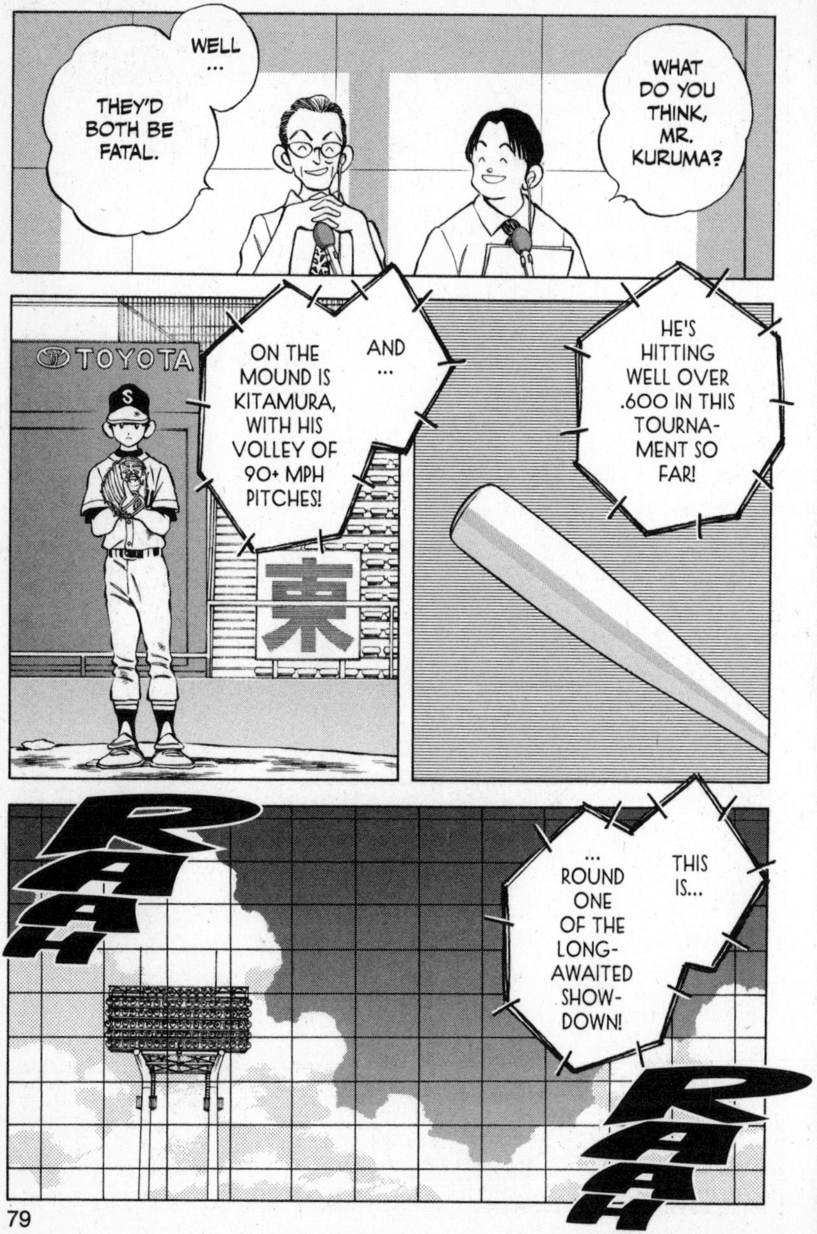

WHAT DO YOU THINK, MR. KURUMA?
WELL ...
THEY'D BOTH BE FATAL.
HE'S HITTING WELL OVER .600 IN THIS TOURNAMENT SO FAR!
AND ...
ON THE MOUND IS KITAMURA, WITH HIS VOLLEY OF 90+ MPH PITCHES!
TOYOTA
東
THIS IS...
... ROUND ONE OF THE LONG-AWAITED SHOWDOWN!
RAAH
RAAH

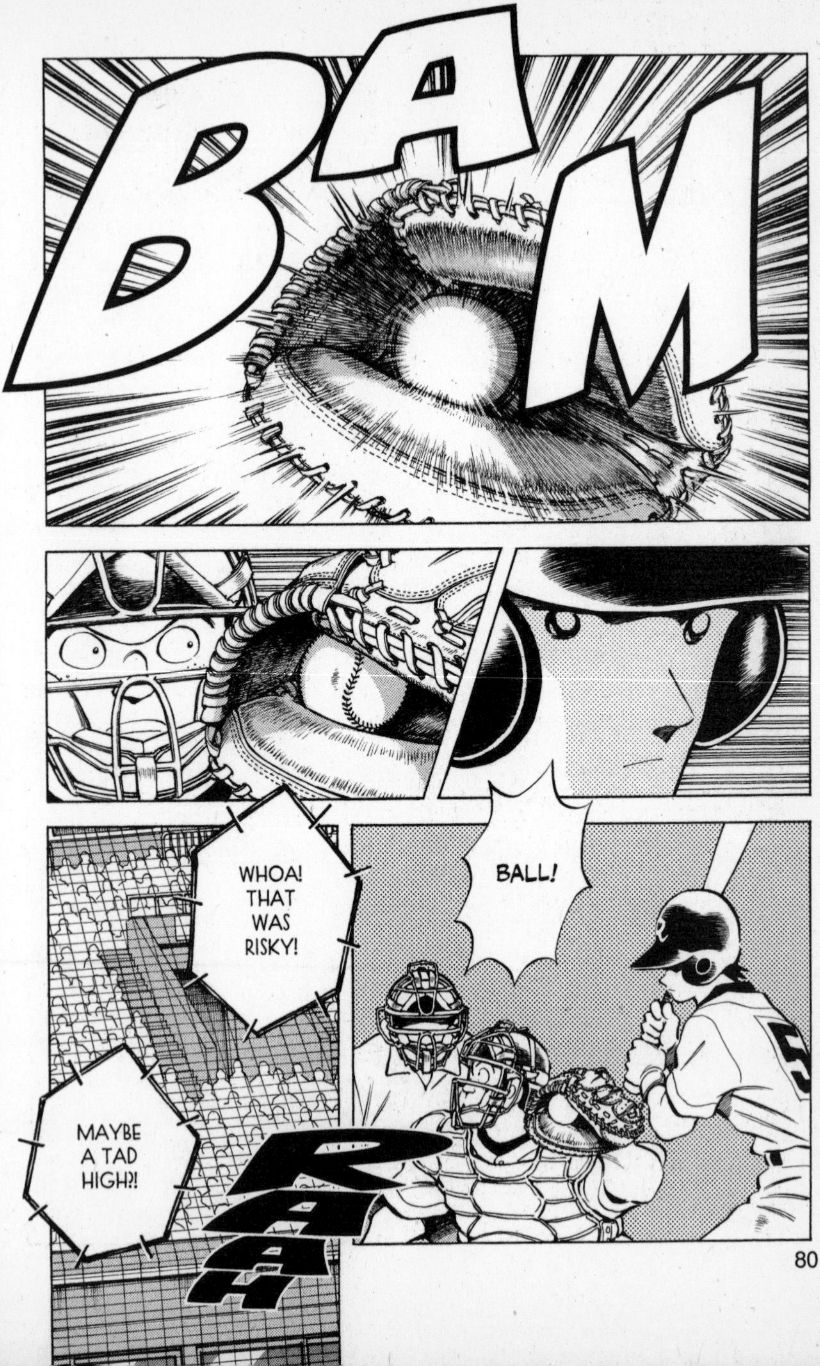
BAM
BALL!
WHOA! THAT WAS RISKY!
MAYBE A TAD HIGH?!
RAAH

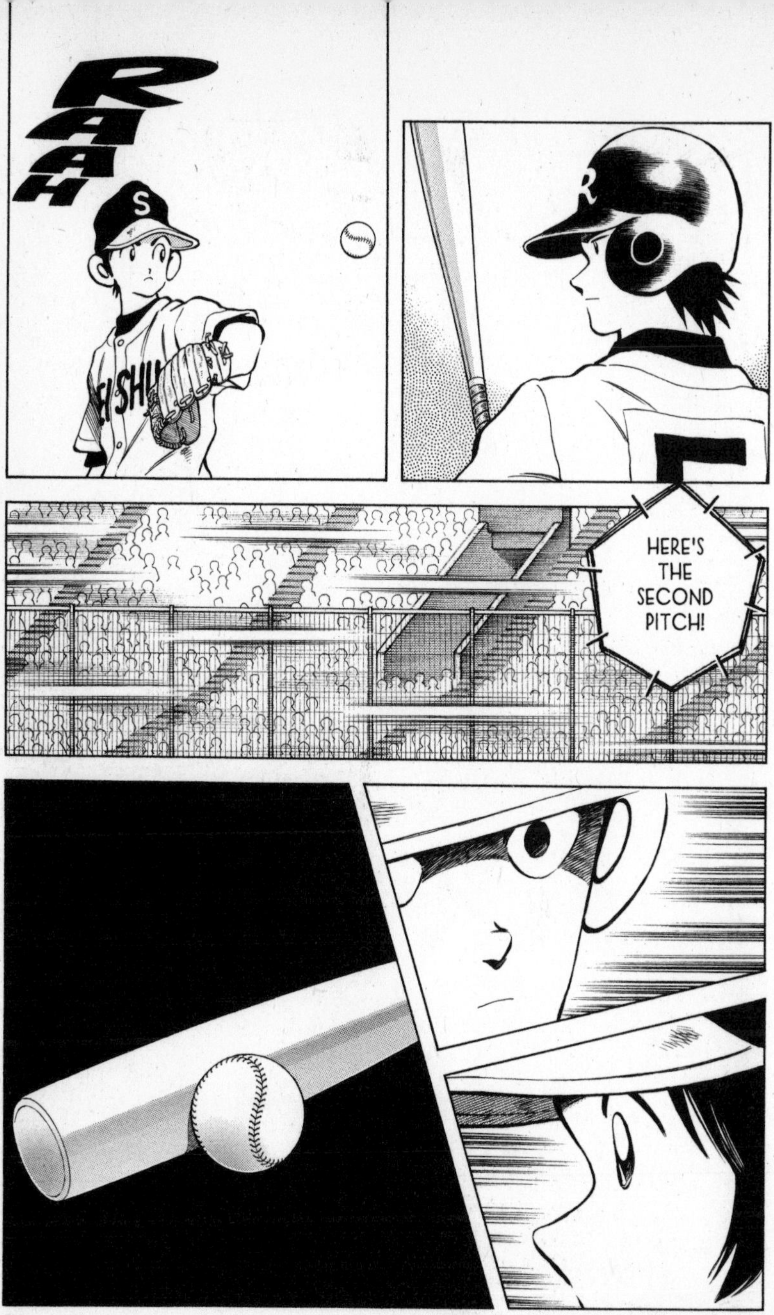
RAAH
HERE'S THE SECOND PITCH!

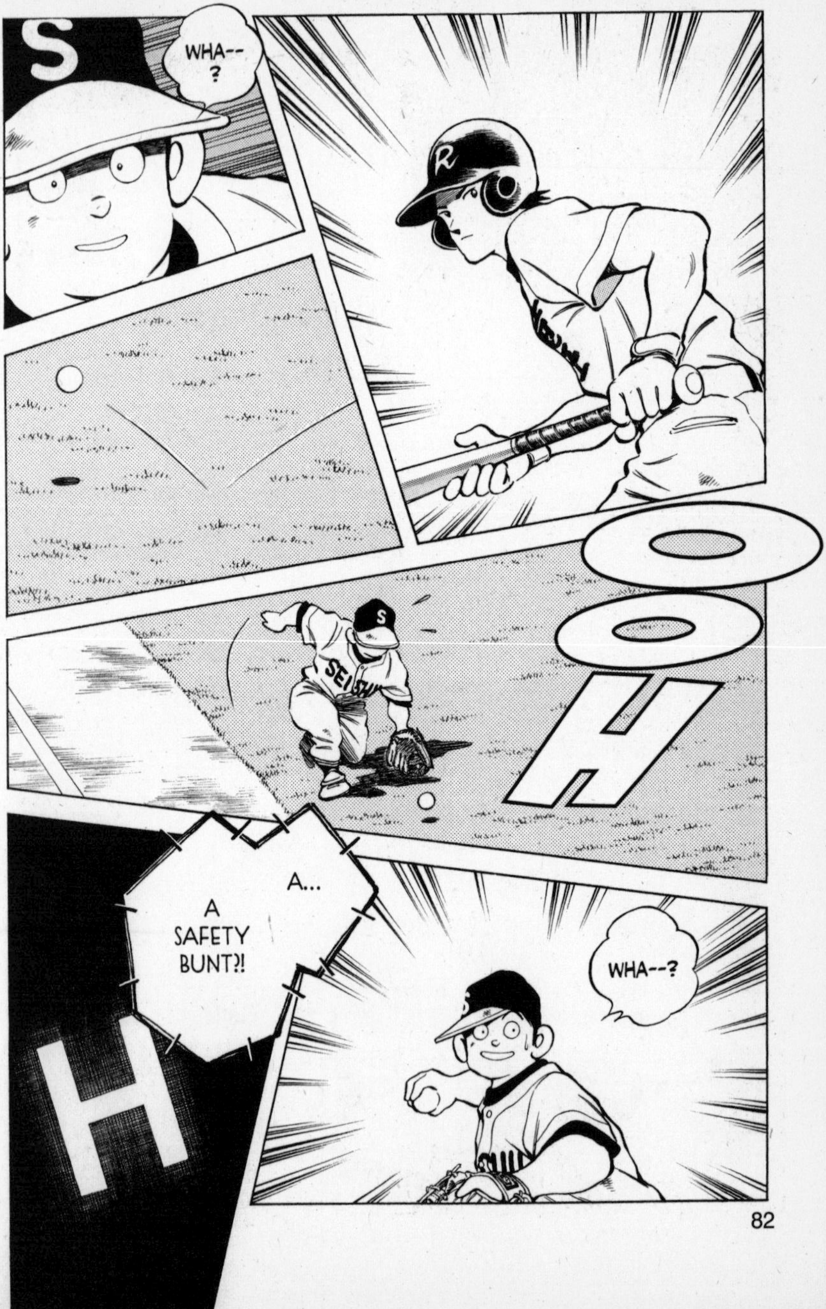
WHA-- ?
OOH
WHA--?
A... A SAFETY BUNT?!
H

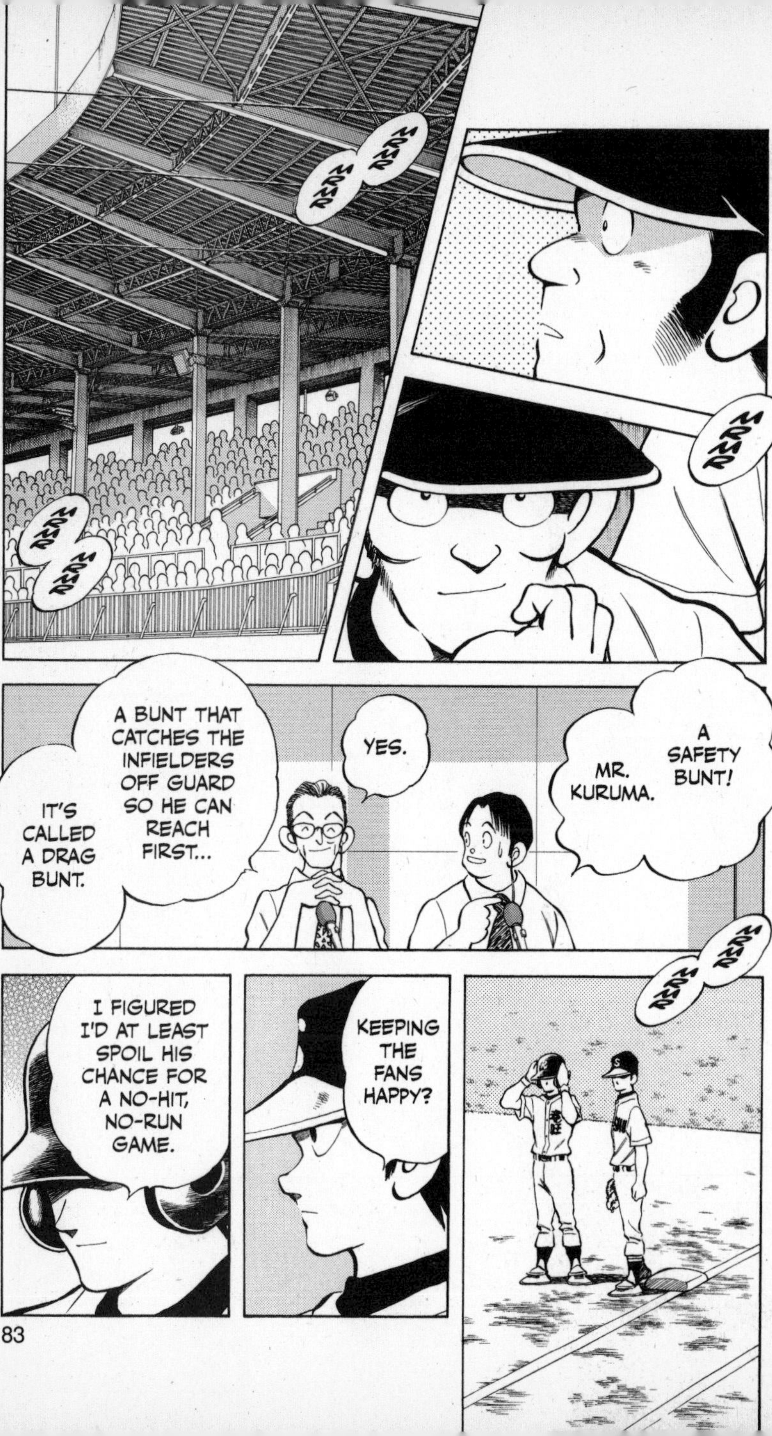
MRMR
MRMR
MRMR
MRMR
MRMR
MRMR. KURUMA. A SAFETY BUNT!
YES.
A BUNT THAT CATCHES THE INFIELDERS OFF GUARD SO HE CAN REACH FIRST...
IT'S CALLED A DRAG BUNT.
MRMR
MRMR
KEEPING THE FANS HAPPY?
I FIGURED I'D AT LEAST SPOIL HIS CHANCE FOR A NO-HIT, NO-RUN GAME.

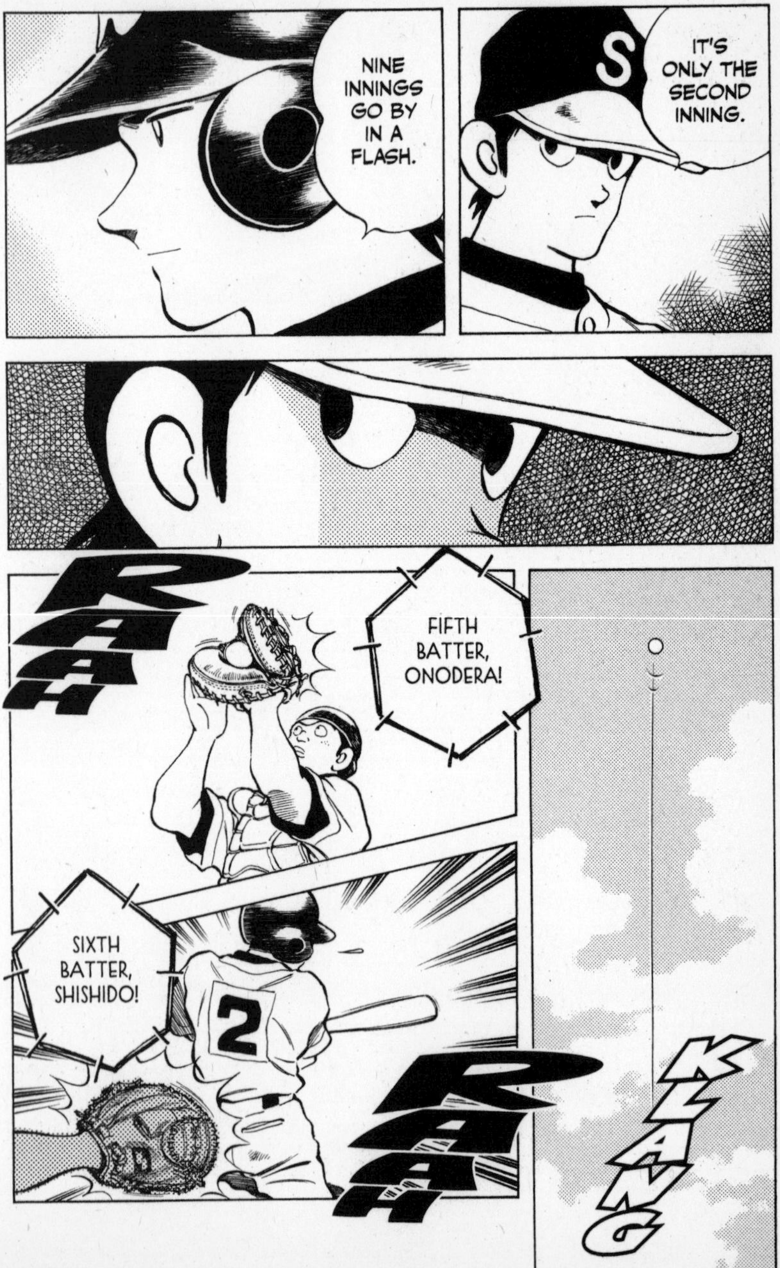
IT'S ONLY THE SECOND INNING.
NINE INNINGS GO BY IN A FLASH.
KLANG
FIFTH BATTER, ONODERA!
RAAH
SIXTH BATTER, SHISHIDO!
RAAH

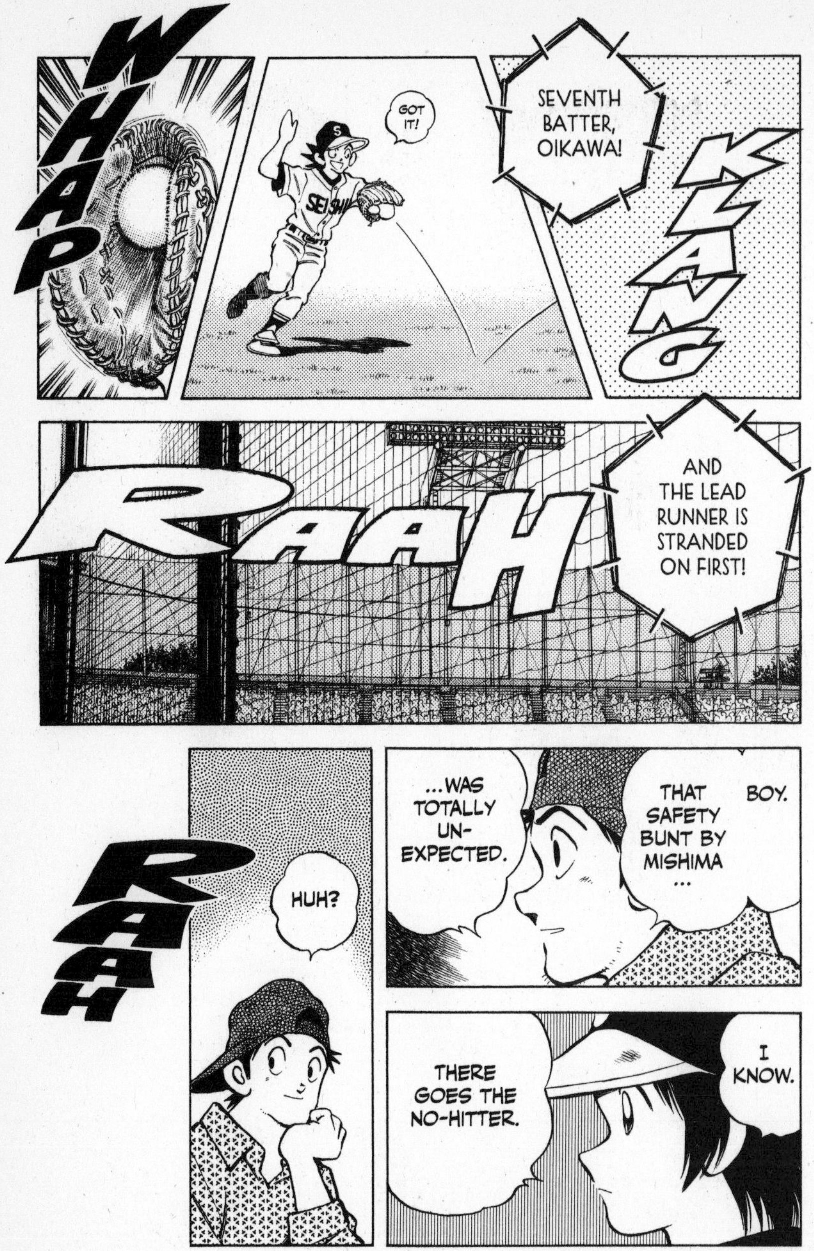
SEVENTH BATTER, OIKAWA!
KLANG
GOT IT!
WHAP
AND THE LEAD RUNNER IS STRANDED ON FIRST!
RAAH
BOY.
THAT SAFETY BUNT BY MISHIMA ...
...WAS TOTALLY UN-EXPECTED.
I KNOW.
THERE GOES THE NO-HITTER.
HUH?
RAAAH

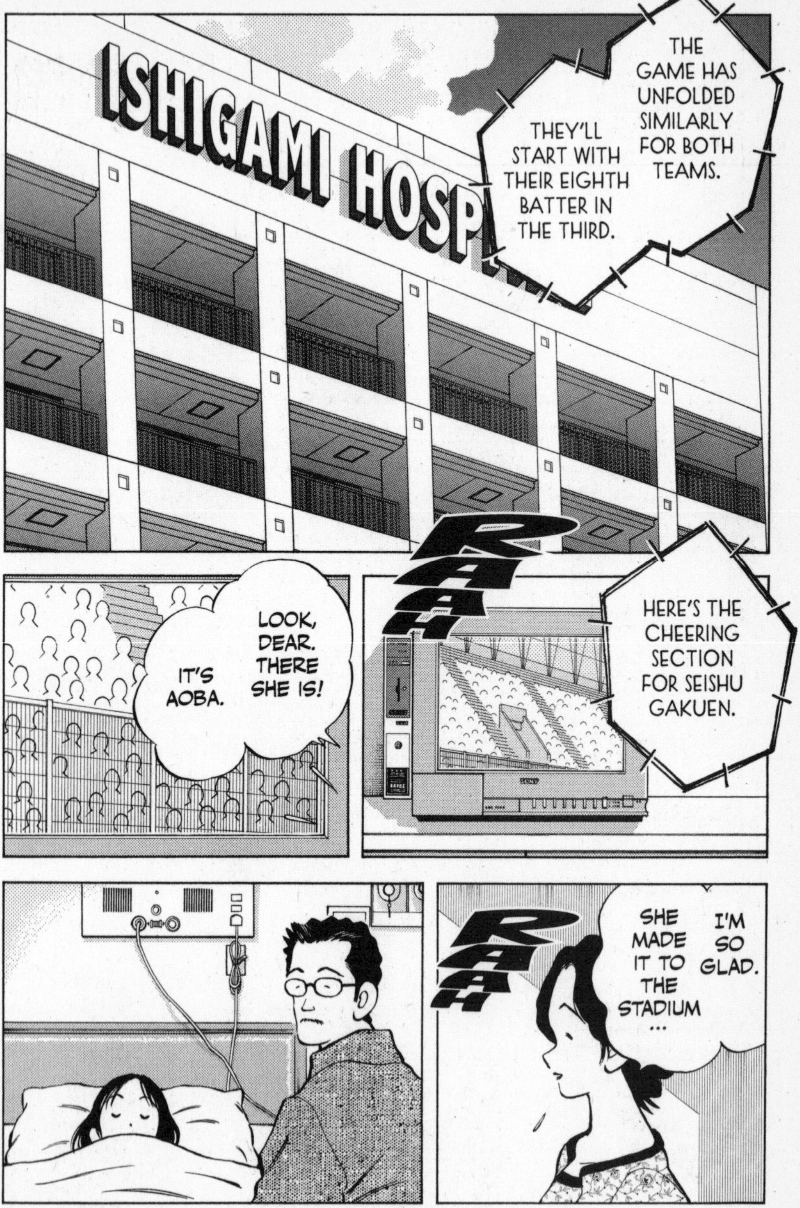
ISHIGAMI HOSP
THE GAME HAS UNFOLDED SIMILARLY FOR BOTH TEAMS.
THEY'LL START WITH THEIR EIGHTH BATTER IN THE THIRD.
RAAH
HERE'S THE CHEERING SECTION FOR SEISHU GAKUEN.
LOOK, DEAR. THERE SHE IS!
IT'S AOBA.
RAAH
I'M SO GLAD.
SHE MADE IT TO THE STADIUM...

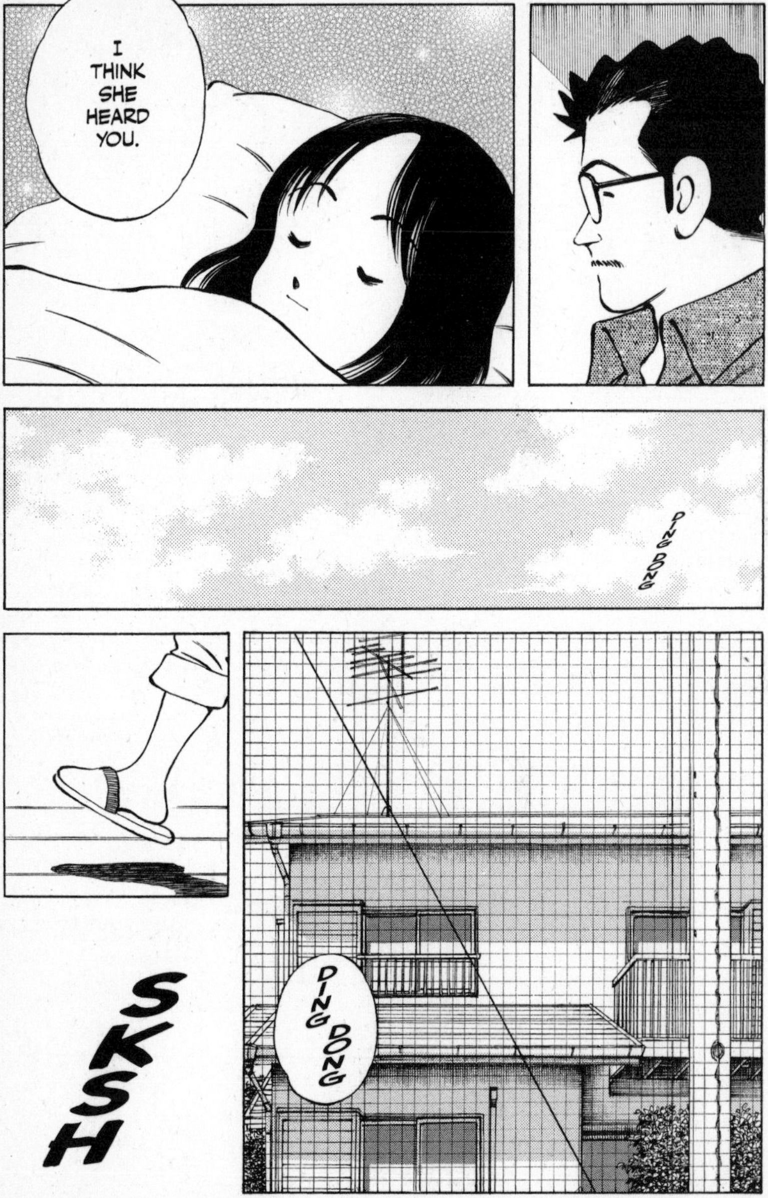
I THINK SHE HEARD YOU.
DING DONG
DING DONG
SKSH

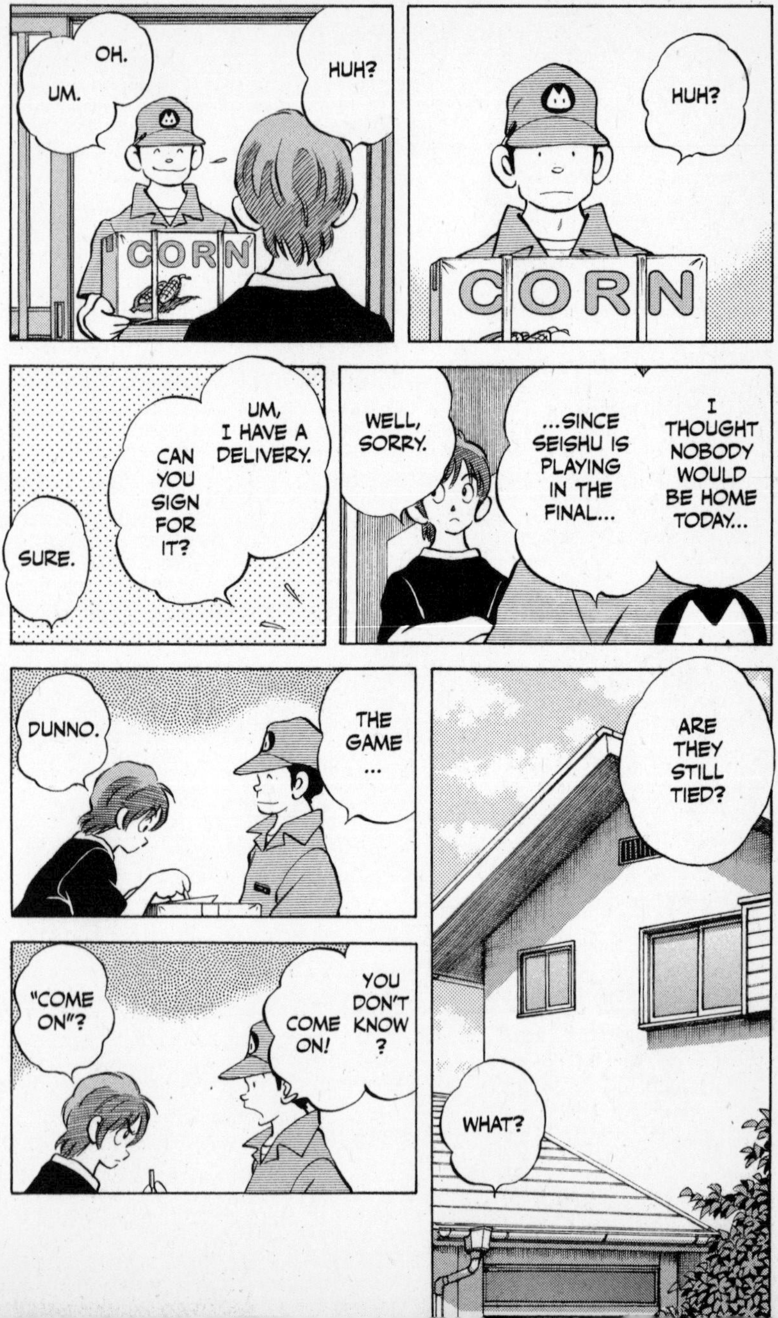
HUH?
HUH?
OH. UM.
I THOUGHT NOBODY WOULD BE HOME TODAY...
...SINCE SEISHU IS PLAYING IN THE FINAL...
WELL, SORRY.
UM, I HAVE A DELIVERY.
CAN YOU SIGN FOR IT?
SURE.
ARE THEY STILL TIED?
WHAT?
THE GAME ...
DUNNO.
YOU DON'T KNOW ?
COME ON!
"COME ON"?

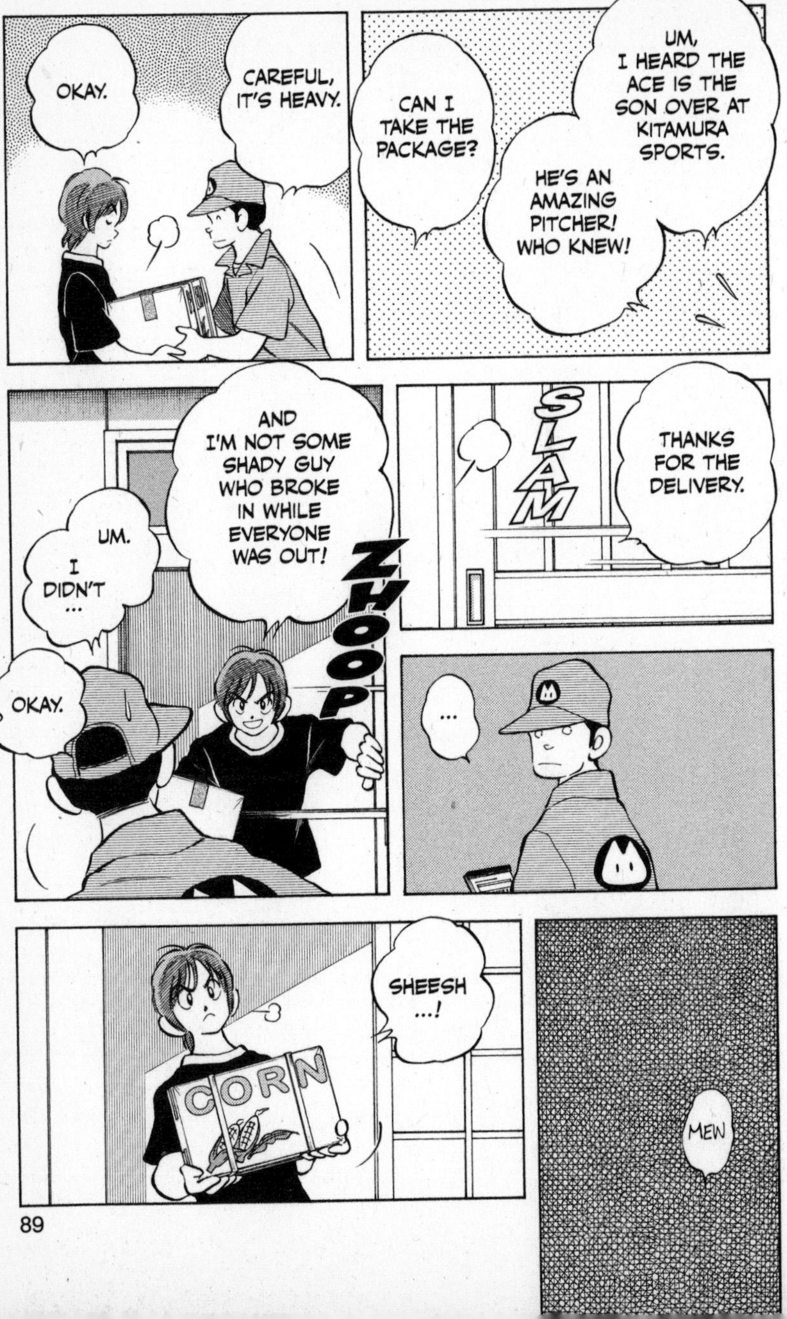
UM, I HEARD THE ACE IS THE SON OVER AT KITAMURA SPORTS.
HE'S AN AMAZING PITCHER! WHO KNEW!
CAN I TAKE THE PACKAGE?
CAREFUL, IT'S HEAVY.
OKAY.
THANKS FOR THE DELIVERY.
SLAM
...
AND I'M NOT SOME SHADY GUY WHO BROKE IN WHILE EVERYONE WAS OUT!
ZHOOOP
UM. I DIDN'T ...
OKAY.
MEW
SHEESH ...!
CORN

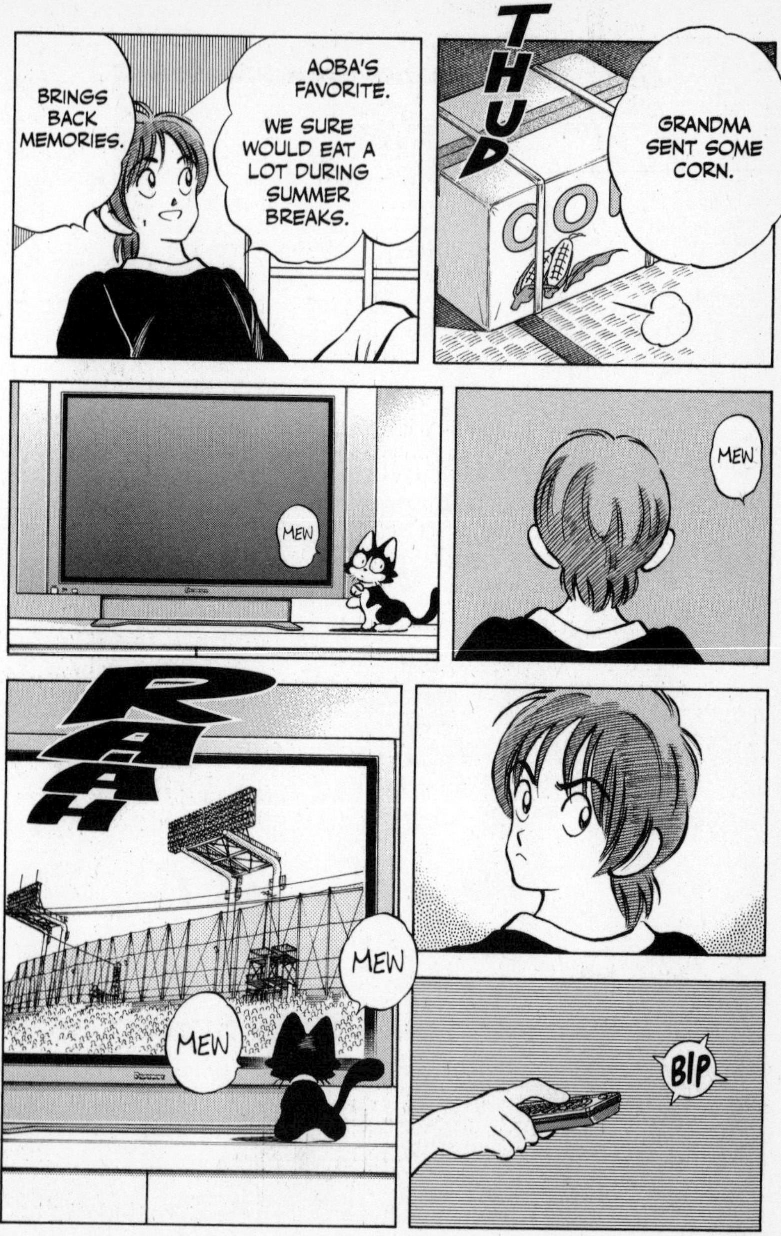
THUD
GRANDMA SENT SOME CORN.
AOBA'S FAVORITE. WE SURE WOULD EAT A LOT DURING SUMMER BREAKS.
BRINGS BACK MEMORIES.
MEW
MEW
BIP
RAAAH
MEW
MEW

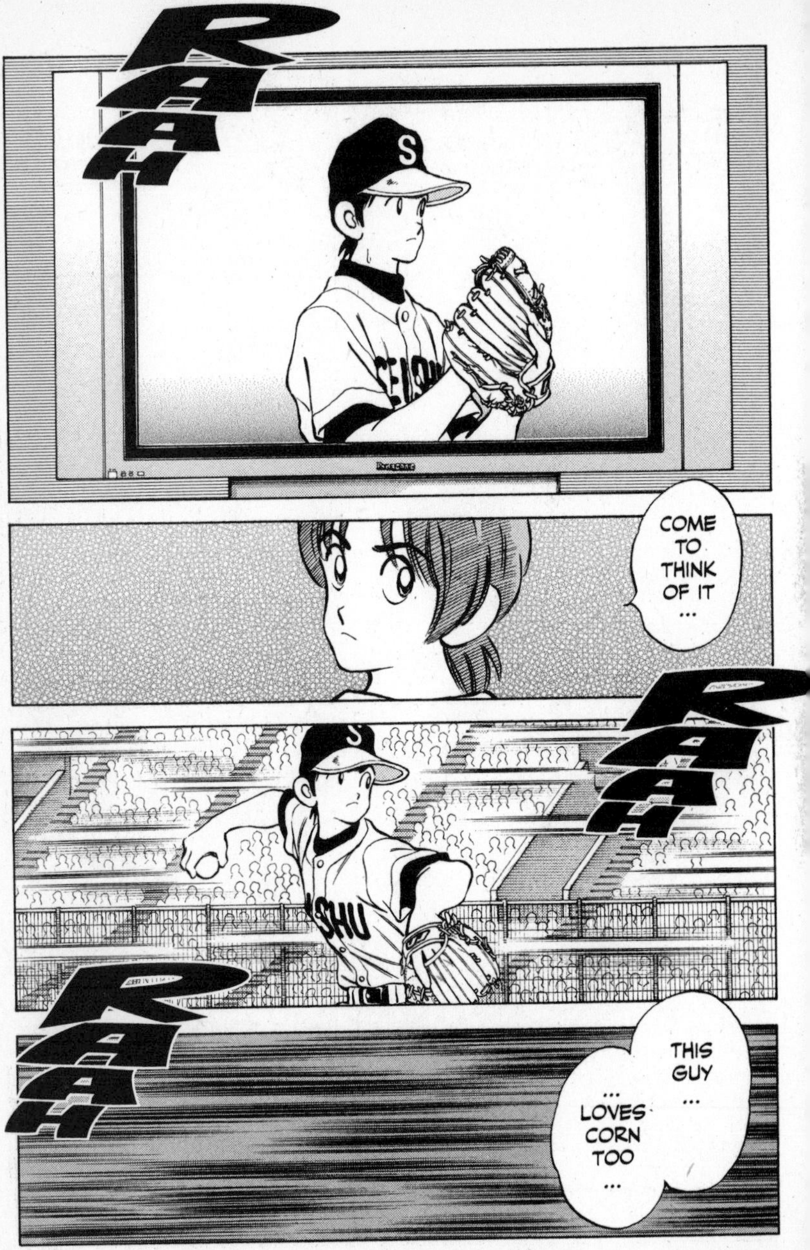
RAAH
COME TO THINK OF IT ...
RAAH
THIS GUY ...
... LOVES CORN TOO ...
RAAH

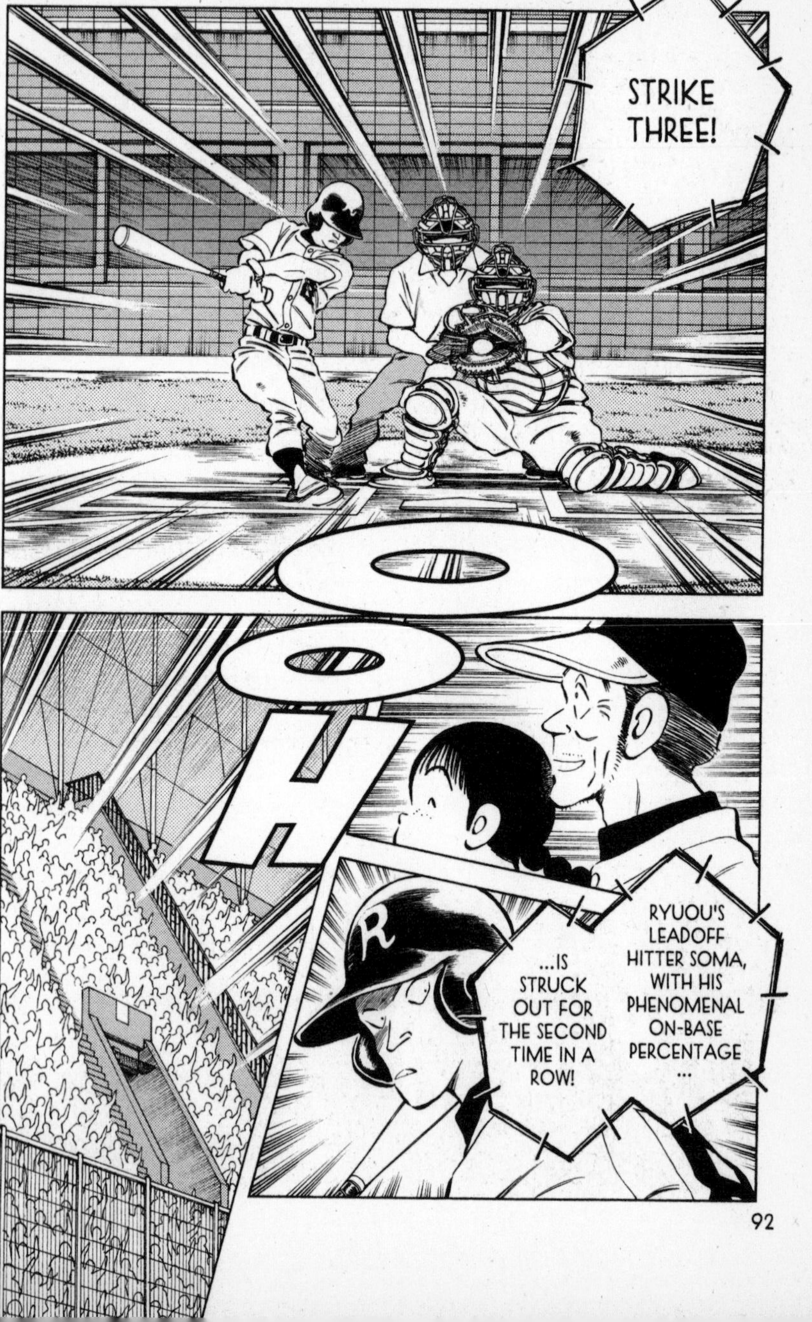
STRIKE THREE!
OOH
RYUOU'S LEADOFF HITTER SOMA, WITH HIS PHENOMENAL ON-BASE PERCENTAGE...
...IS STRUCK OUT FOR THE SECOND TIME IN A ROW!

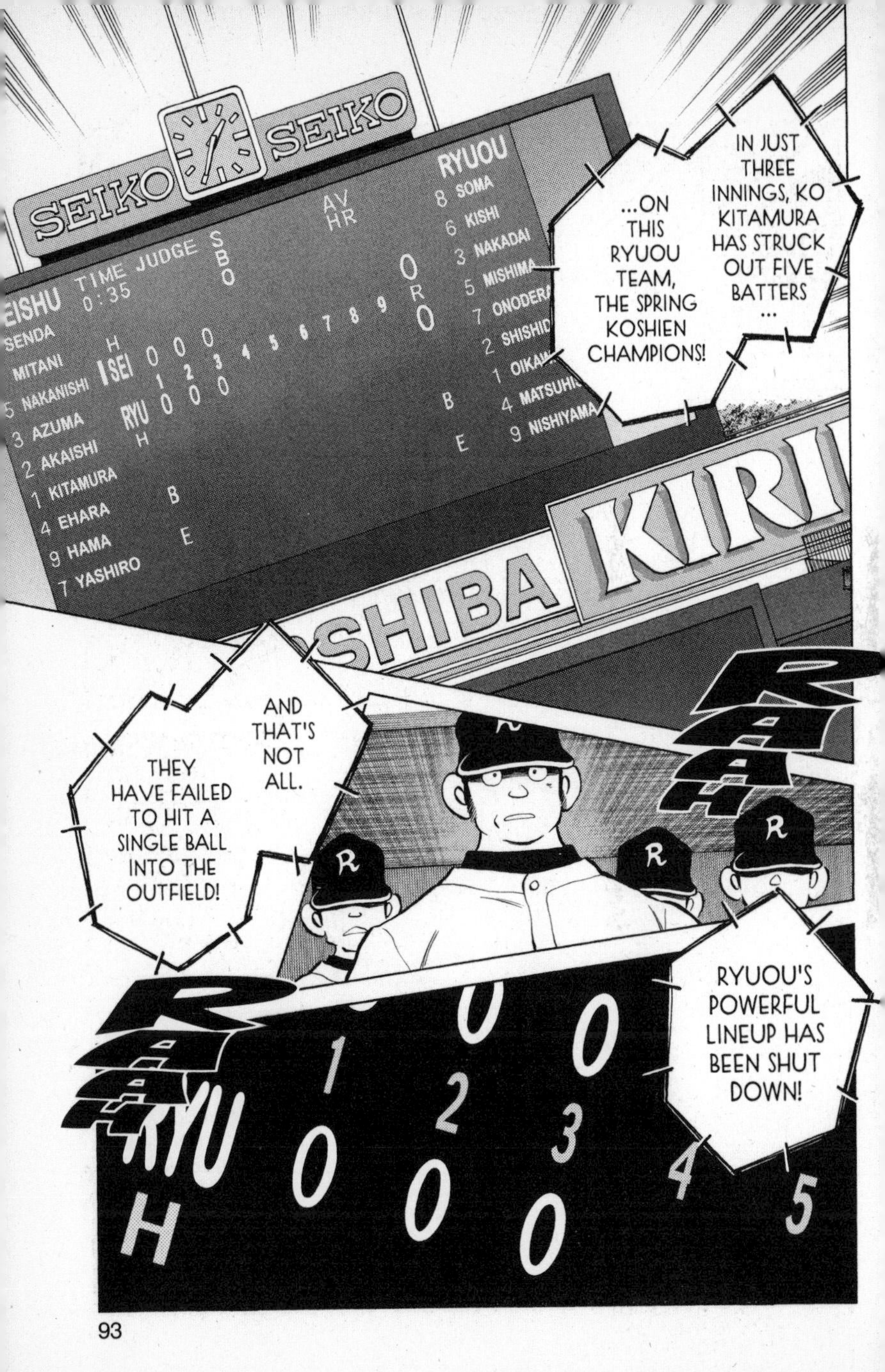
SEIKO
SEIKO
IN JUST THREE INNINGS, KO KITAMURA HAS STRUCK OUT FIVE BATTERS ...
...ON THIS RYUOU TEAM, THE SPRING KOSHIEN CHAMPIONS!
RYUOU
SEISHU
KIRIN
SHIBA
RAAAH
AND THAT'S NOT ALL.
THEY HAVE FAILED TO HIT A SINGLE BALL INTO THE OUTFIELD!
RAAAH
RYUOU'S POWERFUL LINEUP HAS BEEN SHUT DOWN!

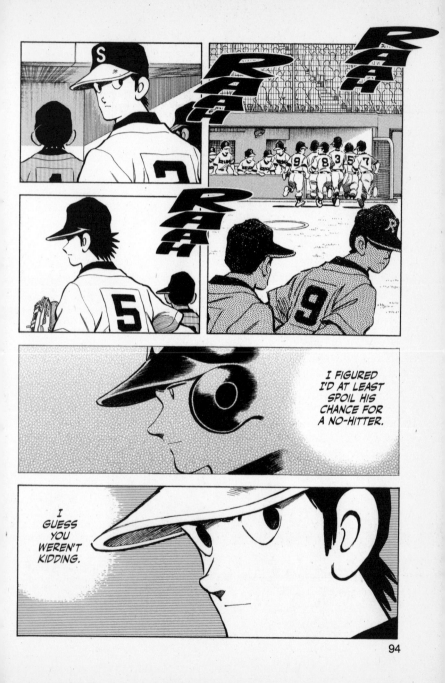

I FIGURED I'D AT LEAST SPOIL HIS CHANCE FOR A NO-HITTER.

I GUESS YOU WEREN'T KIDDING.

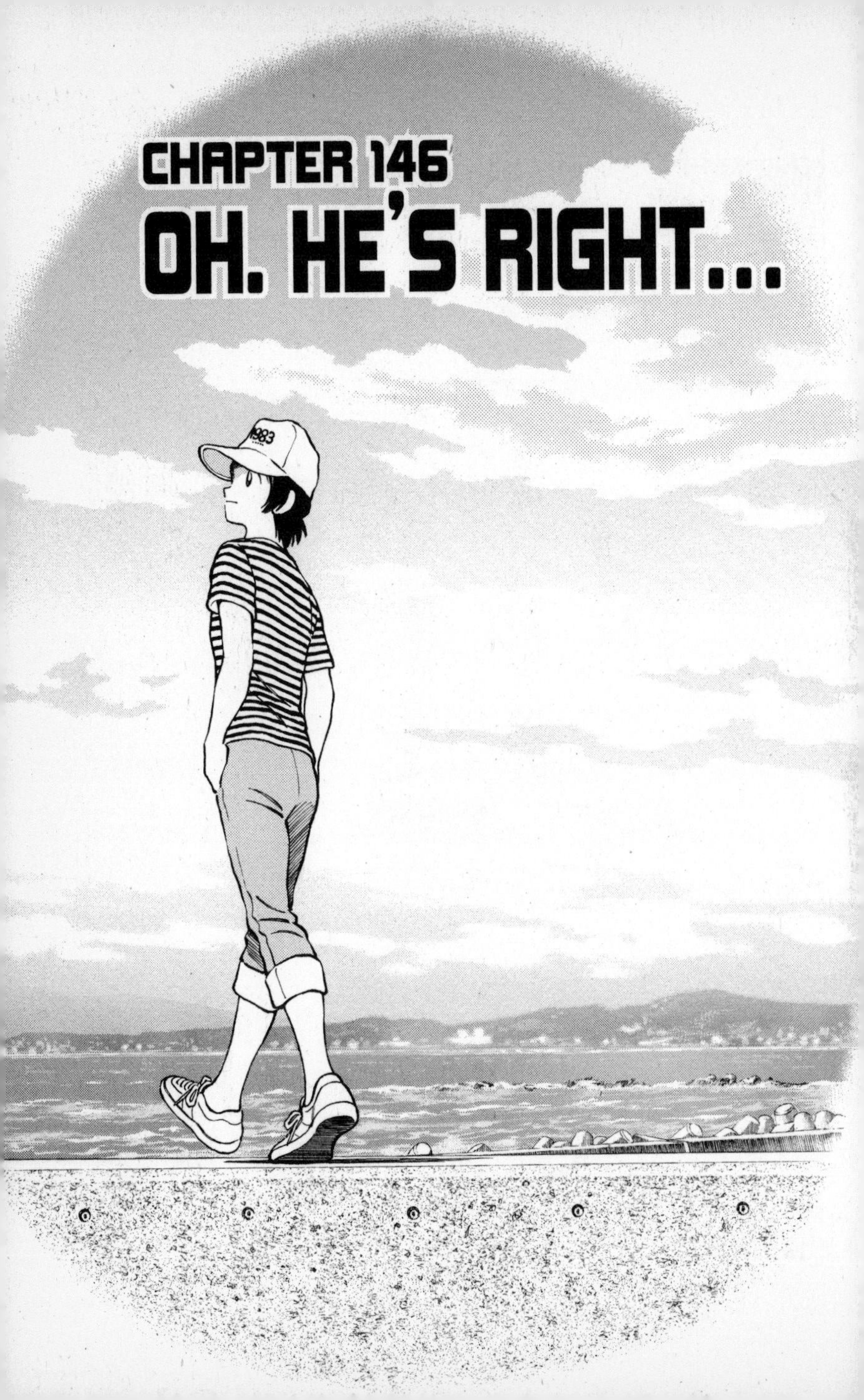
CHAPTER 146
OH. HE'S RIGHT...

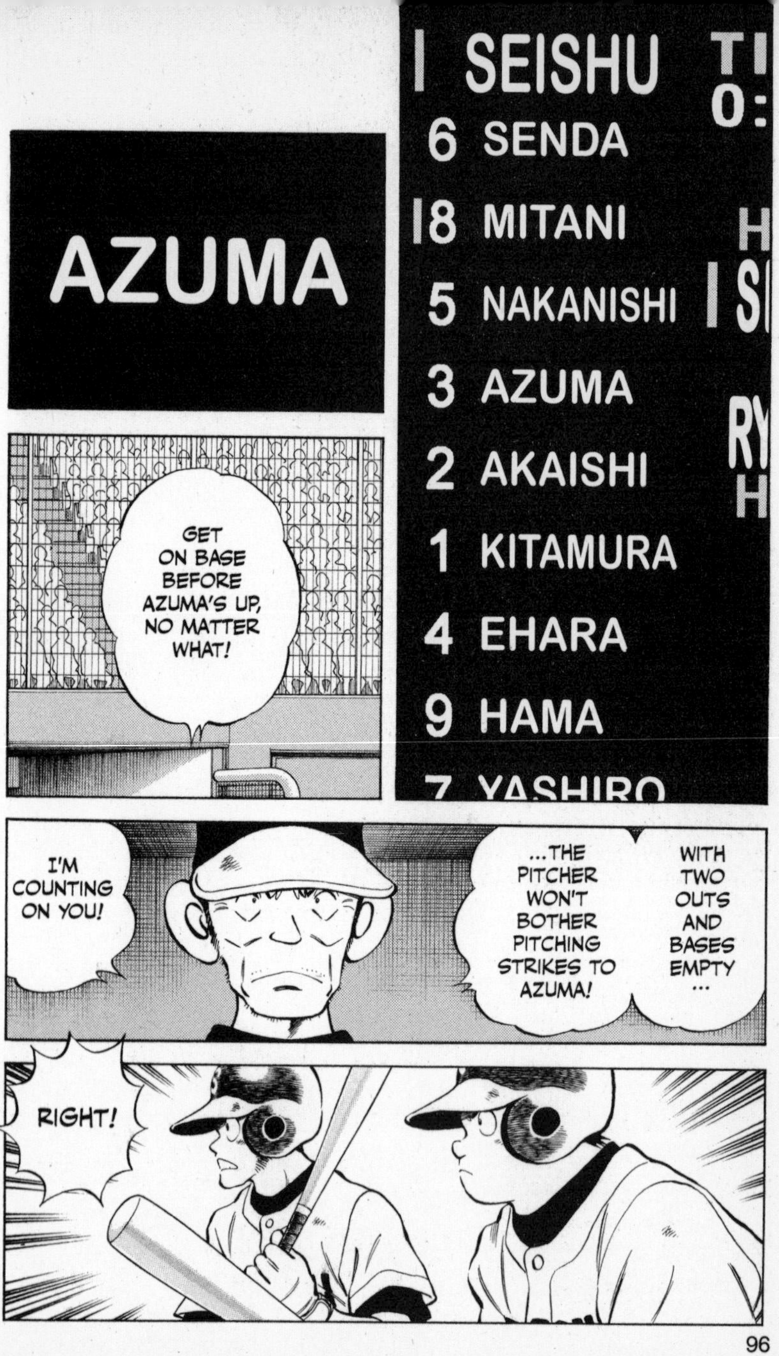

1 SEISHU
6 SENDA
18 MITANI
5 NAKANISHI
3 AZUMA
2 AKAISHI
1 KITAMURA
4 EHARA
9 HAMA
7 YASHIRO
AZUMA
GET ON BASE BEFORE AZUMA'S UP, NO MATTER WHAT!
WITH TWO OUTS AND BASES EMPTY...
...THE PITCHER WON'T BOTHER PITCHING STRIKES TO AZUMA!
I'M COUNTING ON YOU!
RIGHT!

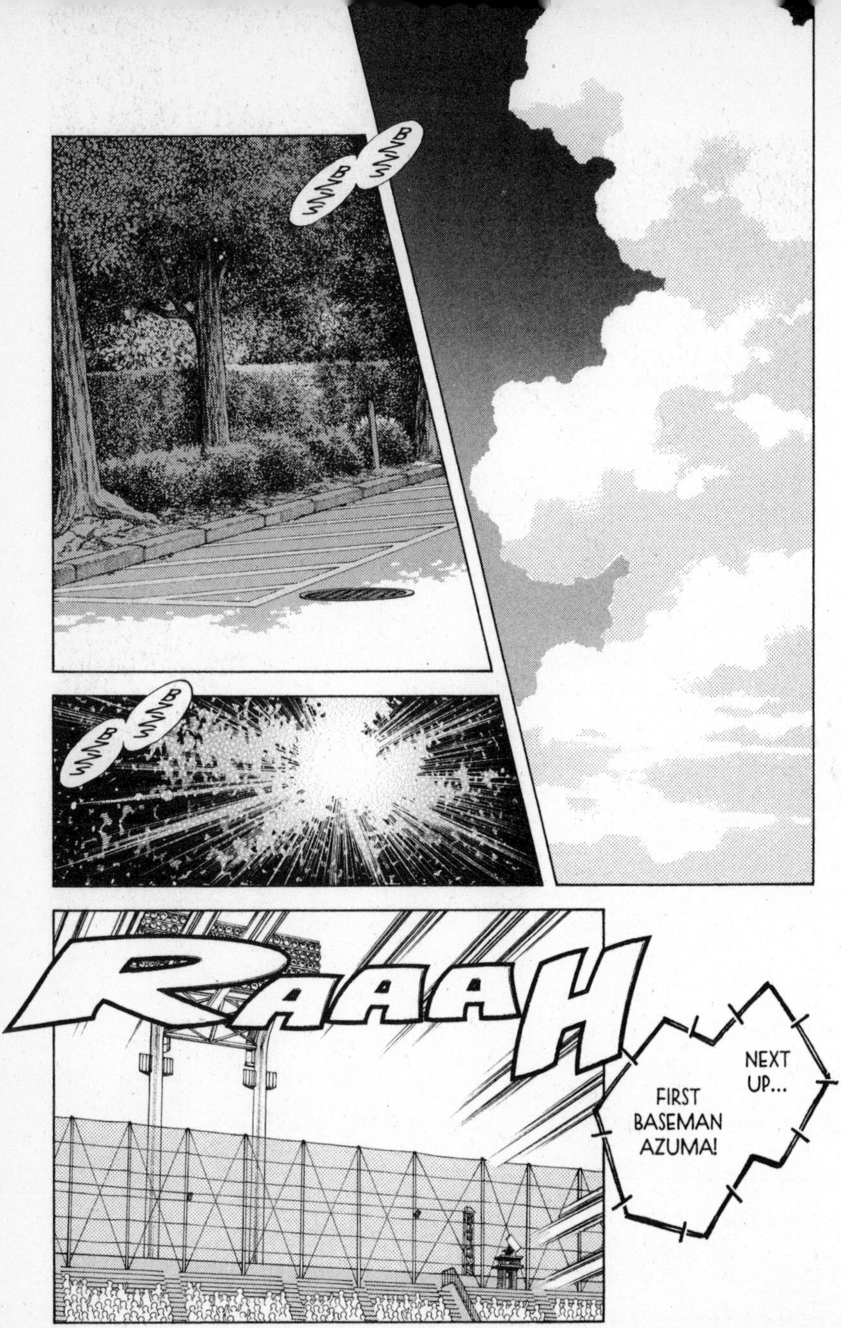
BZZZ
BZZZ
BZZZ
BZZZ
RAAAH
NEXT UP... FIRST BASEMAN AZUMA!

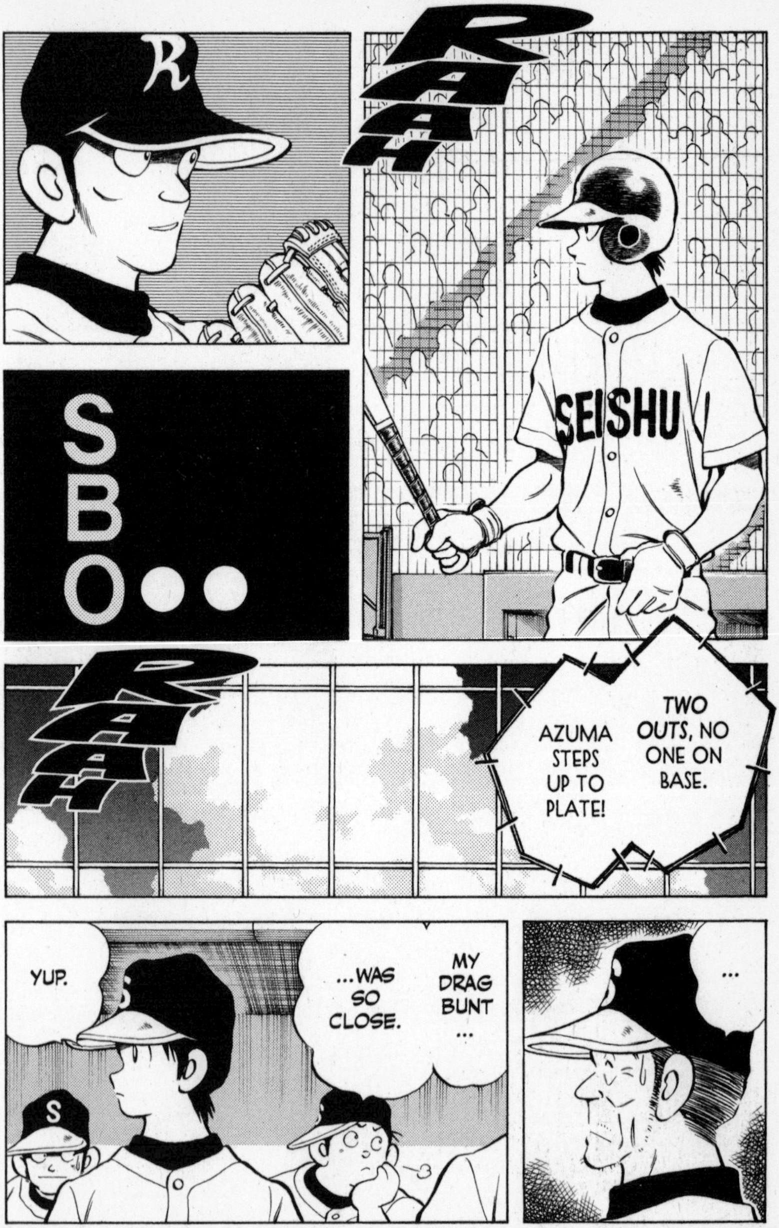
RAAH
SBO
RAAH
TWO OUTS, NO ONE ON BASE.
AZUMA STEPS UP TO PLATE!
...
MY DRAG BUNT ...
...WAS SO CLOSE.
YUP.

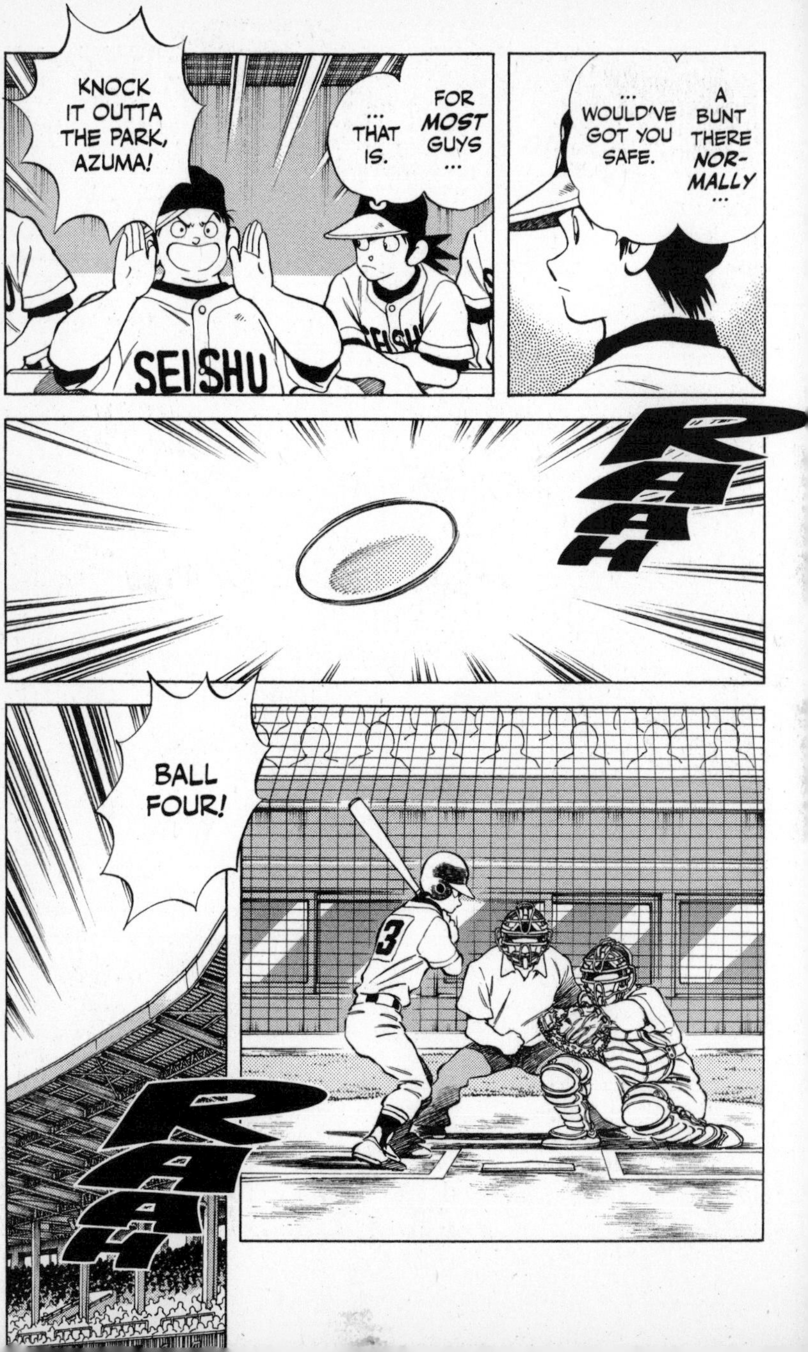
A BUNT THERE NORMALLY ...
... WOULD'VE GOT YOU SAFE.
FOR MOST GUYS ...
... THAT IS.
KNOCK IT OUTTA THE PARK, AZUMA!
RAAAH
BALL FOUR!
RAAAH

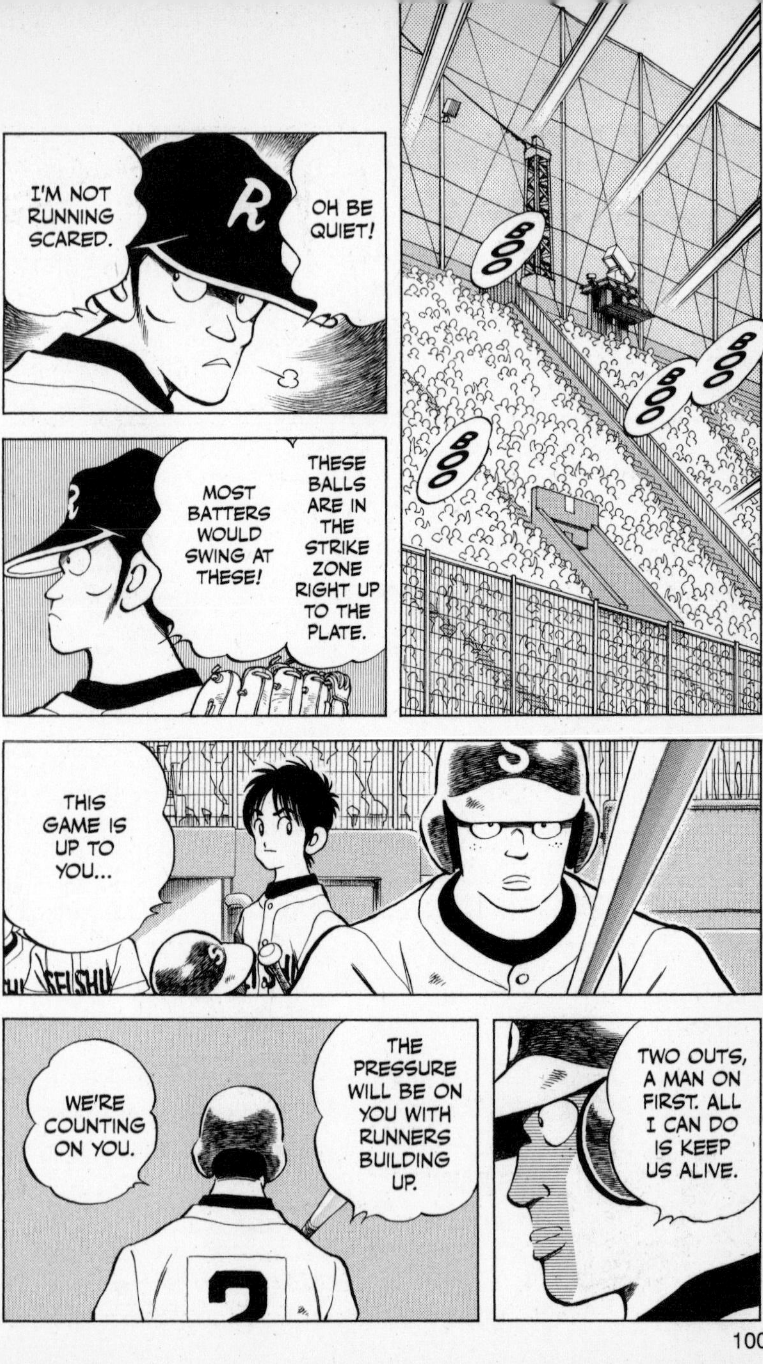
BOO
BOO
BOO
BOO
OH BE QUIET!
I'M NOT RUNNING SCARED.
THESE BALLS ARE IN THE STRIKE ZONE RIGHT UP TO THE PLATE.
MOST BATTERS WOULD SWING AT THESE!
THIS GAME IS UP TO YOU...
SEISHU
TWO OUTS, A MAN ON FIRST. ALL I CAN DO IS KEEP US ALIVE.
THE PRESSURE WILL BE ON YOU WITH RUNNERS BUILDING UP.
WE'RE COUNTING ON YOU.

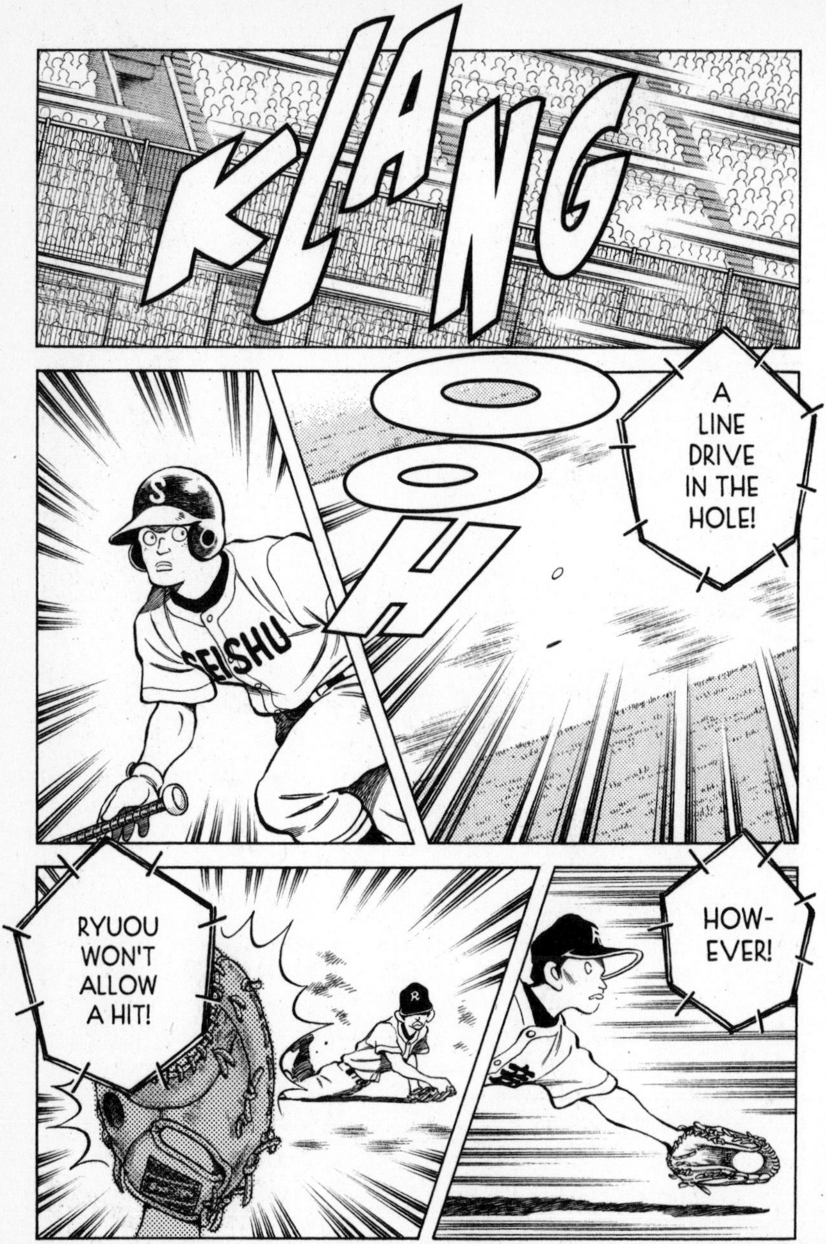
KLANG
OOOH
A LINE DRIVE IN THE HOLE!
HOW-EVER!
RYUOU WON'T ALLOW A HIT!

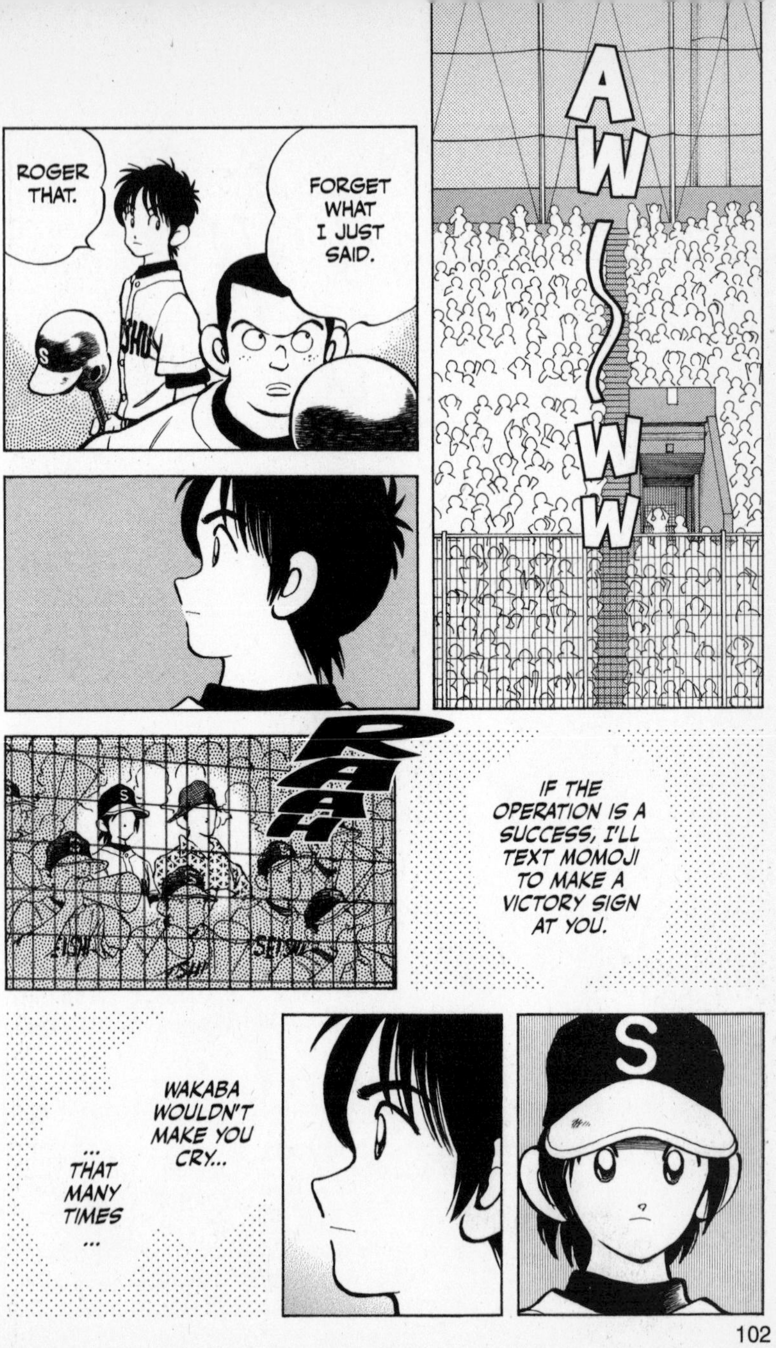
AW~WWW
FORGET WHAT I JUST SAID.
ROGER THAT.
IF THE OPERATION IS A SUCCESS, I'LL TEXT MOMOJI TO MAKE A VICTORY SIGN AT YOU.
RAAAH
WAKABA WOULDN'T MAKE YOU CRY...
...THAT MANY TIMES...

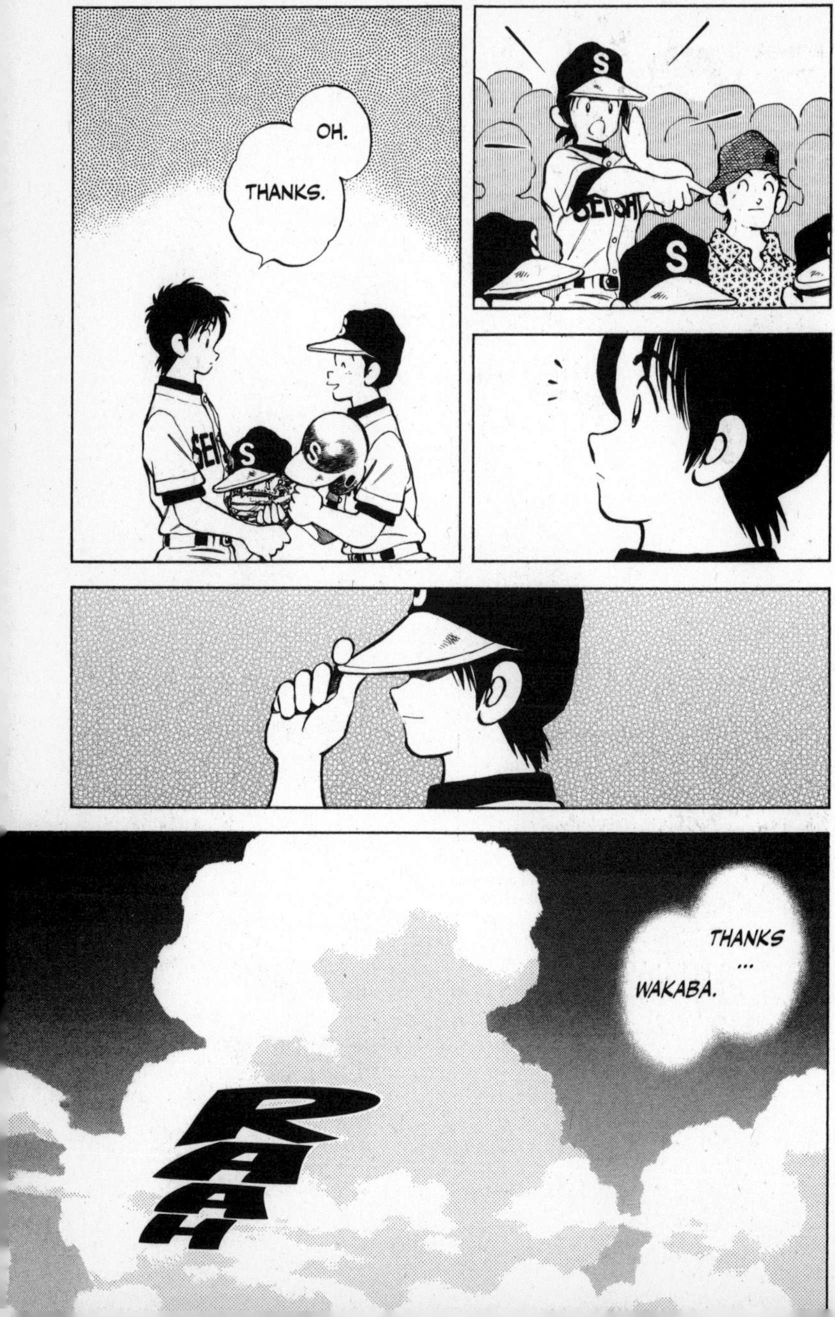
OH.
THANKS.
THANKS ... WAKABA.
RAAAH

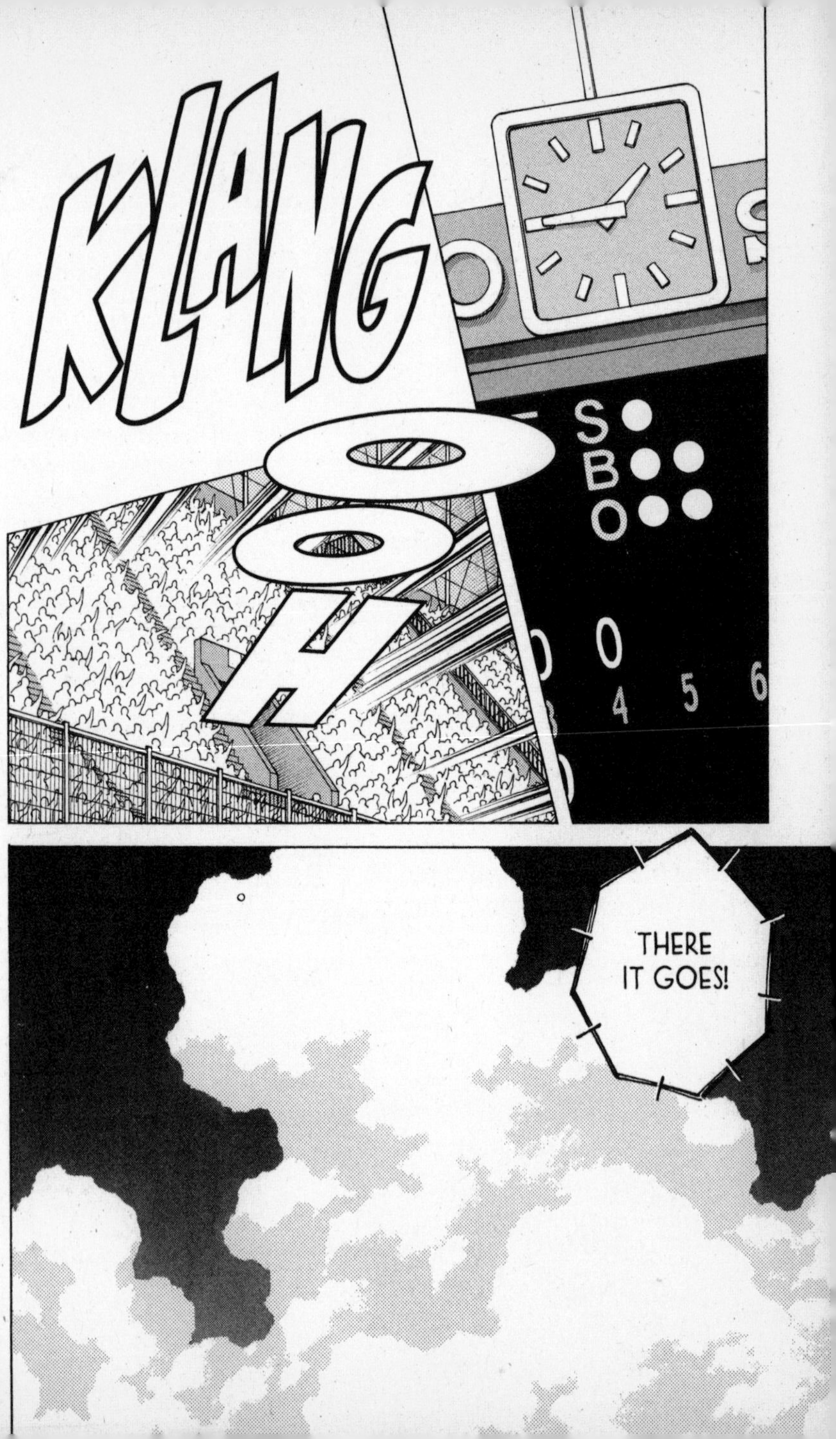
KLANG
OOH
SBO
0
4 5 6
THERE IT GOES!

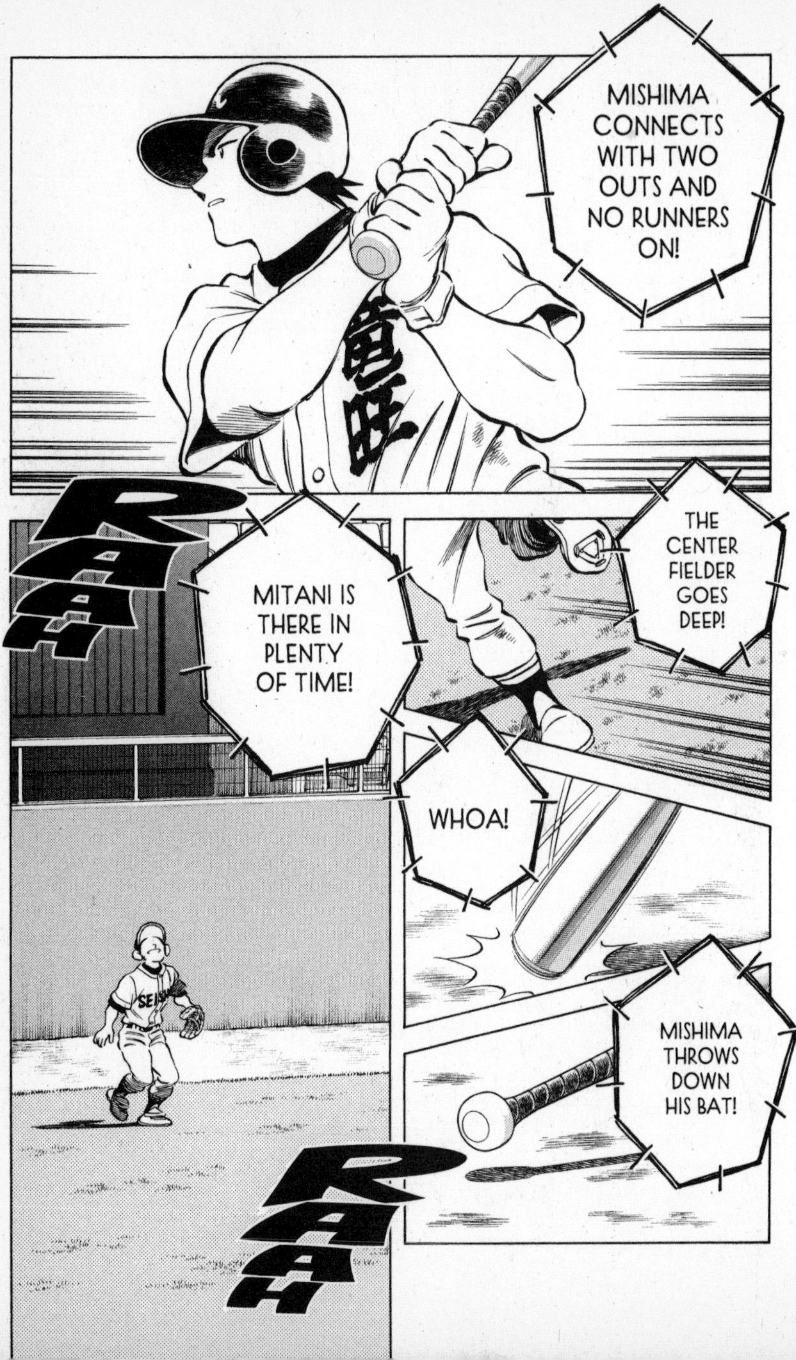
MISHIMA CONNECTS WITH TWO OUTS AND NO RUNNERS ON!
RAAH
THE CENTER FIELDER GOES DEEP!
WHOA!
MISHIMA THROWS DOWN HIS BAT!
MITANI IS THERE IN PLENTY OF TIME!
RAAH

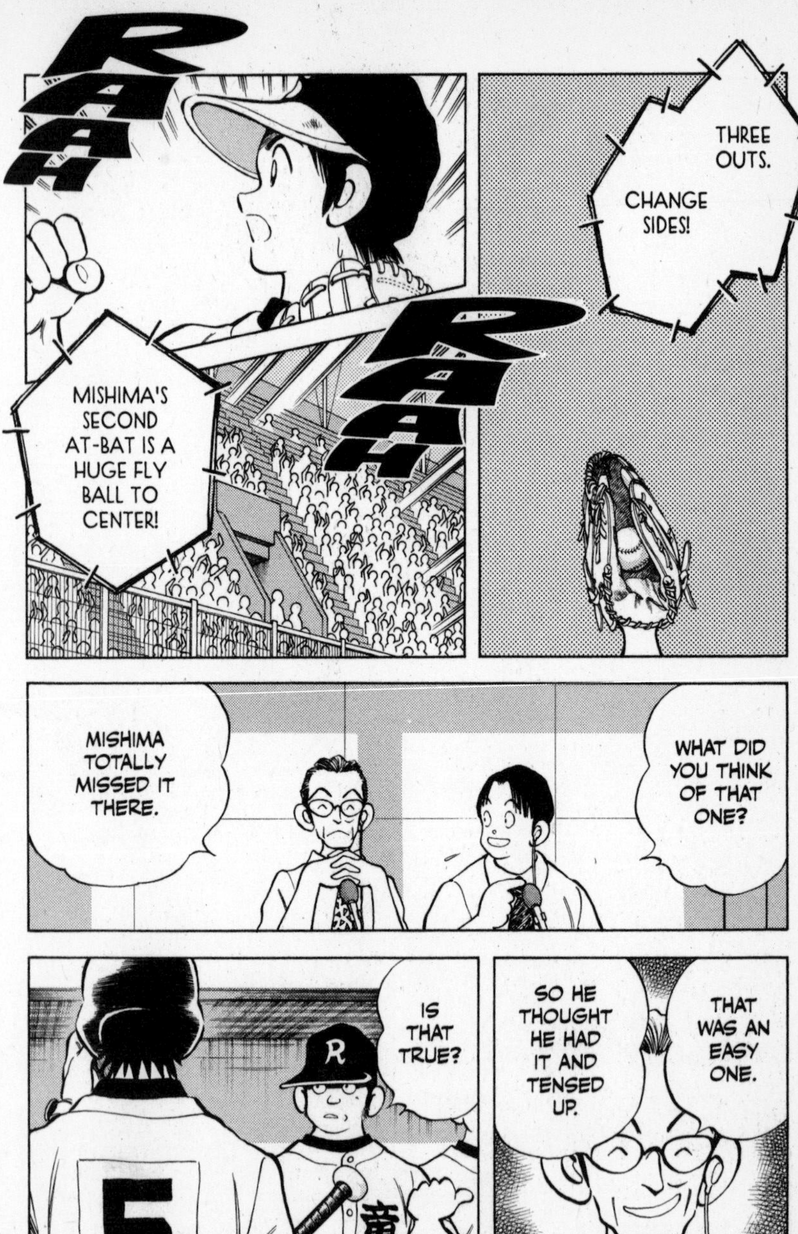
THREE OUTS.
CHANGE SIDES!
RAAH
RAAH
MISHIMA'S SECOND AT-BAT IS A HUGE FLY BALL TO CENTER!
WHAT DID YOU THINK OF THAT ONE?
MISHIMA TOTALLY MISSED IT THERE.
THAT WAS AN EASY ONE.
SO HE THOUGHT HE HAD IT AND TENSED UP.
IS THAT TRUE?

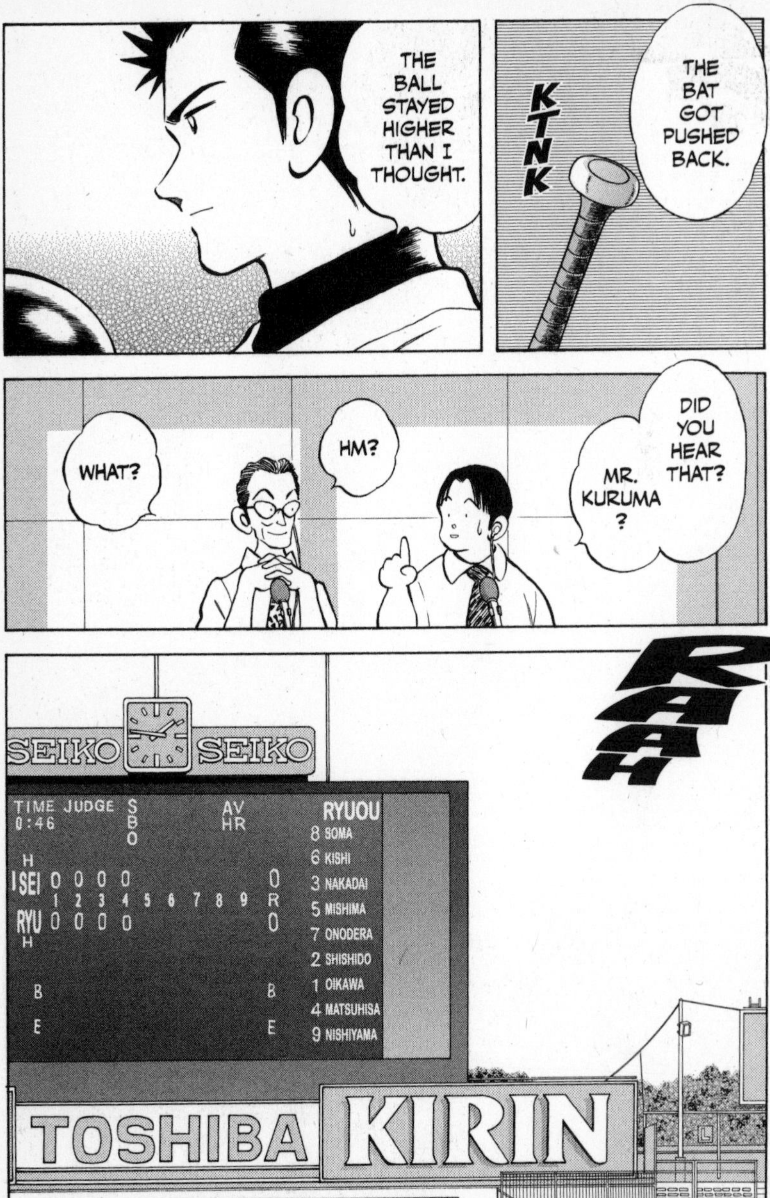
THE BAT GOT PUSHED BACK.
KTNK
THE BALL STAYED HIGHER THAN I THOUGHT.
DID YOU HEAR THAT?
MR. KURUMA?
HM?
WHAT?
RAAAH
SEIKO SEIKO
TIME JUDGE S B O AV HR
0:46
ISEI 0 0 0 0 0
RYU 0 0 0 0 0
RYUOU
8 SOMA
6 KISHI
3 NAKADAI
5 MISHIMA
7 ONODERA
2 SHISHIDO
1 OIKAWA
4 MATSUHISA
9 NISHIYAMA
TOSHIBA
KIRIN

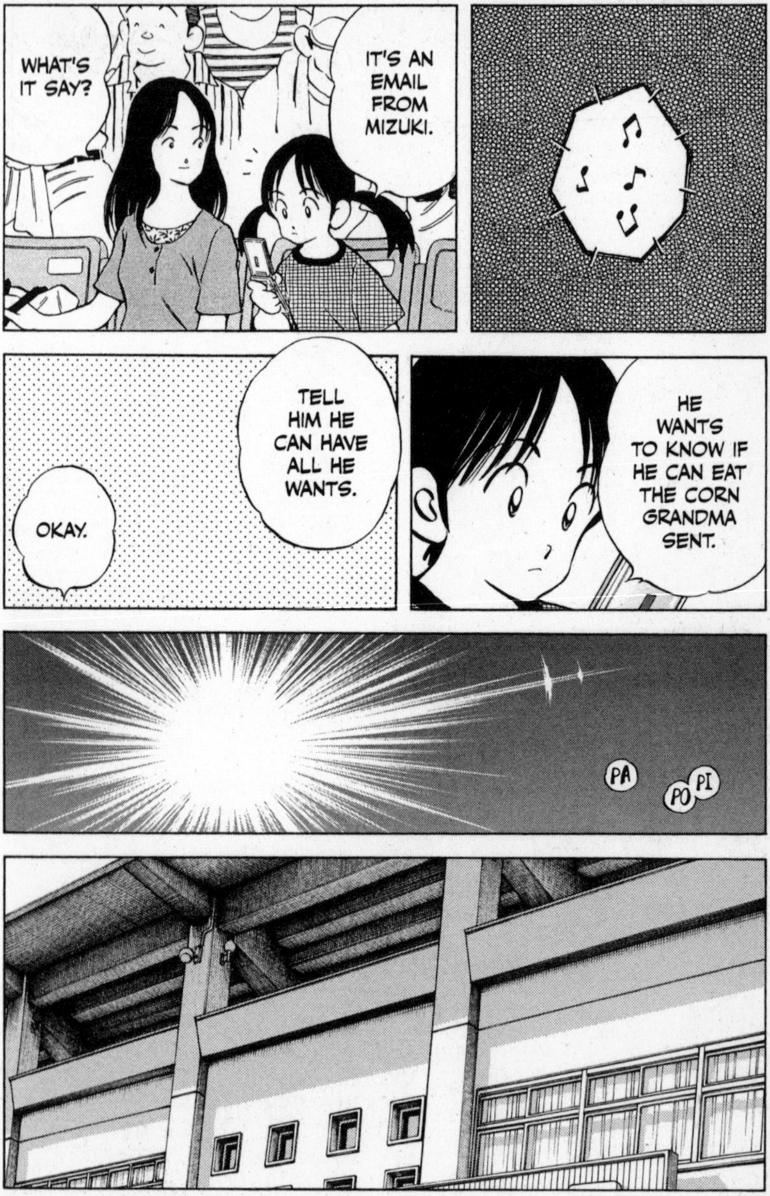
IT'S AN EMAIL FROM MIZUKI.
WHAT'S IT SAY?
HE WANTS TO KNOW IF HE CAN EAT THE CORN GRANDMA SENT.
TELL HIM HE CAN HAVE ALL HE WANTS.
OKAY.
PA
PO
PI

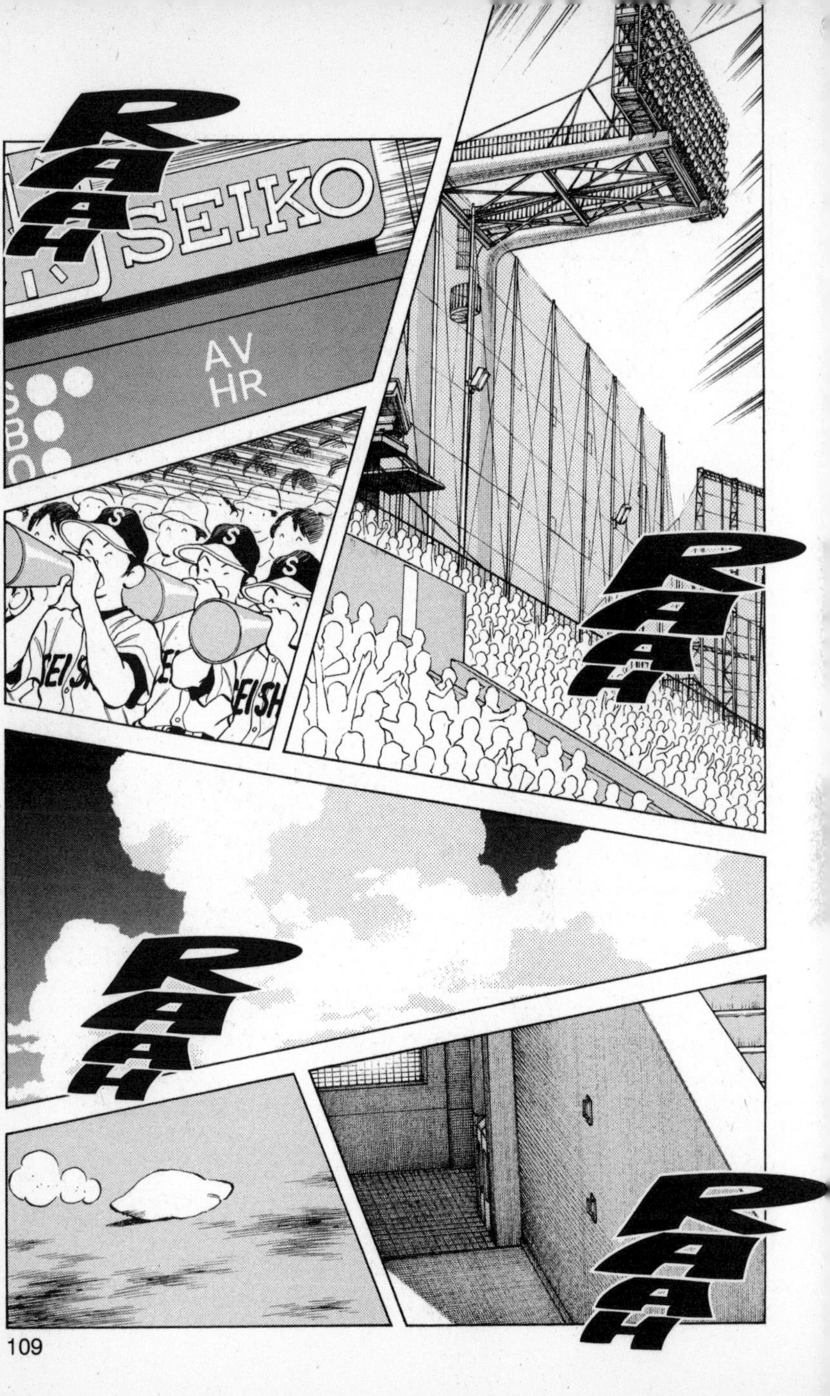
RAAH
RAAH
SEIKO
AV
HR
RAAH
RAAH

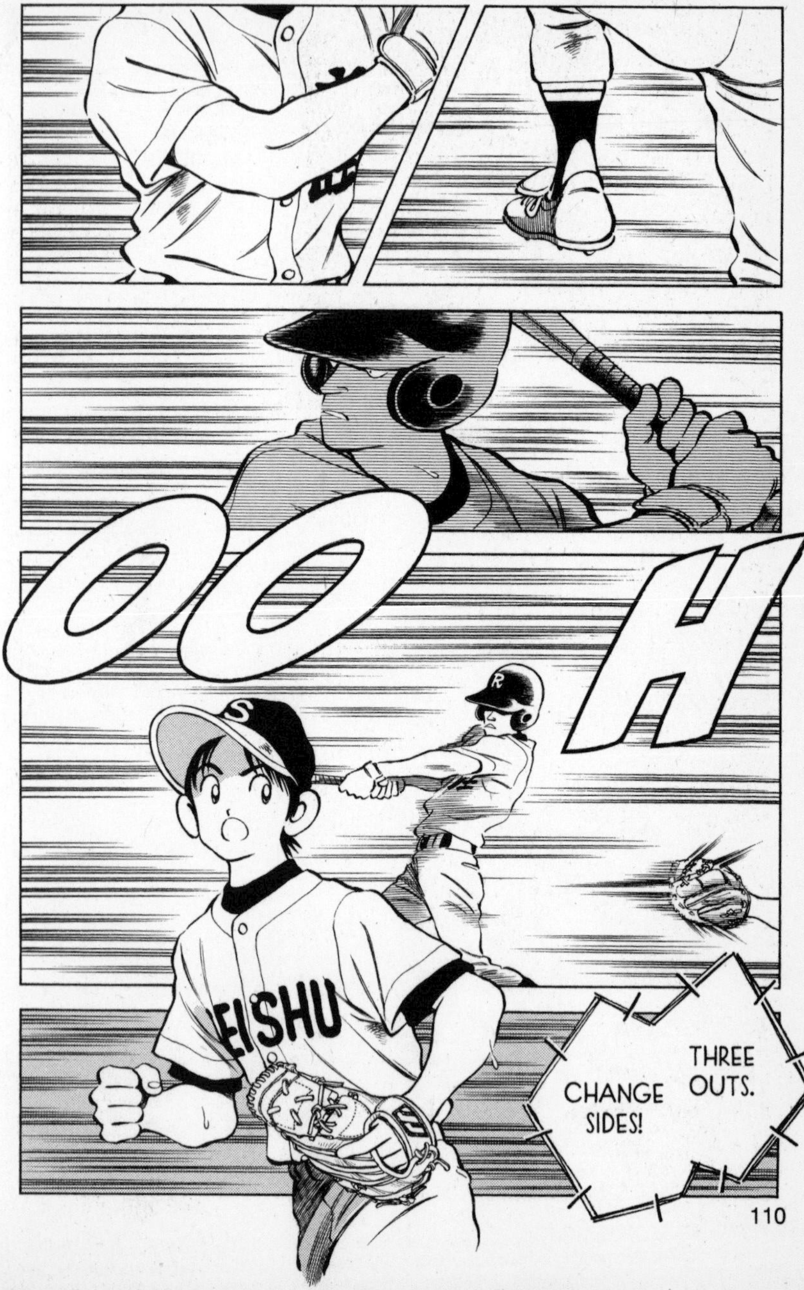
OOH
EISHU
THREE OUTS.
CHANGE SIDES!

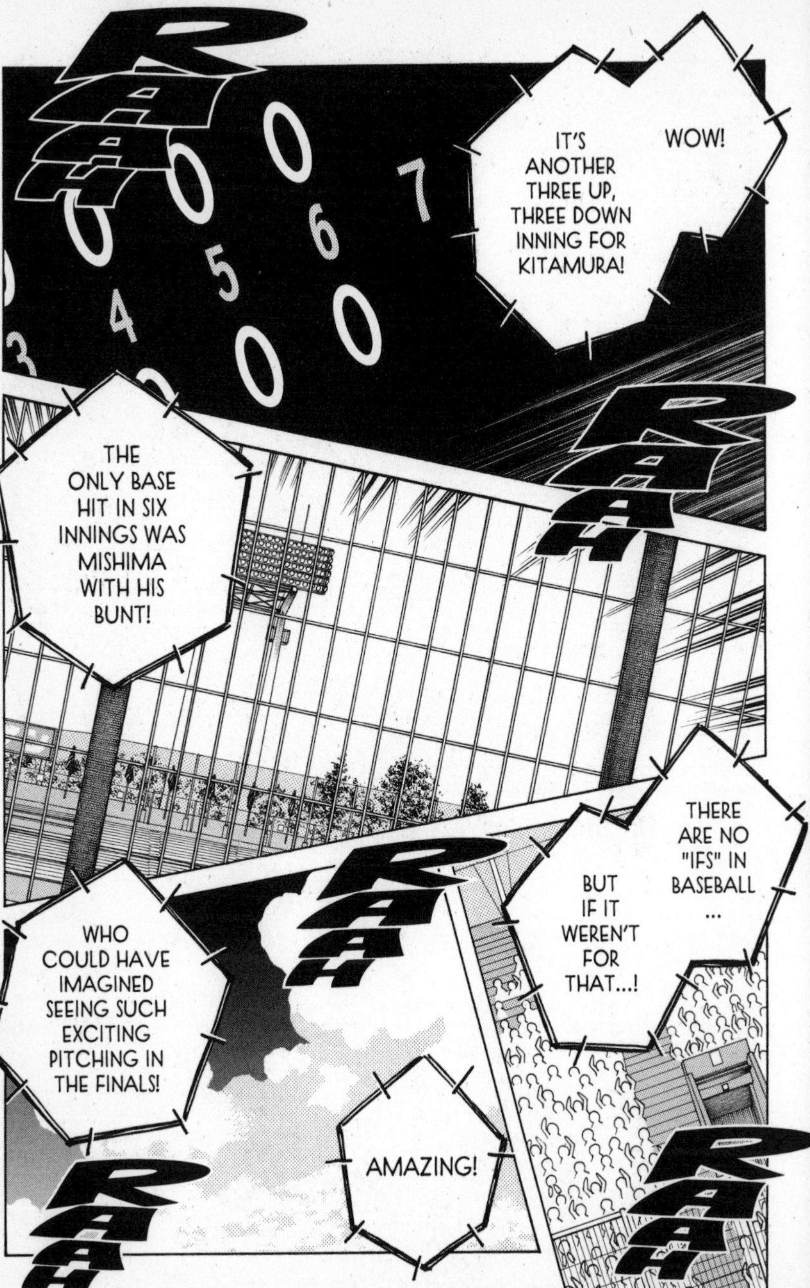
RAAAH
WOW!
IT'S ANOTHER THREE UP, THREE DOWN INNING FOR KITAMURA!
RAAH
THE ONLY BASE HIT IN SIX INNINGS WAS MISHIMA WITH HIS BUNT!
THERE ARE NO "IFS" IN BASEBALL...
BUT IF IT WEREN'T FOR THAT...!
RAAH
RAAAH
WHO COULD HAVE IMAGINED SEEING SUCH EXCITING PITCHING IN THE FINALS!
AMAZING!
RAAAH

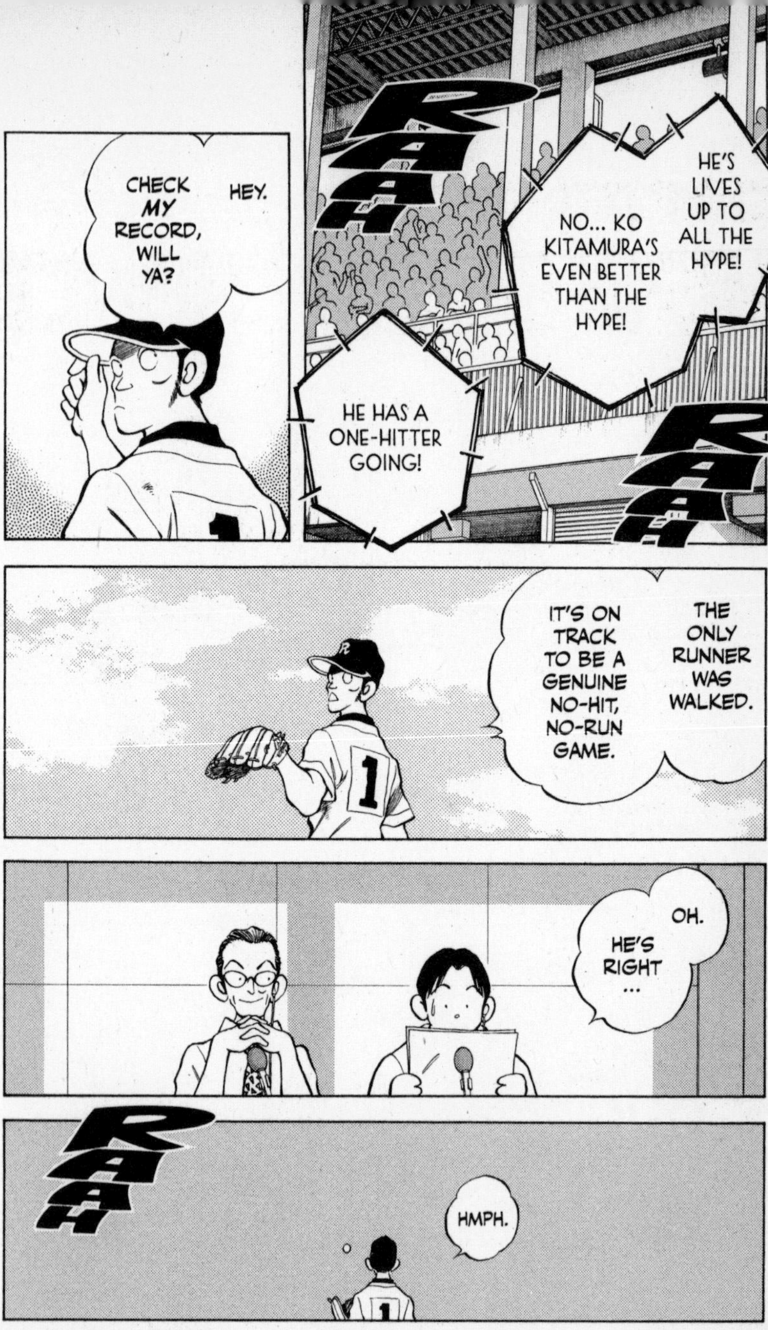
RAAAH
HE'S LIVES UP TO ALL THE HYPE!
NO... KO KITAMURA'S EVEN BETTER THAN THE HYPE!
HE HAS A ONE-HITTER GOING!
RAAAH
HEY.
CHECK *MY* RECORD, WILL YA?
THE ONLY RUNNER WAS WALKED.
IT'S ON TRACK TO BE A GENUINE NO-HIT, NO-RUN GAME.
OH.
HE'S RIGHT ...
RAAH
HMPH.

CHAPTER 147
HERE'S OUR CHANCE

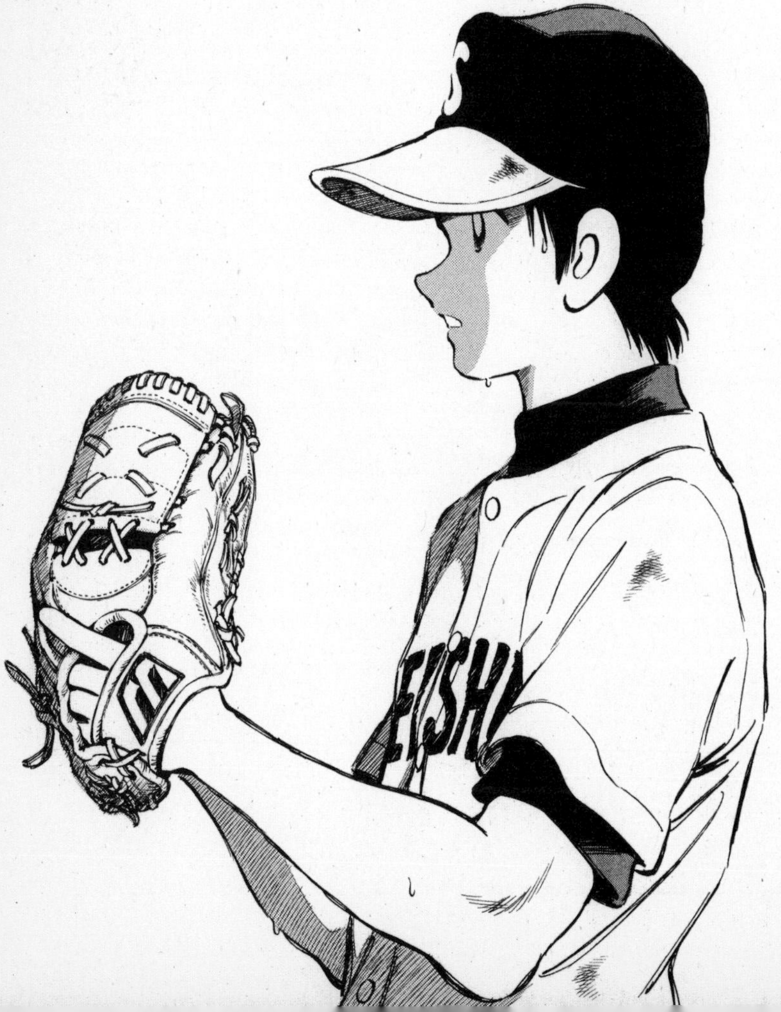

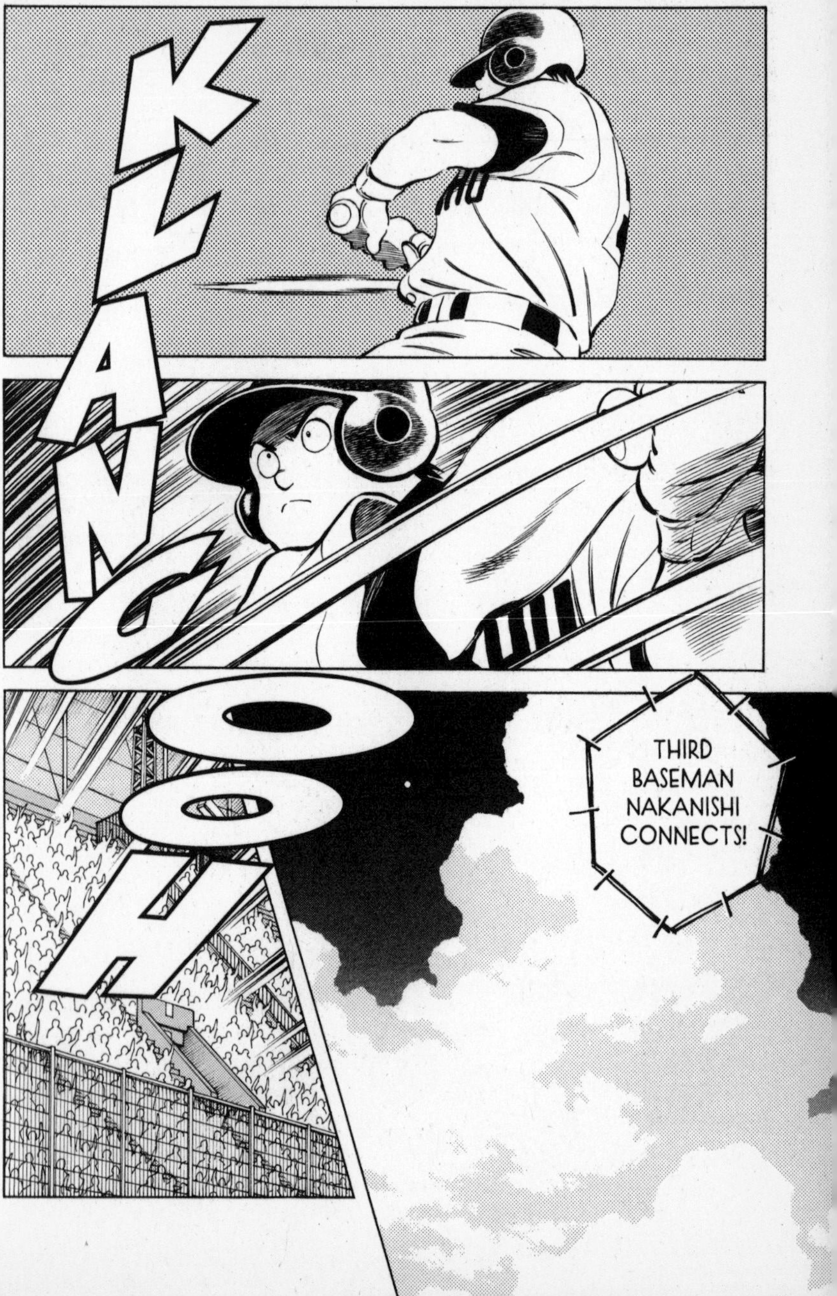
KLANG
OOOH
THIRD BASEMAN NAKANISHI CONNECTS!

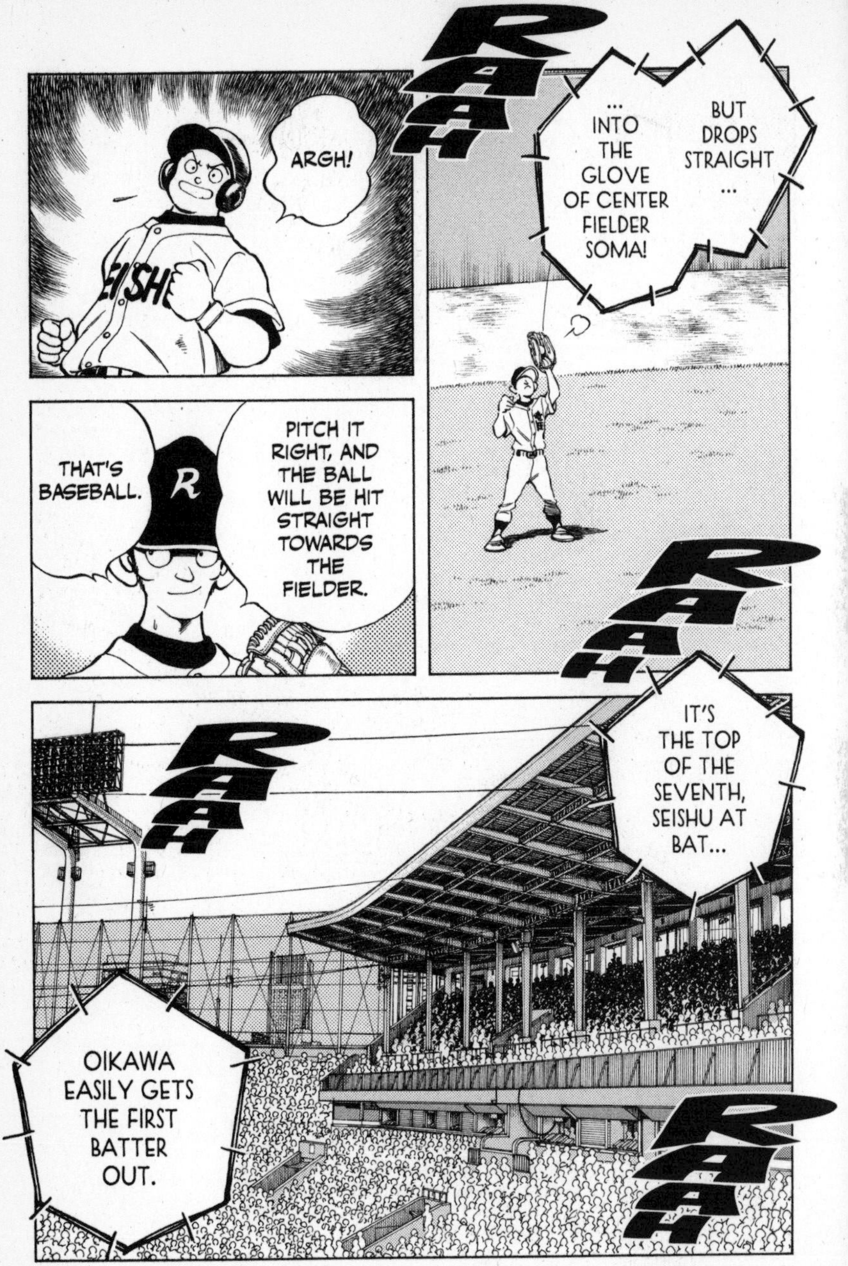
RAAH
BUT DROPS STRAIGHT ...
... INTO THE GLOVE OF CENTER FIELDER SOMA!
RAAH
ARGH!
PITCH IT RIGHT, AND THE BALL WILL BE HIT STRAIGHT TOWARDS THE FIELDER.
THAT'S BASEBALL.
IT'S THE TOP OF THE SEVENTH, SEISHU AT BAT...
RAAH
OIKAWA EASILY GETS THE FIRST BATTER OUT.
RAAH

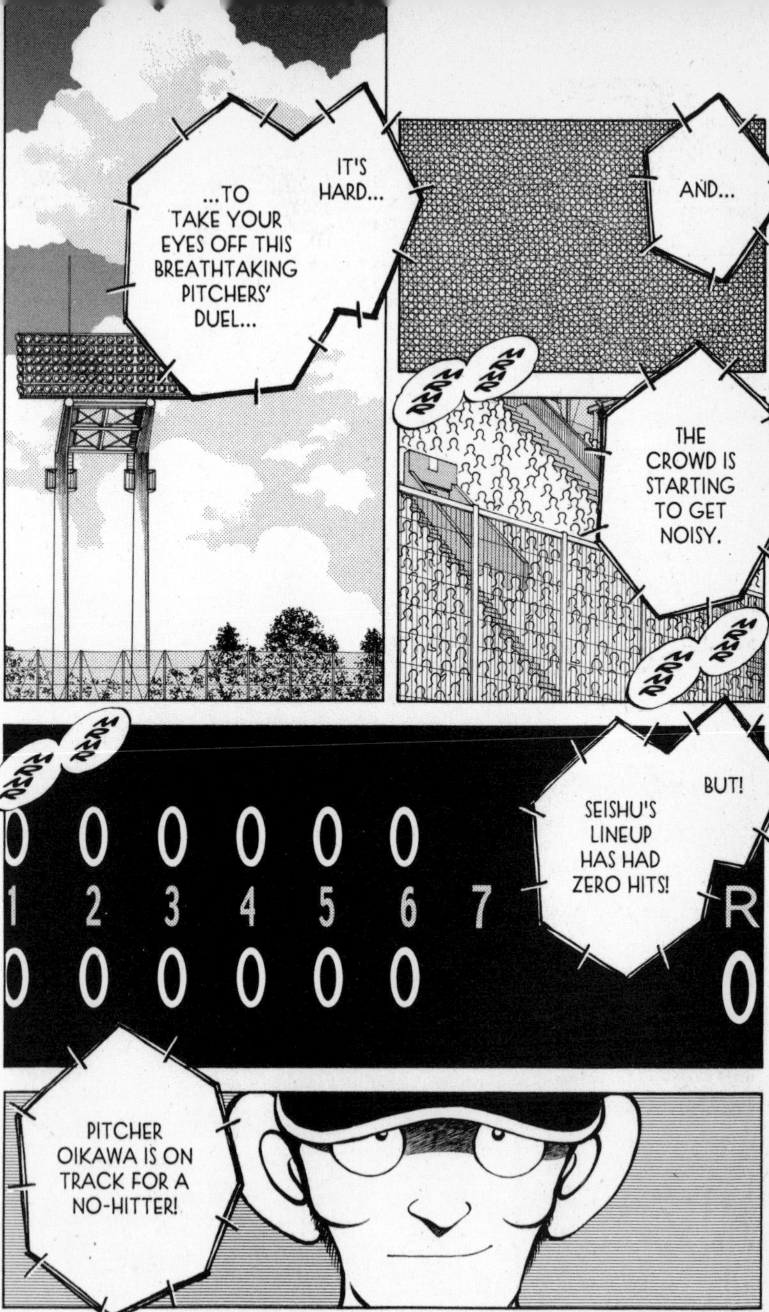
IT'S HARD...
...TO TAKE YOUR EYES OFF THIS BREATHTAKING PITCHERS' DUEL...
AND...
THE CROWD IS STARTING TO GET NOISY.
MRMR
MRMR
MRMR
MRMR
BUT!
SEISHU'S LINEUP HAS HAD ZERO HITS!
MRMR
MRMR
0 0 0 0 0 0
1 2 3 4 5 6 7 R
0 0 0 0 0 0 0
PITCHER OIKAWA IS ON TRACK FOR A NO-HITTER!

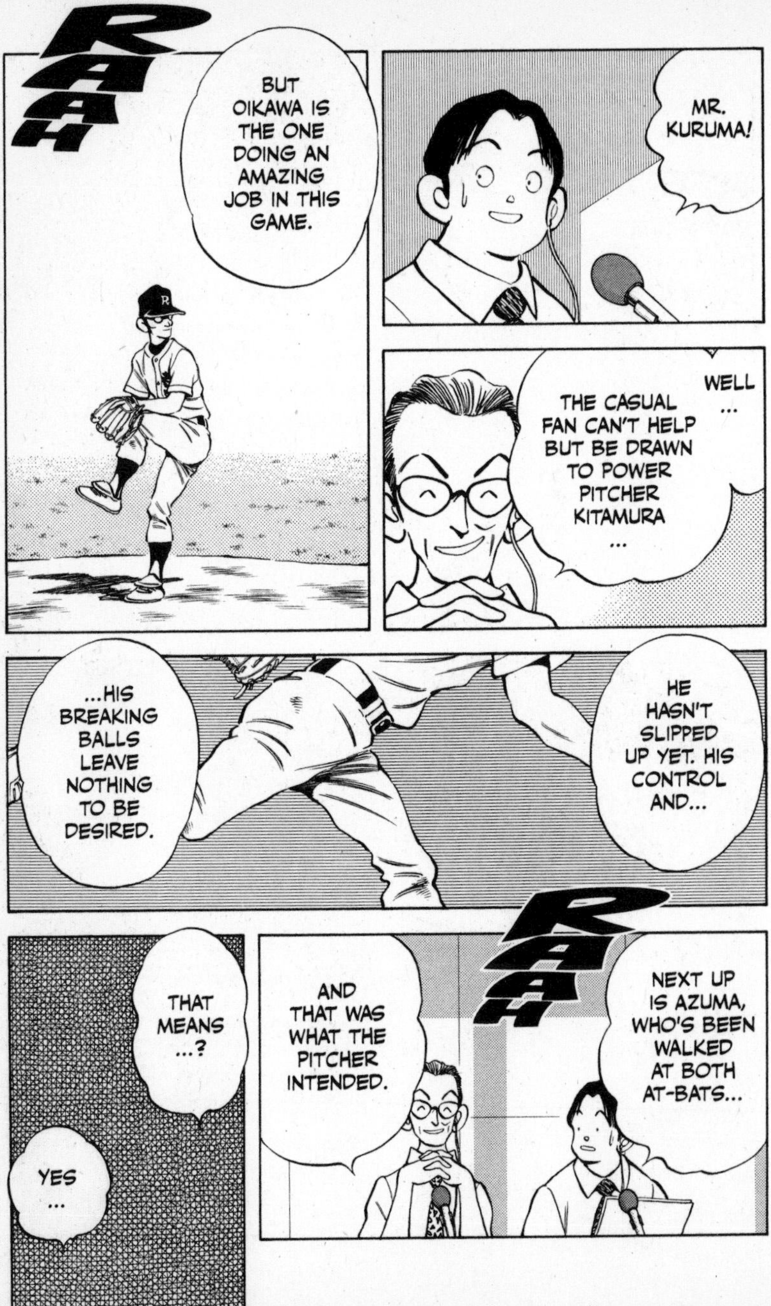
MR. KURUMA!
WELL ...
THE CASUAL FAN CAN'T HELP BUT BE DRAWN TO POWER PITCHER KITAMURA ...
RAAH
BUT OIKAWA IS THE ONE DOING AN AMAZING JOB IN THIS GAME.
HE HASN'T SLIPPED UP YET. HIS CONTROL AND...
...HIS BREAKING BALLS LEAVE NOTHING TO BE DESIRED.
RAAH
NEXT UP IS AZUMA, WHO'S BEEN WALKED AT BOTH AT-BATS...
AND THAT WAS WHAT THE PITCHER INTENDED.
THAT MEANS ...?
YES ...

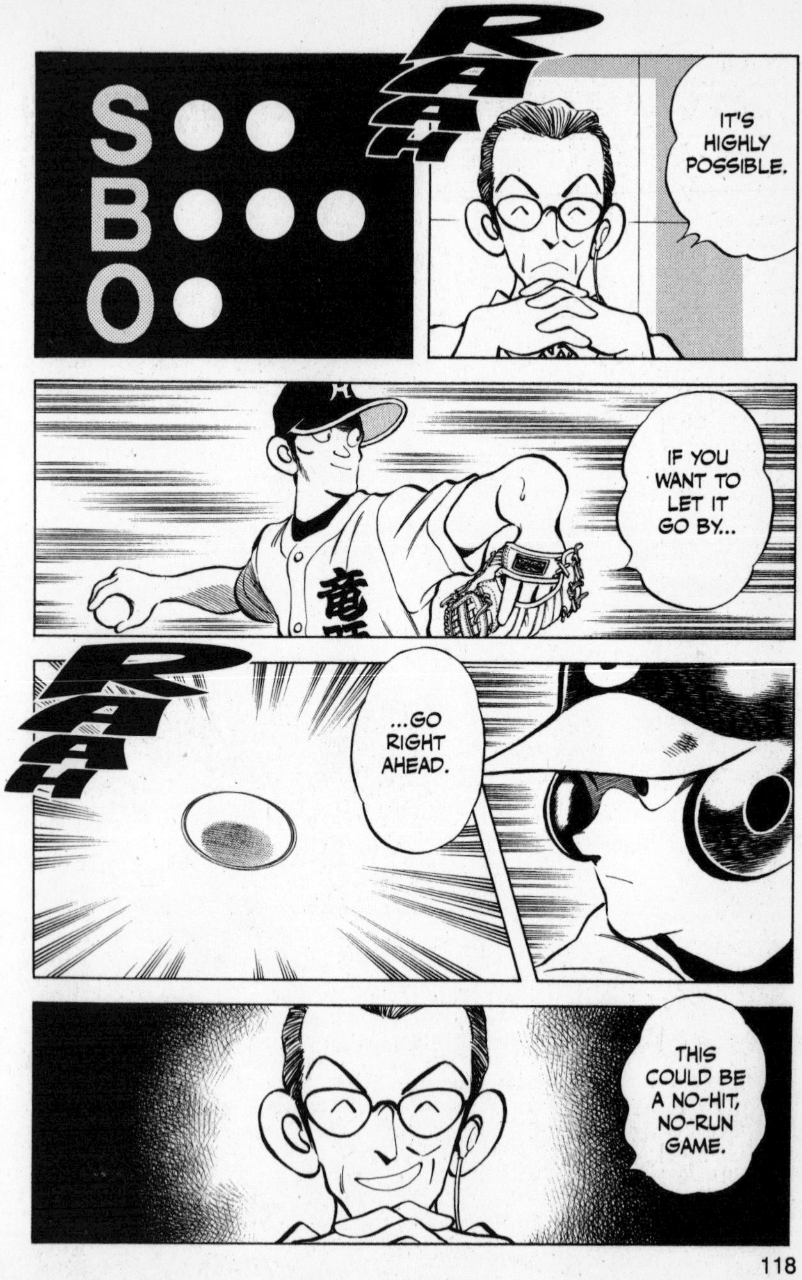
IT'S HIGHLY POSSIBLE.
RAAH
S
B
O
IF YOU WANT TO LET IT GO BY...
...GO RIGHT AHEAD.
RAAH
THIS COULD BE A NO-HIT, NO-RUN GAME.

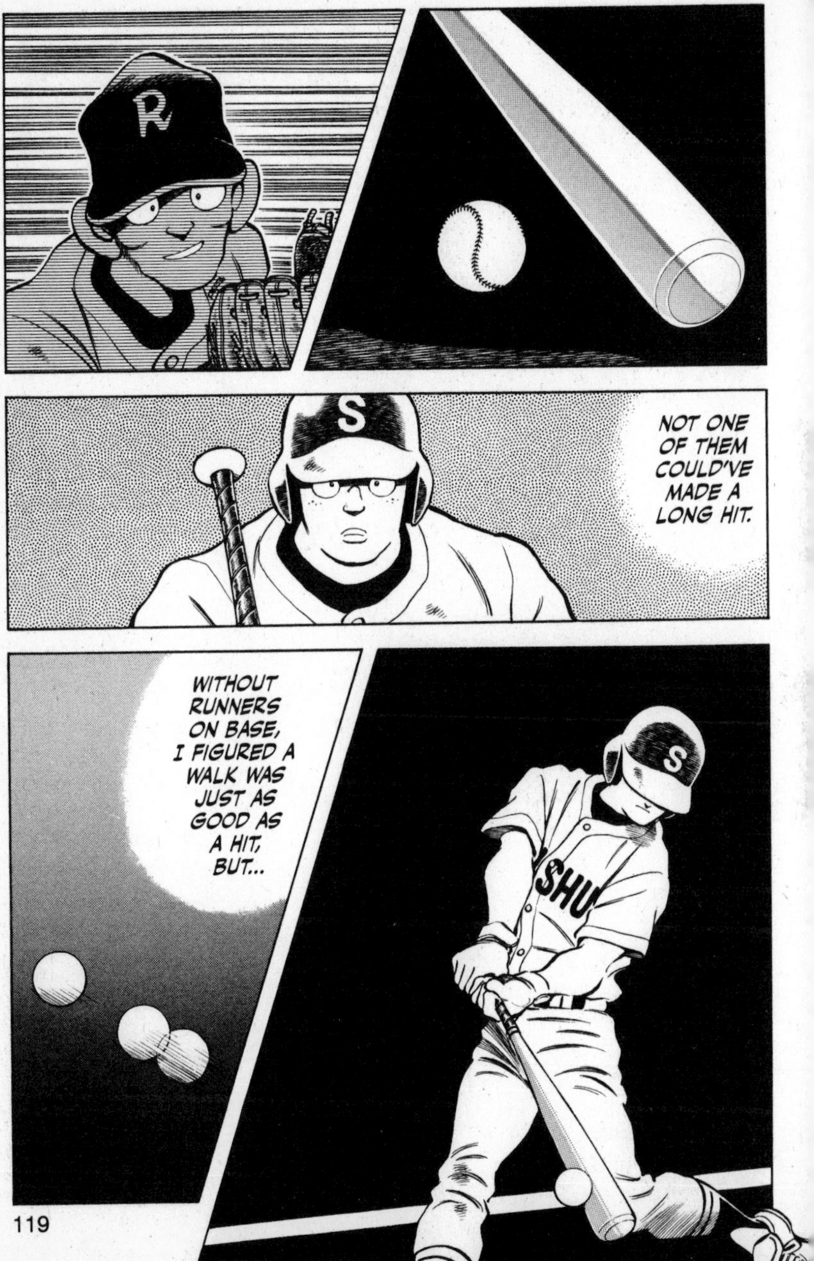
NOT ONE OF THEM COULD'VE MADE A LONG HIT.
WITHOUT RUNNERS ON BASE, I FIGURED A WALK WAS JUST AS GOOD AS A HIT, BUT...

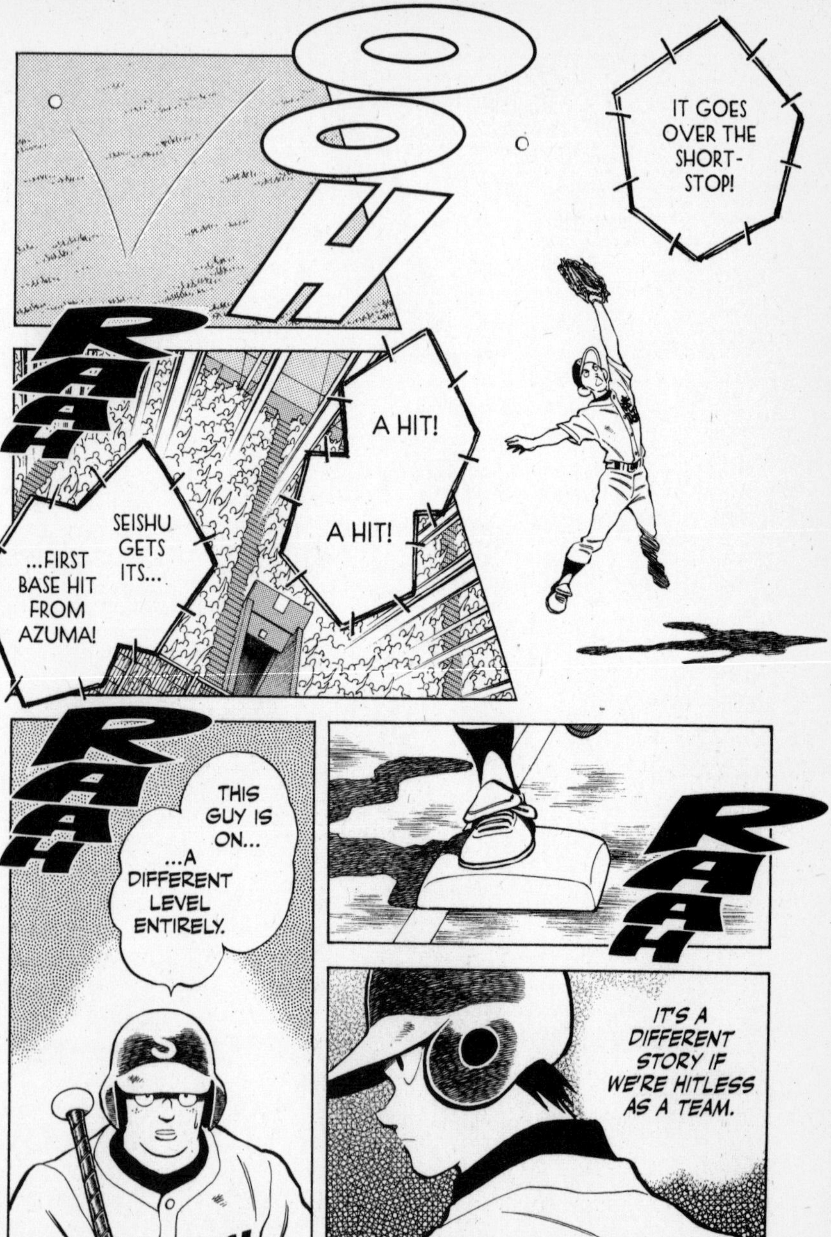
IT GOES OVER THE SHORT-STOP!
OOH
RAAAH
A HIT!
A HIT!
SEISHU GETS ITS...
...FIRST BASE HIT FROM AZUMA!
RAAAH
IT'S A DIFFERENT STORY IF WE'RE HITLESS AS A TEAM.
RAAAH
THIS GUY IS ON...
...A DIFFERENT LEVEL ENTIRELY.

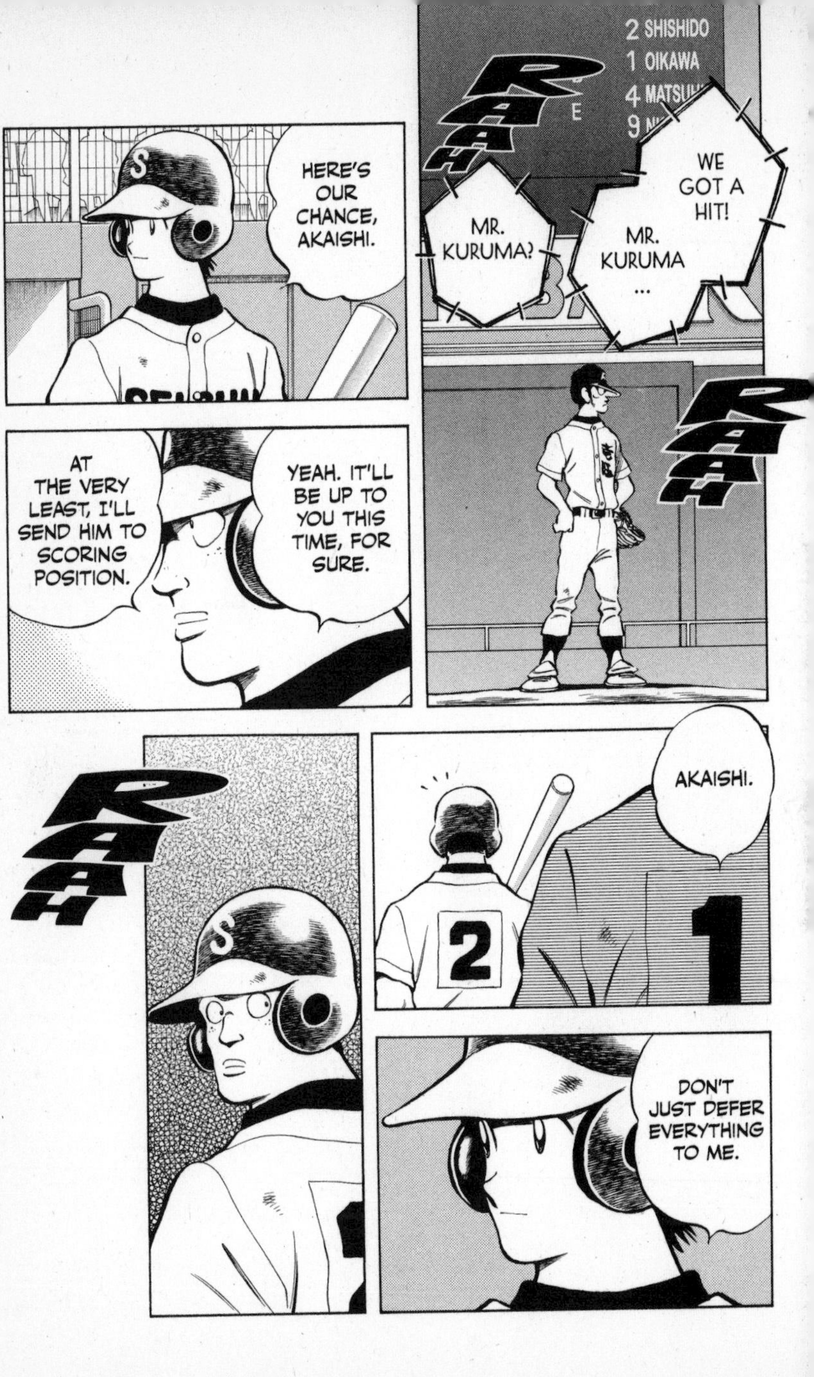
2 SHISHIDO
1 OIKAWA
RAAH
WE GOT A HIT!
MR. KURUMA ...
MR. KURUMA?
HERE'S OUR CHANCE, AKAISHI.
RAAH
YEAH. IT'LL BE UP TO YOU THIS TIME, FOR SURE.
AT THE VERY LEAST, I'LL SEND HIM TO SCORING POSITION.
AKAISHI.
DON'T JUST DEFER EVERYTHING TO ME.
RAAH

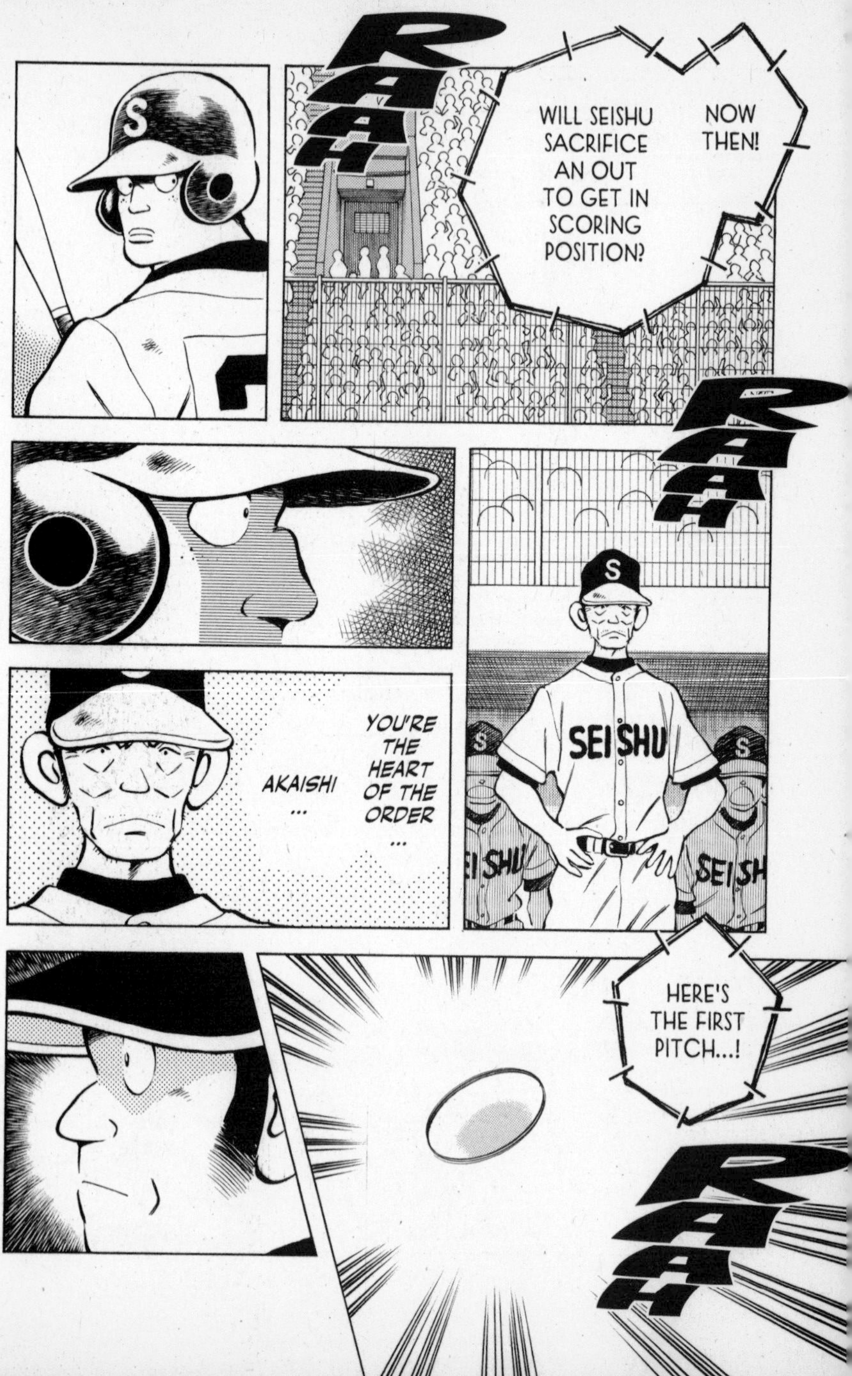
RAAH
NOW THEN!
WILL SEISHU SACRIFICE AN OUT TO GET IN SCORING POSITION?
RAAH
YOU'RE THE HEART OF THE ORDER ...
AKAISHI ...
SEISHU
HERE'S THE FIRST PITCH...!
RAAH

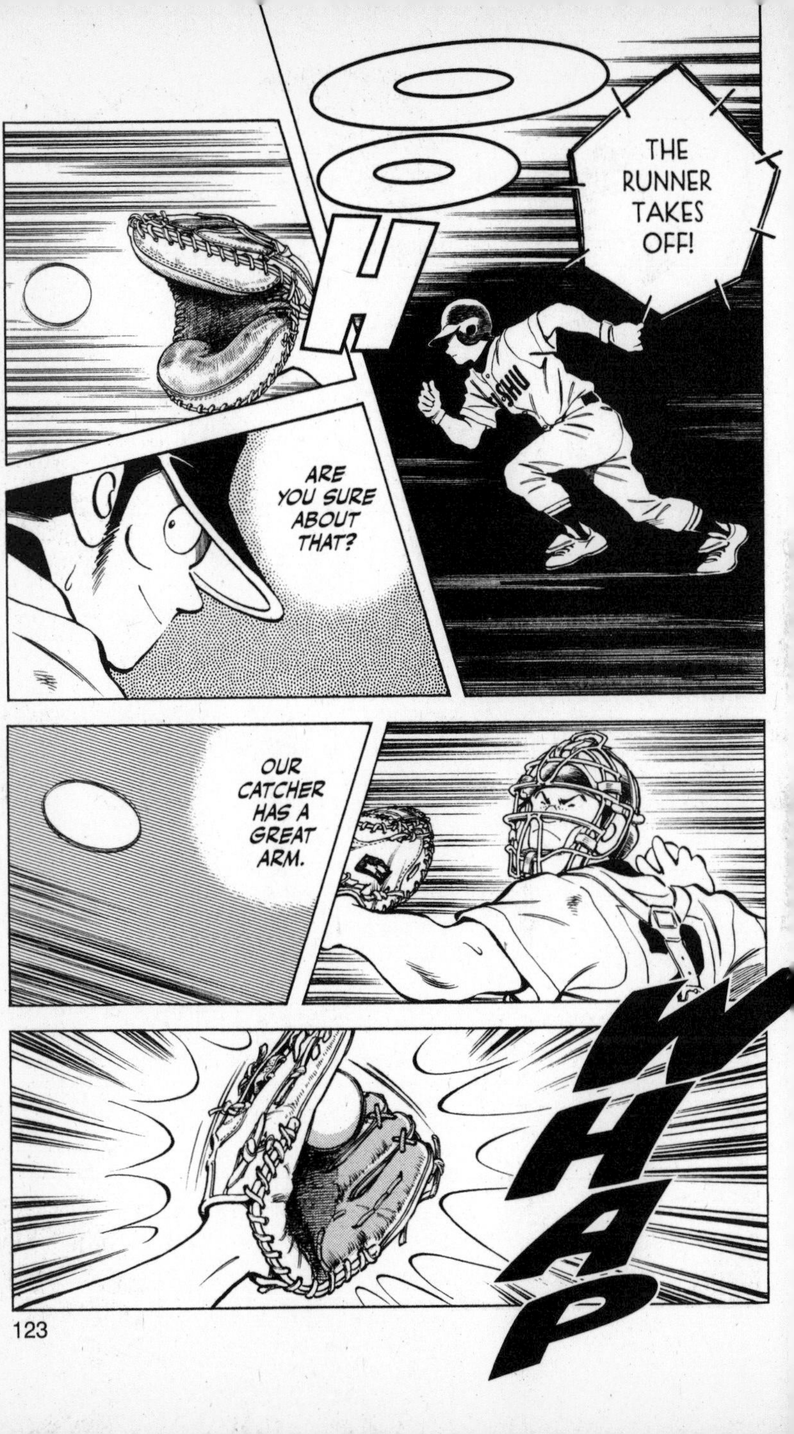
OOH
THE RUNNER TAKES OFF!
ARE YOU SURE ABOUT THAT?
OUR CATCHER HAS A GREAT ARM.
WHAP

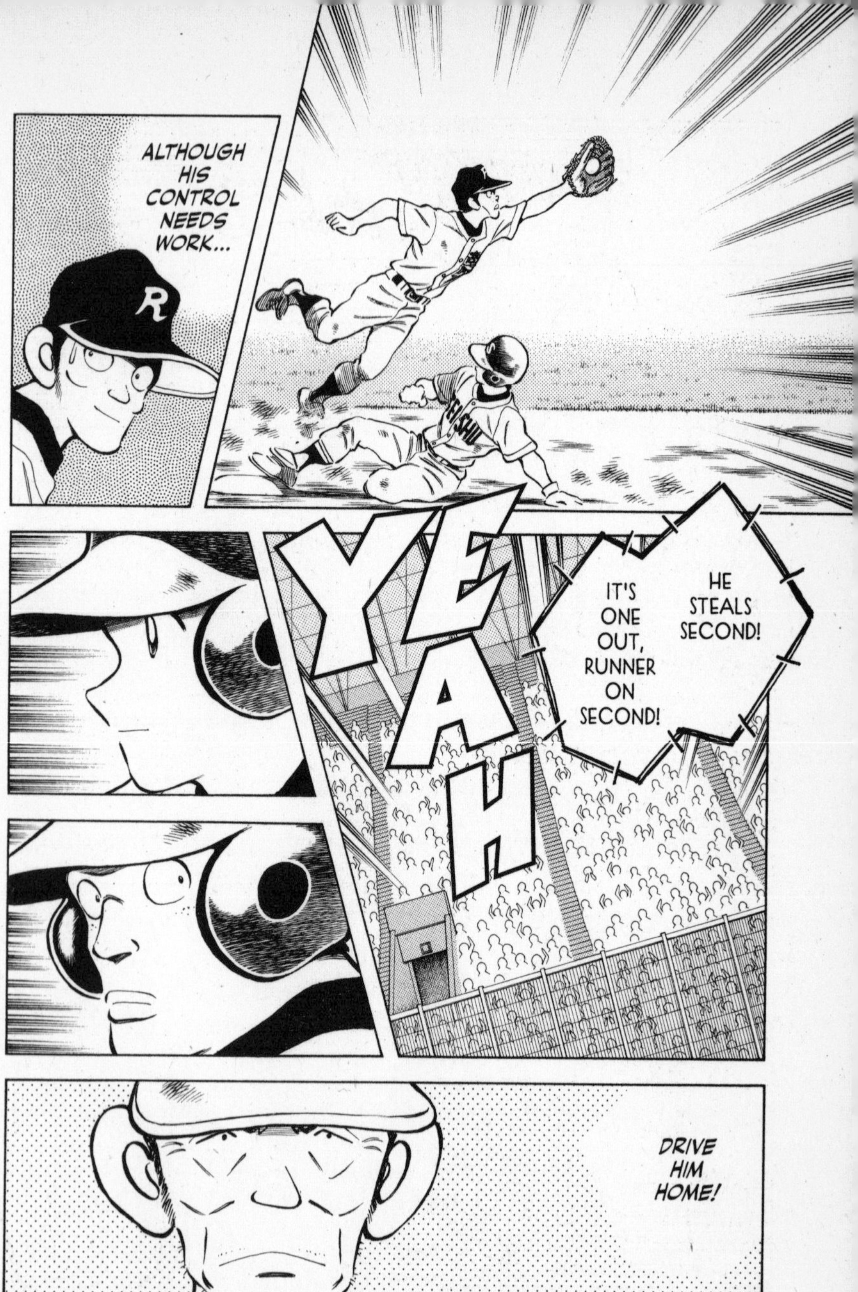
ALTHOUGH HIS CONTROL NEEDS WORK...
YEAH
HE STEALS SECOND!
IT'S ONE OUT, RUNNER ON SECOND!
DRIVE HIM HOME!

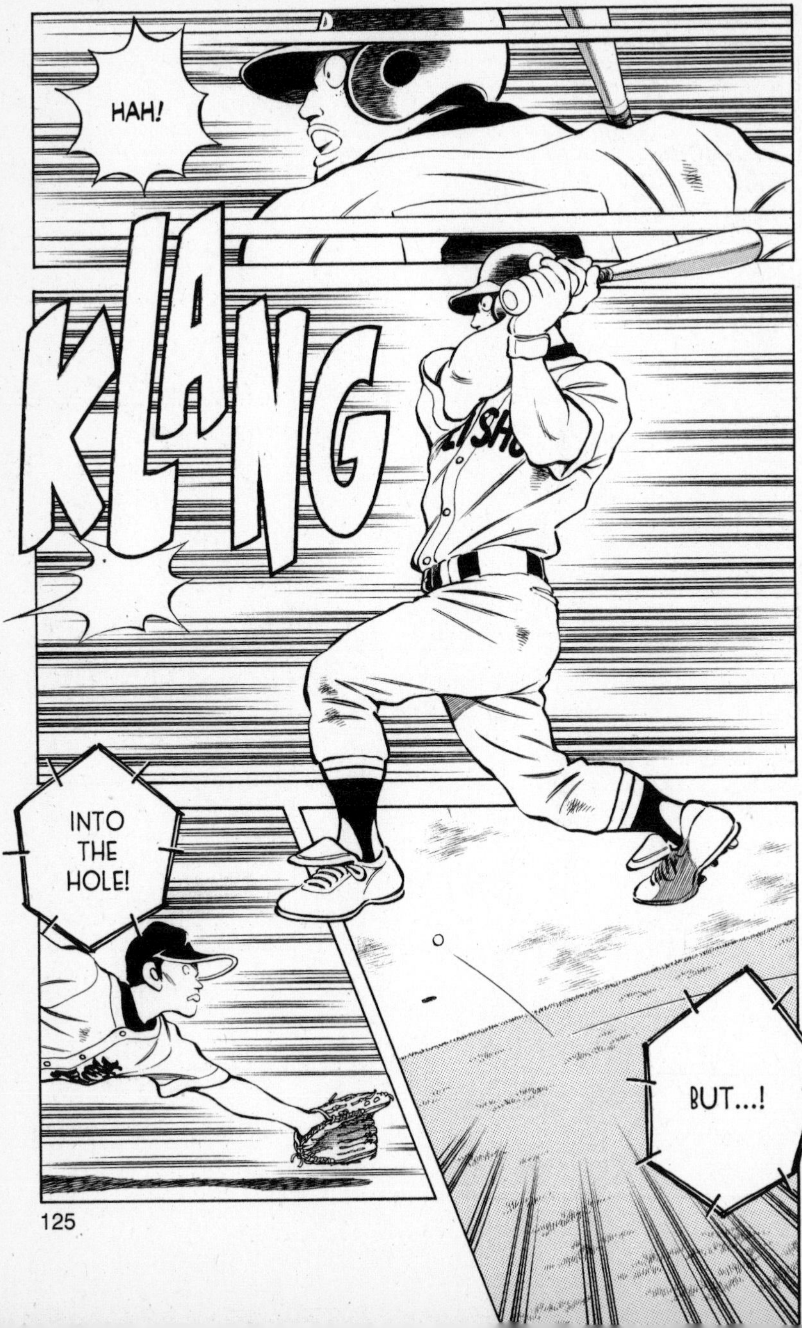
HAH!
KLANG
INTO THE HOLE!
BUT...!

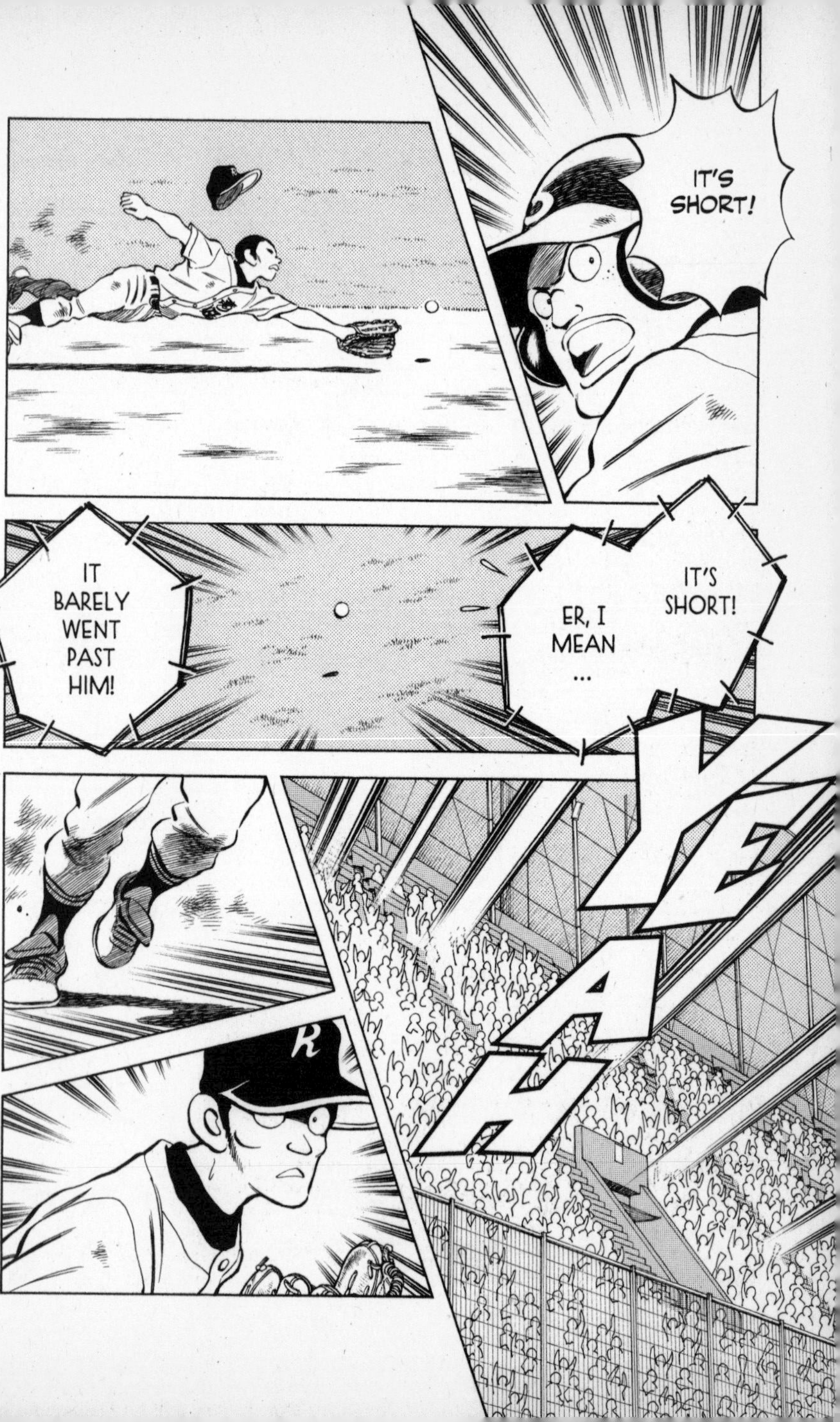
IT'S SHORT!
IT'S SHORT! ER, I MEAN ...
IT BARELY WENT PAST HIM!
YEAH

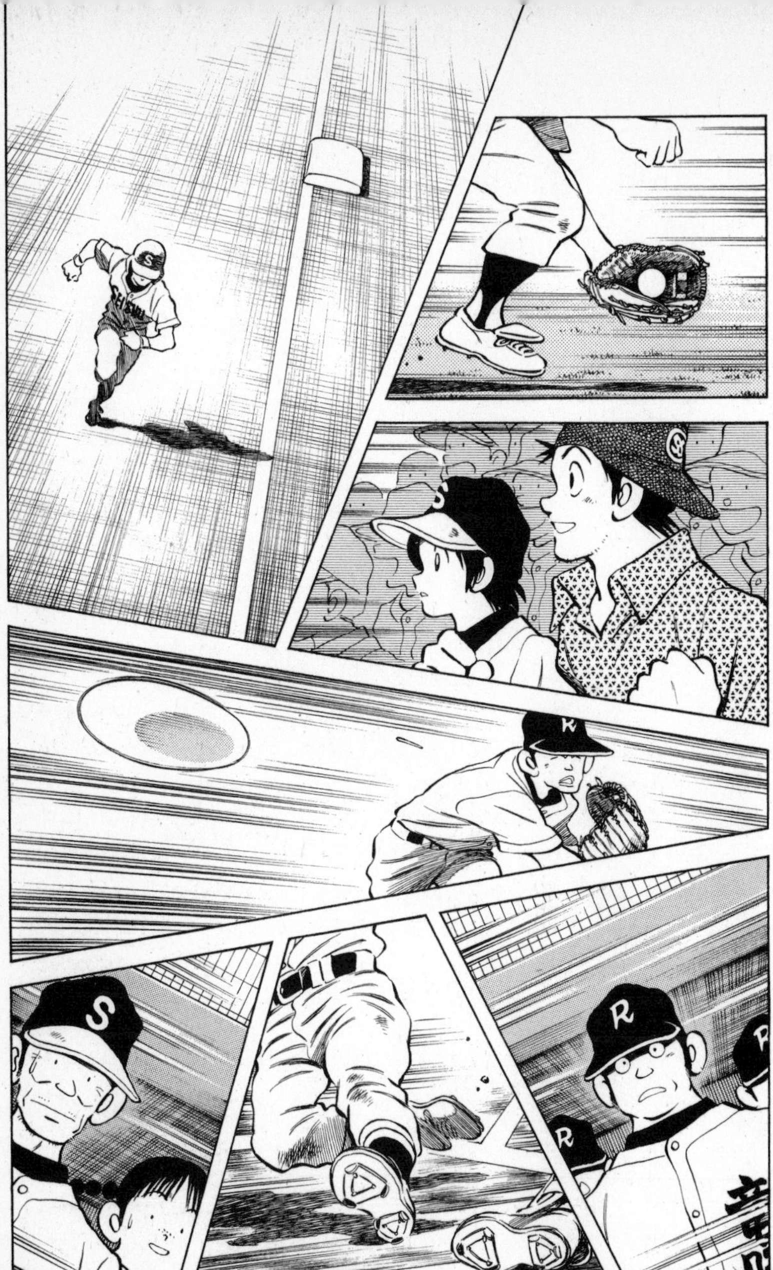

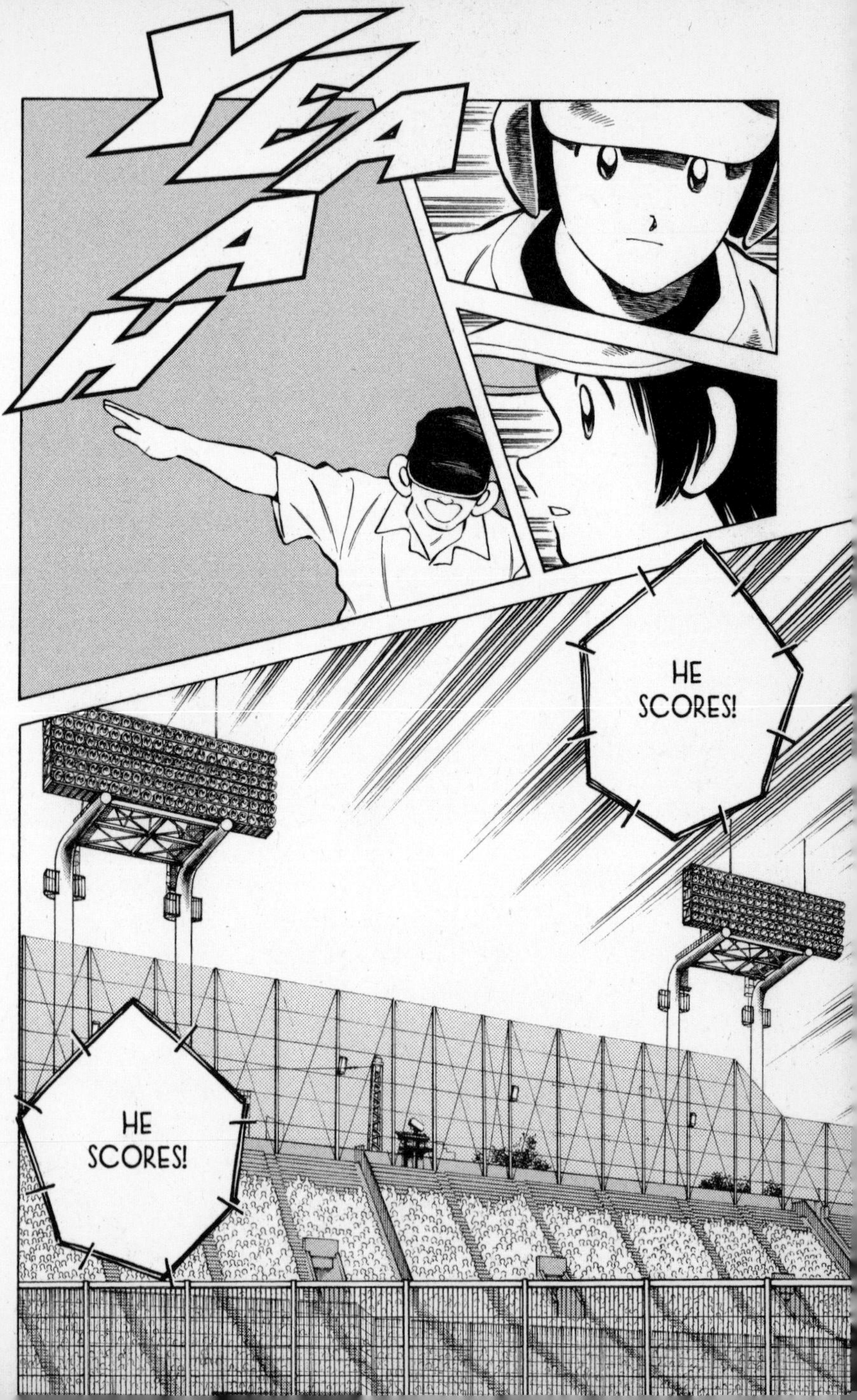
YEAAH
HE SCORES!
HE SCORES!

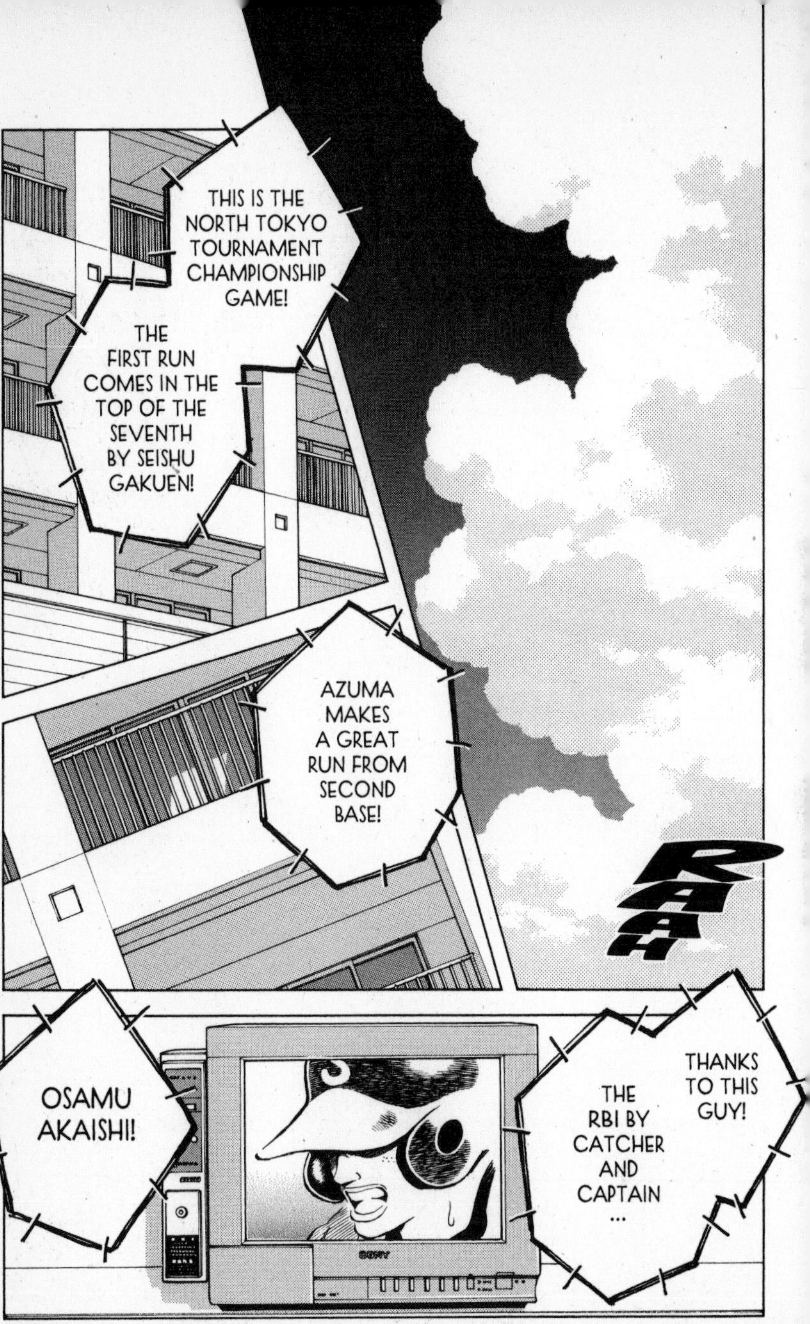
RAAAH
THIS IS THE NORTH TOKYO TOURNAMENT CHAMPIONSHIP GAME!
THE FIRST RUN COMES IN THE TOP OF THE SEVENTH BY SEISHU GAKUEN!
AZUMA MAKES A GREAT RUN FROM SECOND BASE!
THANKS TO THIS GUY!
THE RBI BY CATCHER AND CAPTAIN ...
OSAMU AKAISHI!

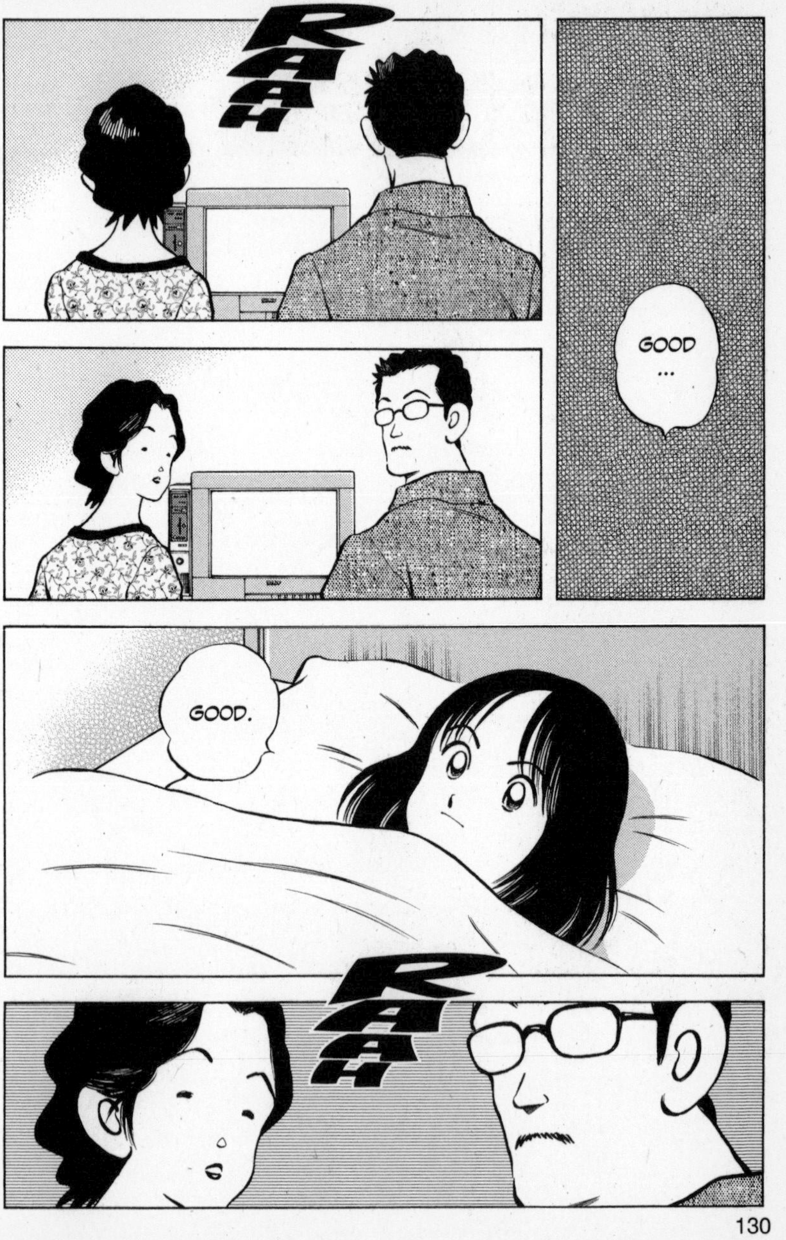
GOOD ...
RAAH
GOOD.
RAAH

CHAPTER 148
HE PROMISED ME

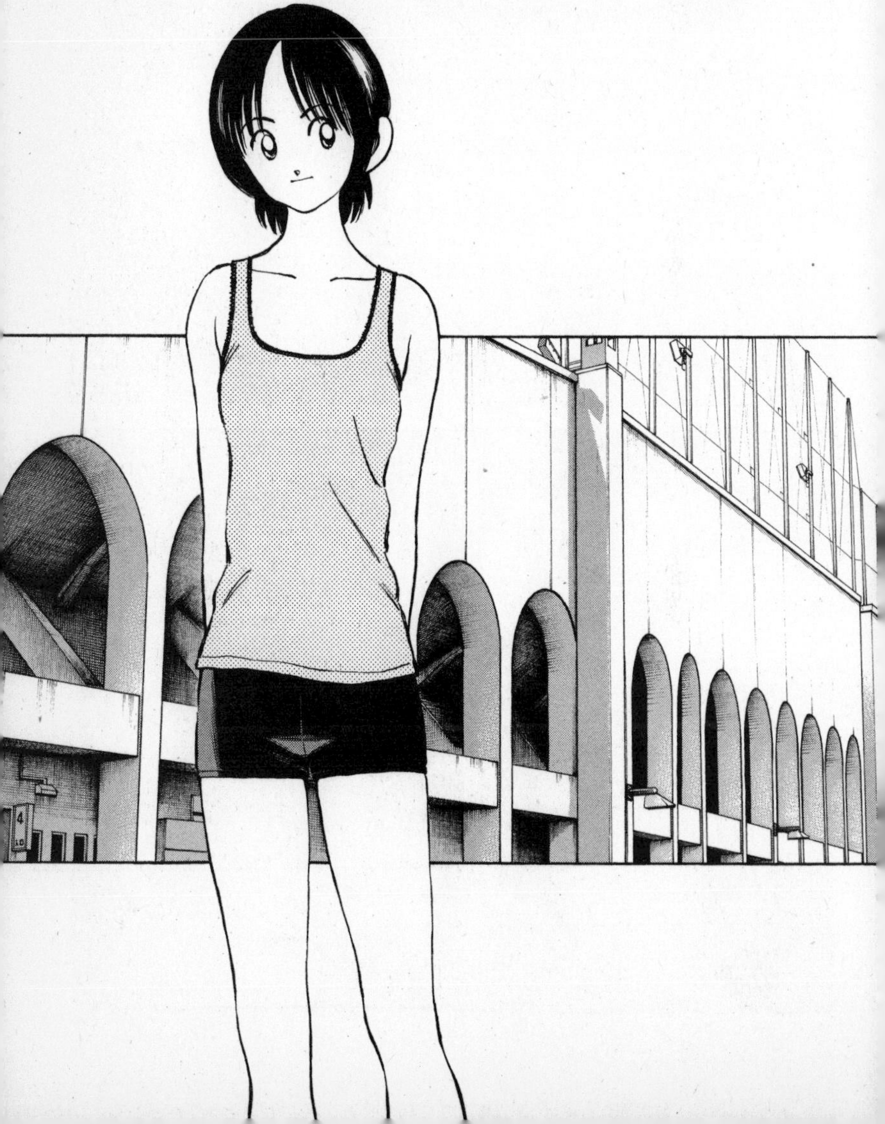

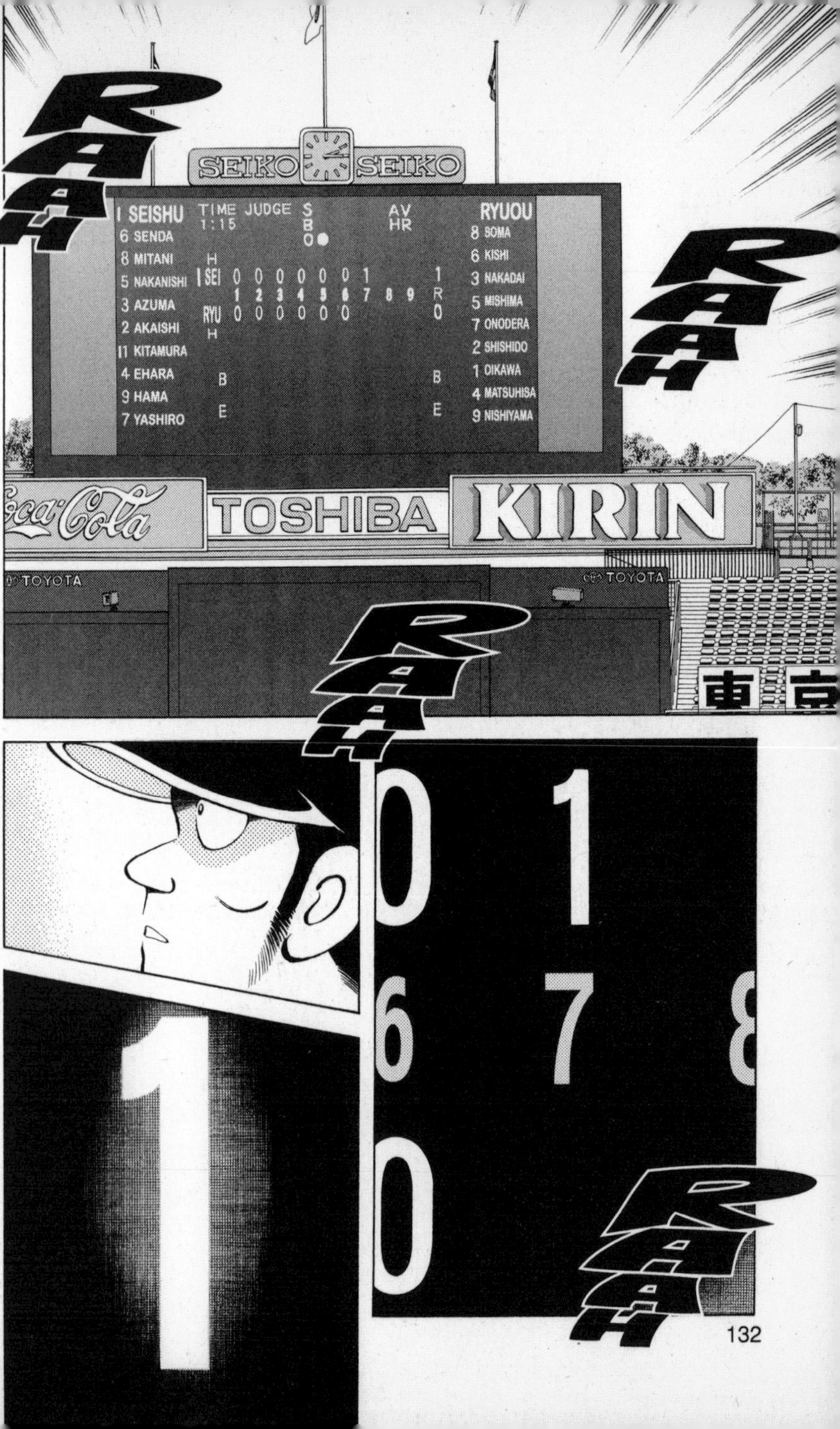
RAAH
RAAH
SEIKO SEIKO
I SEISHU
6 SENDA
8 MITANI
5 NAKANISHI
3 AZUMA
2 AKAISHI
11 KITAMURA
4 EHARA
9 HAMA
7 YASHIRO
RYUOU
8 SOMA
6 KISHI
3 NAKADAI
5 MISHIMA
7 ONODERA
2 SHISHIDO
1 OIKAWA
4 MATSUHISA
9 NISHIYAMA
Coca-Cola
TOSHIBA
KIRIN
TOYOTA
TOYOTA
東京
RAAH
RAAH

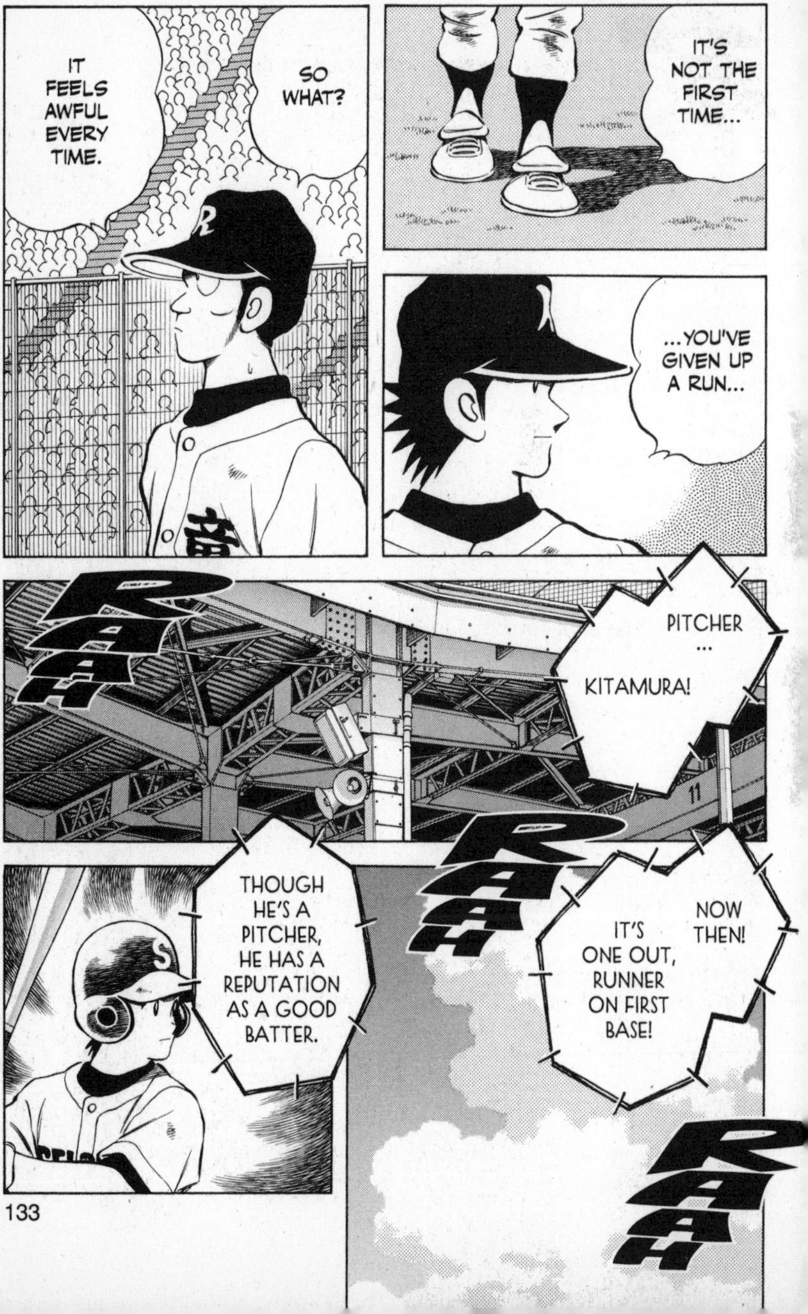
IT'S NOT THE FIRST TIME...
...YOU'VE GIVEN UP A RUN...
SO WHAT?
IT FEELS AWFUL EVERY TIME.
PITCHER ... KITAMURA!
RAAH
RAAH
NOW THEN! IT'S ONE OUT, RUNNER ON FIRST BASE!
RAAH
THOUGH HE'S A PITCHER, HE HAS A REPUTATION AS A GOOD BATTER.

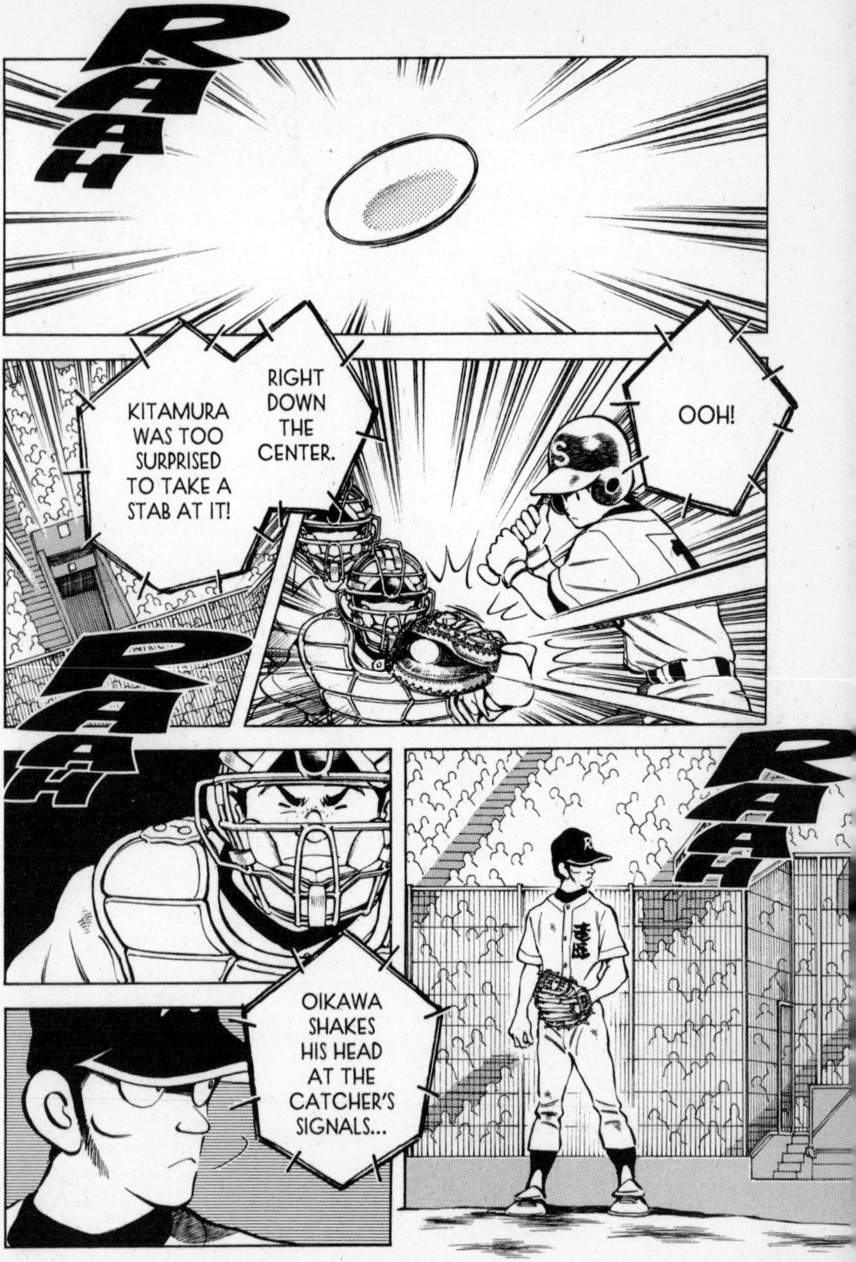
RAAH
OOH!
RIGHT DOWN THE CENTER.
KITAMURA WAS TOO SURPRISED TO TAKE A STAB AT IT!
RAAH
RAAH
OIKAWA SHAKES HIS HEAD AT THE CATCHER'S SIGNALS...

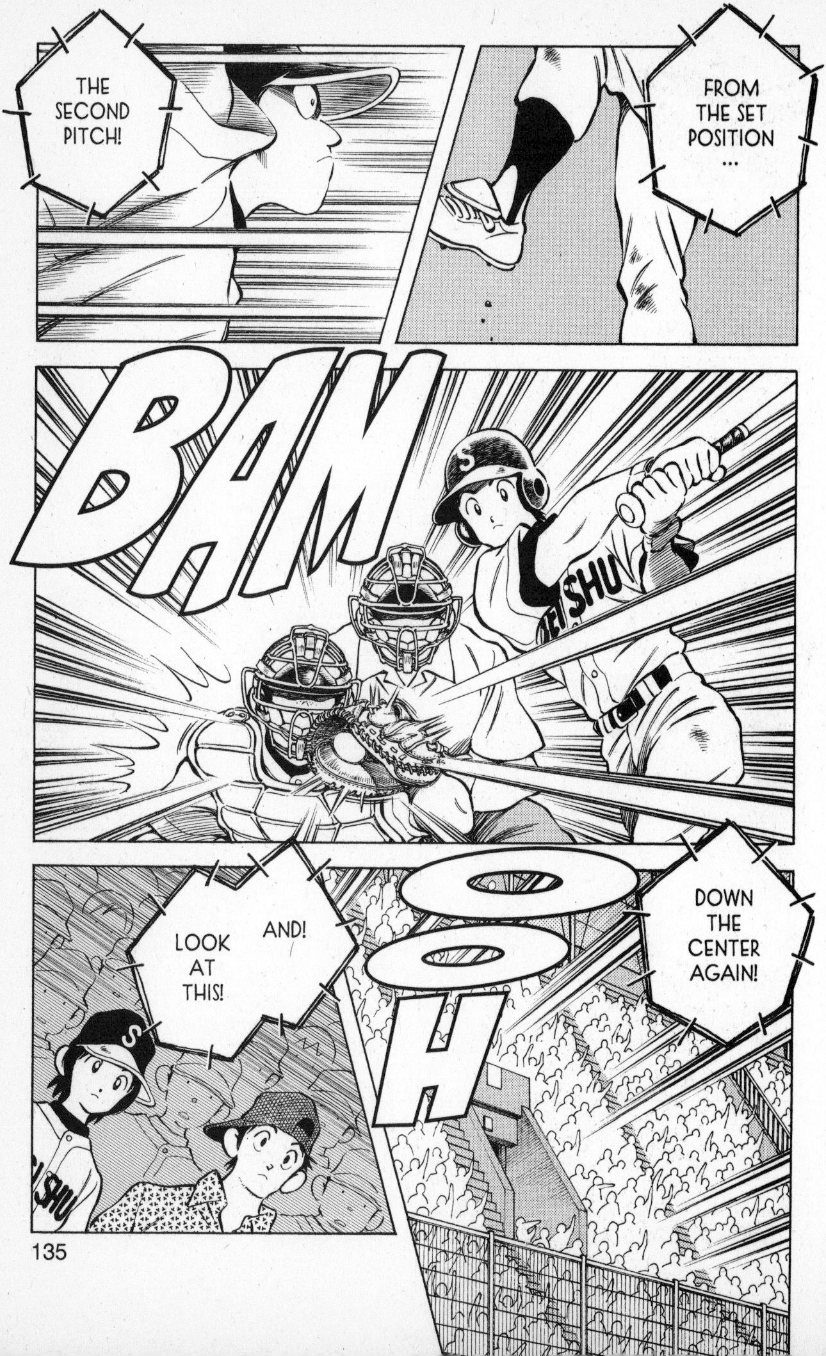
FROM THE SET POSITION ...
THE SECOND PITCH!
BAM
DOWN THE CENTER AGAIN!
OOH
AND!
LOOK AT THIS!

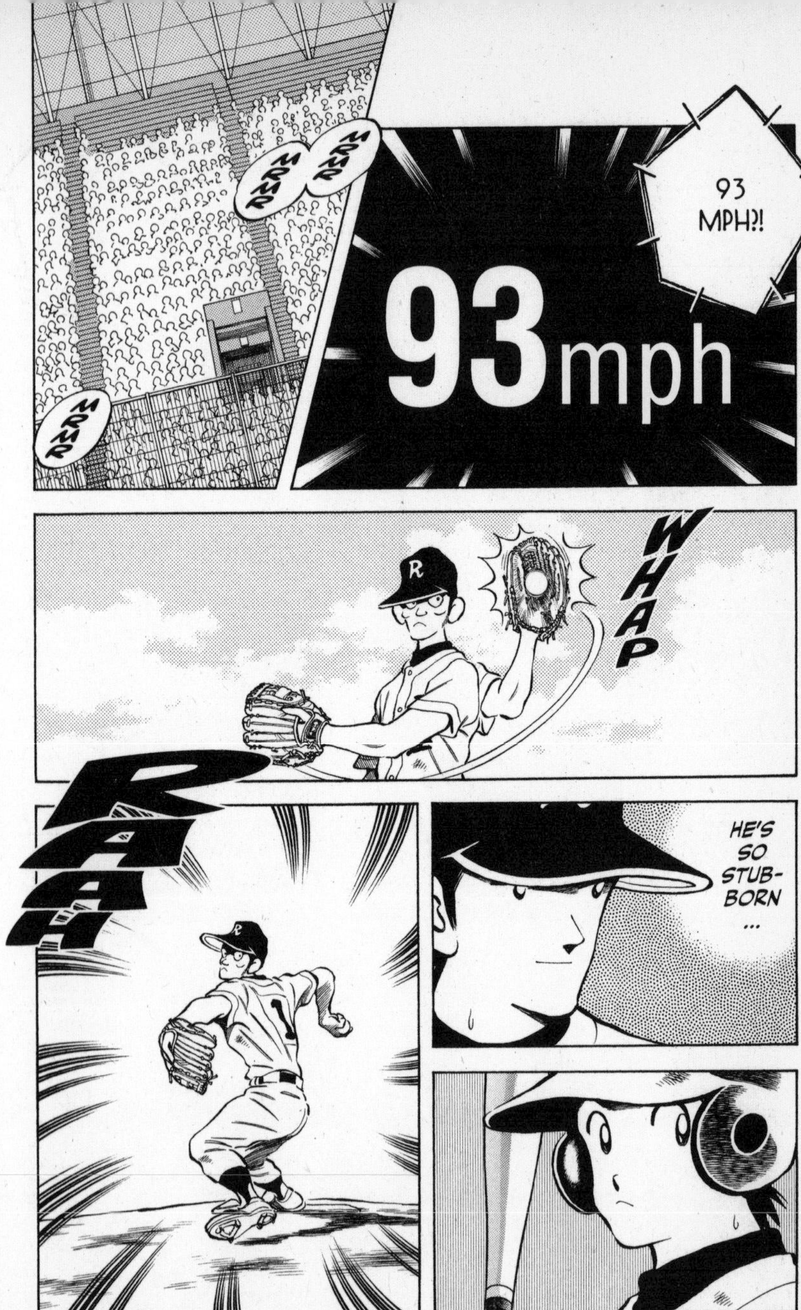
93mph
93 MPH?!
MRMR
MRMR
MRMR
WHAP
HE'S SO STUB-BORN ...
RAAH

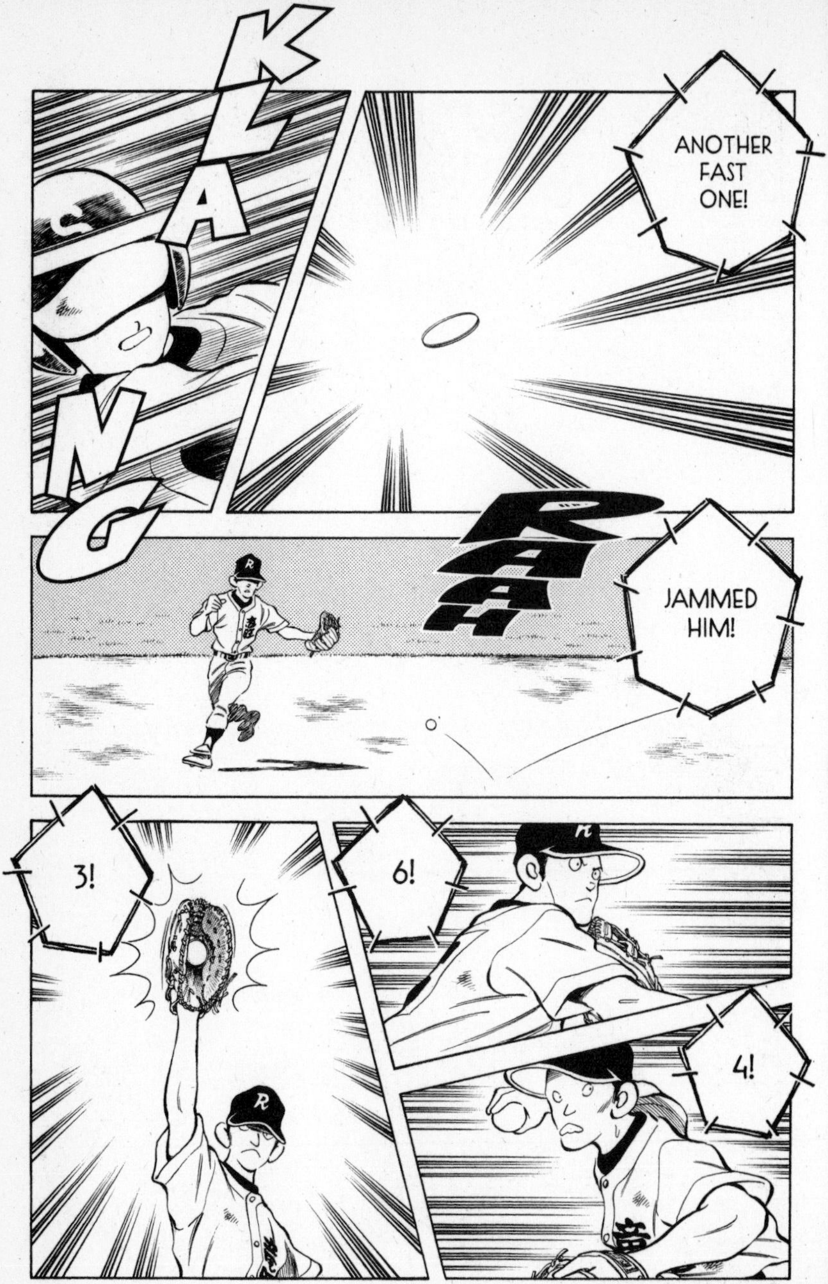
ANOTHER FAST ONE!
KLANG
JAMMED HIM!
RAAH
6!
4!
3!

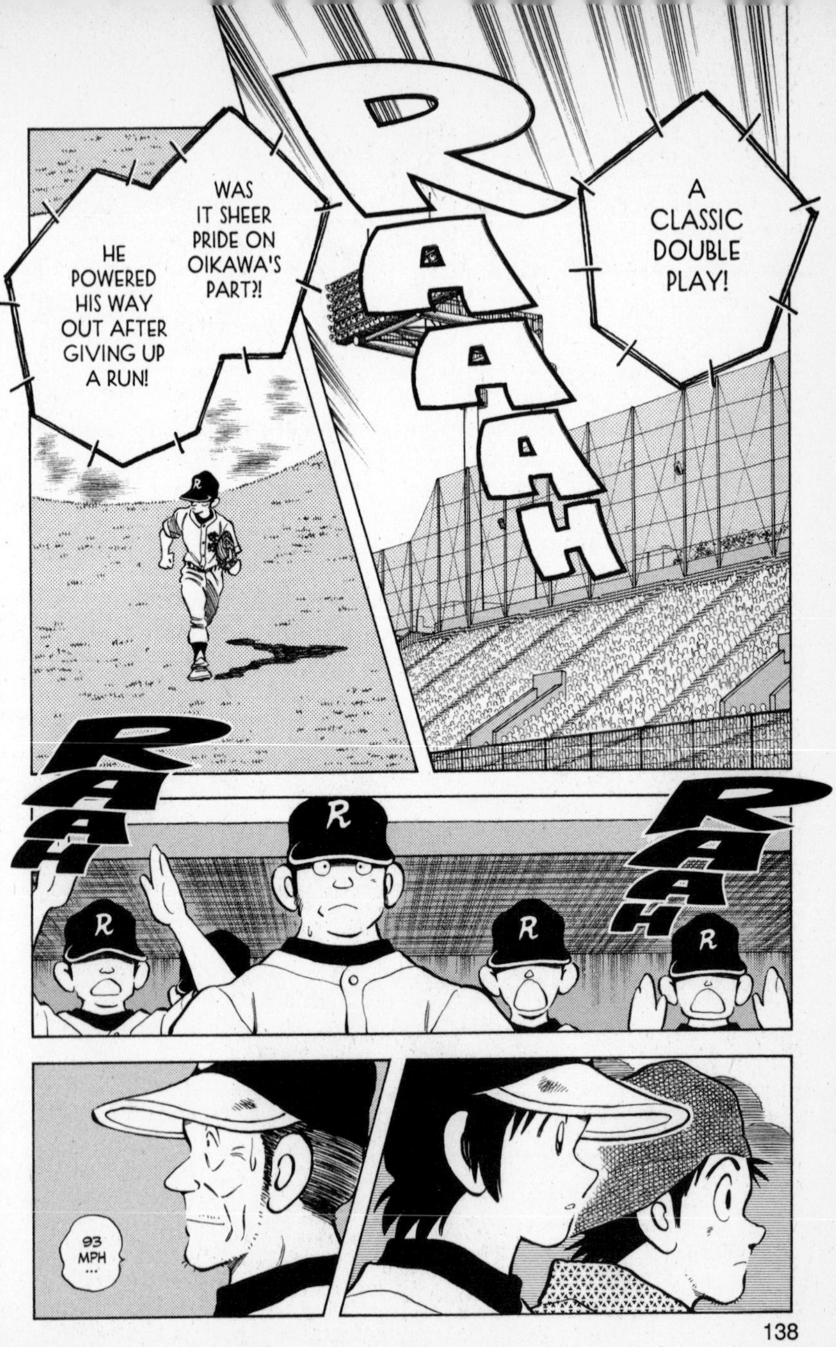
A CLASSIC DOUBLE PLAY!
RAAAH
WAS IT SHEER PRIDE ON OIKAWA'S PART?!
HE POWERED HIS WAY OUT AFTER GIVING UP A RUN!
RAAH
RAAH
93 MPH...

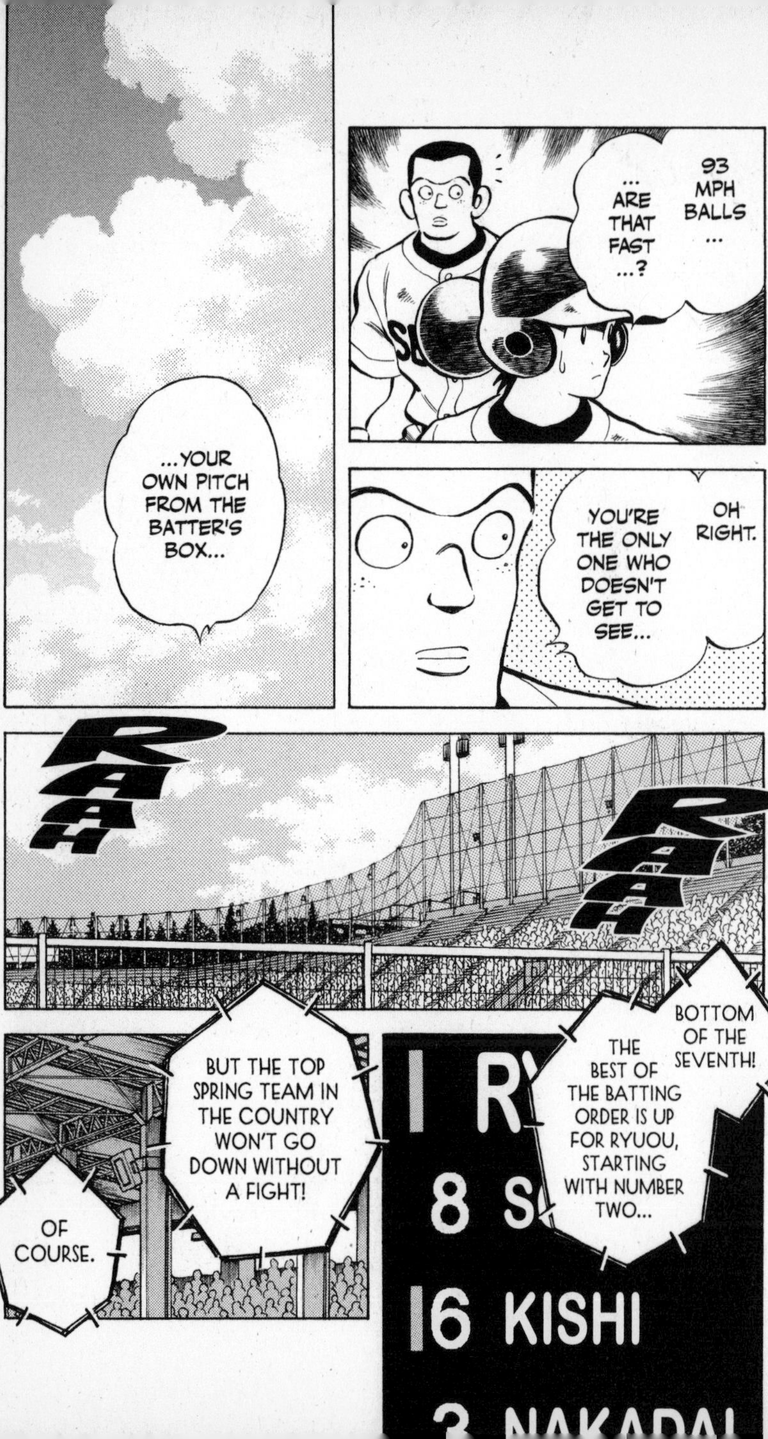
93 MPH BALLS...
...ARE THAT FAST...?
OH RIGHT.
YOU'RE THE ONLY ONE WHO DOESN'T GET TO SEE...
...YOUR OWN PITCH FROM THE BATTER'S BOX...
RAAH
RAAH
BOTTOM OF THE SEVENTH!
THE BEST OF THE BATTING ORDER IS UP FOR RYUOU, STARTING WITH NUMBER TWO...
16 KISHI
BUT THE TOP SPRING TEAM IN THE COUNTRY WON'T GO DOWN WITHOUT A FIGHT!
OF COURSE.

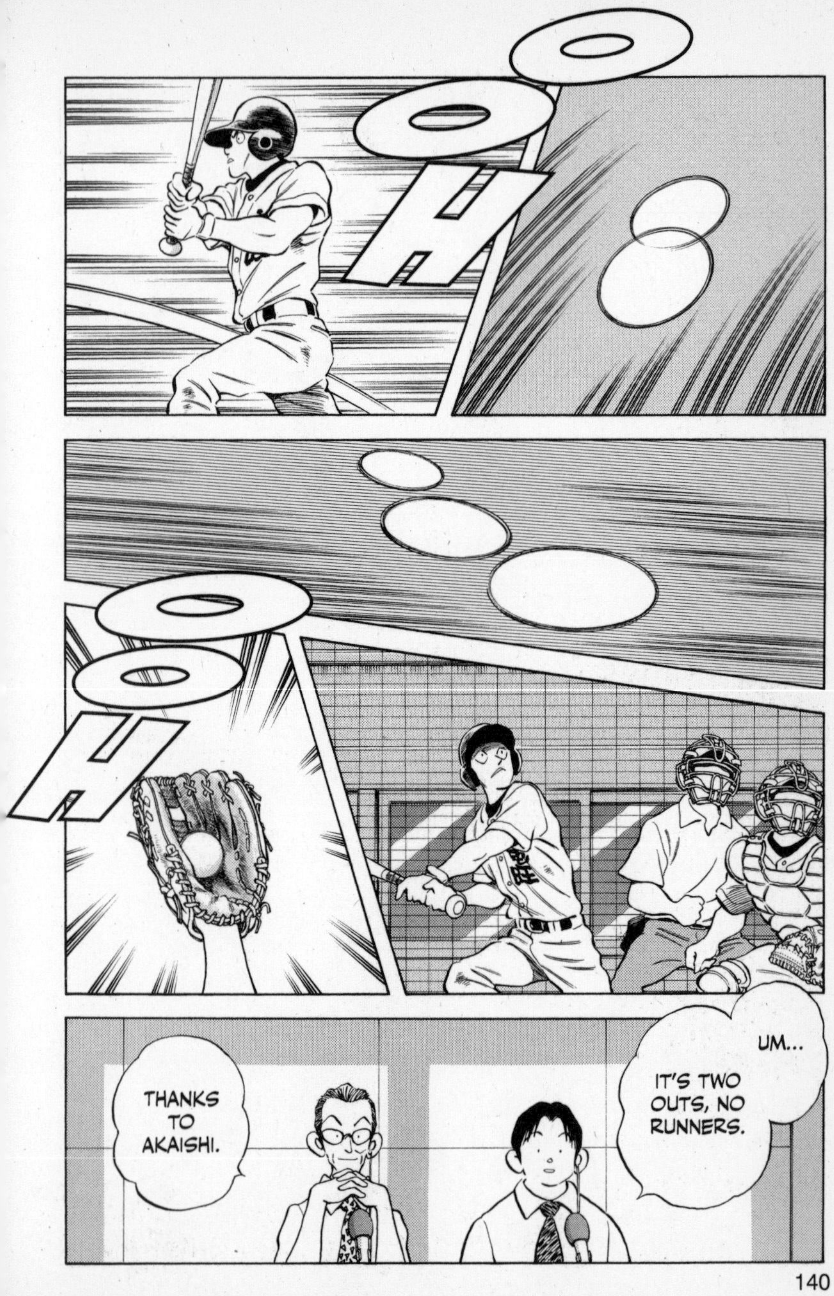
HOO
HOO
UM...
IT'S TWO OUTS, NO RUNNERS.
THANKS TO AKAISHI.

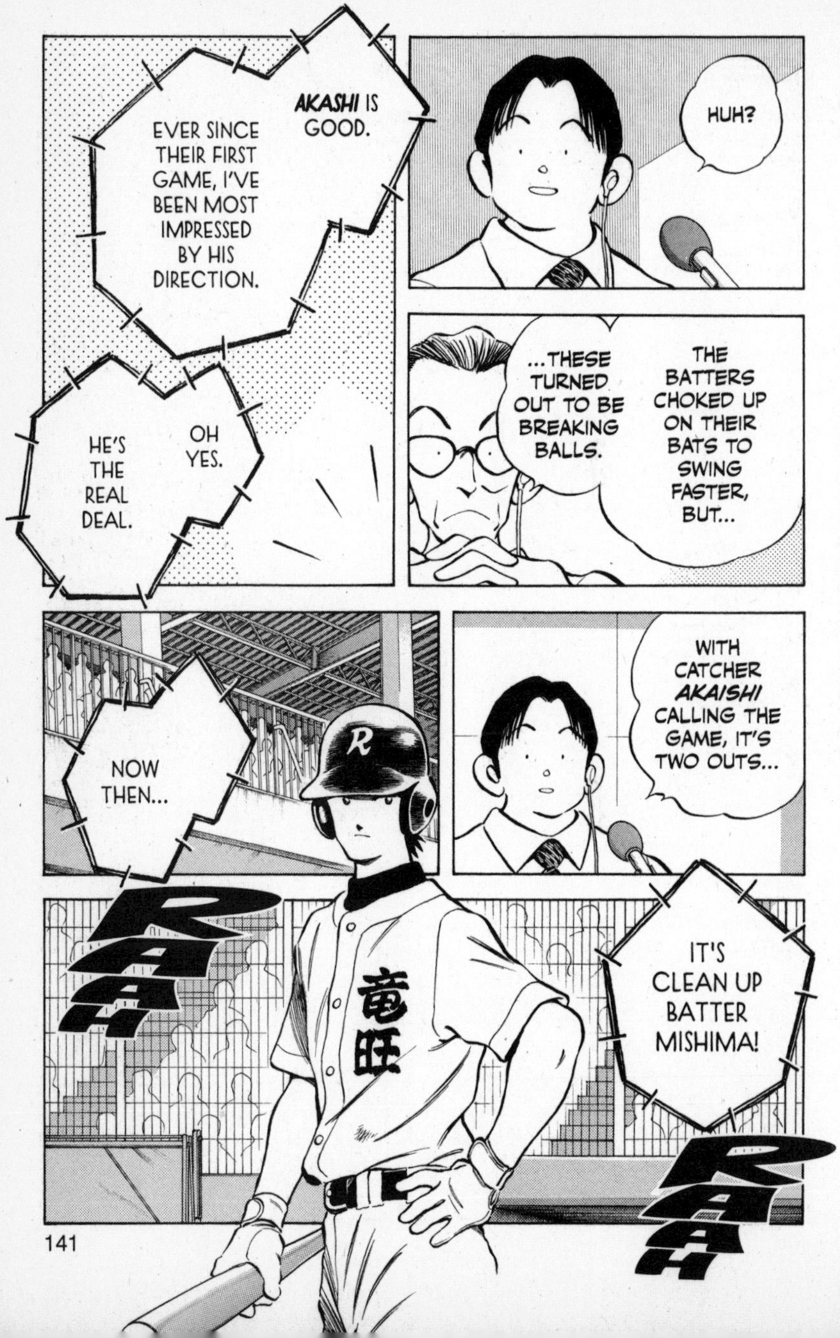
HUH?
AKASHI IS GOOD.
EVER SINCE THEIR FIRST GAME, I'VE BEEN MOST IMPRESSED BY HIS DIRECTION.
THE BATTERS CHOKED UP ON THEIR BATS TO SWING FASTER, BUT...
...THESE TURNED OUT TO BE BREAKING BALLS.
OH YES.
HE'S THE REAL DEAL.
WITH CATCHER AKAISHI CALLING THE GAME, IT'S TWO OUTS...
NOW THEN...
IT'S CLEAN UP BATTER MISHIMA!
RAAH
RAAH

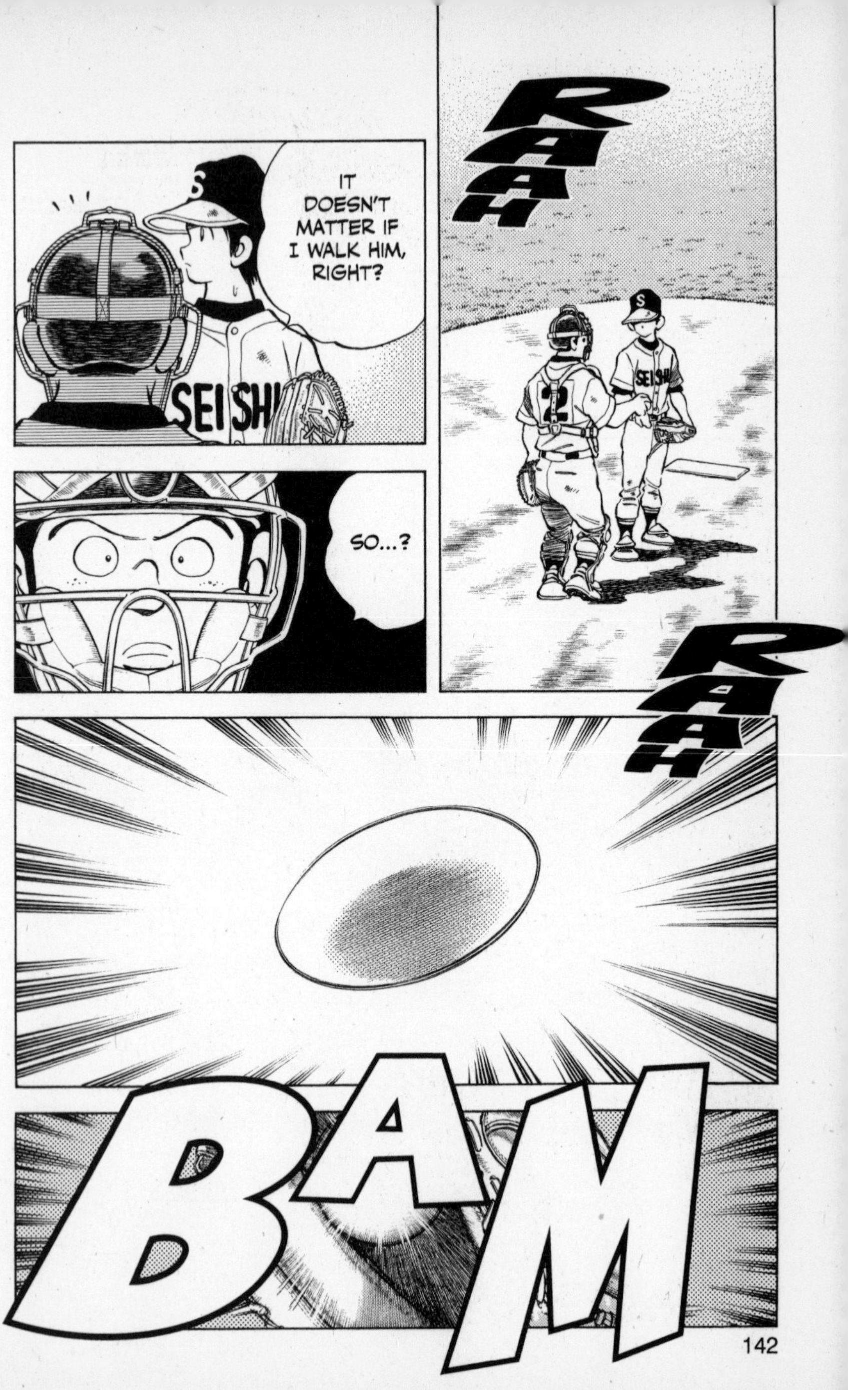
RAAH
IT DOESN'T MATTER IF I WALK HIM, RIGHT?
SO...?
RAAH
BAM

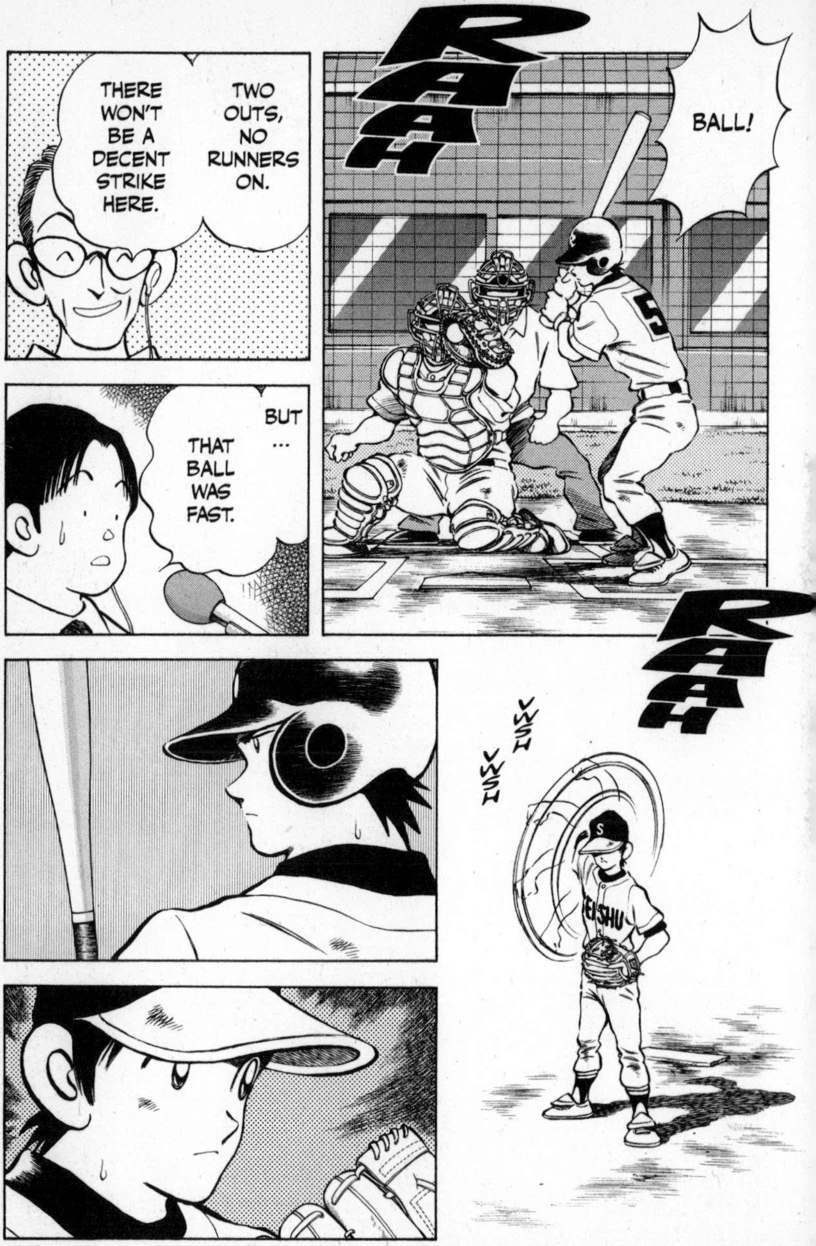

RAAH
BALL!
TWO OUTS, NO RUNNERS ON.
THERE WON'T BE A DECENT STRIKE HERE.
BUT...
THAT BALL WAS FAST.
RAAH
VWSH
VWSH

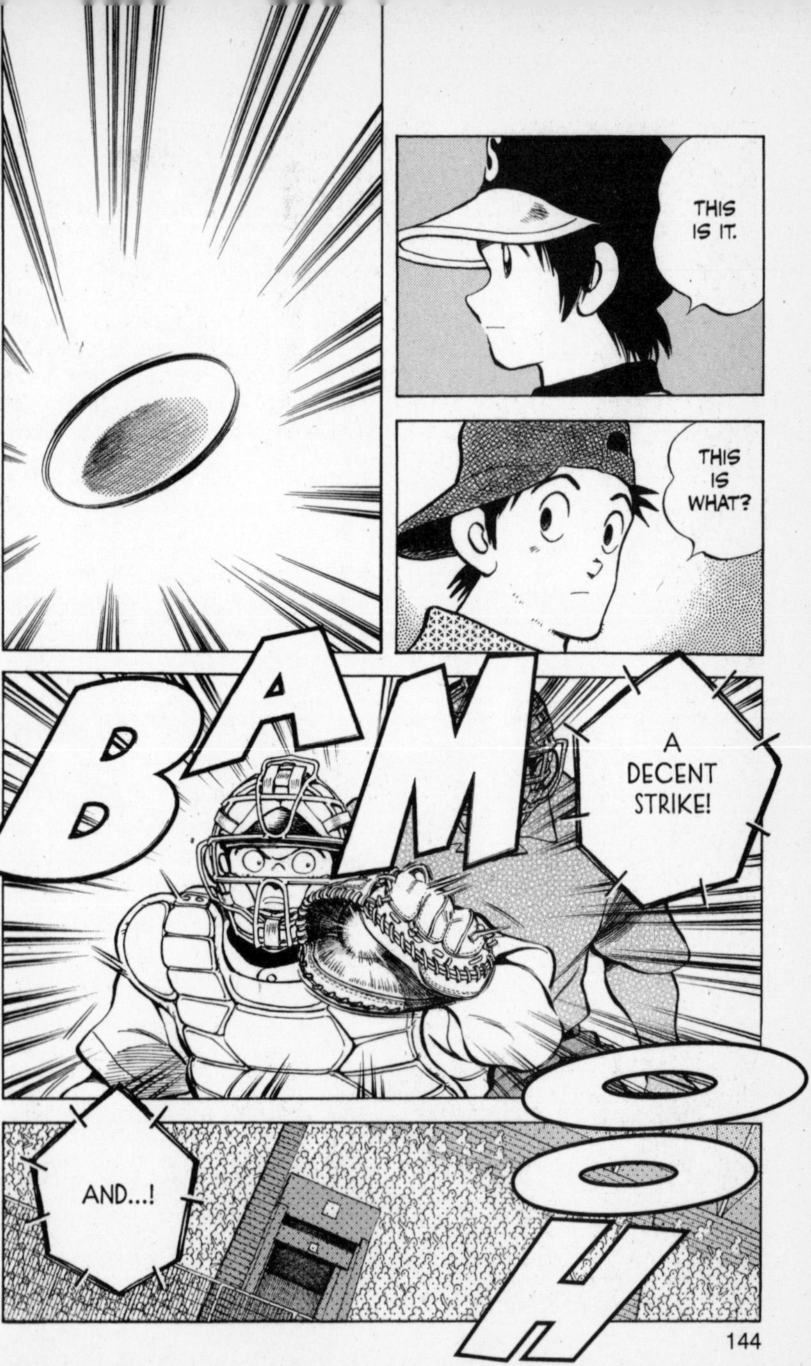
THIS IS IT.
THIS IS WHAT?
A DECENT STRIKE!
BAM
OOH
AND...!

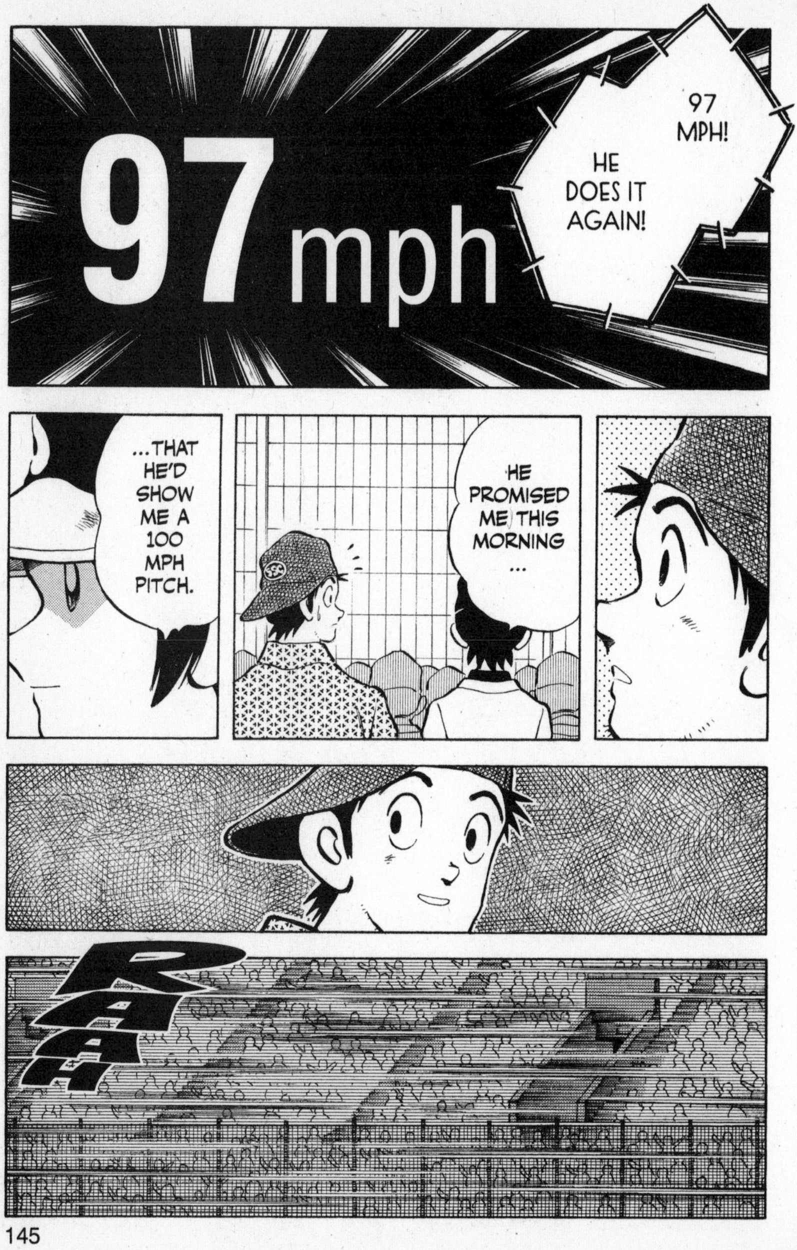
97 mph
97 MPH! HE DOES IT AGAIN!
HE PROMISED ME THIS MORNING...
...THAT HE'D SHOW ME A 100 MPH PITCH.
RAAAH

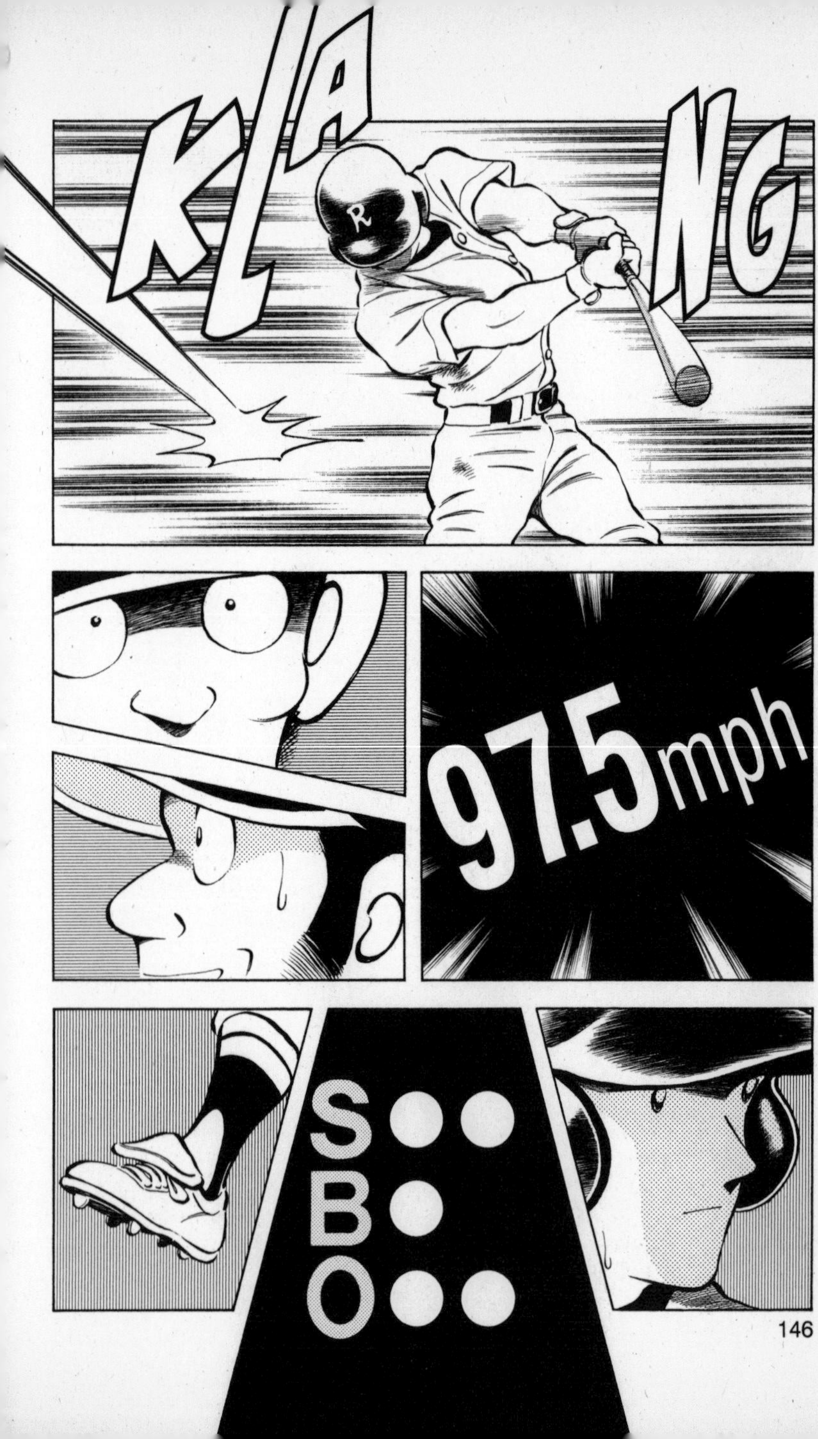
KLANG
97.5mph
S
B
O

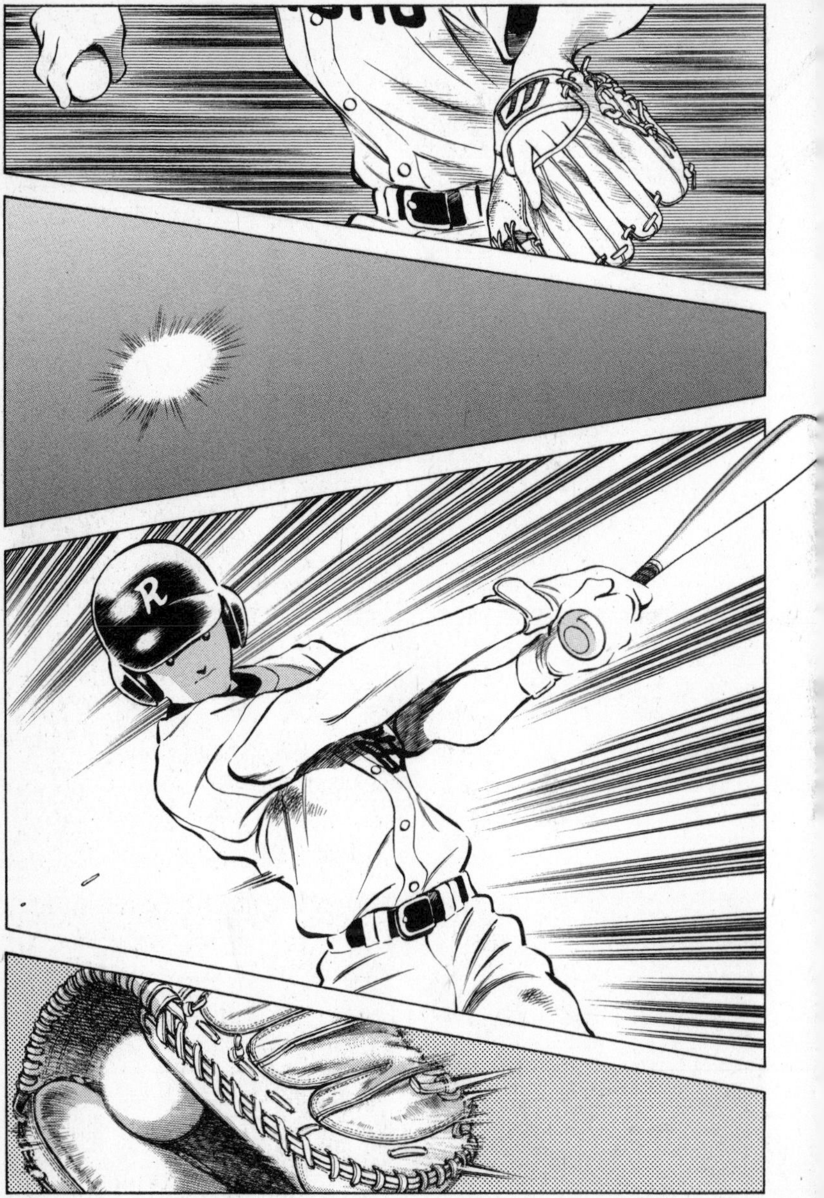

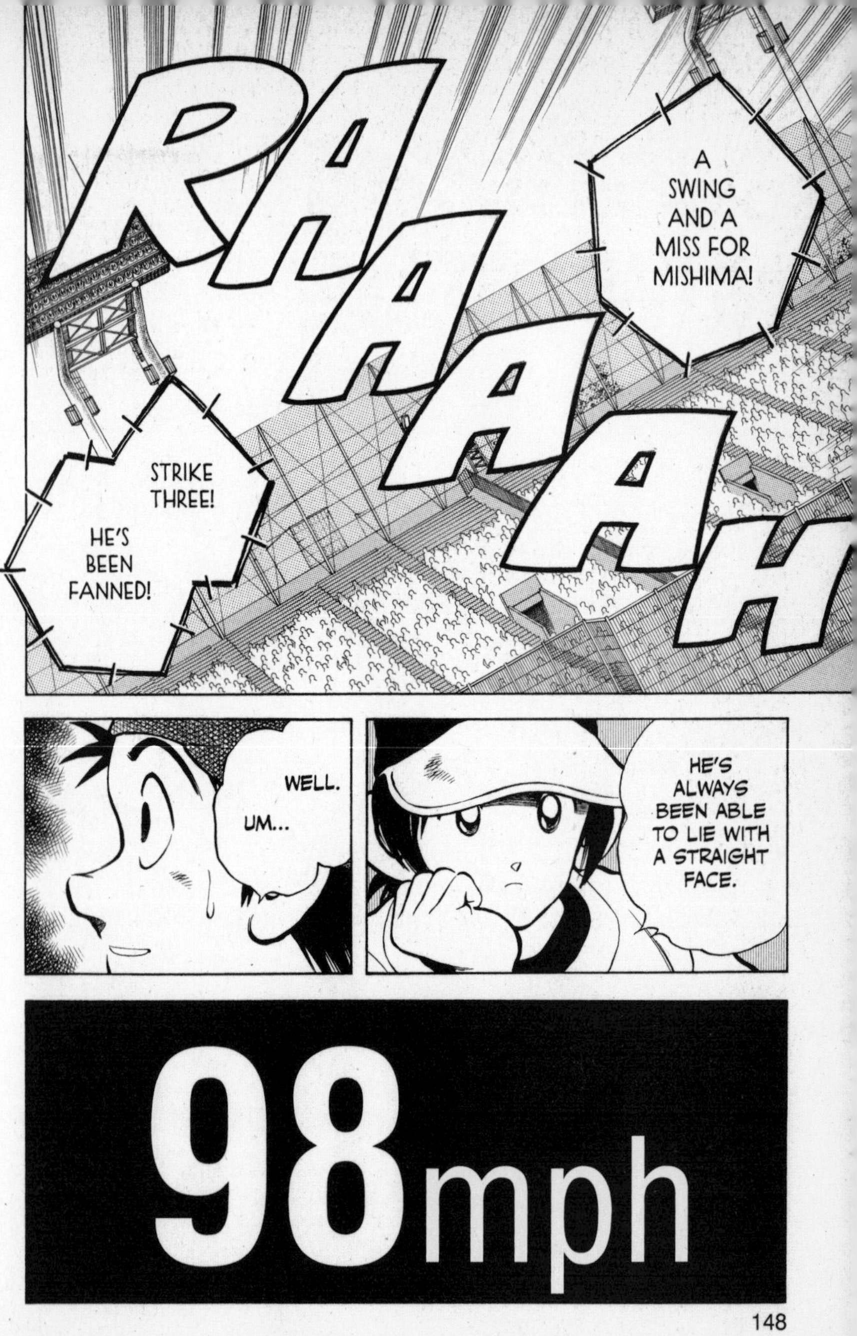
RAAAAH
A SWING AND A MISS FOR MISHIMA!
STRIKE THREE!
HE'S BEEN FANNED!
HE'S ALWAYS BEEN ABLE TO LIE WITH A STRAIGHT FACE.
WELL.
UM...

98mph

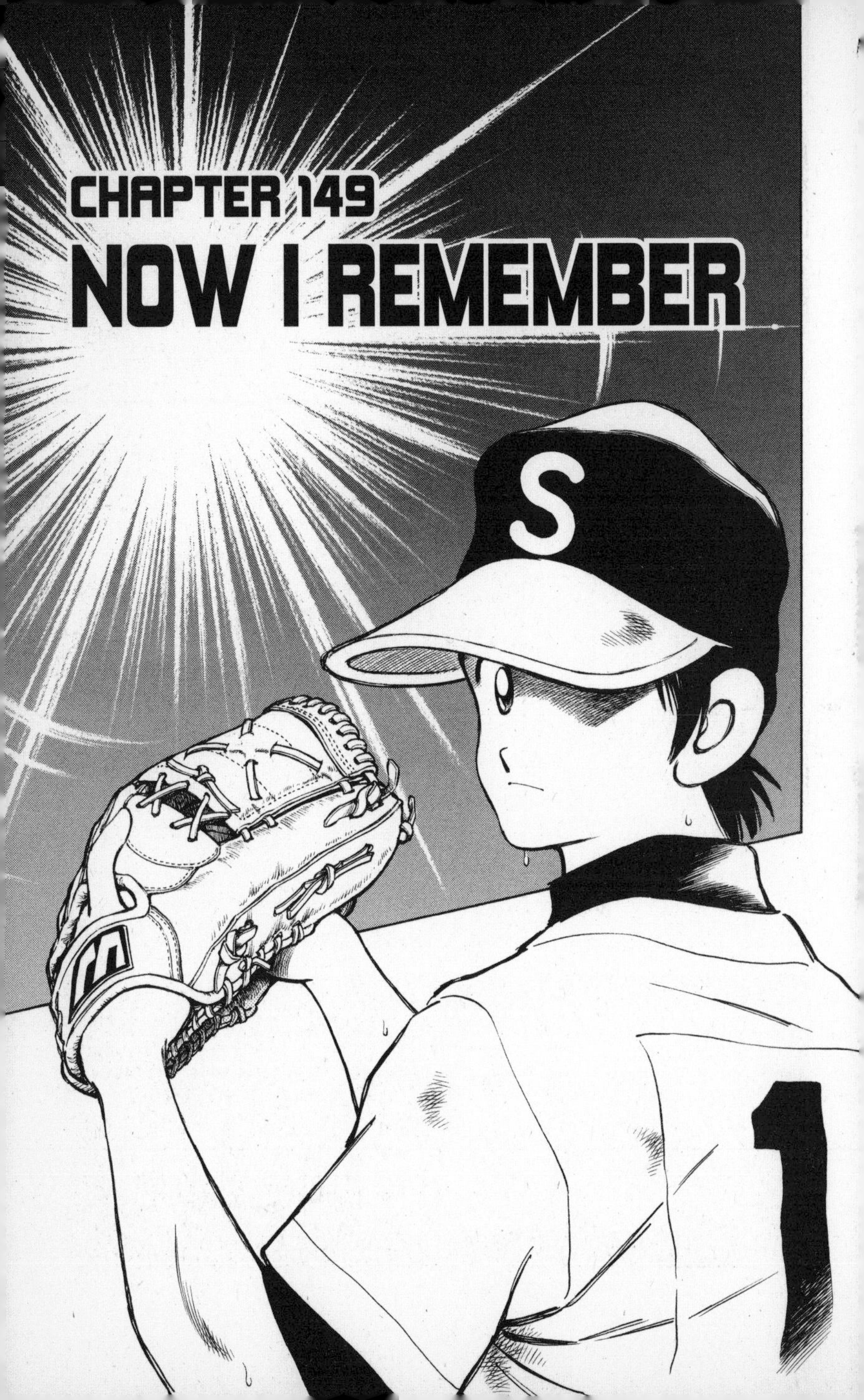
CHAPTER 149
NOW I REMEMBER

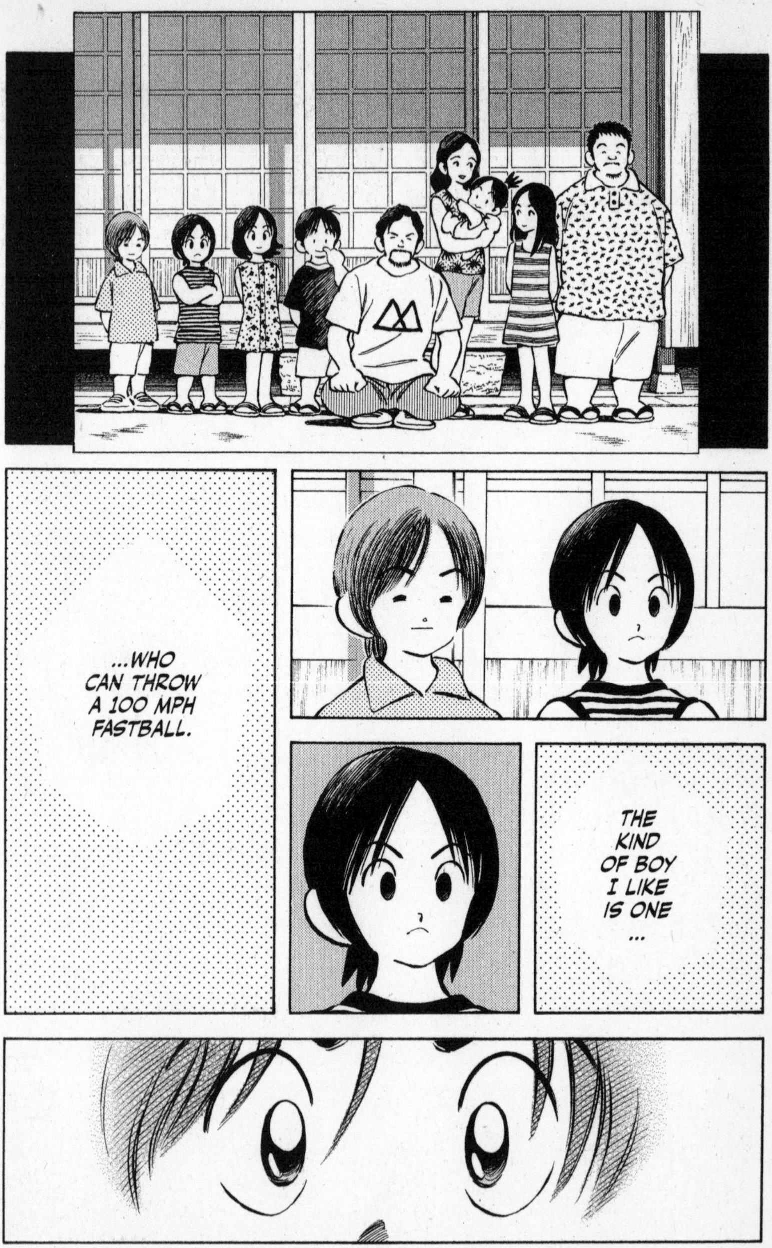
THE KIND OF BOY I LIKE IS ONE ...
...WHO CAN THROW A 100 MPH FASTBALL.

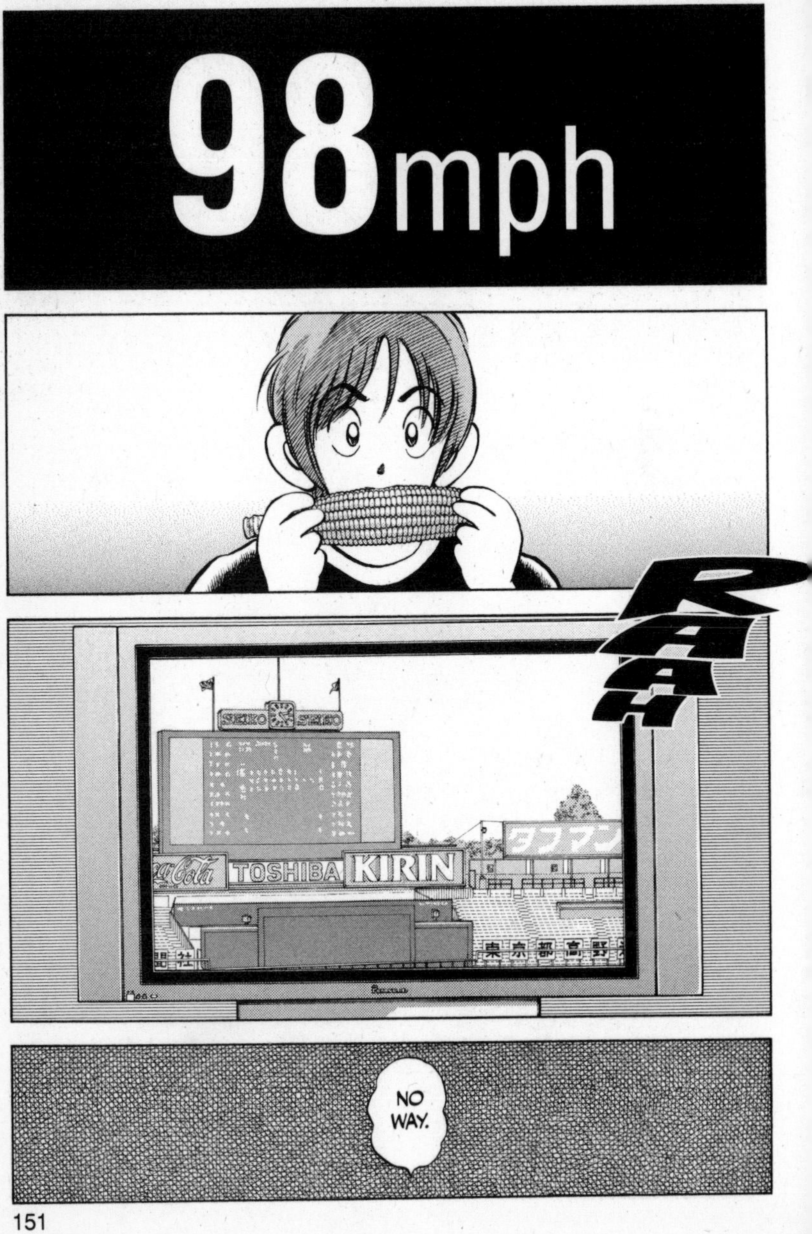
98mph
NO WAY.

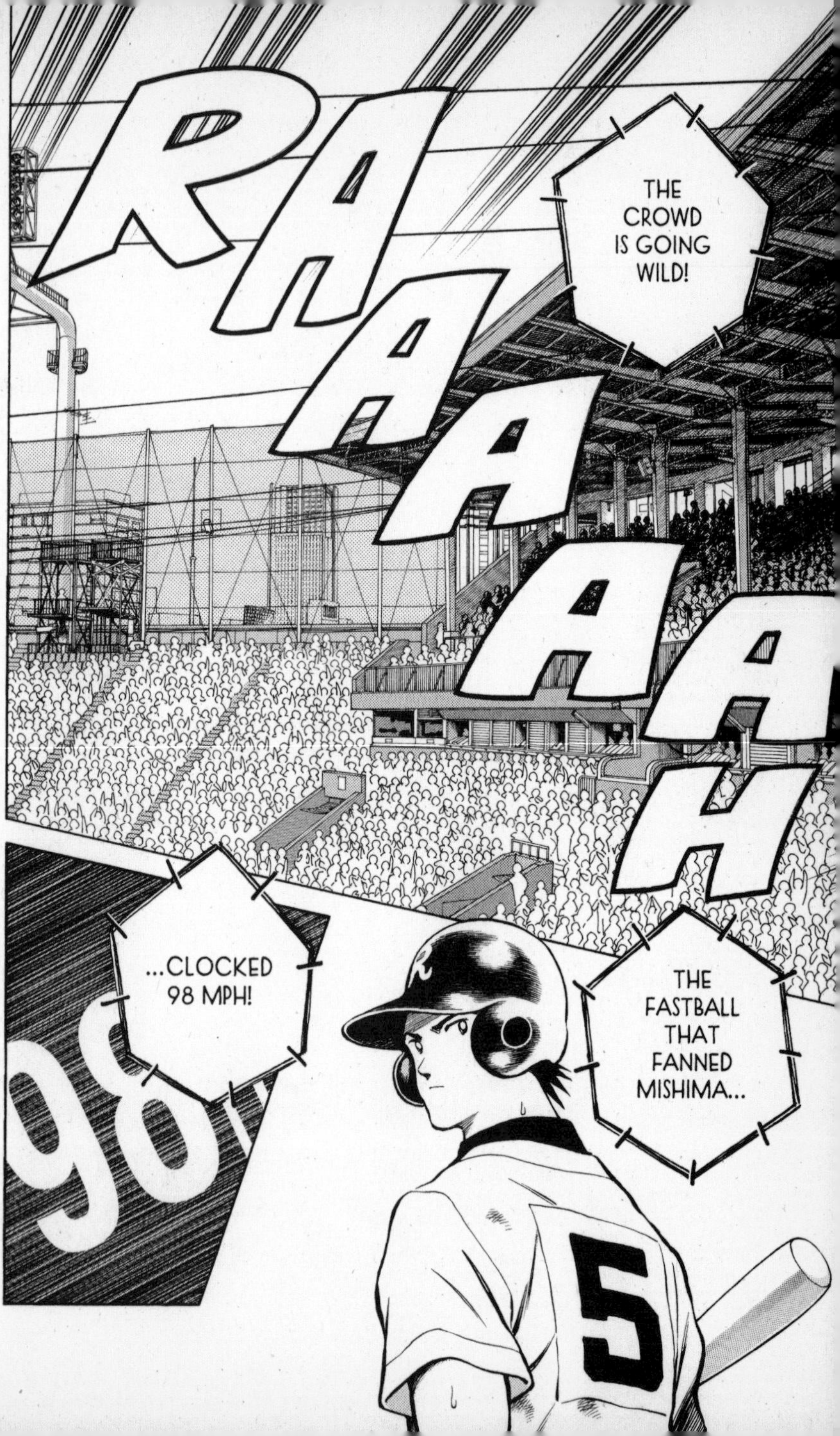
RAAAAAH
THE CROWD IS GOING WILD!
THE FASTBALL THAT FANNED MISHIMA...
...CLOCKED 98 MPH!
98

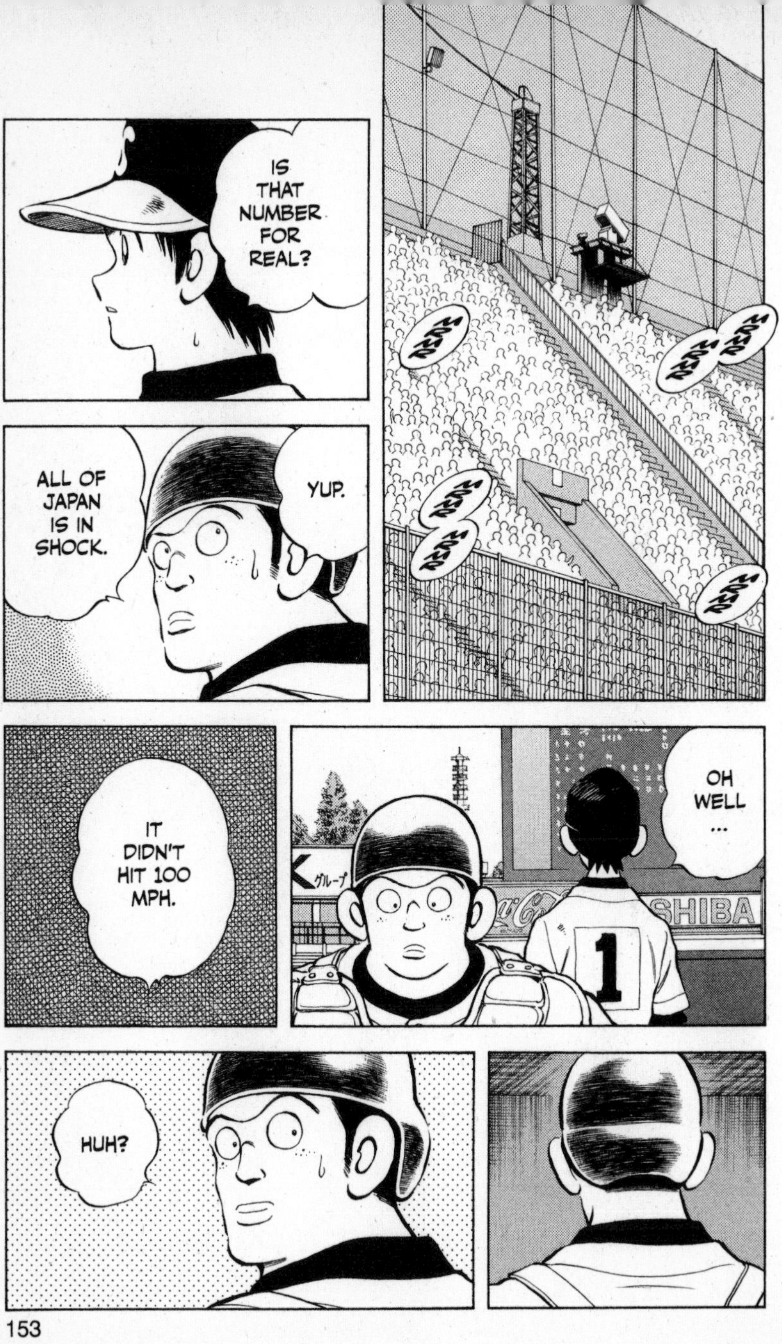
MRMR
MRMR
MRMR
MRMR
MRMR
IS THAT NUMBER FOR REAL?
YUP.
ALL OF JAPAN IS IN SHOCK.
OH WELL ...
IT DIDN'T HIT 100 MPH.
HUH?

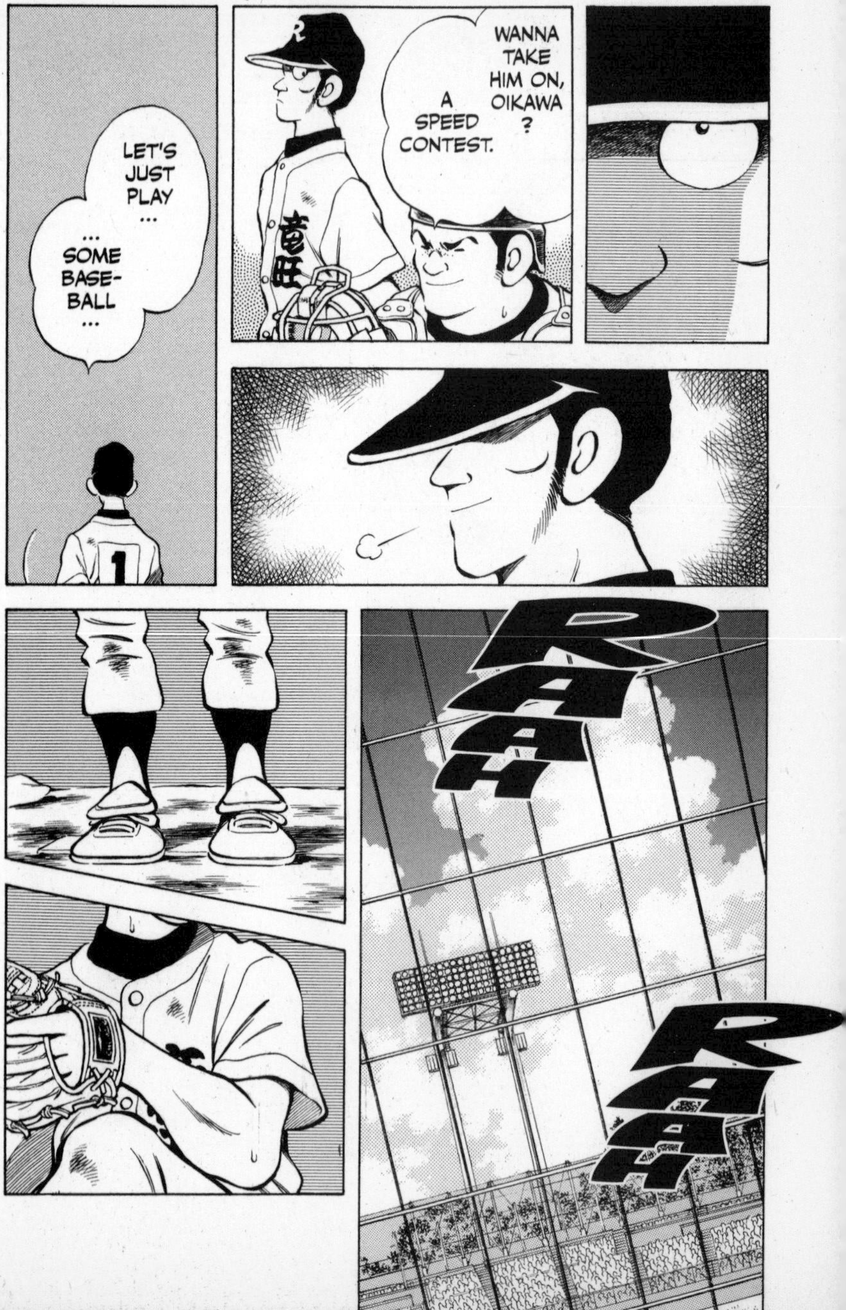
WANNA TAKE HIM ON, OIKAWA?
A SPEED CONTEST.
LET'S JUST PLAY ...
... SOME BASE-BALL ...
RAAH
RAAH

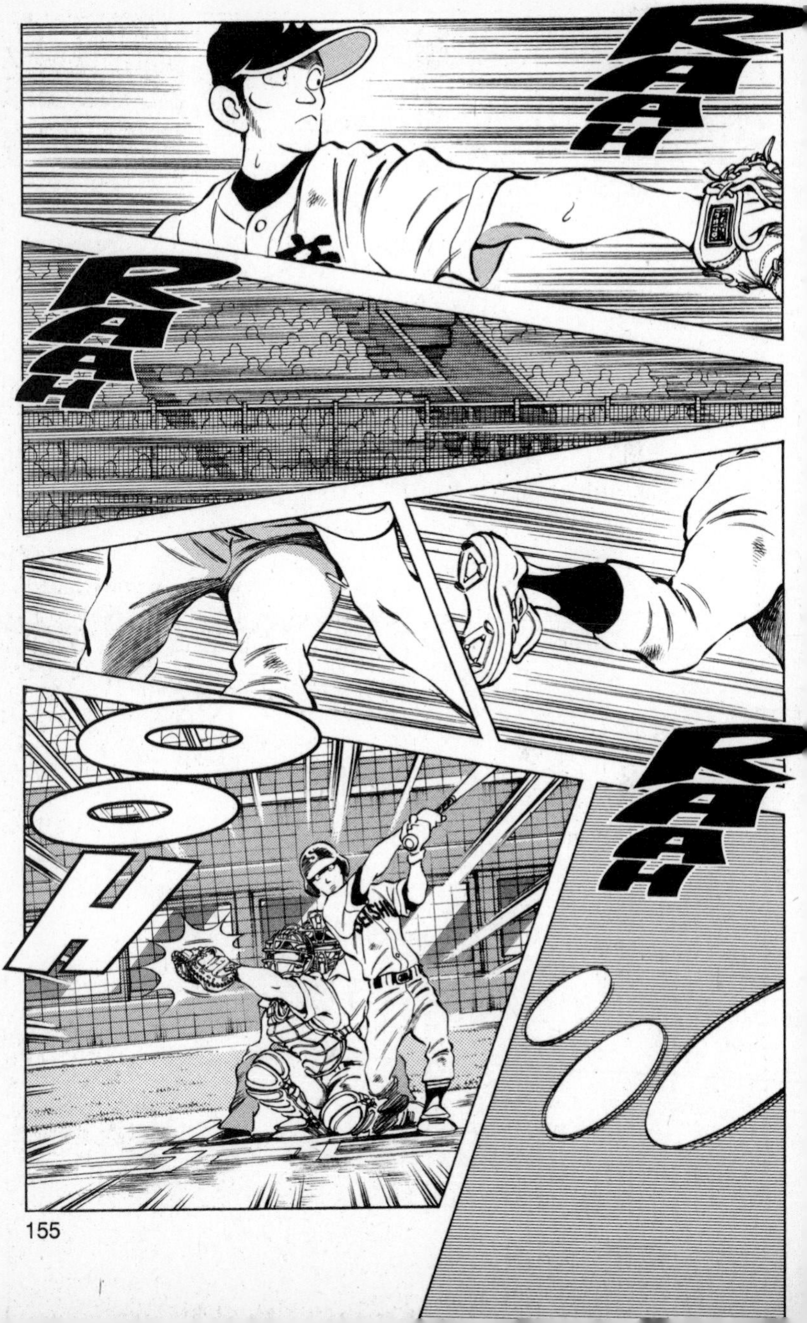
RAAH
RAAH
RAAH
OOOH

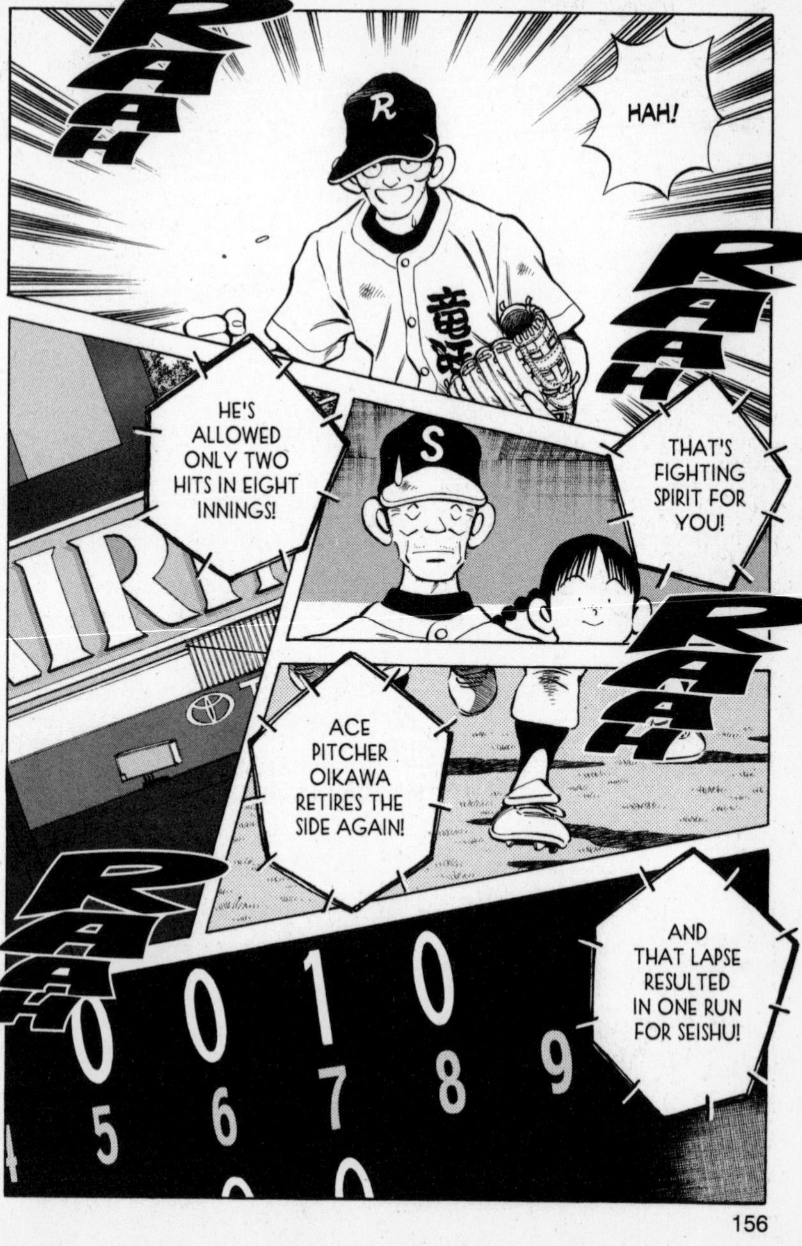
HAH!
RAAH
RAAH
THAT'S FIGHTING SPIRIT FOR YOU!
HE'S ALLOWED ONLY TWO HITS IN EIGHT INNINGS!
RAAH
ACE PITCHER OIKAWA RETIRES THE SIDE AGAIN!
AND THAT LAPSE RESULTED IN ONE RUN FOR SEISHU!
RAAH

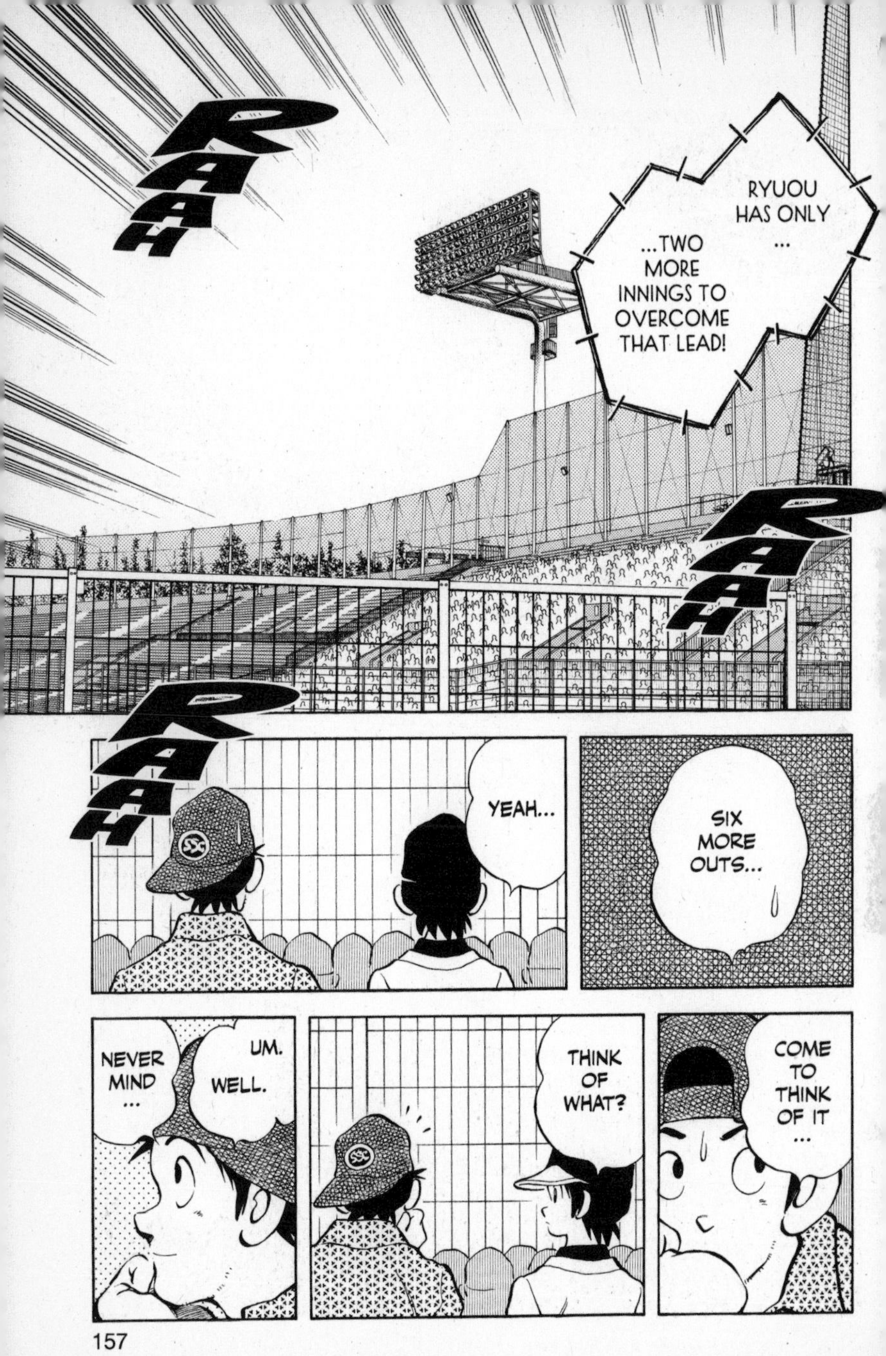
RYUOU HAS ONLY ...
...TWO MORE INNINGS TO OVERCOME THAT LEAD!
RAAH
RAAH
RAAH
SIX MORE OUTS...
YEAH...
COME TO THINK OF IT ...
THINK OF WHAT?
UM. WELL.
NEVER MIND ...

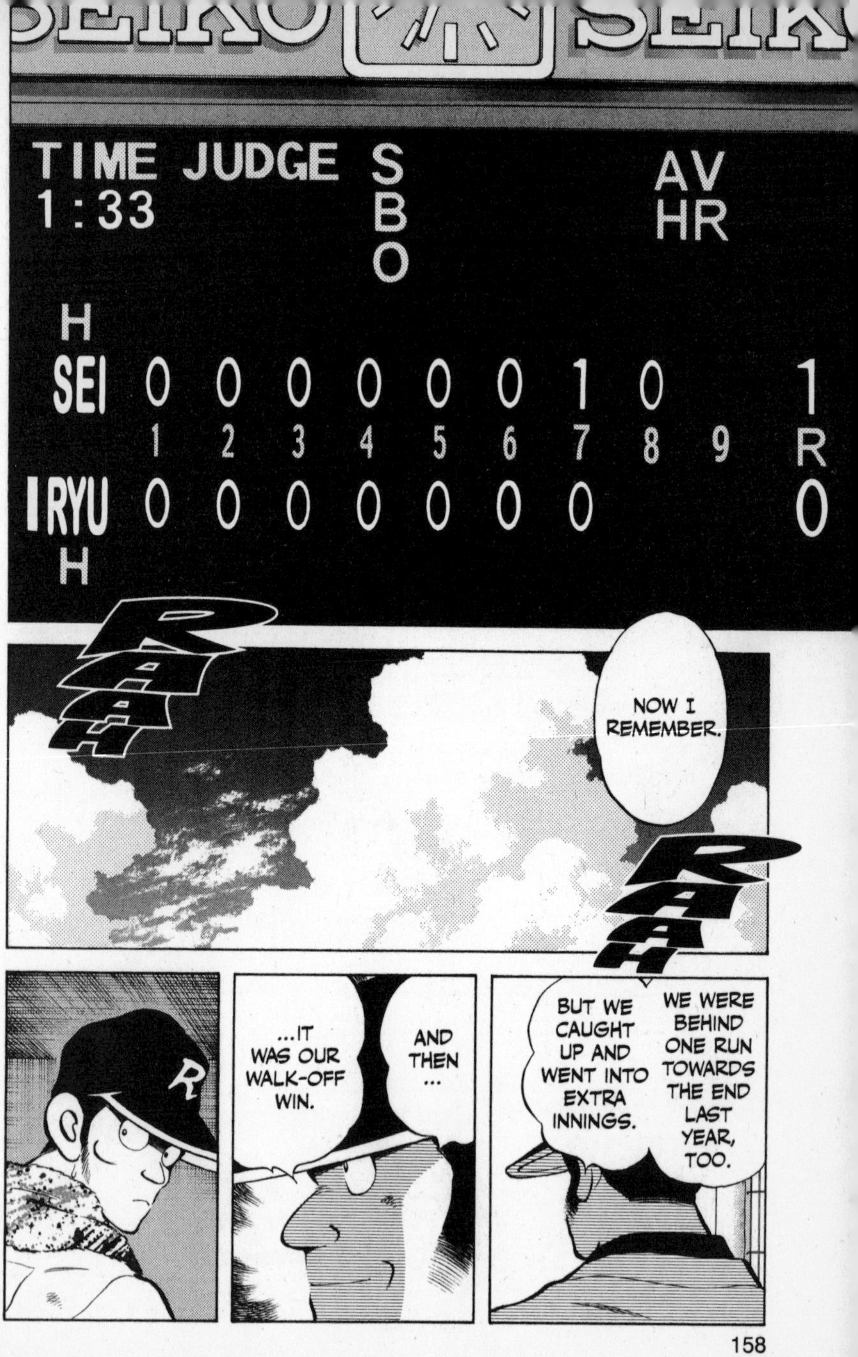
TIME JUDGE
1:33
S
B
O
AV
HR
H
SEI 0 0 0 0 0 0 1 0 1
1 2 3 4 5 6 7 8 9 R
IRYU 0 0 0 0 0 0 0 0
H
RAAH
RAAAH
NOW I REMEMBER.
WE WERE BEHIND ONE RUN TOWARDS THE END LAST YEAR, TOO.
BUT WE CAUGHT UP AND WENT INTO EXTRA INNINGS.
AND THEN...
...IT WAS OUR WALK-OFF WIN.

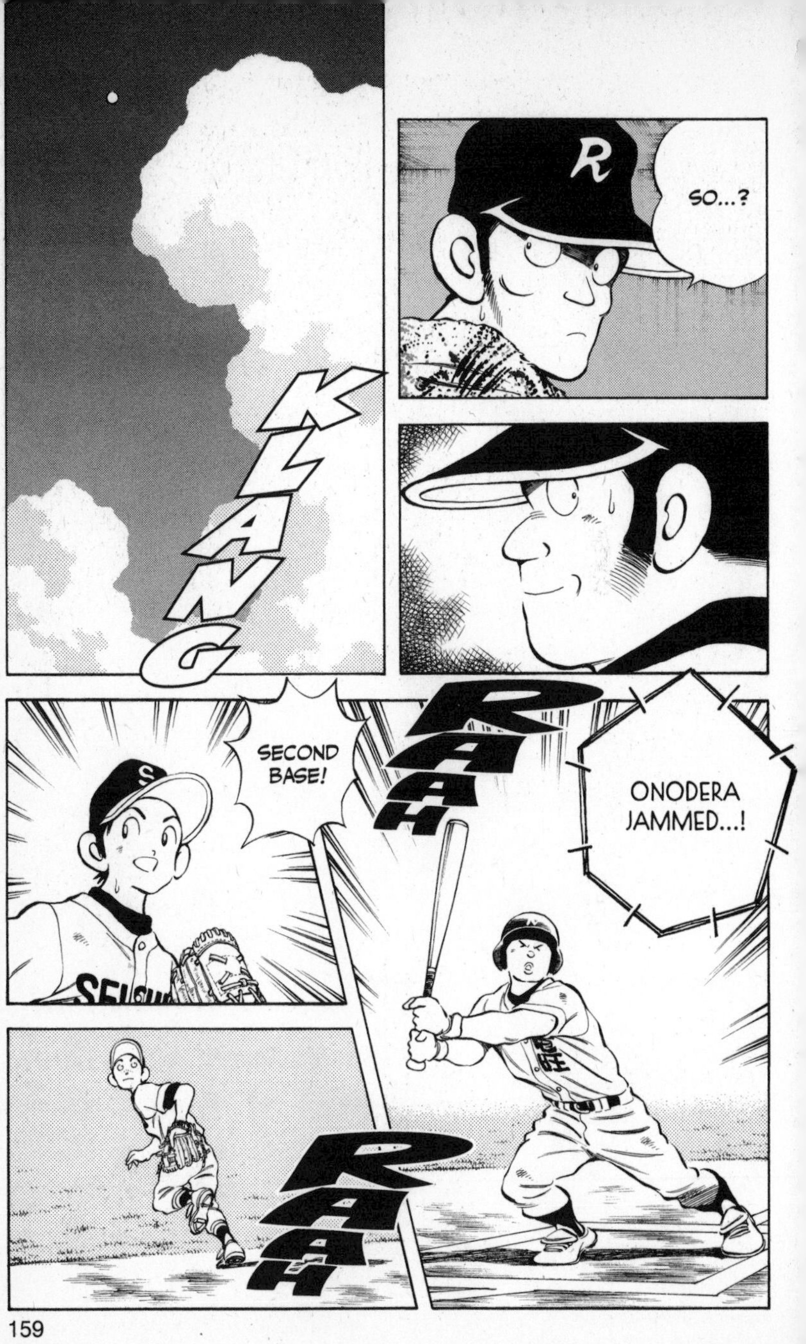
SO...?
KLANG
RAAH
ONODERA JAMMED...!
SECOND BASE!
RAAH

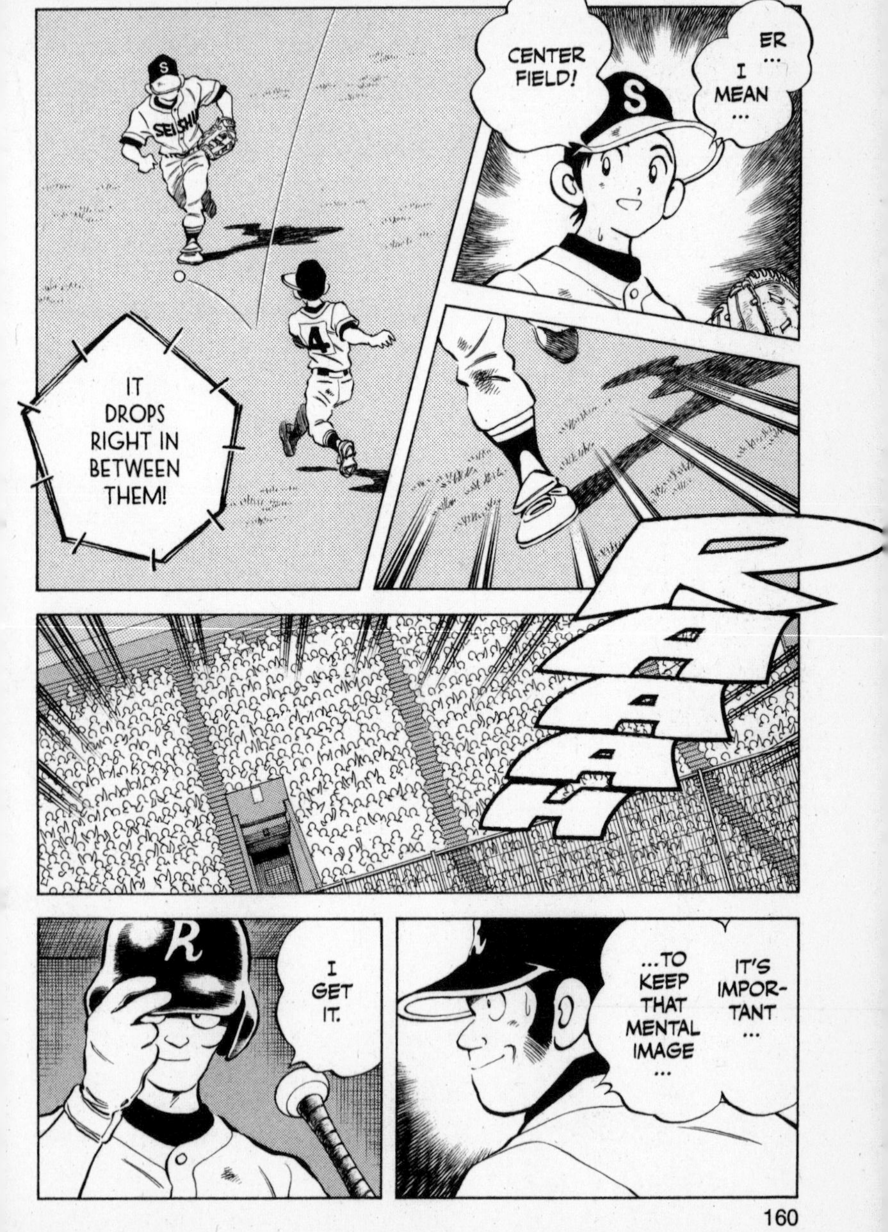
CENTER FIELD!
ER ... I MEAN ...
RAAAH
IT DROPS RIGHT IN BETWEEN THEM!
IT'S IMPORTANT ...
...TO KEEP THAT MENTAL IMAGE ...
I GET IT.

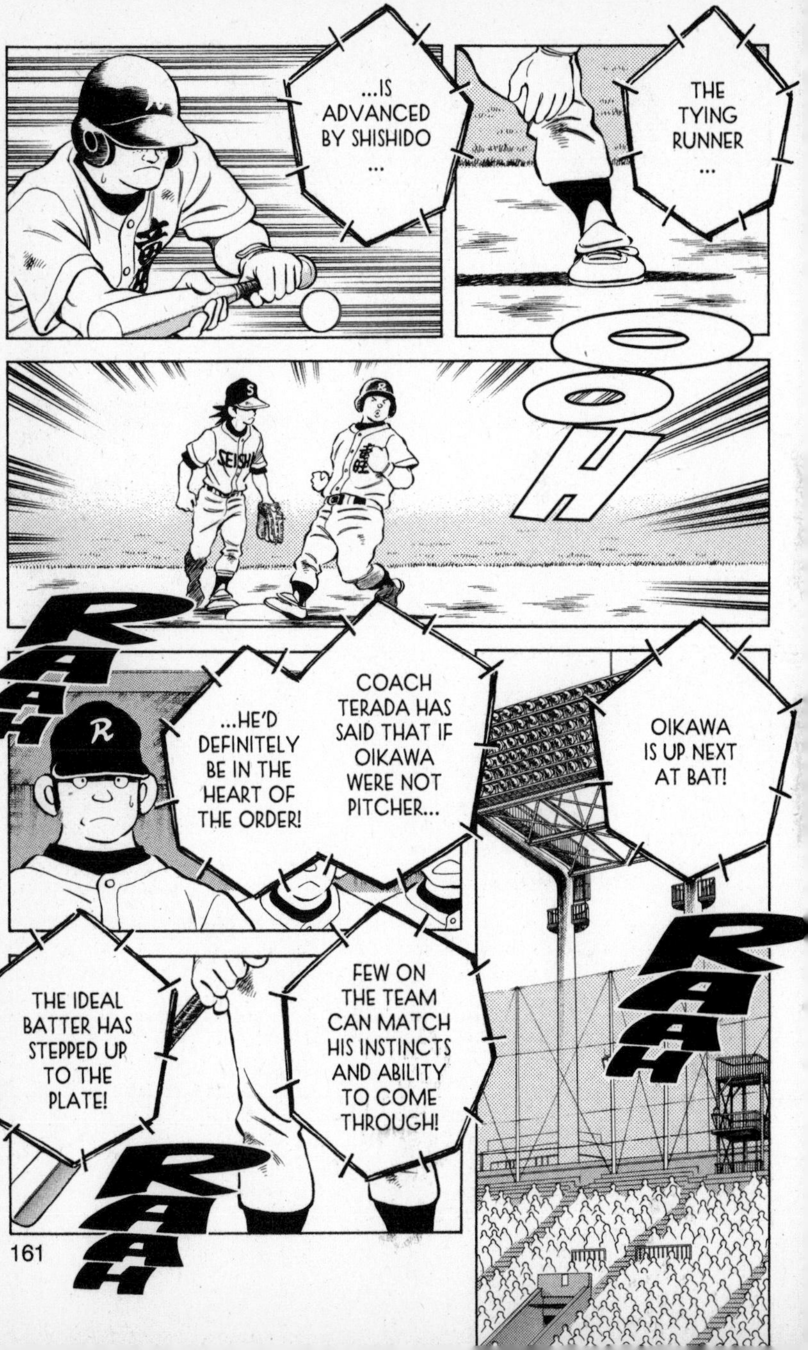
THE TYING RUNNER ...
...IS ADVANCED BY SHISHIDO ...
OOOH
RAAAH
OIKAWA IS UP NEXT AT BAT!
COACH TERADA HAS SAID THAT IF OIKAWA WERE NOT PITCHER...
...HE'D DEFINITELY BE IN THE HEART OF THE ORDER!
RAAAH
FEW ON THE TEAM CAN MATCH HIS INSTINCTS AND ABILITY TO COME THROUGH!
THE IDEAL BATTER HAS STEPPED UP TO THE PLATE!
RAAAH

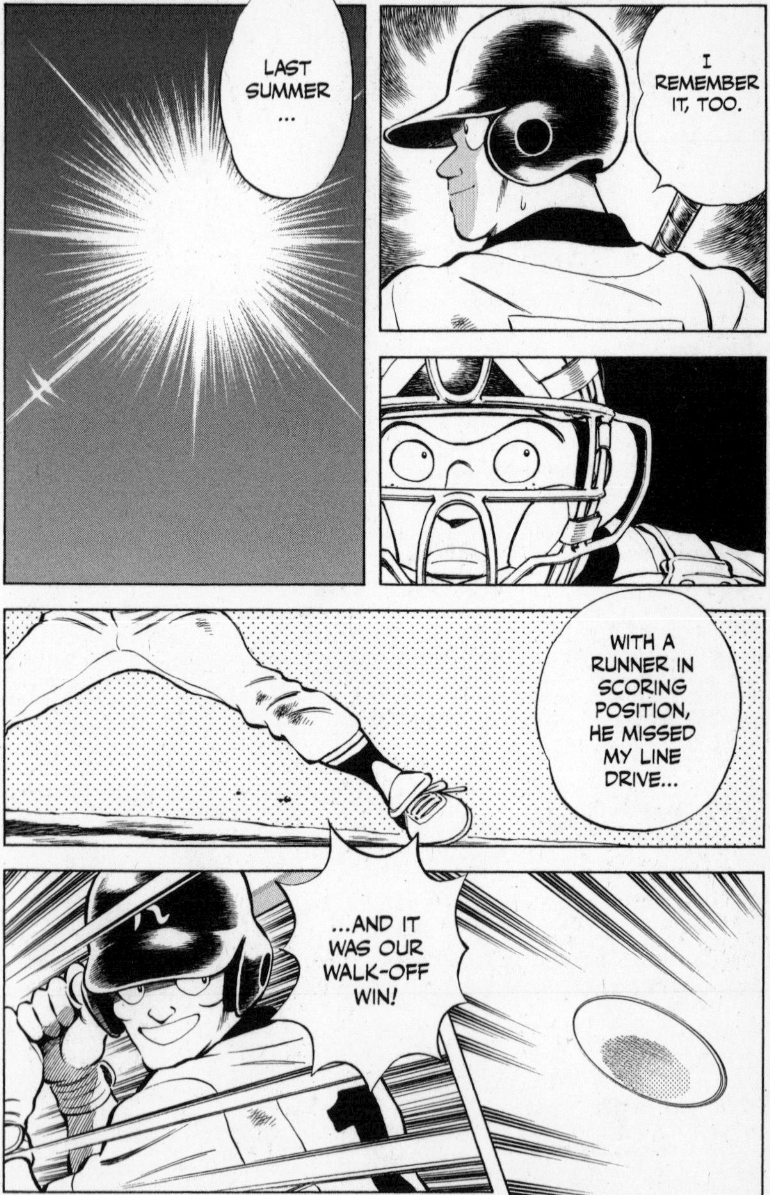
I REMEMBER IT, TOO.
LAST SUMMER ...
WITH A RUNNER IN SCORING POSITION, HE MISSED MY LINE DRIVE...
...AND IT WAS OUR WALK-OFF WIN!

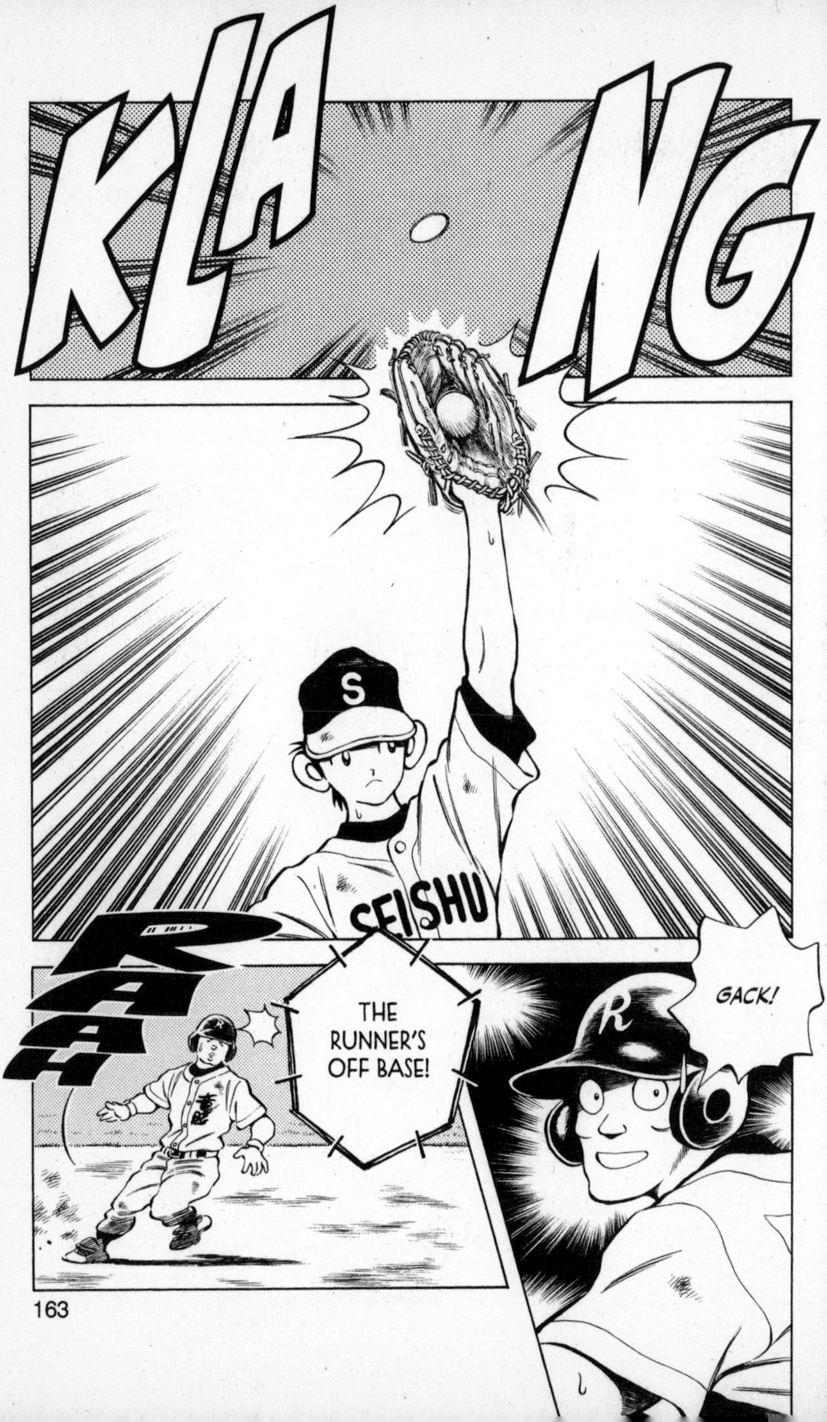
KLA-NG
SEISHU
GACK!
THE RUNNER'S OFF BASE!
RAAAH

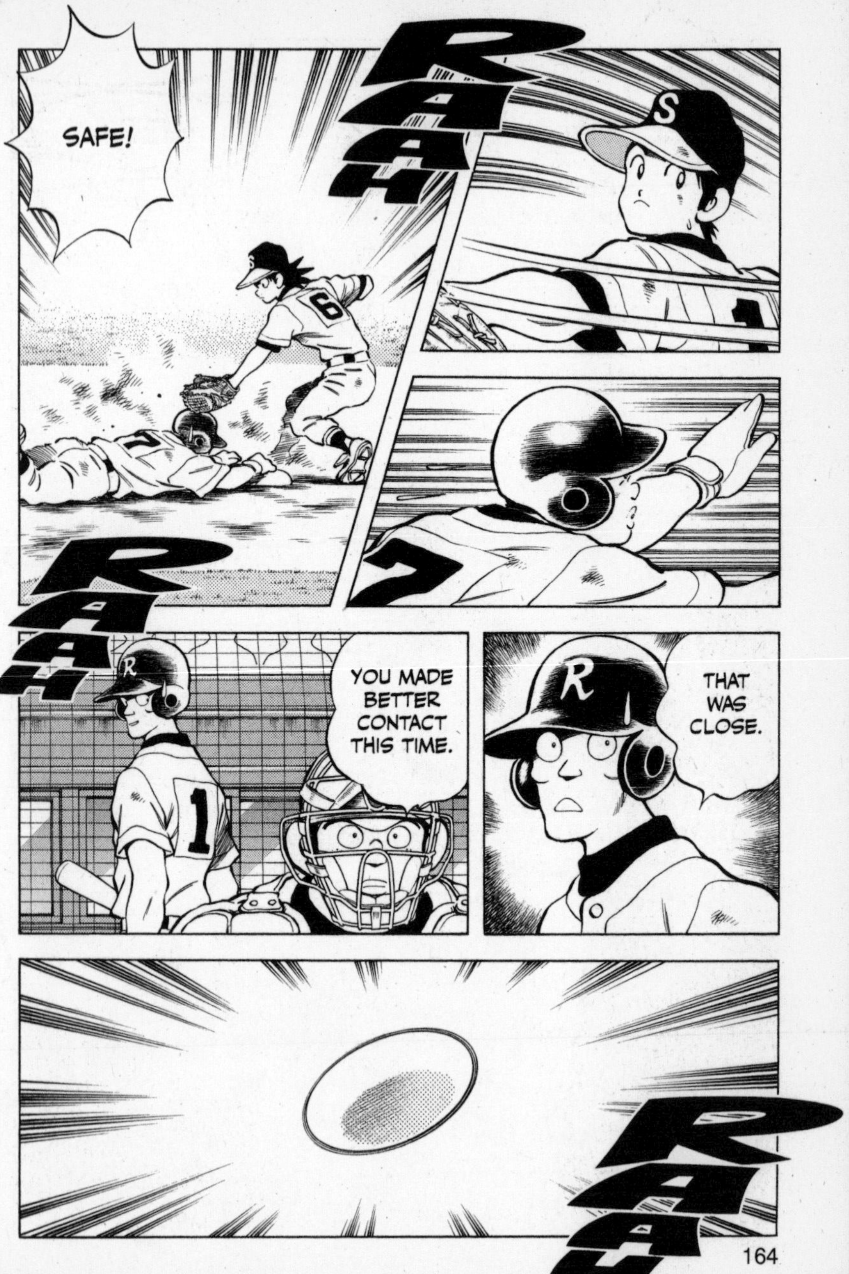
RAAH
SAFE!
RAAH
THAT WAS CLOSE.
YOU MADE BETTER CONTACT THIS TIME.
RAAH

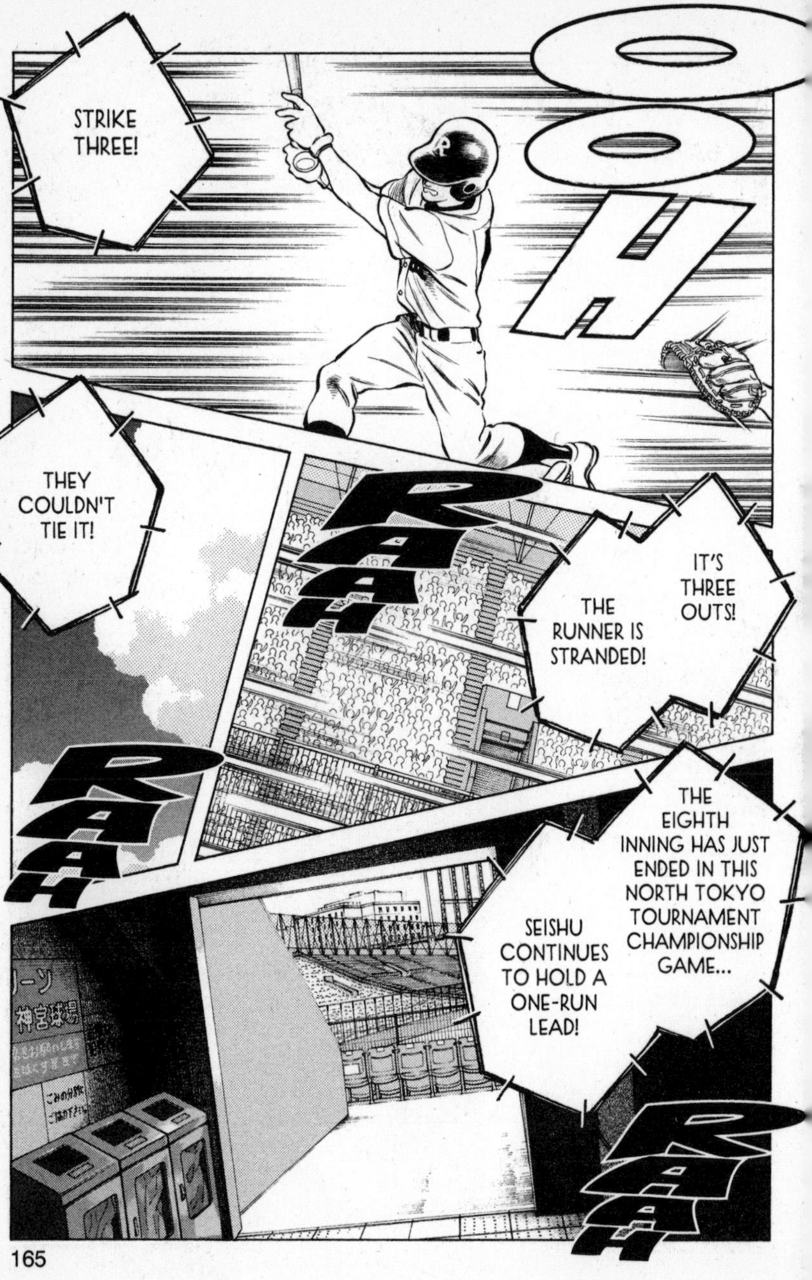
OOH
STRIKE THREE!
IT'S THREE OUTS!
THE RUNNER IS STRANDED!
RAAAH
THEY COULDN'T TIE IT!
RAAAH
THE EIGHTH INNING HAS JUST ENDED IN THIS NORTH TOKYO TOURNAMENT CHAMPIONSHIP GAME...
SEISHU CONTINUES TO HOLD A ONE-RUN LEAD!
RAAAH

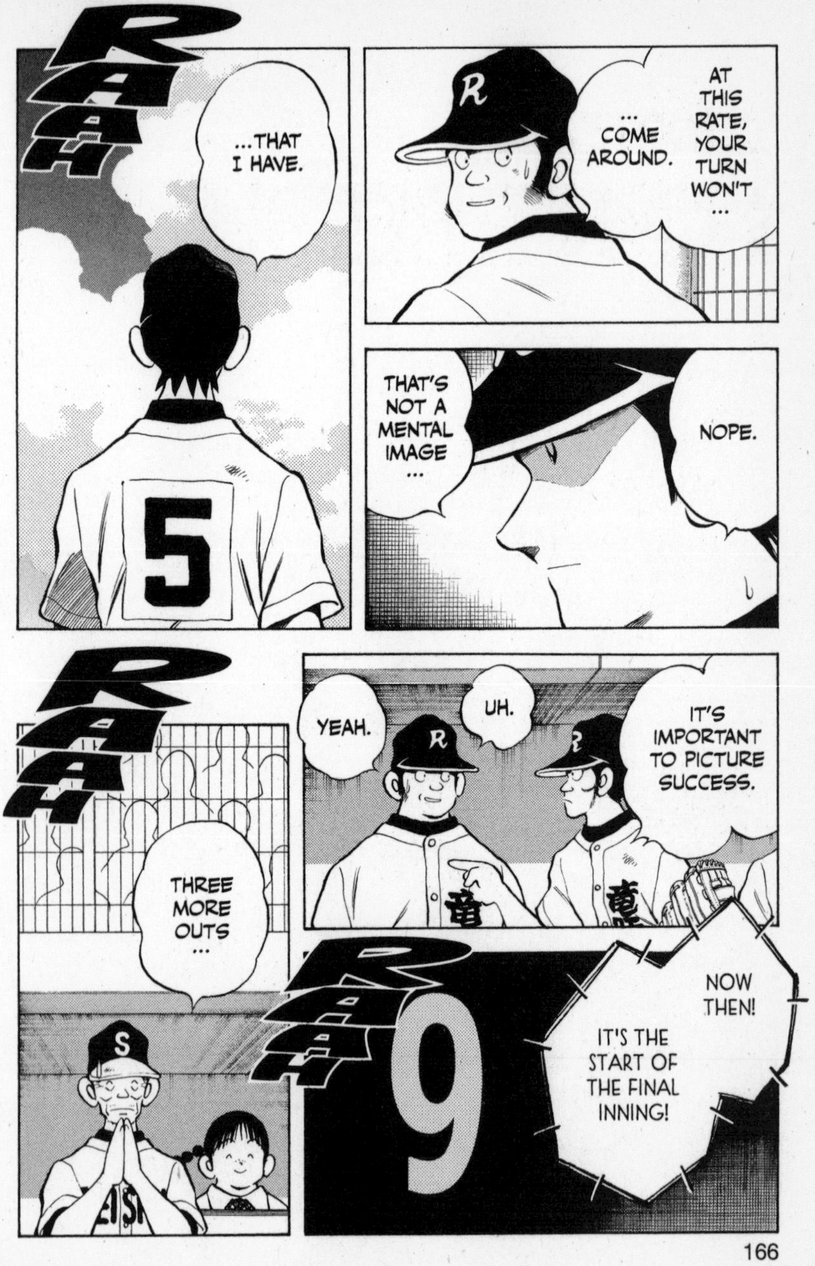
AT THIS RATE, YOUR TURN WON'T ...
... COME AROUND.
NOPE.
THAT'S NOT A MENTAL IMAGE ...
RAAH
...THAT I HAVE.
IT'S IMPORTANT TO PICTURE SUCCESS.
UH.
YEAH.
RAAAH
THREE MORE OUTS ...
NOW THEN!
IT'S THE START OF THE FINAL INNING!
9
RAAH

CHAPTER 150
I CAN'T RECALL

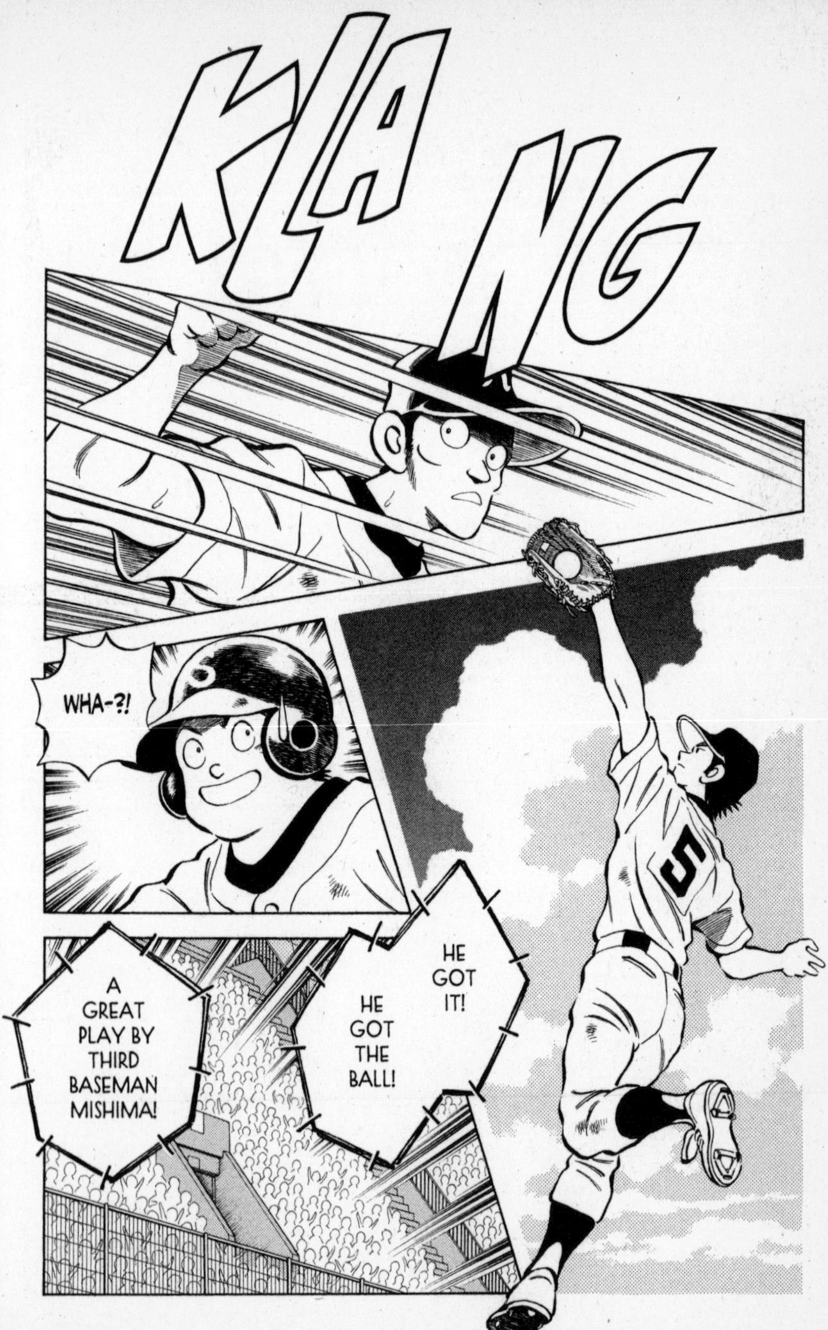
KLANG
WHA-?!
HE GOT IT!
HE GOT THE BALL!
A GREAT PLAY BY THIRD BASEMAN MISHIMA!

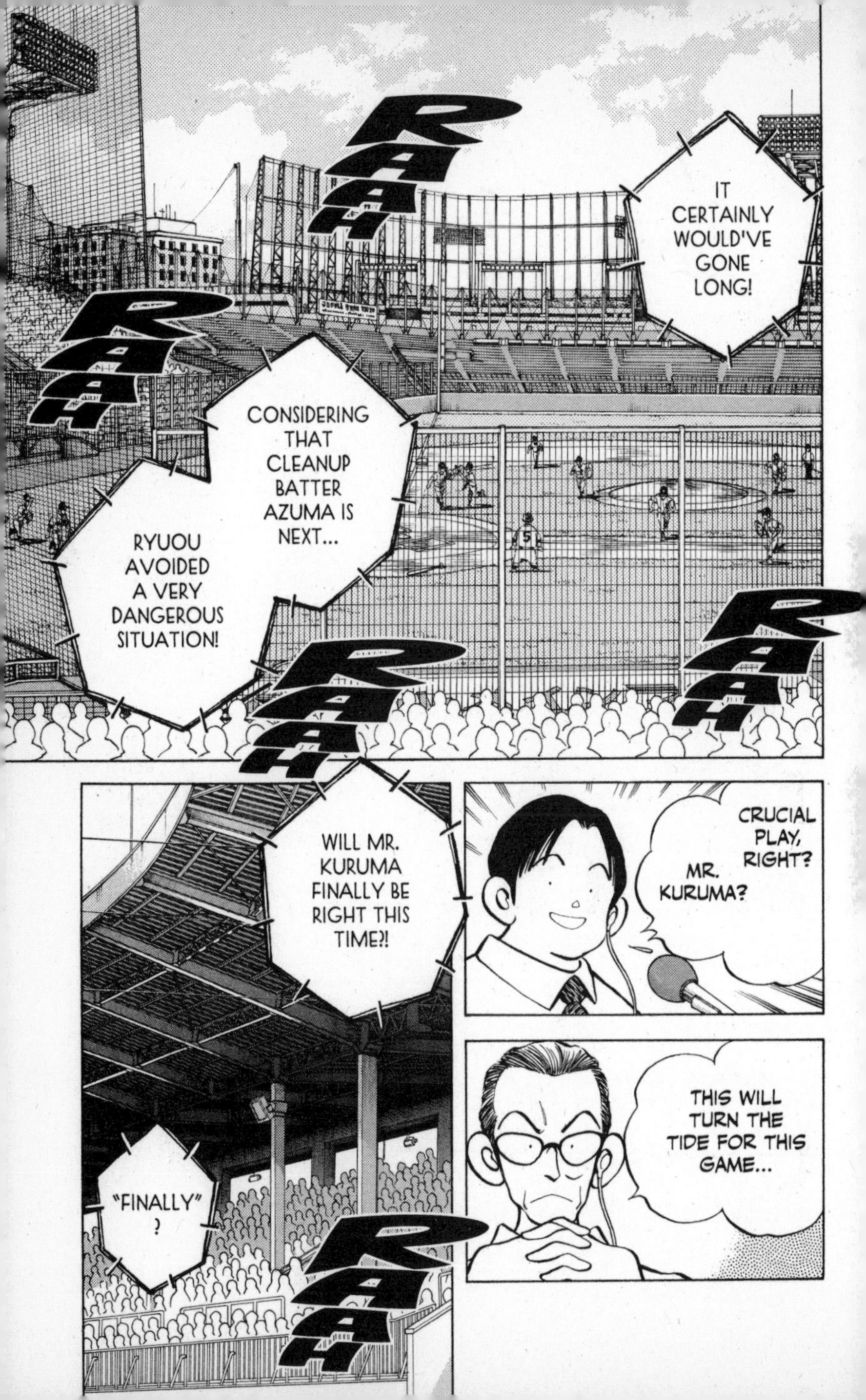
IT CERTAINLY WOULD'VE GONE LONG!
RAAH
RAAH
CONSIDERING THAT CLEANUP BATTER AZUMA IS NEXT...
RAAH
RAAH
RYUOU AVOIDED A VERY DANGEROUS SITUATION!
CRUCIAL PLAY, RIGHT?
MR. KURUMA?
THIS WILL TURN THE TIDE FOR THIS GAME...
WILL MR. KURUMA FINALLY BE RIGHT THIS TIME?!
"FINALLY" ?
RAAH

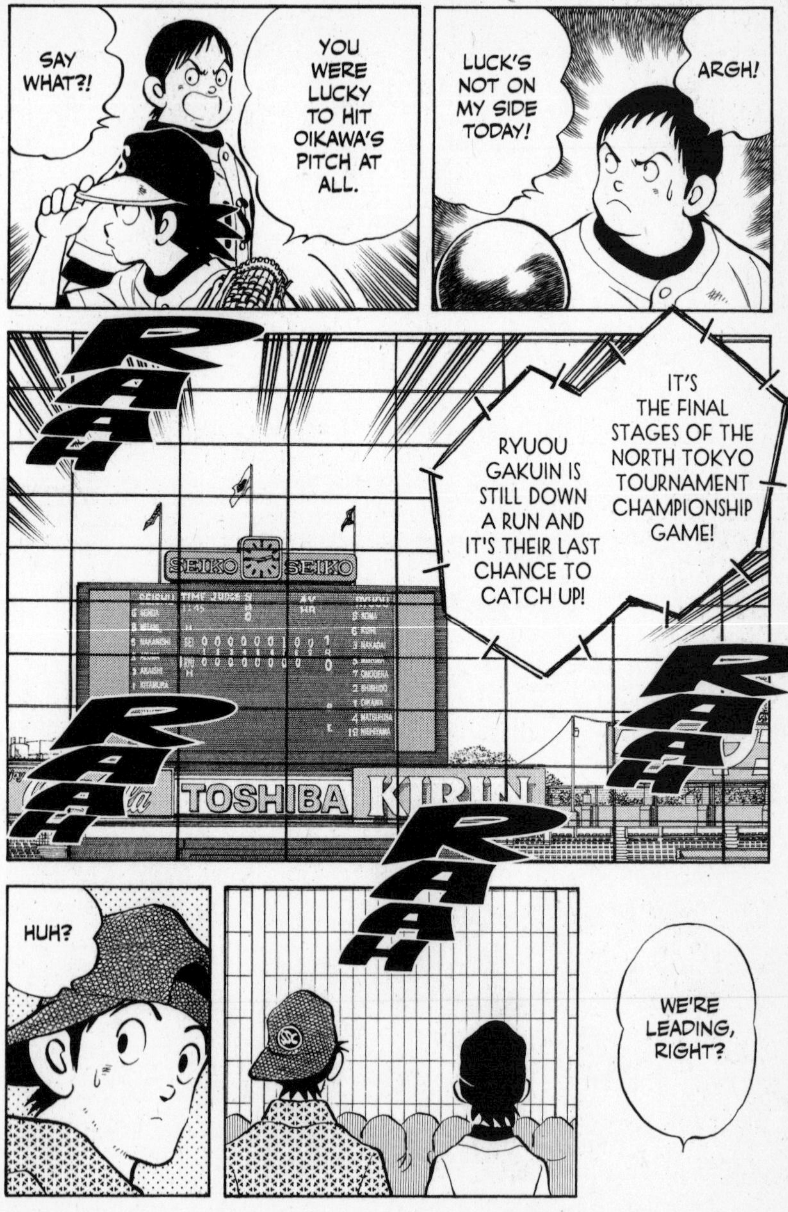
ARGH!
LUCK'S NOT ON MY SIDE TODAY!
YOU WERE LUCKY TO HIT OIKAWA'S PITCH AT ALL.
SAY WHAT?!
RAAH
IT'S THE FINAL STAGES OF THE NORTH TOKYO TOURNAMENT CHAMPIONSHIP GAME!
RYUOU GAKUIN IS STILL DOWN A RUN AND IT'S THEIR LAST CHANCE TO CATCH UP!
SEIKO
SEIKO
TOSHIBA
KIRIN
RAAH
RAAH
RAAH
WE'RE LEADING, RIGHT?
HUH?

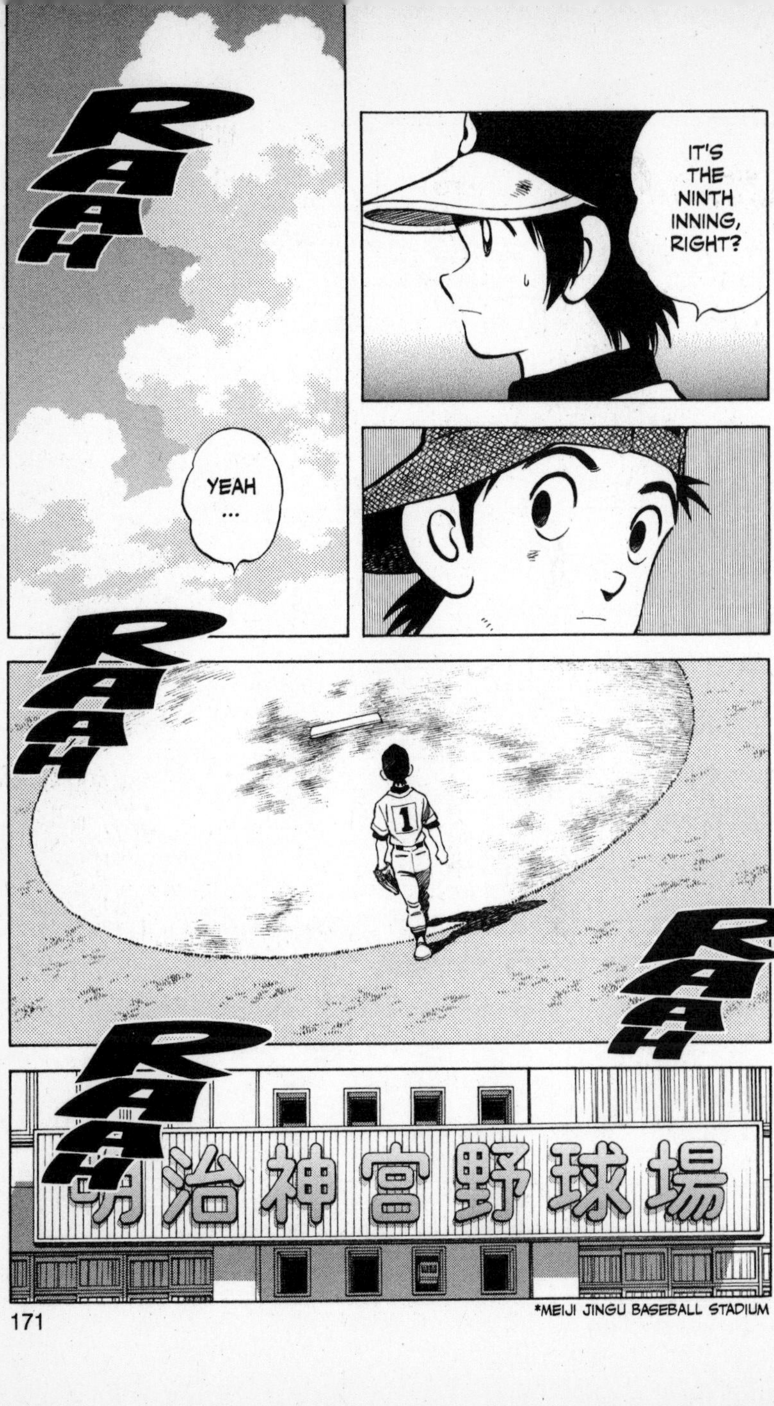
IT'S THE NINTH INNING, RIGHT?
RAAH
YEAH ...
RAAH
RAAH
RAAH
明治神宮野球場
*MEIJI JINGU BASEBALL STADIUM

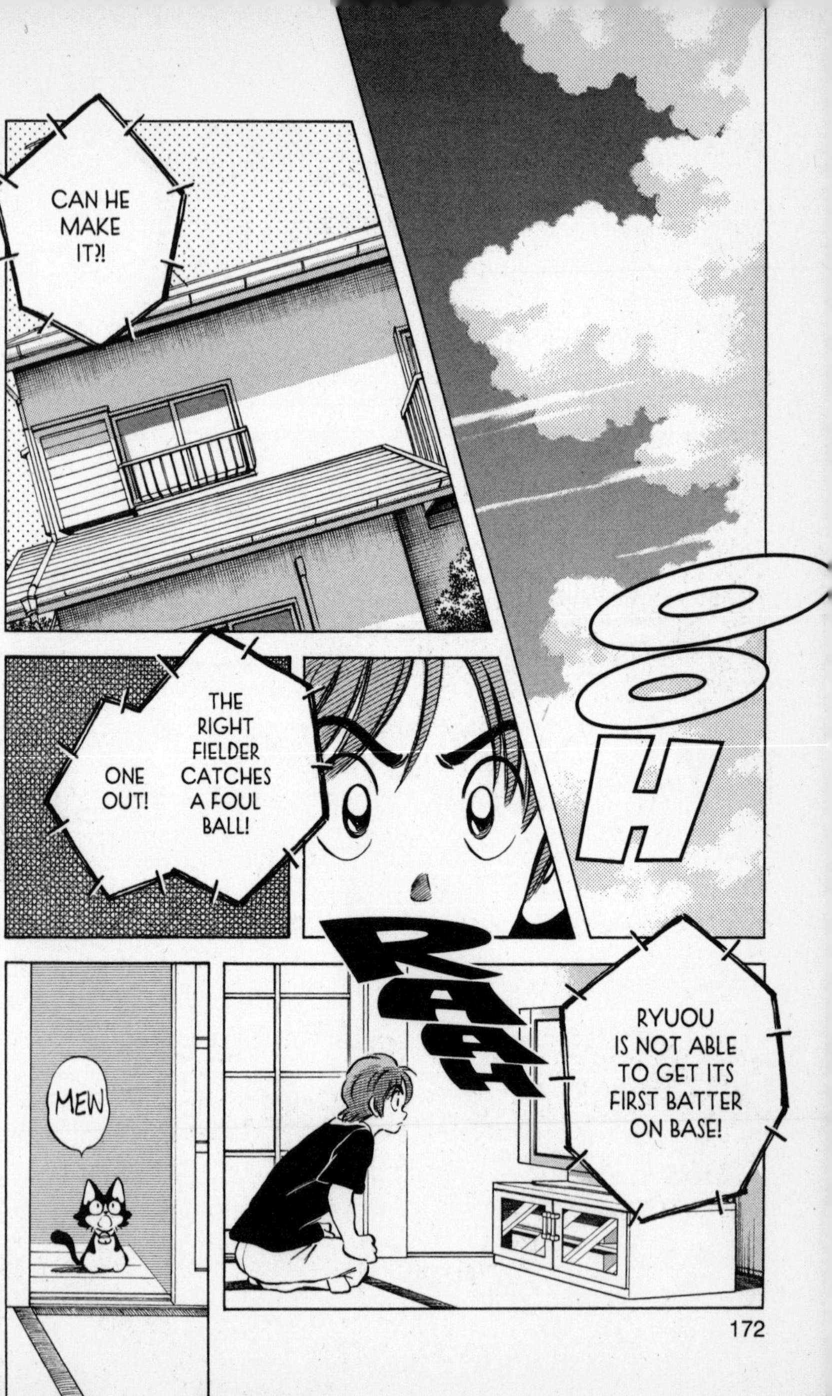
OOHH
CAN HE MAKE IT?!
THE RIGHT FIELDER CATCHES A FOUL BALL!
ONE OUT!
RAAH
RYUOU IS NOT ABLE TO GET ITS FIRST BATTER ON BASE!
MEW

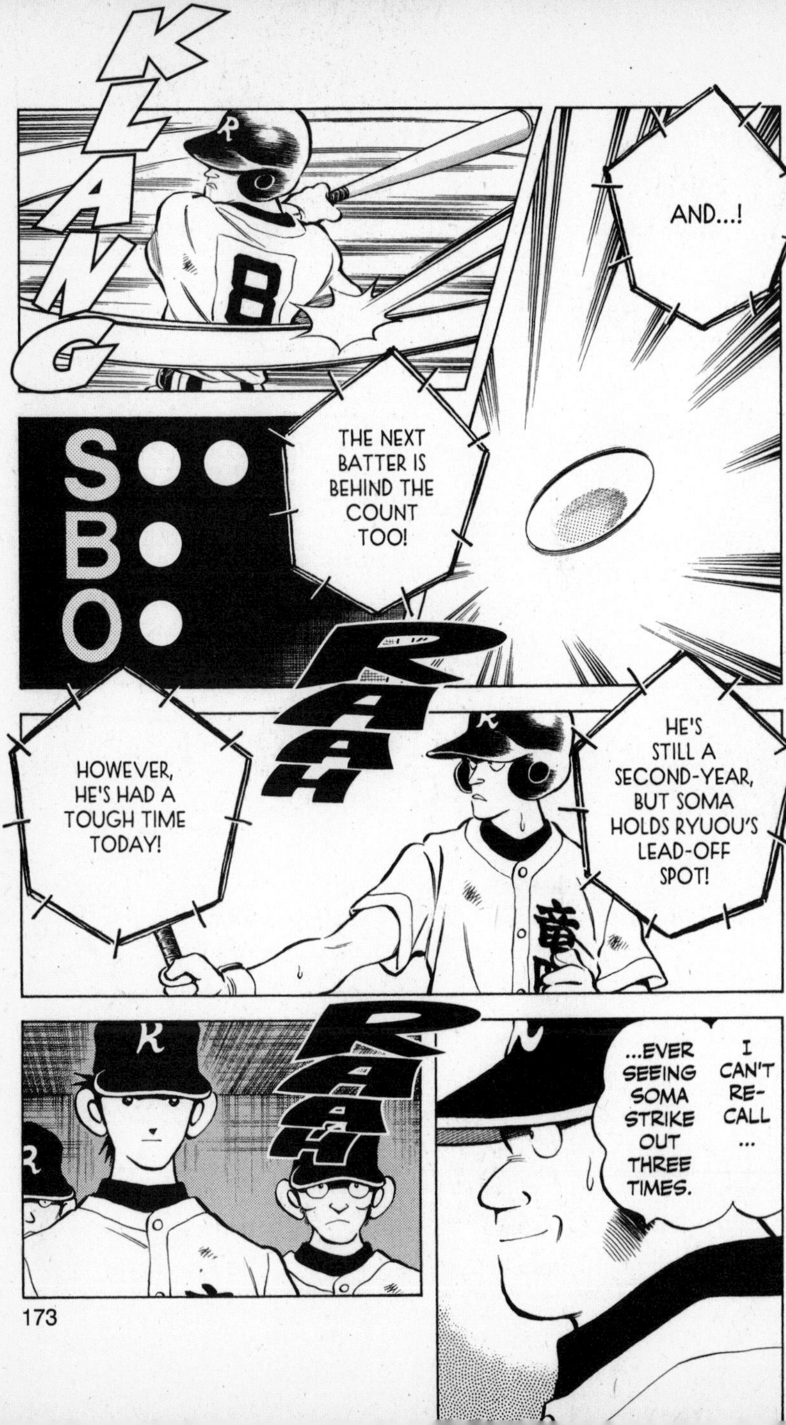
AND...!
THE NEXT BATTER IS BEHIND THE COUNT TOO!
KLANG
S
B
O
HE'S STILL A SECOND-YEAR, BUT SOMA HOLDS RYUOU'S LEAD-OFF SPOT!
HOWEVER, HE'S HAD A TOUGH TIME TODAY!
RAAH
I CAN'T RECALL...
...EVER SEEING SOMA STRIKE OUT THREE TIMES.
RAAH

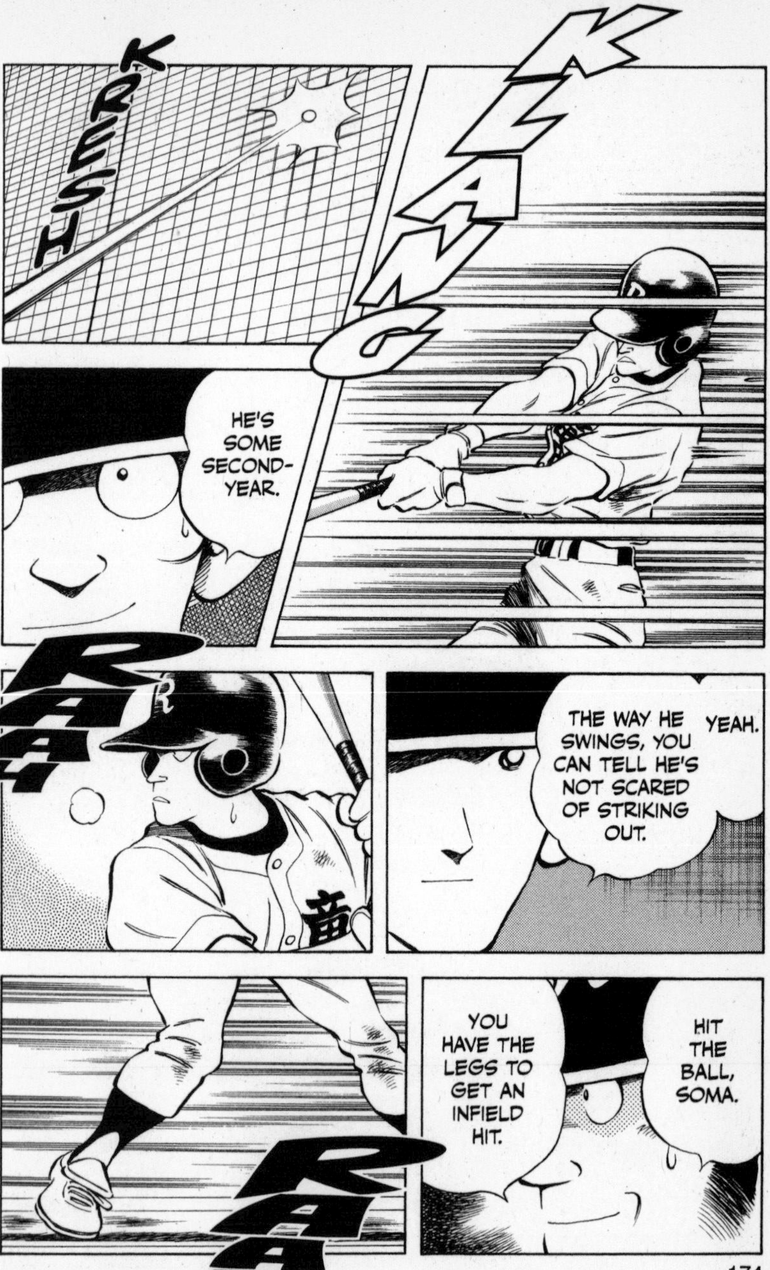
KLANG
KRESH
HE'S SOME SECOND-YEAR.
YEAH.
THE WAY HE SWINGS, YOU CAN TELL HE'S NOT SCARED OF STRIKING OUT.
RAAH
HIT THE BALL, SOMA.
YOU HAVE THE LEGS TO GET AN INFIELD HIT.
RAAH

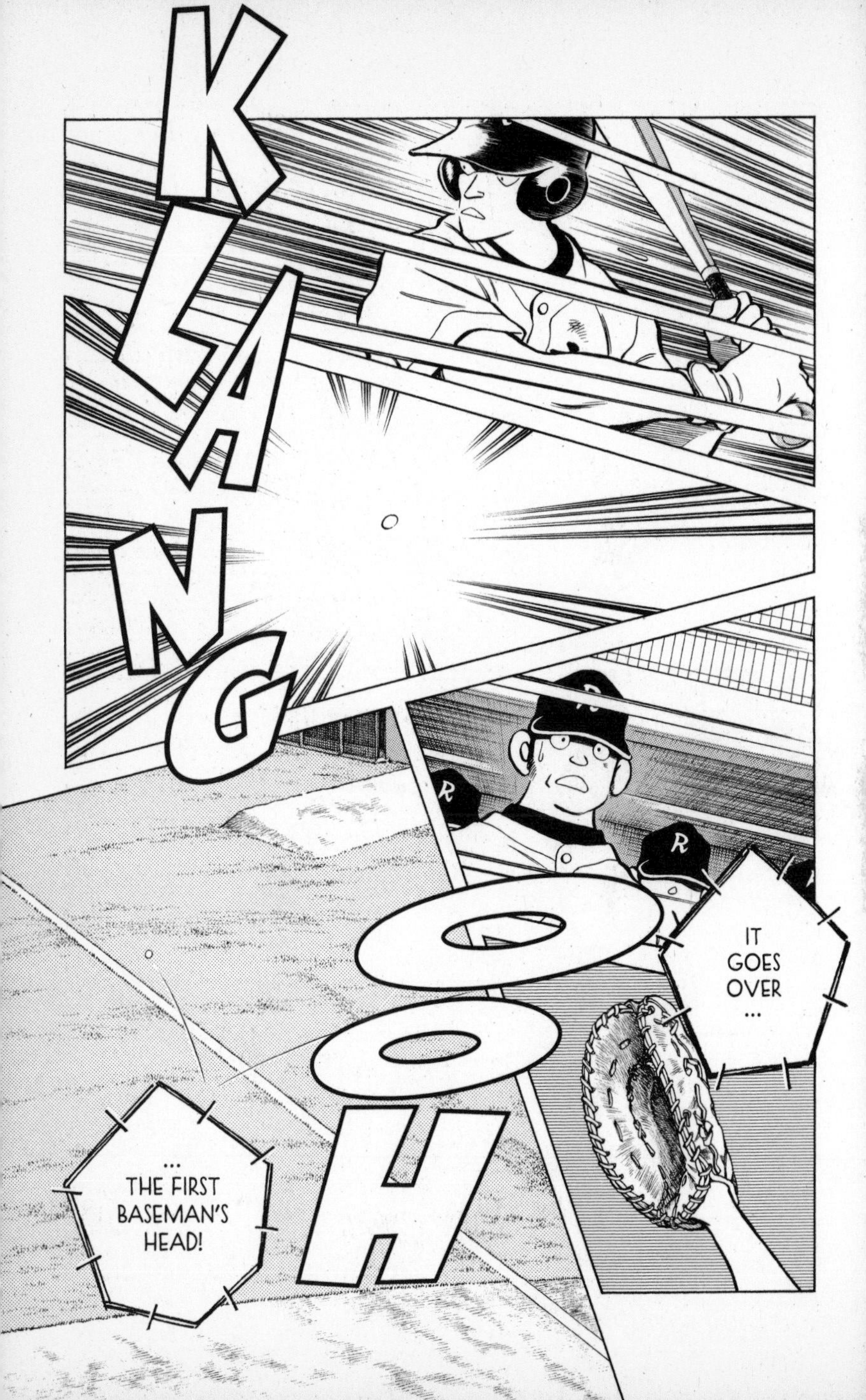
KLANG
IT GOES OVER ...
OOH
... THE FIRST BASEMAN'S HEAD!

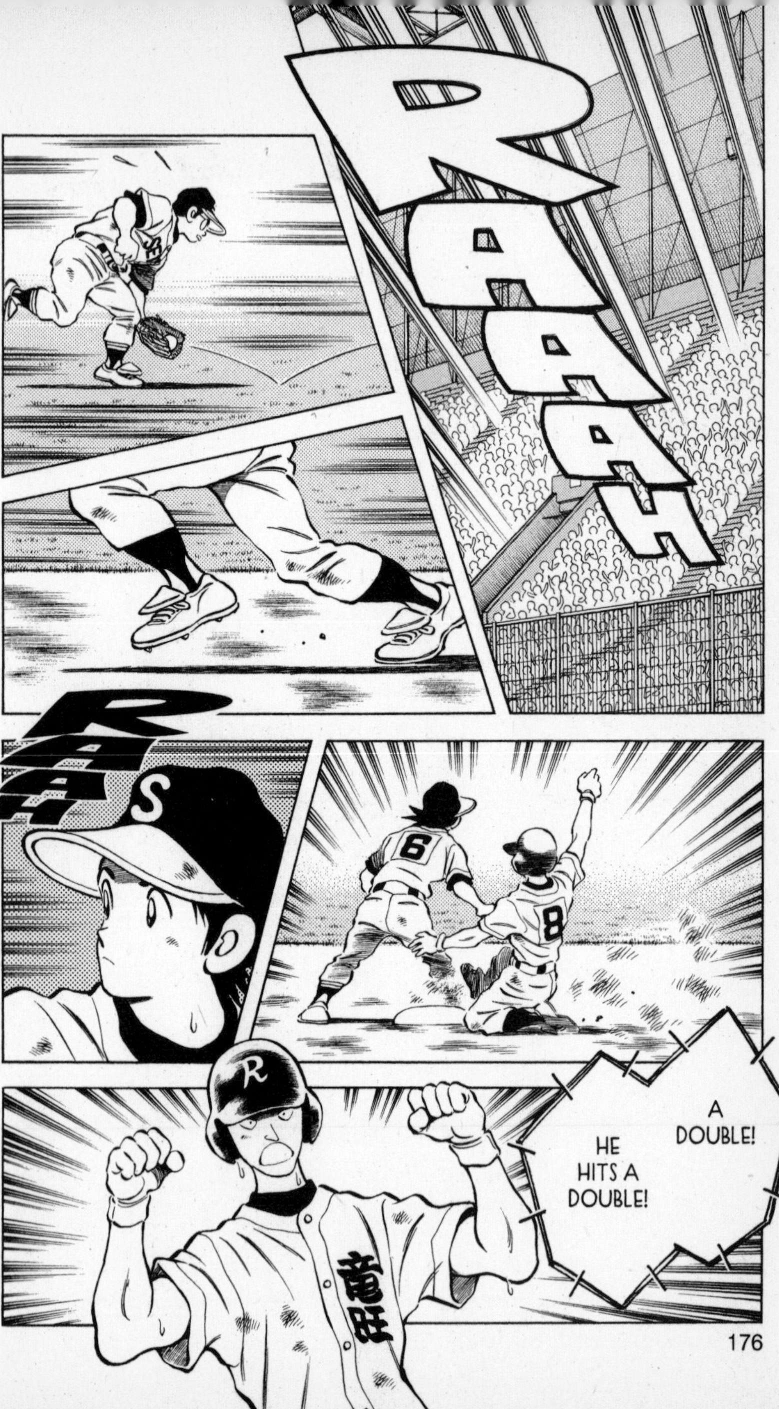
RAAAAH
RAAAH
A DOUBLE!
HE HITS A DOUBLE!
竜旺

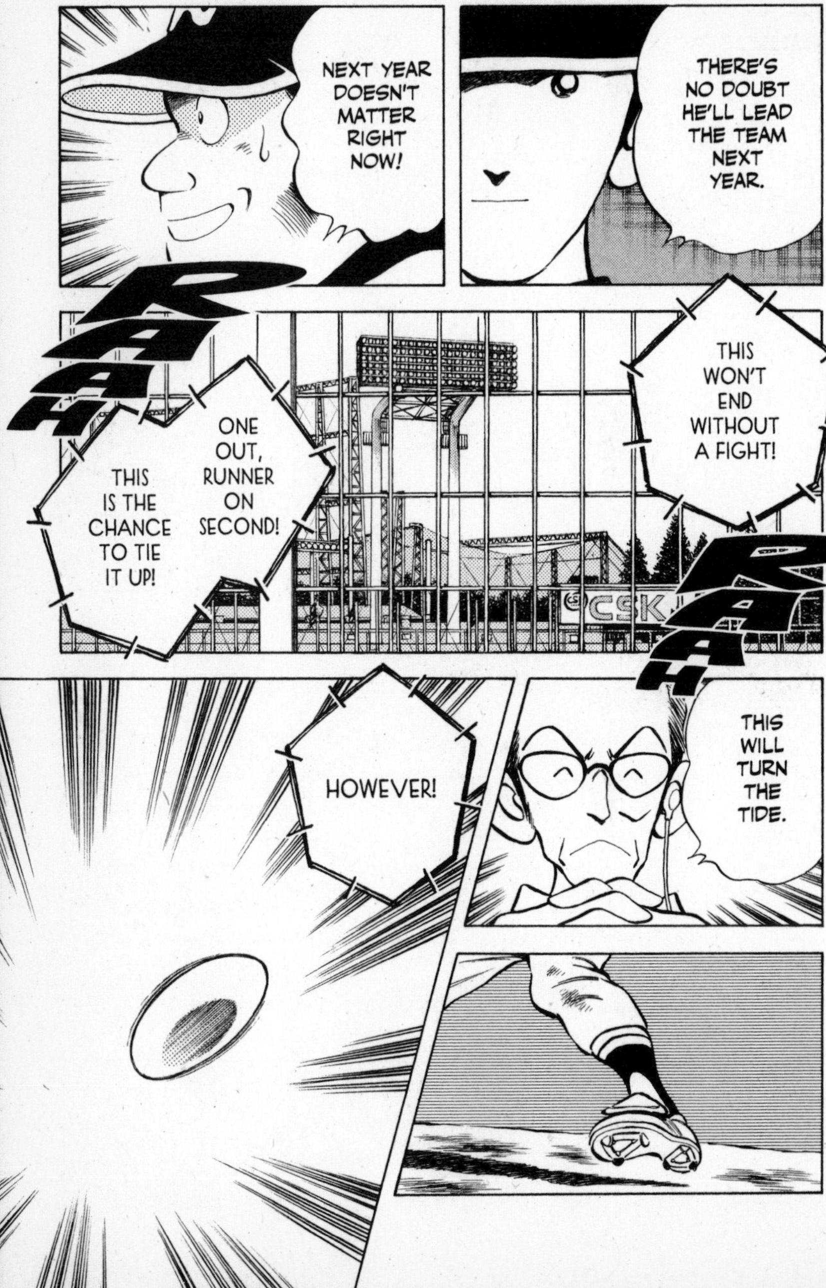
THERE'S NO DOUBT HE'LL LEAD THE TEAM NEXT YEAR.
NEXT YEAR DOESN'T MATTER RIGHT NOW!
RAAH
THIS WON'T END WITHOUT A FIGHT!
ONE OUT, RUNNER ON SECOND!
THIS IS THE CHANCE TO TIE IT UP!
RAAH
THIS WILL TURN THE TIDE.
HOWEVER!

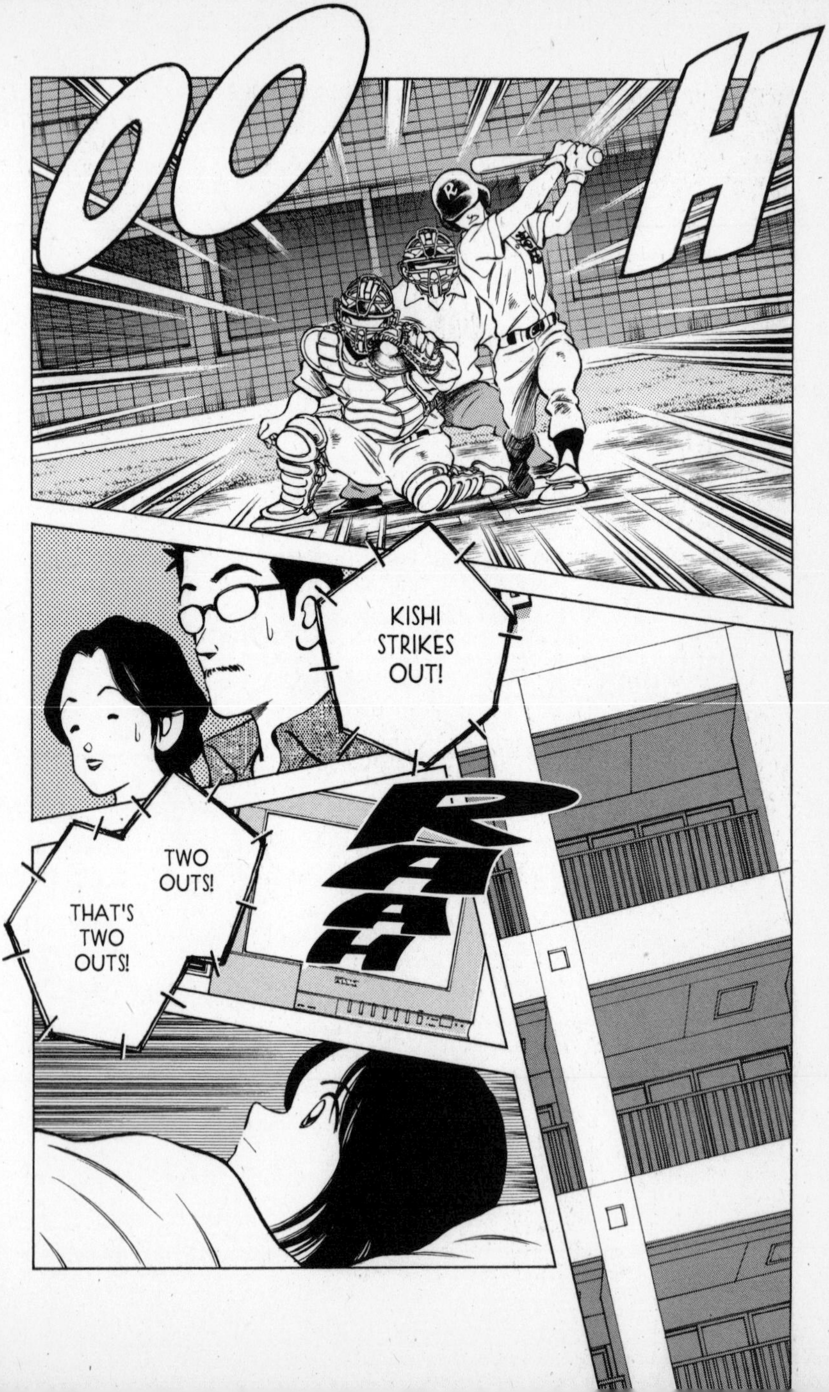
OOOH
KISHI STRIKES OUT!
RAAAH
TWO OUTS!
THAT'S TWO OUTS!

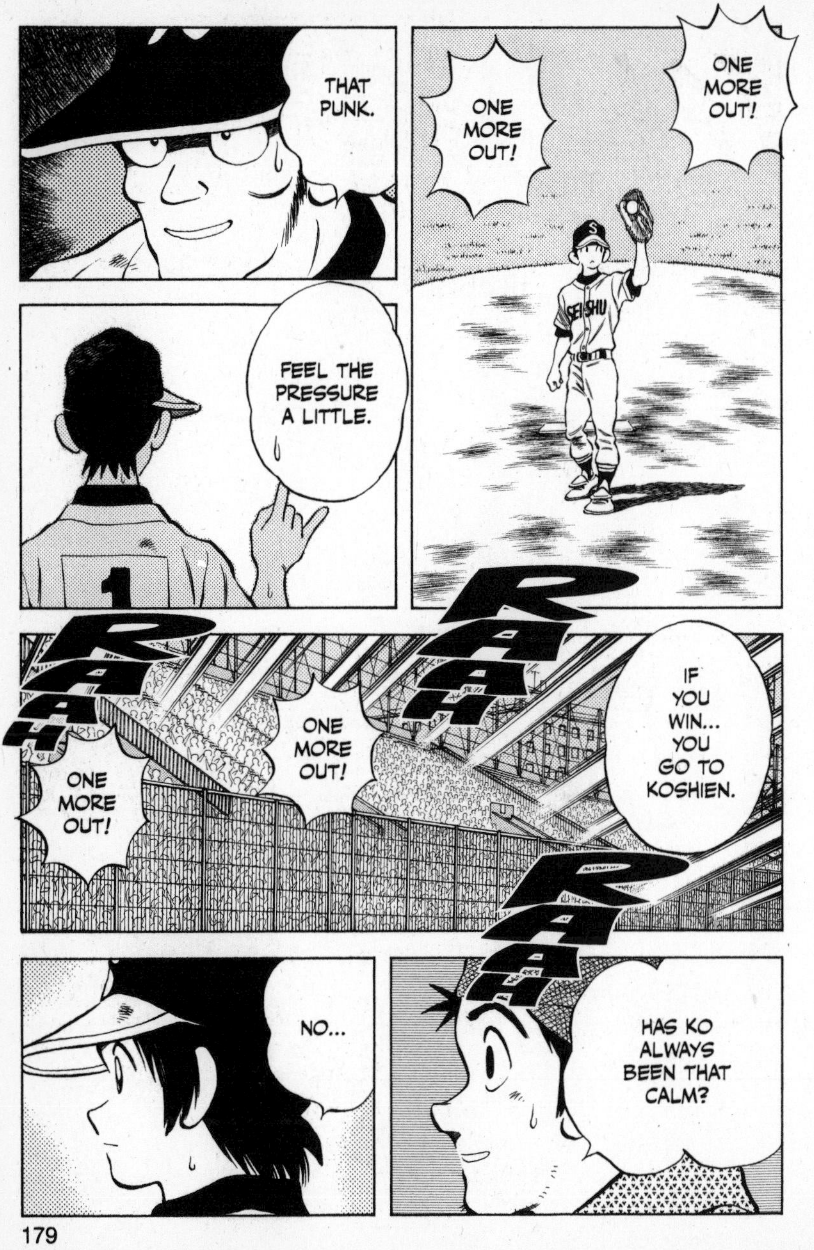
ONE MORE OUT!
ONE MORE OUT!
THAT PUNK.
FEEL THE PRESSURE A LITTLE.
RAAAH
IF YOU WIN... YOU GO TO KOSHIEN.
RAAAH
ONE MORE OUT!
ONE MORE OUT!
RAAAH
HAS KO ALWAYS BEEN THAT CALM?
NO...

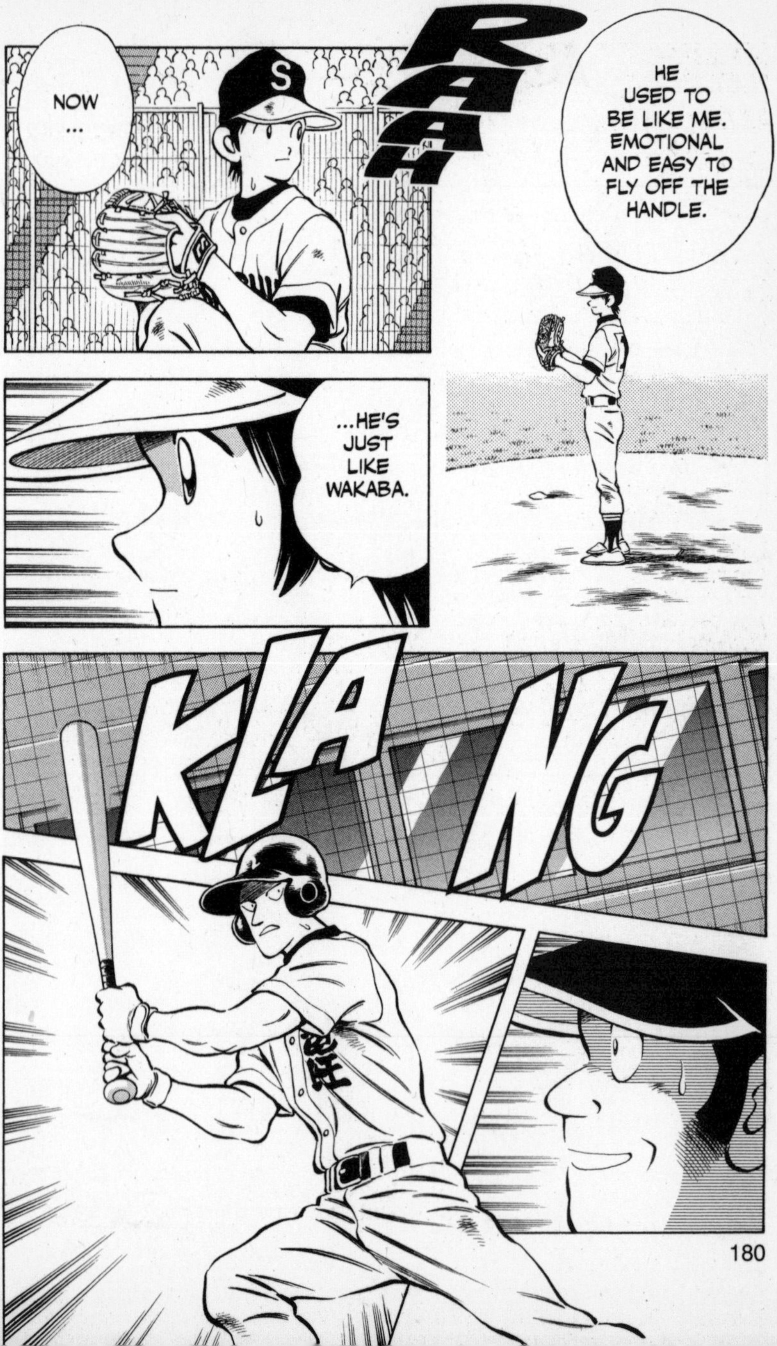
HE USED TO BE LIKE ME. EMOTIONAL AND EASY TO FLY OFF THE HANDLE.
RAAAH
NOW ...
...HE'S JUST LIKE WAKABA.
KLANG

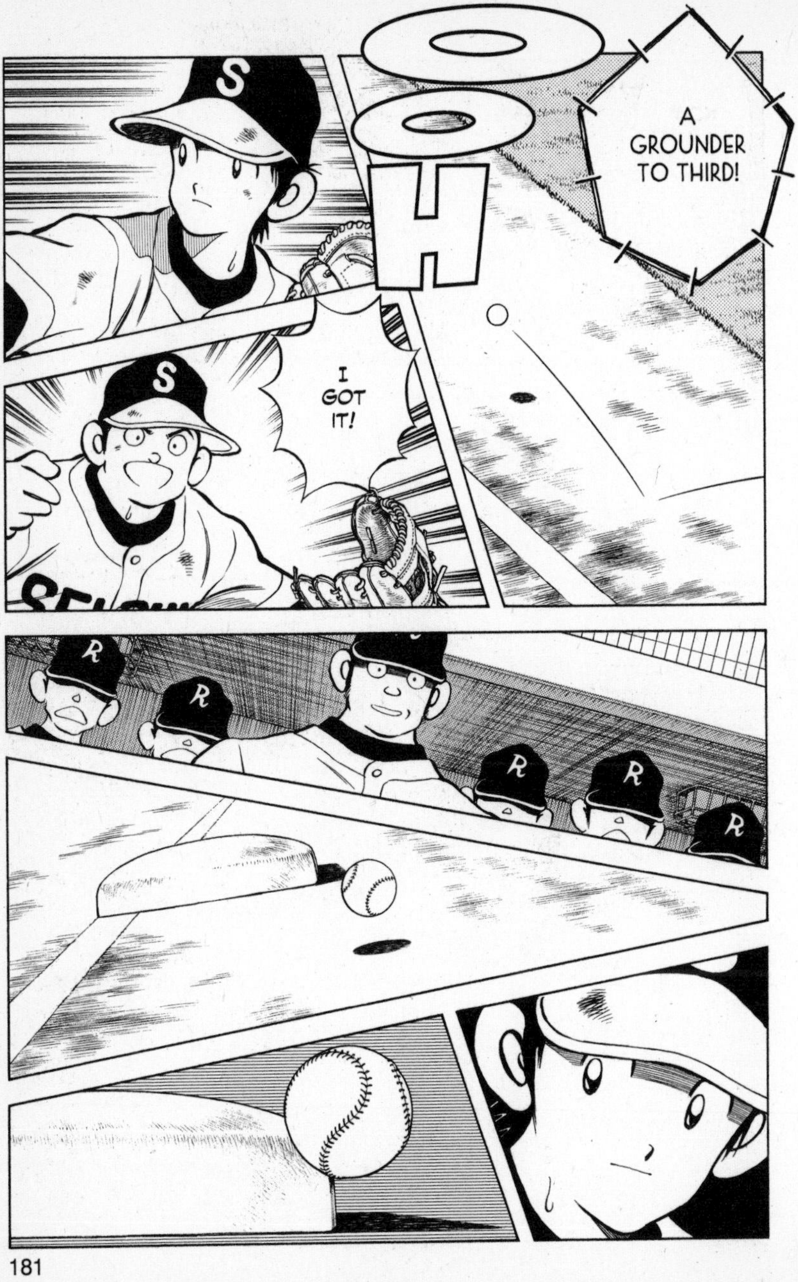
A GROUNDER TO THIRD!
OOH
I GOT IT!

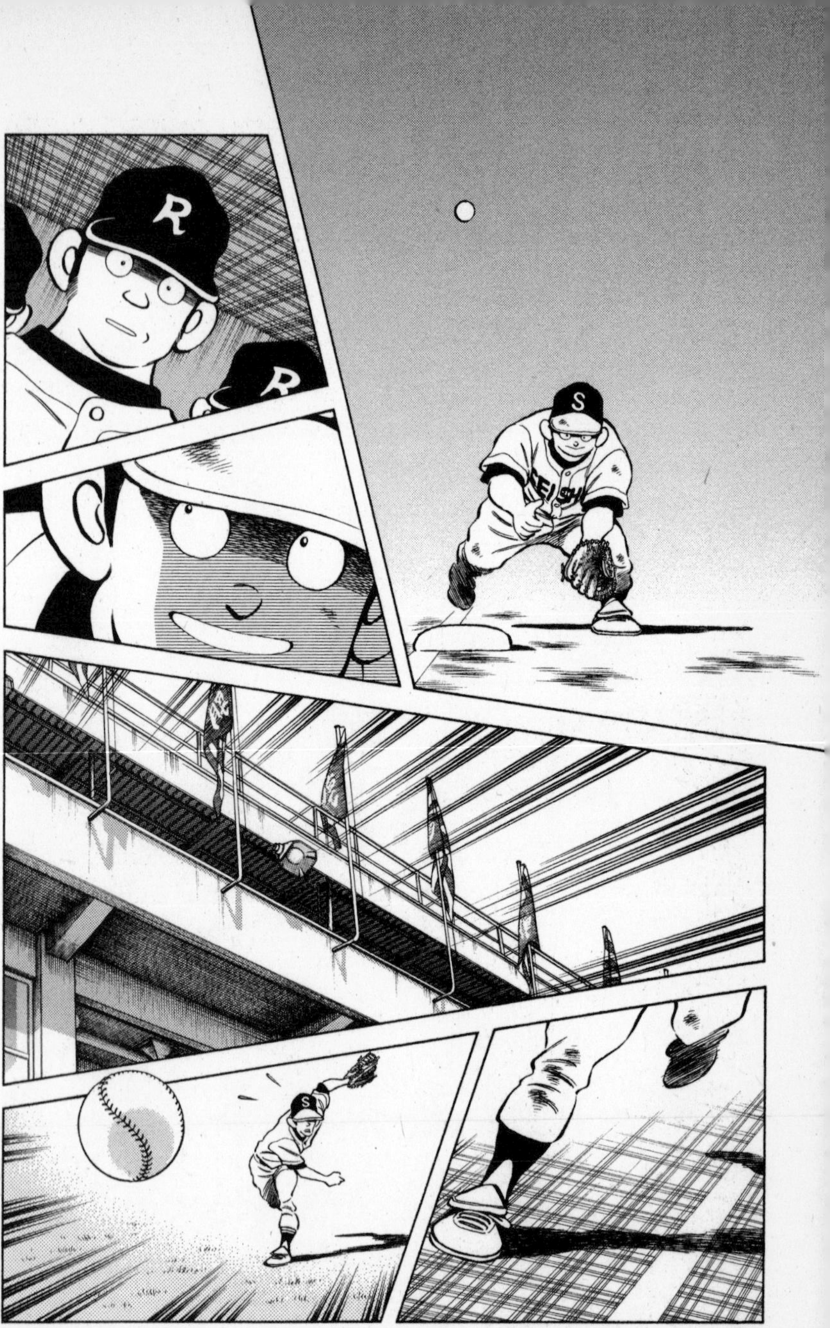

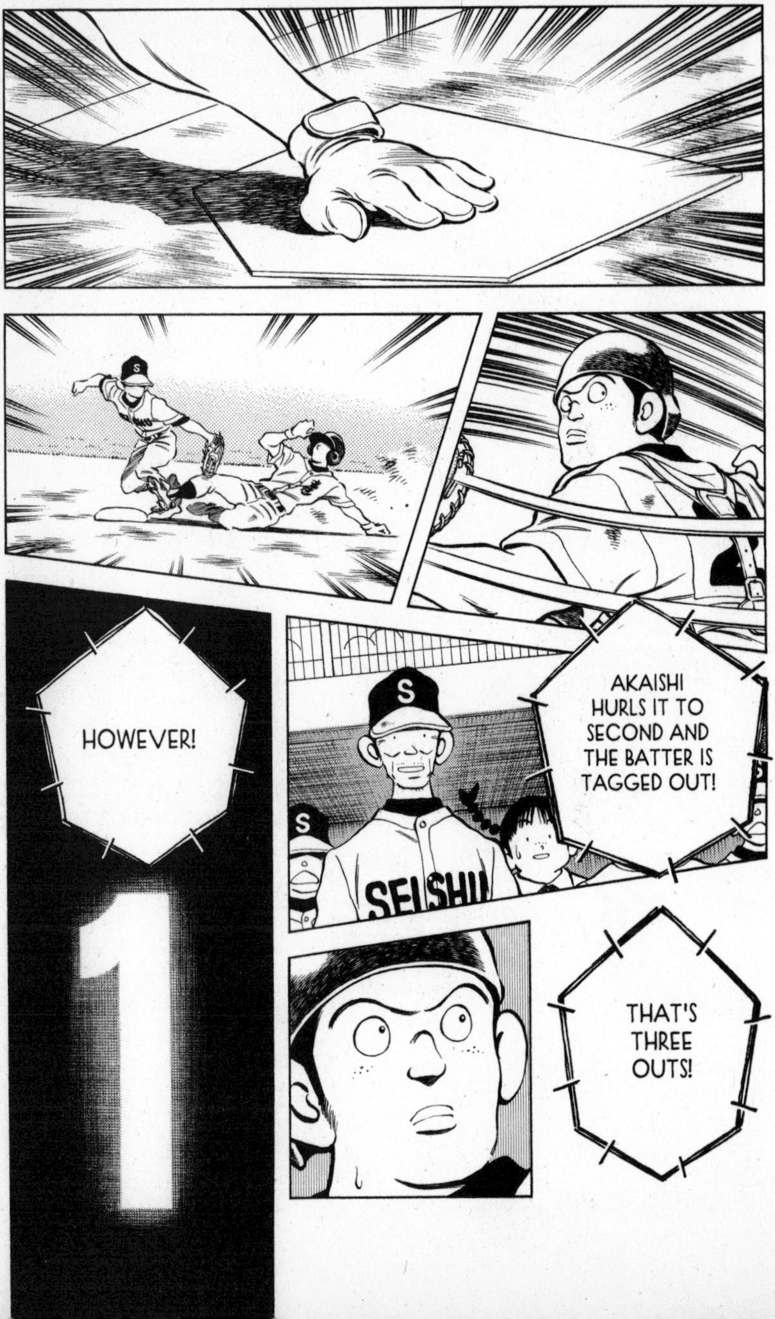
AKAISHI HURLS IT TO SECOND AND THE BATTER IS TAGGED OUT!
SEISHU
THAT'S THREE OUTS!
HOWEVER!
1

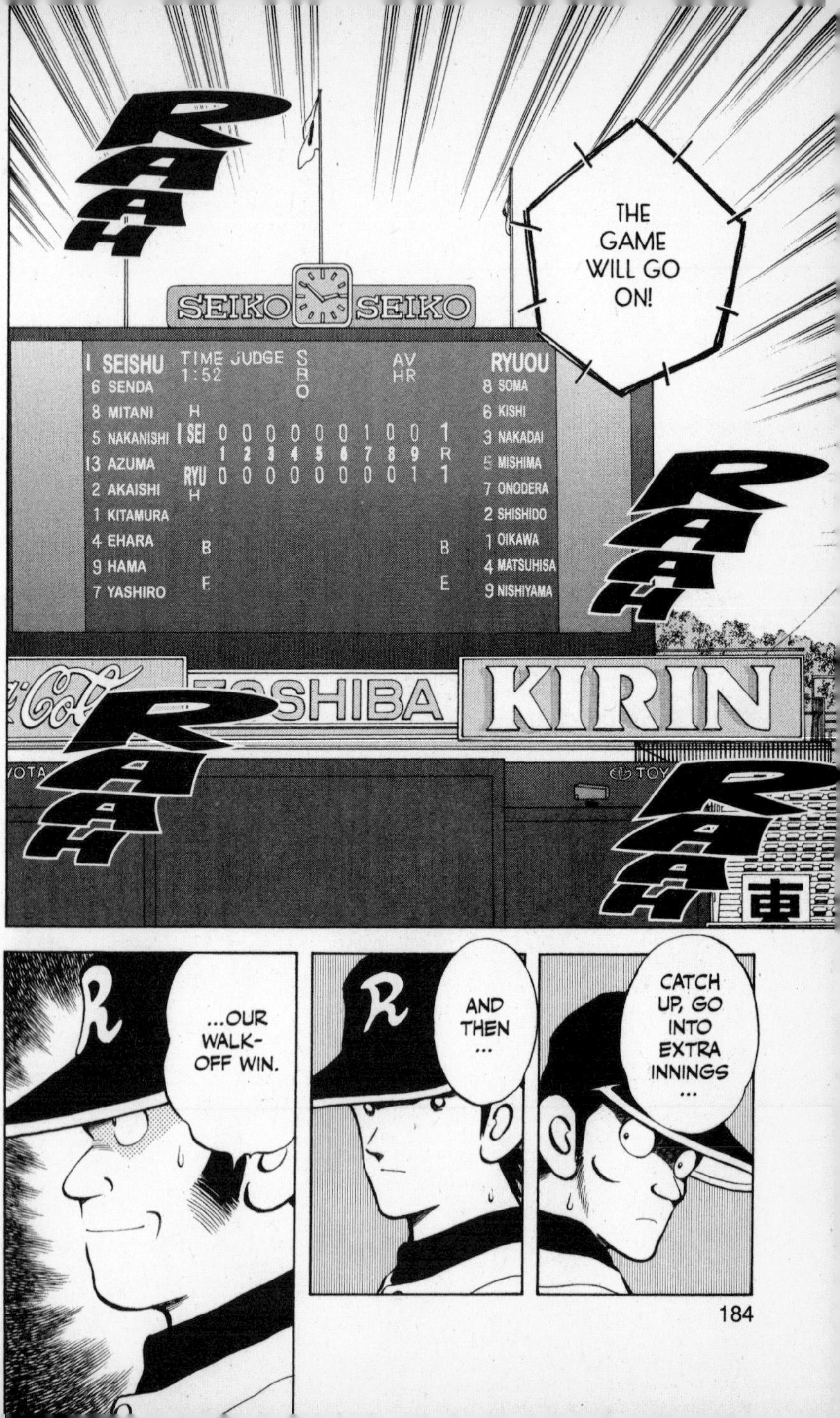
RAAH
THE GAME WILL GO ON!
SEIKO SEIKO
1 SEISHU
TIME 1:52
JUDGE
S B O
AV HR
RYUOU
6 SENDA
8 MITANI
5 NAKANISHI
13 AZUMA
2 AKAISHI
1 KITAMURA
4 EHARA
9 HAMA
7 YASHIRO
1 SEI 0 0 0 0 0 0 1 0 0 1
1 2 3 4 5 6 7 8 9 R
RYU 0 0 0 0 0 0 0 0 1 1
8 SOMA
6 KISHI
3 NAKADAI
5 MISHIMA
7 ONODERA
2 SHISHIDO
1 OIKAWA
4 MATSUHISA
9 NISHIYAMA
RAAH
KIRIN
SHIBA
RAAH
RAAH
CATCH UP, GO INTO EXTRA INNINGS ...
AND THEN ...
...OUR WALK-OFF WIN.

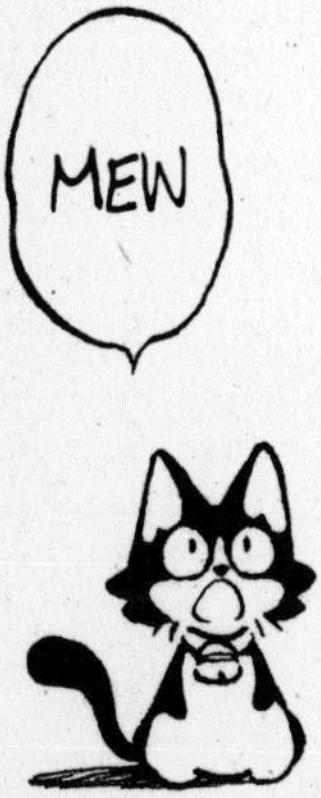
MEW

Cross✿Game

17

Story & Art by
Mitsuru Adachi

CHAPTER 151
HE WAS CRYING

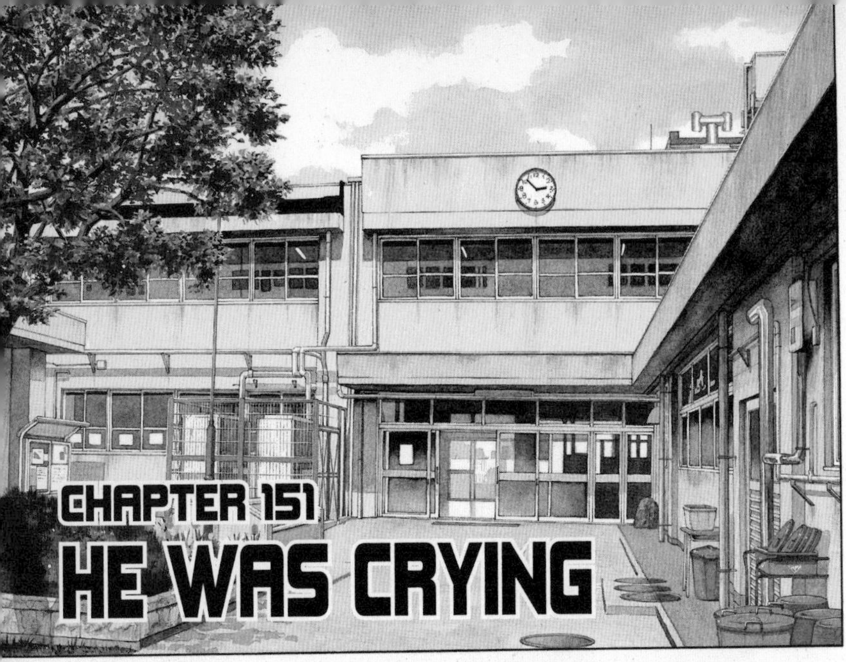

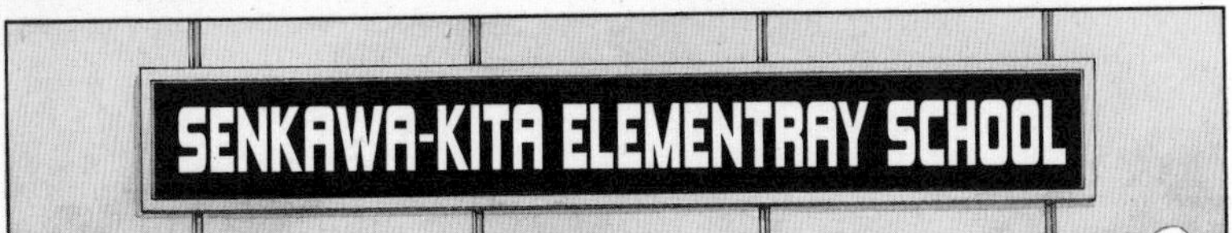
SENKAWA-KITA ELEMENTRAY SCHOOL

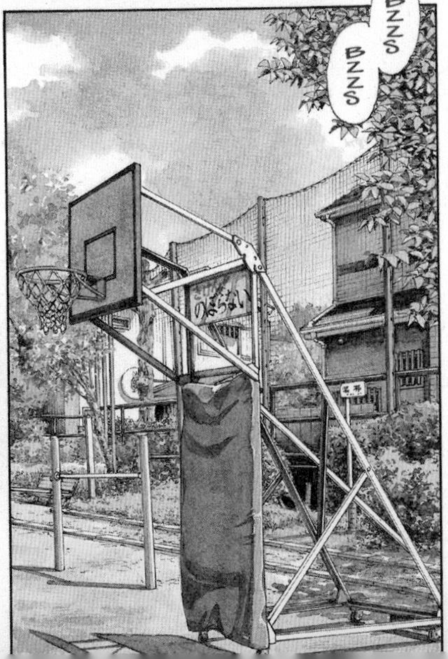
BZZS
BZZS

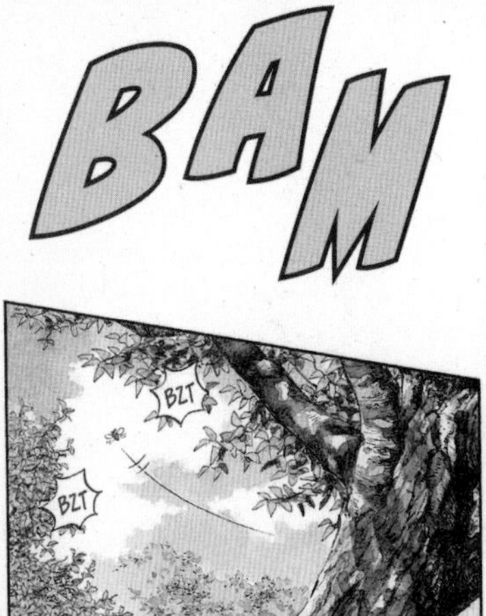
BAM
BZT
BZT

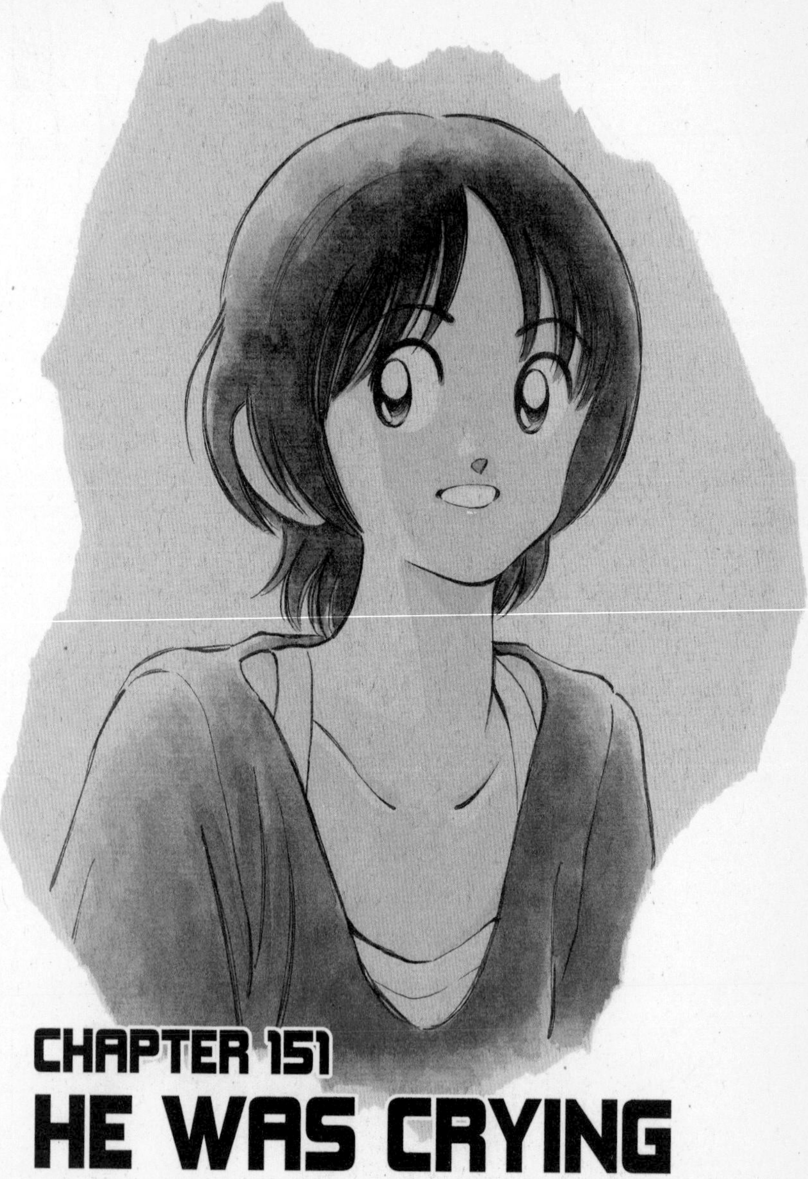

CHAPTER 151
HE WAS CRYING

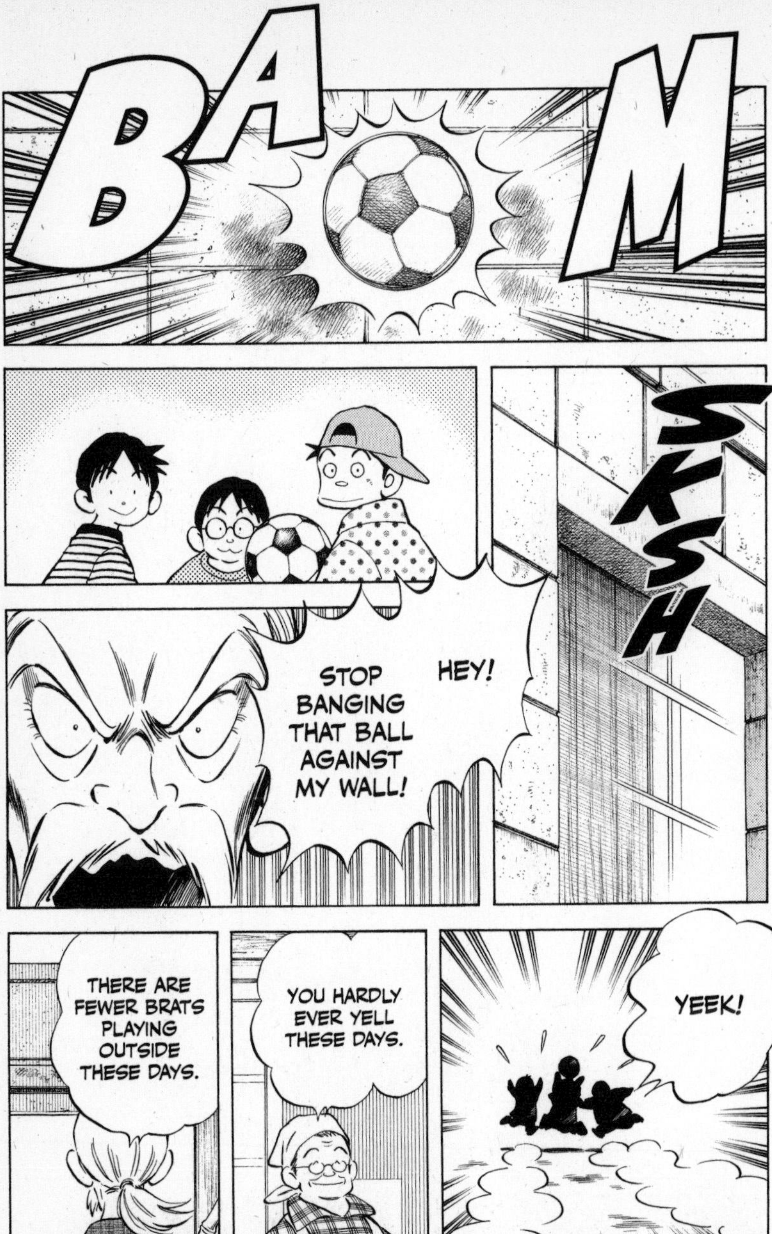
BAM
SKSH
HEY!
STOP BANGING THAT BALL AGAINST MY WALL!
YEEK!
YOU HARDLY EVER YELL THESE DAYS.
THERE ARE FEWER BRATS PLAYING OUTSIDE THESE DAYS.

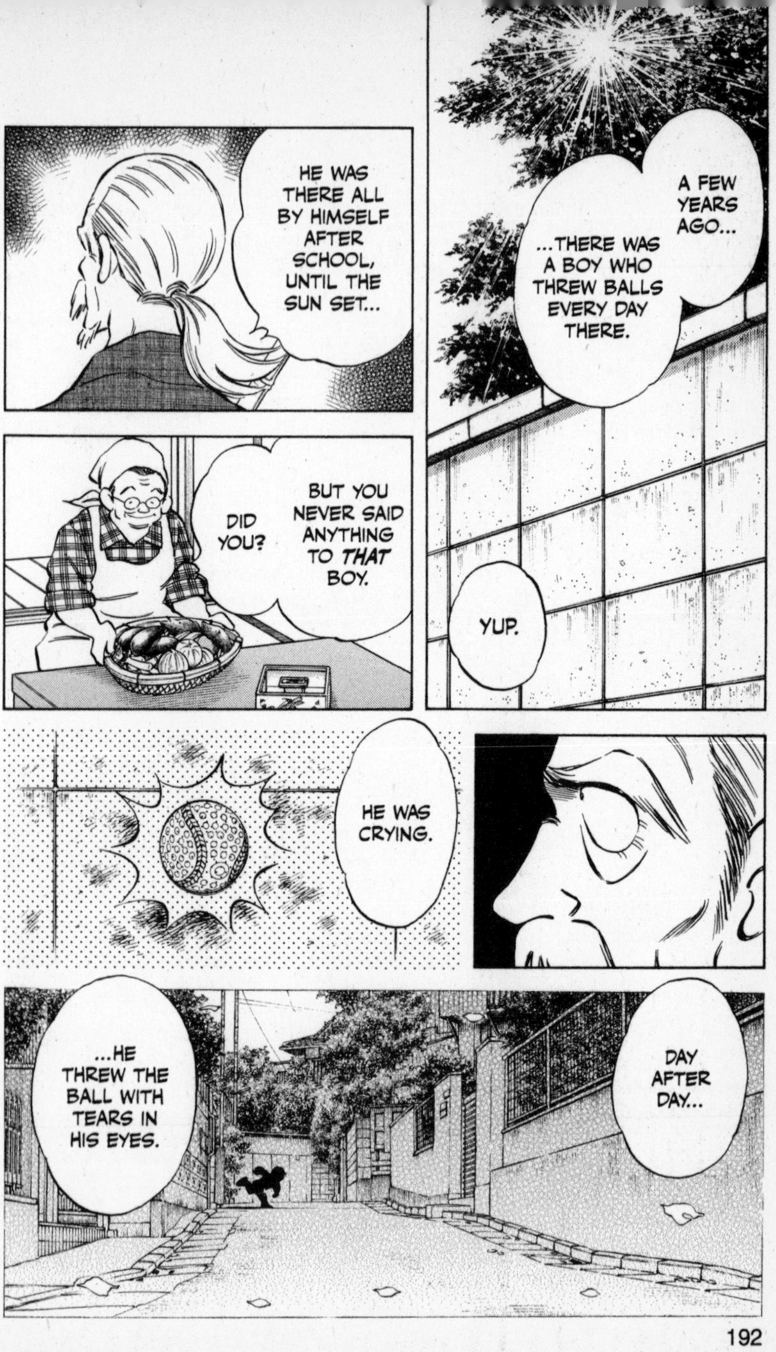
A FEW YEARS AGO...
...THERE WAS A BOY WHO THREW BALLS EVERY DAY THERE.
YUP.
HE WAS THERE ALL BY HIMSELF AFTER SCHOOL, UNTIL THE SUN SET...
BUT YOU NEVER SAID ANYTHING TO THAT BOY.
DID YOU?
HE WAS CRYING.
DAY AFTER DAY...
...HE THREW THE BALL WITH TEARS IN HIS EYES.

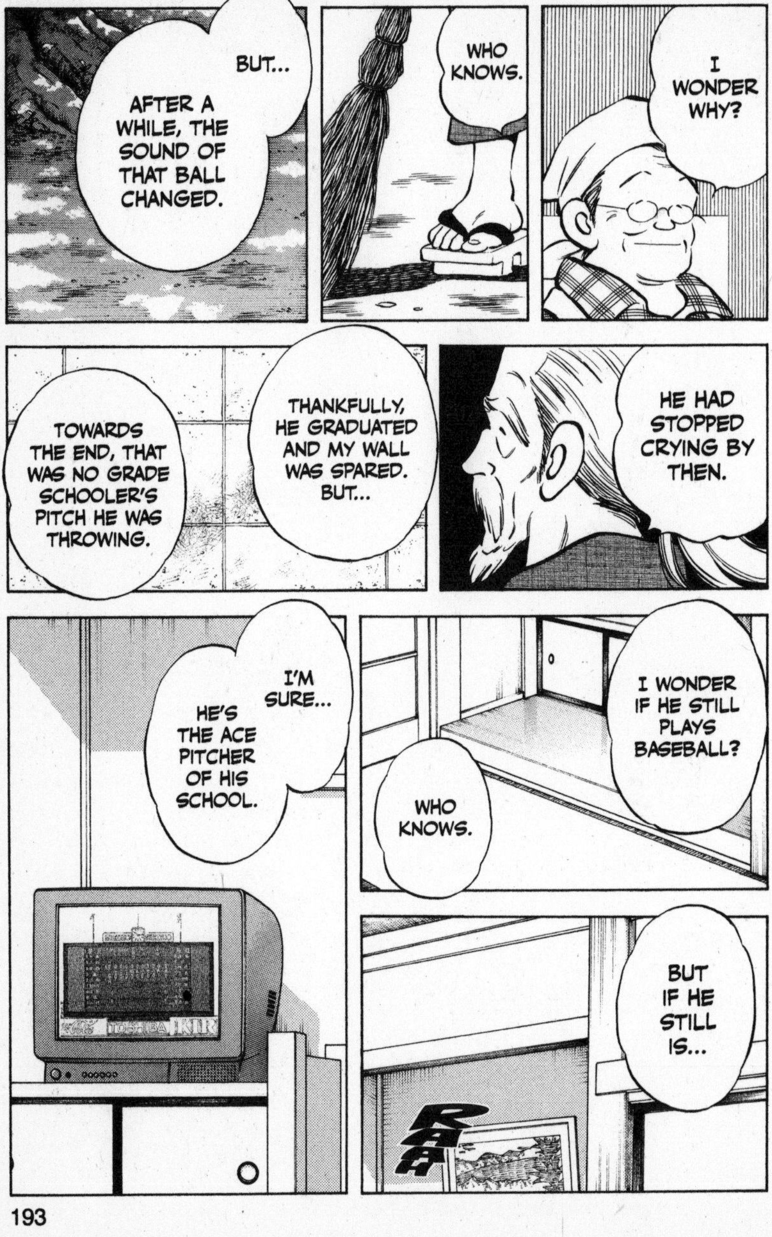
I WONDER WHY?
WHO KNOWS.
BUT...
AFTER A WHILE, THE SOUND OF THAT BALL CHANGED.
HE HAD STOPPED CRYING BY THEN.
THANKFULLY, HE GRADUATED AND MY WALL WAS SPARED. BUT...
TOWARDS THE END, THAT WAS NO GRADE SCHOOLER'S PITCH HE WAS THROWING.
I WONDER IF HE STILL PLAYS BASEBALL?
WHO KNOWS.
BUT IF HE STILL IS...
RAAA
I'M SURE...
HE'S THE ACE PITCHER OF HIS SCHOOL.
TOSHIBA

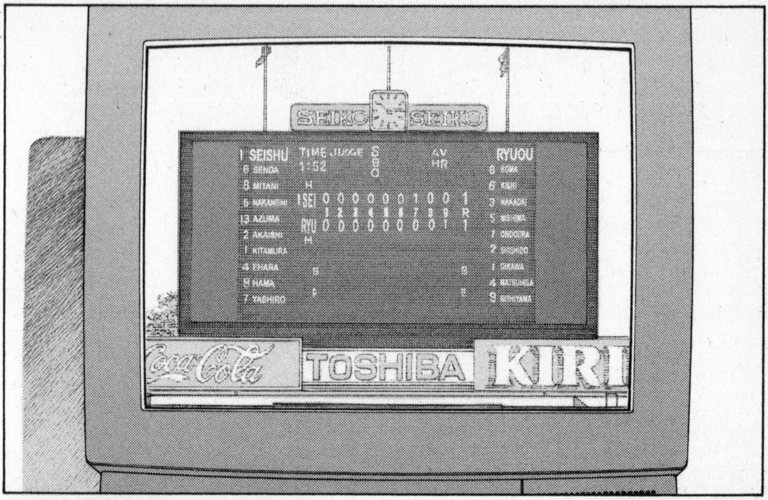
SEIKO SEIKO
Coca-Cola
TOSHIBA
KIRI

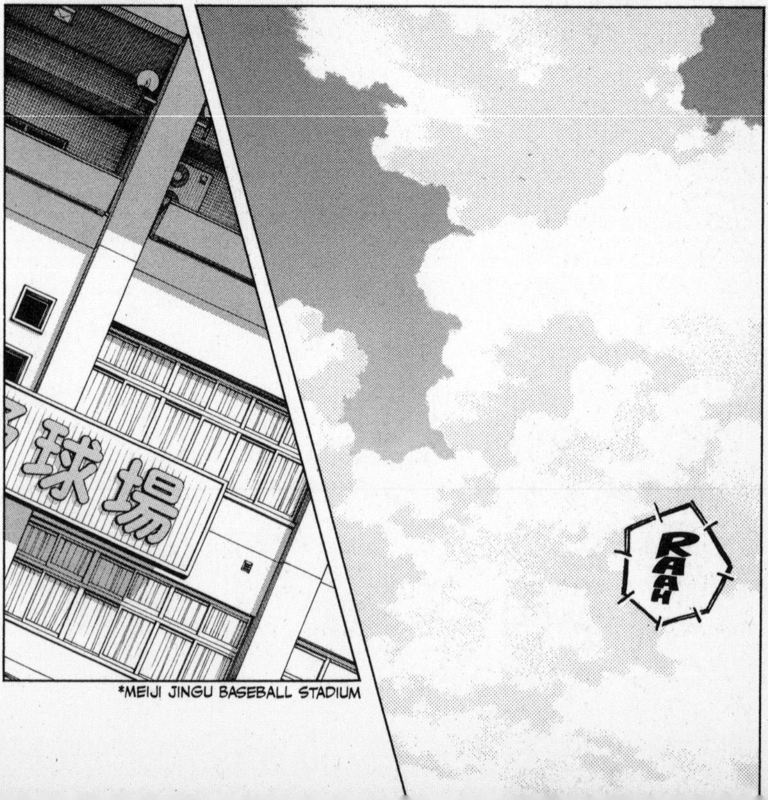
RAAH
球場

*MEIJI JINGU BASEBALL STADIUM

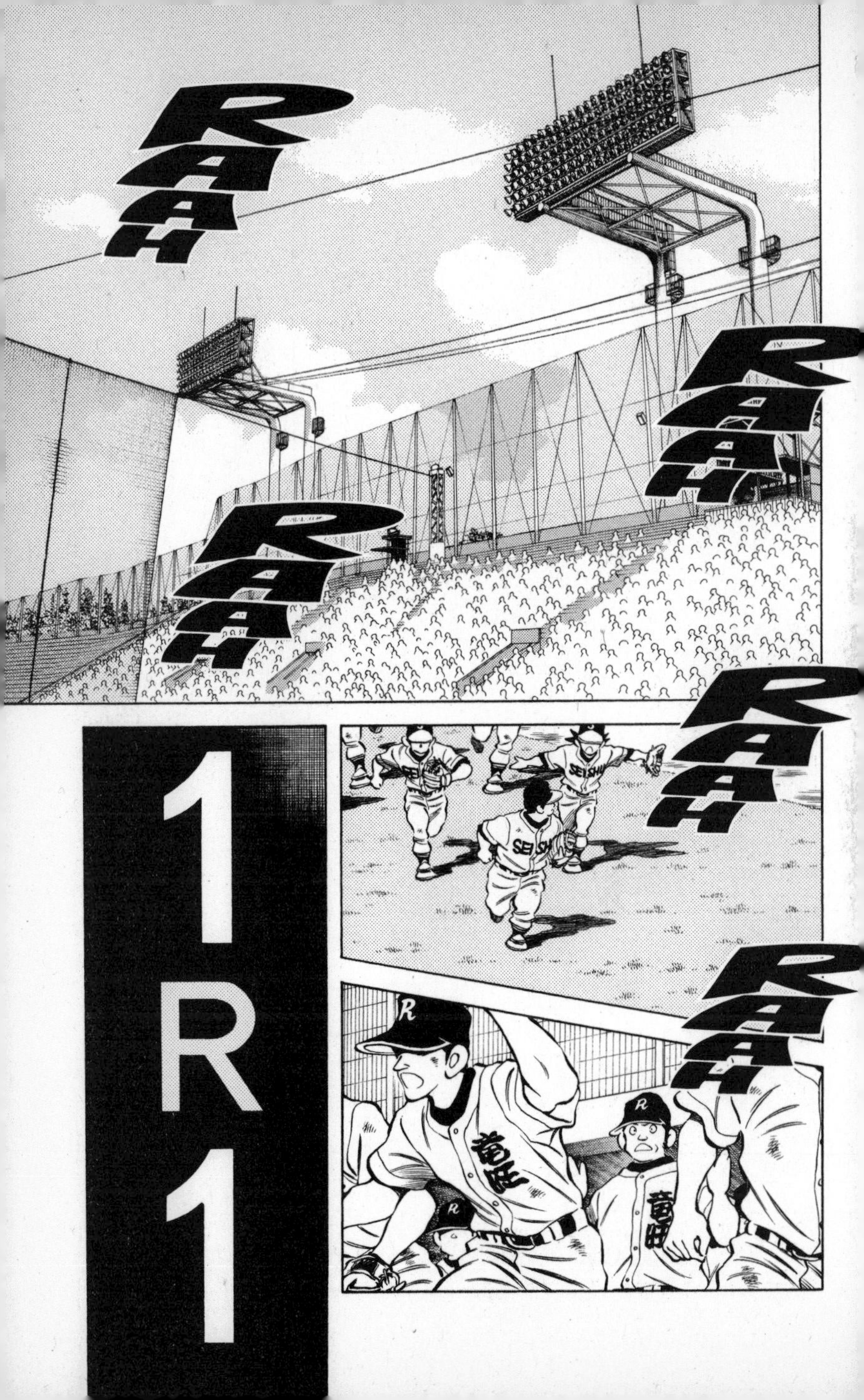
RAAH
RAAH
RAAH
RAAH
SEISHU
SEISHU
RAAH
1R1

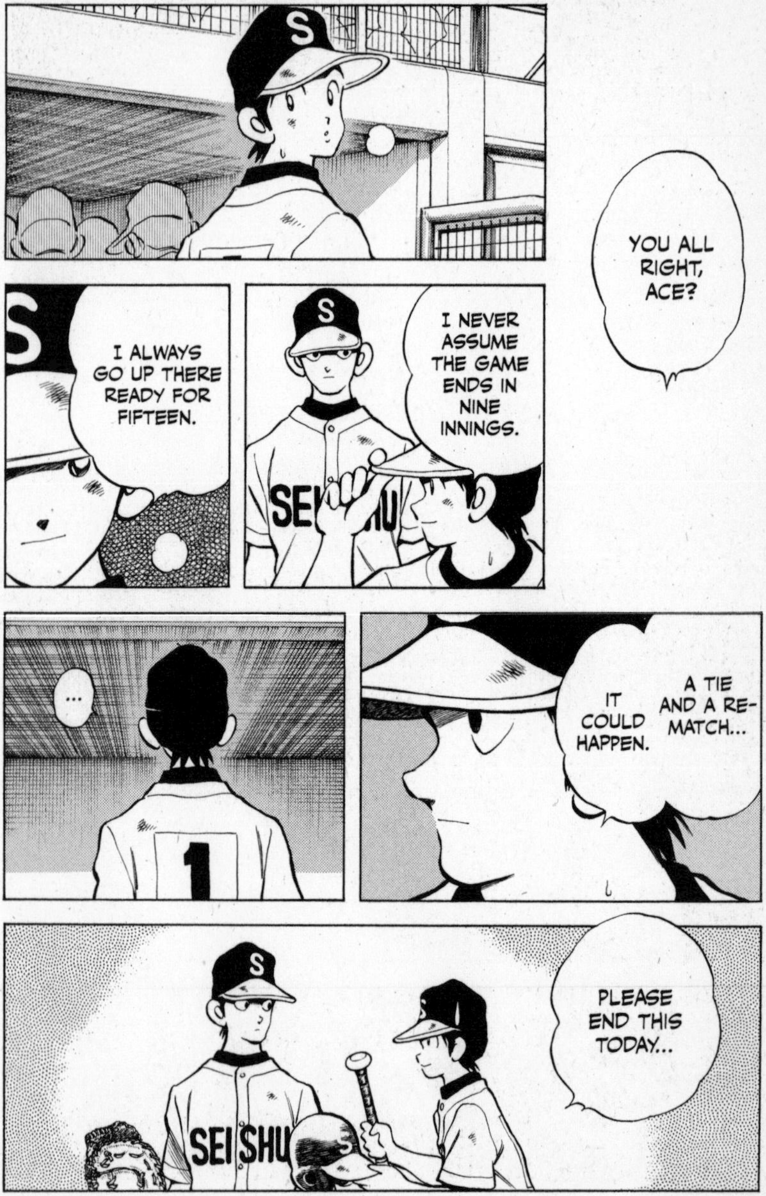
YOU ALL RIGHT, ACE?
I NEVER ASSUME THE GAME ENDS IN NINE INNINGS.
I ALWAYS GO UP THERE READY FOR FIFTEEN.
A TIE AND A RE-MATCH...
IT COULD HAPPEN.
...
PLEASE END THIS TODAY...

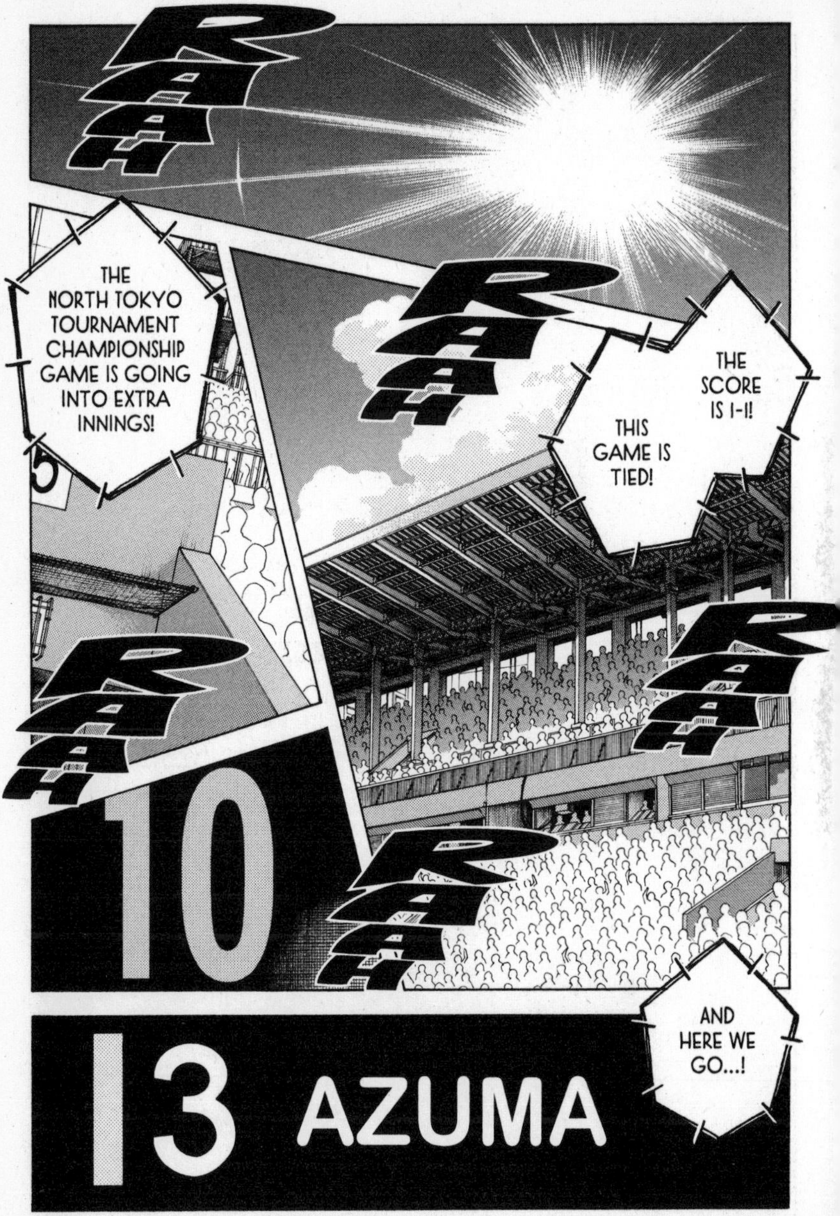
RAAAH
RAAAH
THE SCORE IS 1-1!
THIS GAME IS TIED!
RAAAH
RAAAH
THE NORTH TOKYO TOURNAMENT CHAMPIONSHIP GAME IS GOING INTO EXTRA INNINGS!
RAAAH
10
13 AZUMA
AND HERE WE GO...!

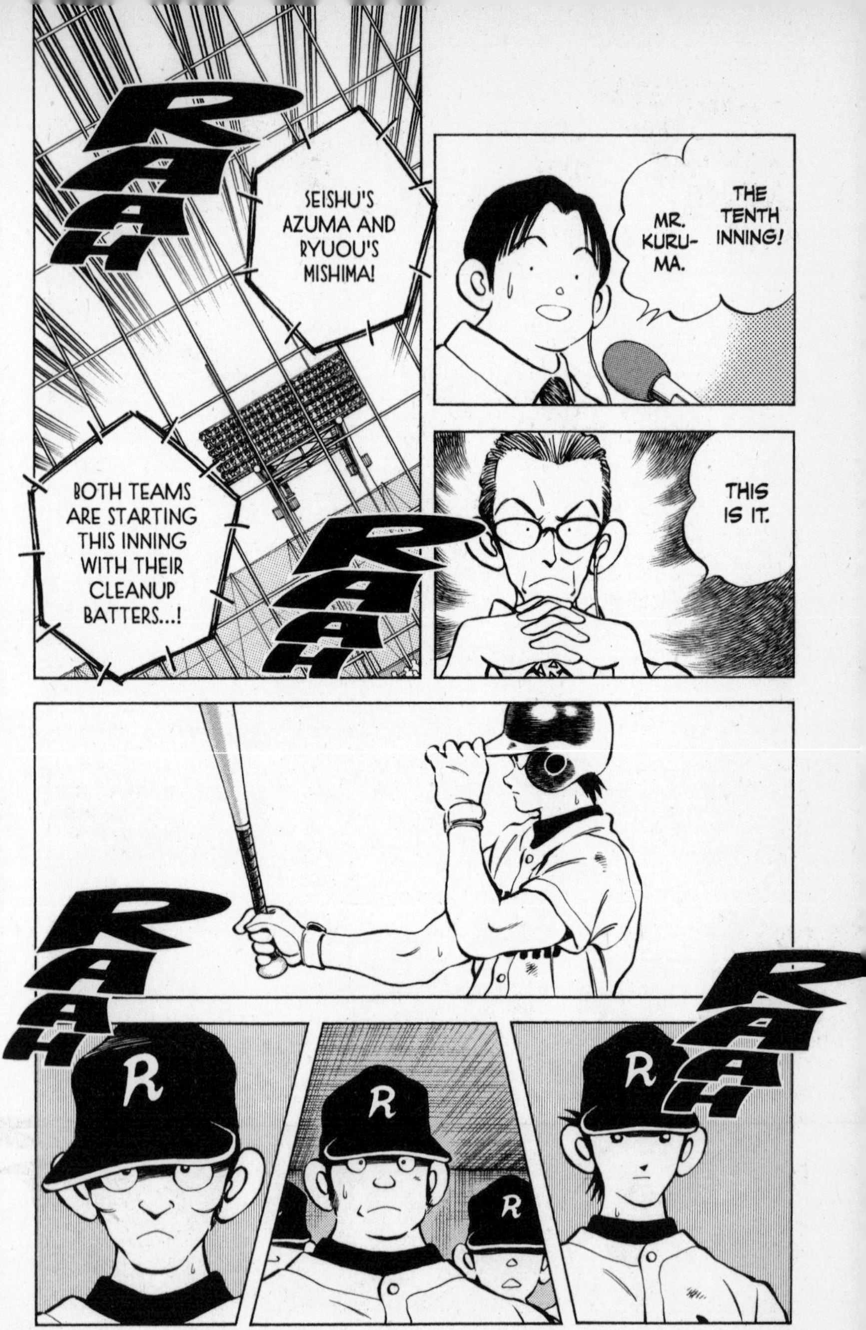
THE TENTH INNING!
MR. KURUMA.
THIS IS IT.
RAAH
SEISHU'S AZUMA AND RYUOU'S MISHIMA!
RAAH
BOTH TEAMS ARE STARTING THIS INNING WITH THEIR CLEANUP BATTERS...!
RAAH
RAAH

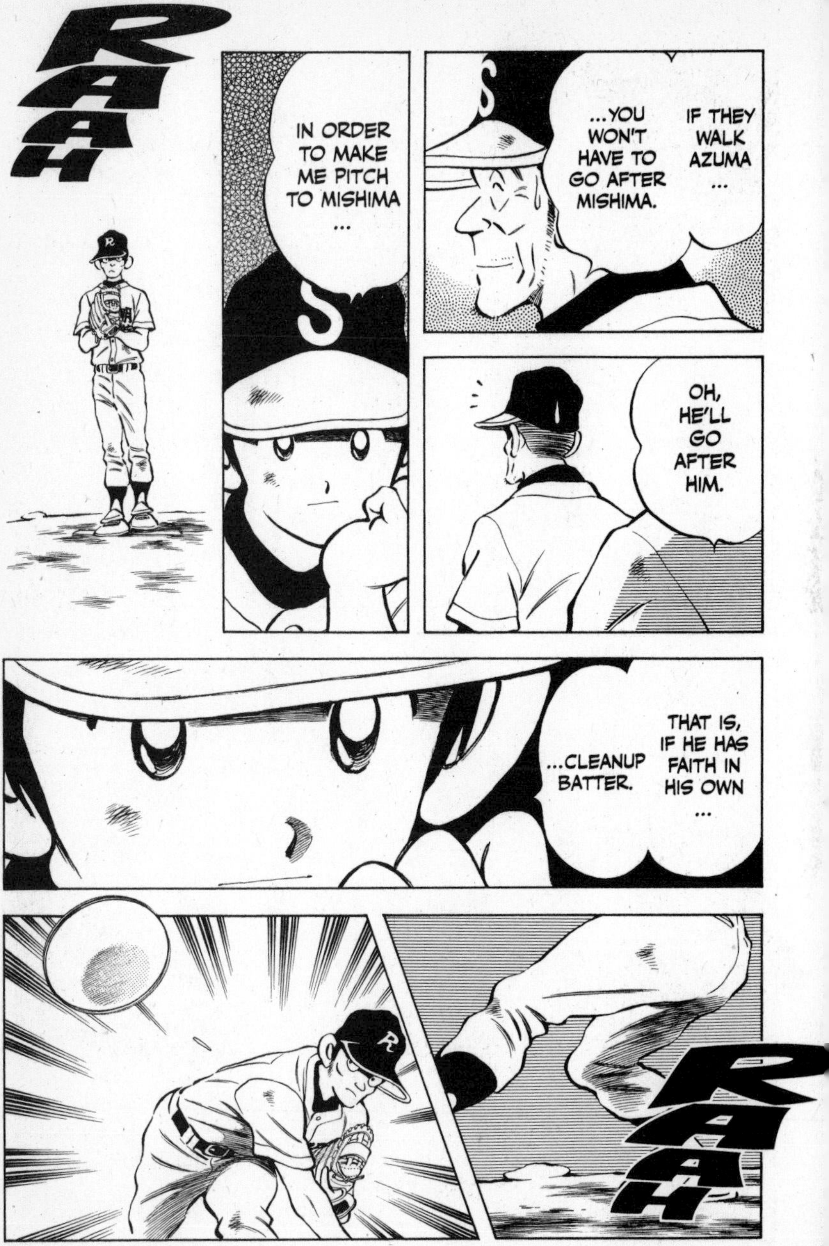
IF THEY WALK AZUMA ...
...YOU WON'T HAVE TO GO AFTER MISHIMA.
OH, HE'LL GO AFTER HIM.
IN ORDER TO MAKE ME PITCH TO MISHIMA ...
RAAH
THAT IS, IF HE HAS FAITH IN HIS OWN ...
...CLEANUP BATTER.
RAAH

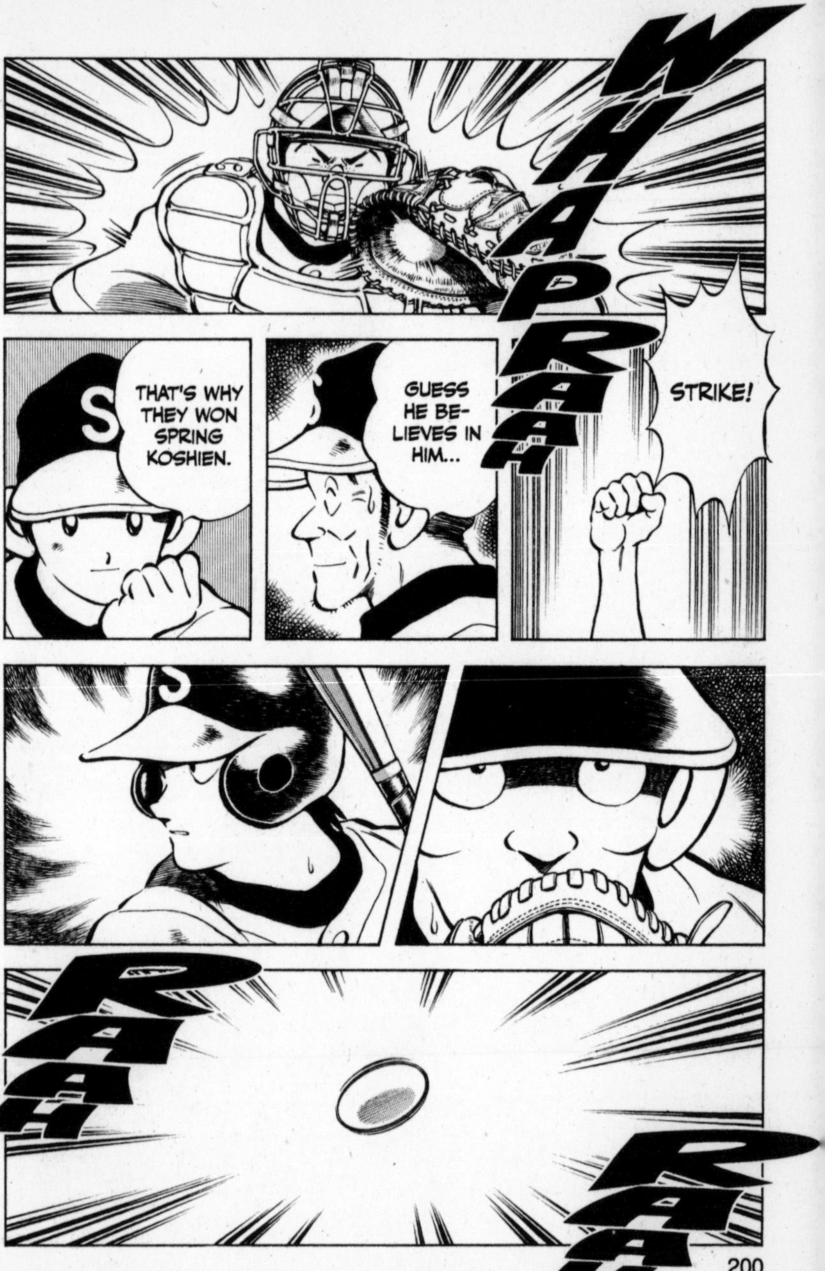
WHAPRAAH
STRIKE!
GUESS HE BE-LIEVES IN HIM...
THAT'S WHY THEY WON SPRING KOSHIEN.
RAAH
RAAH

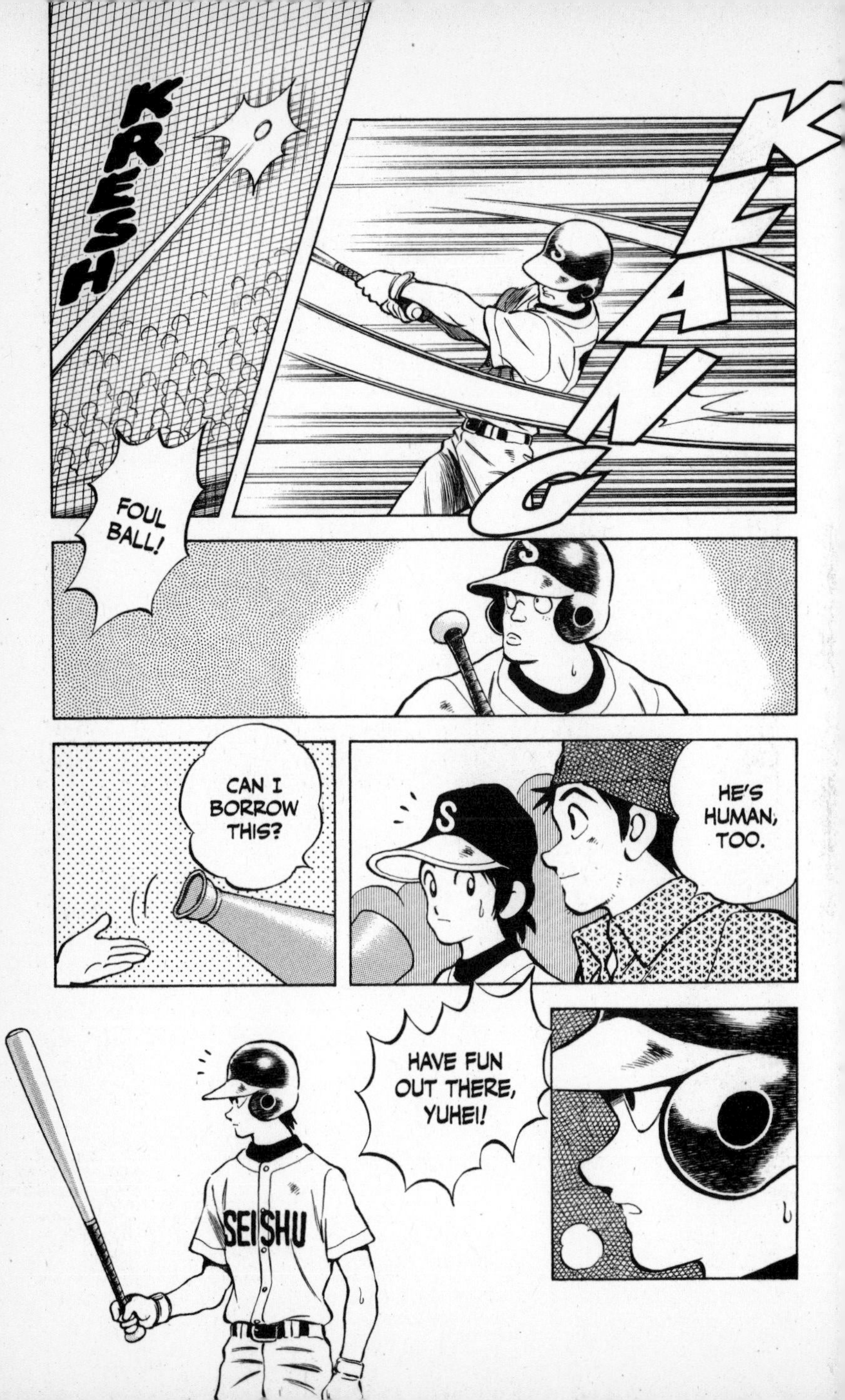
KLANG
KRESH
FOUL BALL!
HE'S HUMAN, TOO.
CAN I BORROW THIS?
HAVE FUN OUT THERE, YUHEI!
SEISHU

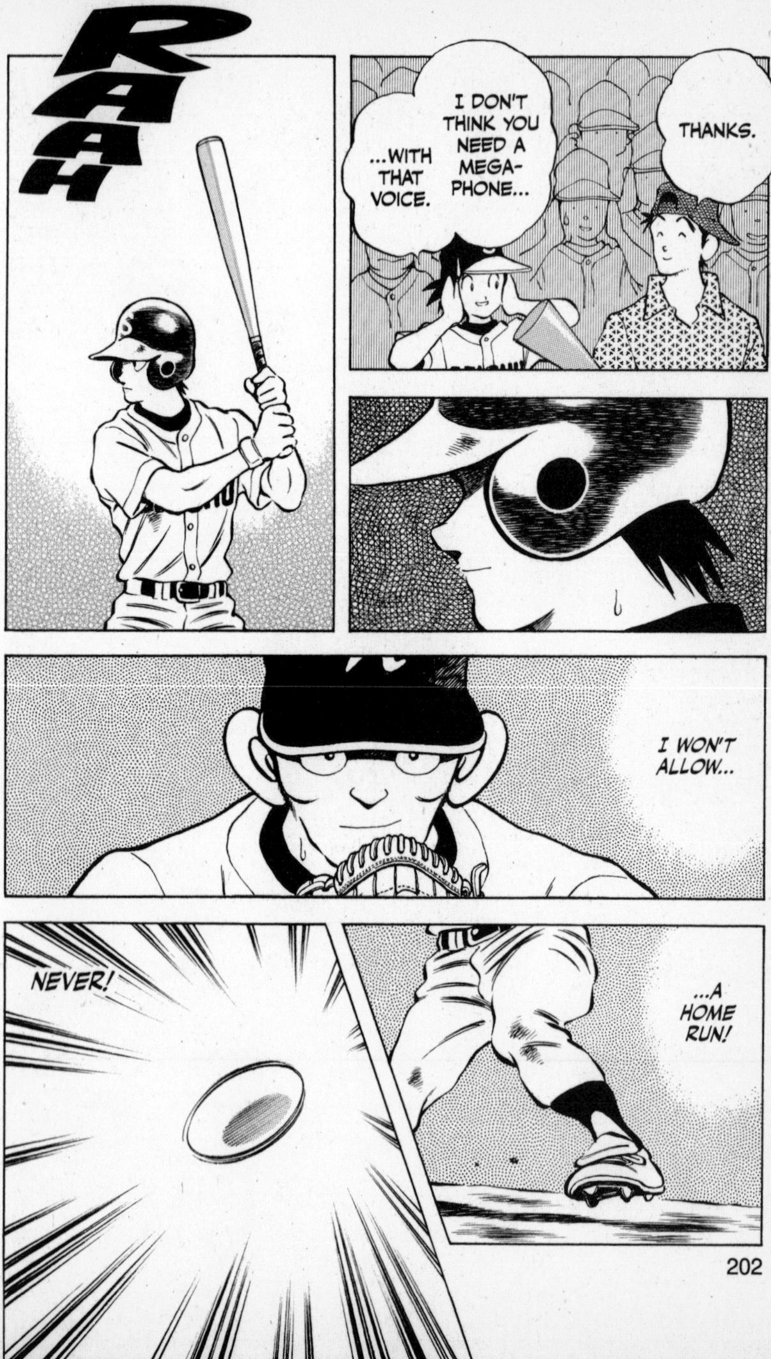

I DON'T THINK YOU NEED A MEGA-PHONE...
...WITH THAT VOICE.
THANKS.
RAAAH
I WON'T ALLOW...
...A HOME RUN!
NEVER!

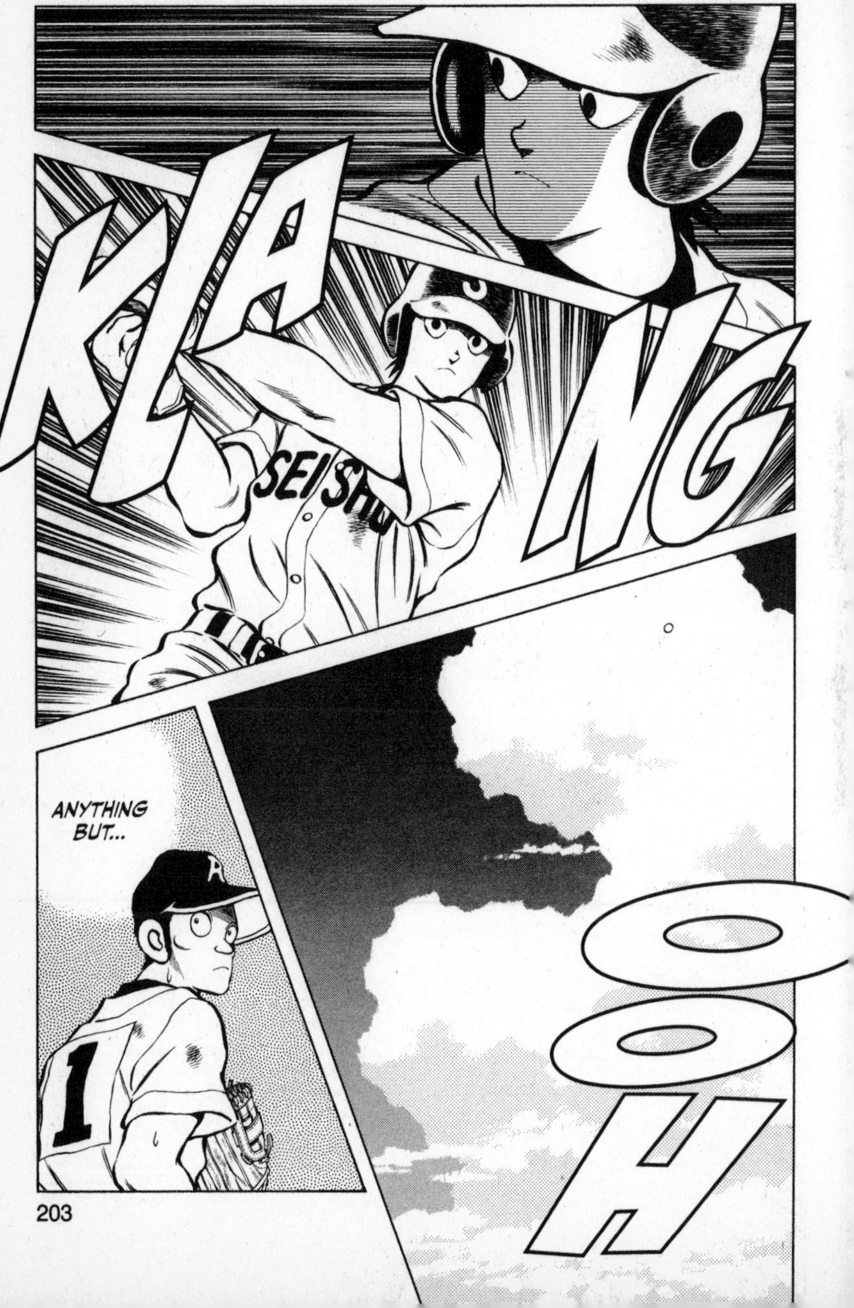
KLANG
ANYTHING BUT...
OOOH

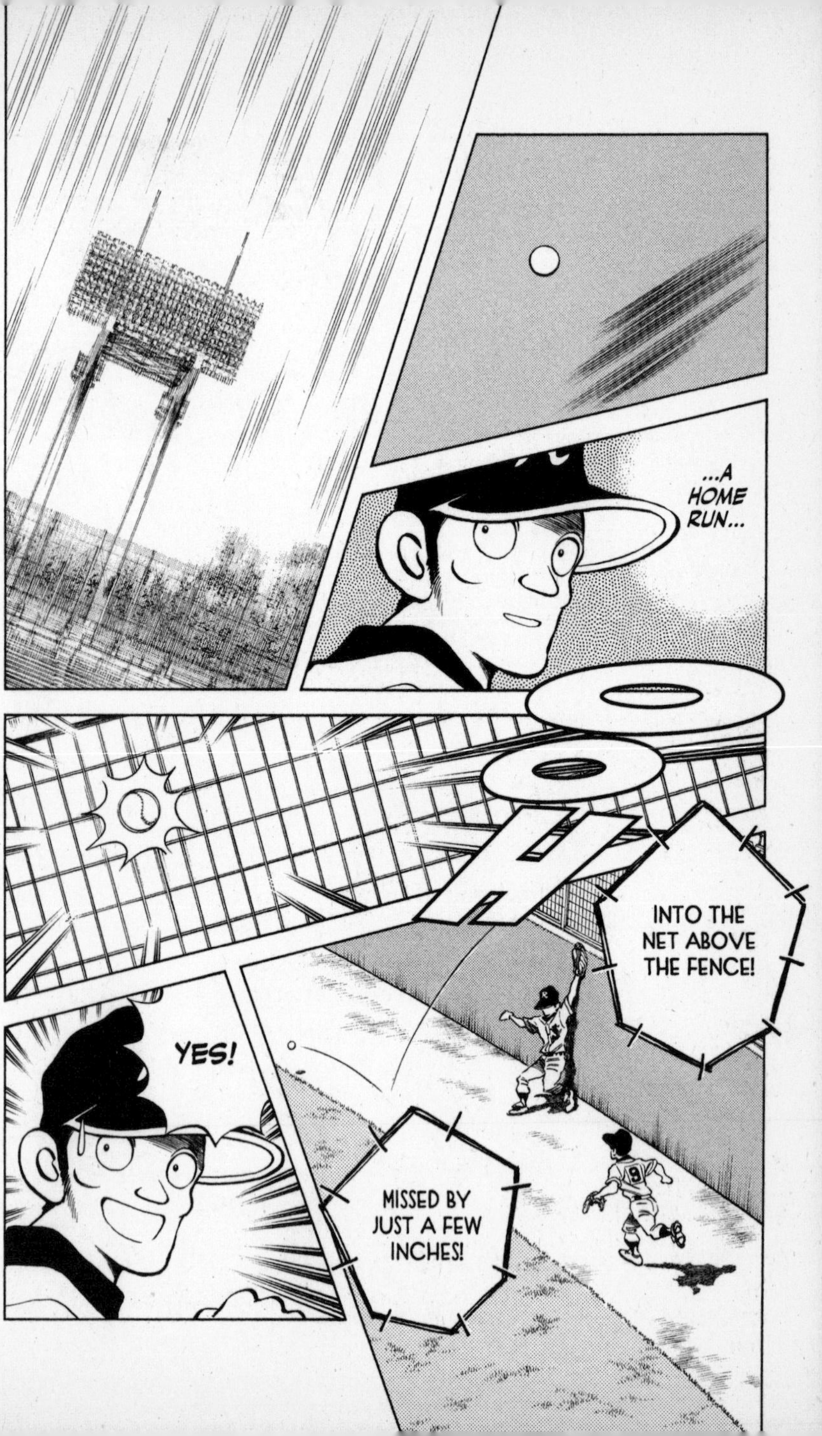
...A HOME RUN...
HOO
INTO THE NET ABOVE THE FENCE!
MISSED BY JUST A FEW INCHES!
YES!

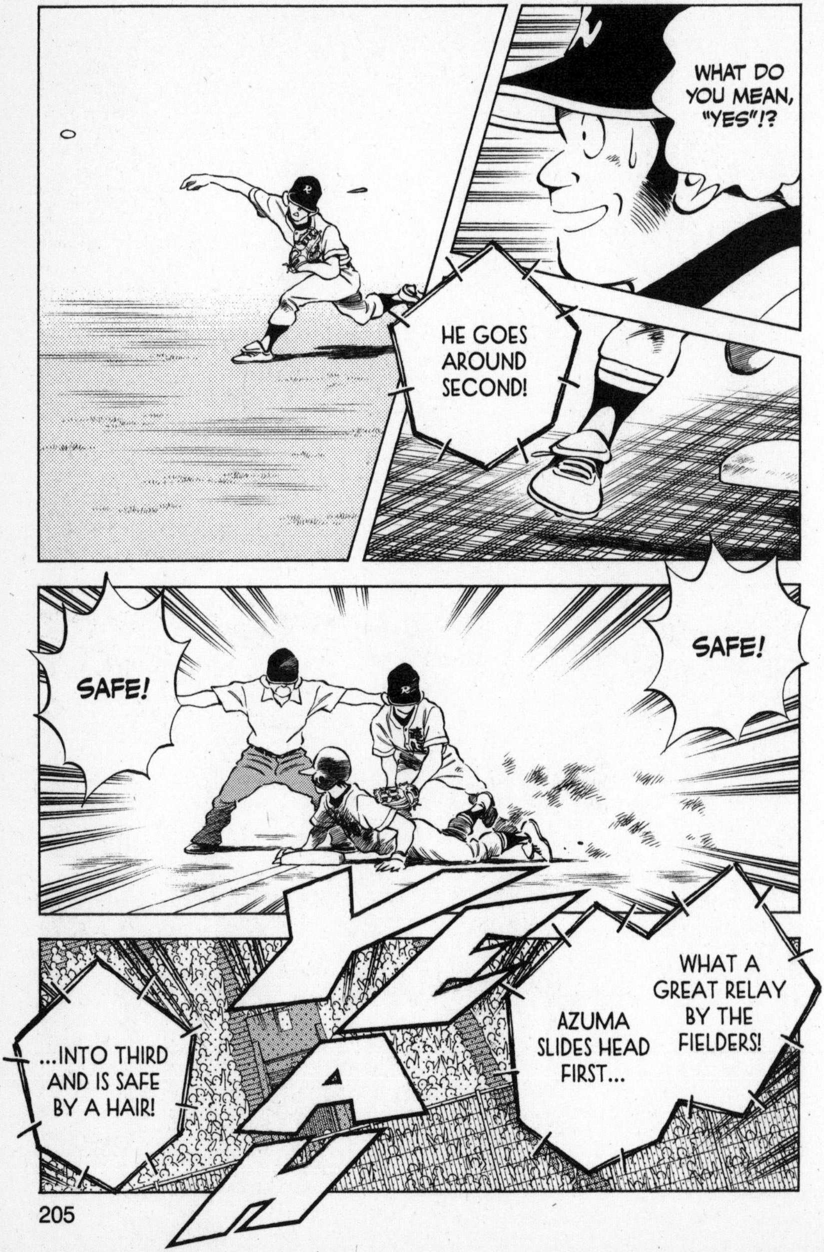
WHAT DO YOU MEAN, "YES"!?
HE GOES AROUND SECOND!
SAFE!
SAFE!
WHAT A GREAT RELAY BY THE FIELDERS!
AZUMA SLIDES HEAD FIRST...
YEAH
...INTO THIRD AND IS SAFE BY A HAIR!

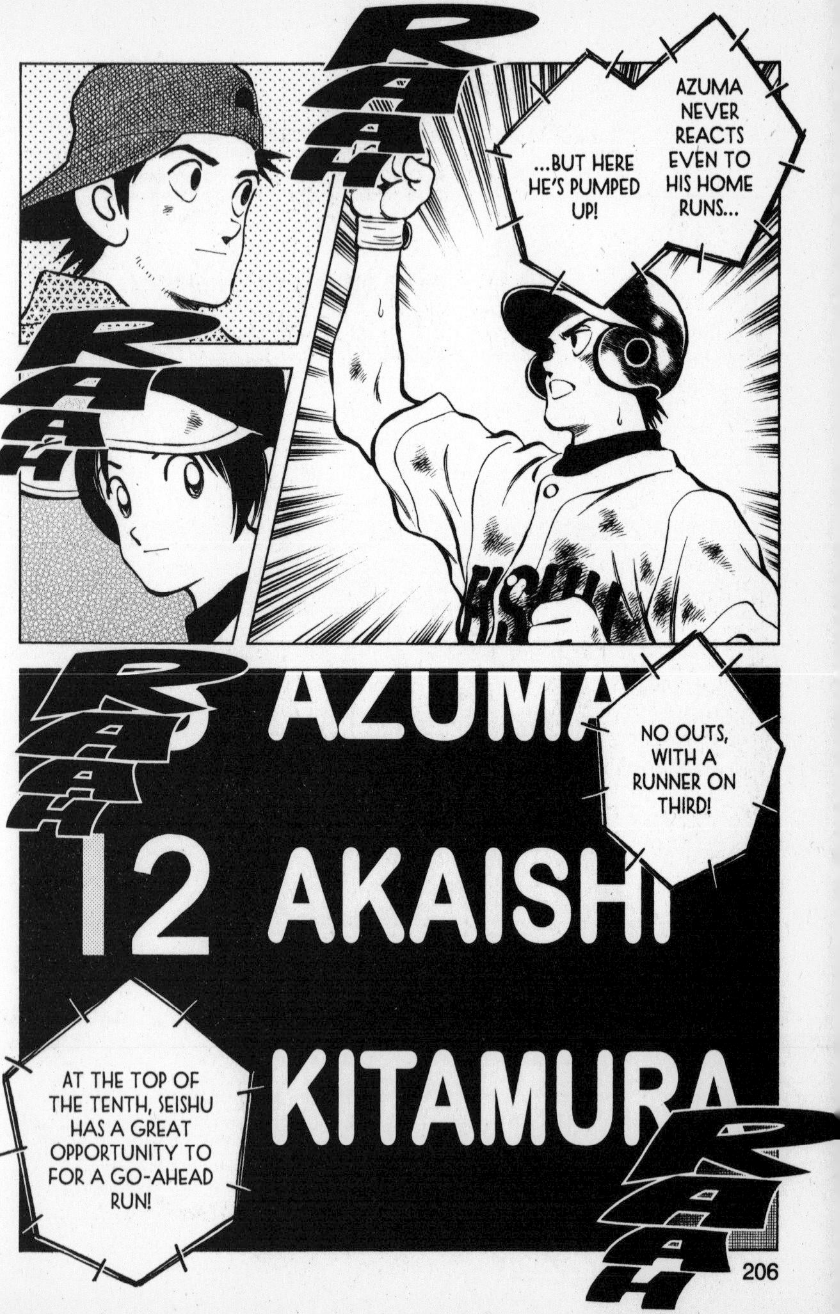
AZUMA NEVER REACTS EVEN TO HIS HOME RUNS...
...BUT HERE HE'S PUMPED UP!
AZUMA
12 AKAISHI
KITAMURA
NO OUTS, WITH A RUNNER ON THIRD!
AT THE TOP OF THE TENTH, SEISHU HAS A GREAT OPPORTUNITY TO FOR A GO-AHEAD RUN!

CHAPTER 152
I AGREE

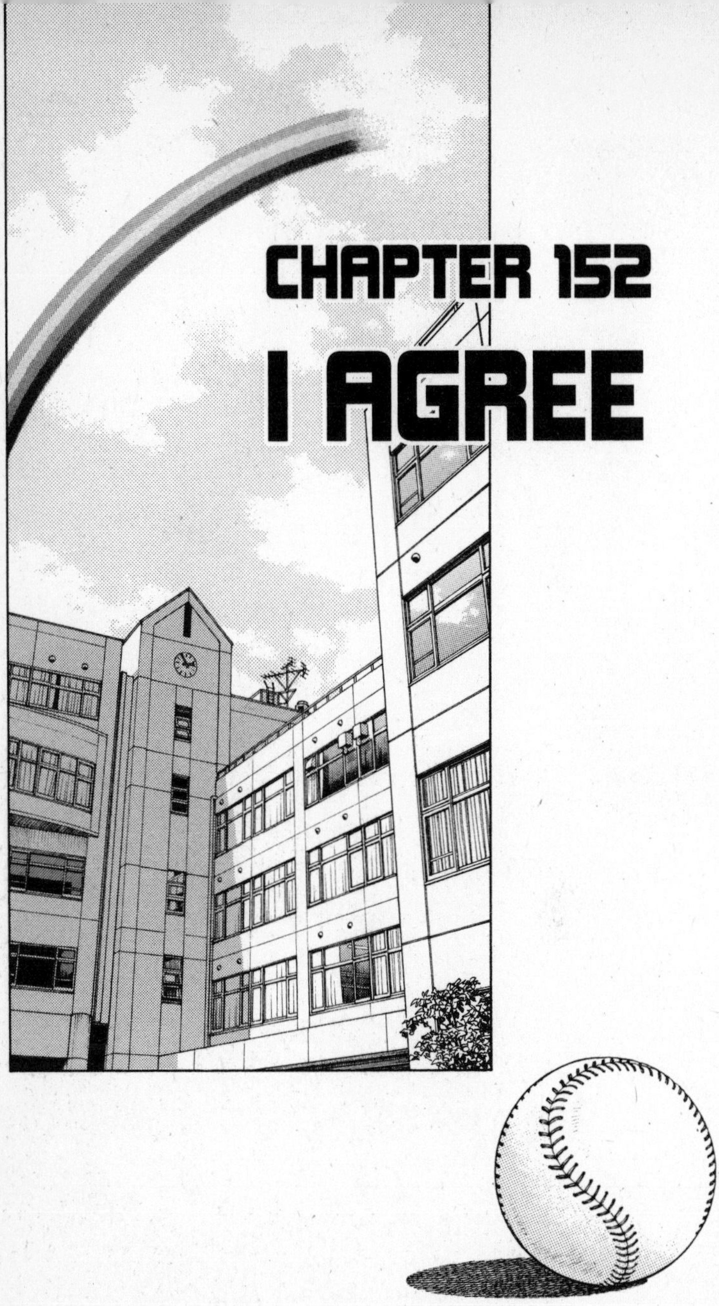

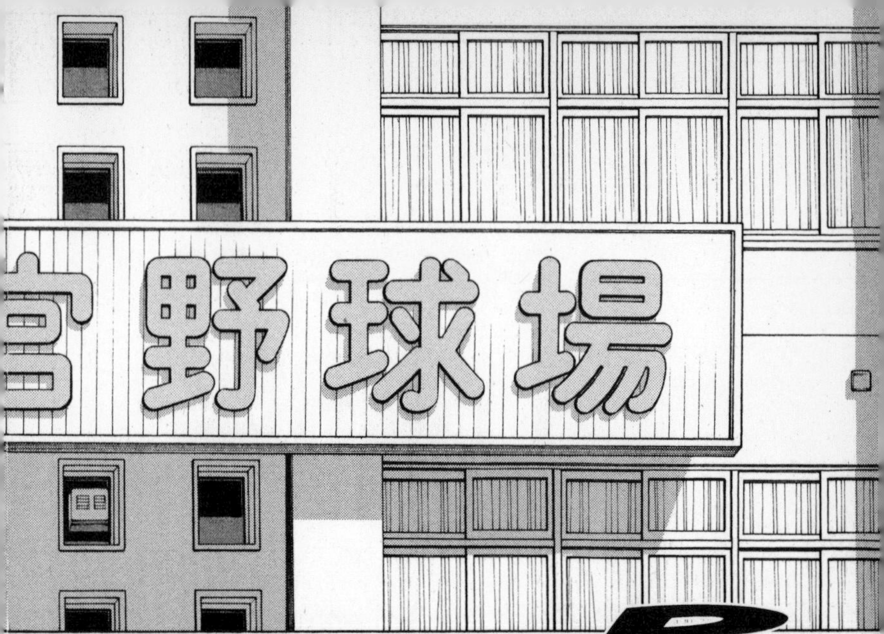
野球場

*MEIJI JINGU BASEBALL STADIUM

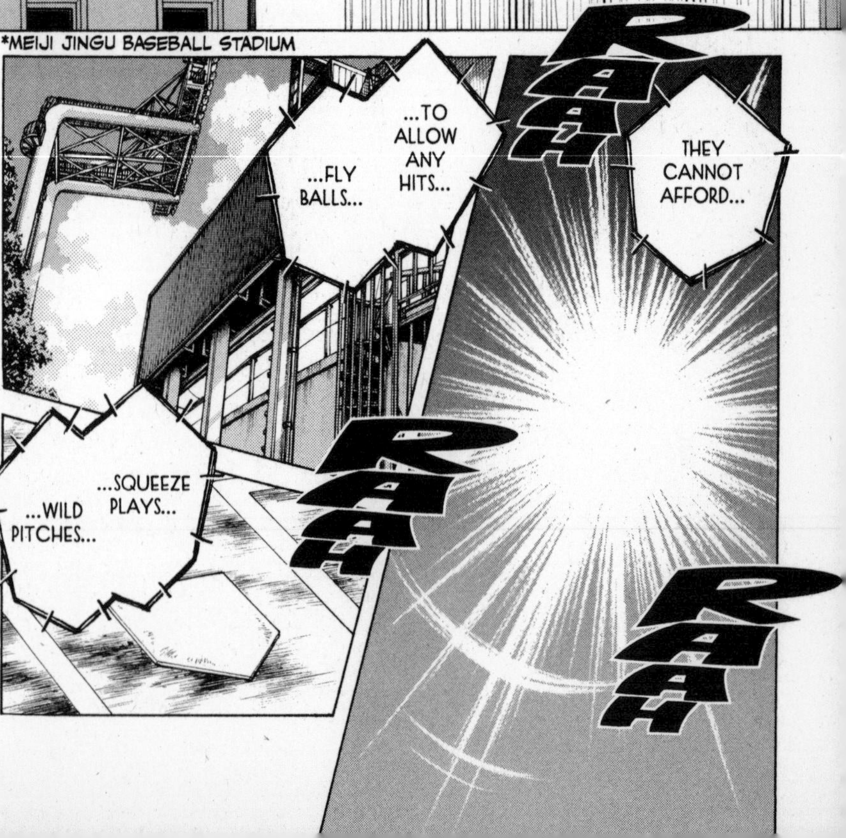
RAAH
THEY CANNOT AFFORD...
...TO ALLOW ANY HITS...
...FLY BALLS...
RAAH
...SQUEEZE PLAYS...
...WILD PITCHES...
RAAH

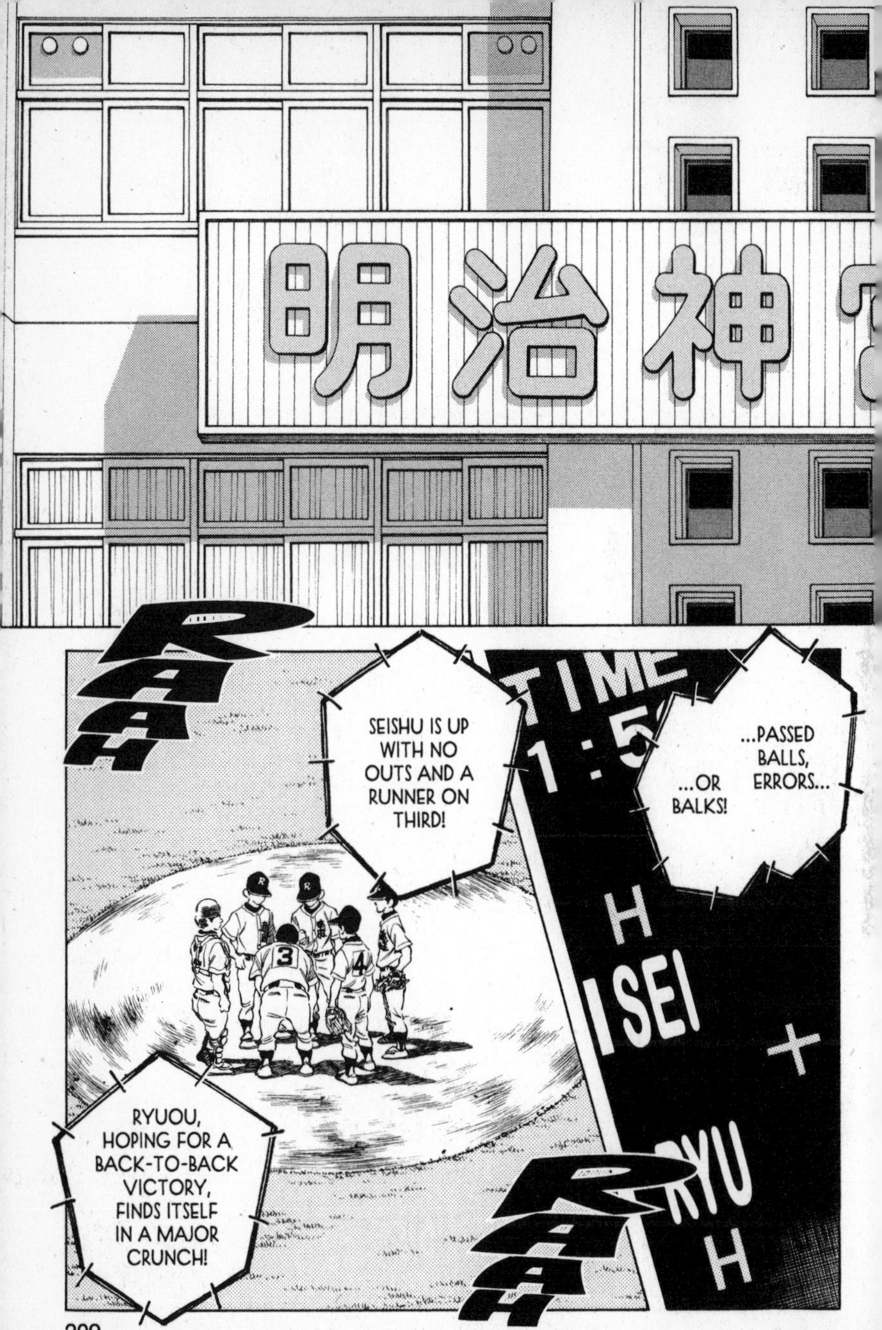
明治神
TIME
1 : 5
H
SEI
RYU
H
...PASSED BALLS, ERRORS...
...OR BALKS!
RAAAH
SEISHU IS UP WITH NO OUTS AND A RUNNER ON THIRD!
RAAAH
RYUOU, HOPING FOR A BACK-TO-BACK VICTORY, FINDS ITSELF IN A MAJOR CRUNCH!

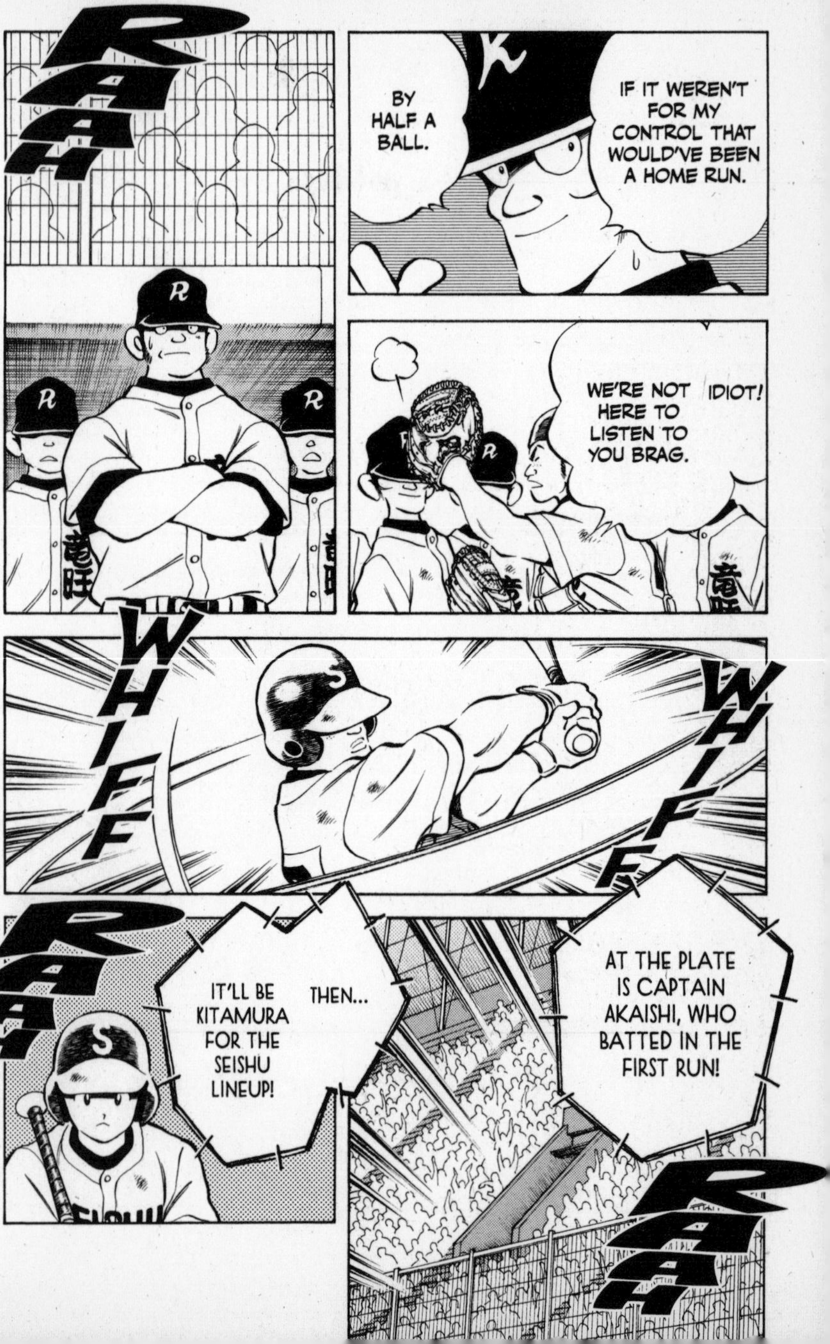
IF IT WEREN'T FOR MY CONTROL THAT WOULD'VE BEEN A HOME RUN.
BY HALF A BALL.
RAAAH
IDIOT!
WE'RE NOT HERE TO LISTEN TO YOU BRAG.
WHIFFF
WHIFFF
AT THE PLATE IS CAPTAIN AKAISHI, WHO BATTED IN THE FIRST RUN!
RAAA
THEN...
IT'LL BE KITAMURA FOR THE SEISHU LINEUP!
RAAAH

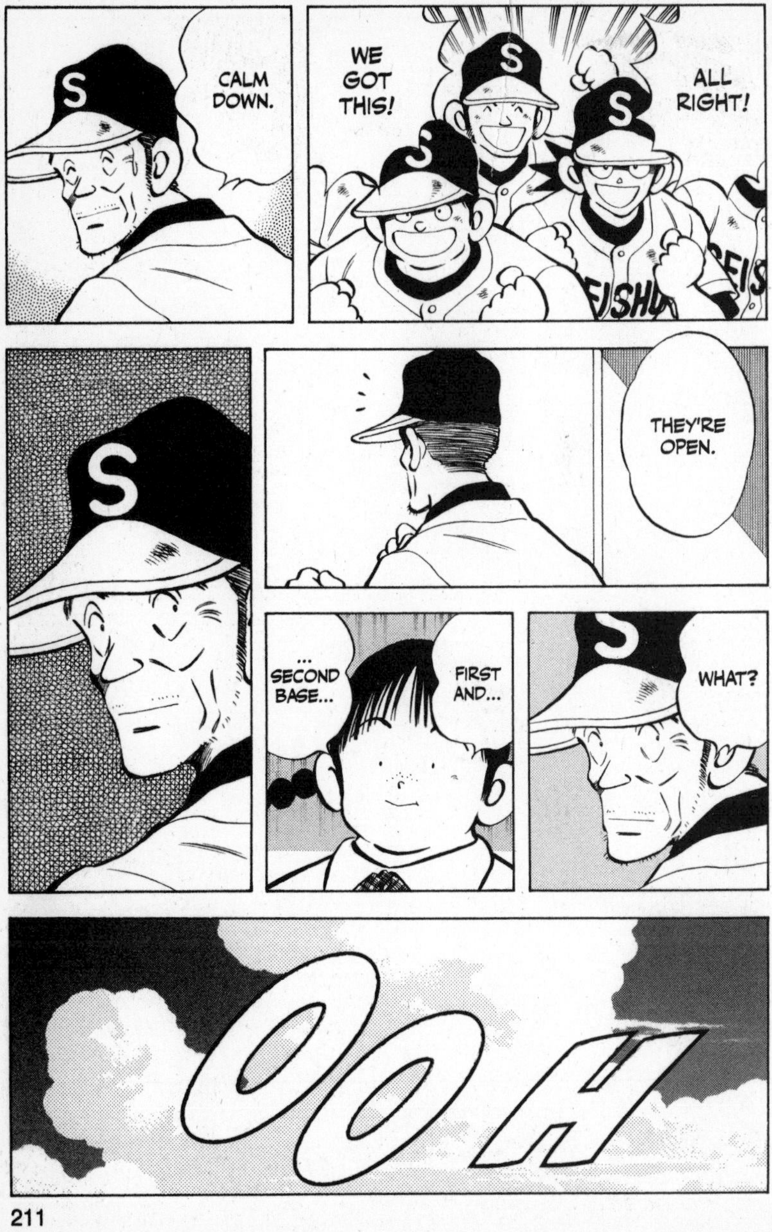
ALL RIGHT!
WE GOT THIS!
CALM DOWN.
THEY'RE OPEN.
WHAT?
FIRST AND...
... SECOND BASE...
OOH

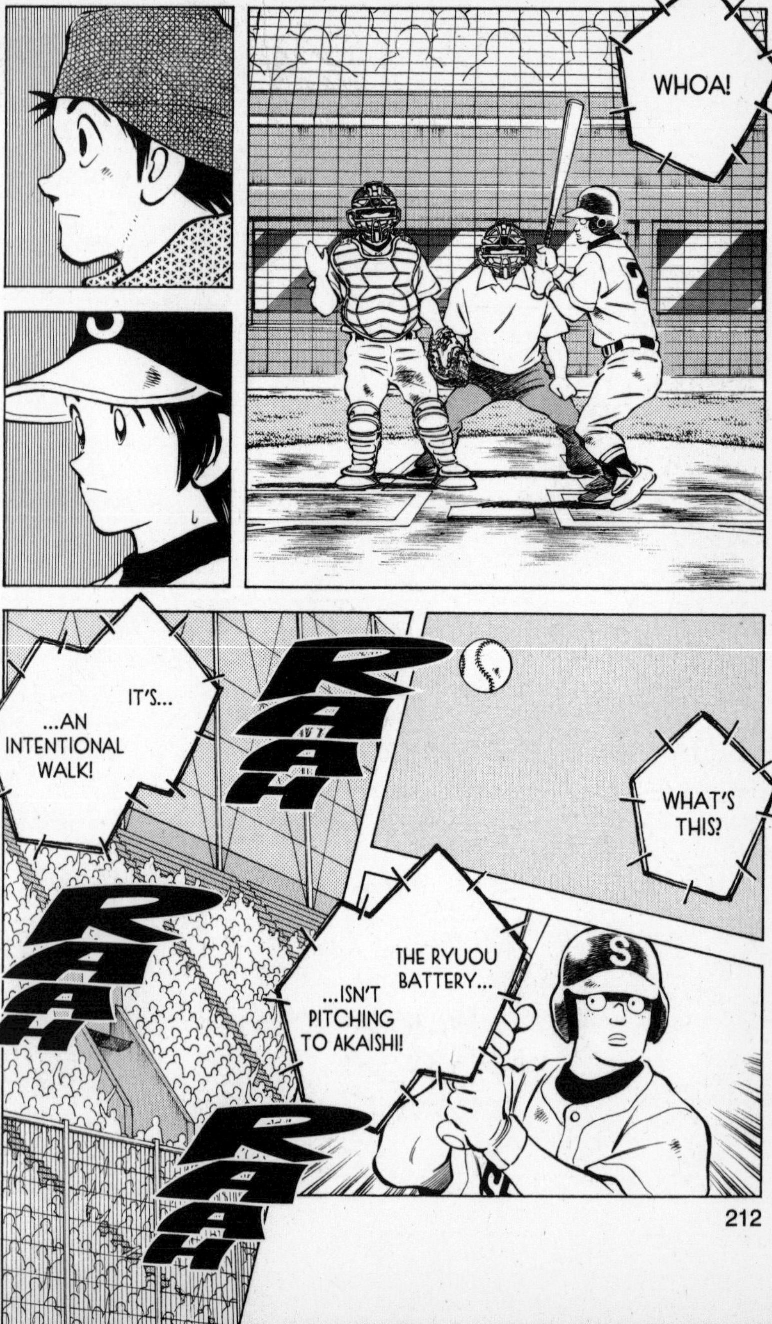
WHOA!
WHAT'S THIS?
THE RYUOU BATTERY...
...ISN'T PITCHING TO AKAISHI!
IT'S...
...AN INTENTIONAL WALK!
RAAAH
RAAAH
RAAAH

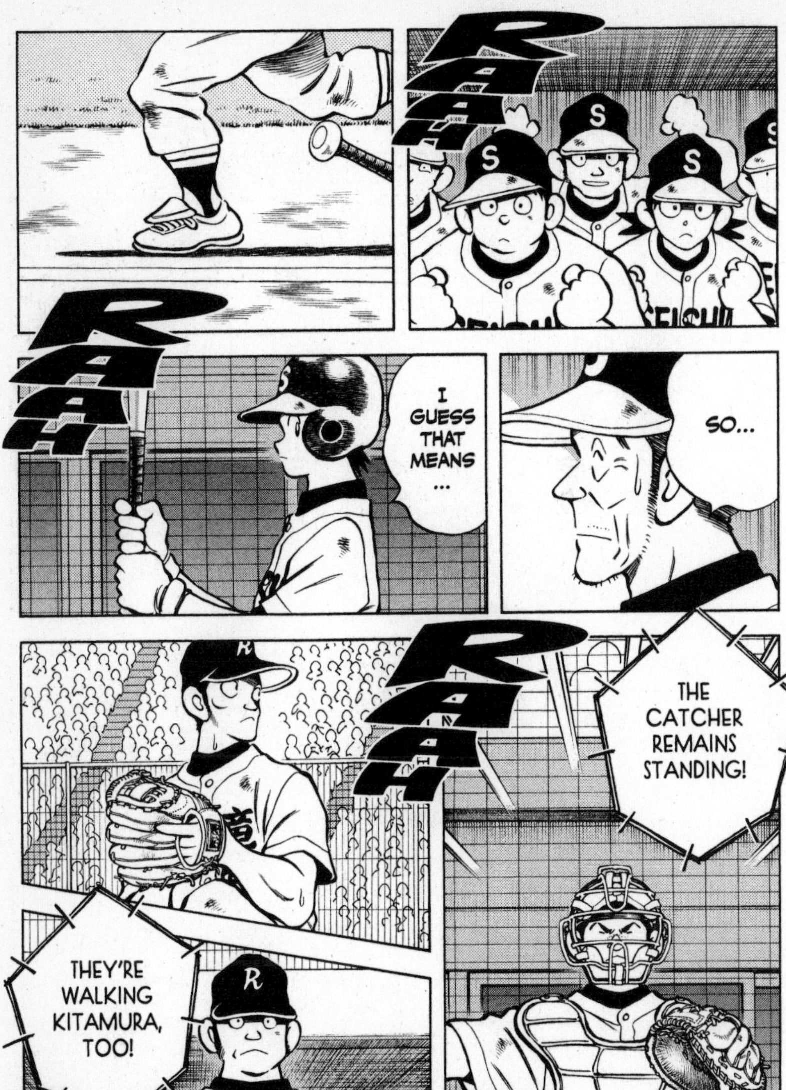
RAAAH
SO...
I GUESS THAT MEANS ...
RAAAH
RAAAH
THE CATCHER REMAINS STANDING!
THEY'RE WALKING KITAMURA, TOO!

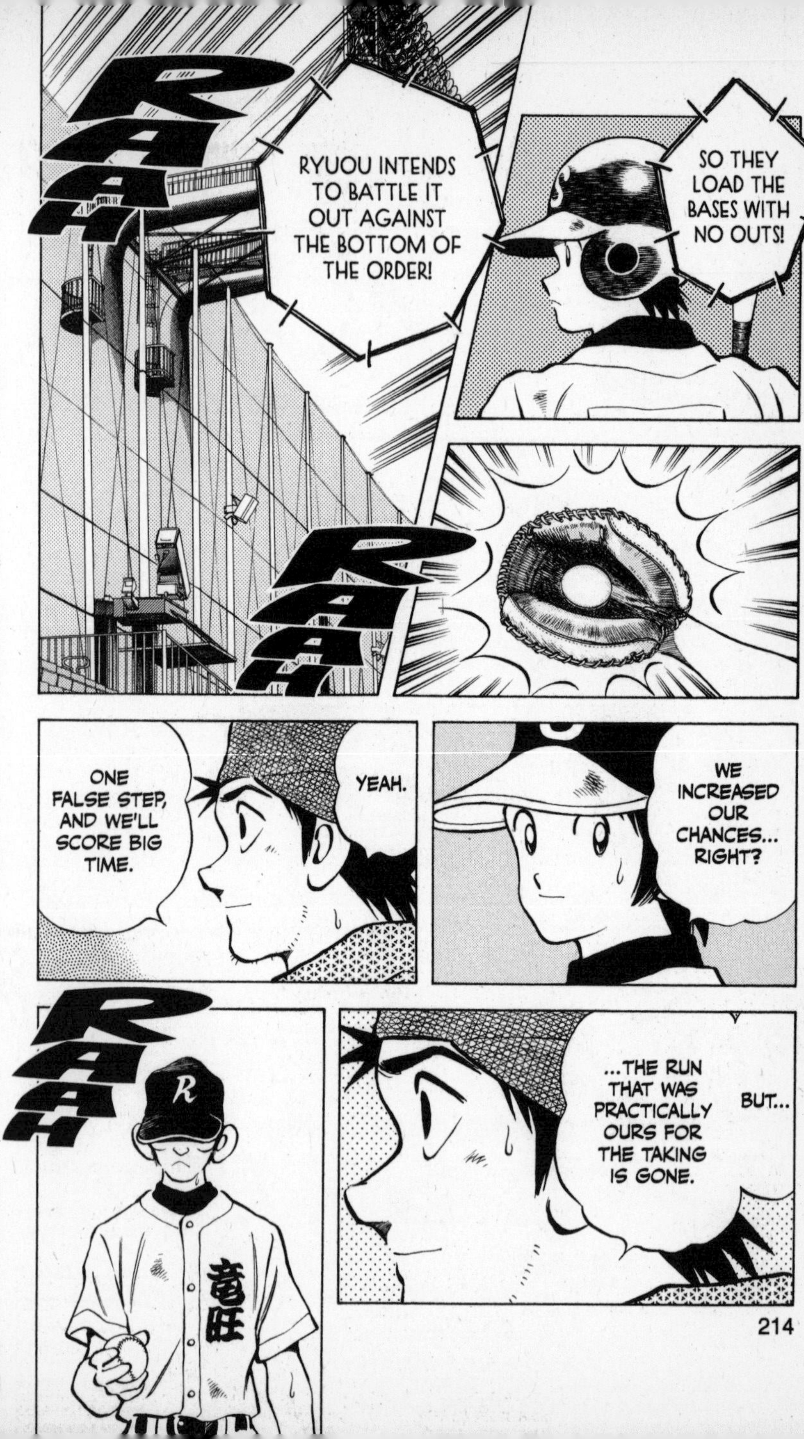
SO THEY LOAD THE BASES WITH NO OUTS!
RAAH
RYUOU INTENDS TO BATTLE IT OUT AGAINST THE BOTTOM OF THE ORDER!
RAAH
WE INCREASED OUR CHANCES... RIGHT?
YEAH.
ONE FALSE STEP, AND WE'LL SCORE BIG TIME.
BUT...
...THE RUN THAT WAS PRACTICALLY OURS FOR THE TAKING IS GONE.
RAAH

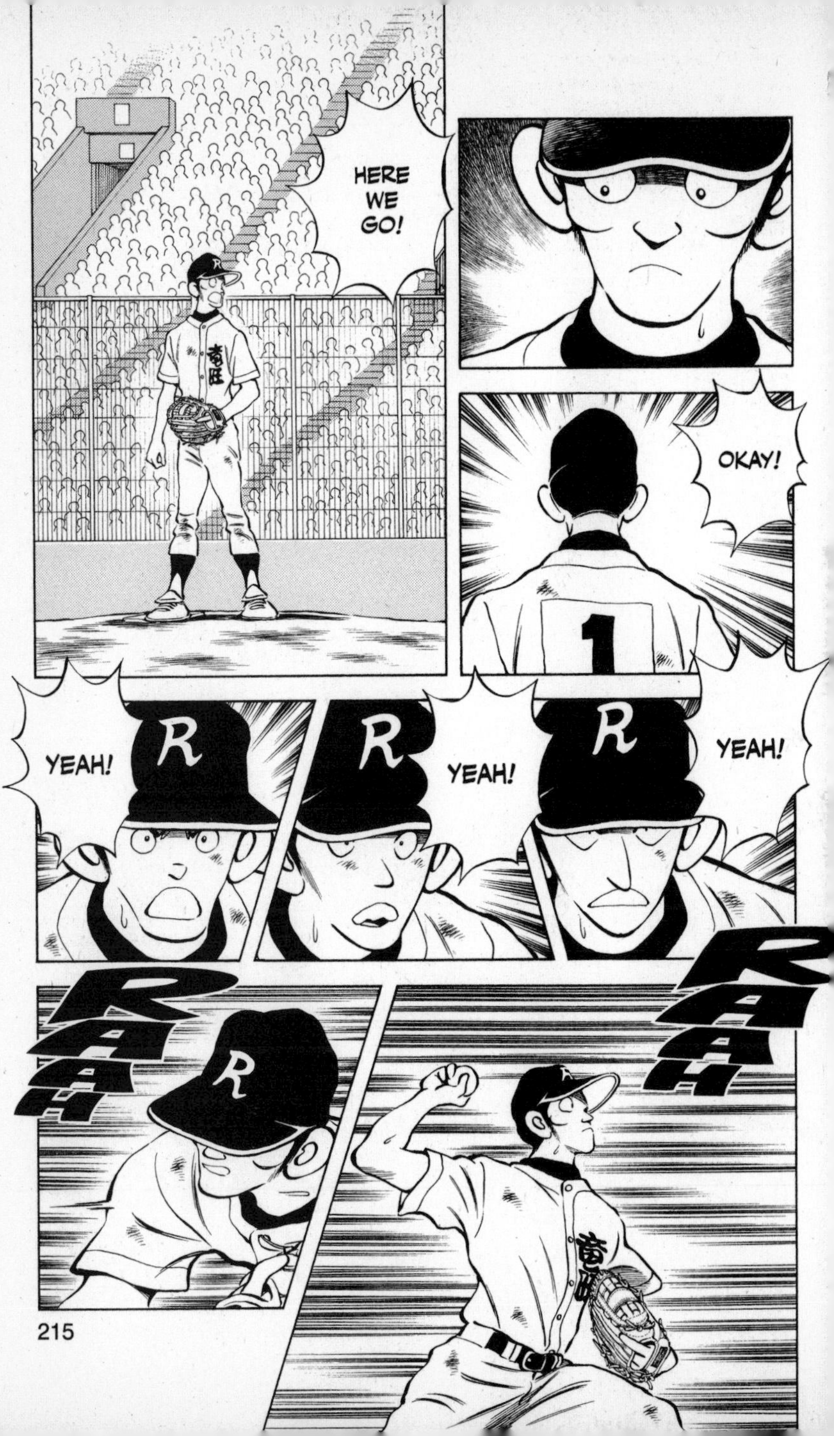
OKAY!
HERE WE GO!
YEAH!
YEAH!
YEAH!
RAAAH
RAAAH

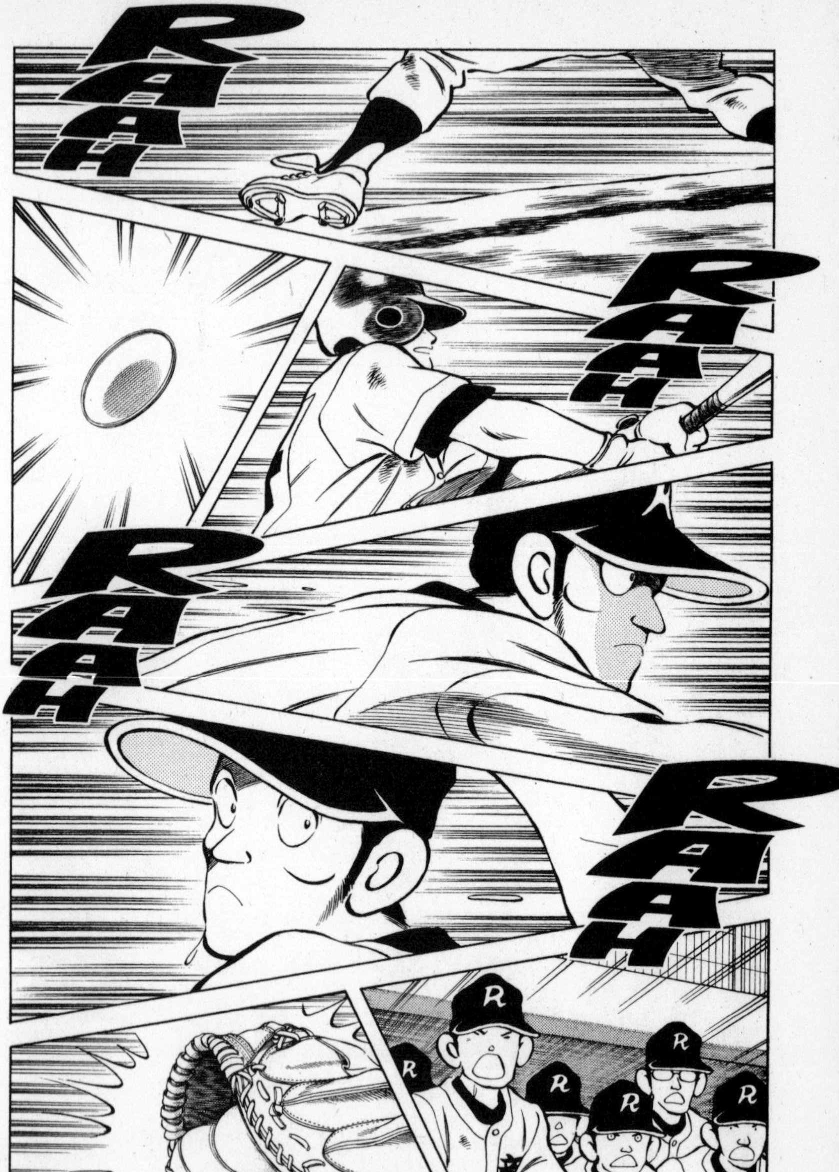
RAAH
RAAH
RAAH
RAAH

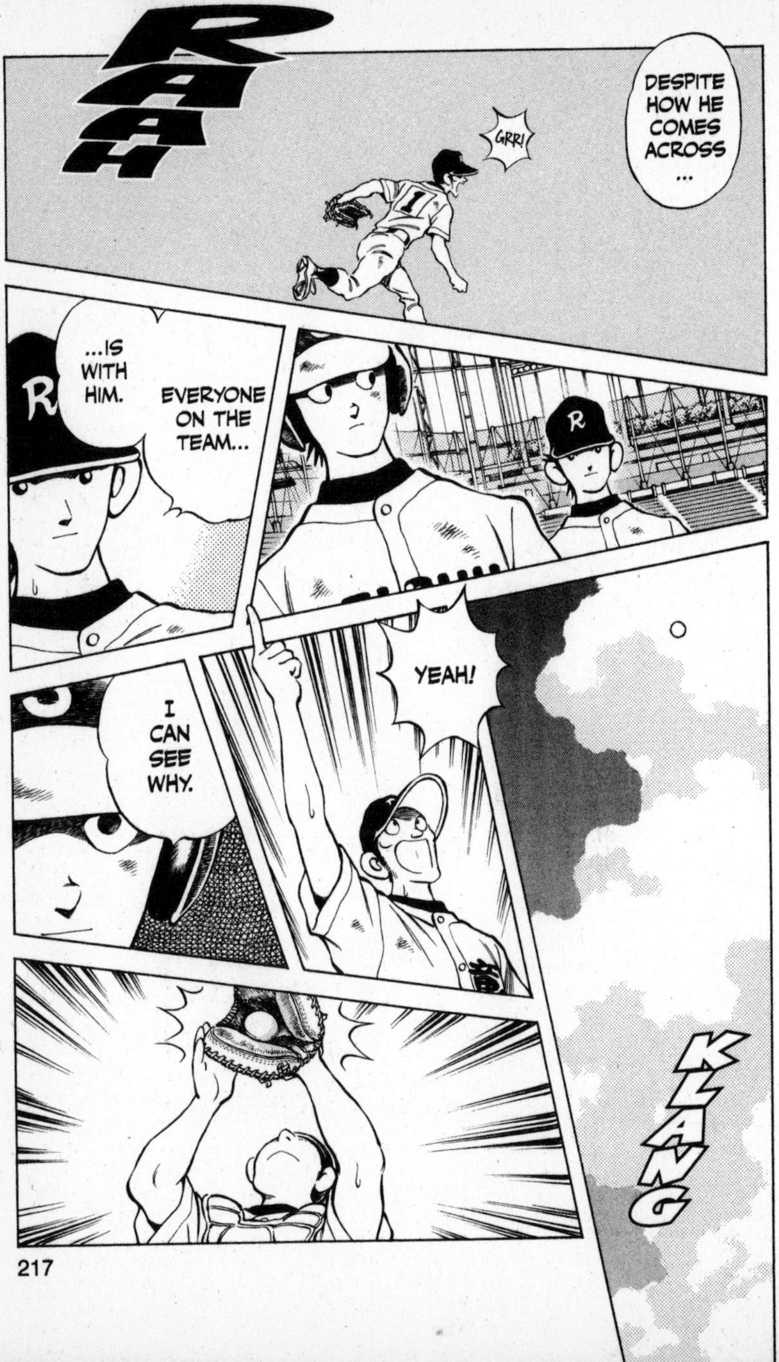
RAAH
DESPITE HOW HE COMES ACROSS...
GRR!
EVERYONE ON THE TEAM...
...IS WITH HIM.
KLANG
YEAH!
I CAN SEE WHY.

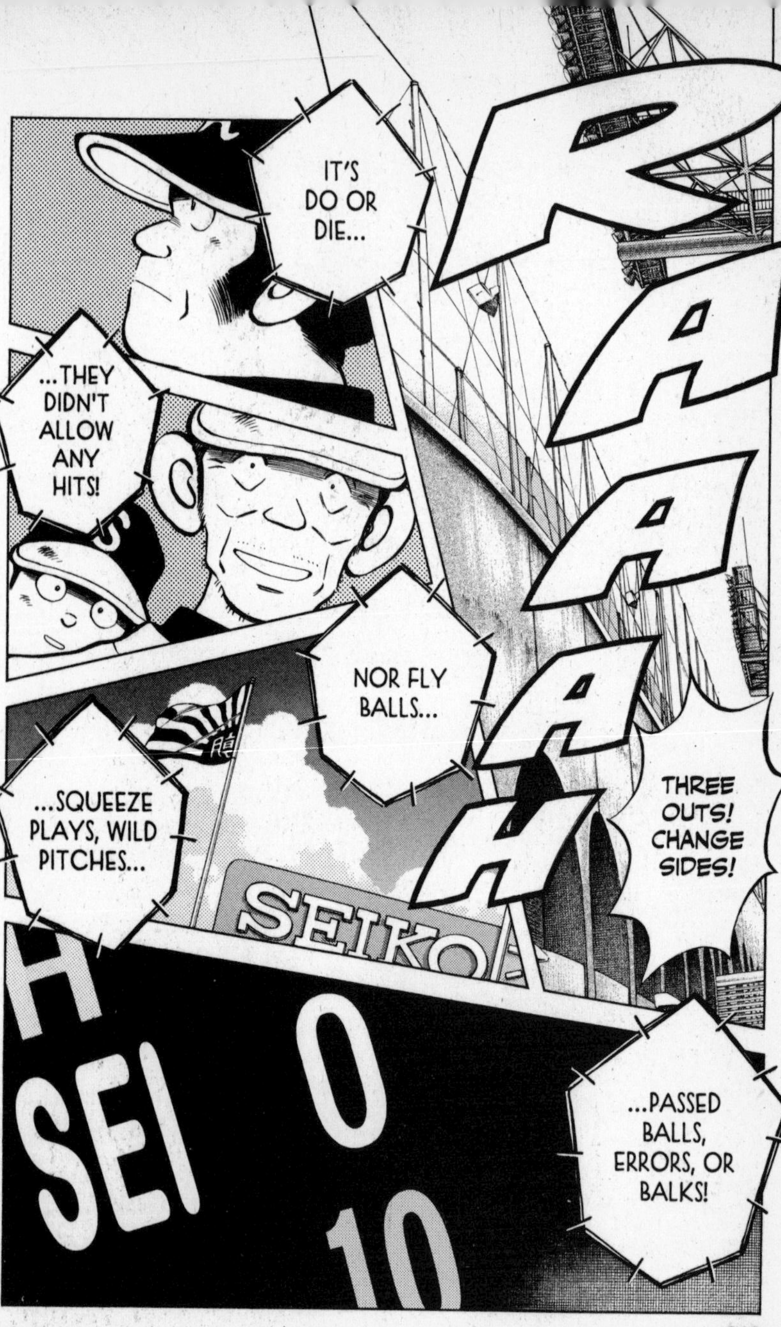
RAAAH
THREE OUTS! CHANGE SIDES!
IT'S DO OR DIE...
...THEY DIDN'T ALLOW ANY HITS!
NOR FLY BALLS...
...SQUEEZE PLAYS, WILD PITCHES...
SEIKO
H
SEI 0
10
...PASSED BALLS, ERRORS, OR BALKS!

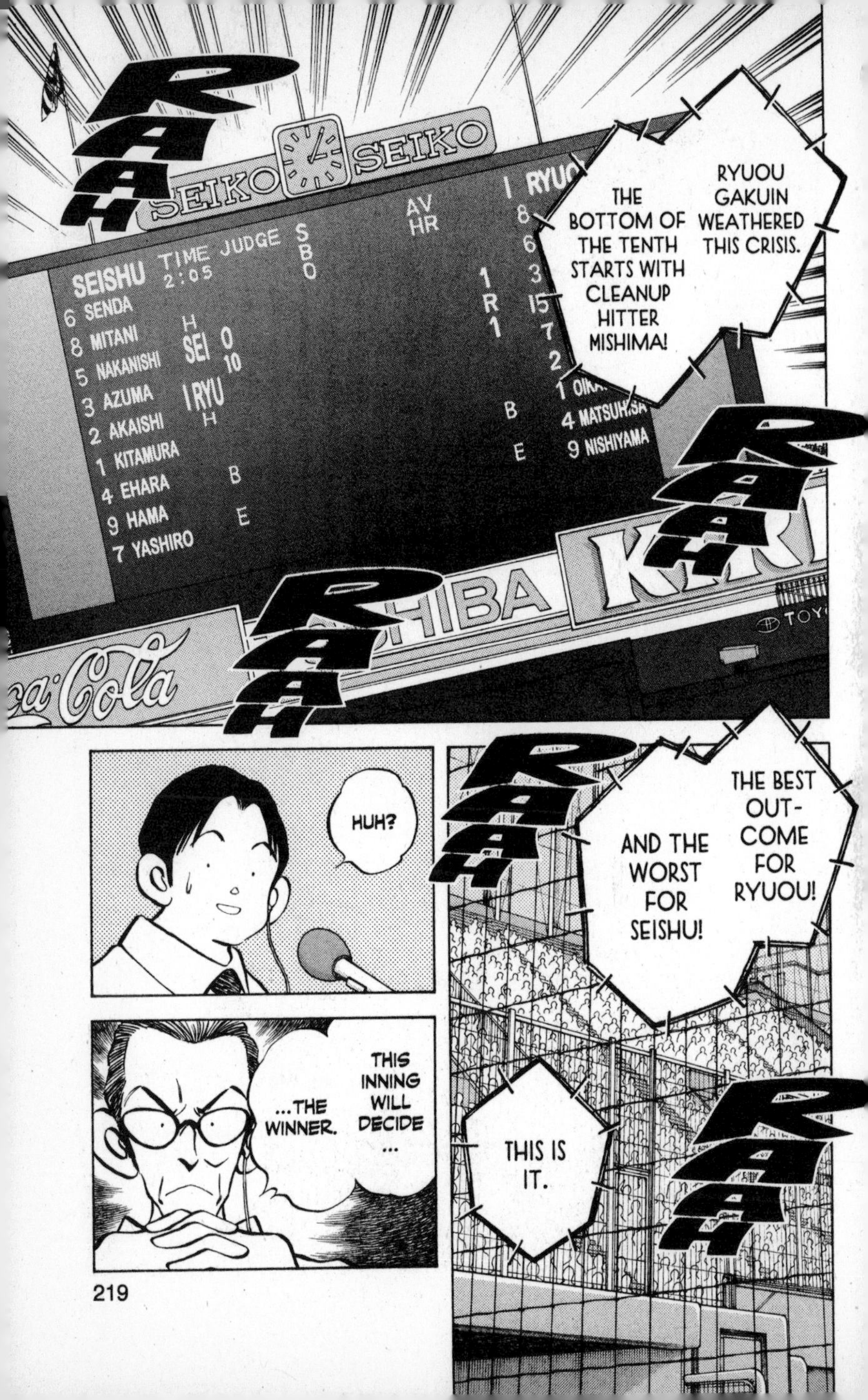
RAAH
SEIKO SEIKO
SEISHU TIME 2:05 JUDGE
6 SENDA
8 MITANI
5 NAKANISHI
3 AZUMA
2 AKAISHI
1 KITAMURA
4 EHARA
9 HAMA
7 YASHIRO
SEI 0
RYU 10
4 MATSUHISA
9 NISHIYAMA
RYUOU GAKUIN WEATHERED THIS CRISIS.
THE BOTTOM OF THE TENTH STARTS WITH CLEANUP HITTER MISHIMA!
RAAH
RAAH
HIBA
Coca-Cola
RAAH
THE BEST OUT-COME FOR RYUOU!
AND THE WORST FOR SEISHU!
RAAH
THIS IS IT.
HUH?
THIS INNING WILL DECIDE ...
...THE WINNER.

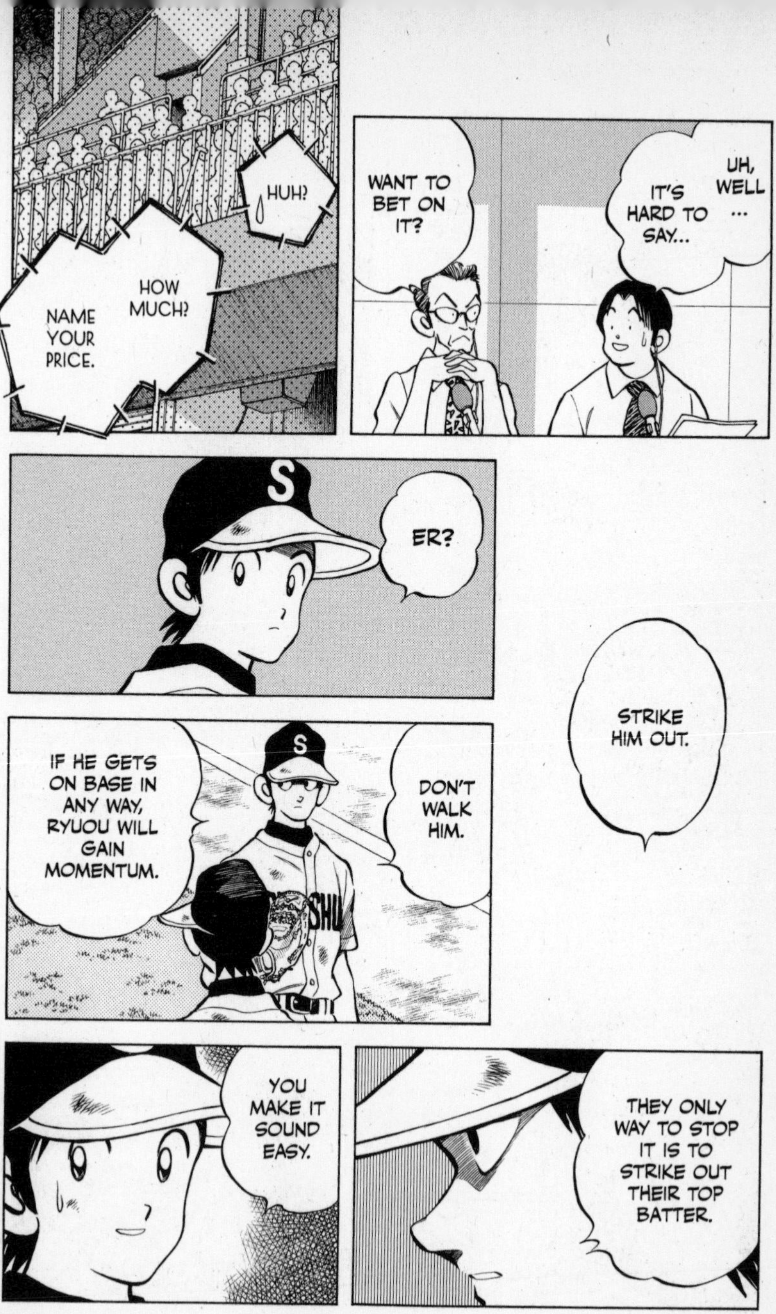
UH, WELL ...
IT'S HARD TO SAY...
WANT TO BET ON IT?
HUH?
HOW MUCH?
NAME YOUR PRICE.
ER?
STRIKE HIM OUT.
DON'T WALK HIM.
IF HE GETS ON BASE IN ANY WAY, RYUOU WILL GAIN MOMENTUM.
THEY ONLY WAY TO STOP IT IS TO STRIKE OUT THEIR TOP BATTER.
YOU MAKE IT SOUND EASY.

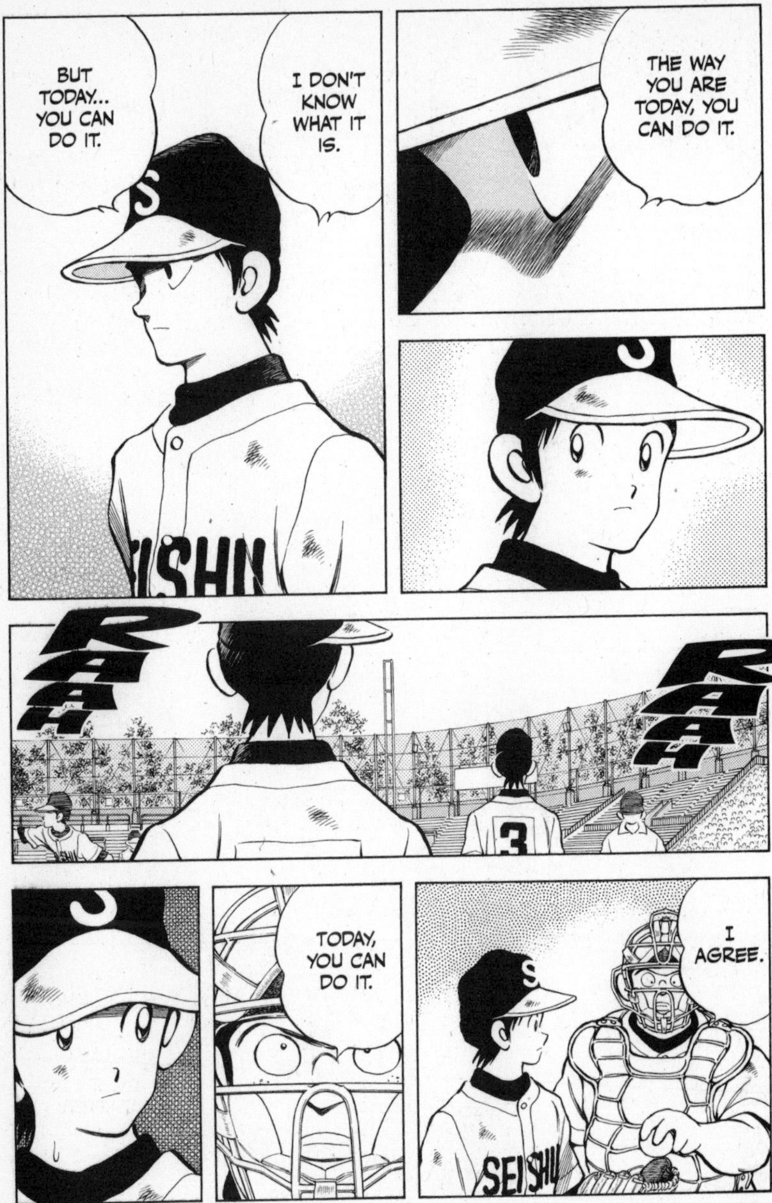
THE WAY YOU ARE TODAY, YOU CAN DO IT.
I DON'T KNOW WHAT IT IS.
BUT TODAY... YOU CAN DO IT.
RAAH
RAAH
I AGREE.
TODAY, YOU CAN DO IT.

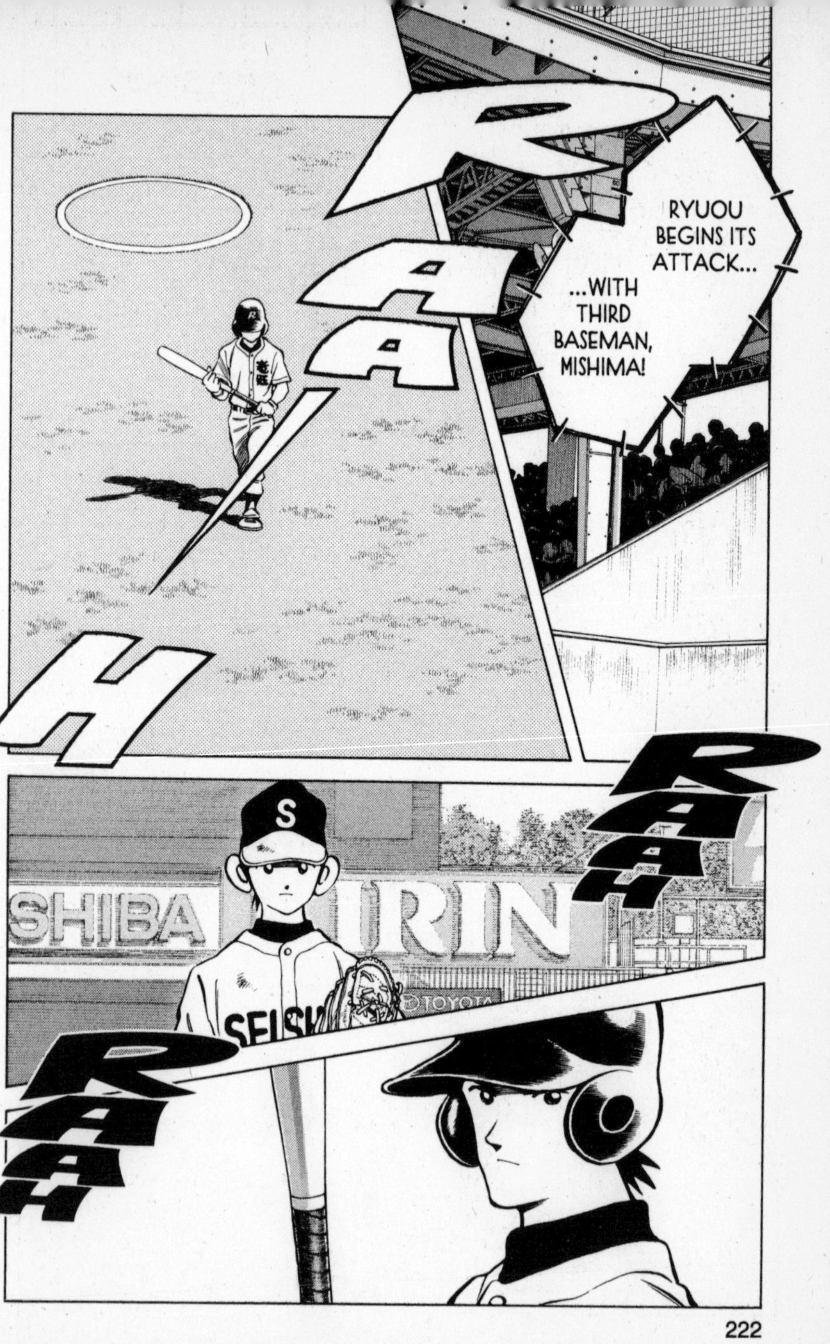
RAAH
RYUOU BEGINS ITS ATTACK...
...WITH THIRD BASEMAN, MISHIMA!
RAAH
SHIBA
TOYOTA
RAAH

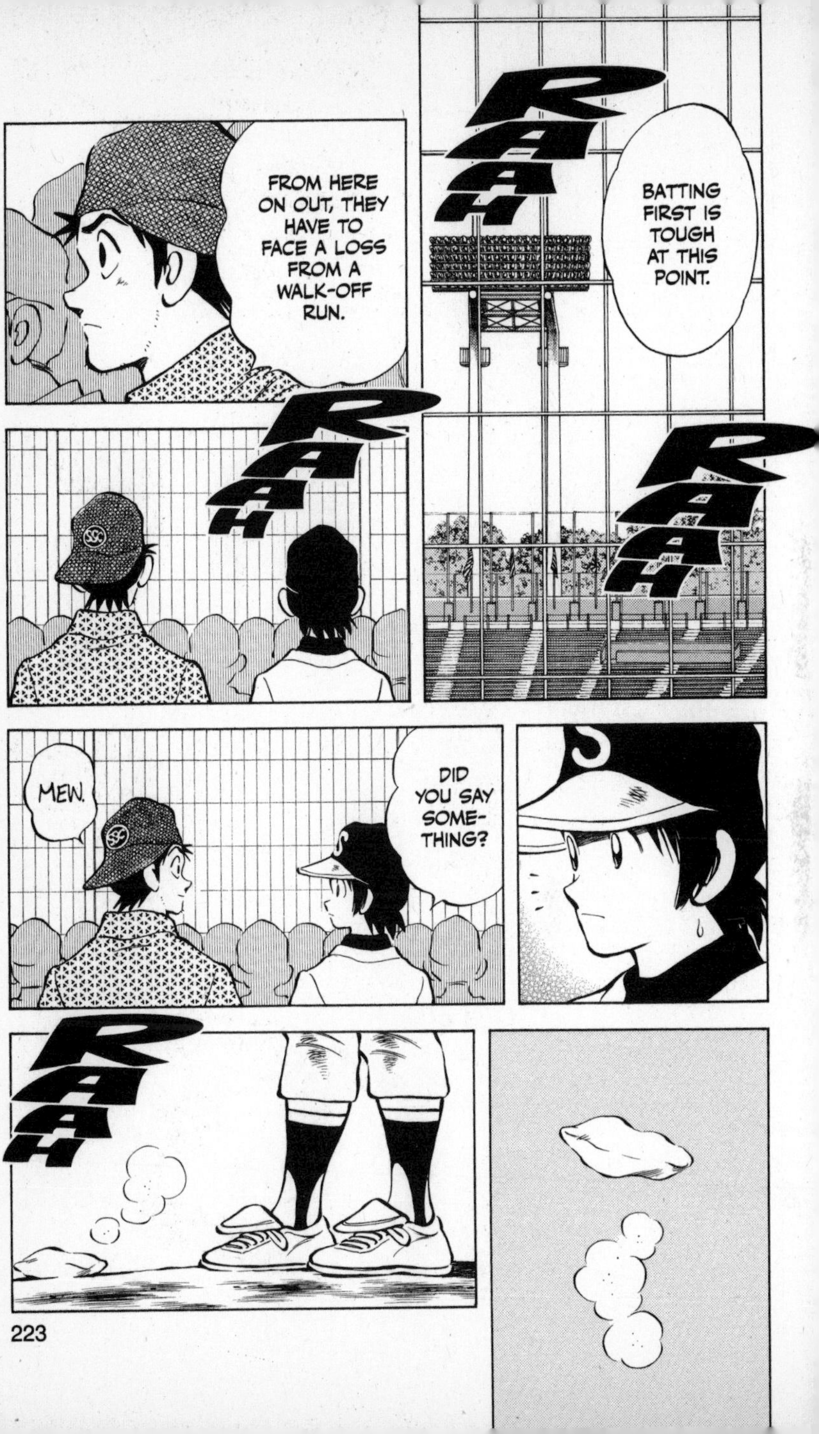
RAAH
BATTING FIRST IS TOUGH AT THIS POINT.
FROM HERE ON OUT, THEY HAVE TO FACE A LOSS FROM A WALK-OFF RUN.
RAAH
RAAH
DID YOU SAY SOME-THING?
MEW.
RAAH

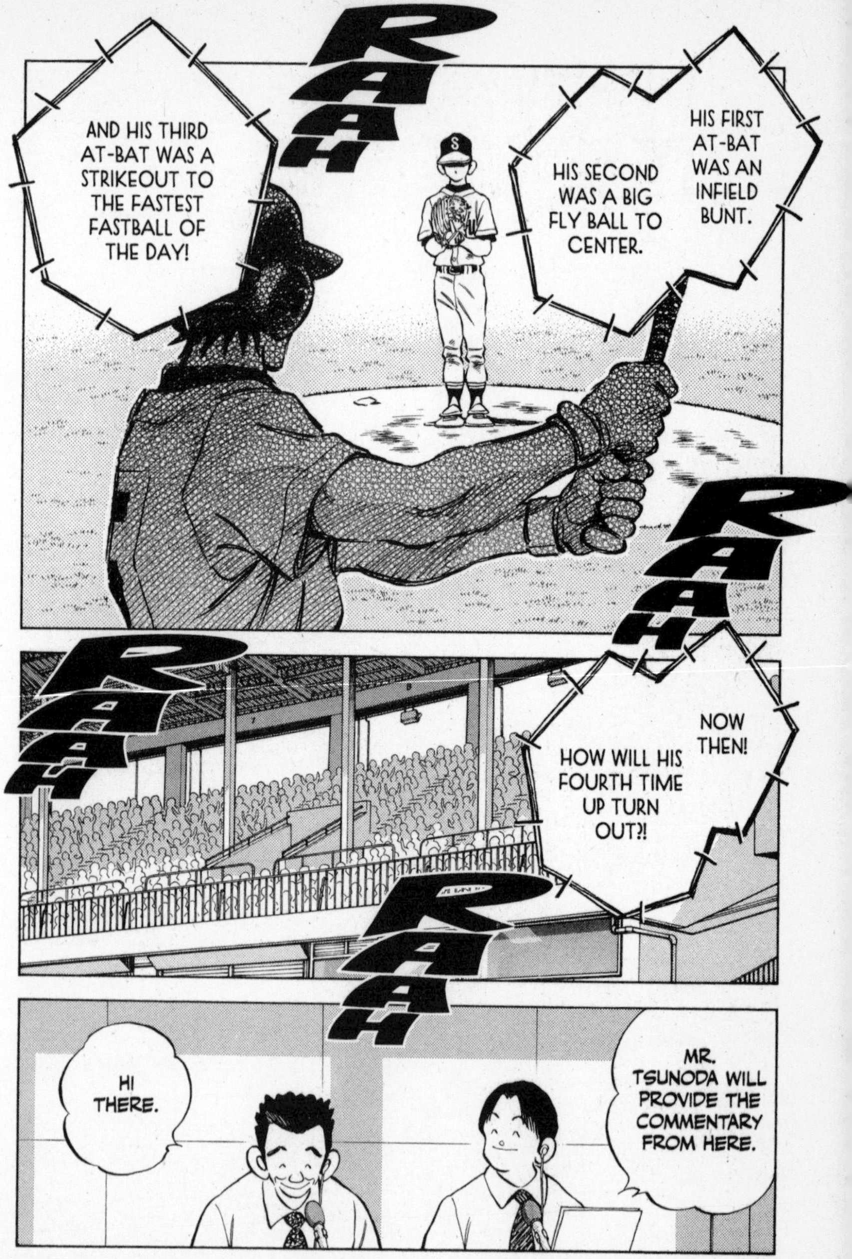
RAAH
HIS FIRST AT-BAT WAS AN INFIELD BUNT.
HIS SECOND WAS A BIG FLY BALL TO CENTER.
AND HIS THIRD AT-BAT WAS A STRIKEOUT TO THE FASTEST FASTBALL OF THE DAY!
RAAH
NOW THEN!
HOW WILL HIS FOURTH TIME UP TURN OUT?!
RAAH
RAAH
MR. TSUNODA WILL PROVIDE THE COMMENTARY FROM HERE.
HI THERE.

CHAPTER 153
IT'S NOT FAIR

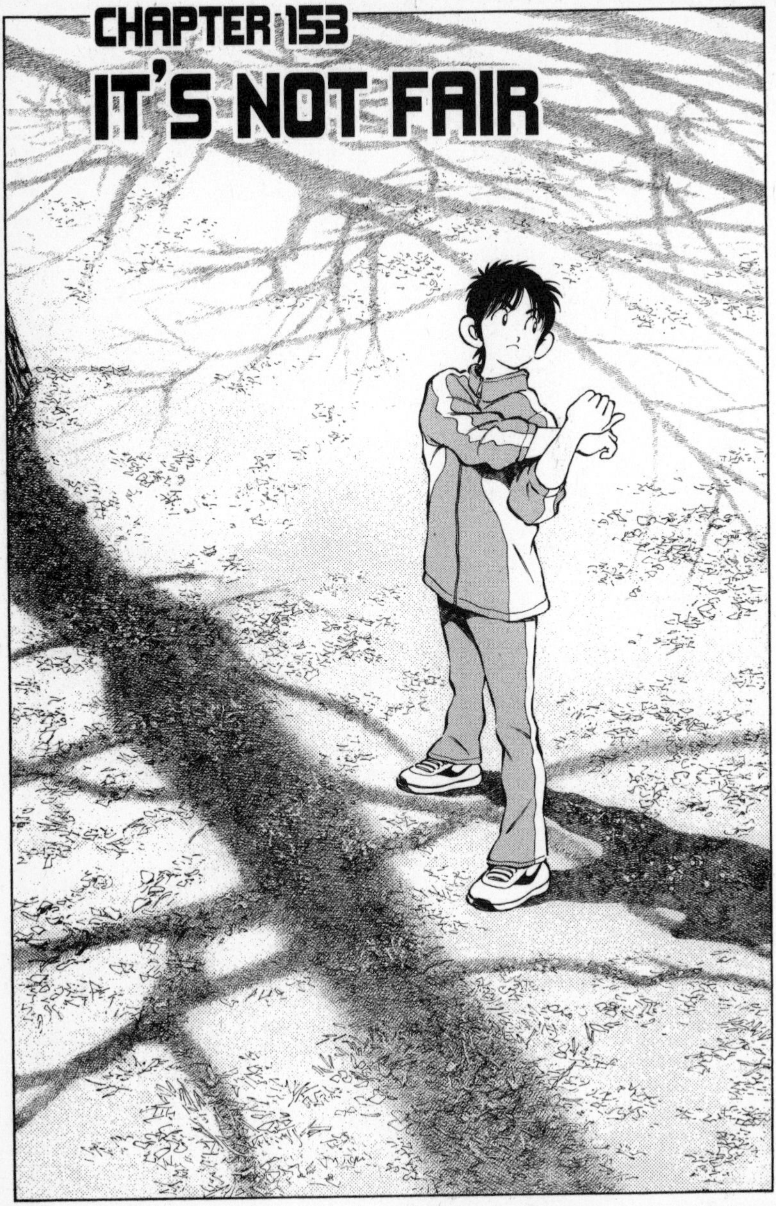

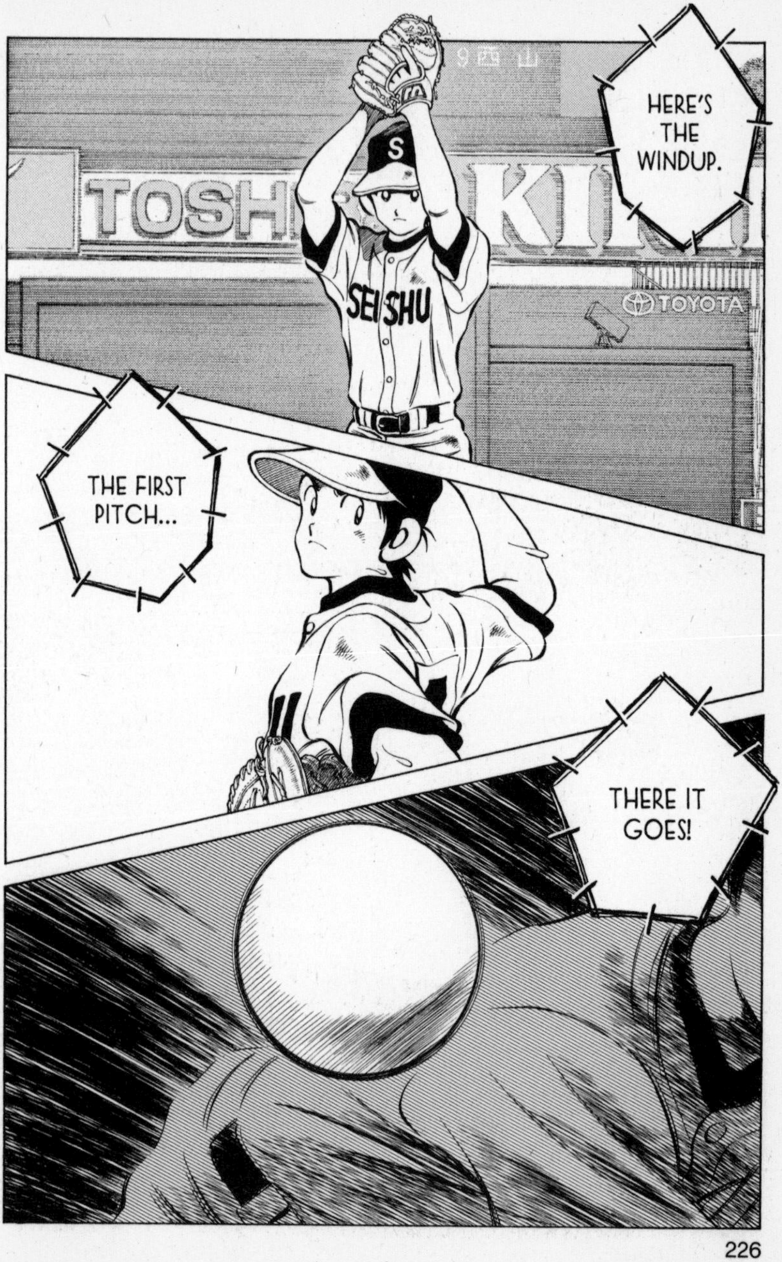
HERE'S THE WINDUP.
SEISHU
TOYOTA
THE FIRST PITCH...
THERE IT GOES!

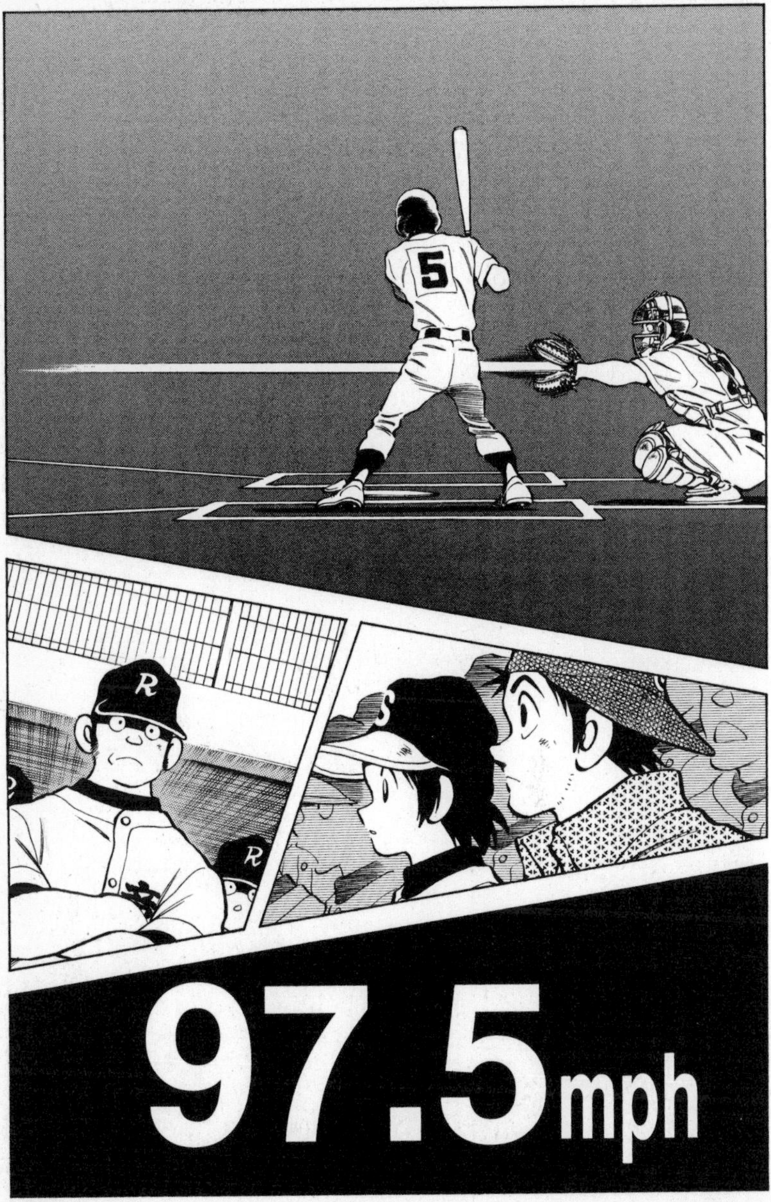
97.5mph

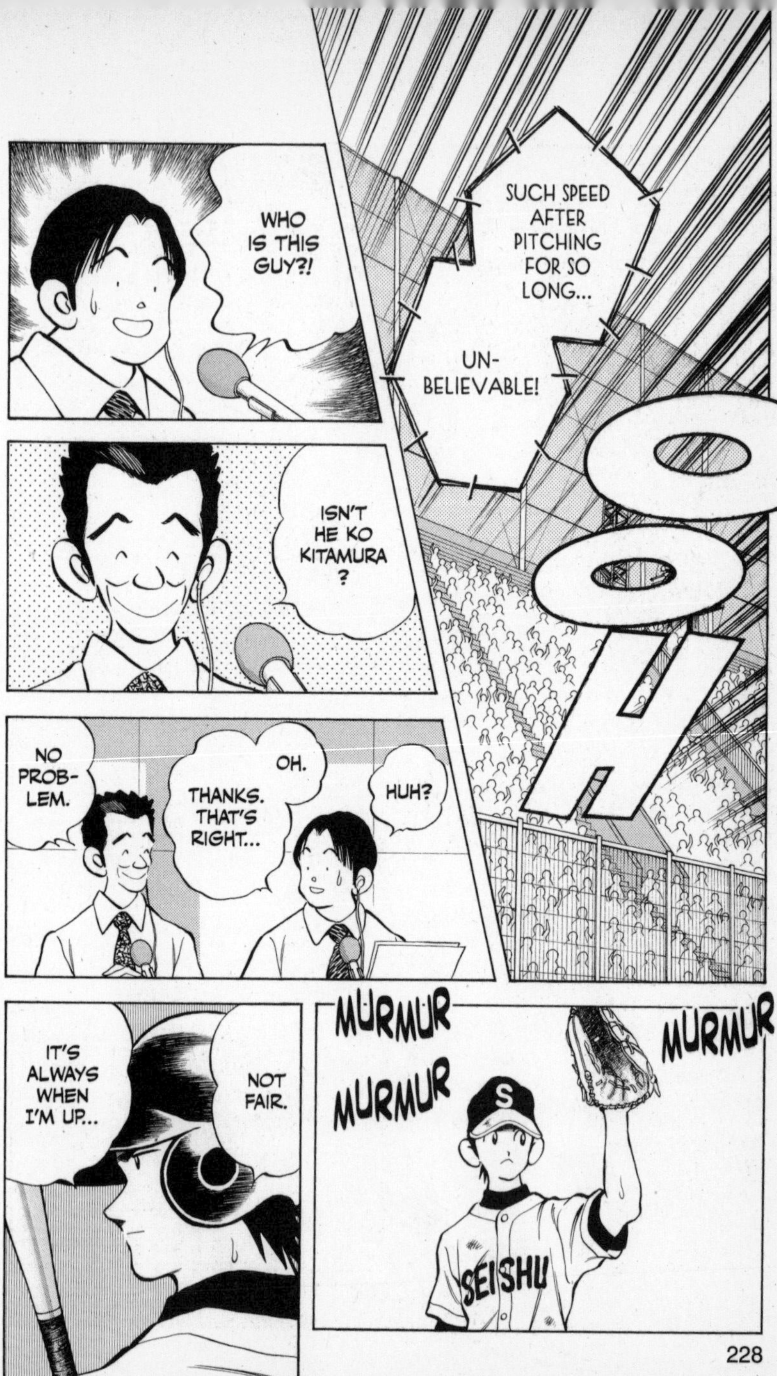
SUCH SPEED AFTER PITCHING FOR SO LONG...
UN-BELIEVABLE!
OOH
WHO IS THIS GUY?!
ISN'T HE KO KITAMURA?
HUH?
OH.
THANKS. THAT'S RIGHT...
NO PROB-LEM.
MURMUR
MURMUR
MURMUR
SEISHU
NOT FAIR.
IT'S ALWAYS WHEN I'M UP...

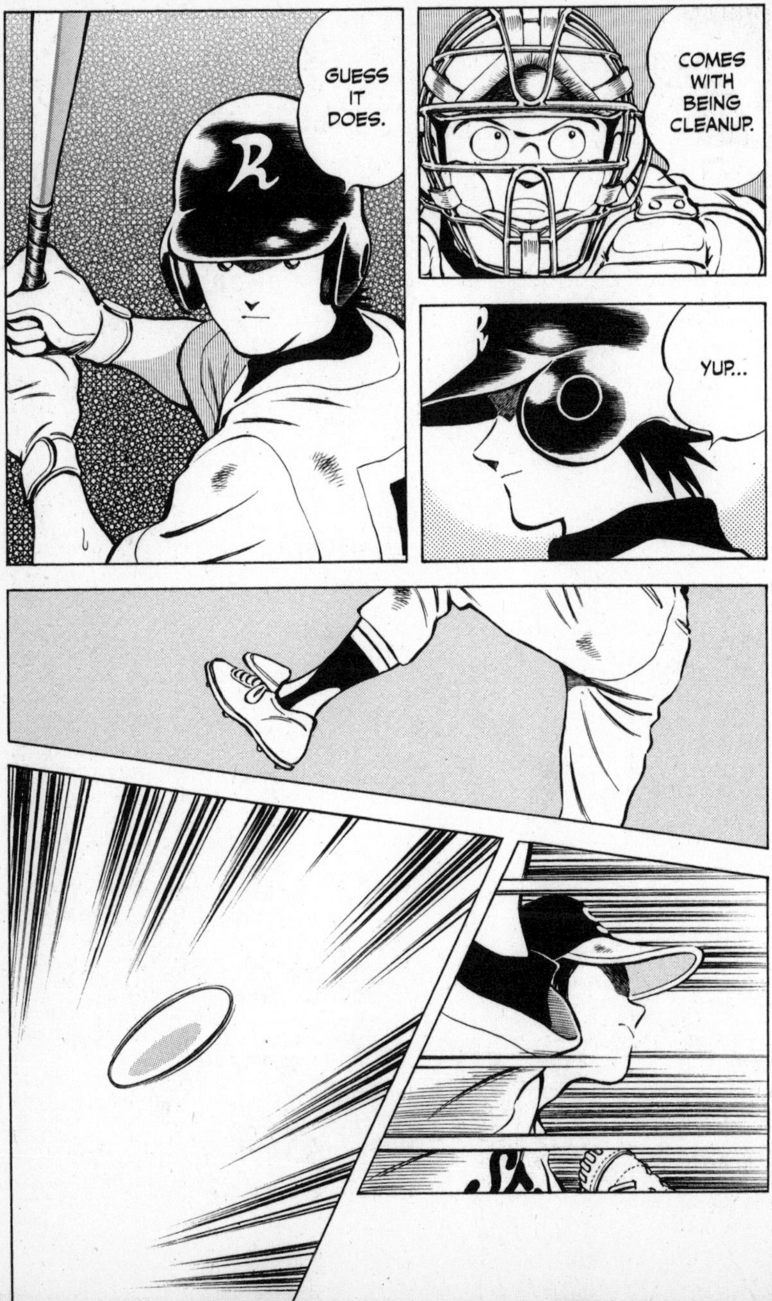
COMES WITH BEING CLEANUP.
YUP...
GUESS IT DOES.

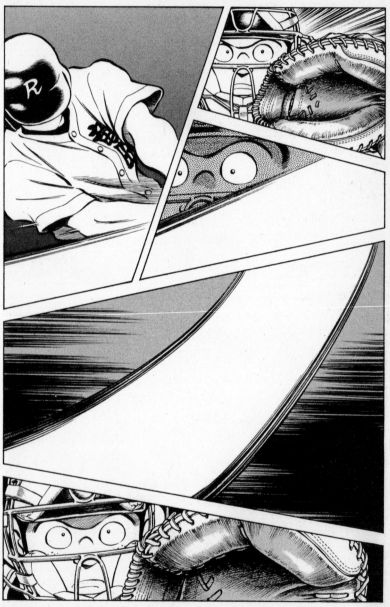

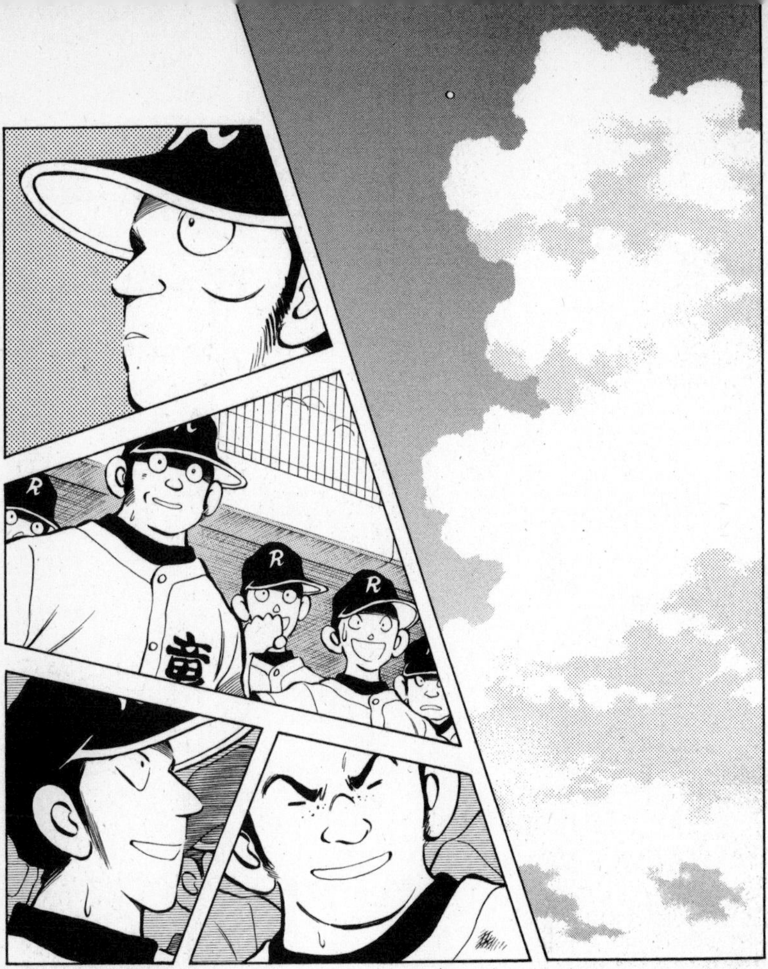
竜

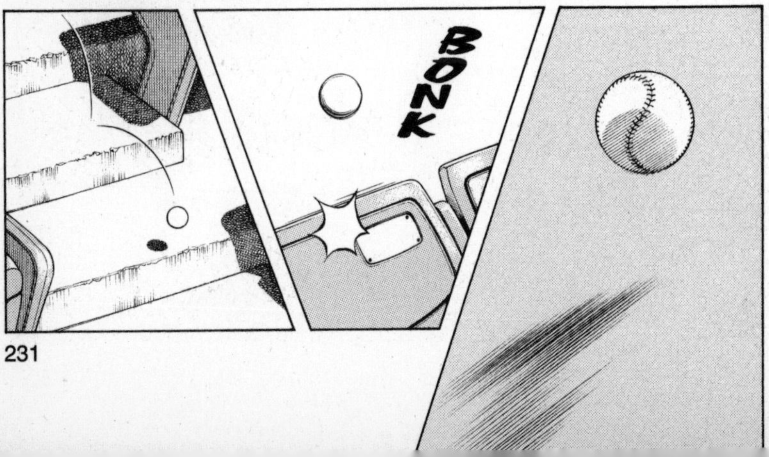
BONK

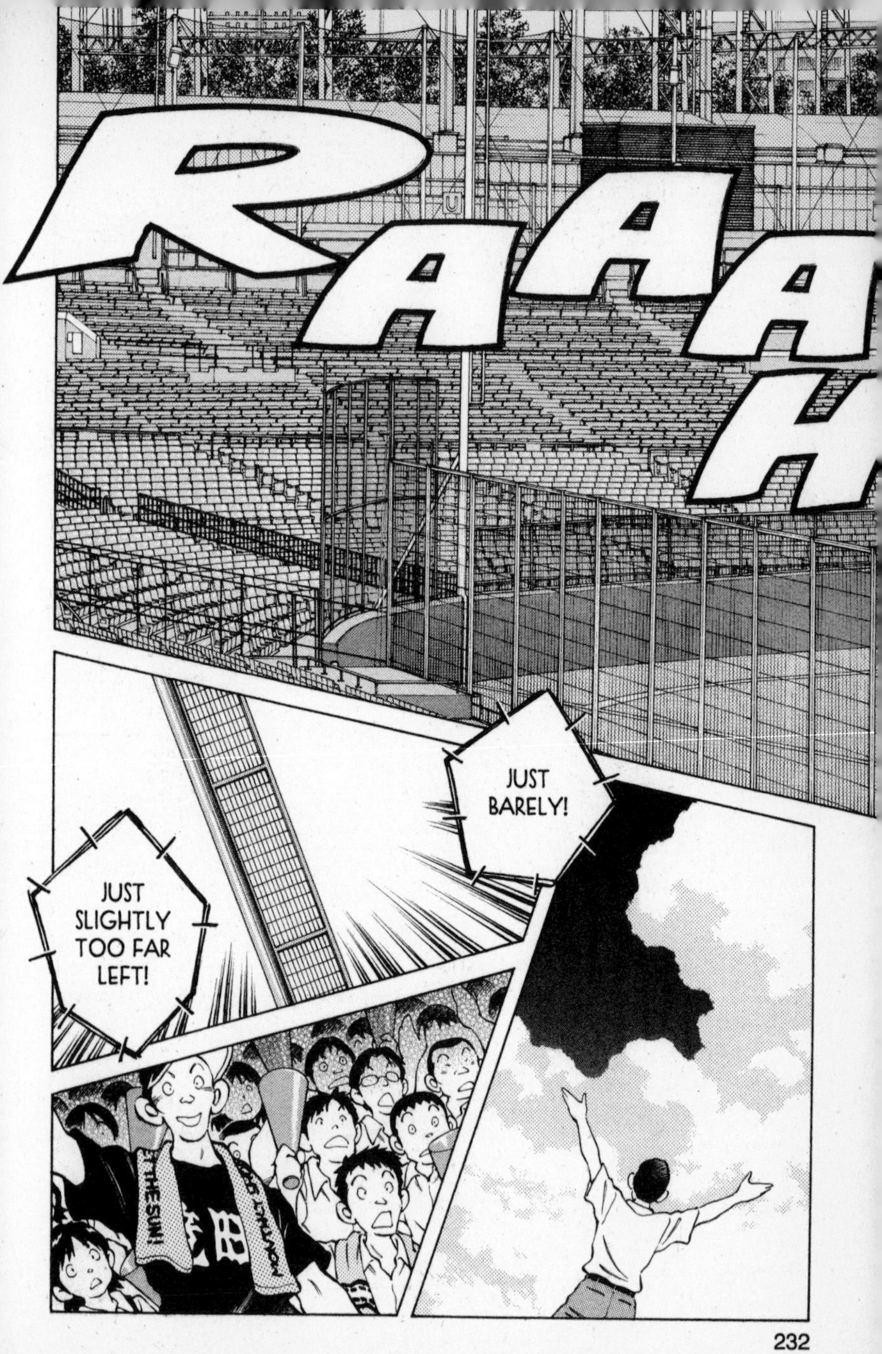
RAAAH
JUST BARELY!
JUST SLIGHTLY TOO FAR LEFT!

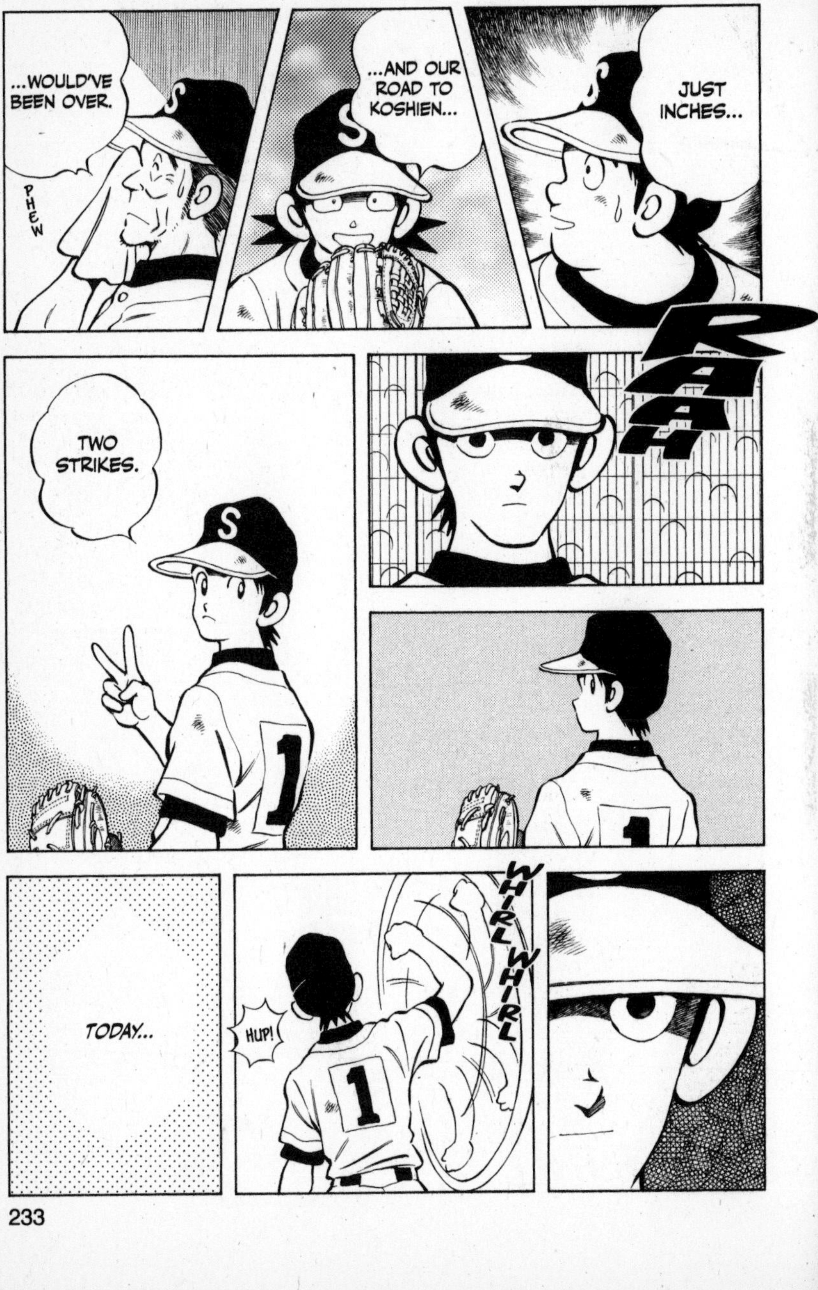
JUST INCHES...
...AND OUR ROAD TO KOSHIEN...
PHEW
...WOULD'VE BEEN OVER.
RAAAH
TWO STRIKES.
WHIRL WHIRL
HUP!
TODAY...

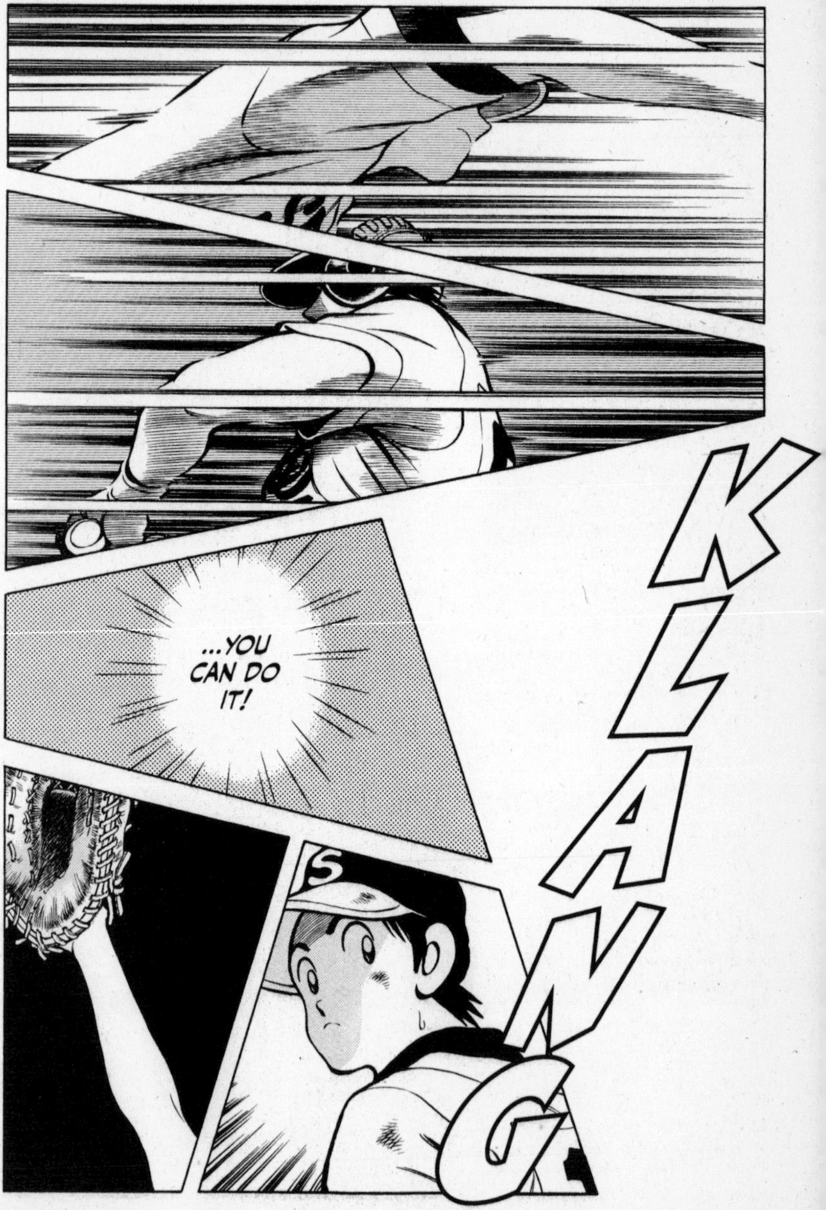
...YOU CAN DO IT!
KLANG

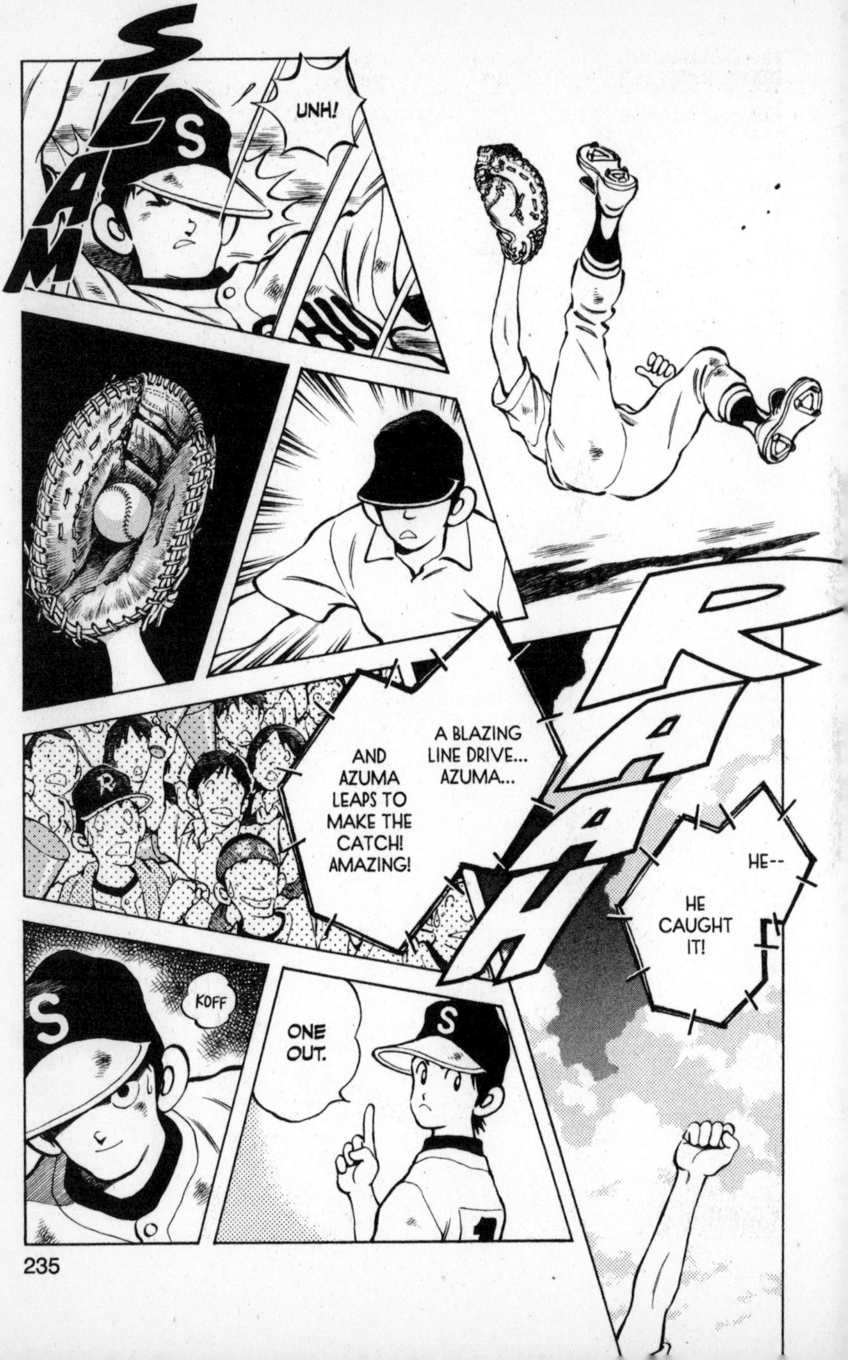
UNH!
SLAM
HE--
HE CAUGHT IT!
RAAH
A BLAZING LINE DRIVE... AZUMA...
AND AZUMA LEAPS TO MAKE THE CATCH! AMAZING!
ONE OUT.
KOFF

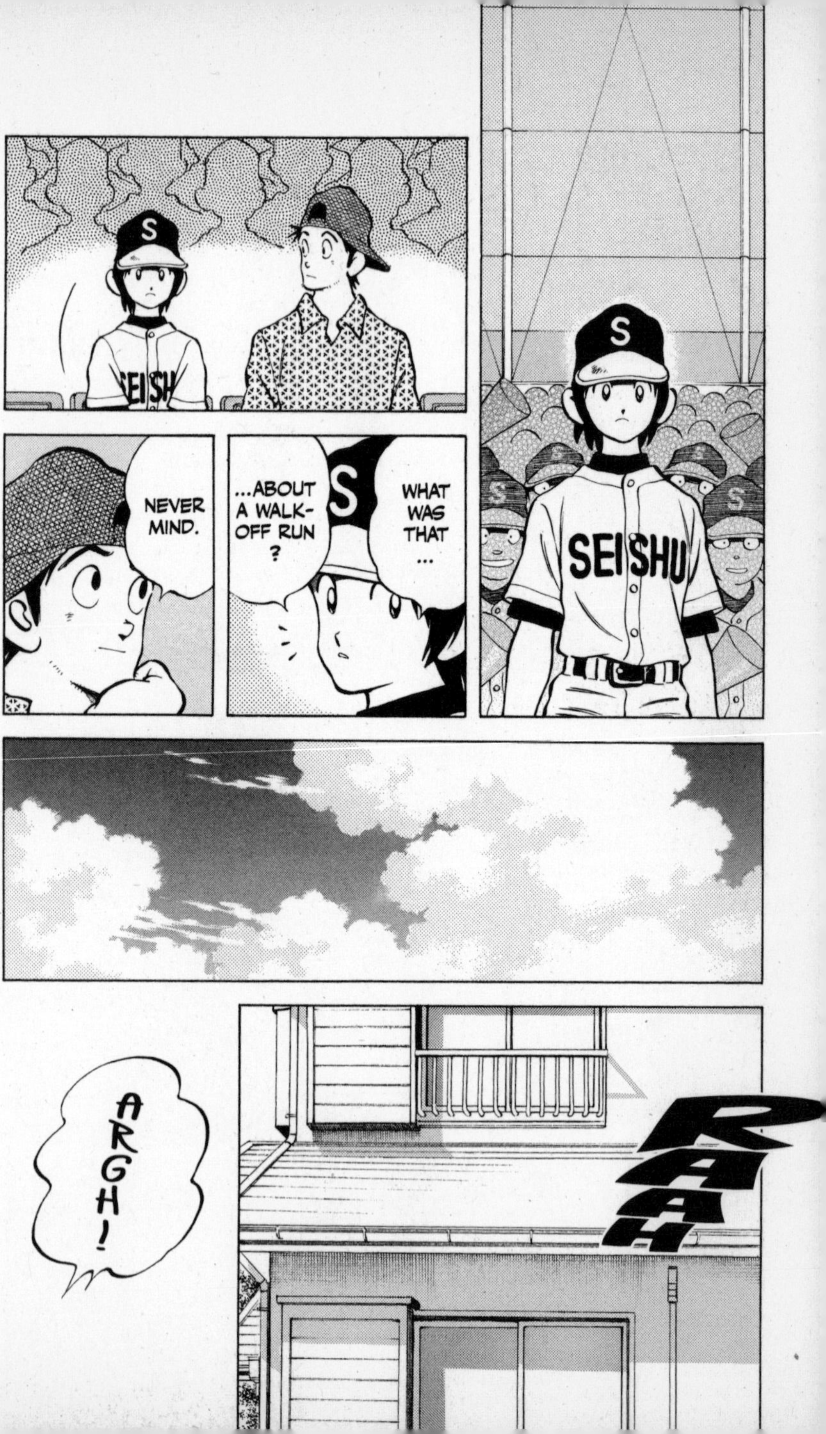
WHAT WAS THAT ...
...ABOUT A WALK-OFF RUN ?
NEVER MIND.
RAAH
ARGH!

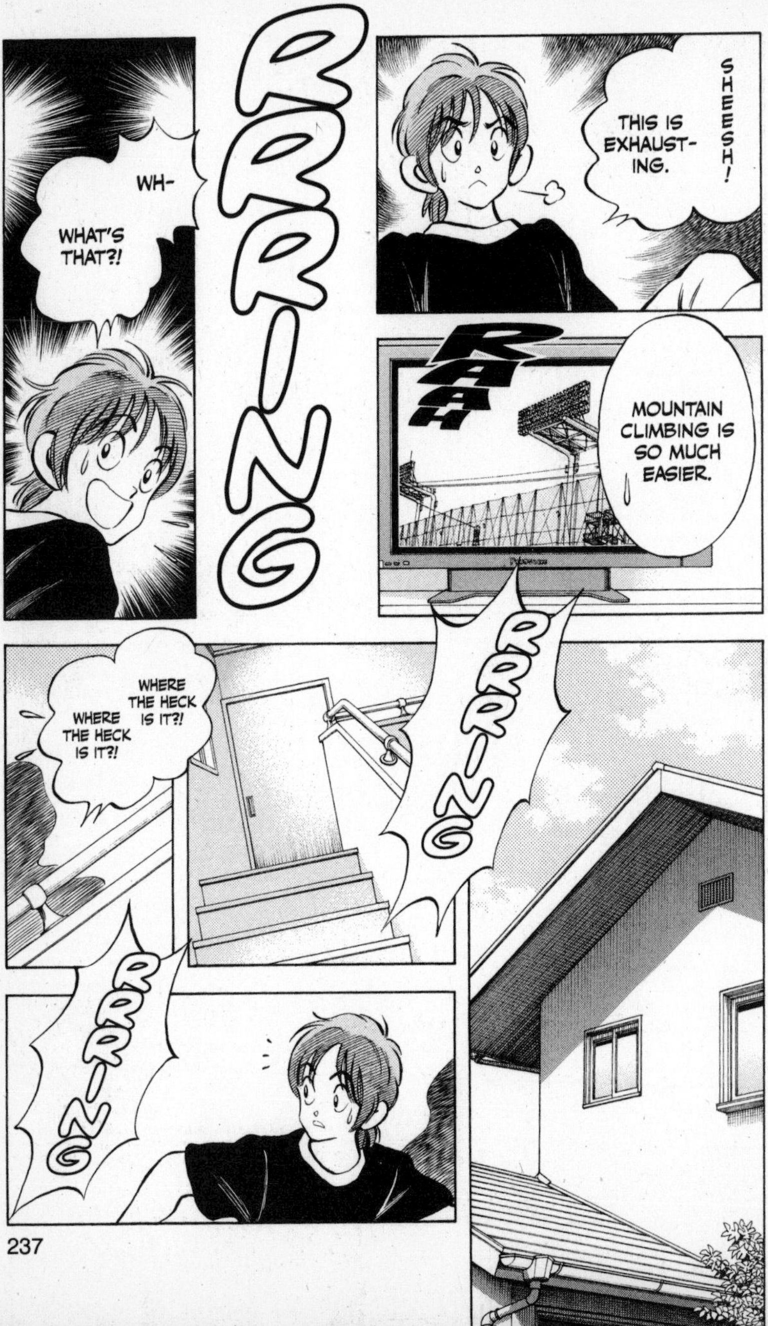
SHEESH!
THIS IS EXHAUST-ING.
RAAAH
MOUNTAIN CLIMBING IS SO MUCH EASIER.
RRRING
WH-
WHAT'S THAT?!
RRRING
WHERE THE HECK IS IT?!
WHERE THE HECK IS IT?!
RRRING

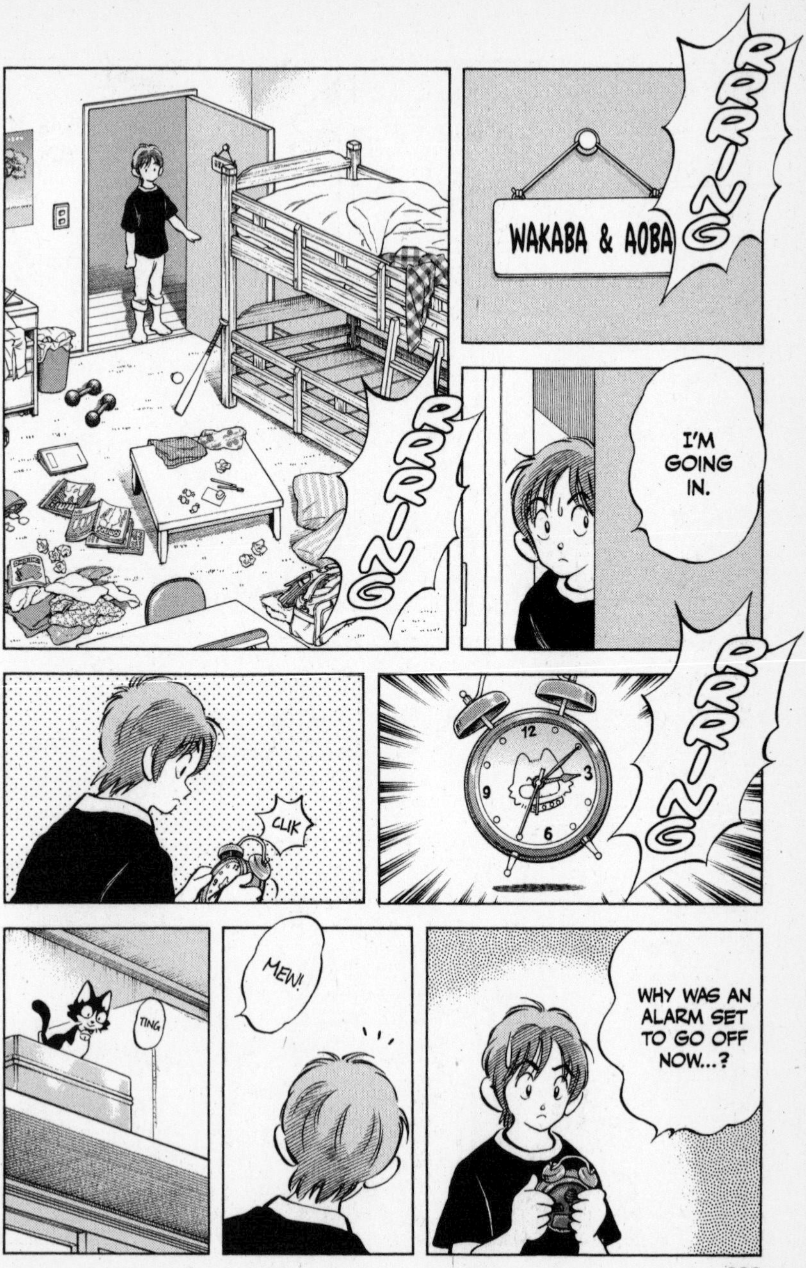
WAKABA & AOBA
RRRING
I'M GOING IN.
RRRING
RRRING
CLIK
WHY WAS AN ALARM SET TO GO OFF NOW...?
MEW!
TING

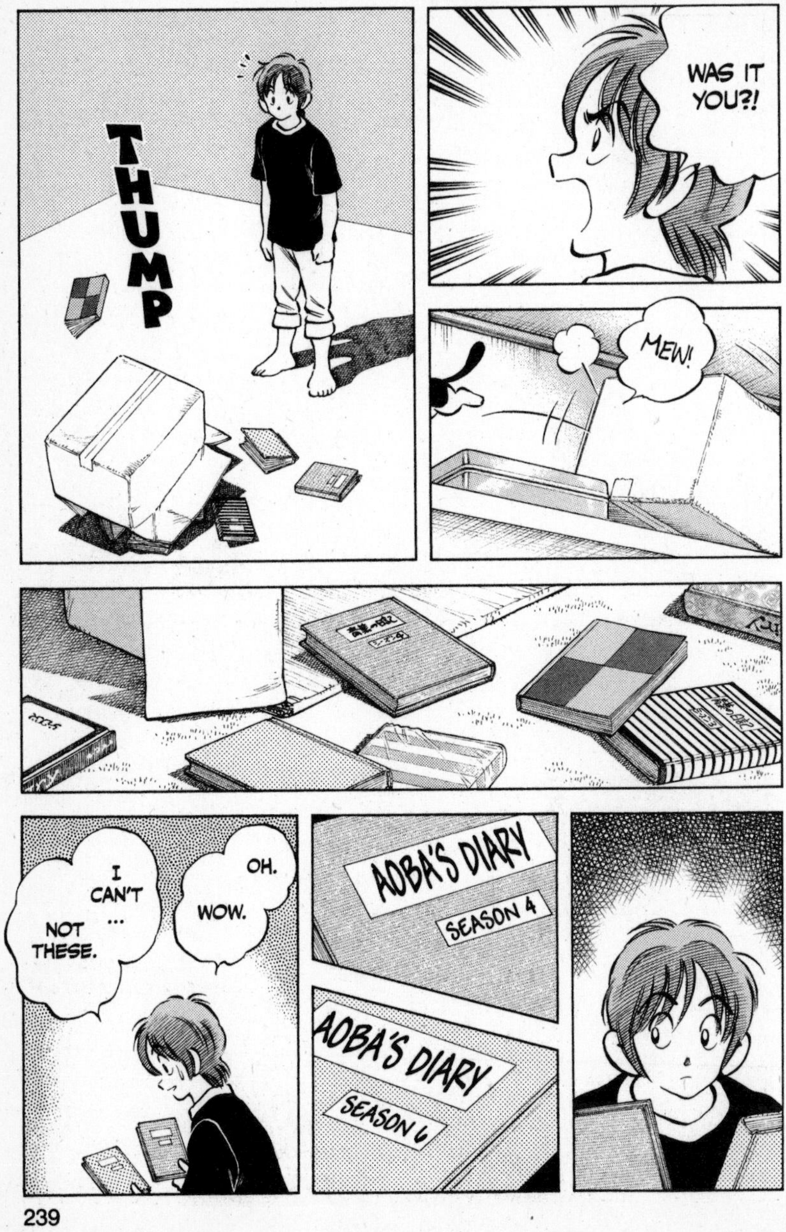
WAS IT YOU?!
MEW!
THUMP
AOBA'S DIARY
SEASON 4
AOBA'S DIARY
SEASON 6
OH. WOW.
I CAN'T ... NOT THESE.

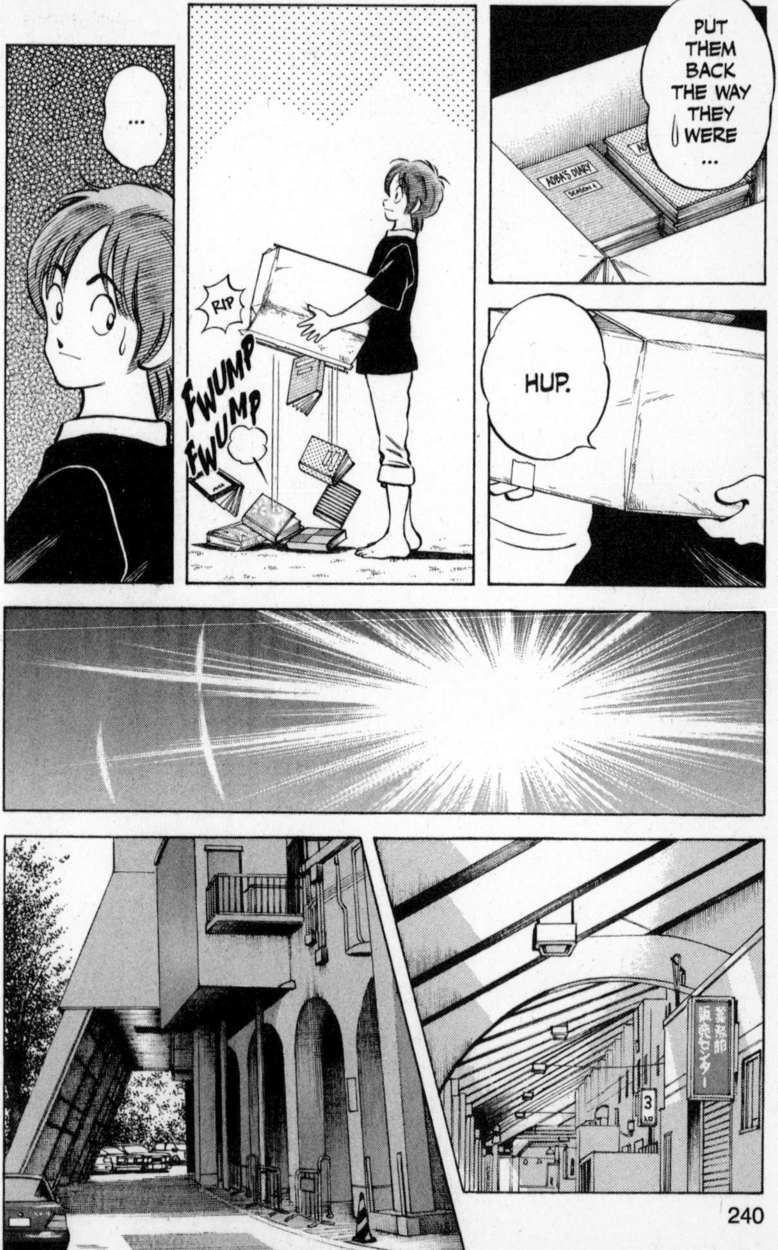
PUT THEM BACK THE WAY THEY WERE ...
HUP.
RIP
FWUMP FWUMP
...

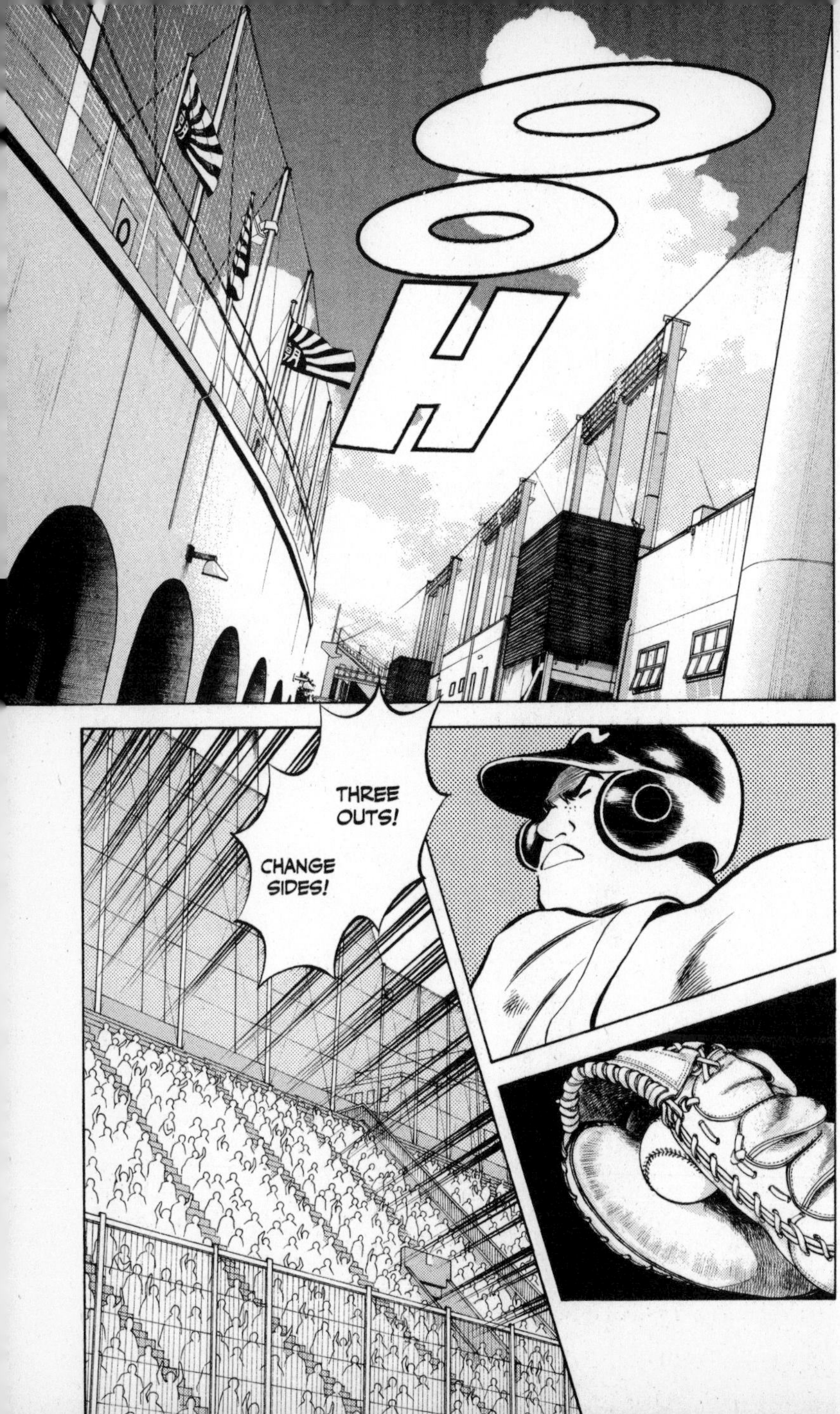
OOH
THREE OUTS! CHANGE SIDES!

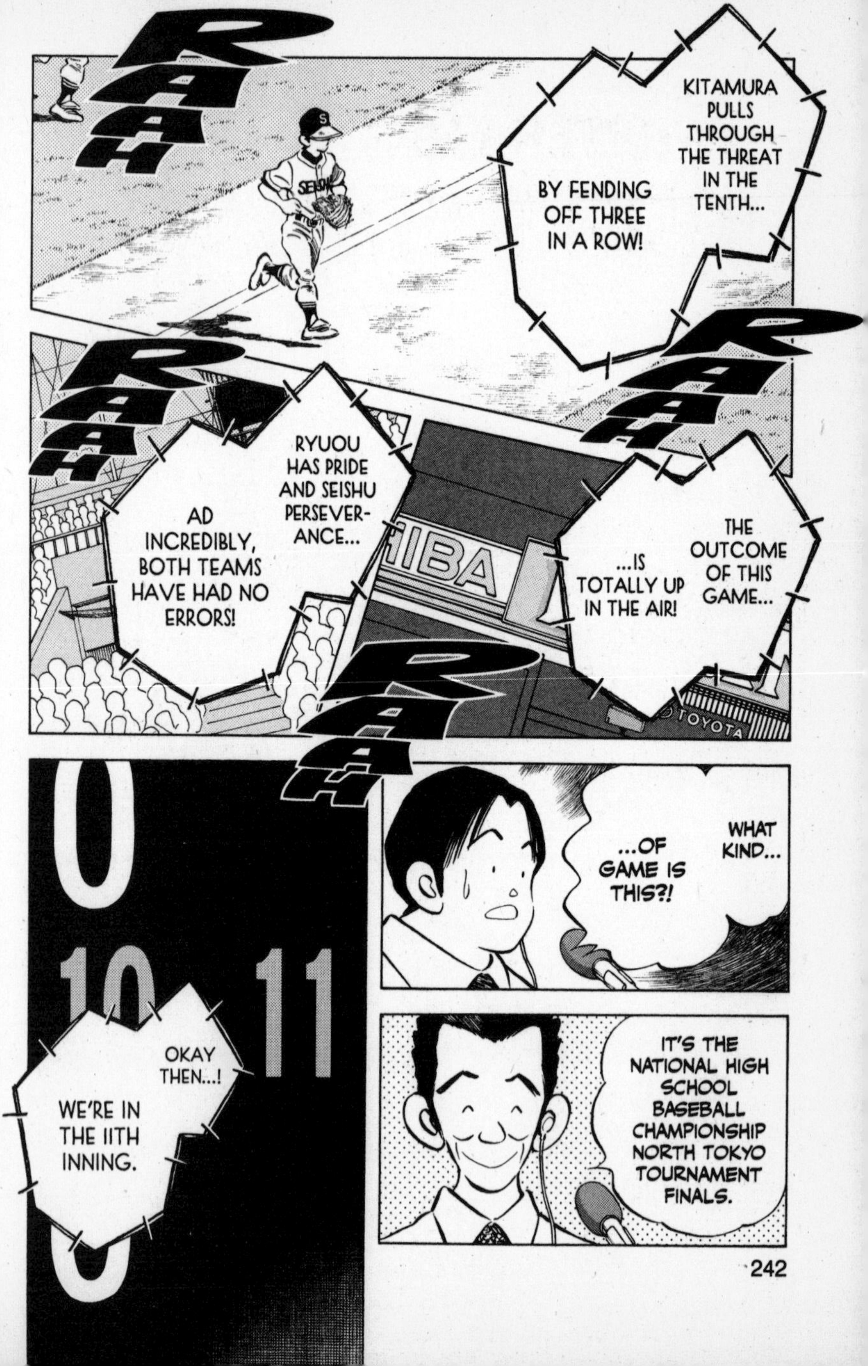
KITAMURA PULLS THROUGH THE THREAT IN THE TENTH...
BY FENDING OFF THREE IN A ROW!
RAAAH
RAAAH
THE OUTCOME OF THIS GAME...
...IS TOTALLY UP IN THE AIR!
RYUOU HAS PRIDE AND SEISHU PERSEVERANCE...
AD INCREDIBLY, BOTH TEAMS HAVE HAD NO ERRORS!
RAAAH
TOYOTA
WHAT KIND...
...OF GAME IS THIS?!
IT'S THE NATIONAL HIGH SCHOOL BASEBALL CHAMPIONSHIP NORTH TOKYO TOURNAMENT FINALS.
OKAY THEN...!
WE'RE IN THE 11TH INNING.

CHAPTER 154
DON'T FORGET

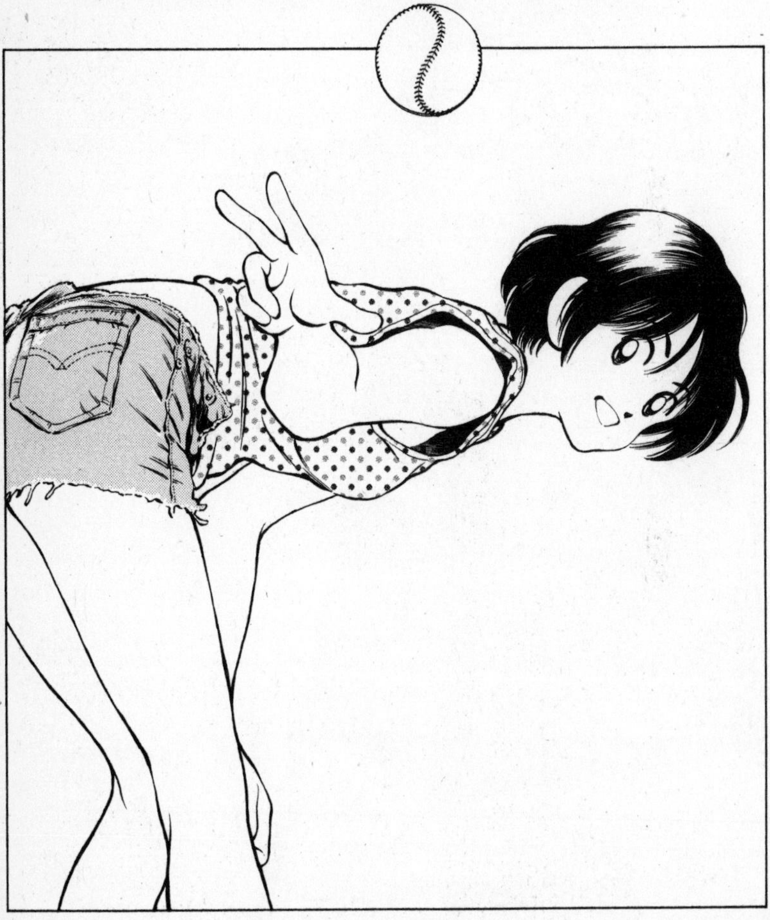

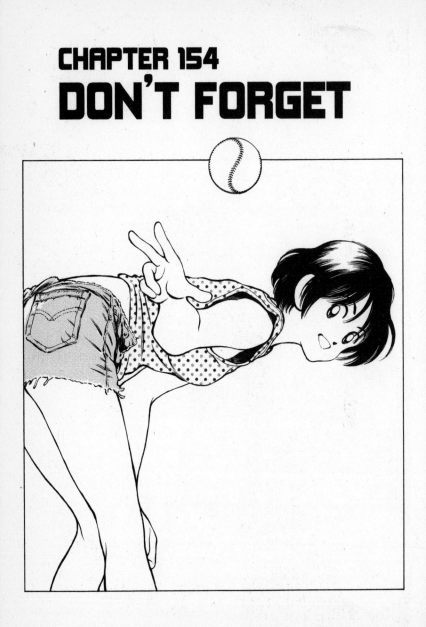

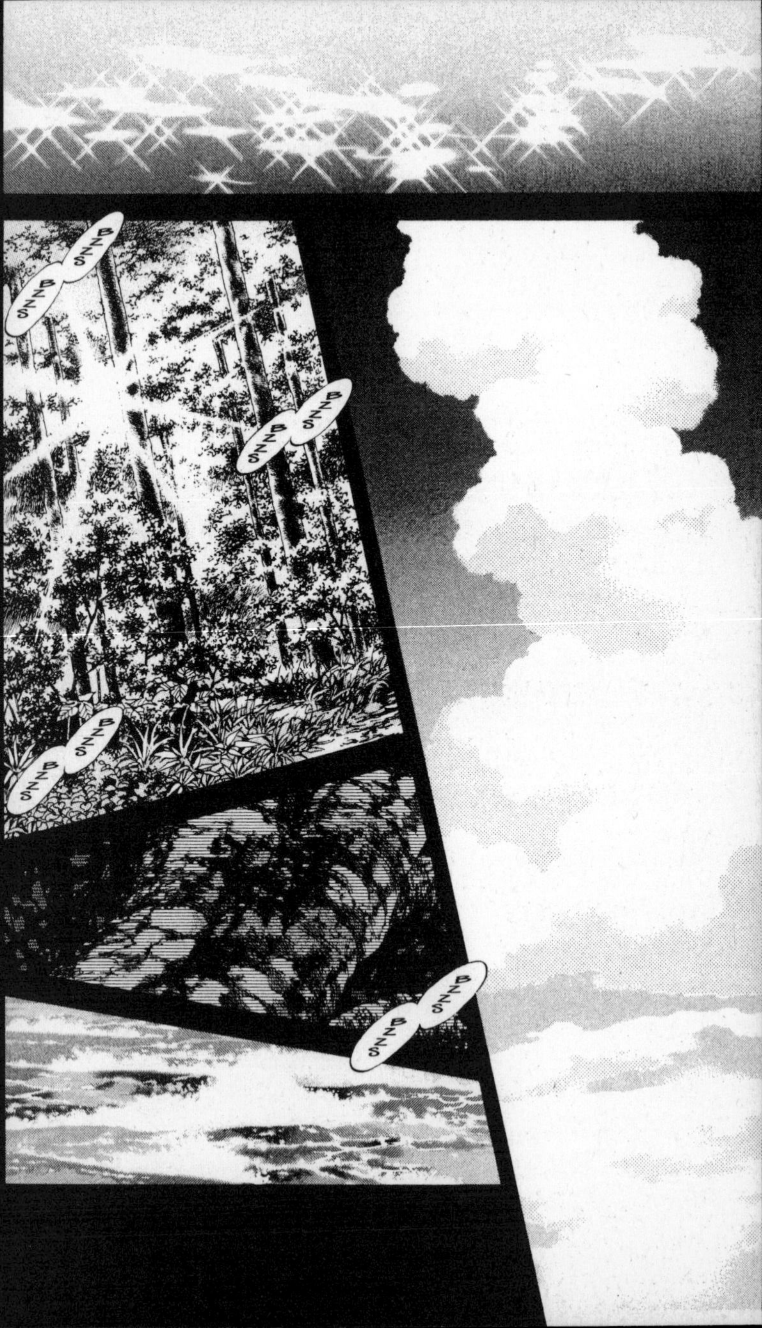
BZZS
BZZS
BZZS
BZZS
BZZS
BZZS
BZZS
BZZS

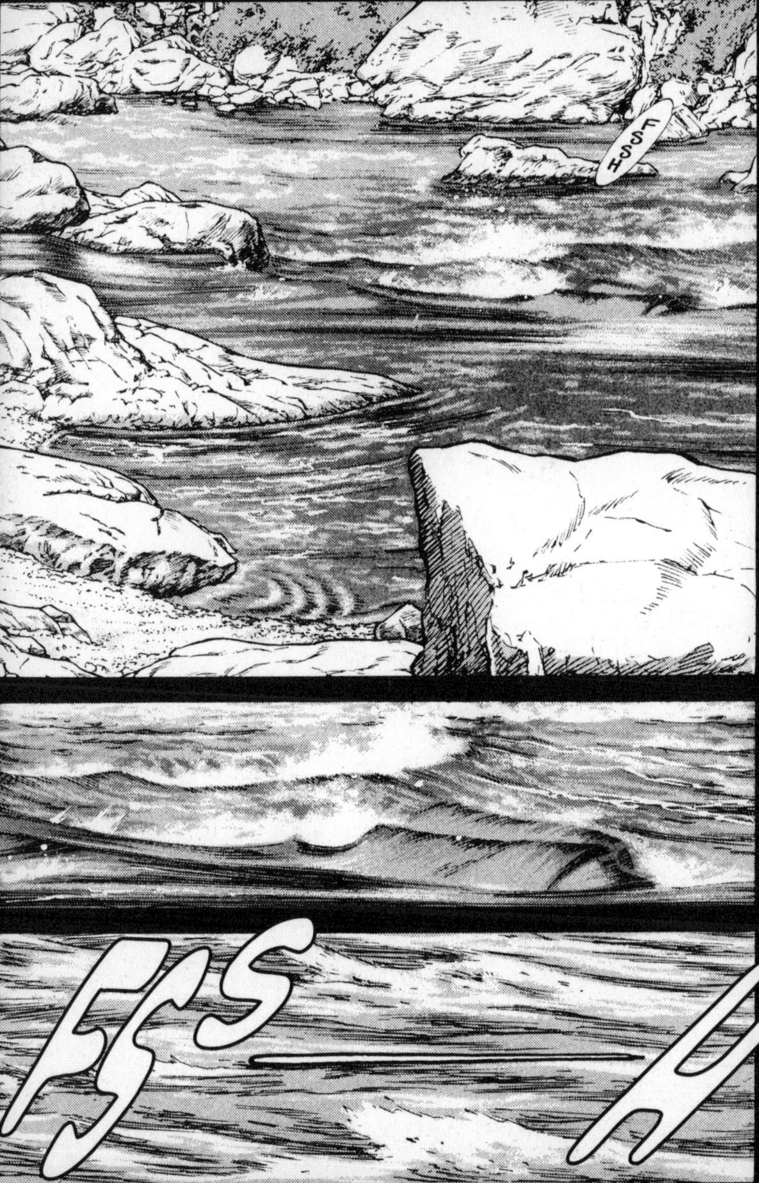
FSSH
FSS—H

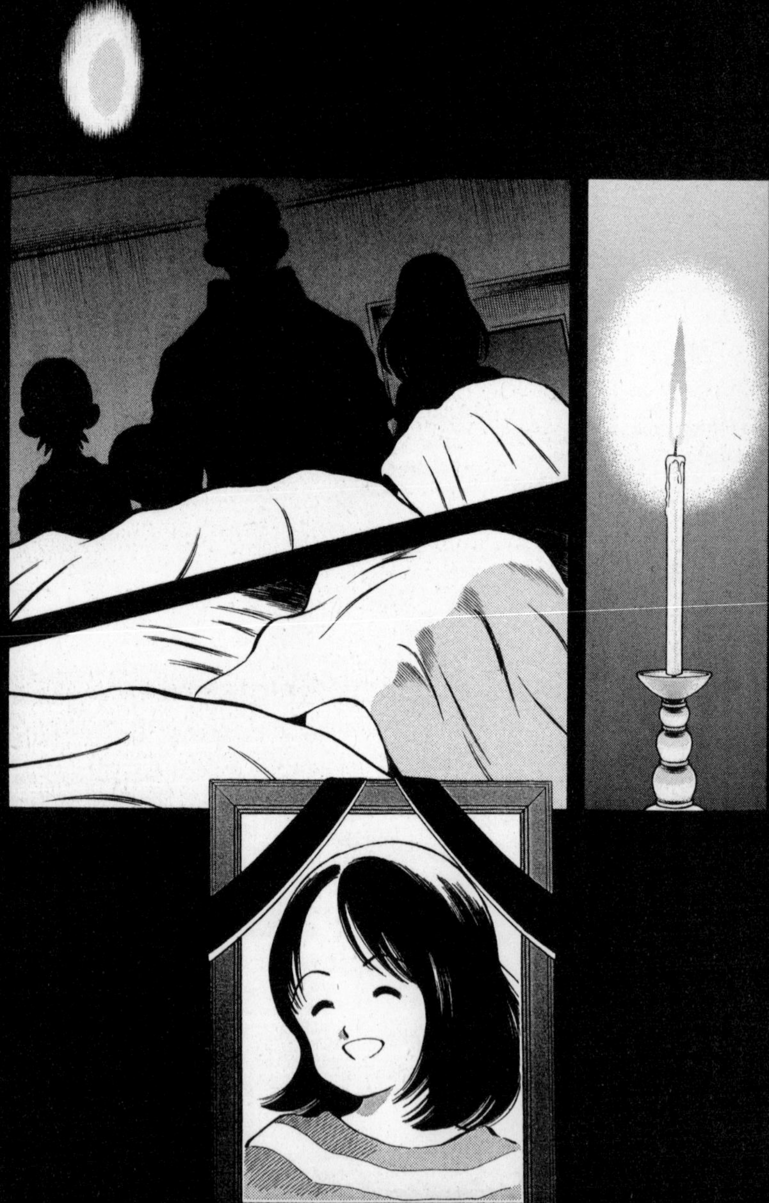

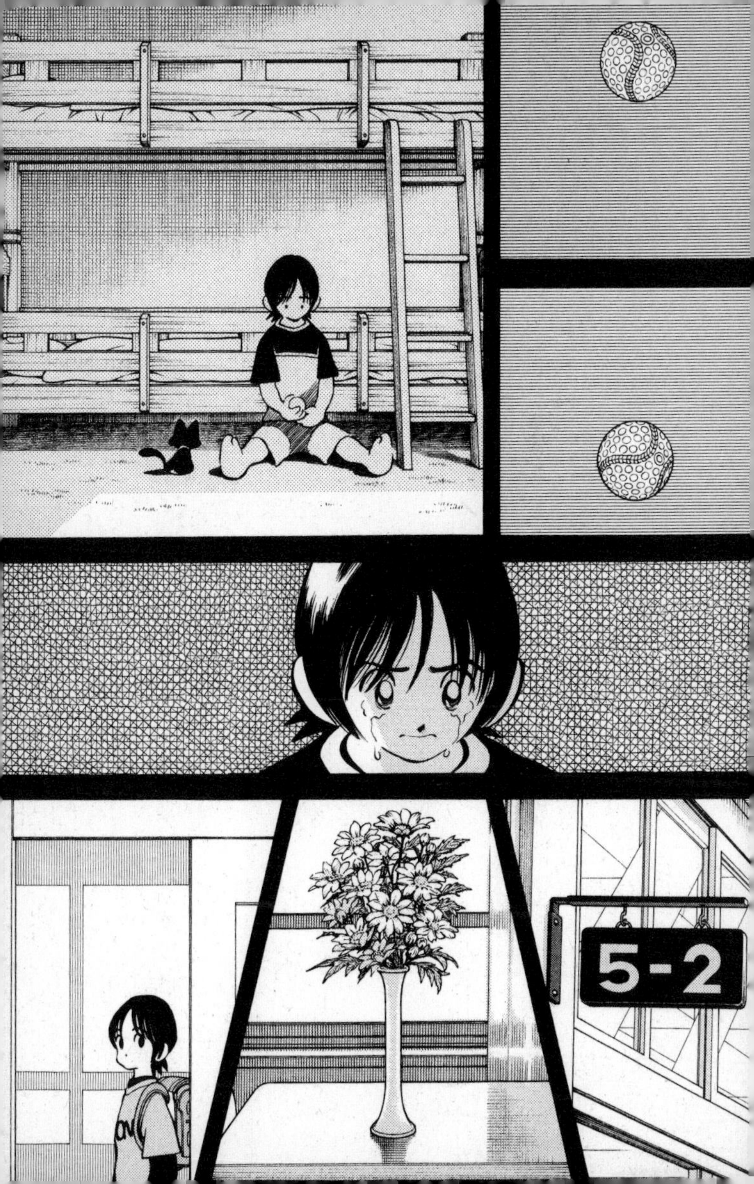
5-2

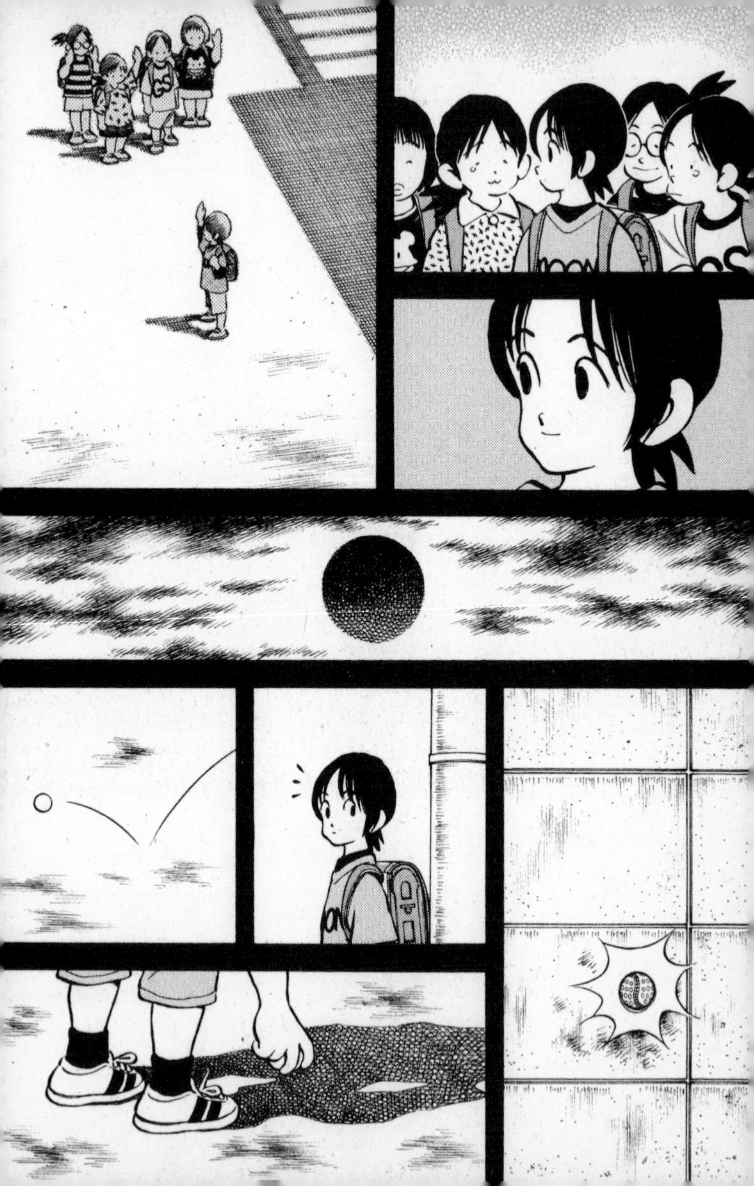

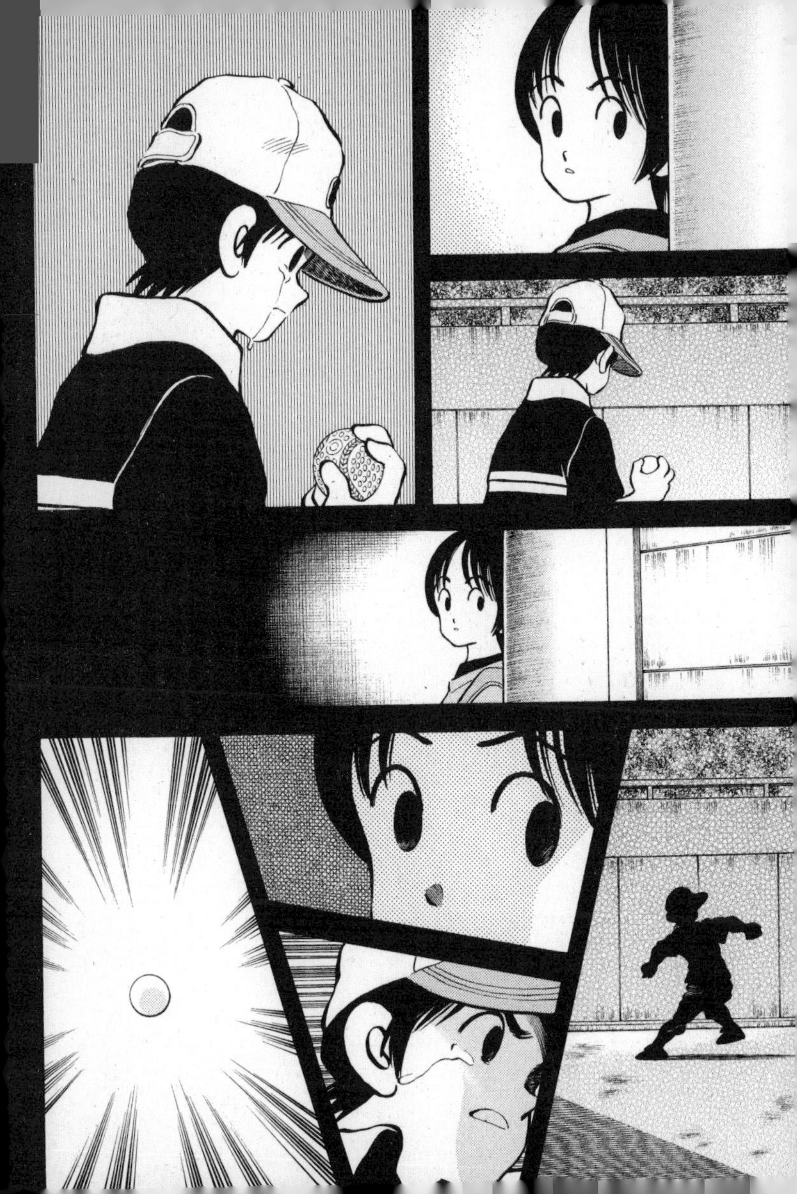

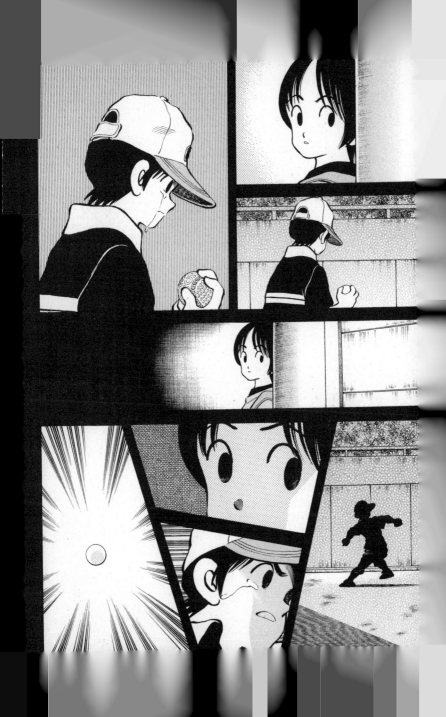

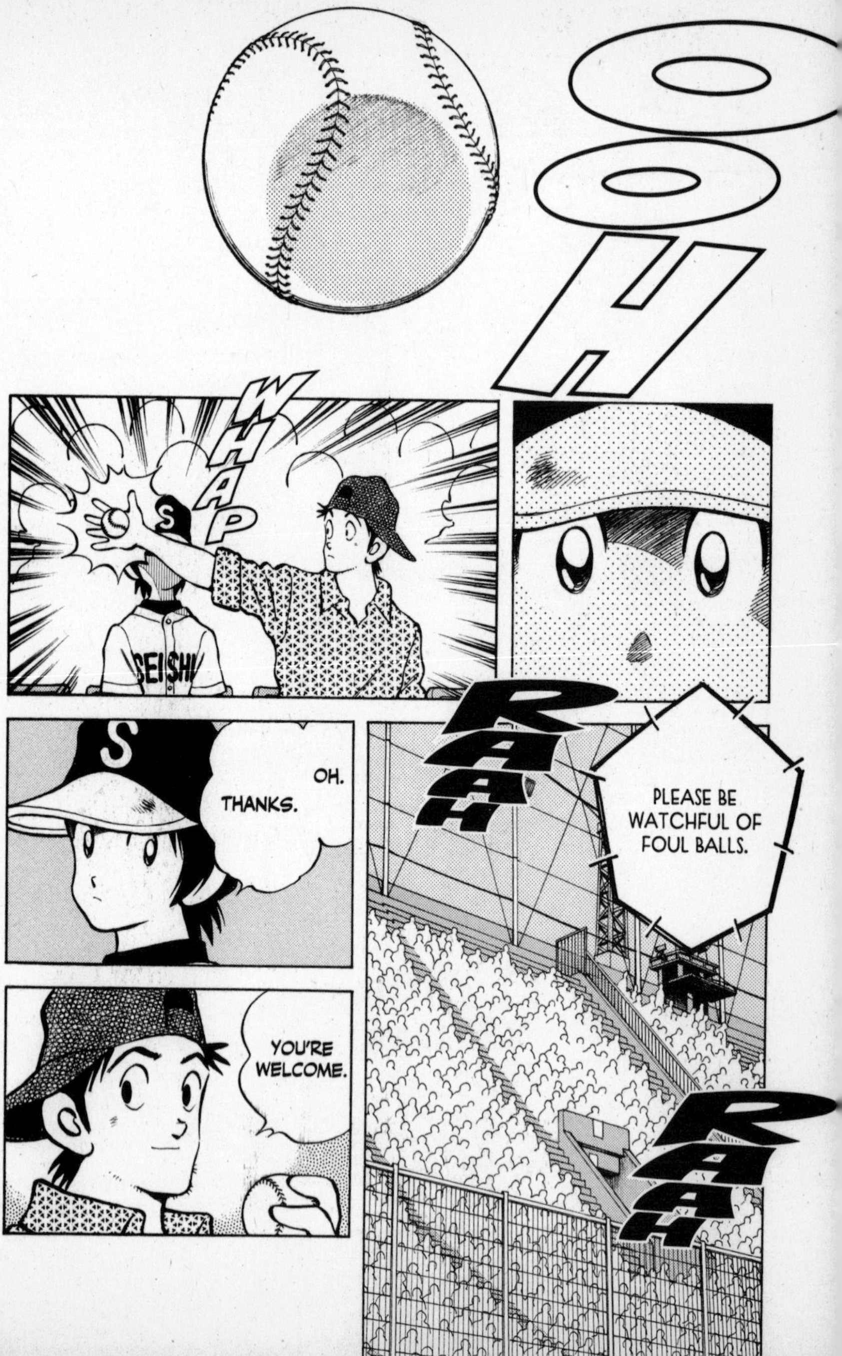
OOH
WHAP
RAAH
PLEASE BE WATCHFUL OF FOUL BALLS.
RAAH
OH. THANKS.
YOU'RE WELCOME.

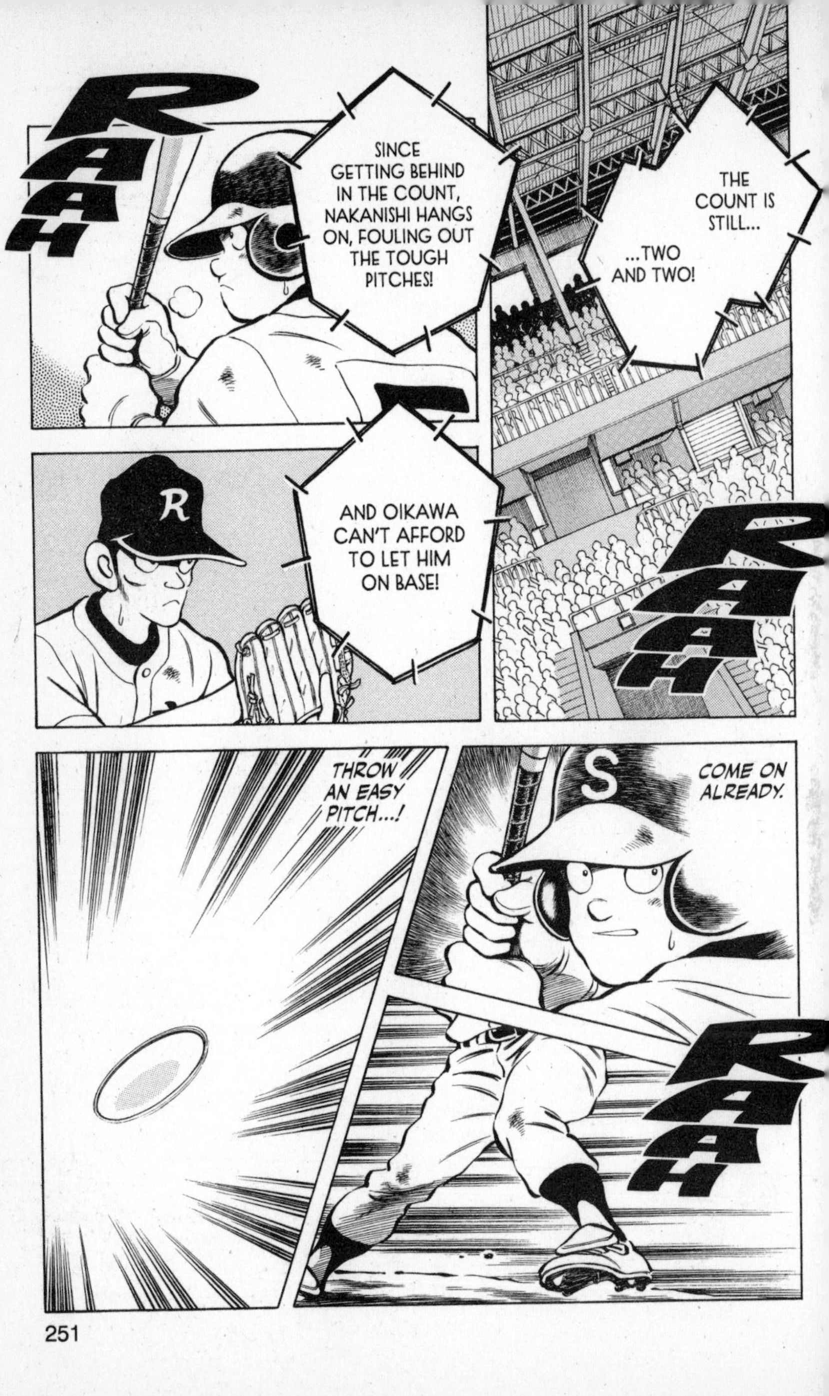
THE COUNT IS STILL...
...TWO AND TWO!
RAAH
RAAH
SINCE GETTING BEHIND IN THE COUNT, NAKANISHI HANGS ON, FOULING OUT THE TOUGH PITCHES!
AND OIKAWA CAN'T AFFORD TO LET HIM ON BASE!
COME ON ALREADY.
RAAH
THROW AN EASY PITCH...!

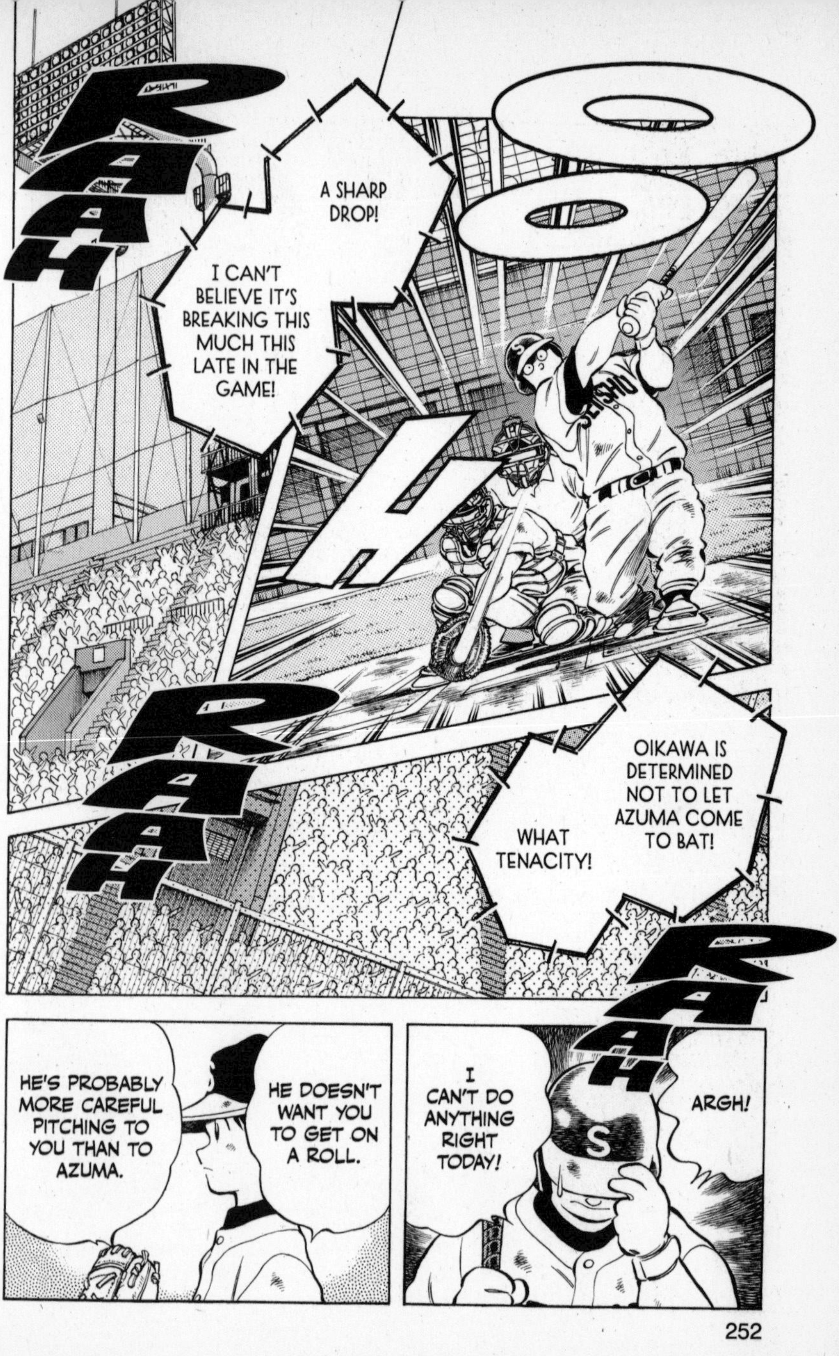
RAAAH
A SHARP DROP!
I CAN'T BELIEVE IT'S BREAKING THIS MUCH THIS LATE IN THE GAME!
RAAAH
OIKAWA IS DETERMINED NOT TO LET AZUMA COME TO BAT!
WHAT TENACITY!
RAAAH
ARGH!
I CAN'T DO ANYTHING RIGHT TODAY!
HE DOESN'T WANT YOU TO GET ON A ROLL.
HE'S PROBABLY MORE CAREFUL PITCHING TO YOU THAN TO AZUMA.

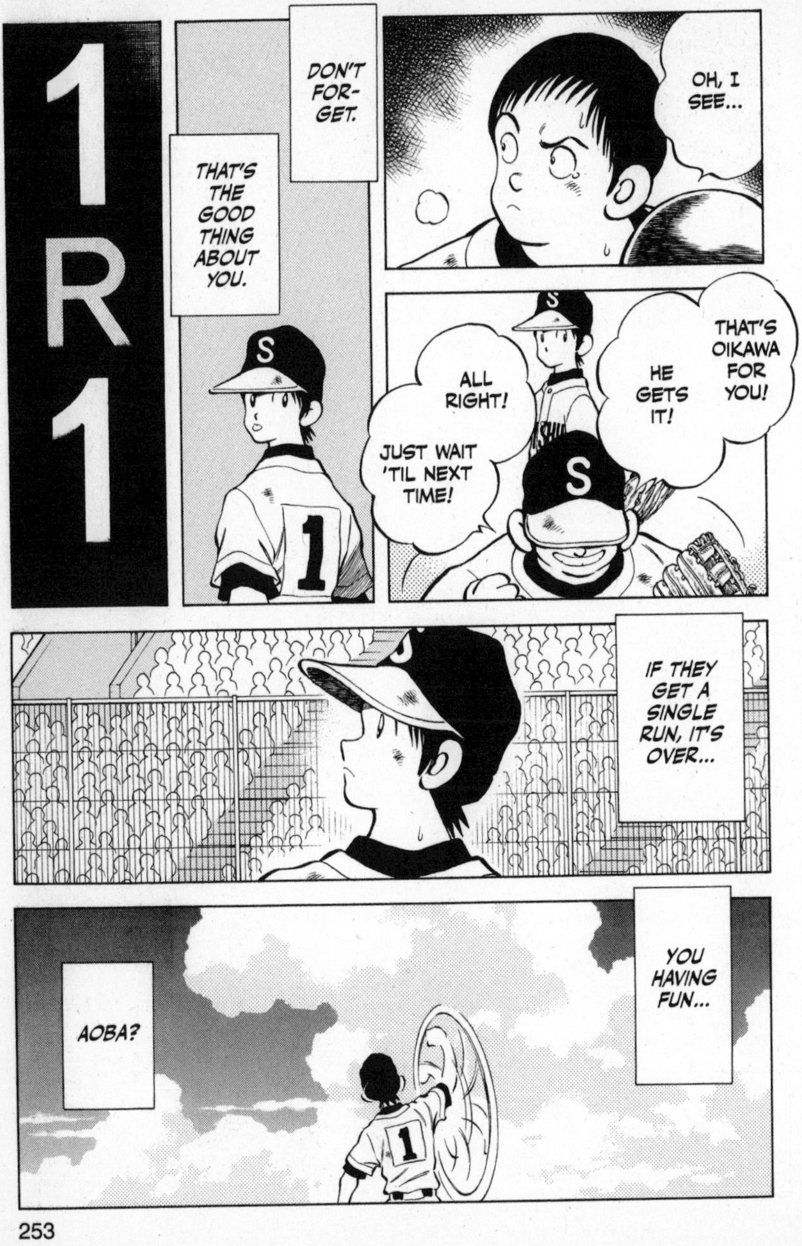
OH, I SEE...
THAT'S OIKAWA FOR YOU!
HE GETS IT!
ALL RIGHT!
JUST WAIT 'TIL NEXT TIME!
DON'T FOR-GET.
THAT'S THE GOOD THING ABOUT YOU.
1R1
IF THEY GET A SINGLE RUN, IT'S OVER...
YOU HAVING FUN...
AOBA?

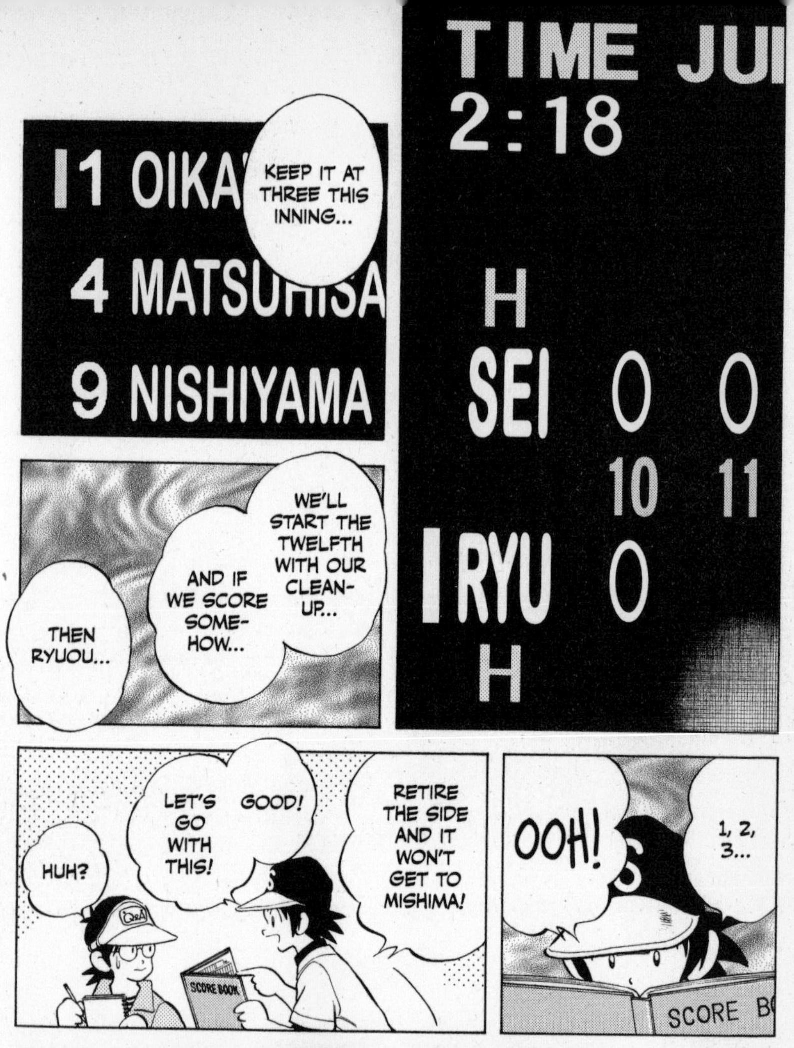
TIME JU
2:18
H
SEI 0 0
10 11
RYU 0
H
11 OIKA
4 MATSUHISA
9 NISHIYAMA
KEEP IT AT THREE THIS INNING...
WE'LL START THE TWELFTH WITH OUR CLEAN-UP...
AND IF WE SCORE SOME-HOW...
THEN RYUOU...
1, 2, 3...
OOH!
SCORE B
RETIRE THE SIDE AND IT WON'T GET TO MISHIMA!
GOOD!
LET'S GO WITH THIS!
HUH?
SCORE BOOK
WHEN IT'S OVER, REMEMBER TO TELL KO HE DID A GOOD JOB.
BOOK

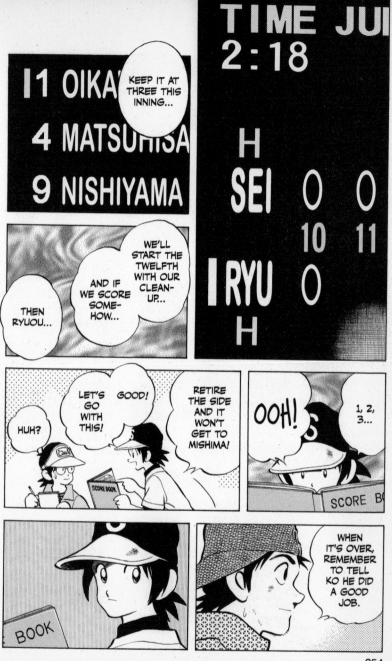

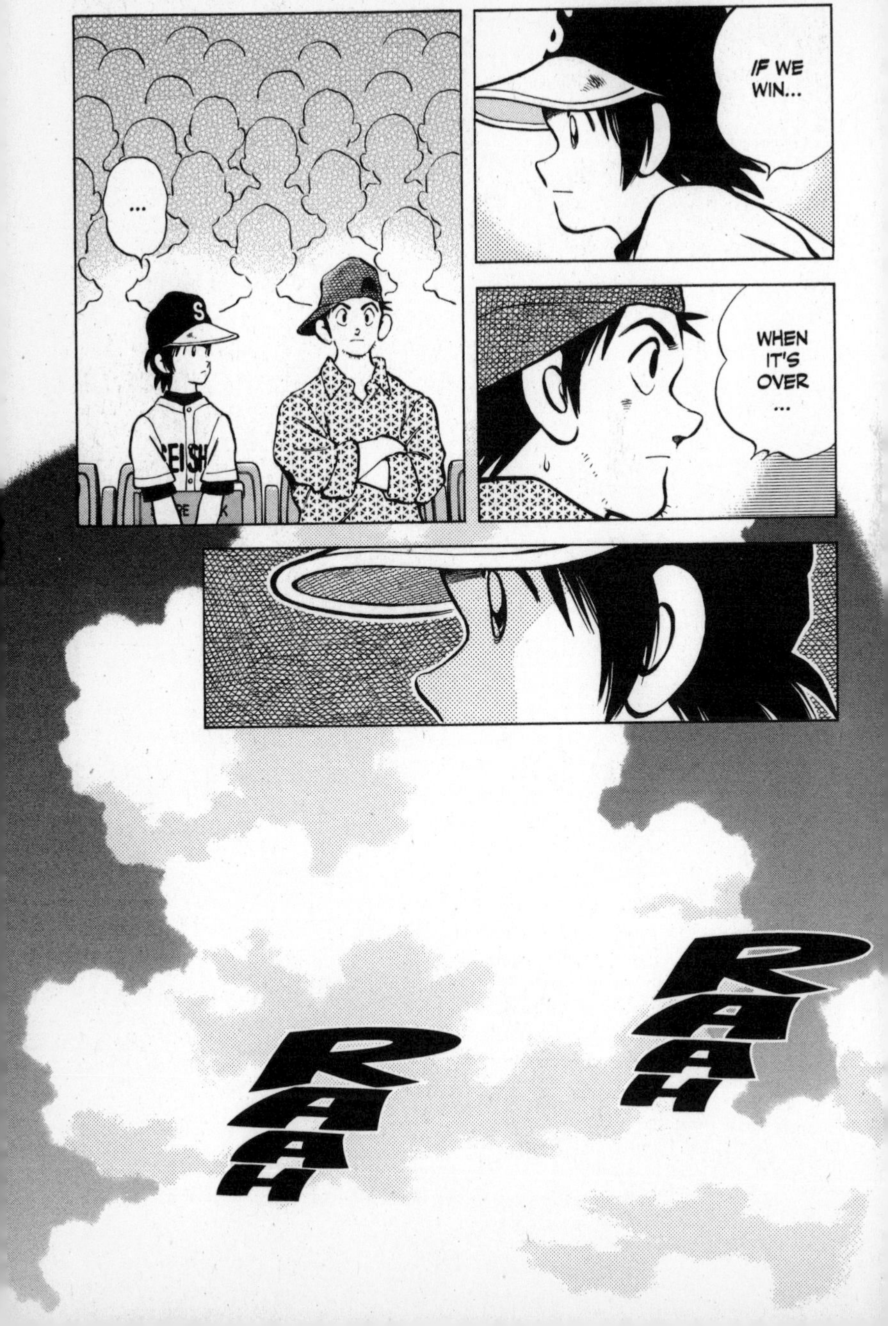
IF WE WIN...
WHEN IT'S OVER ...
...
RAAH
RAAH

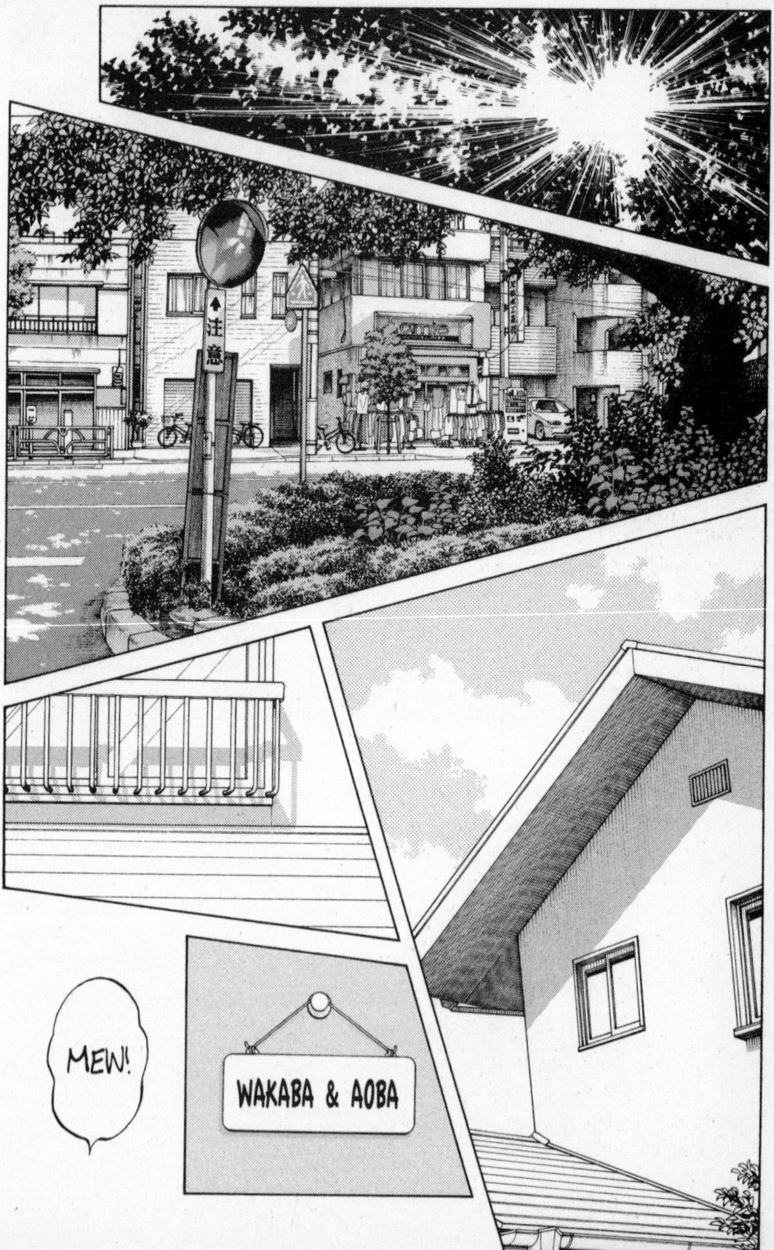
注意
WAKABA & AOBA
MEW!

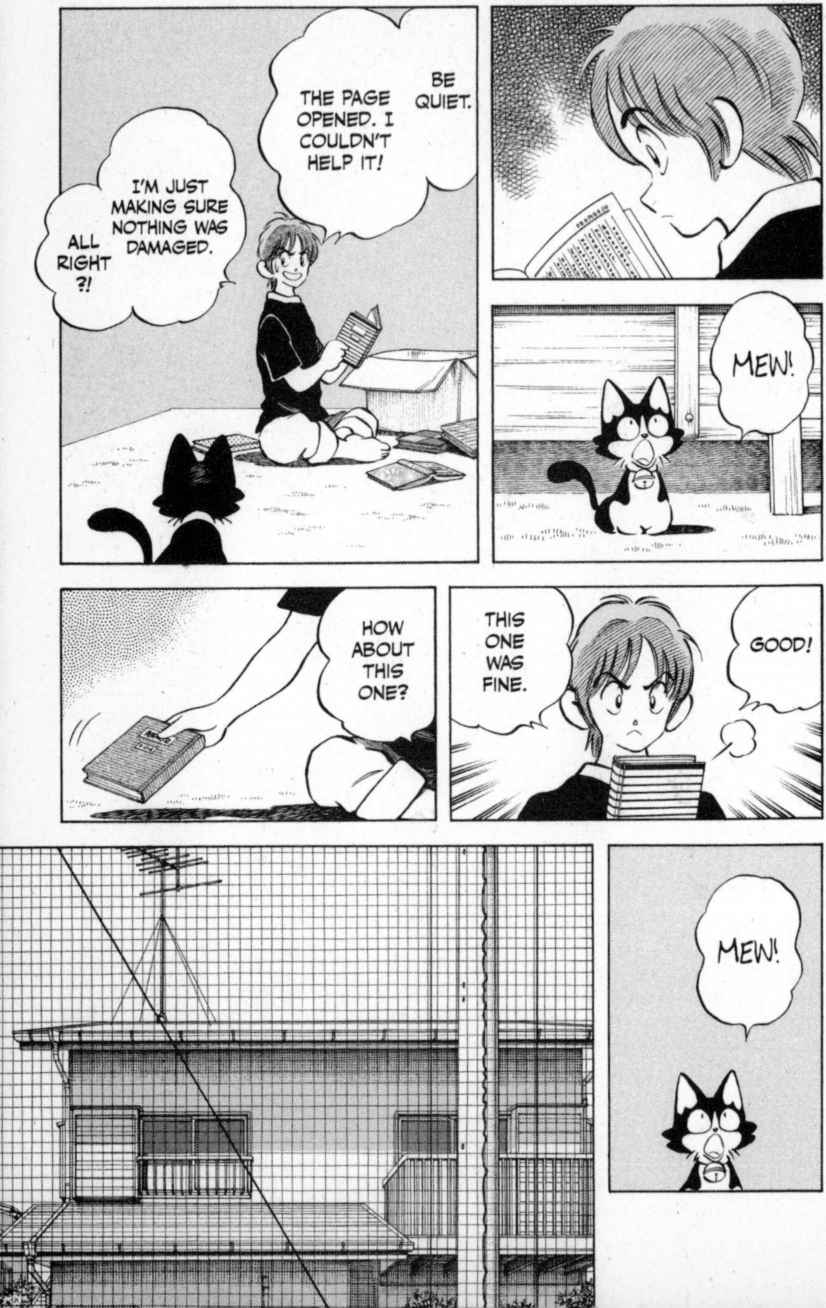
MEW!
BE QUIET.
THE PAGE OPENED. I COULDN'T HELP IT!
I'M JUST MAKING SURE NOTHING WAS DAMAGED.
ALL RIGHT?!
GOOD!
THIS ONE WAS FINE.
HOW ABOUT THIS ONE?
MEW!

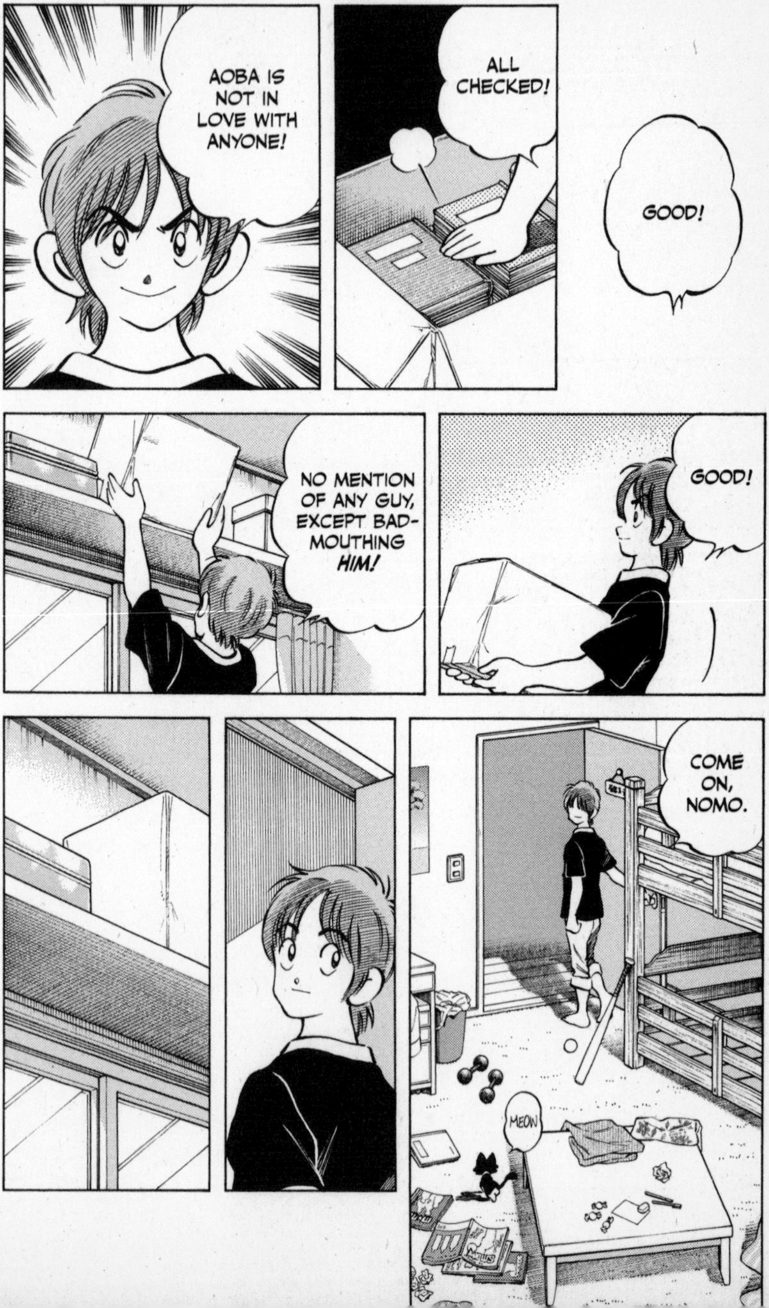
GOOD!
ALL CHECKED!
AOBA IS NOT IN LOVE WITH ANYONE!
GOOD!
NO MENTION OF ANY GUY, EXCEPT BAD-MOUTHING *HIM!*
COME ON, NOMO.
MEOW

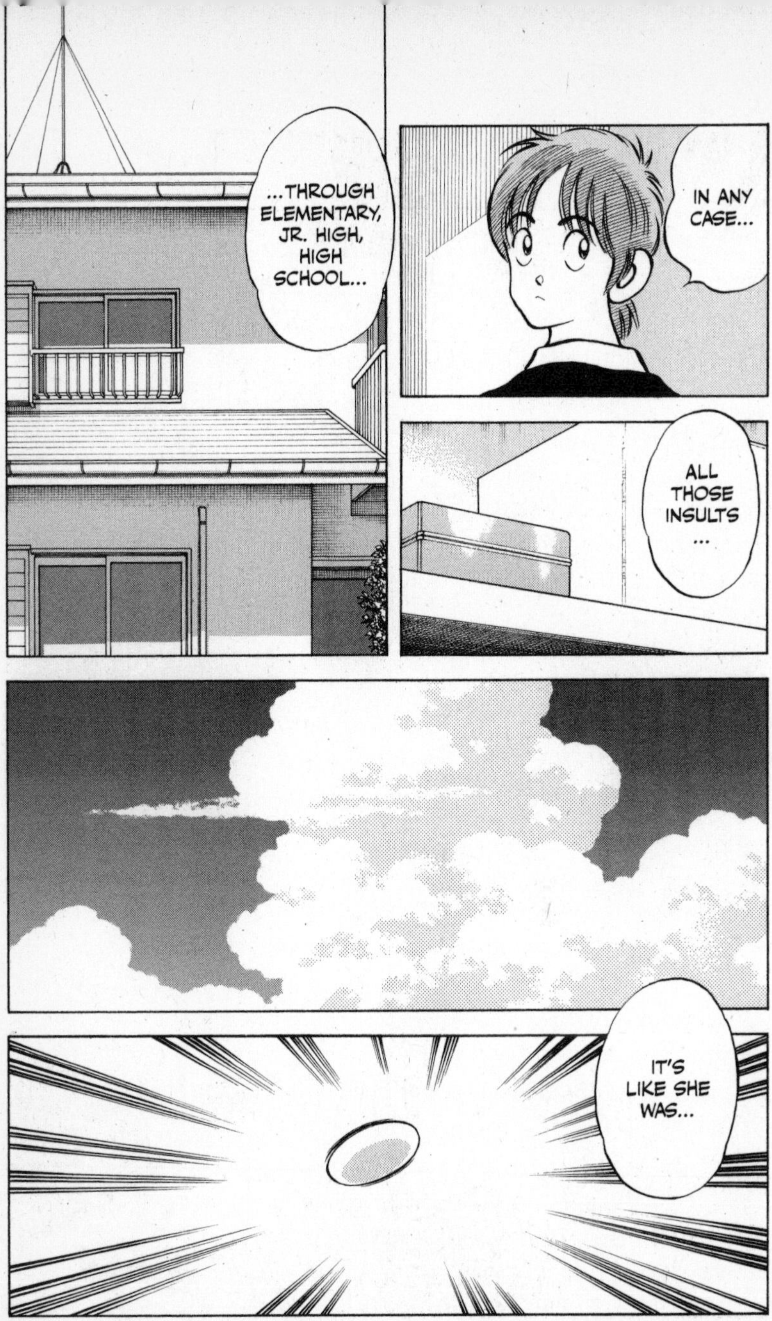
IN ANY CASE...
ALL THOSE INSULTS ...
...THROUGH ELEMENTARY, JR. HIGH, HIGH SCHOOL...
IT'S LIKE SHE WAS...

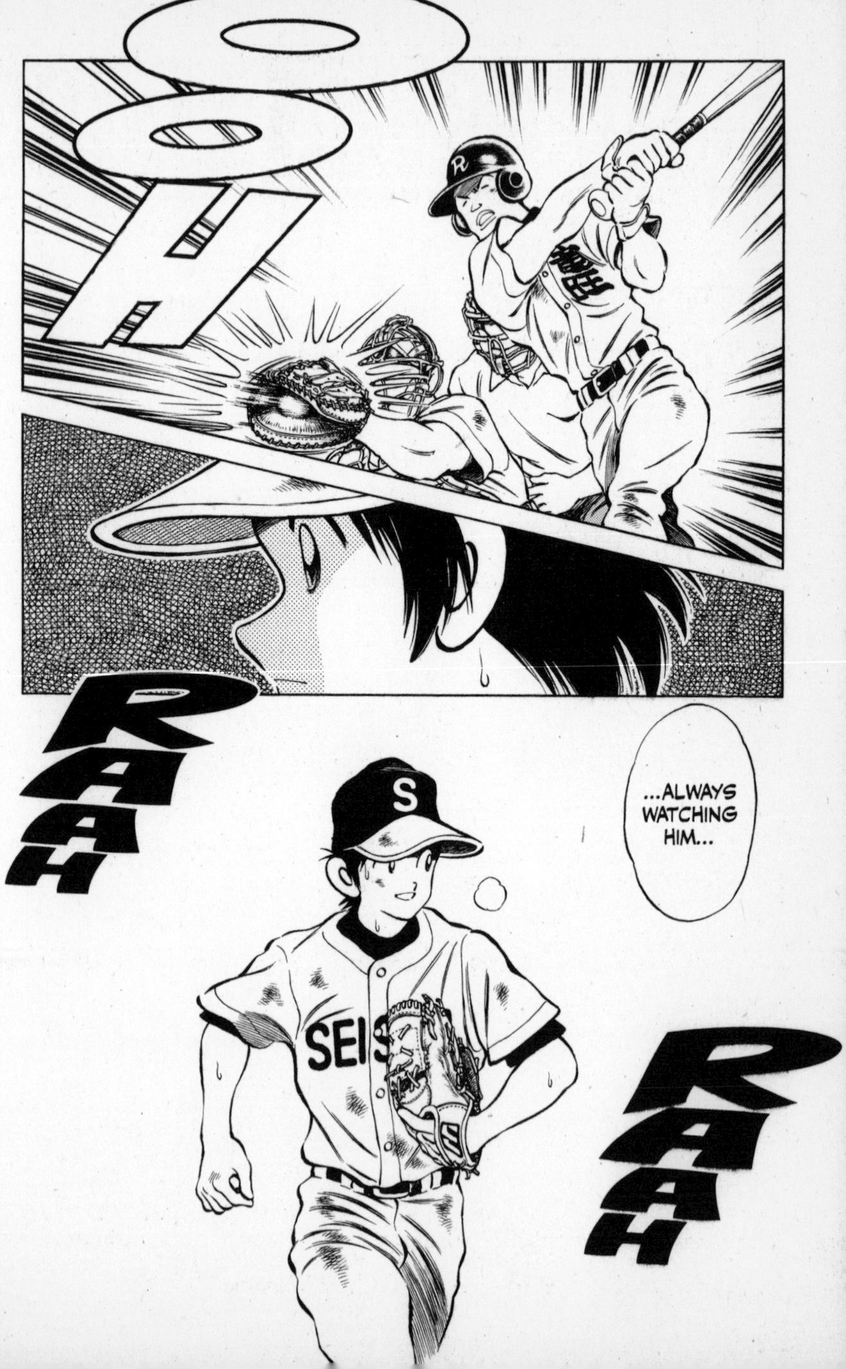
RAAH
...ALWAYS WATCHING HIM...
RAAH
SEIS

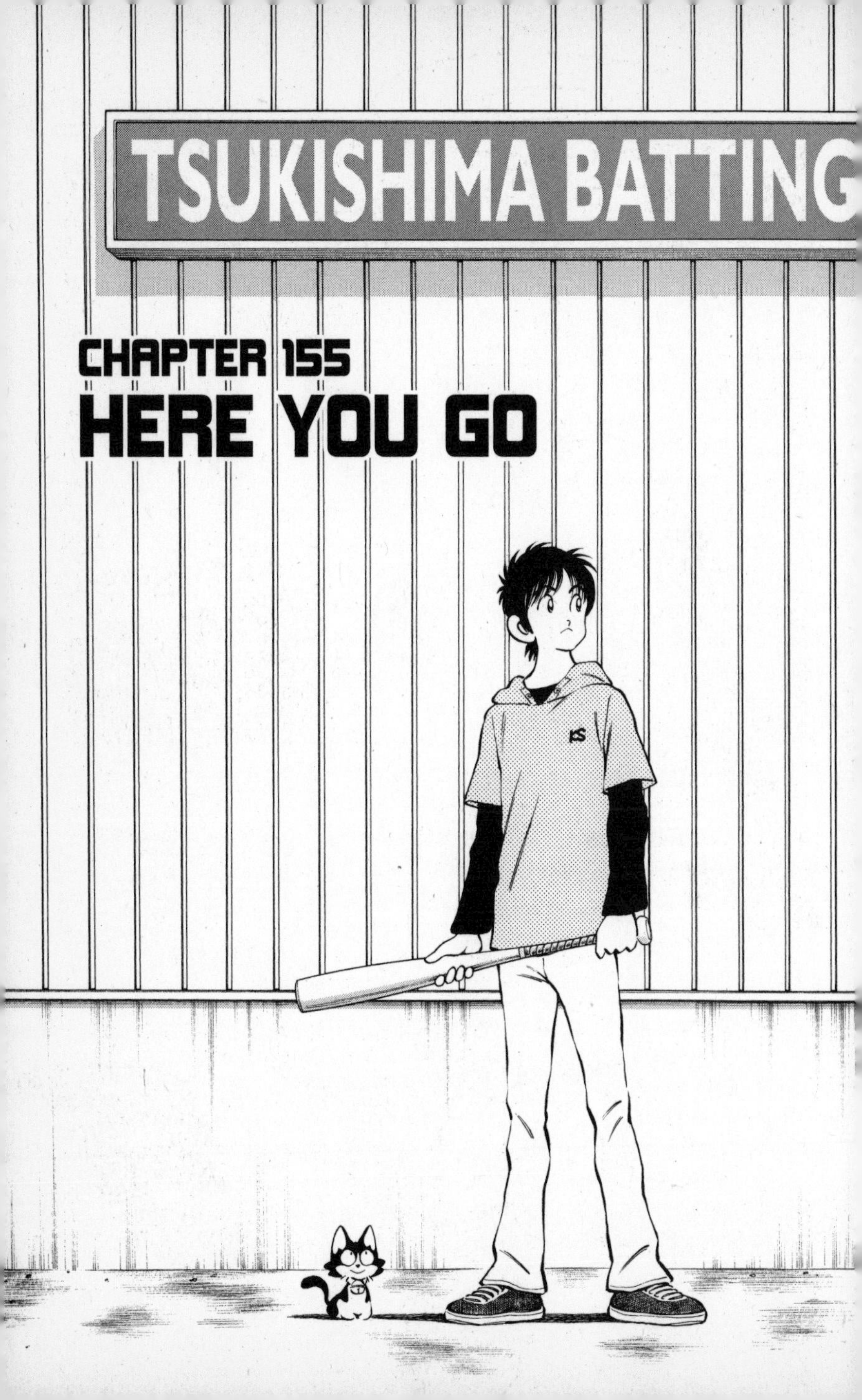
TSUKISHIMA BATTING
CHAPTER 155
HERE YOU GO

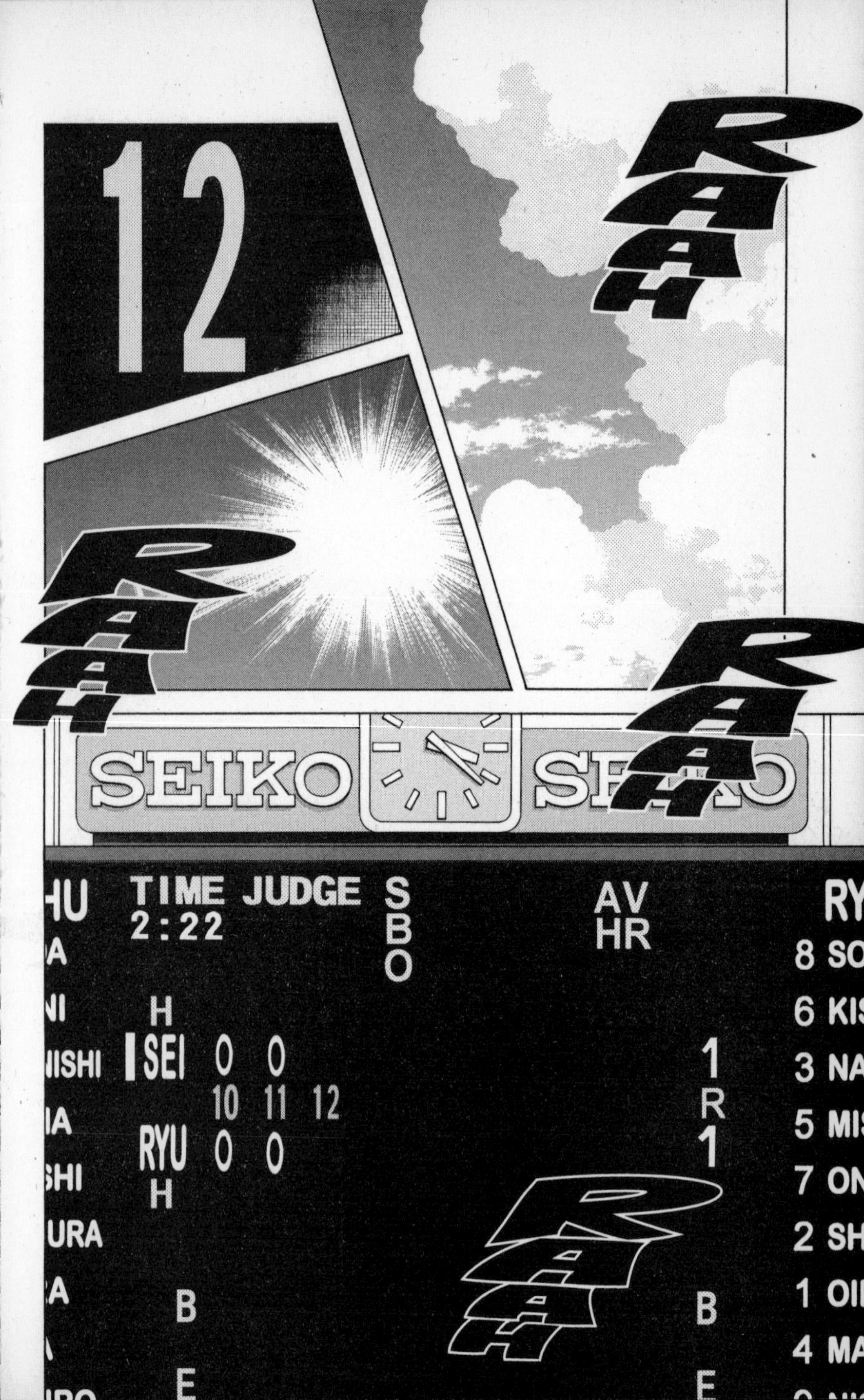
RAAH
12
RAAH
SEIKO
RAAH
TIME JUDGE
2:22
S
B
O
AV
HR
H
SEI 0 0 1
10 11 12 R
RYU 0 0 1
H
B
B
E
E
8 SO
6 KIS
3 NA
5 MIS
7 ON
2 SH
1 OI
4 MA
RAAH

13 AZUMA

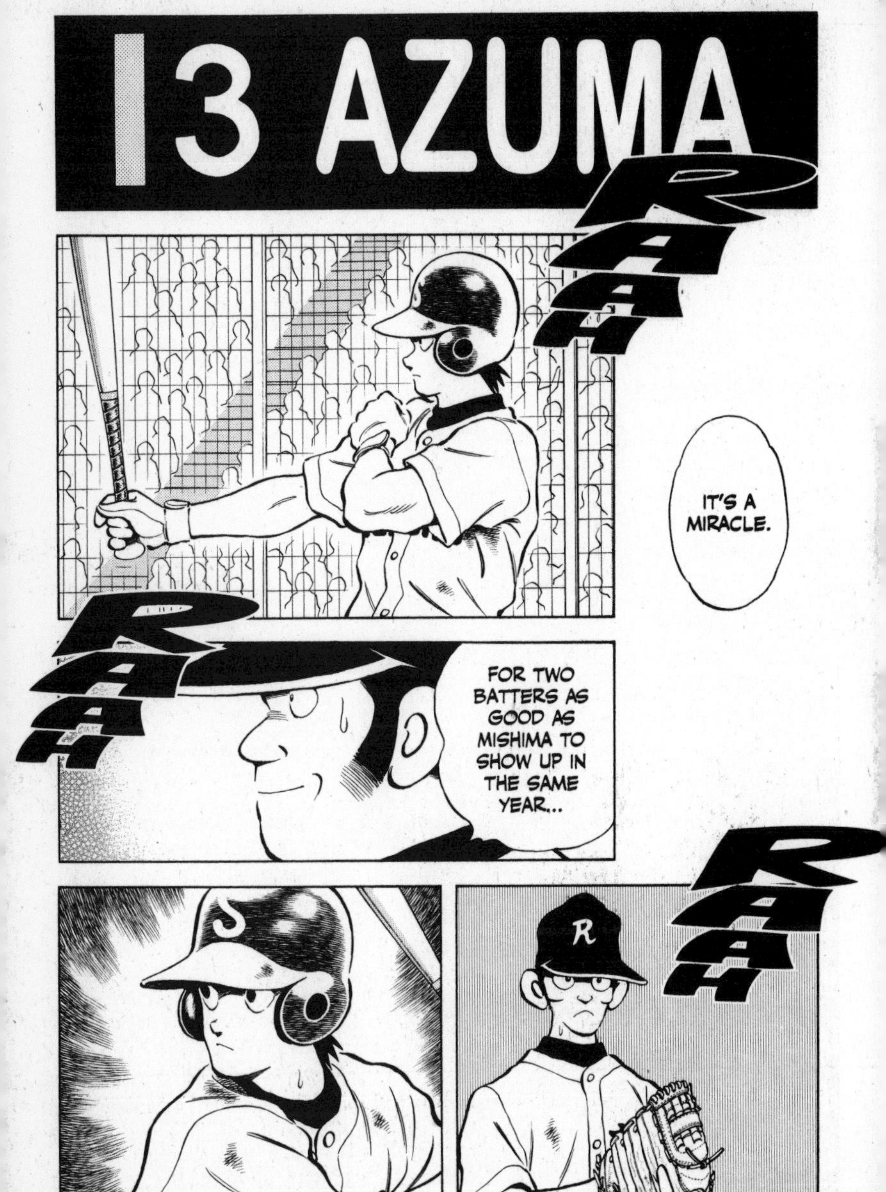
RAAH
IT'S A MIRACLE.
RAAH
FOR TWO BATTERS AS GOOD AS MISHIMA TO SHOW UP IN THE SAME YEAR...
RAAH

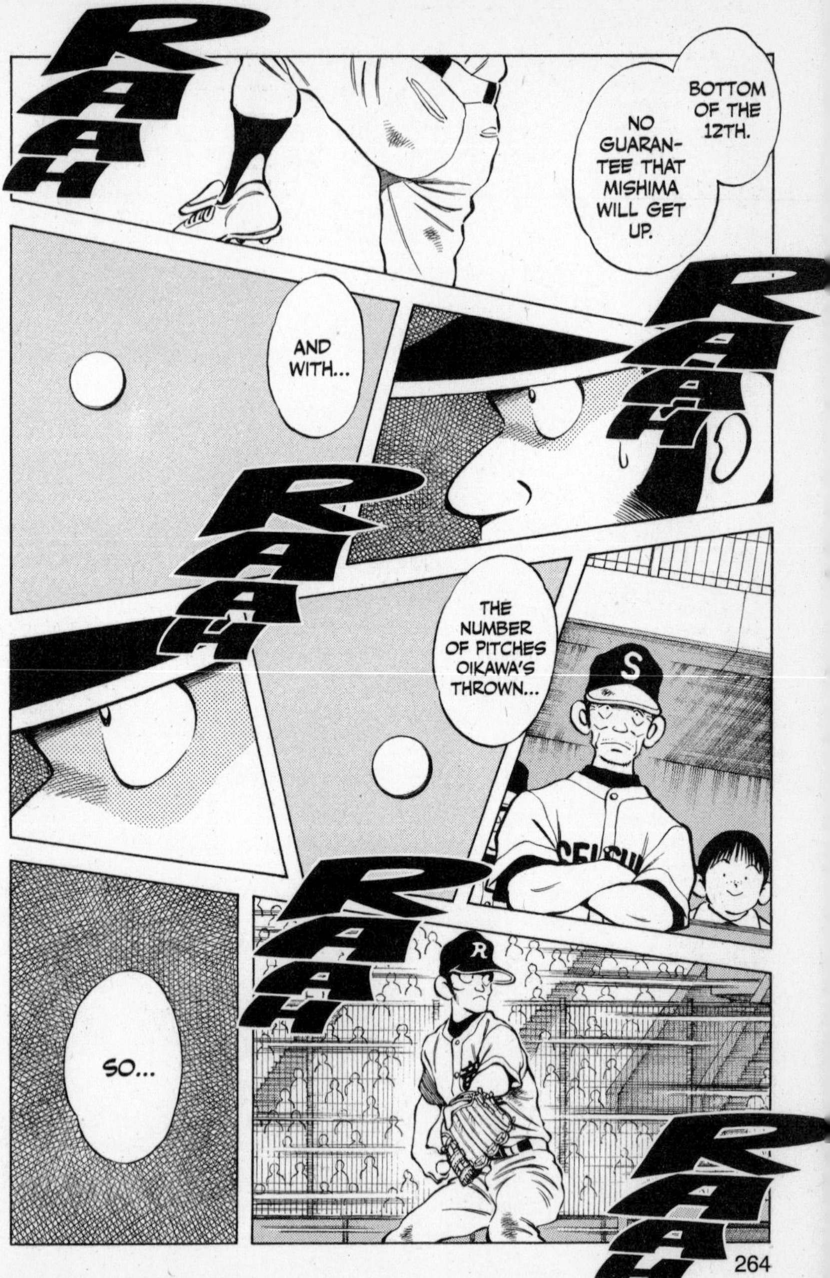
RAAH
BOTTOM OF THE 12TH.
NO GUARAN-TEE THAT MISHIMA WILL GET UP.
RAAH
AND WITH...
RAAH
THE NUMBER OF PITCHES OIKAWA'S THROWN...
RAAH
RAAH
SO...

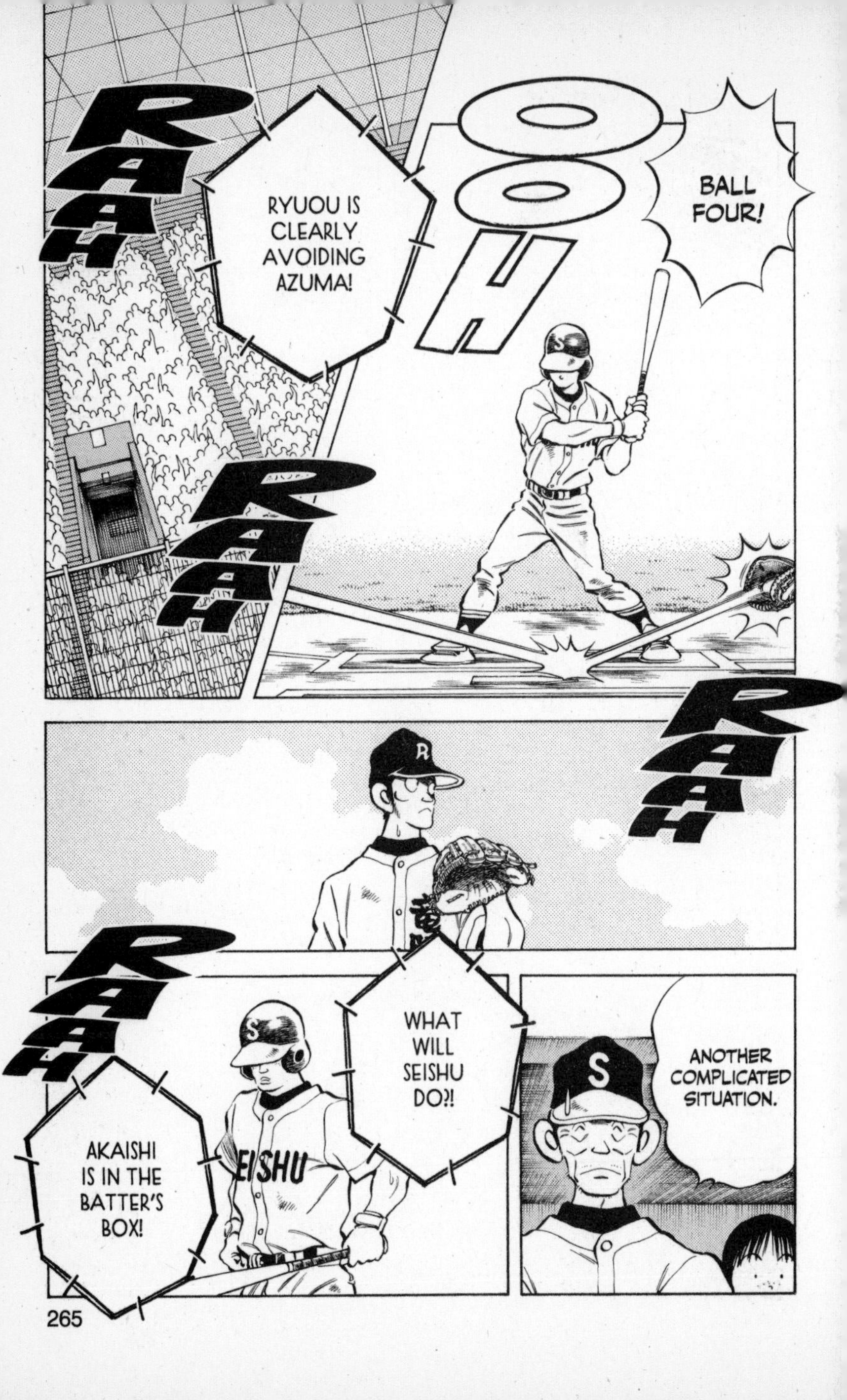
BALL FOUR!
OOH
RAAH
RYUOU IS CLEARLY AVOIDING AZUMA!
RAAH
RAAH
ANOTHER COMPLICATED SITUATION.
WHAT WILL SEISHU DO?!
RAAH
AKAISHI IS IN THE BATTER'S BOX!

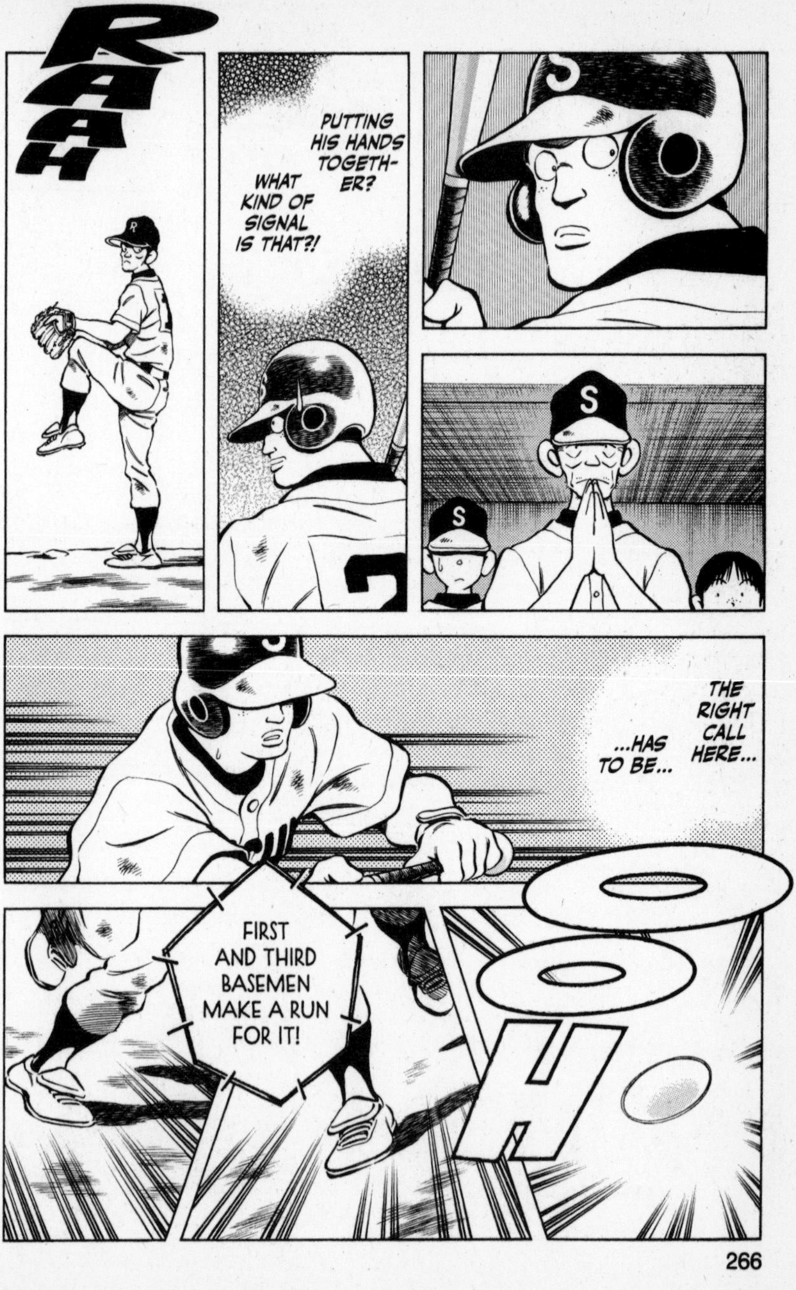
PUTTING HIS HANDS TOGETH-ER?
WHAT KIND OF SIGNAL IS THAT?!
RAAH
THE RIGHT CALL HERE...
...HAS TO BE...
FIRST AND THIRD BASEMEN MAKE A RUN FOR IT!
OOH

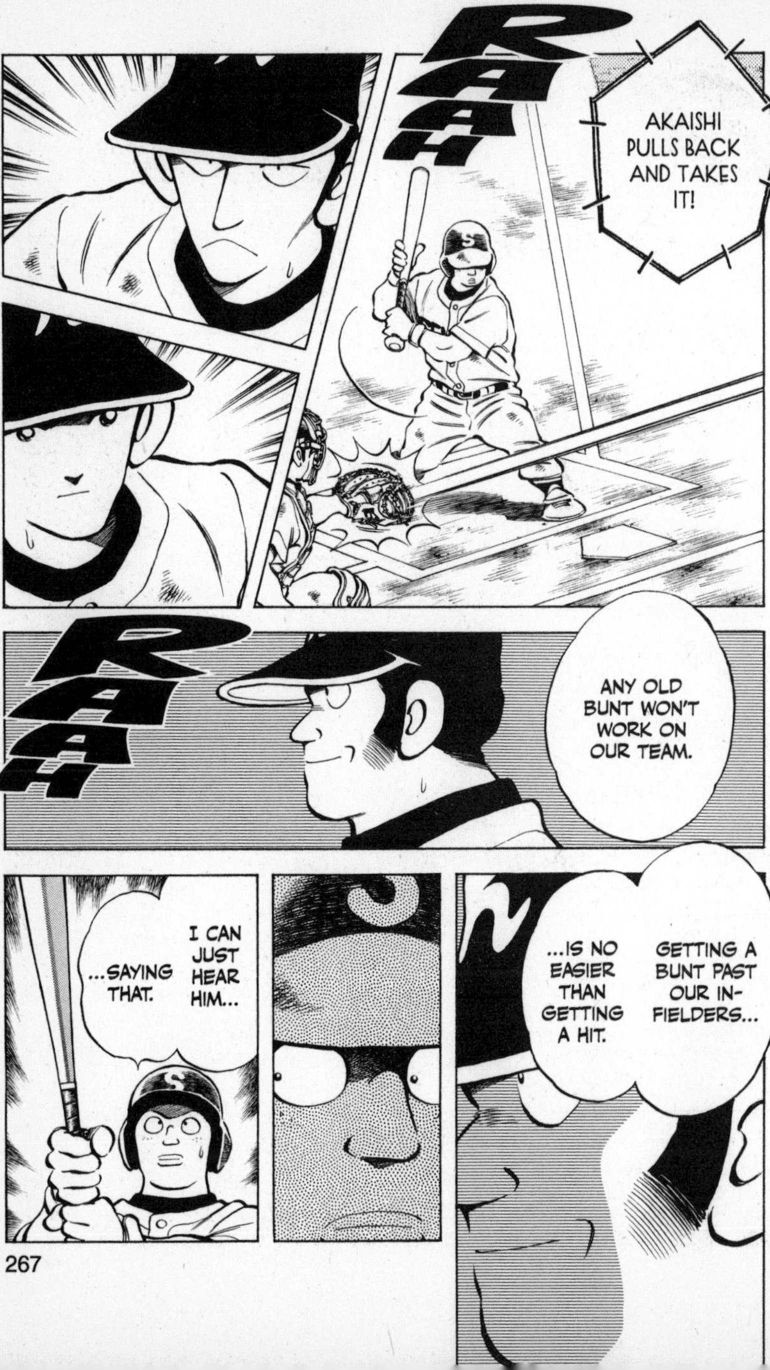
RAAH
AKAISHI PULLS BACK AND TAKES IT!
RAAH
ANY OLD BUNT WON'T WORK ON OUR TEAM.
GETTING A BUNT PAST OUR IN-FIELDERS...
...IS NO EASIER THAN GETTING A HIT.
I CAN JUST HEAR HIM...
...SAYING THAT.

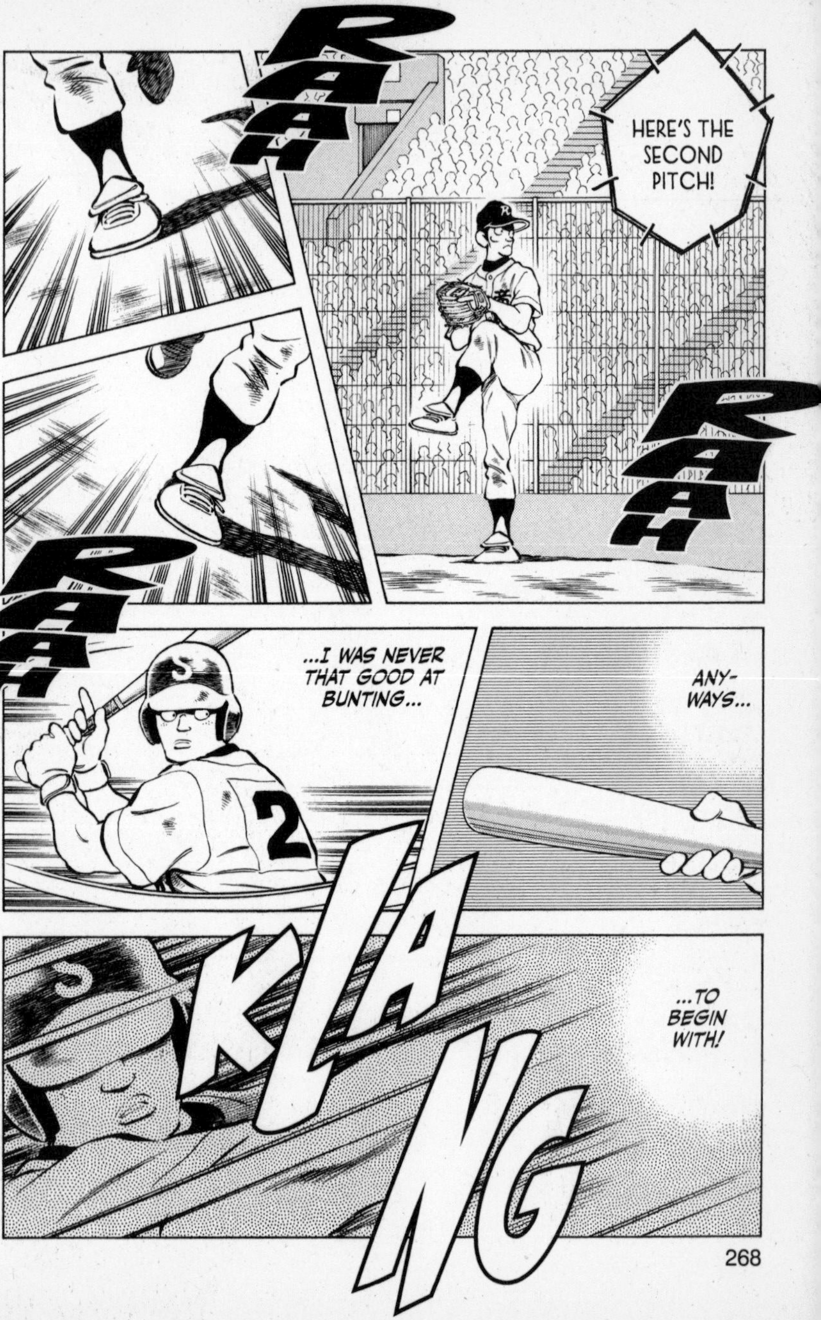
HERE'S THE SECOND PITCH!
RAAAH
RAAAH
RAAAH
ANY-WAYS...
...I WAS NEVER THAT GOOD AT BUNTING...
...TO BEGIN WITH!
KLANG

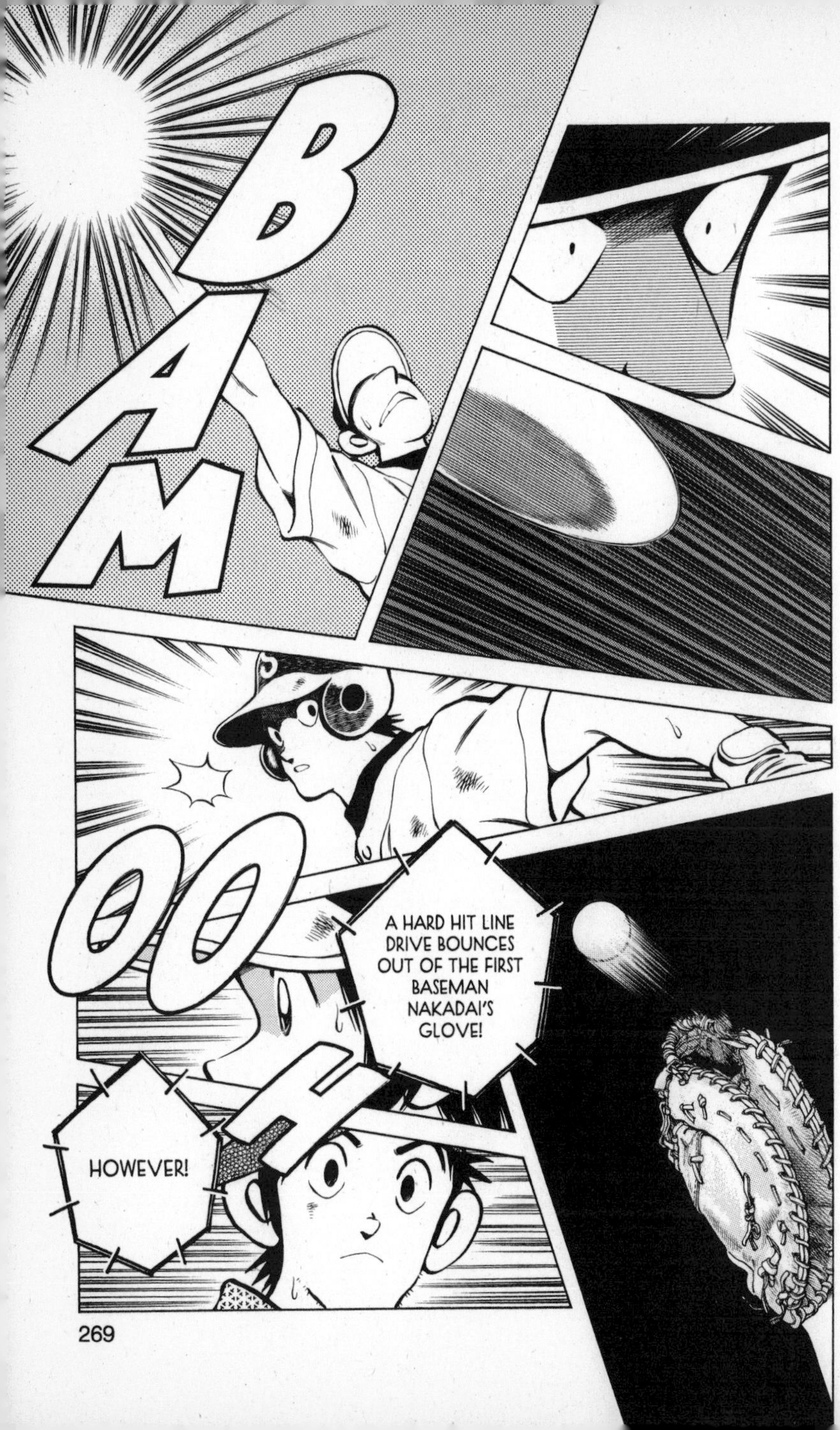
BAM
A HARD HIT LINE DRIVE BOUNCES OUT OF THE FIRST BASEMAN NAKADAI'S GLOVE!
OOH
HOWEVER!

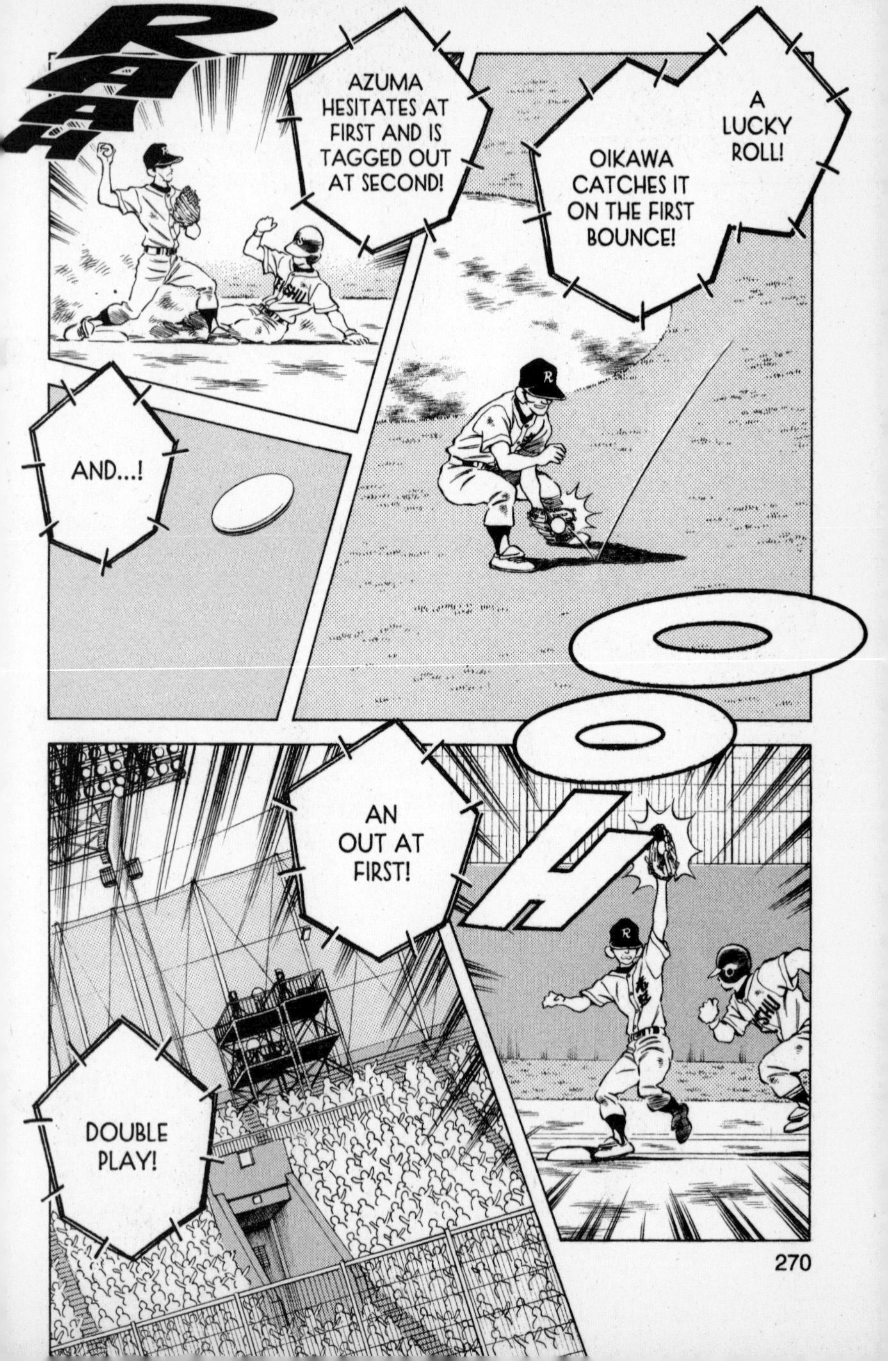
A LUCKY ROLL!
OIKAWA CATCHES IT ON THE FIRST BOUNCE!
RAAH
AZUMA HESITATES AT FIRST AND IS TAGGED OUT AT SECOND!
AND...!
OOH
AN OUT AT FIRST!
DOUBLE PLAY!

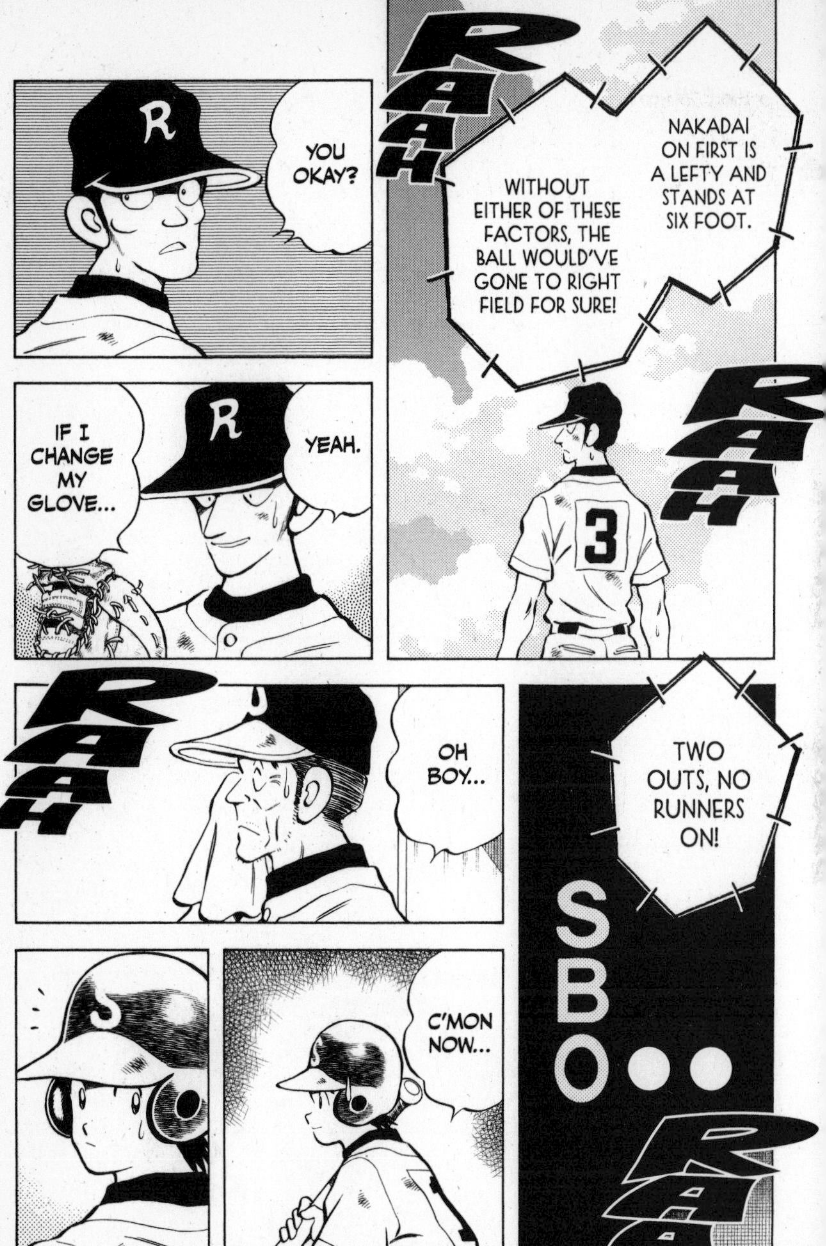
RAAH
NAKADAI ON FIRST IS A LEFTY AND STANDS AT SIX FOOT.
WITHOUT EITHER OF THESE FACTORS, THE BALL WOULD'VE GONE TO RIGHT FIELD FOR SURE!
RAAH
YOU OKAY?
YEAH.
IF I CHANGE MY GLOVE...
TWO OUTS, NO RUNNERS ON!
SBO
RAAH
OH BOY...
RAAH
C'MON NOW...

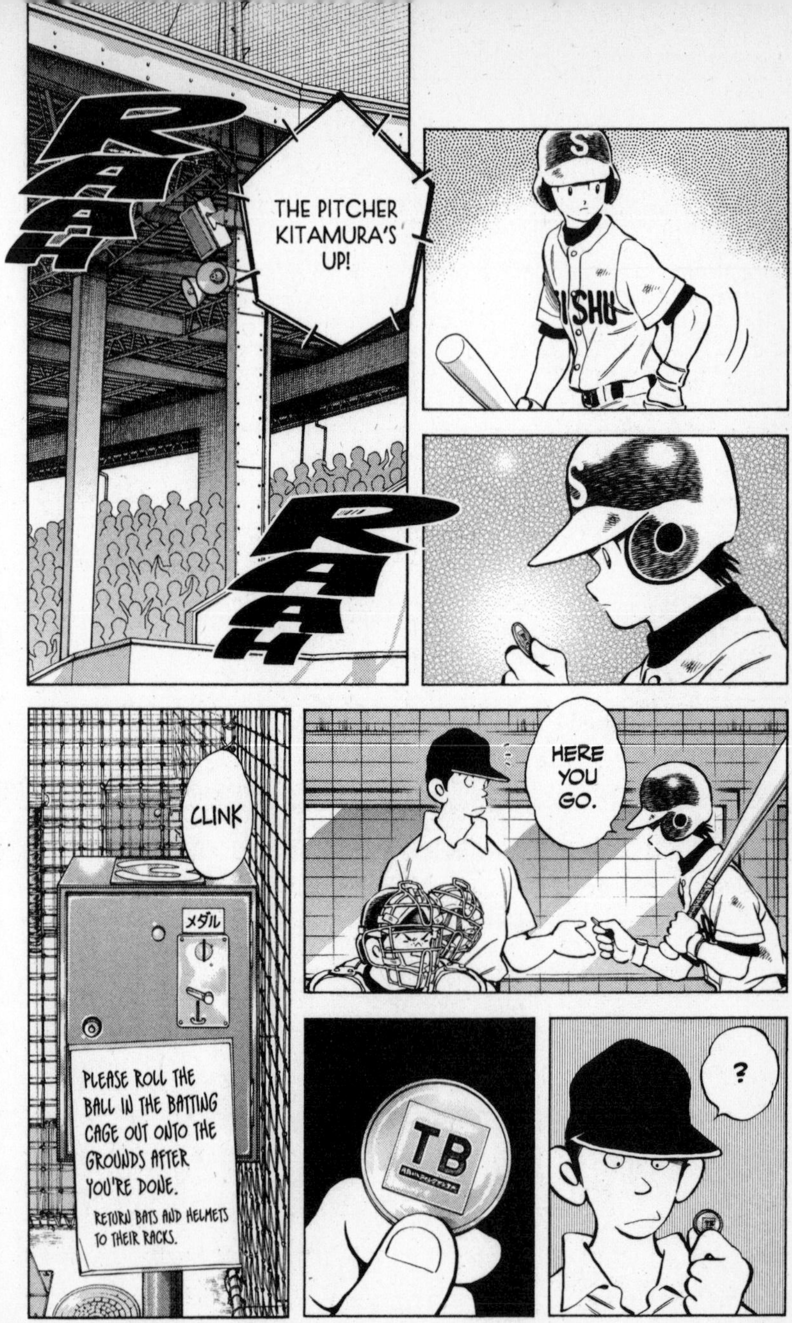
SHU
RAAH
THE PITCHER KITAMURA'S UP!
RAAH
HERE YOU GO.
?
TB
CLINK
メダル
PLEASE ROLL THE BALL IN THE BATTING CAGE OUT ONTO THE GROUNDS AFTER YOU'RE DONE.
RETURN BATS AND HELMETS TO THEIR RACKS.

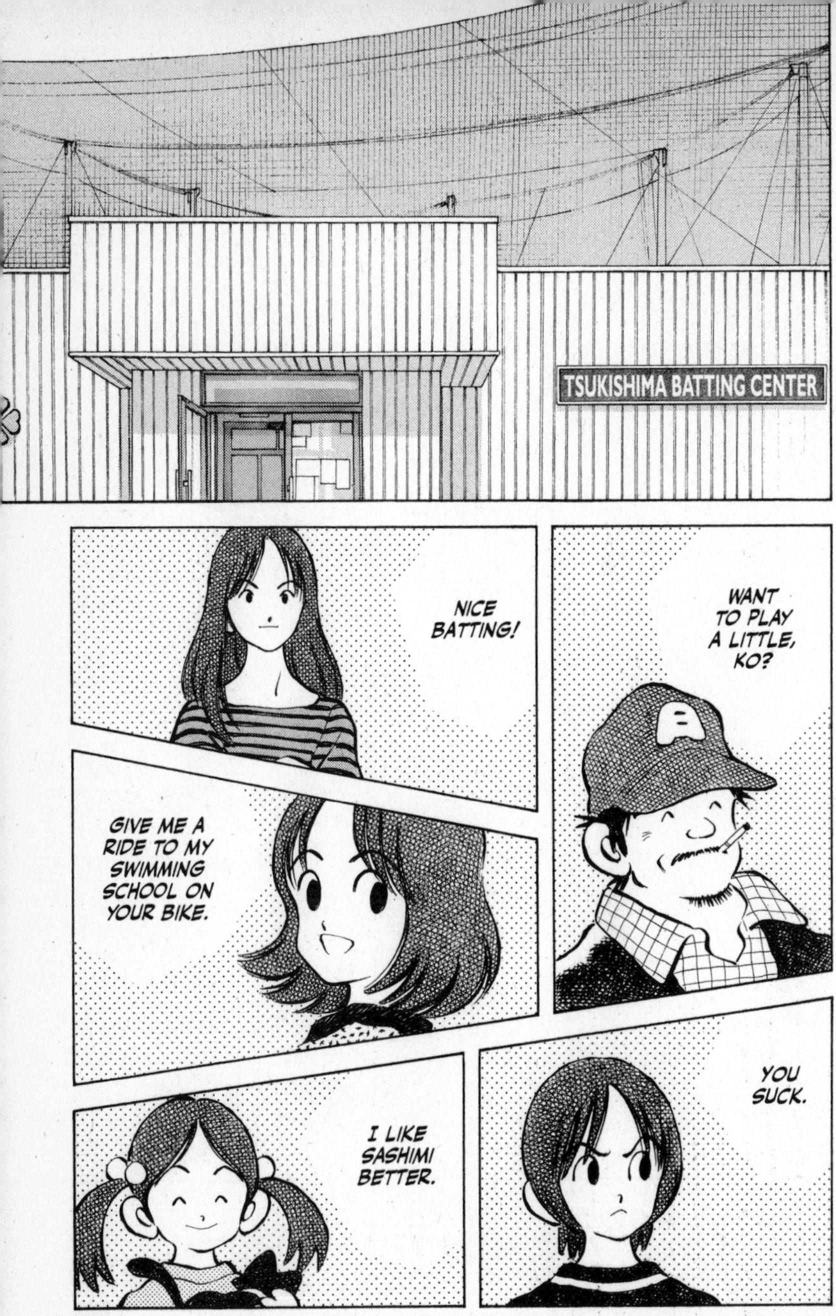
TSUKISHIMA BATTING CENTER
WANT TO PLAY A LITTLE, KO?
NICE BATTING!
GIVE ME A RIDE TO MY SWIMMING SCHOOL ON YOUR BIKE.
YOU SUCK.
I LIKE SASHIMI BETTER.

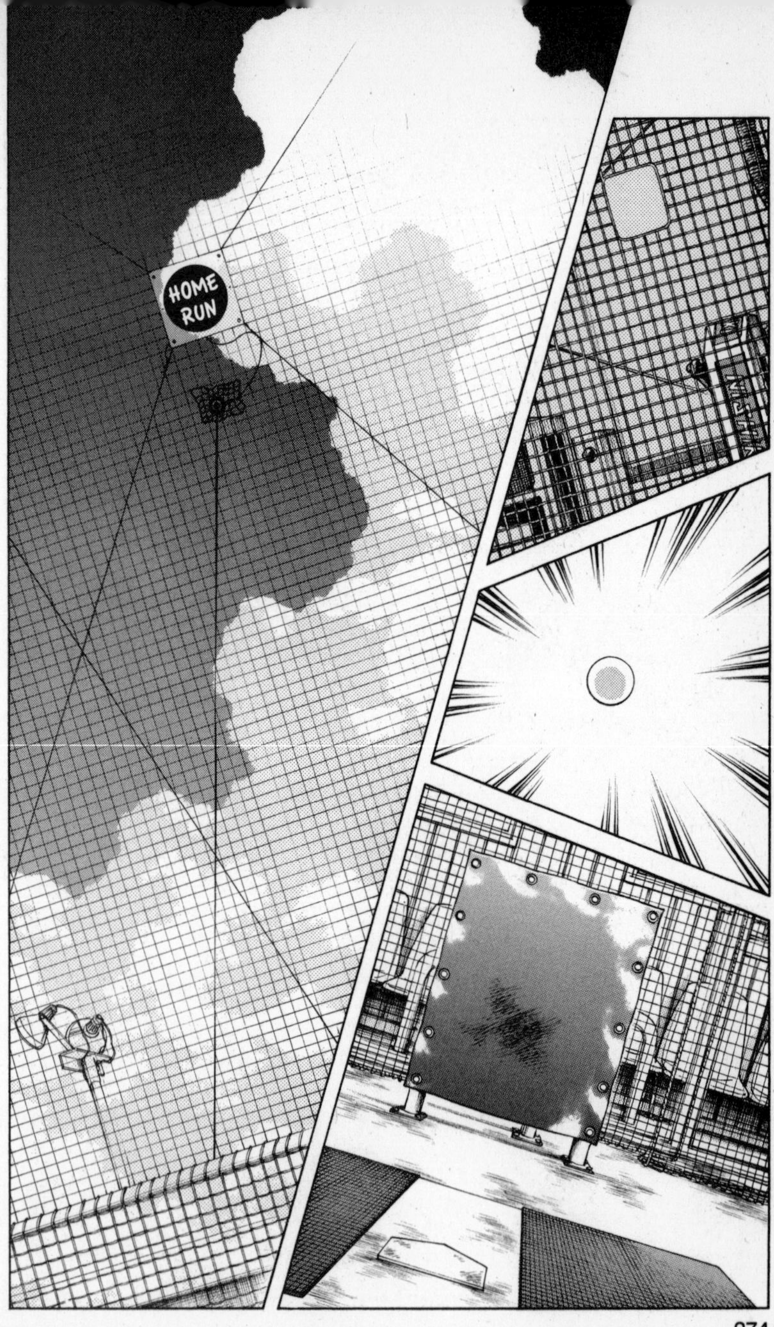
HOME RUN

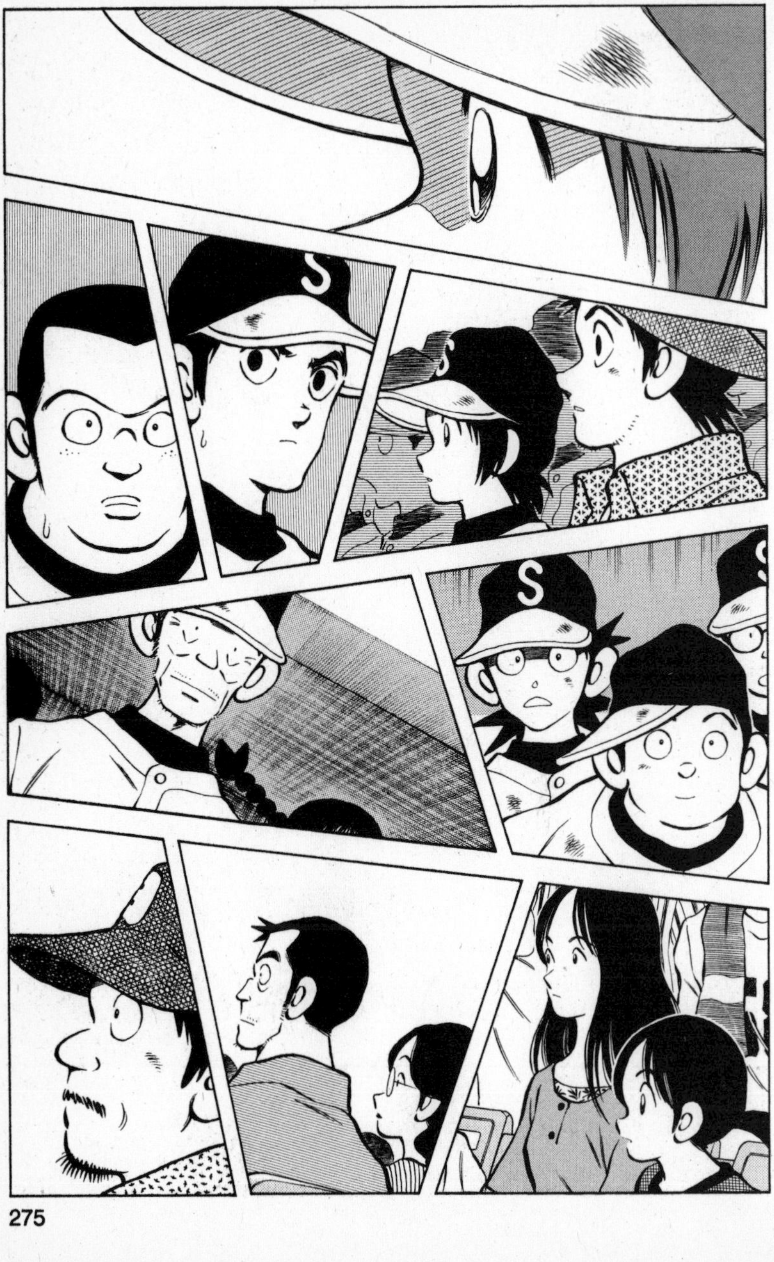

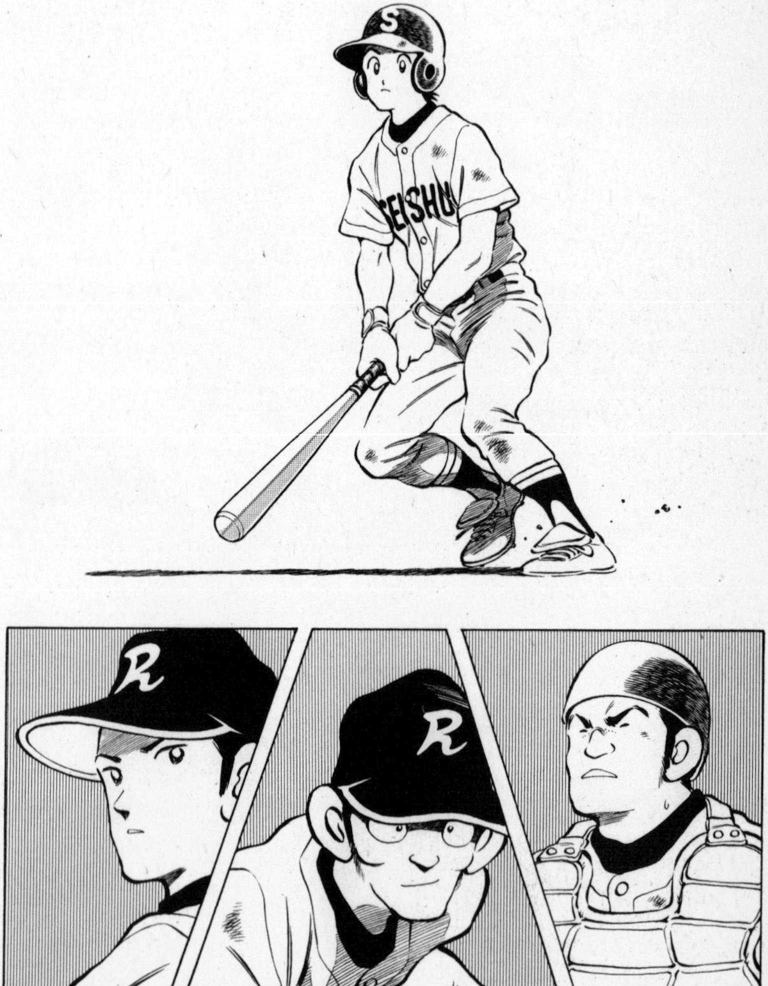

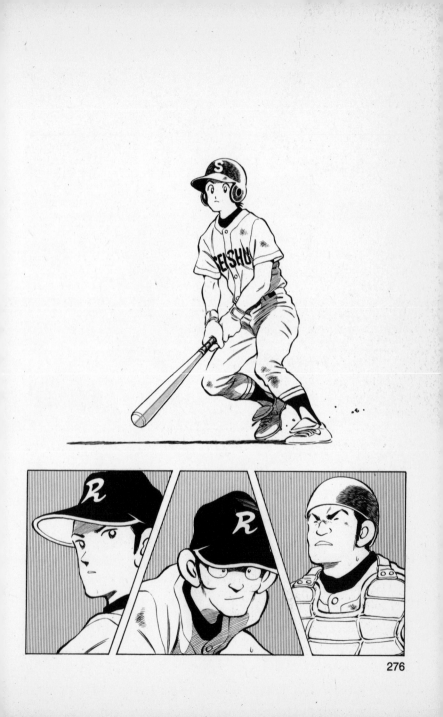

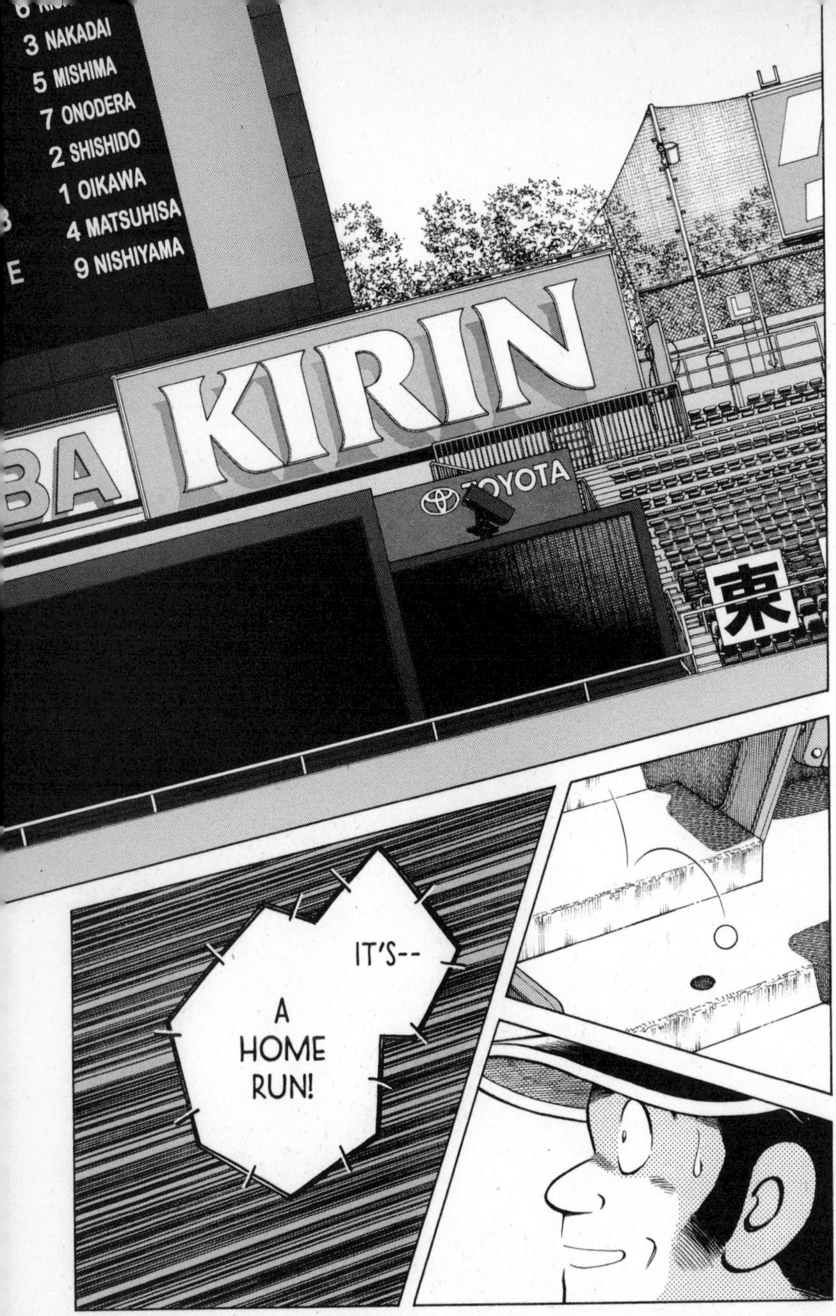
3 NAKADAI
5 MISHIMA
7 ONODERA
2 SHISHIDO
1 OIKAWA
4 MATSUHISA
9 NISHIYAMA
KIRIN
TOYOTA
IT'S--
A HOME RUN!

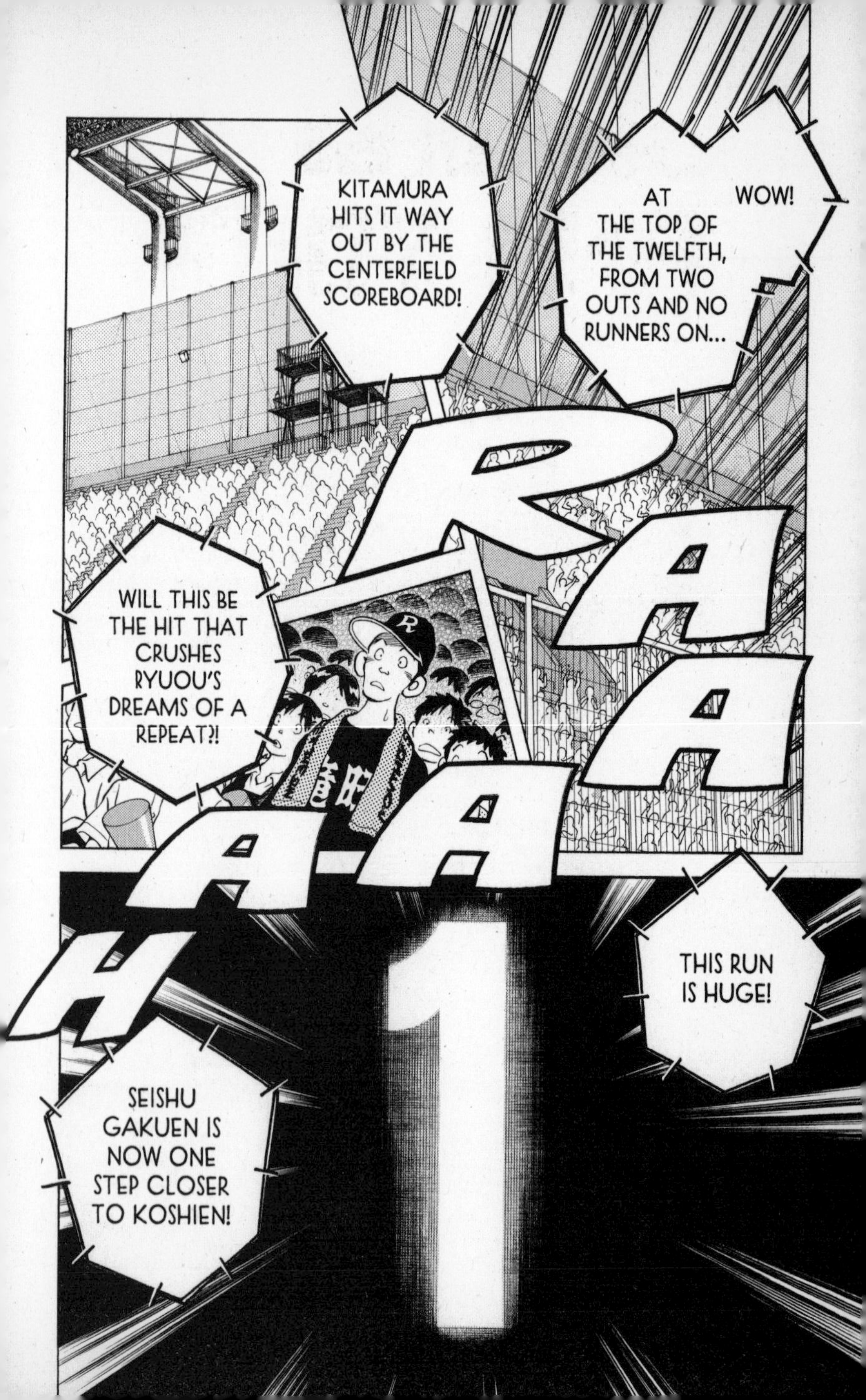
WOW!
AT THE TOP OF THE TWELFTH, FROM TWO OUTS AND NO RUNNERS ON...
KITAMURA HITS IT WAY OUT BY THE CENTERFIELD SCOREBOARD!
WILL THIS BE THE HIT THAT CRUSHES RYUOU'S DREAMS OF A REPEAT?!
RAAAAH
THIS RUN IS HUGE!
SEISHU GAKUEN IS NOW ONE STEP CLOSER TO KOSHIEN!
1

CHAPTER 156
AND YOU?

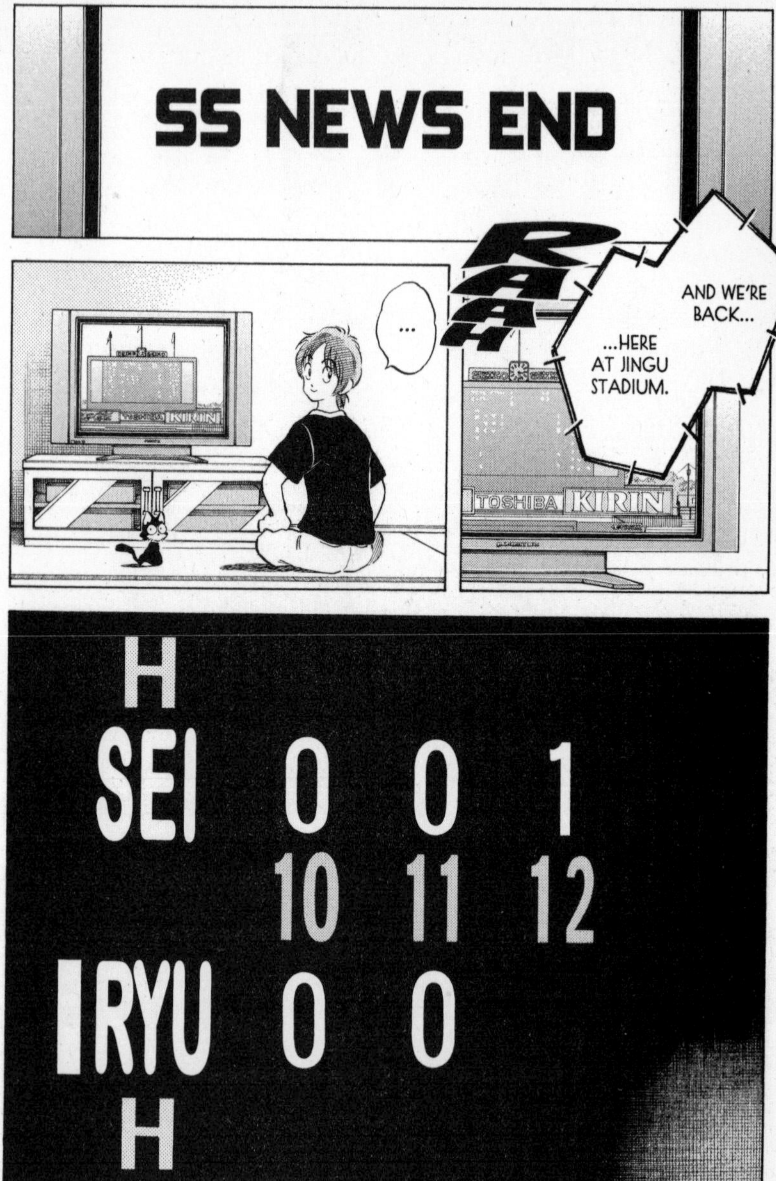
SS NEWS END
RAAAH
AND WE'RE BACK...
...HERE AT JINGU STADIUM.
TOSHIBA
KIRIN
...
H
SEI 0 0 1
10 11 12
IRYU 0 0
H

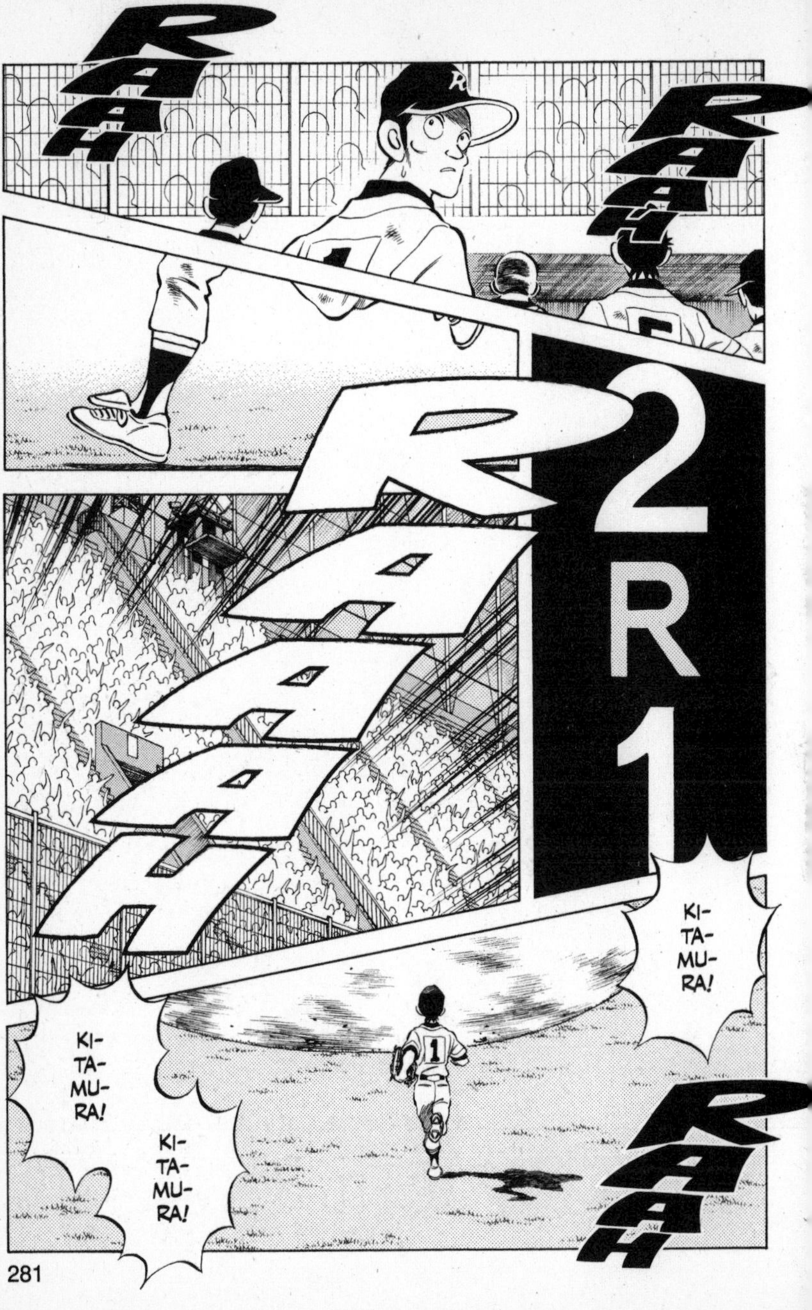
RAAH
RAAH
2R1
RAAAH
KI-TA-MU-RA!
RAAH
KI-TA-MU-RA!
KI-TA-MU-RA!

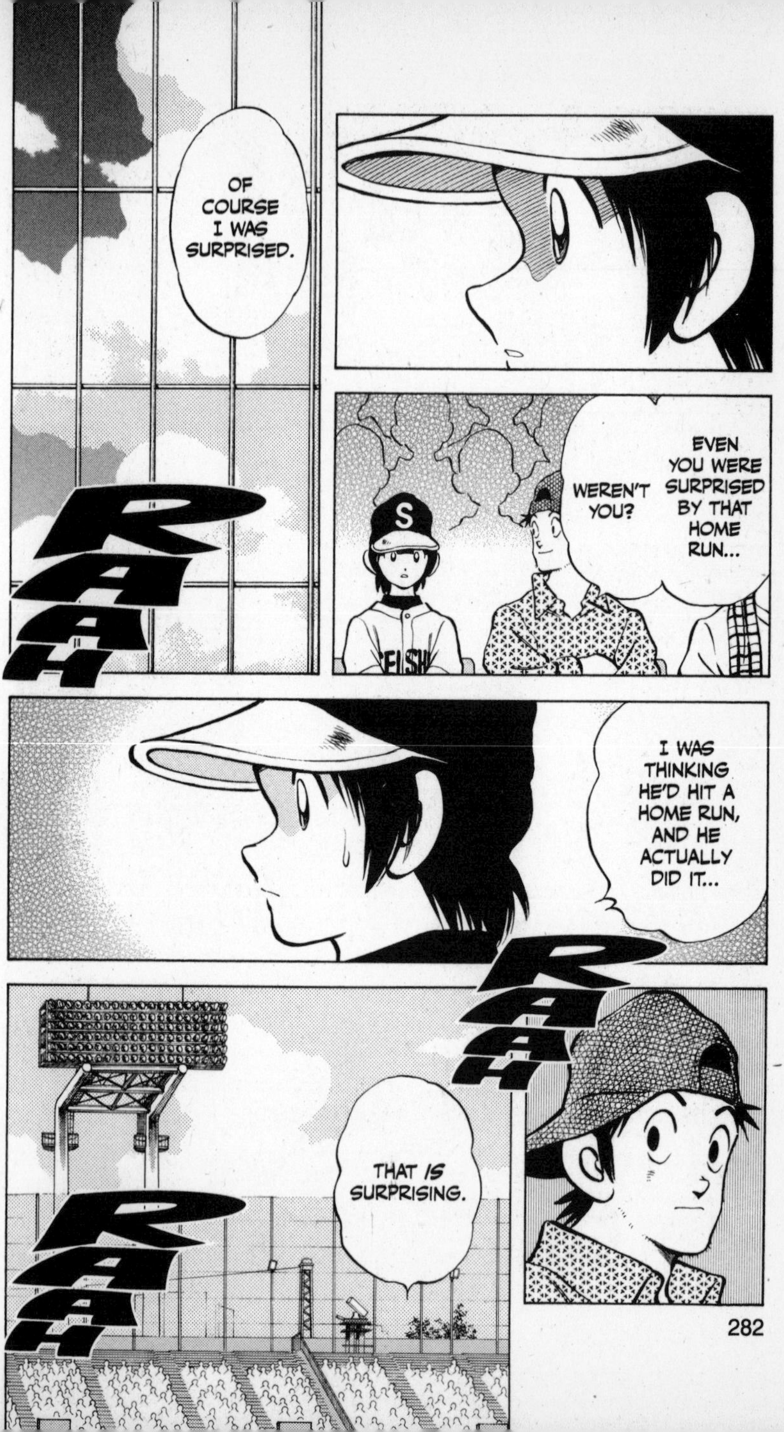
EVEN YOU WERE SURPRISED BY THAT HOME RUN...
WEREN'T YOU?
OF COURSE I WAS SURPRISED.
RAAAH
I WAS THINKING HE'D HIT A HOME RUN, AND HE ACTUALLY DID IT...
RAAAH
THAT *IS* SURPRISING.
RAAAH

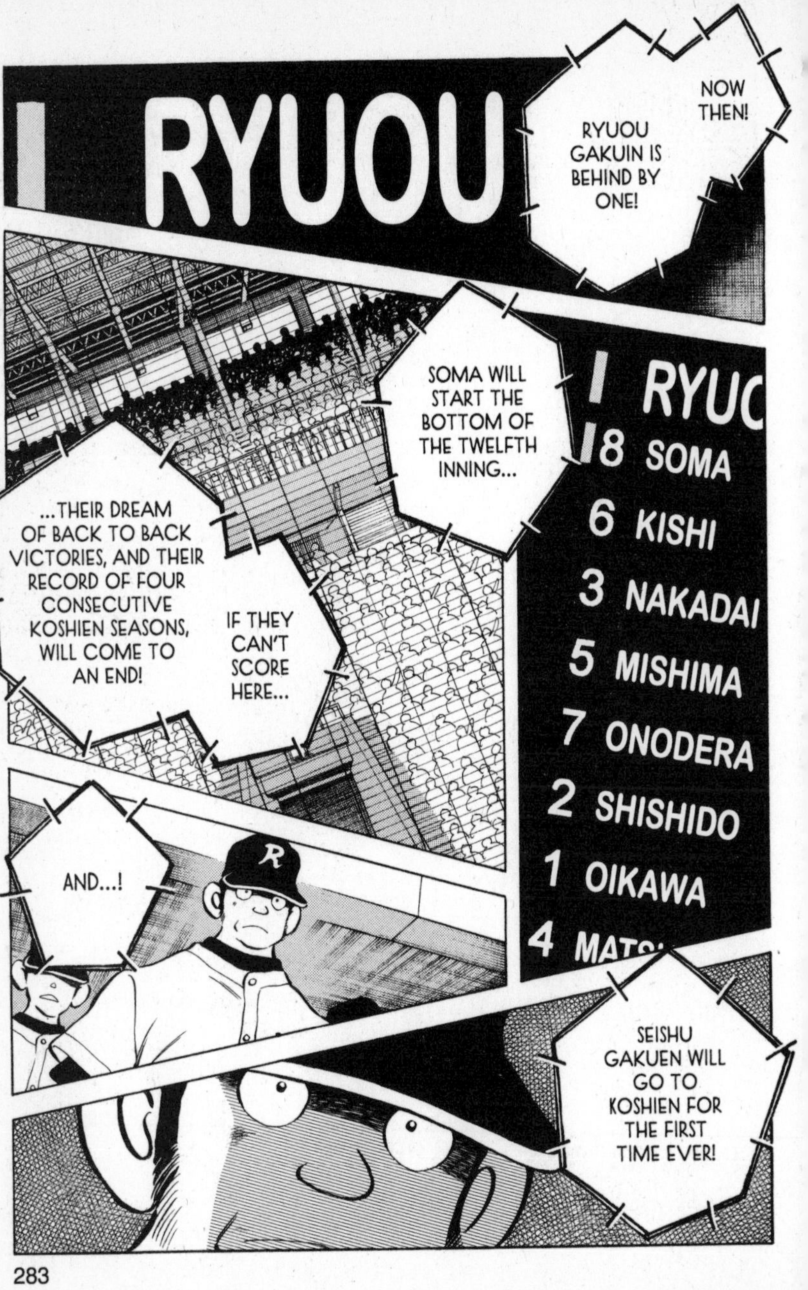
RYUOU
NOW THEN!
RYUOU GAKUIN IS BEHIND BY ONE!
SOMA WILL START THE BOTTOM OF THE TWELFTH INNING...
8 SOMA
6 KISHI
3 NAKADAI
5 MISHIMA
7 ONODERA
2 SHISHIDO
1 OIKAWA
IF THEY CAN'T SCORE HERE...
...THEIR DREAM OF BACK TO BACK VICTORIES, AND THEIR RECORD OF FOUR CONSECUTIVE KOSHIEN SEASONS, WILL COME TO AN END!
AND...!
SEISHU GAKUEN WILL GO TO KOSHIEN FOR THE FIRST TIME EVER!

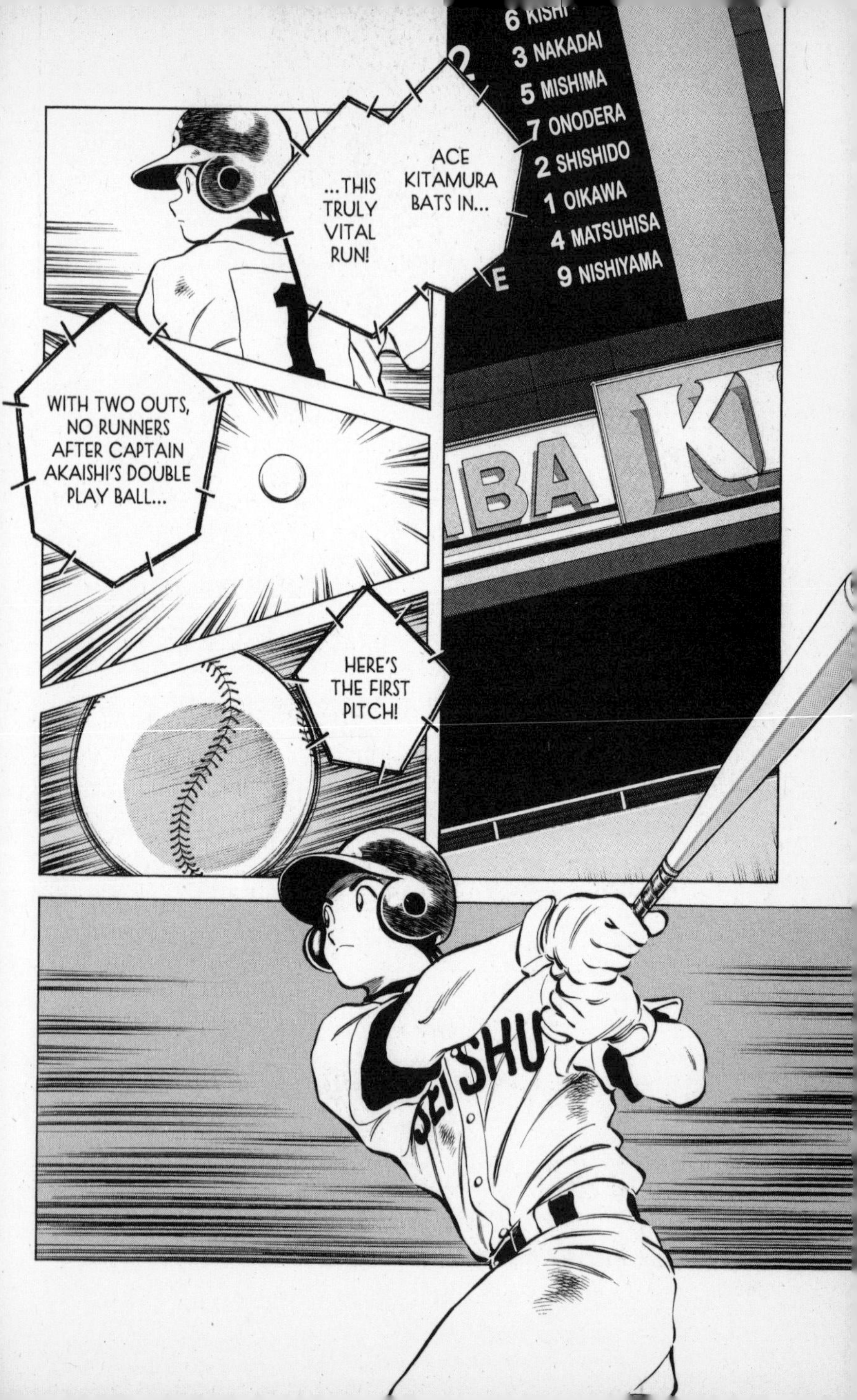
6 KISHI
3 NAKADAI
5 MISHIMA
7 ONODERA
2 SHISHIDO
1 OIKAWA
4 MATSUHISA
9 NISHIYAMA
ACE KITAMURA BATS IN...
...THIS TRULY VITAL RUN!
WITH TWO OUTS, NO RUNNERS AFTER CAPTAIN AKAISHI'S DOUBLE PLAY BALL...
HERE'S THE FIRST PITCH!
SEISHU

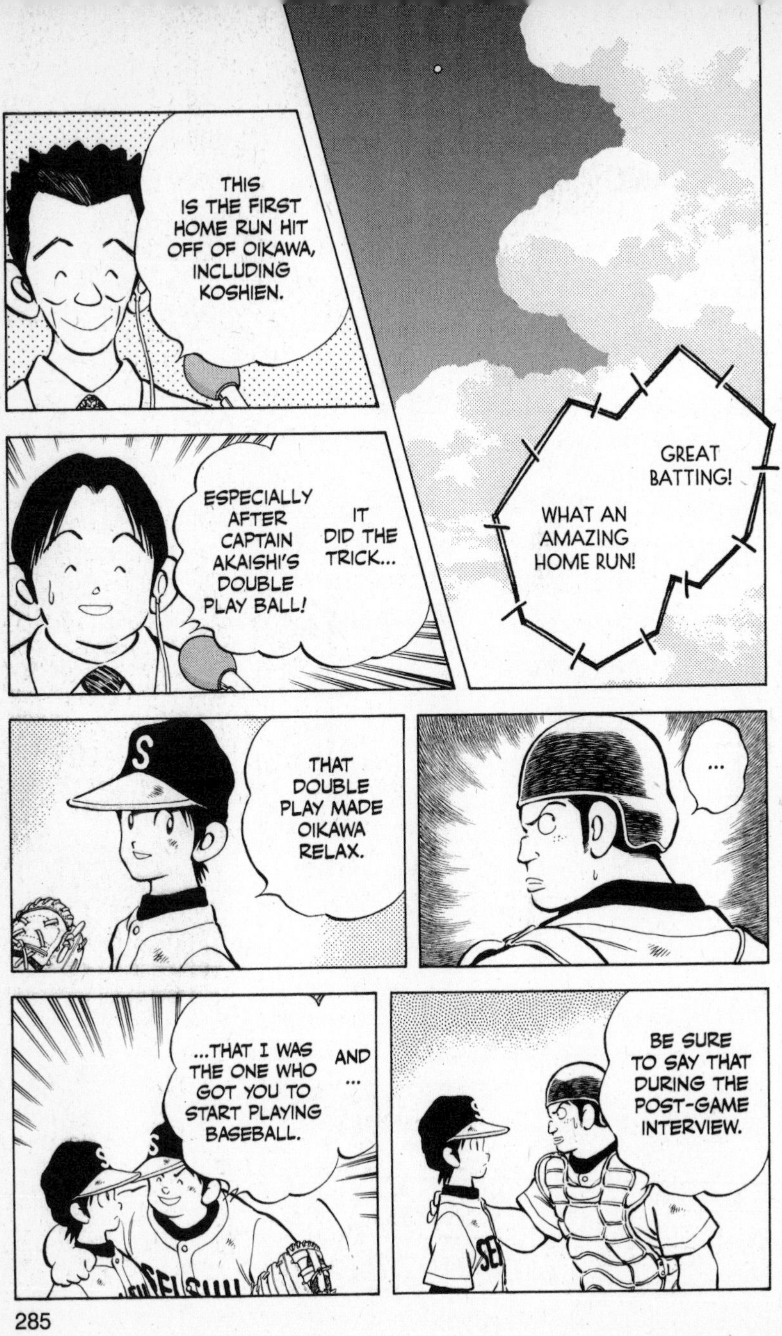
GREAT BATTING!
WHAT AN AMAZING HOME RUN!
THIS IS THE FIRST HOME RUN HIT OFF OF OIKAWA, INCLUDING KOSHIEN.
IT DID THE TRICK...
ESPECIALLY AFTER CAPTAIN AKAISHI'S DOUBLE PLAY BALL!
...
THAT DOUBLE PLAY MADE OIKAWA RELAX.
BE SURE TO SAY THAT DURING THE POST-GAME INTERVIEW.
AND...
...THAT I WAS THE ONE WHO GOT YOU TO START PLAYING BASEBALL.

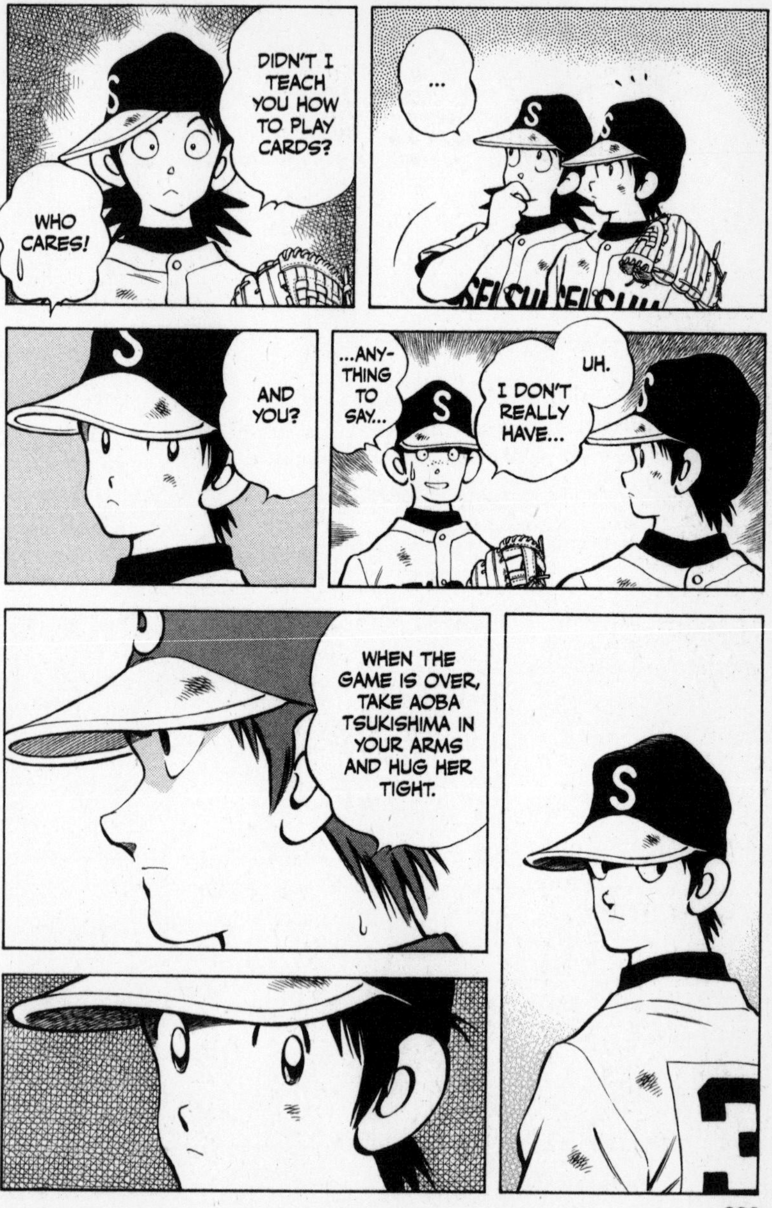
...
DIDN'T I TEACH YOU HOW TO PLAY CARDS?
WHO CARES!
UH. I DON'T REALLY HAVE...
...ANY-THING TO SAY...
AND YOU?
WHEN THE GAME IS OVER, TAKE AOBA TSUKISHIMA IN YOUR ARMS AND HUG HER TIGHT.

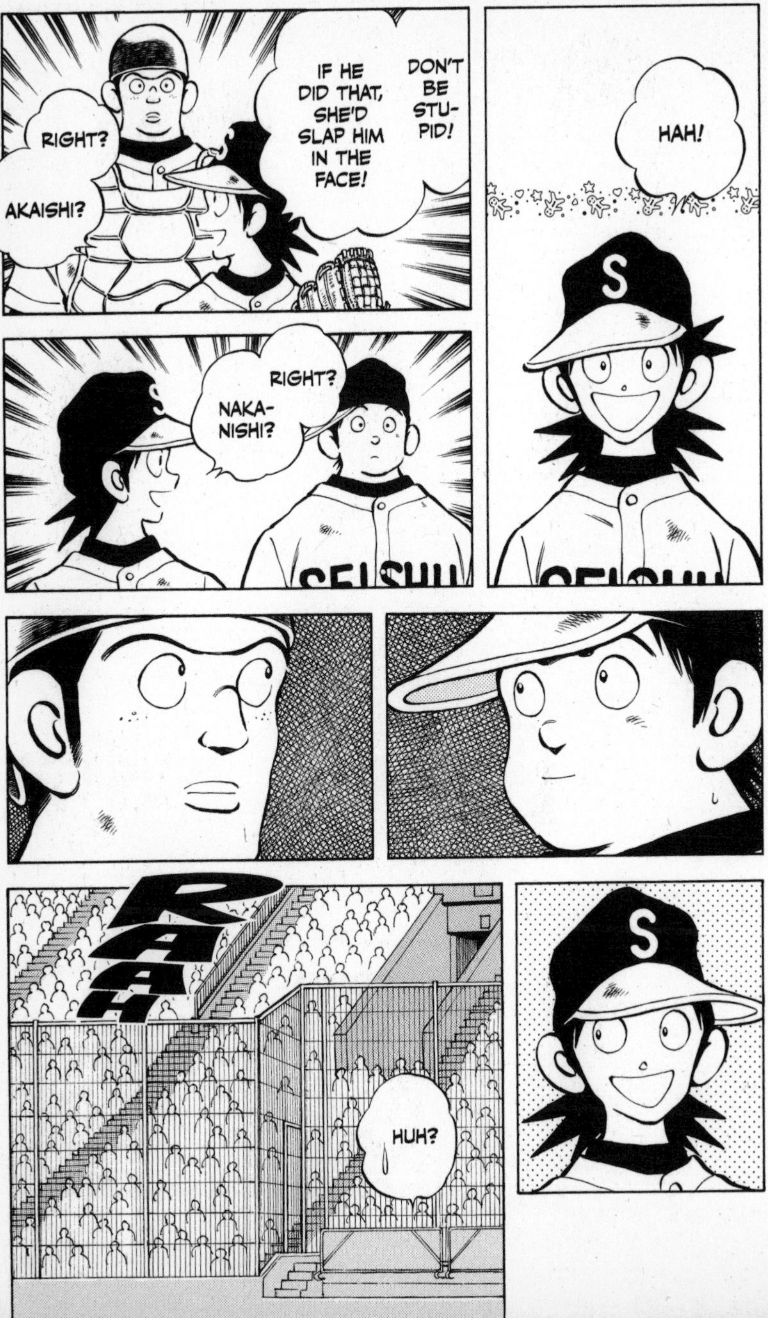
HAH!
DON'T BE STU-PID!
IF HE DID THAT, SHE'D SLAP HIM IN THE FACE!
RIGHT?
AKAISHI?
RIGHT?
NAKA-NISHI?
SEISHU
SEISHU
RAAAH
HUH?

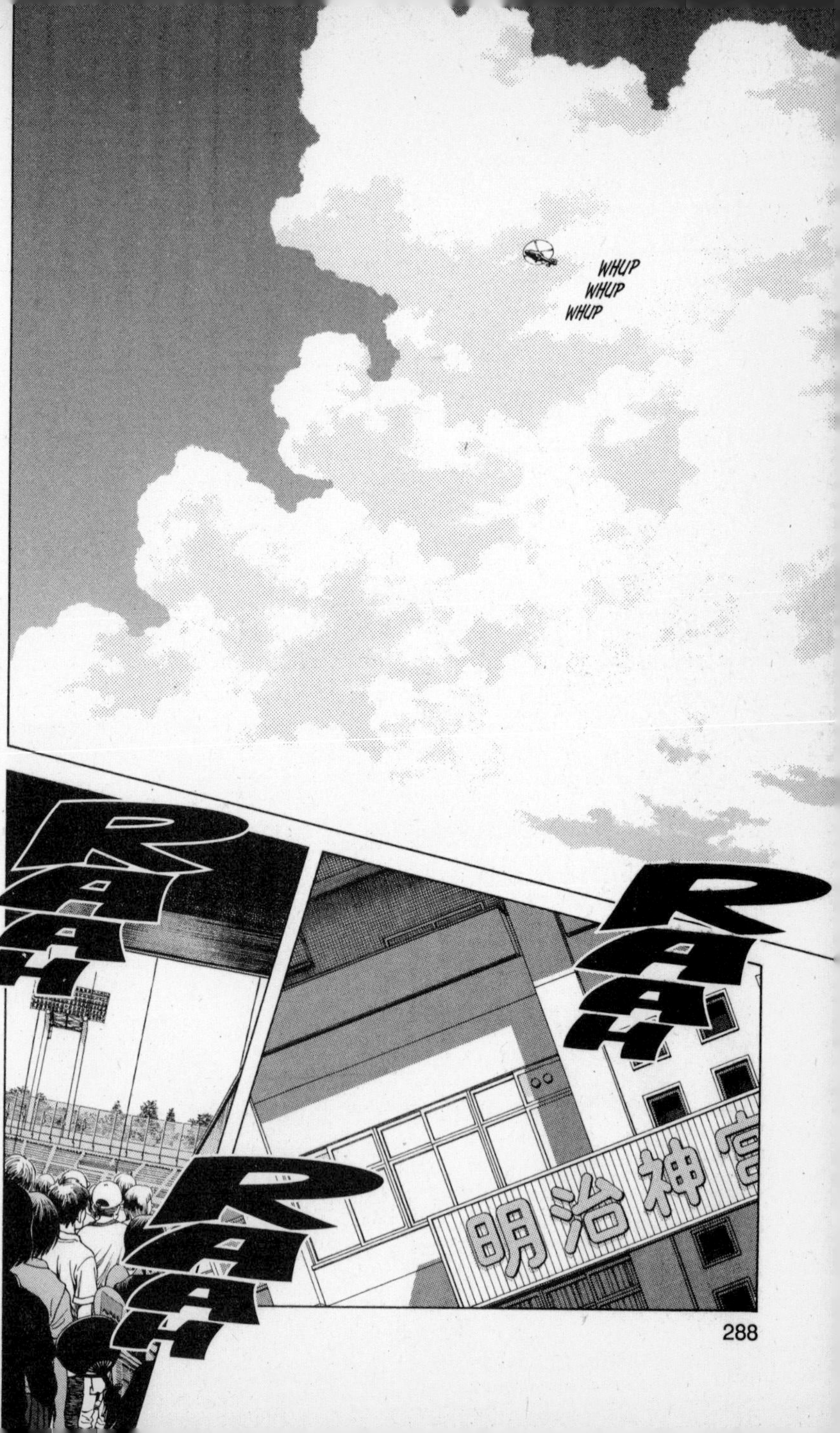
WHUP
WHUP
WHUP
RAAH
明治神
RAAH
RAAH

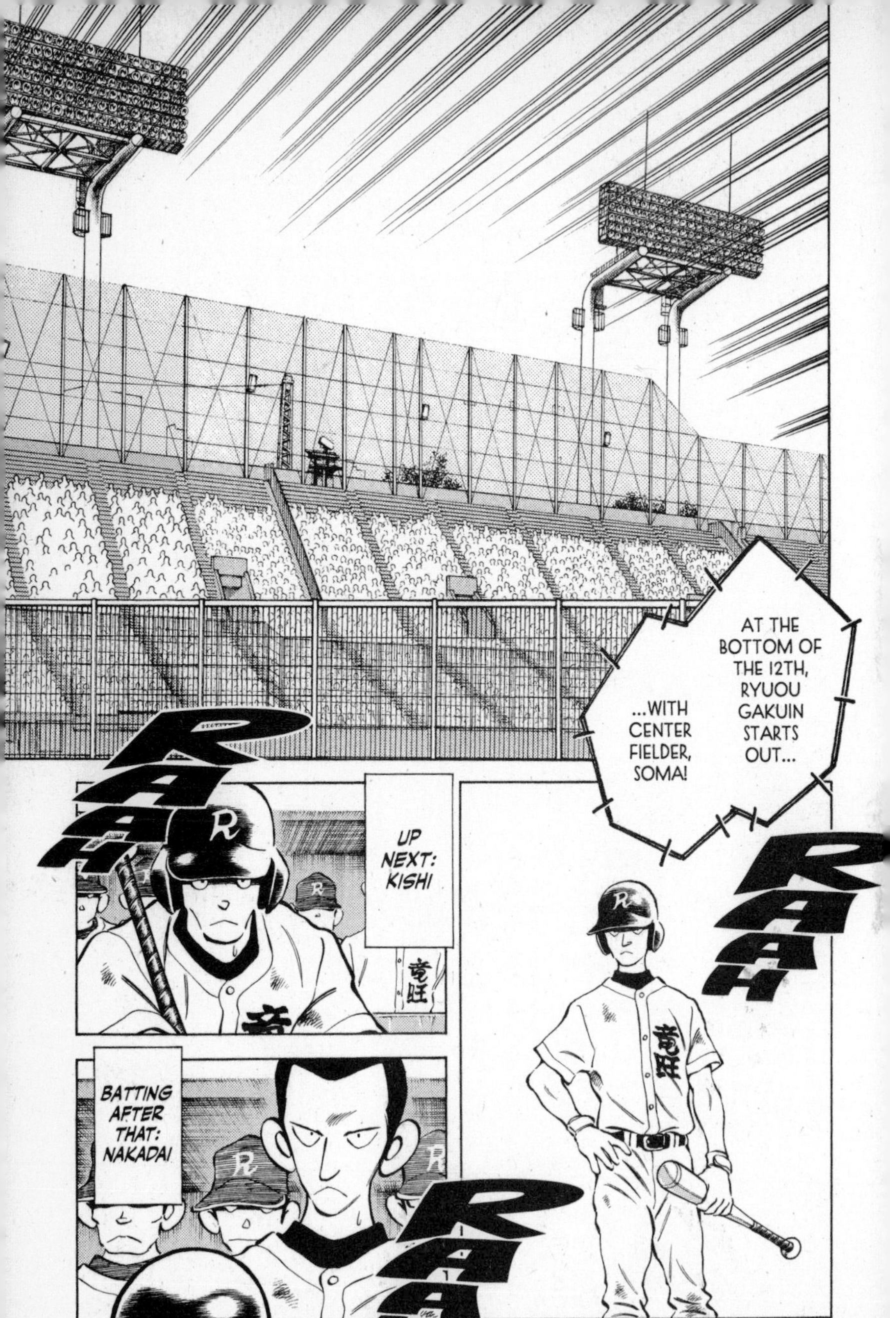

AT THE BOTTOM OF THE 12TH, RYUOU GAKUIN STARTS OUT...
...WITH CENTER FIELDER, SOMA!
RAAH
RAAH
UP NEXT: KISHI
BATTING AFTER THAT: NAKADAI
RAAH

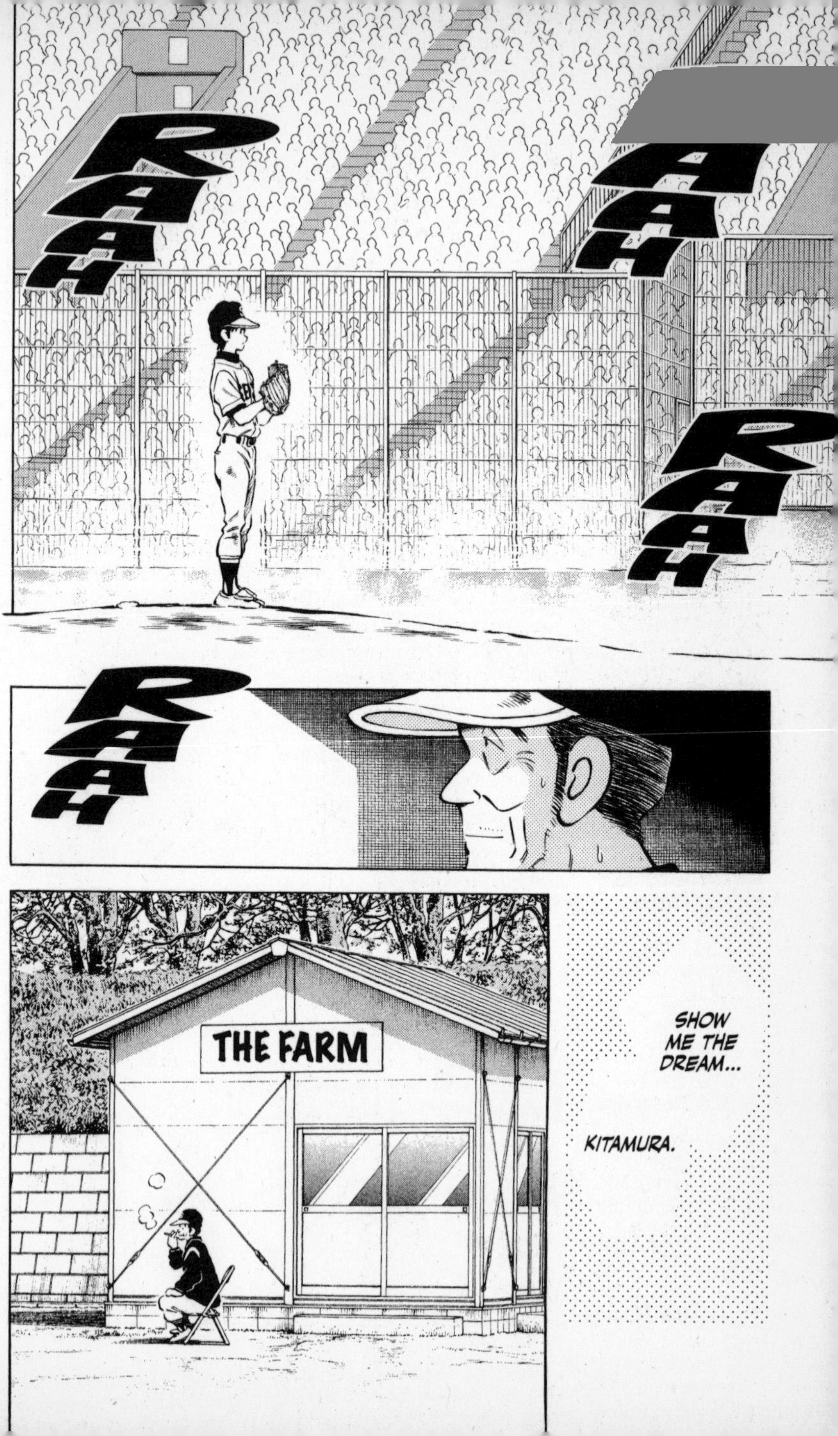
AAH
RAAH
RAAH
RAAH
SHOW ME THE DREAM...
KITAMURA.
THE FARM

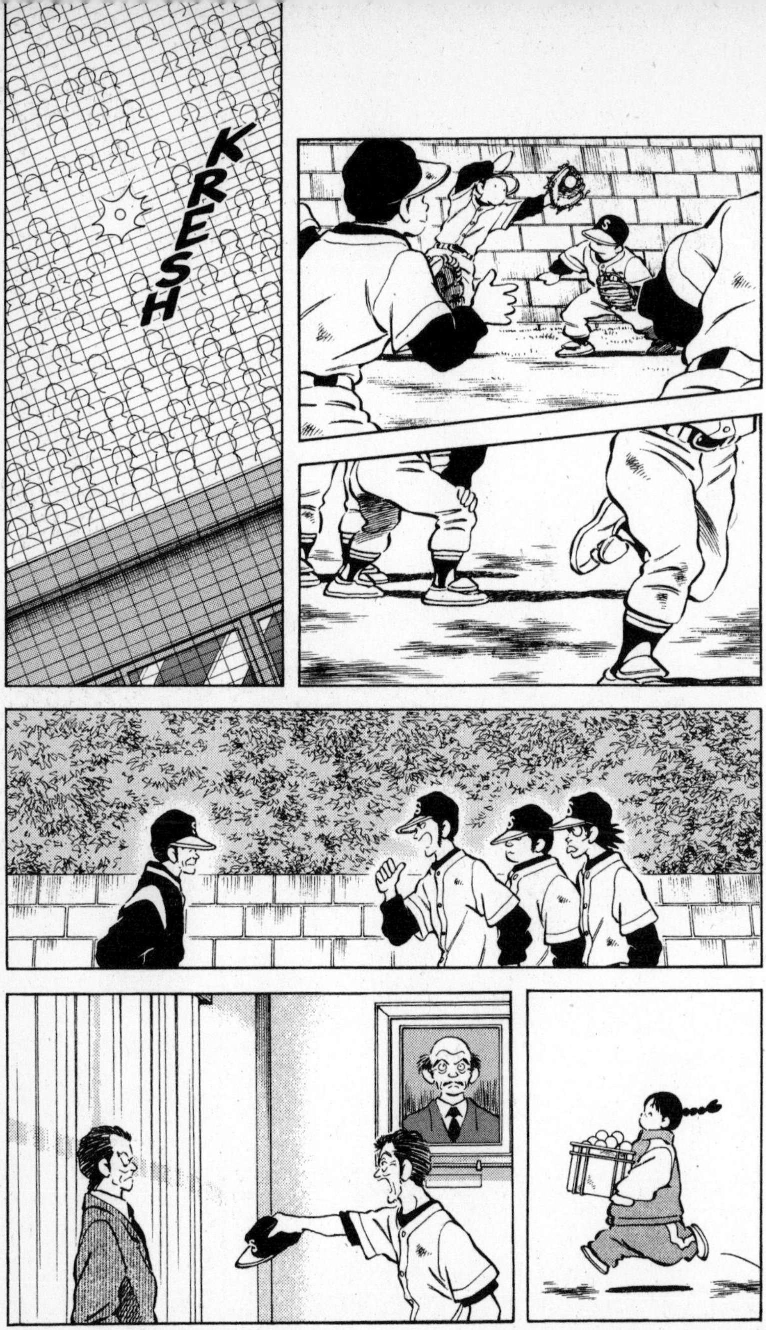
KRESH

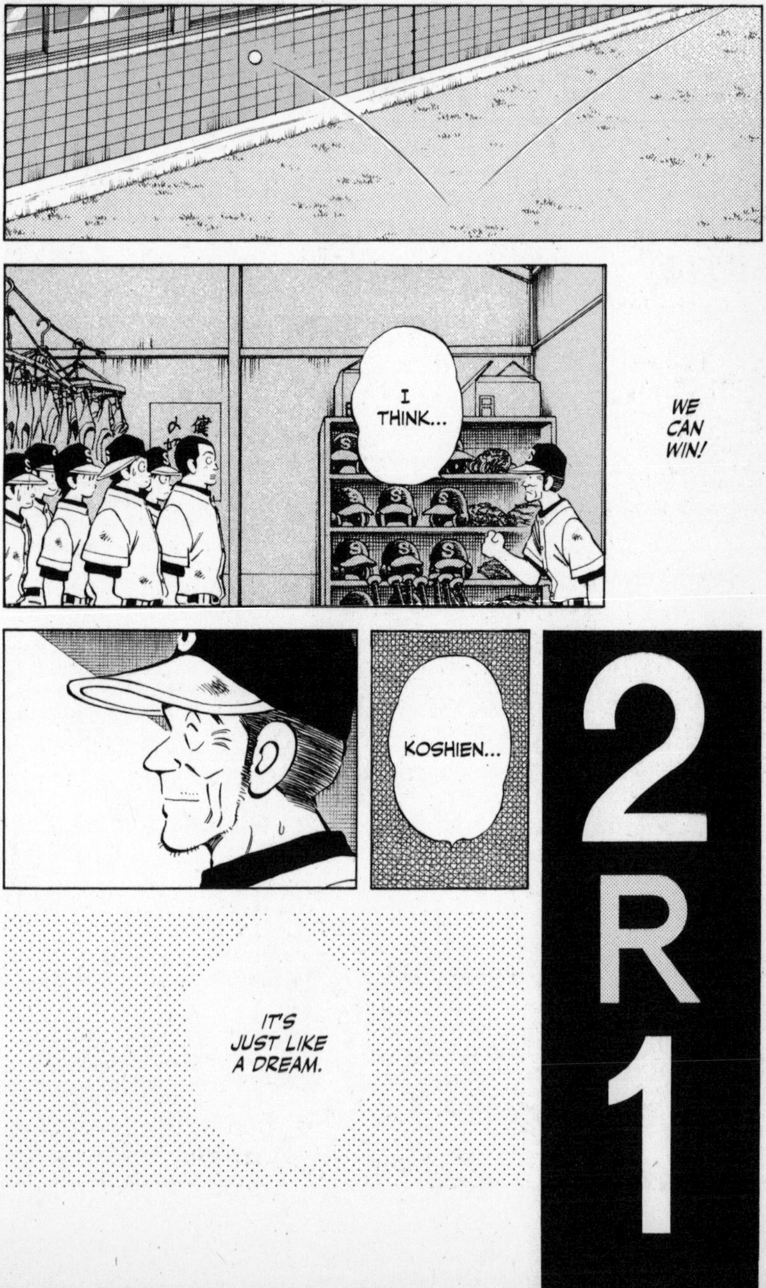
I THINK...
WE CAN WIN!
2R1
KOSHIEN...
IT'S JUST LIKE A DREAM.

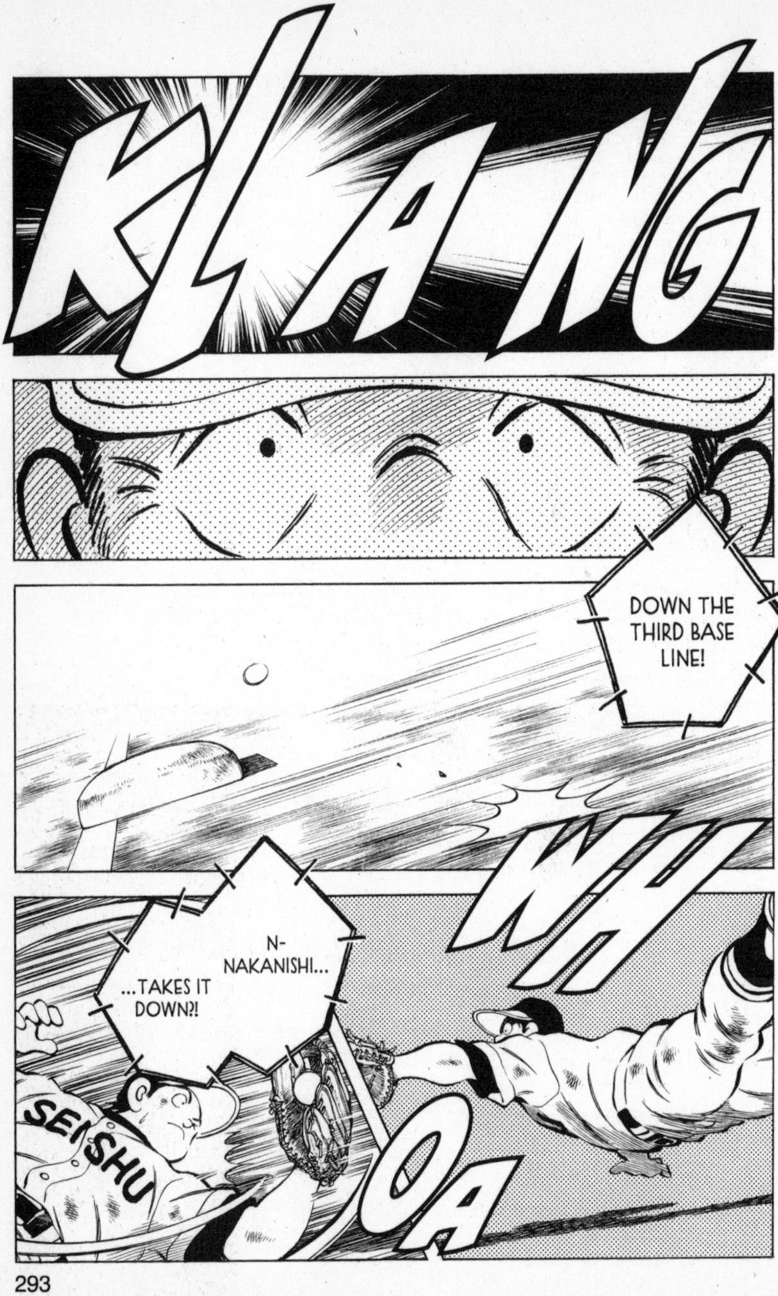
KLANG
DOWN THE THIRD BASE LINE!
WHOA
N-NAKANISHI...
...TAKES IT DOWN?!
SEISHU

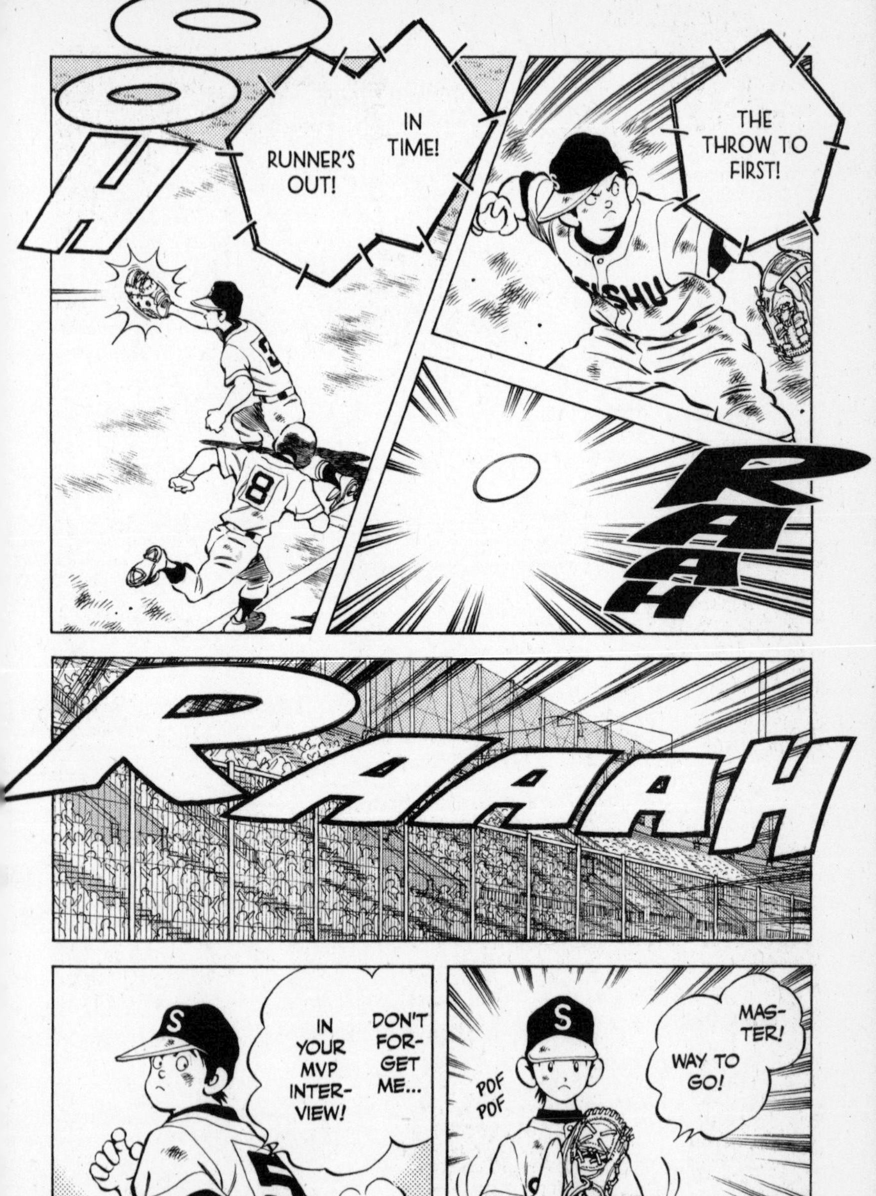
THE THROW TO FIRST!
RAAH
IN TIME!
RUNNER'S OUT!
OOOH
RAAAH
MAS-TER!
WAY TO GO!
POF POF
DON'T FOR-GET ME...
IN YOUR MVP INTER-VIEW!

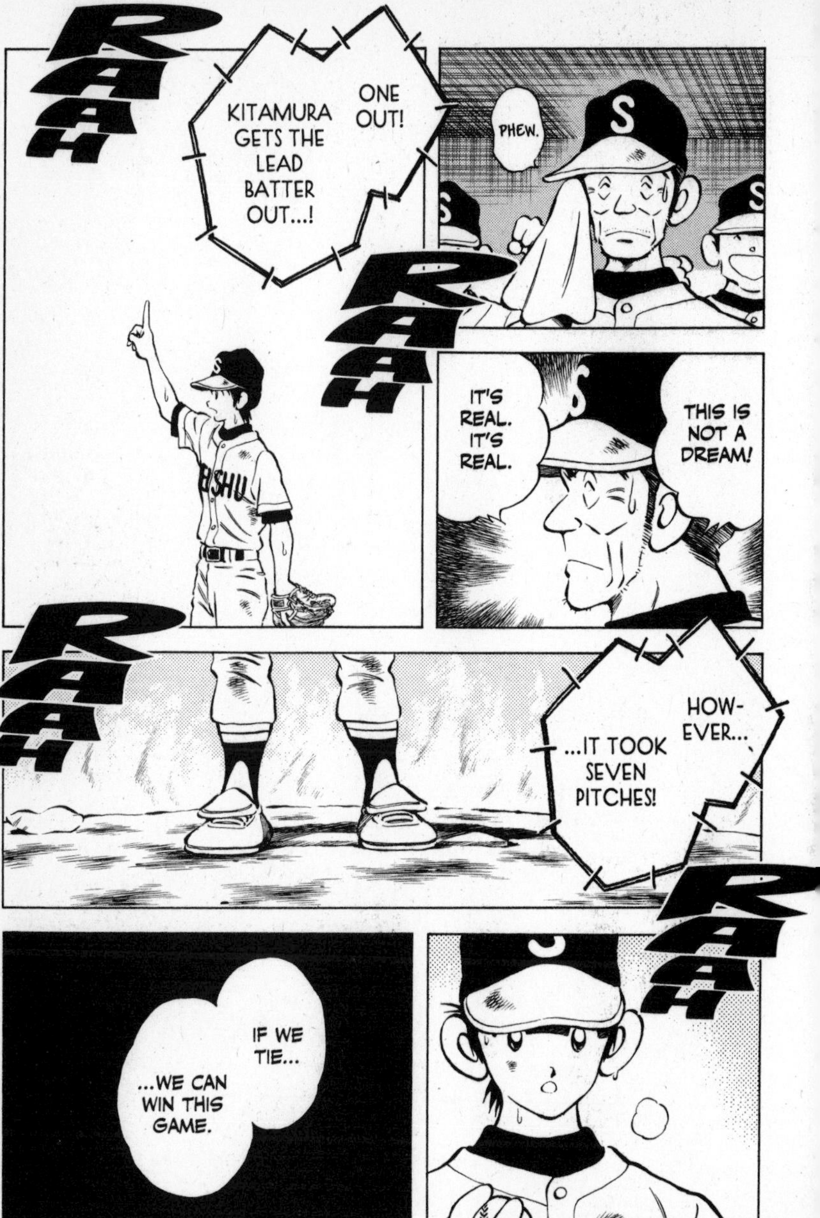
PHEW.
THIS IS NOT A DREAM!
IT'S REAL. IT'S REAL.
RAAH
ONE OUT!
KITAMURA GETS THE LEAD BATTER OUT...!
RAAH
HOW-EVER...
...IT TOOK SEVEN PITCHES!
RAAH
RAAH
IF WE TIE...
...WE CAN WIN THIS GAME.

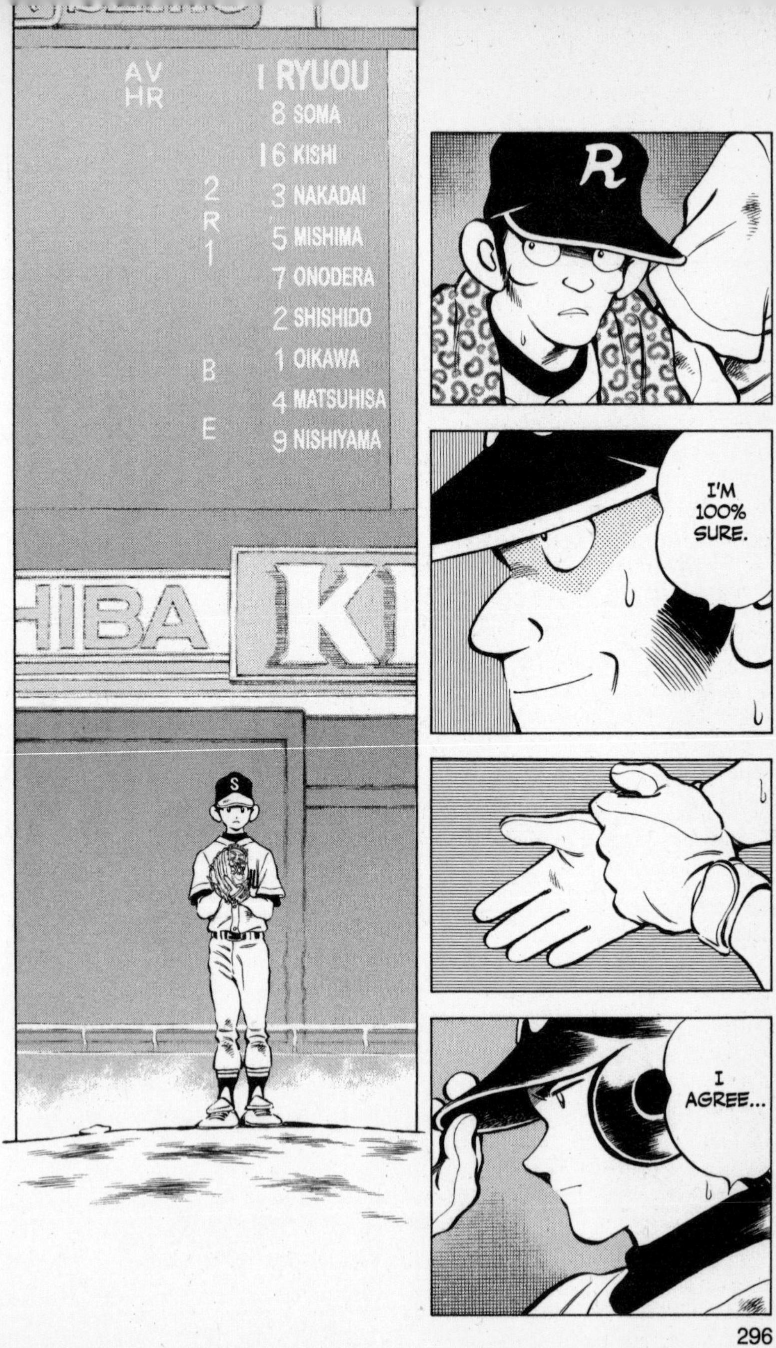
I'M 100% SURE.
I AGREE...
AV
HR
1 RYUOU
8 SOMA
16 KISHI
2 3 NAKADAI
R 5 MISHIMA
1 7 ONODERA
2 SHISHIDO
B 1 OIKAWA
4 MATSUHISA
E 9 NISHIYAMA
HIBA
K

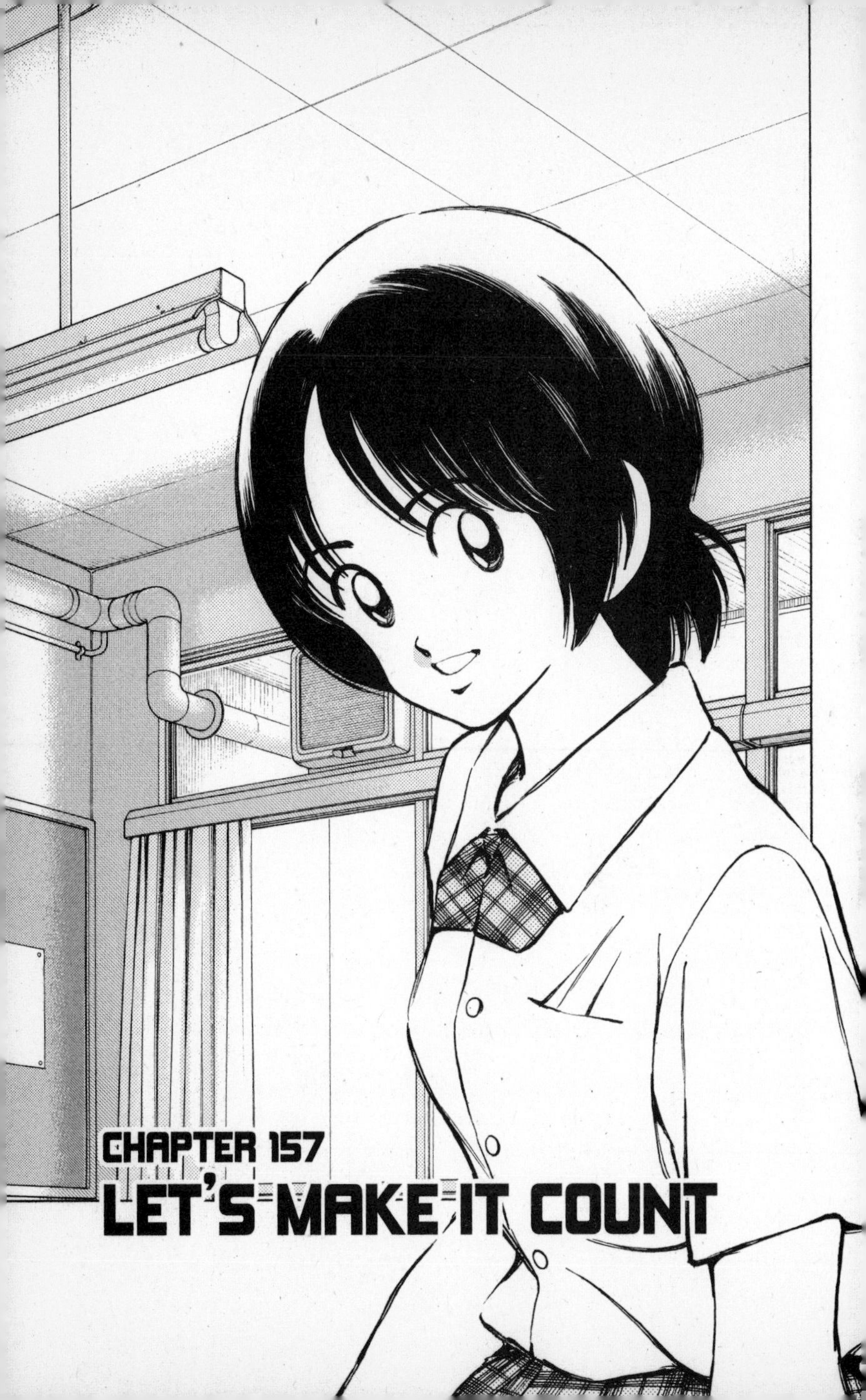
CHAPTER 157
LET'S MAKE IT COUNT

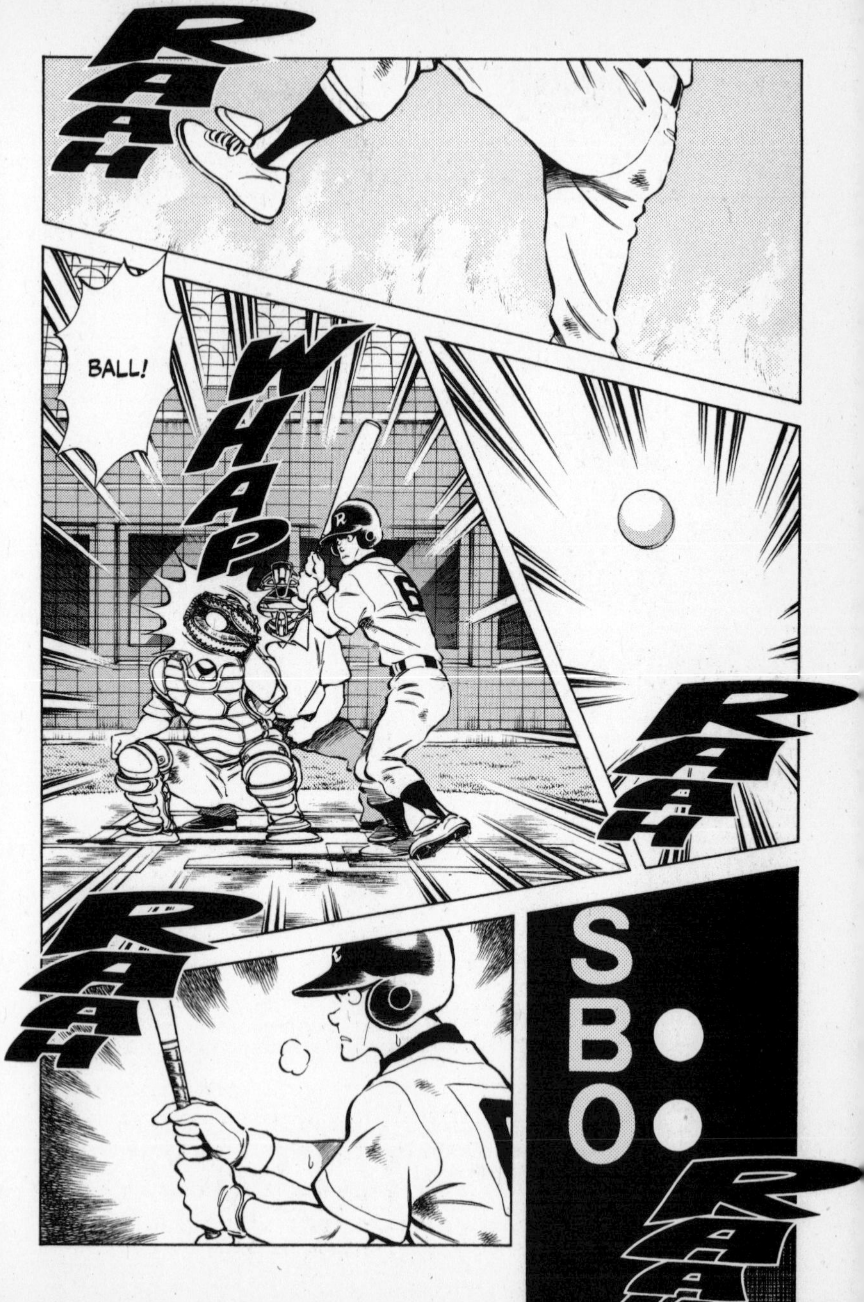
RAAH
RAAH
WHAP
BALL!
S
B
O
RAAH
RAAH

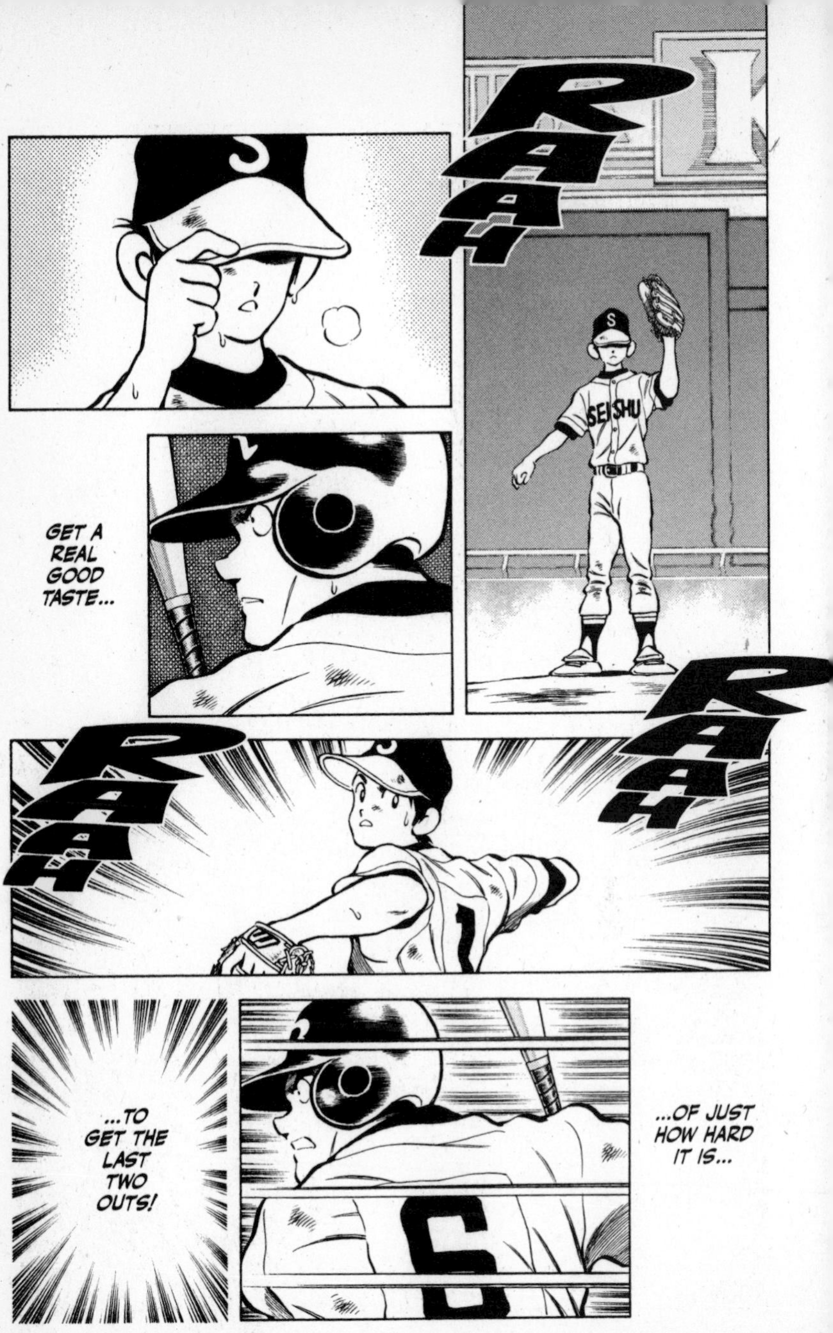
RAAH
GET A REAL GOOD TASTE...
RAAH
RAAH
...OF JUST HOW HARD IT IS...
...TO GET THE LAST TWO OUTS!

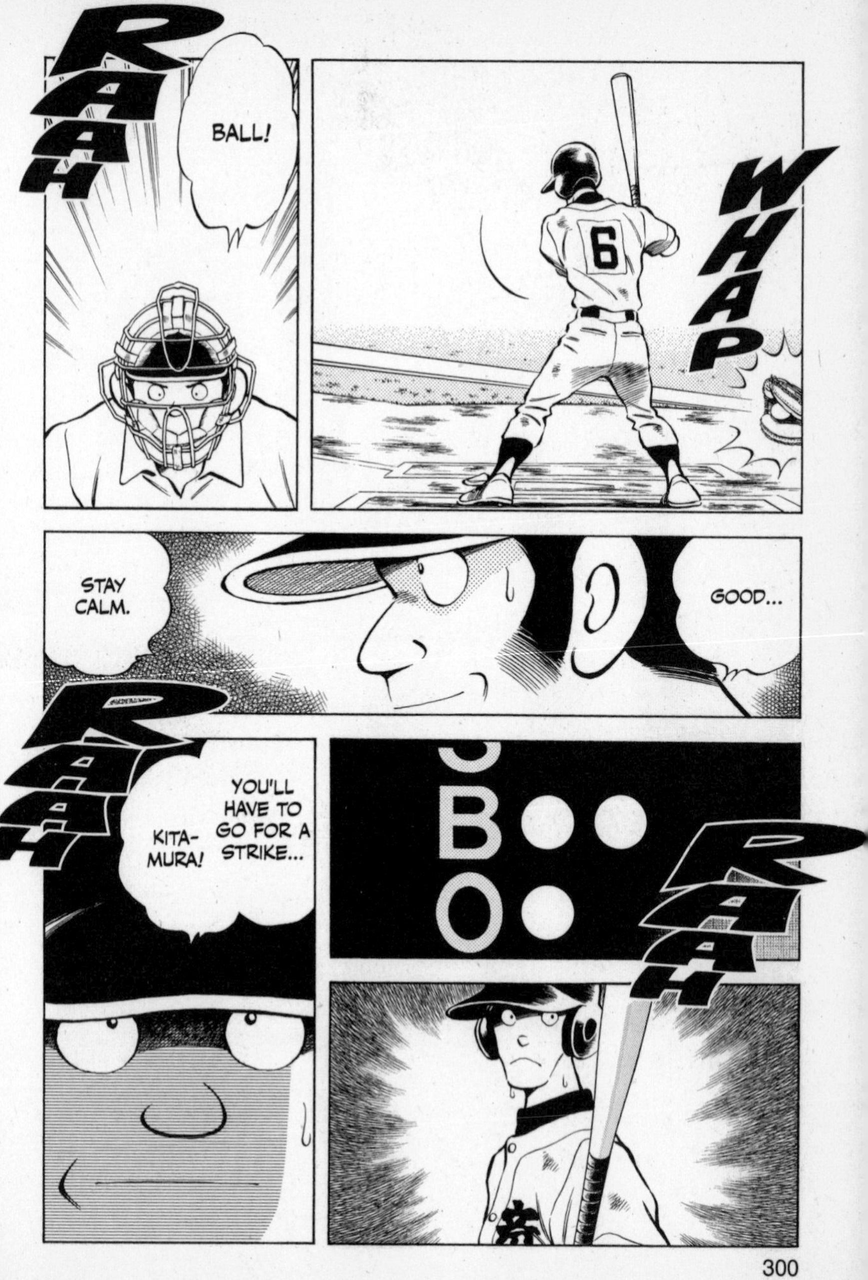
WHAP
BALL!
RAAH
GOOD...
STAY CALM.
B
O
RAAH
RAAH
KITA-MURA! YOU'LL HAVE TO GO FOR A STRIKE...

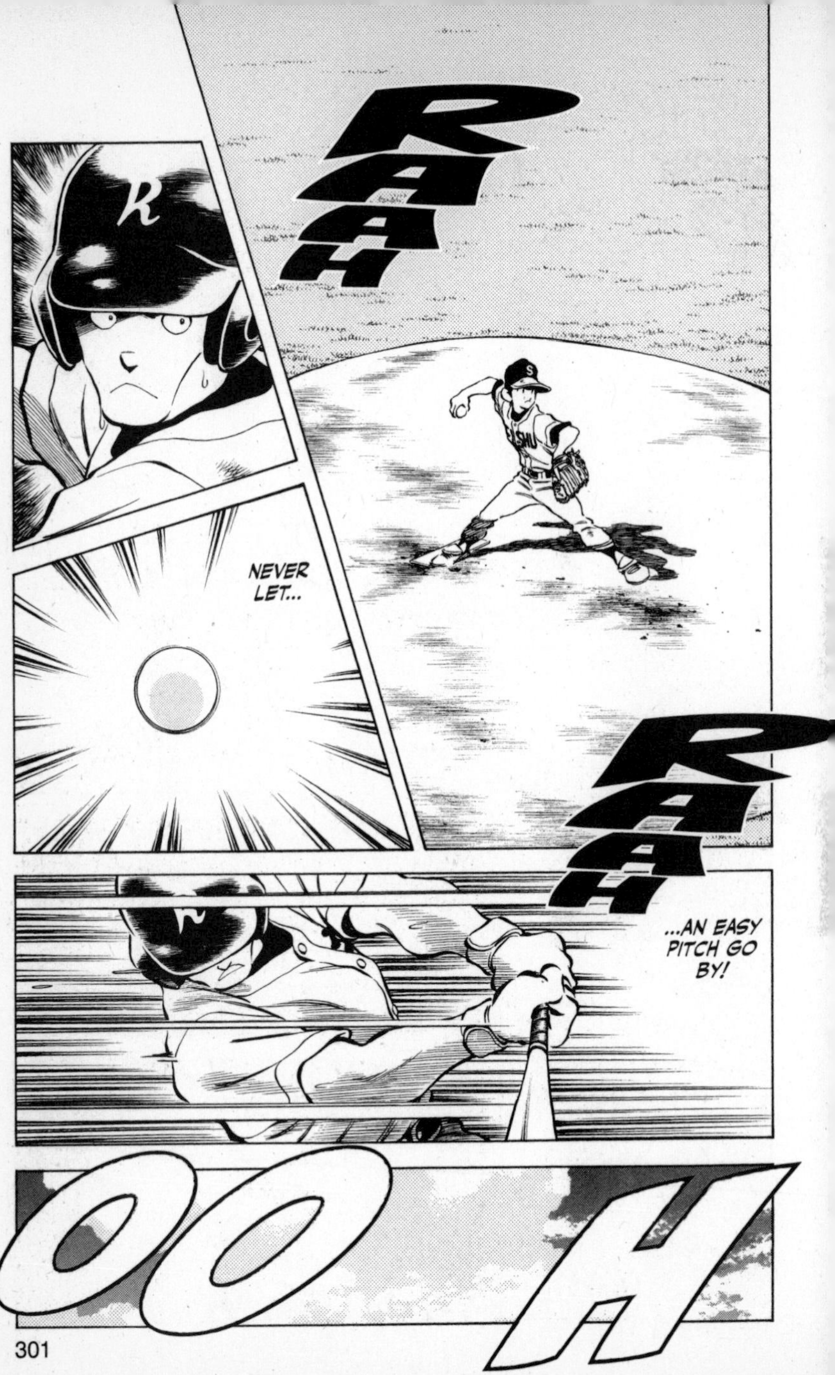
RAAH
RAAH
NEVER LET...
...AN EASY PITCH GO BY!
OOH

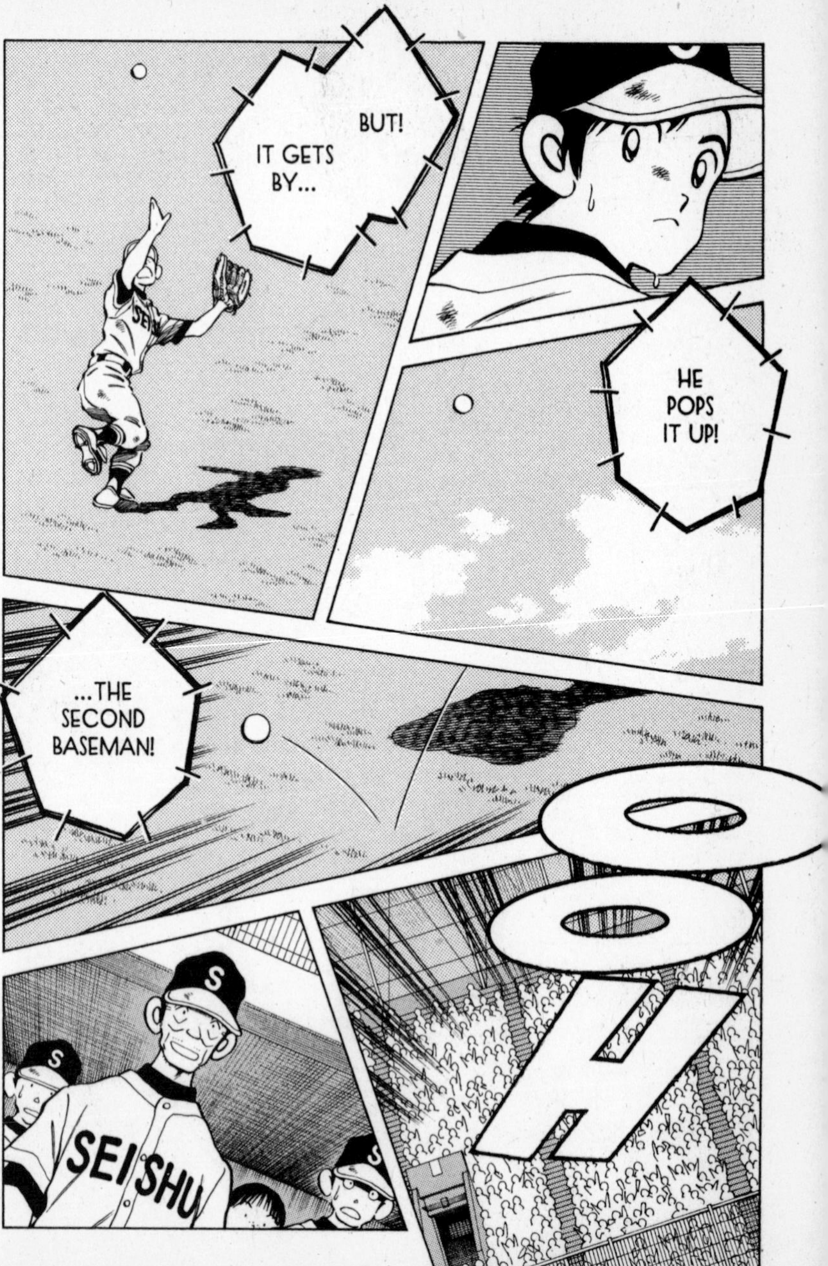
HE POPS IT UP!
BUT! IT GETS BY...
...THE SECOND BASEMAN!
OOH
SEISHU

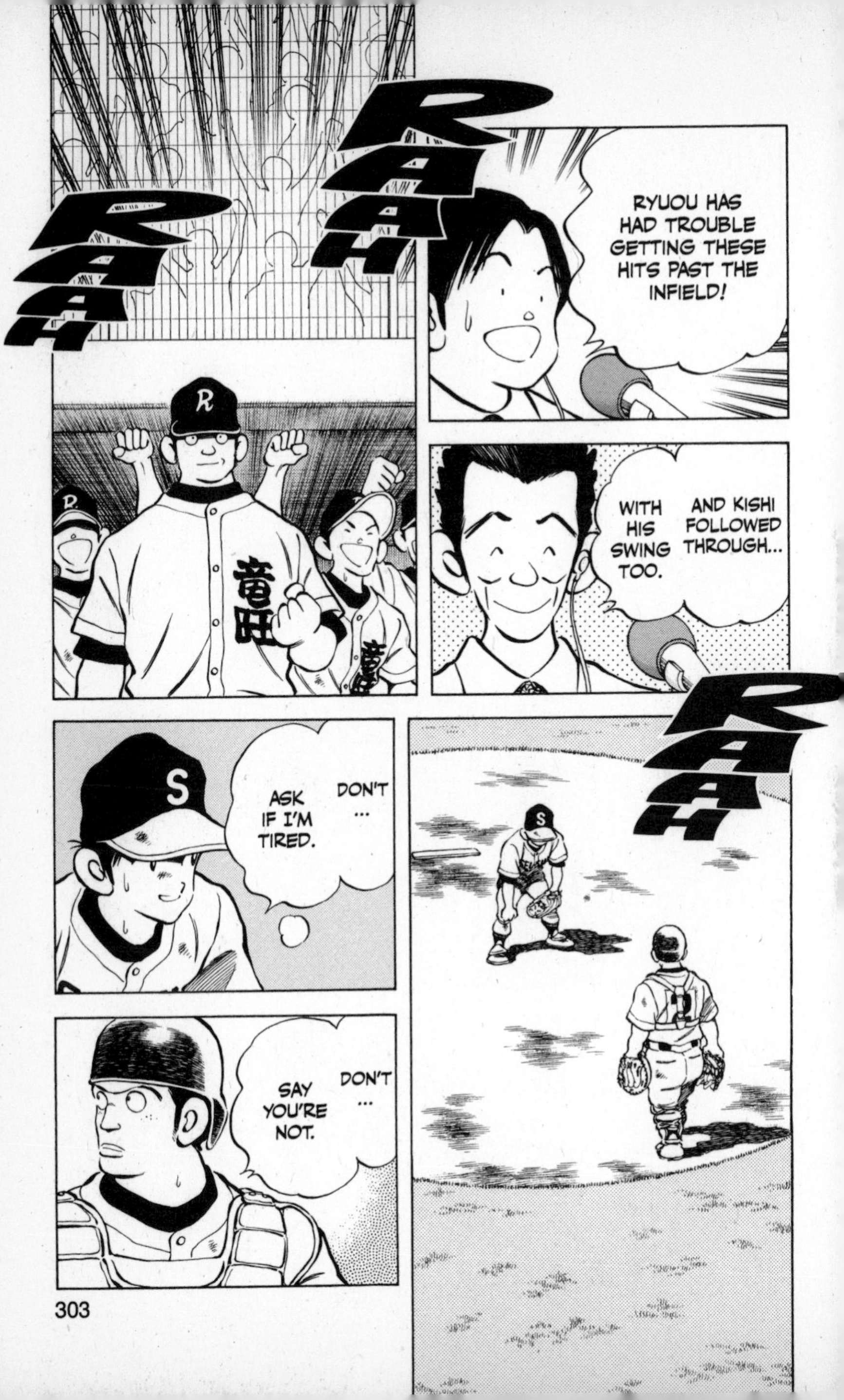
RYUOU HAS HAD TROUBLE GETTING THESE HITS PAST THE INFIELD!
RAAH
RAAH
AND KISHI FOLLOWED THROUGH...
WITH HIS SWING TOO.
RAAH
DON'T...
ASK IF I'M TIRED.
DON'T...
SAY YOU'RE NOT.

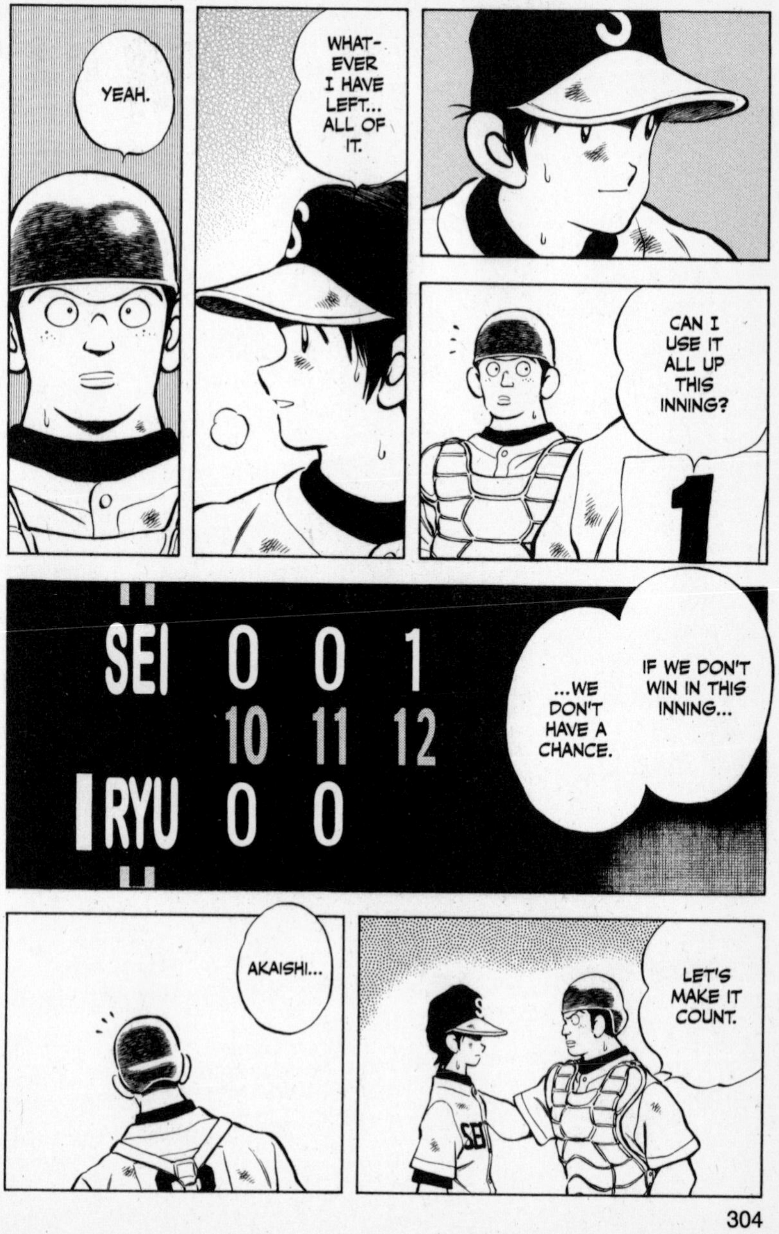
CAN I USE IT ALL UP THIS INNING?
WHAT-EVER I HAVE LEFT... ALL OF IT.
YEAH.
IF WE DON'T WIN IN THIS INNING...
...WE DON'T HAVE A CHANCE.
SEI 0 0 1
10 11 12
RYU 0 0
LET'S MAKE IT COUNT.
AKAISHI...

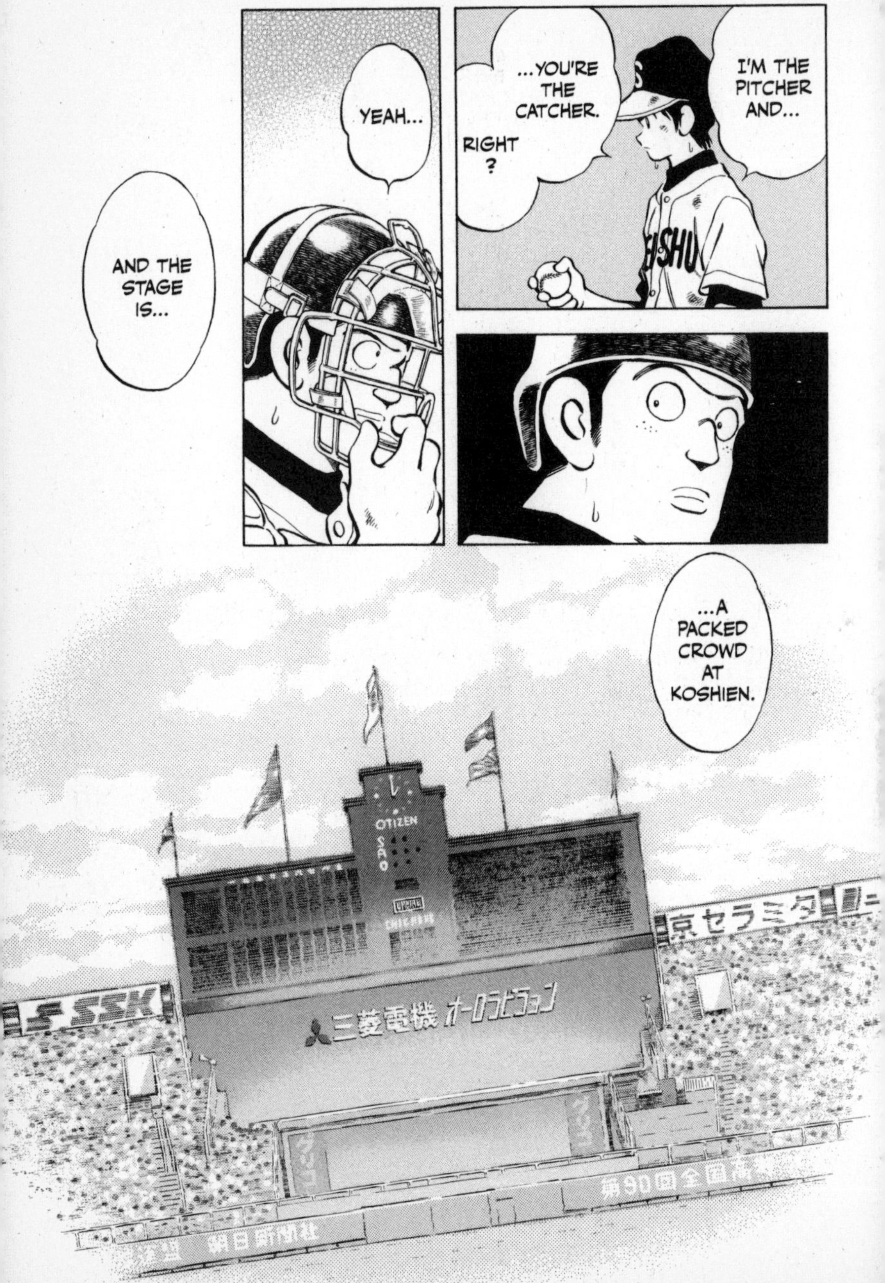
I'M THE PITCHER AND...
...YOU'RE THE CATCHER.
RIGHT?
YEAH...
AND THE STAGE IS...
...A PACKED CROWD AT KOSHIEN.
SSK
京セラミタ
三菱電機 オーロラビジョン
第90回全国
朝日新聞社

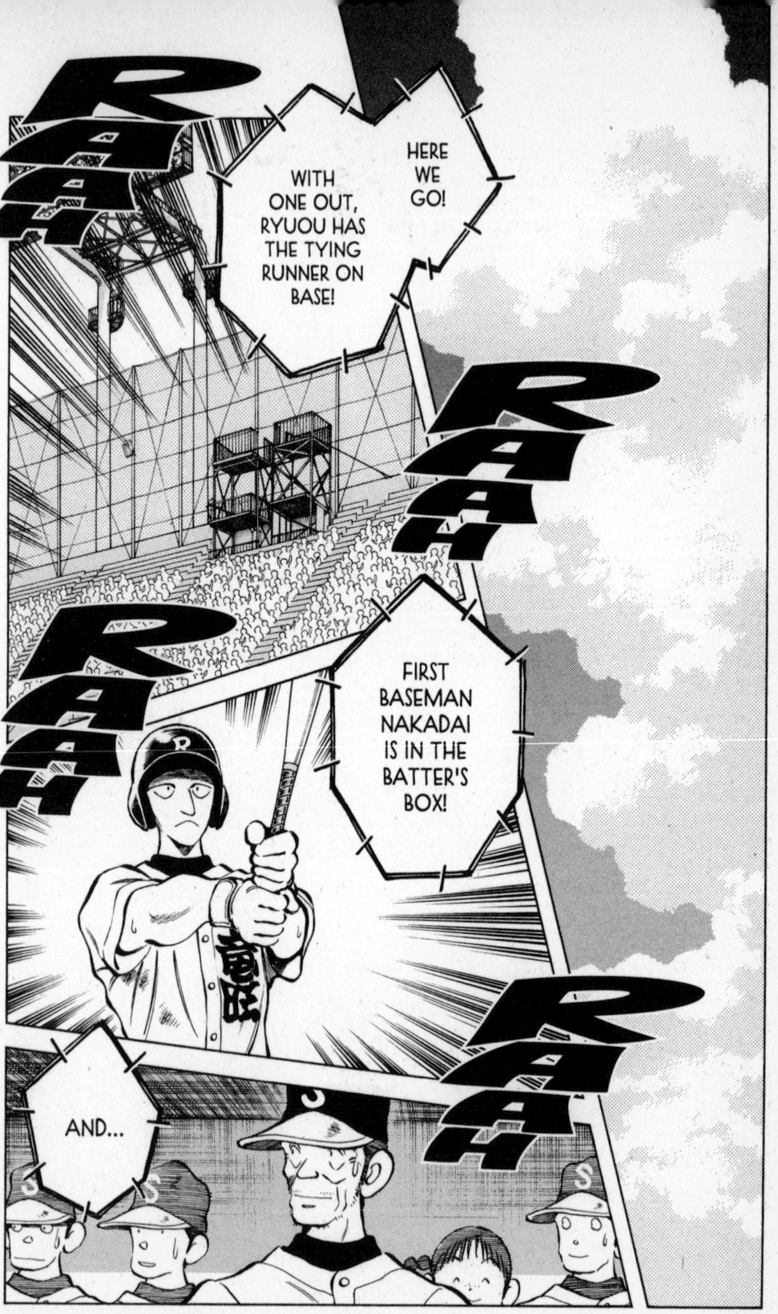
HERE WE GO!
WITH ONE OUT, RYUOU HAS THE TYING RUNNER ON BASE!
RAAAH
RAAH
FIRST BASEMAN NAKADAI IS IN THE BATTER'S BOX!
RAAAH
RAAAH
AND...

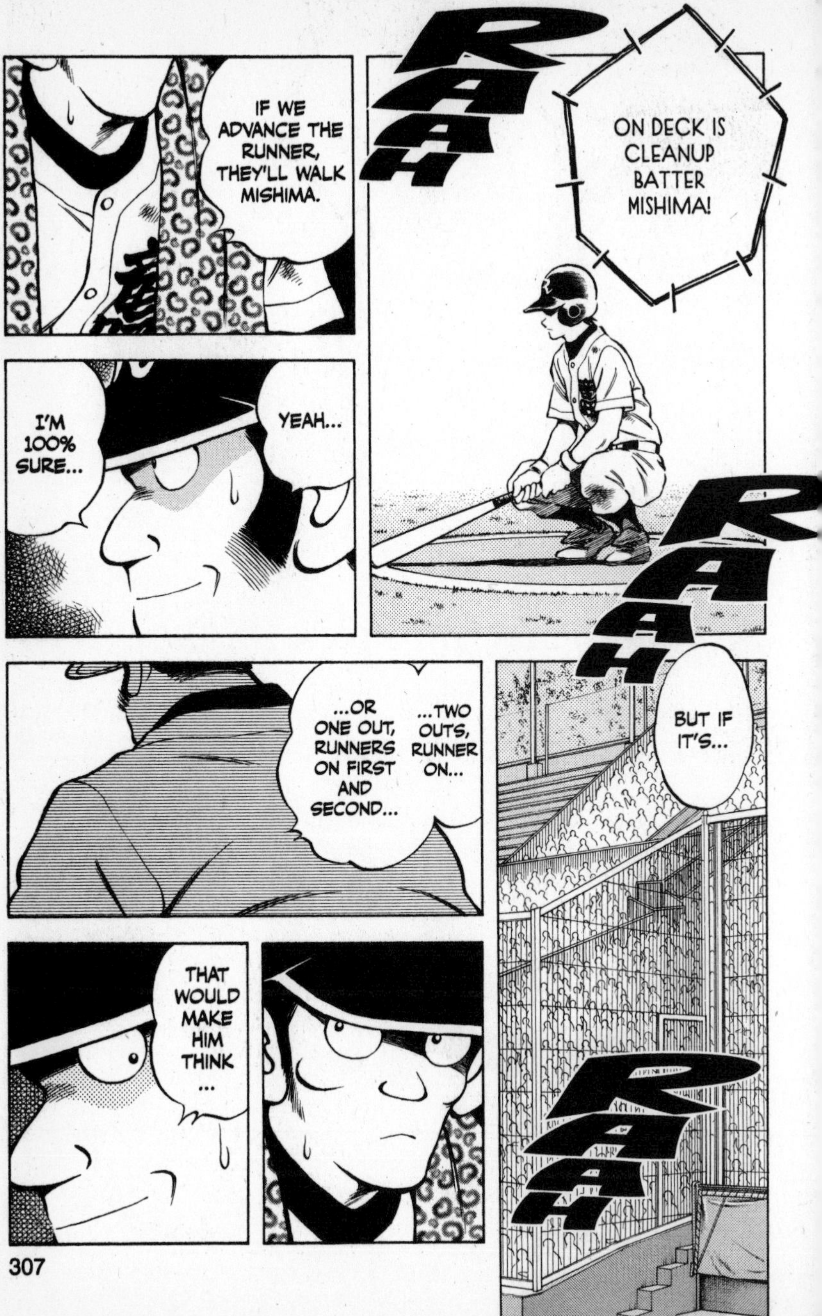
RAAH
ON DECK IS CLEANUP BATTER MISHIMA!
RAAH
IF WE ADVANCE THE RUNNER, THEY'LL WALK MISHIMA.
YEAH...
I'M 100% SURE...
BUT IF IT'S...
RAAH
...TWO OUTS, RUNNER ON...
...OR ONE OUT, RUNNERS ON FIRST AND SECOND...
THAT WOULD MAKE HIM THINK...

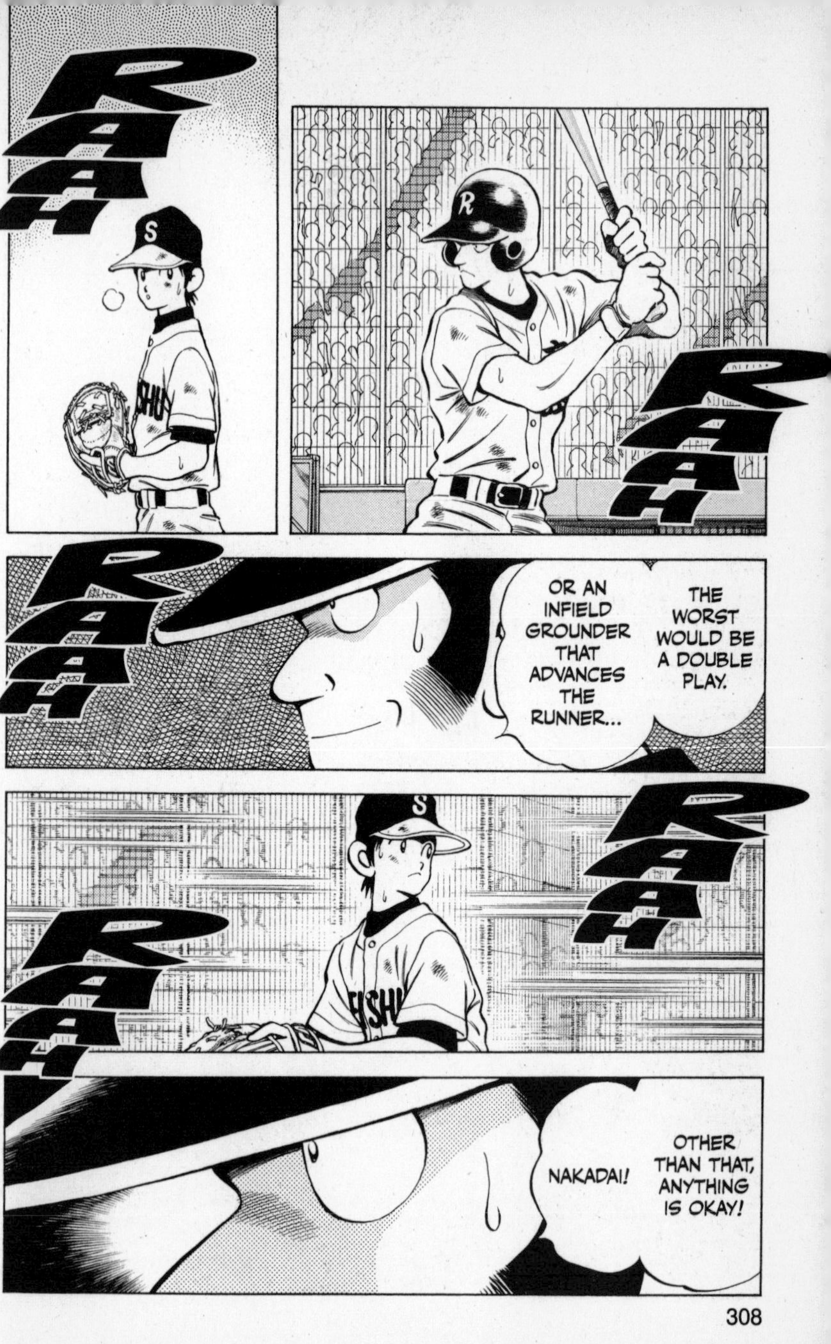
RAAH
RAAH
THE WORST WOULD BE A DOUBLE PLAY.
OR AN INFIELD GROUNDER THAT ADVANCES THE RUNNER...
RAAH
RAAH
RAAH
OTHER THAN THAT, ANYTHING IS OKAY!
NAKADAI!

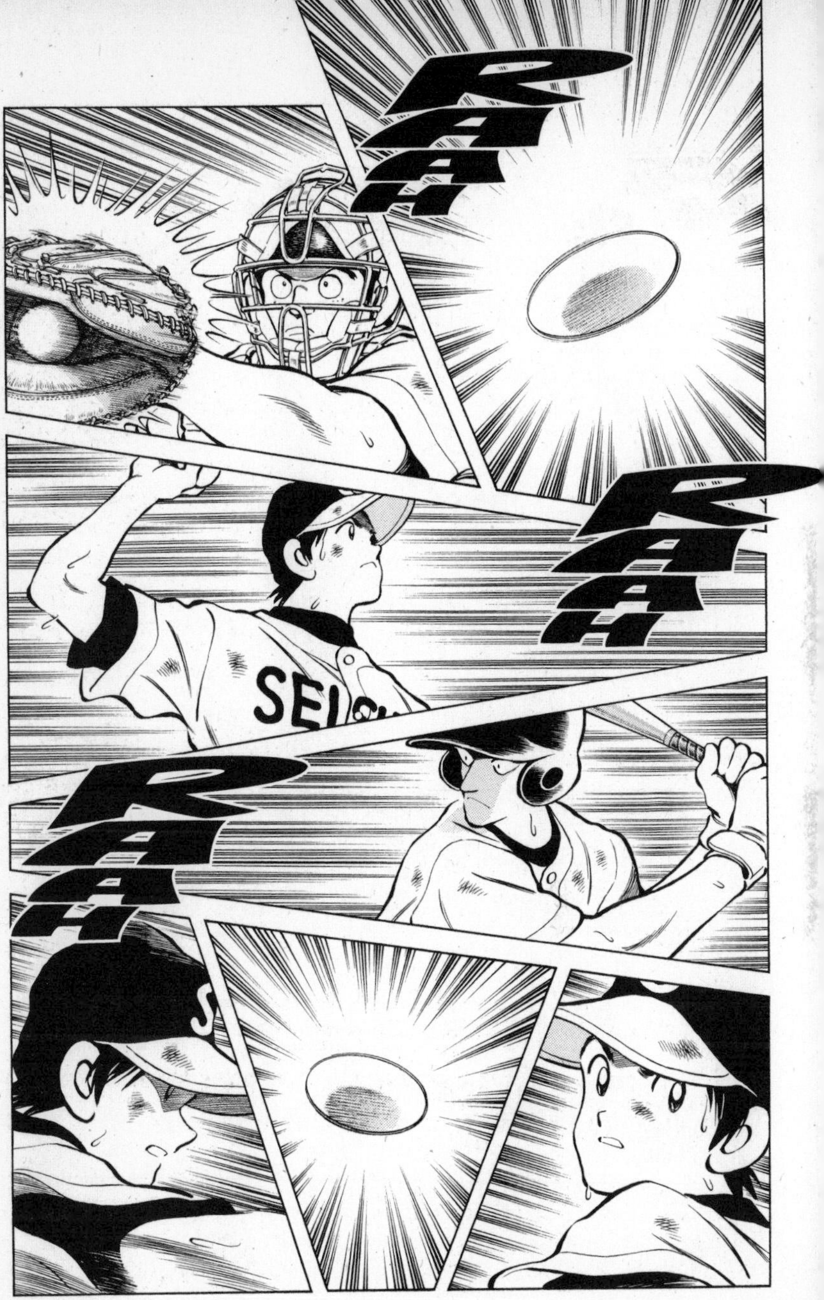
RAAH
RAAH
RAAH

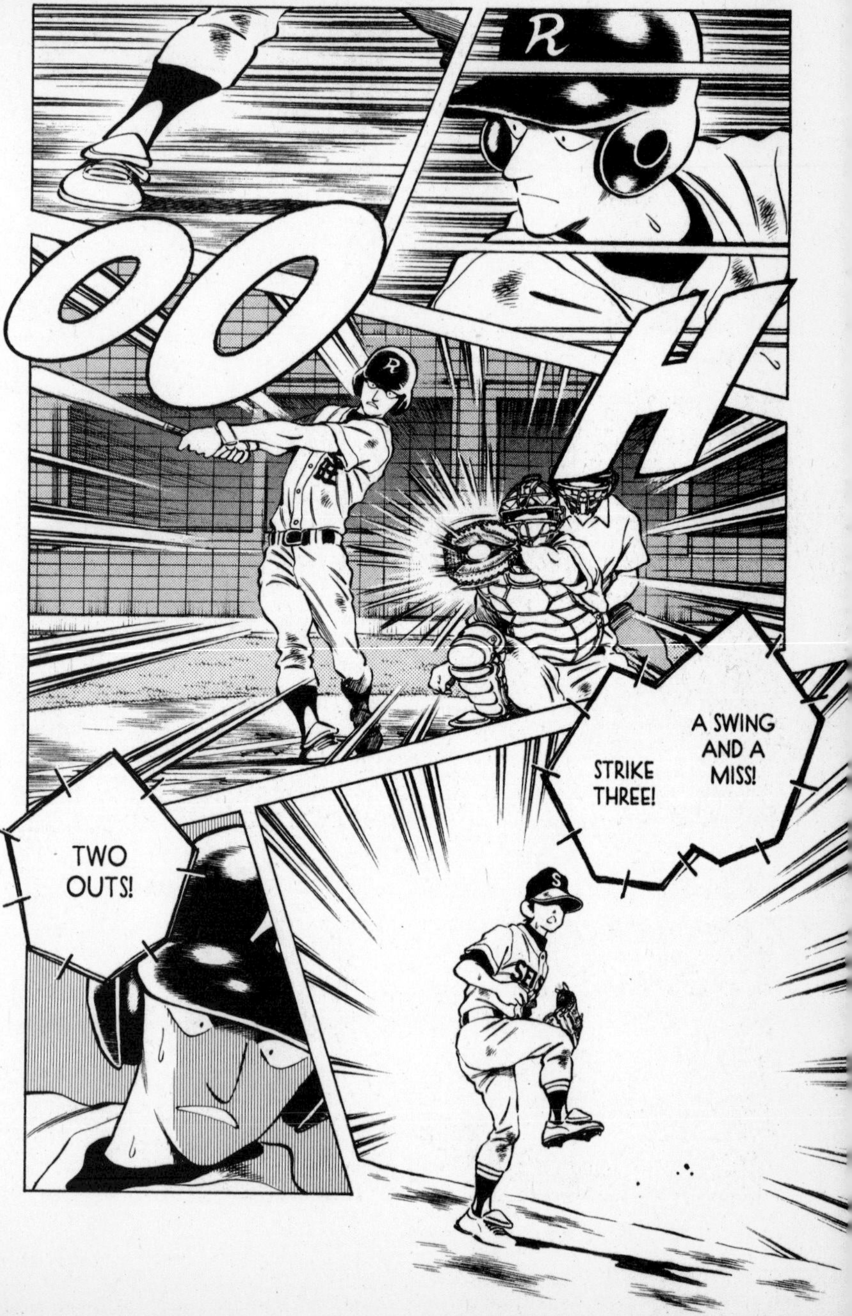
OOH
A SWING AND A MISS!
STRIKE THREE!
TWO OUTS!

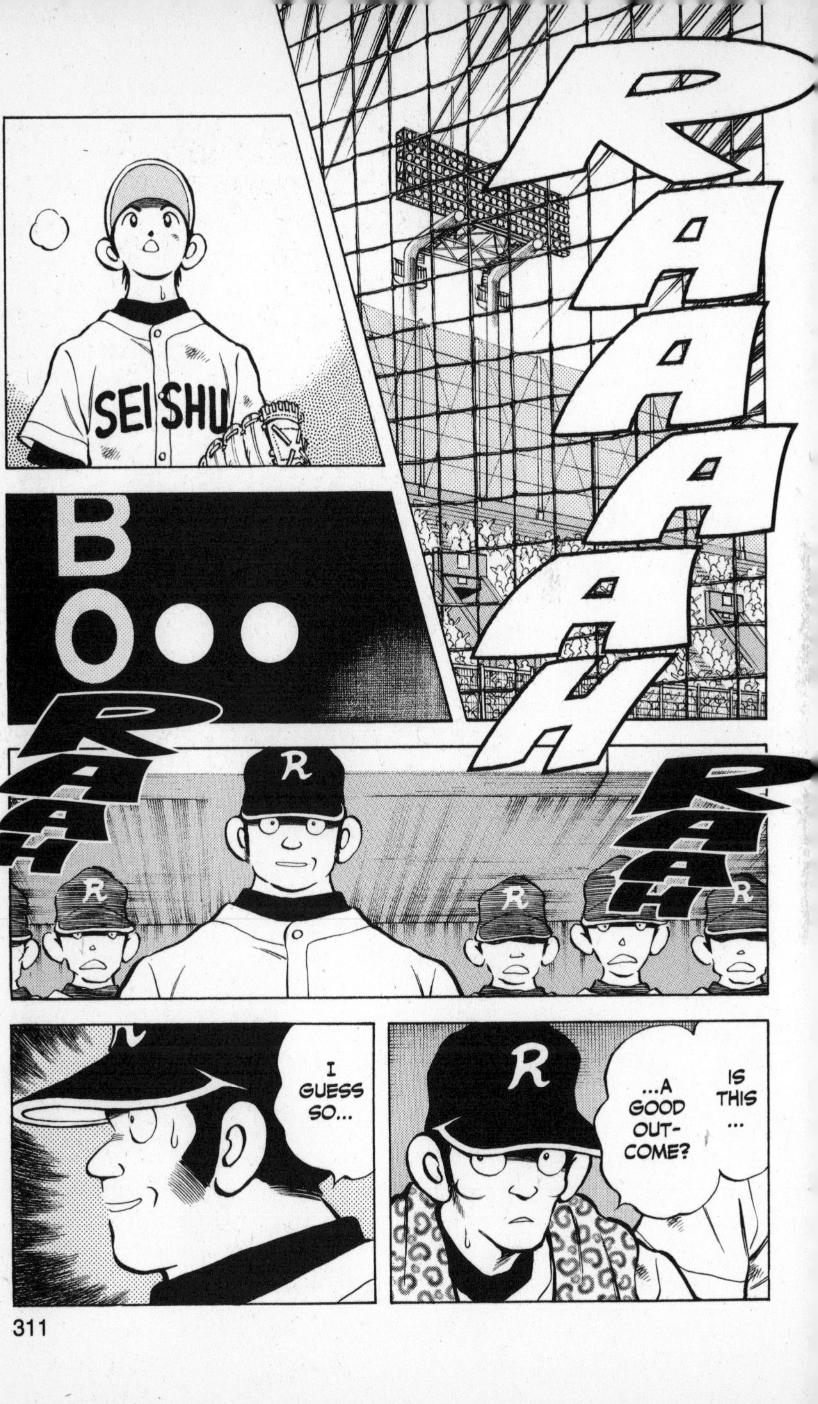
RAAAAH
SEISHU
B
O
R
RAAAH
RAAAH
IS THIS...
...A GOOD OUTCOME?
R
I GUESS SO...

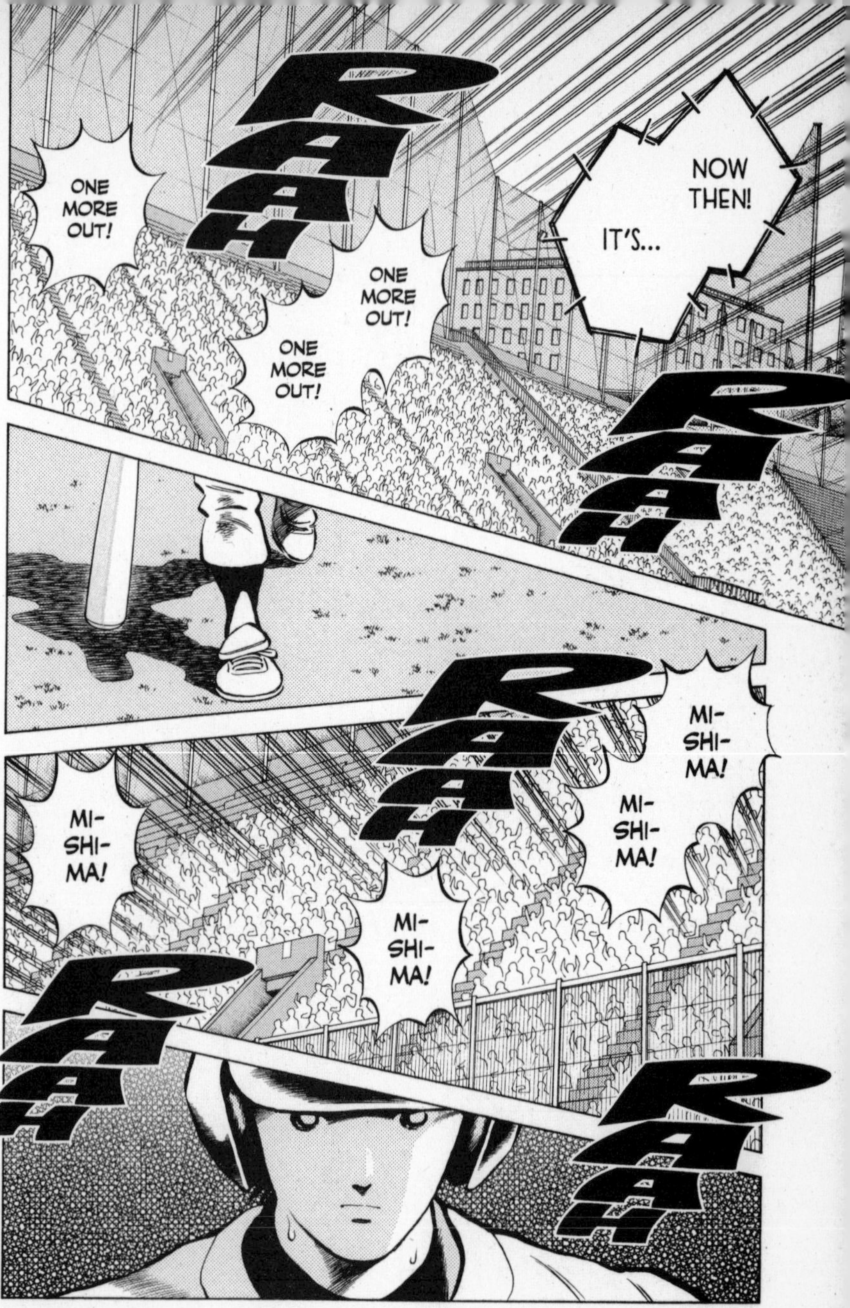
NOW THEN!
IT'S...
RAAH
RAAH
ONE MORE OUT!
ONE MORE OUT!
ONE MORE OUT!
MI-SHI-MA!
RAAH
MI-SHI-MA!
MI-SHI-MA!
MI-SHI-MA!
RAAH
RAAH

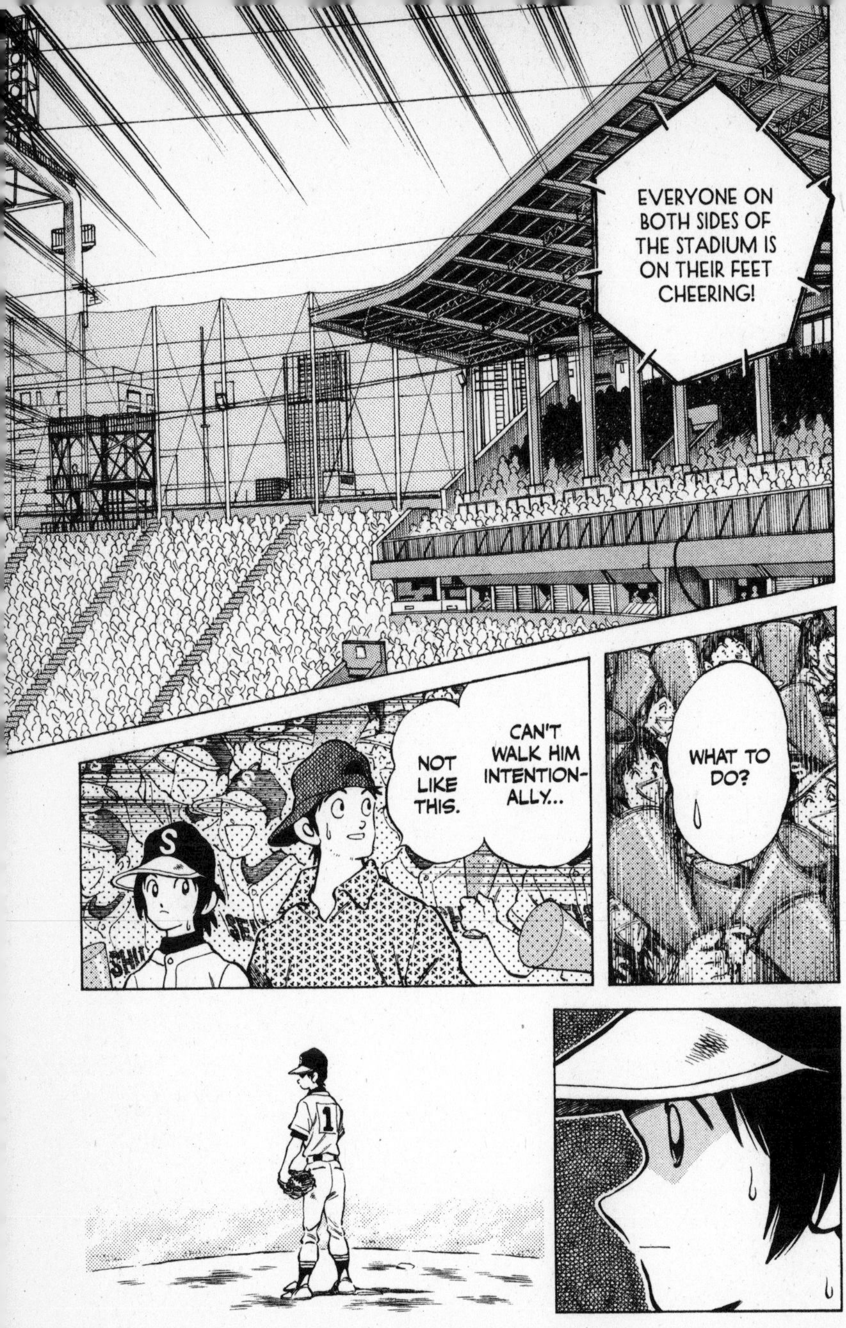
EVERYONE ON BOTH SIDES OF THE STADIUM IS ON THEIR FEET CHEERING!
WHAT TO DO?
CAN'T WALK HIM INTENTION-ALLY...
NOT LIKE THIS.

CAN I
LIE?

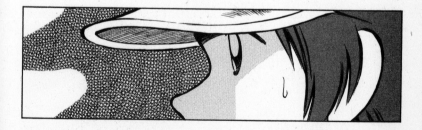

SURE.

CHAPTER 158
LET'S DO THIS

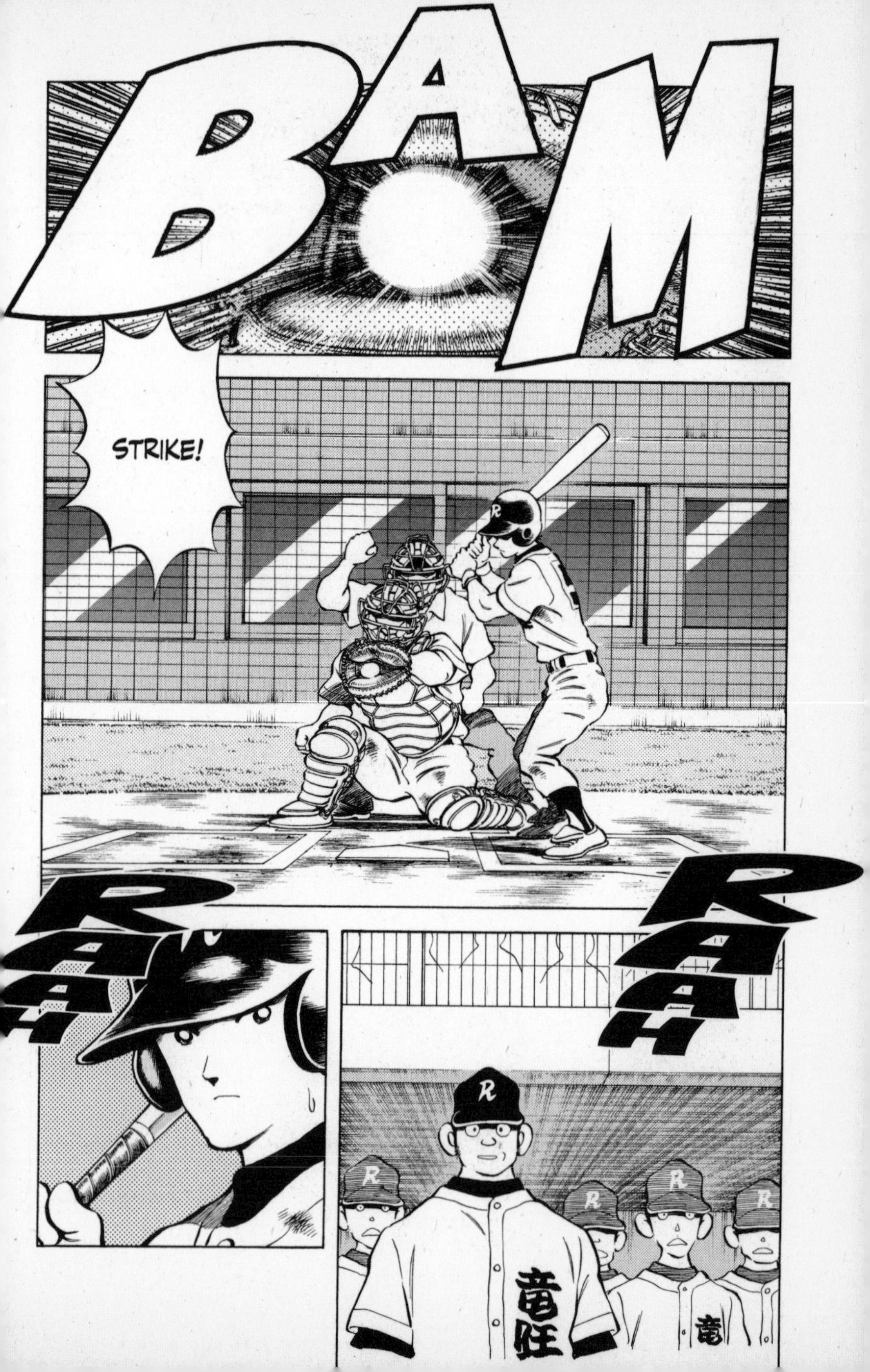
BAM
STRIKE!
RAAH
竜旺
竜
RAAH

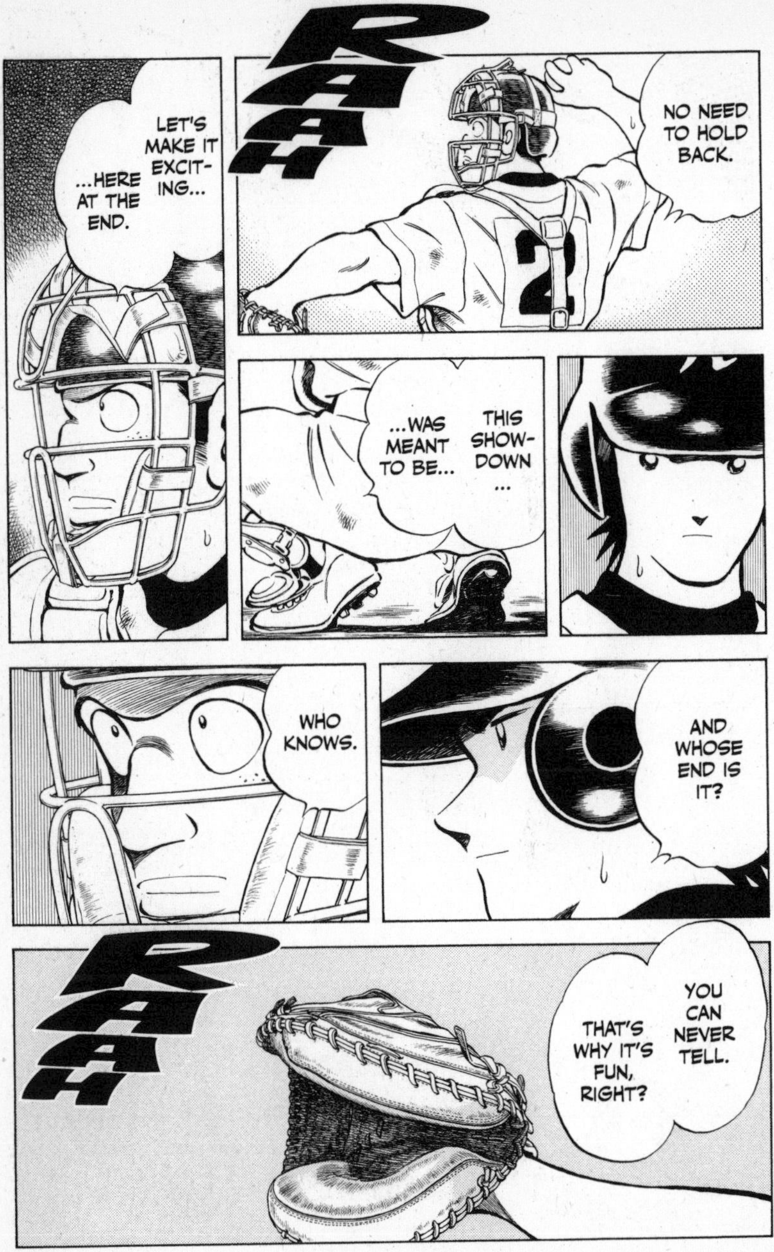
RAAAH
NO NEED TO HOLD BACK.
THIS SHOWDOWN...
...WAS MEANT TO BE...
LET'S MAKE IT EXCITING...
...HERE AT THE END.
AND WHOSE END IS IT?
WHO KNOWS.
YOU CAN NEVER TELL.
THAT'S WHY IT'S FUN, RIGHT?
RAAAH

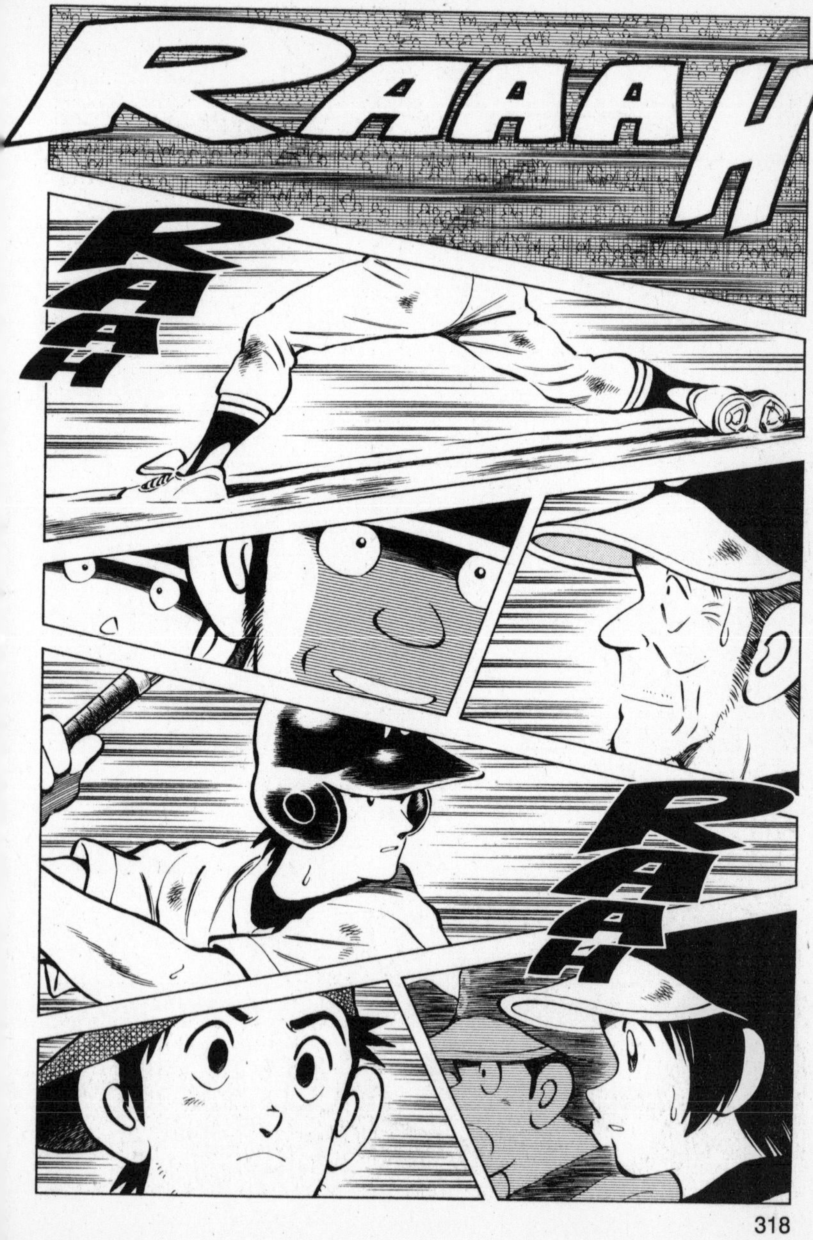
RAAAH
RAAAH
RAAAH

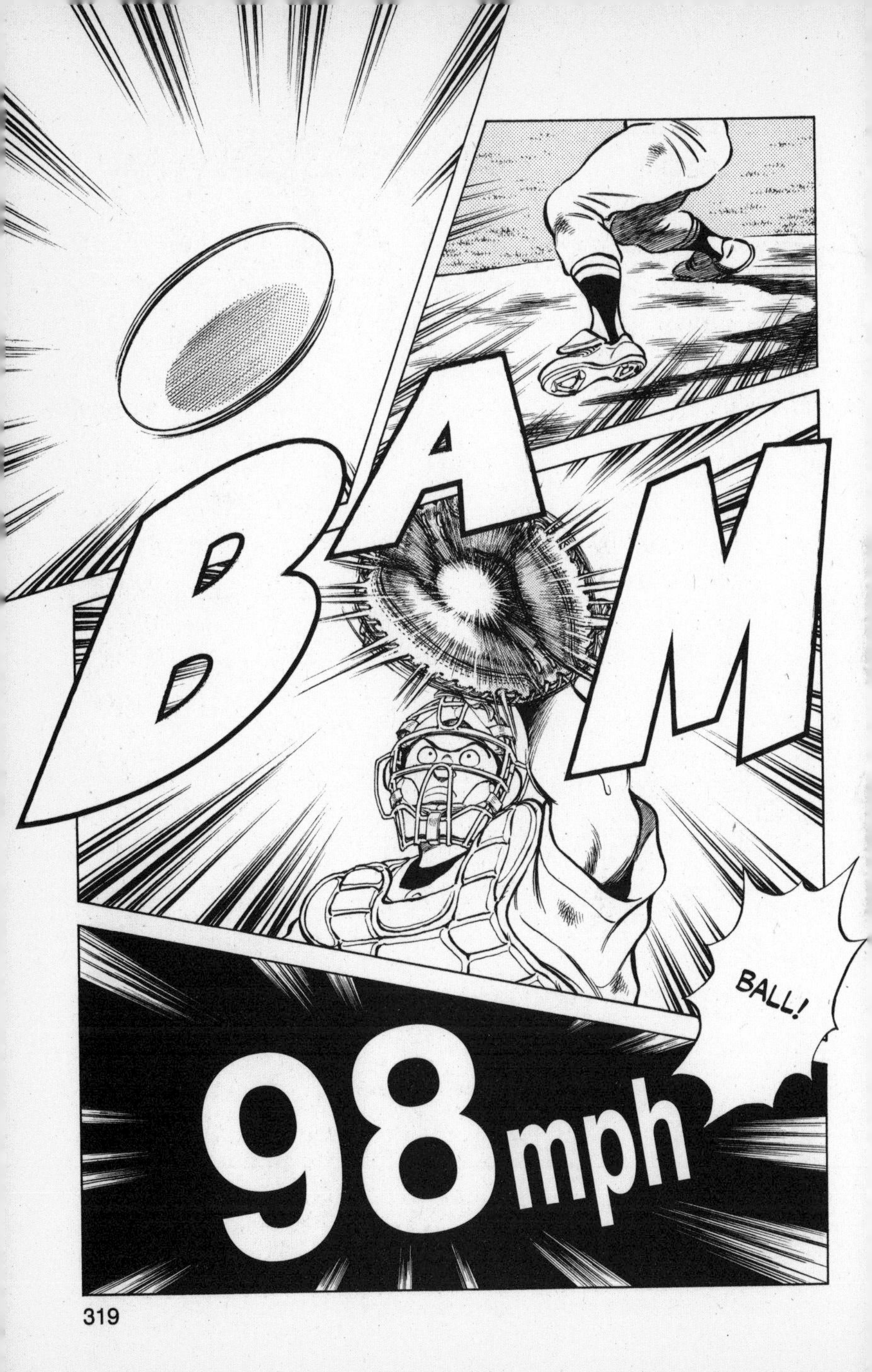
BAM
BALL!
98mph

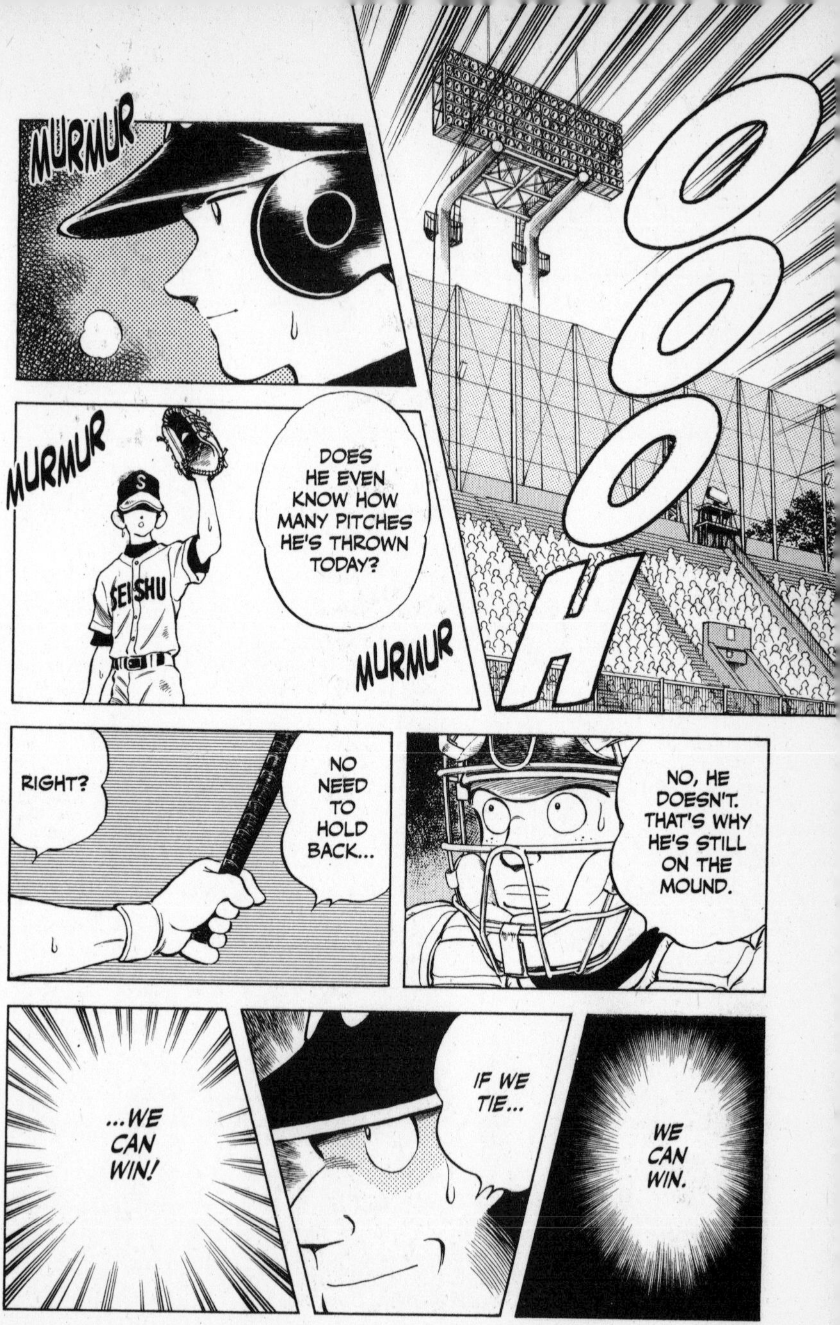
OOOOH
MURMUR
MURMUR
DOES HE EVEN KNOW HOW MANY PITCHES HE'S THROWN TODAY?
MURMUR
NO, HE DOESN'T. THAT'S WHY HE'S STILL ON THE MOUND.
NO NEED TO HOLD BACK...
RIGHT?
WE CAN WIN.
IF WE TIE...
...WE CAN WIN!

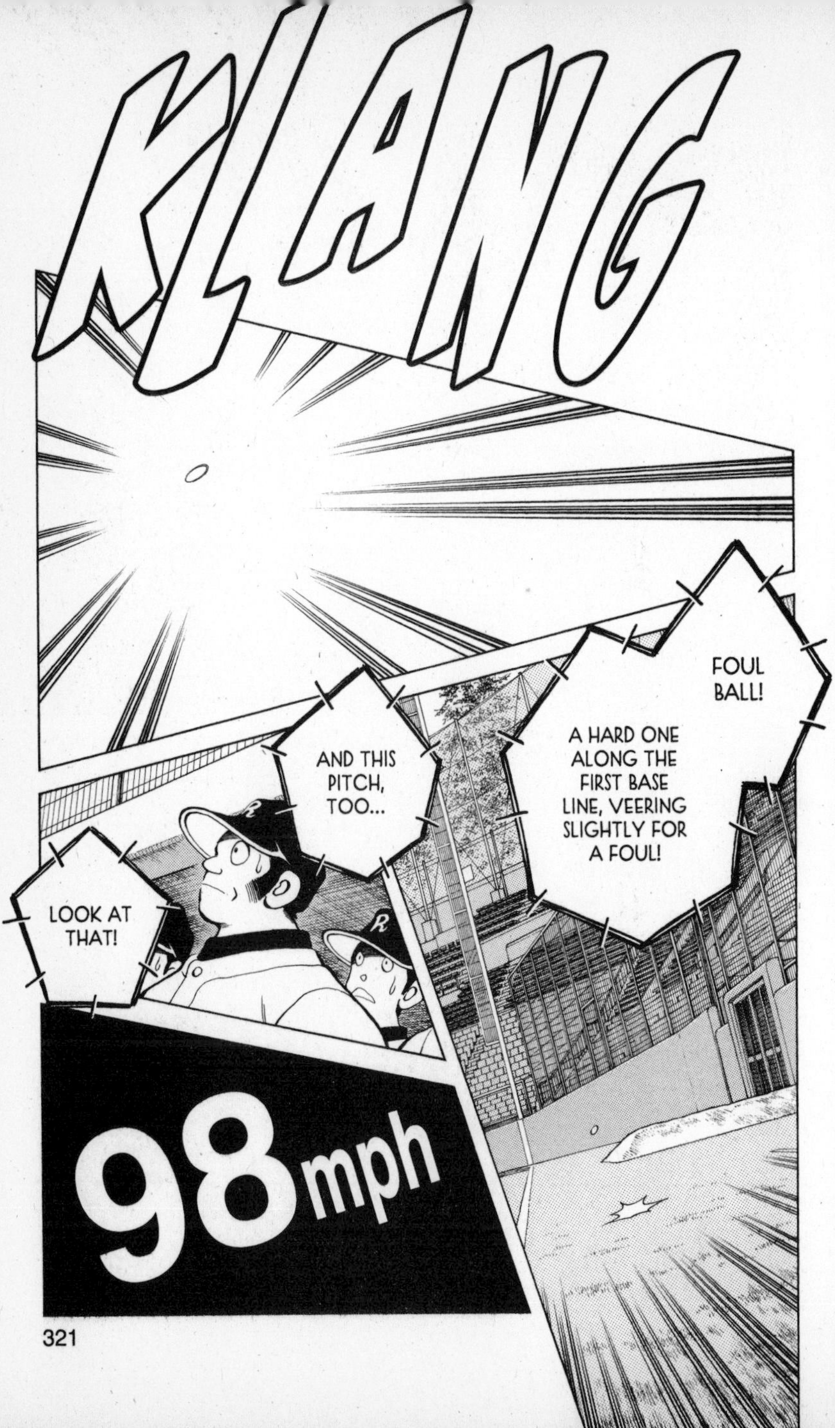
KLANG
FOUL BALL!
A HARD ONE ALONG THE FIRST BASE LINE, VEERING SLIGHTLY FOR A FOUL!
AND THIS PITCH, TOO...
LOOK AT THAT!
98mph

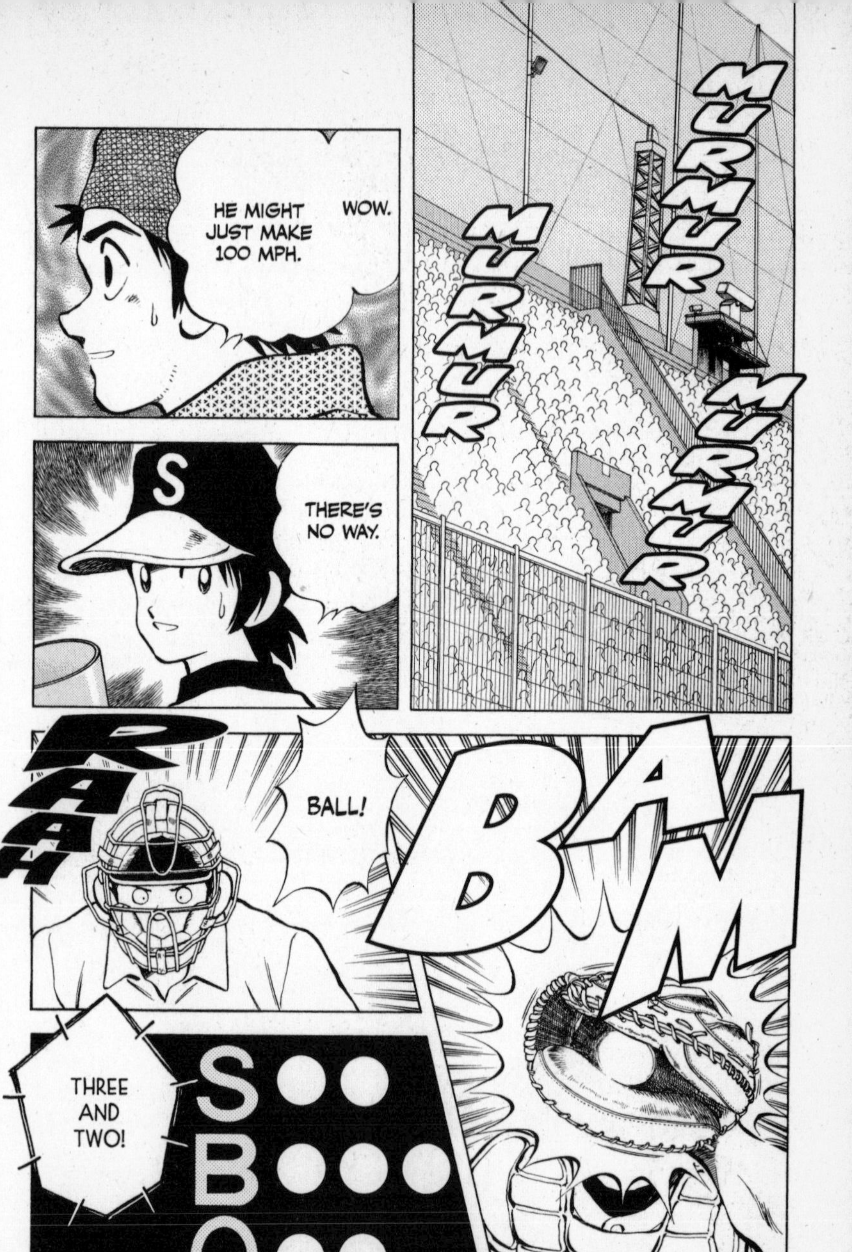
MURMUR
MURMUR
MURMUR
MURMUR
WOW.
HE MIGHT JUST MAKE 100 MPH.
THERE'S NO WAY.
BAM
BALL!
RAAAH
THREE AND TWO!
S
B
O

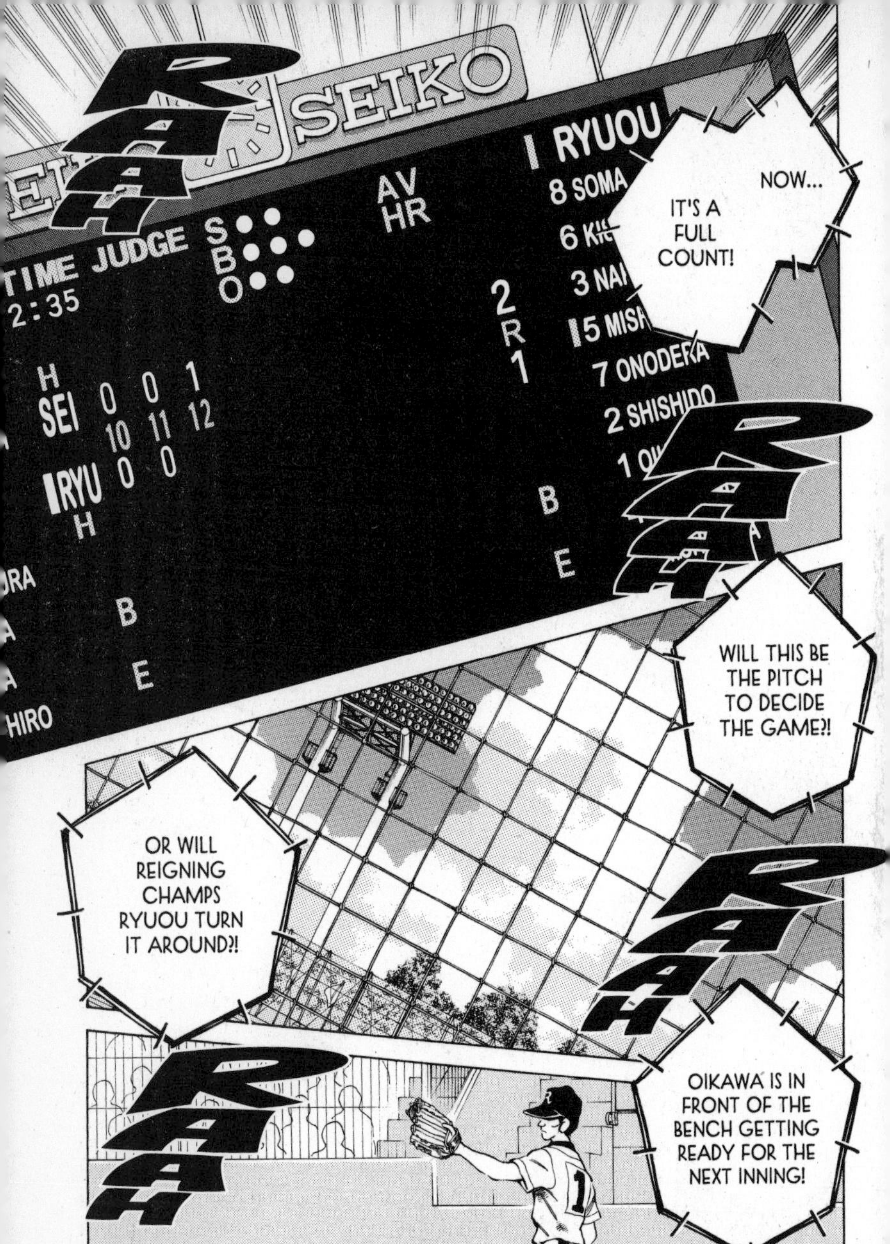
RAAH
SEIKO
NOW...
IT'S A FULL COUNT!
RAAH
WILL THIS BE THE PITCH TO DECIDE THE GAME?!
OR WILL REIGNING CHAMPS RYUOU TURN IT AROUND?!
RAAH
OIKAWA IS IN FRONT OF THE BENCH GETTING READY FOR THE NEXT INNING!
RAAH

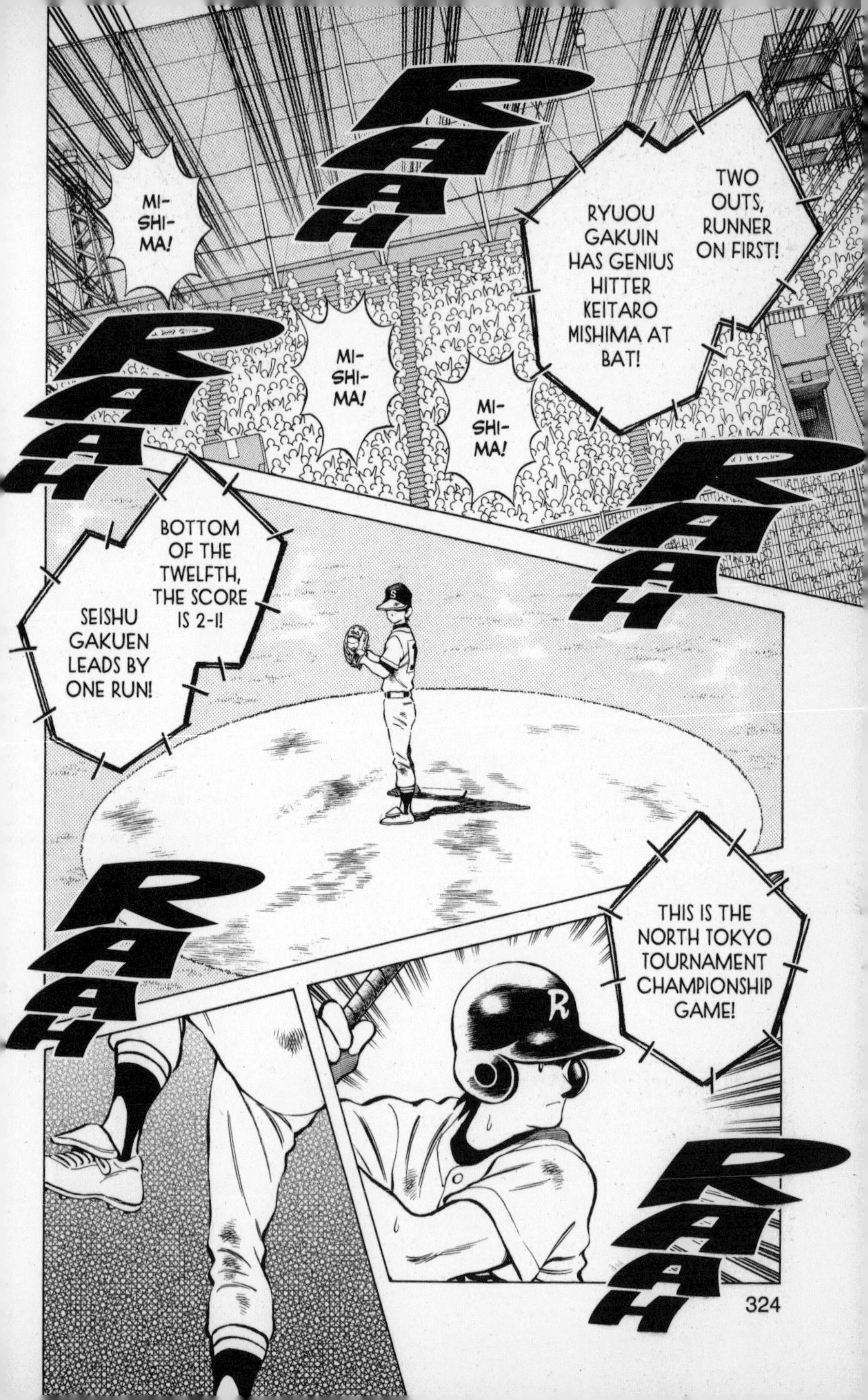
RAAH
TWO OUTS, RUNNER ON FIRST! RYUOU GAKUIN HAS GENIUS HITTER KEITARO MISHIMA AT BAT!
RAAH
MI-SHI-MA!
MI-SHI-MA!
MI-SHI-MA!
RAAH
RAAH
BOTTOM OF THE TWELFTH, THE SCORE IS 2-1! SEISHU GAKUEN LEADS BY ONE RUN!
RAAH
THIS IS THE NORTH TOKYO TOURNAMENT CHAMPIONSHIP GAME!
RAAH

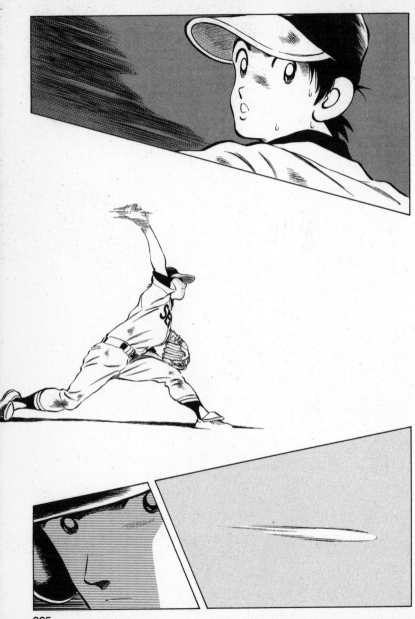

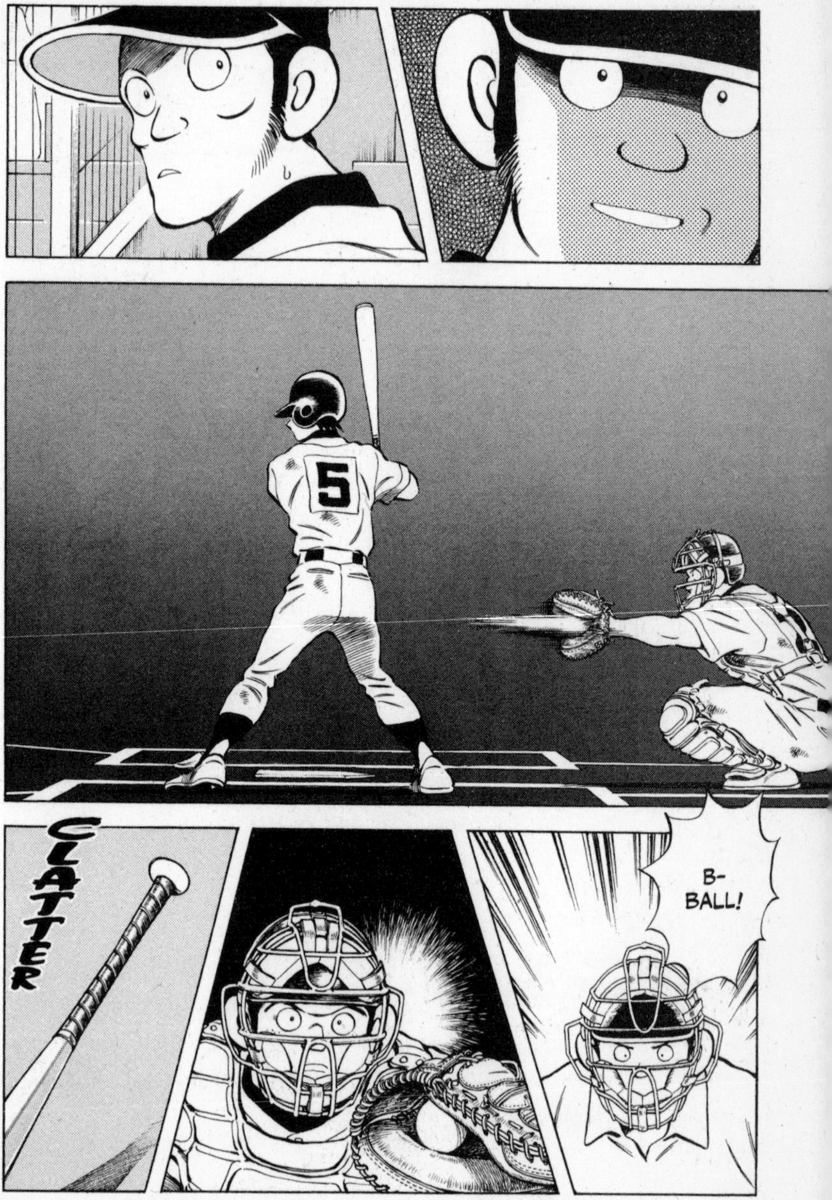
B-
BALL!
CLATTER

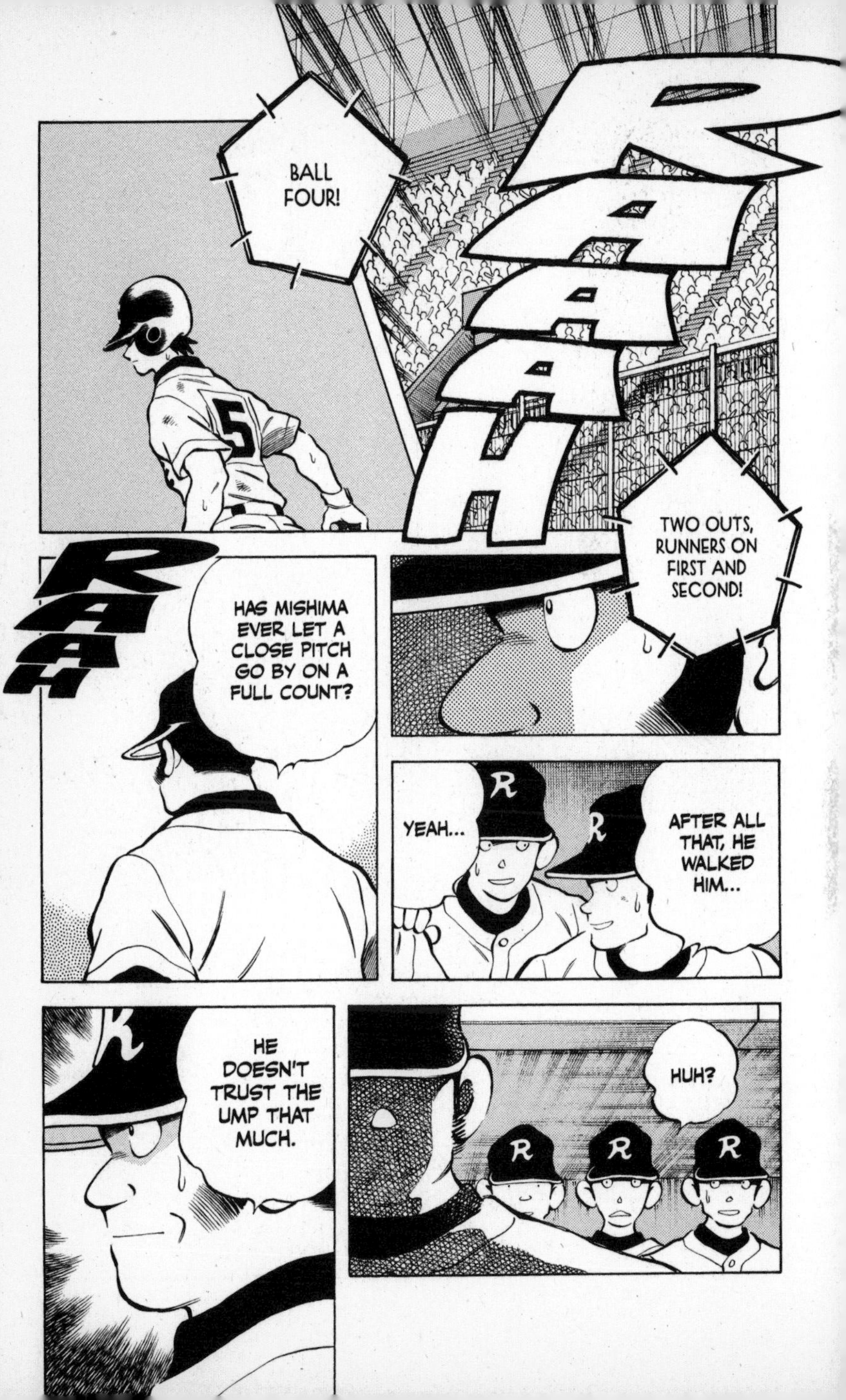
RAAAH
BALL FOUR!
TWO OUTS, RUNNERS ON FIRST AND SECOND!
AFTER ALL THAT, HE WALKED HIM...
YEAH...
RAAAH
HAS MISHIMA EVER LET A CLOSE PITCH GO BY ON A FULL COUNT?
HUH?
HE DOESN'T TRUST THE UMP THAT MUCH.

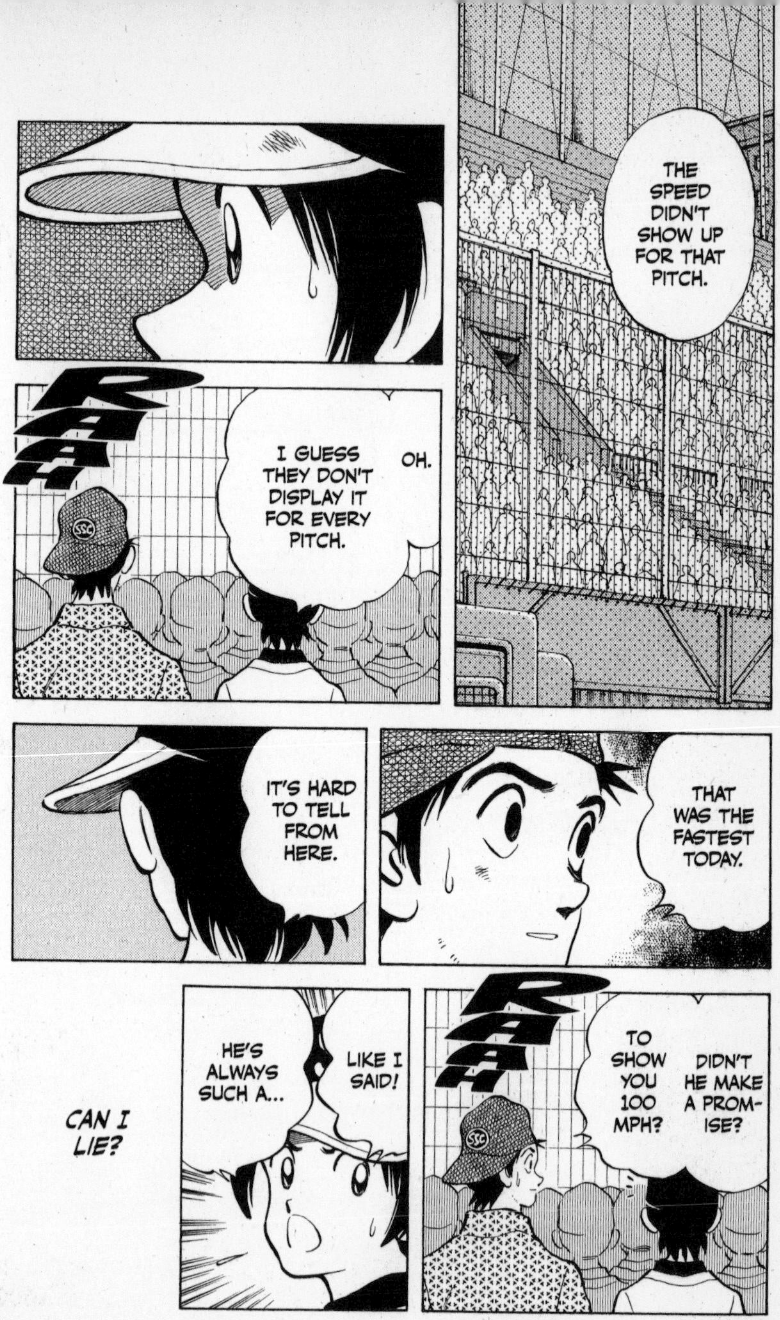
THE SPEED DIDN'T SHOW UP FOR THAT PITCH.
RAAA
OH.
I GUESS THEY DON'T DISPLAY IT FOR EVERY PITCH.
THAT WAS THE FASTEST TODAY.
IT'S HARD TO TELL FROM HERE.
RAAA
DIDN'T HE MAKE A PROM-ISE?
TO SHOW YOU 100 MPH?
LIKE I SAID!
HE'S ALWAYS SUCH A...
CAN I LIE?

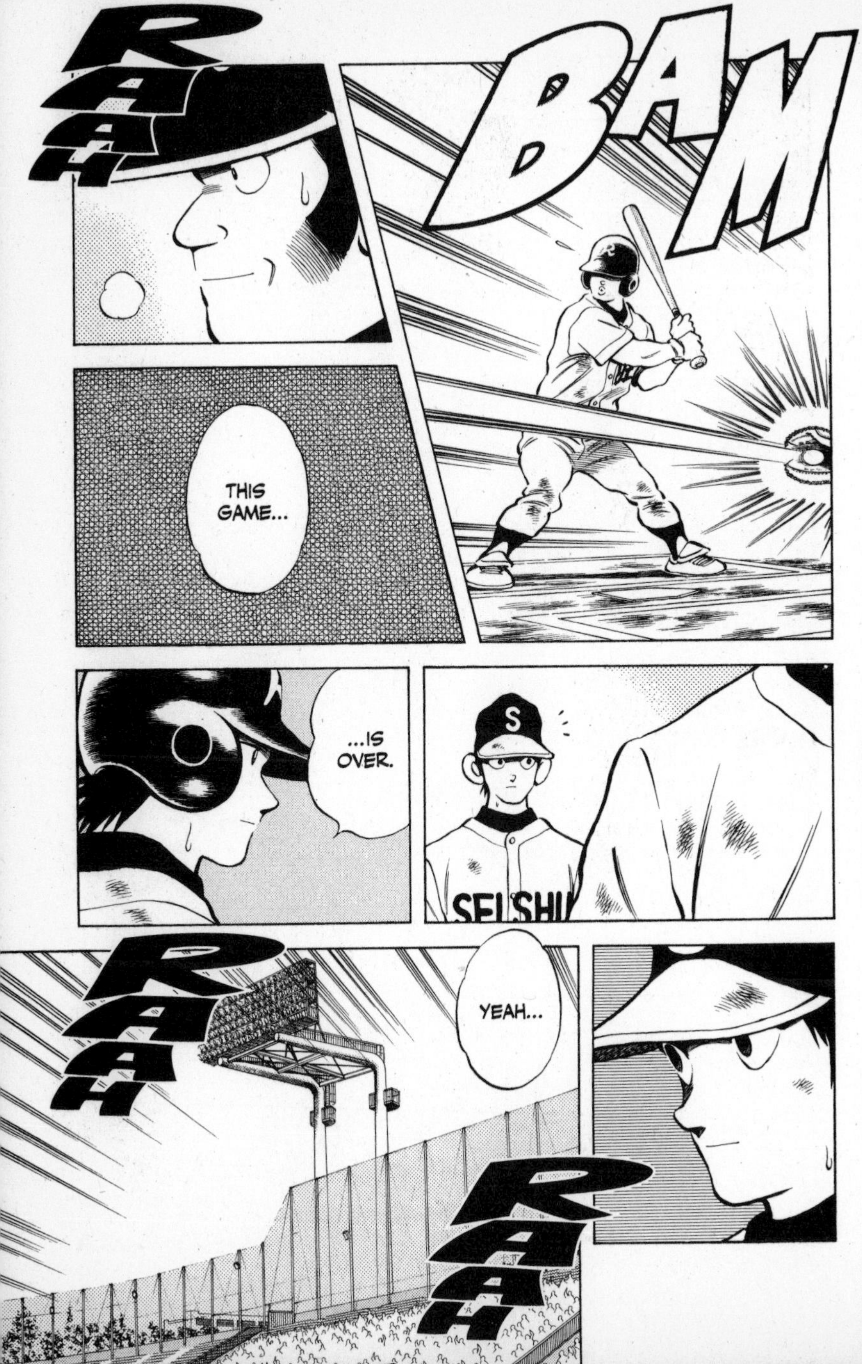
BAM
RAAAH
THIS GAME...
SEISHU
...IS OVER.
YEAH...
RAAAH
RAAAH

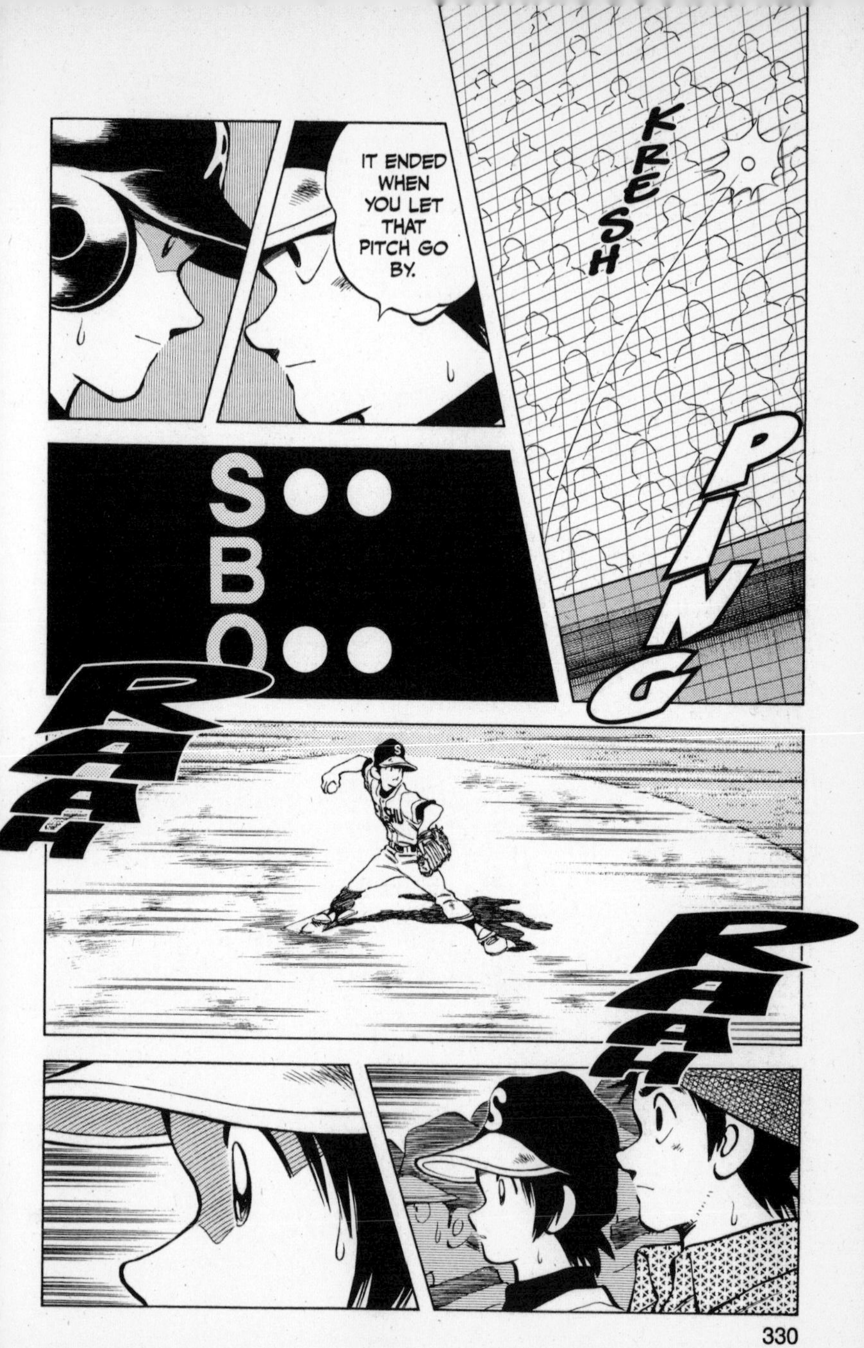
KRESH
PING
IT ENDED WHEN YOU LET THAT PITCH GO BY.
S
B
RAAAH
RAAAH

I'M GOING TO KOSHIEN!

I'M GOING TO PITCH 100 MPH!

AND...

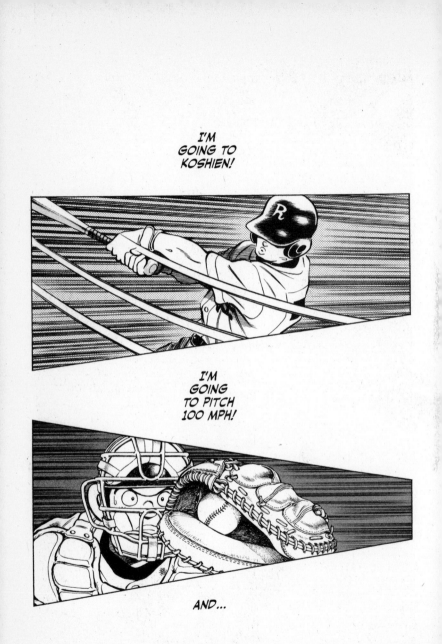

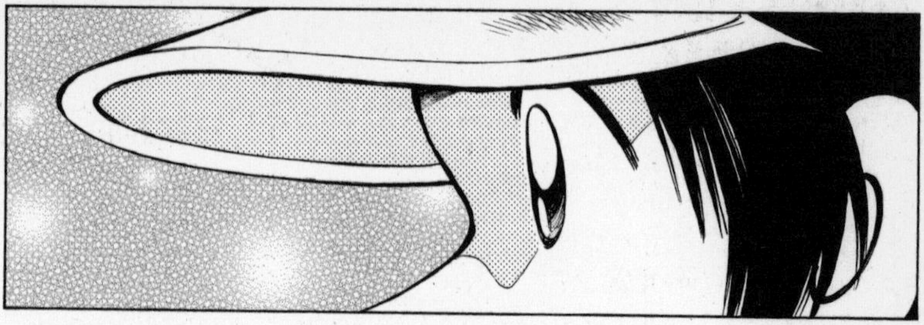

I LOVE AOBA TSUKISHIMA MORE THAN ANYTHING...

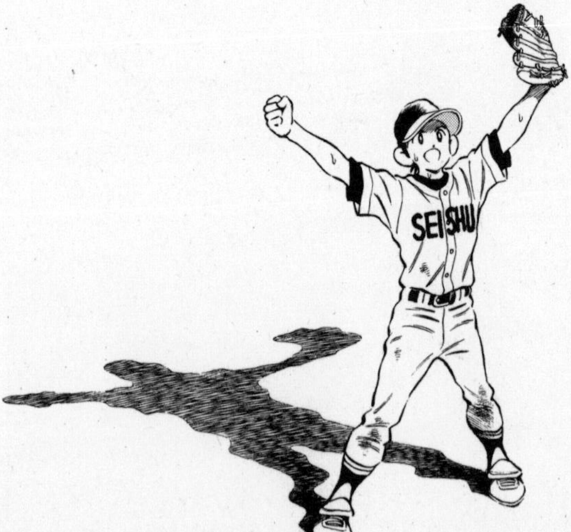
SEISHU

CHAPTER 159
I KNOW

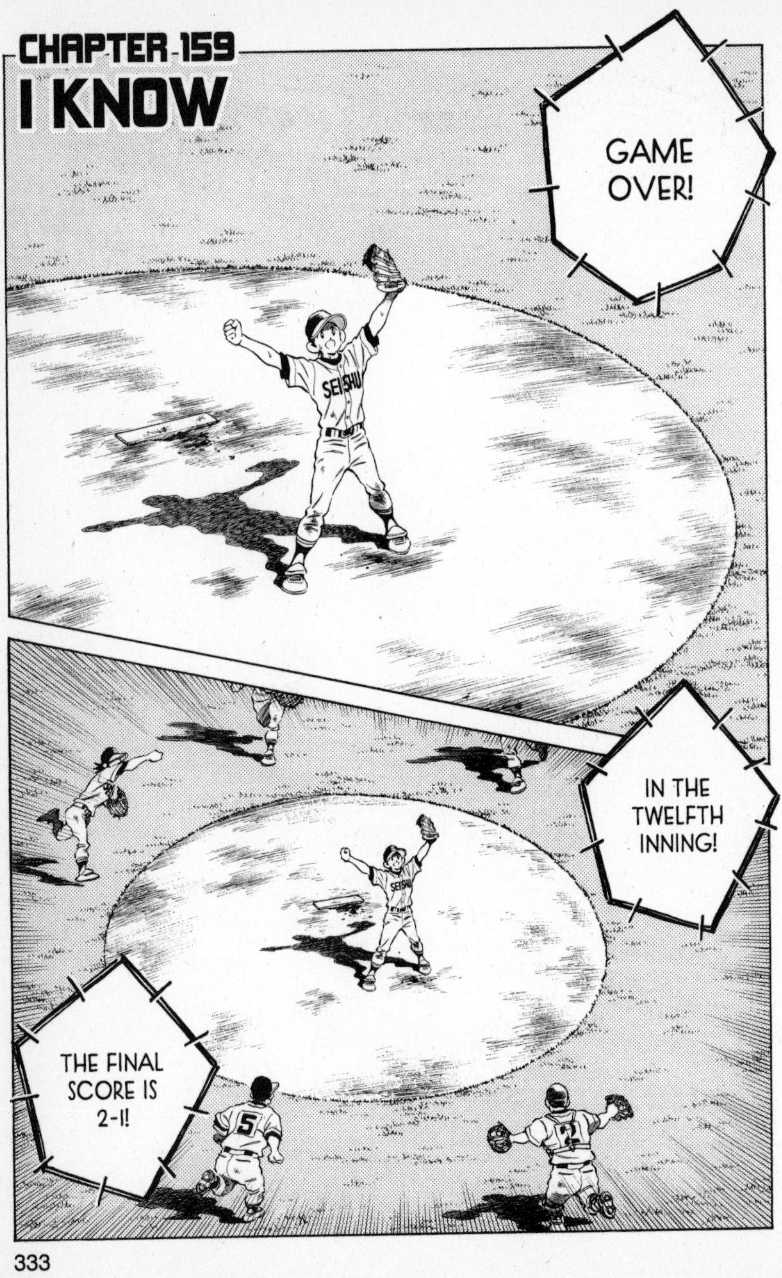
GAME OVER!
IN THE TWELFTH INNING!
THE FINAL SCORE IS 2-1!

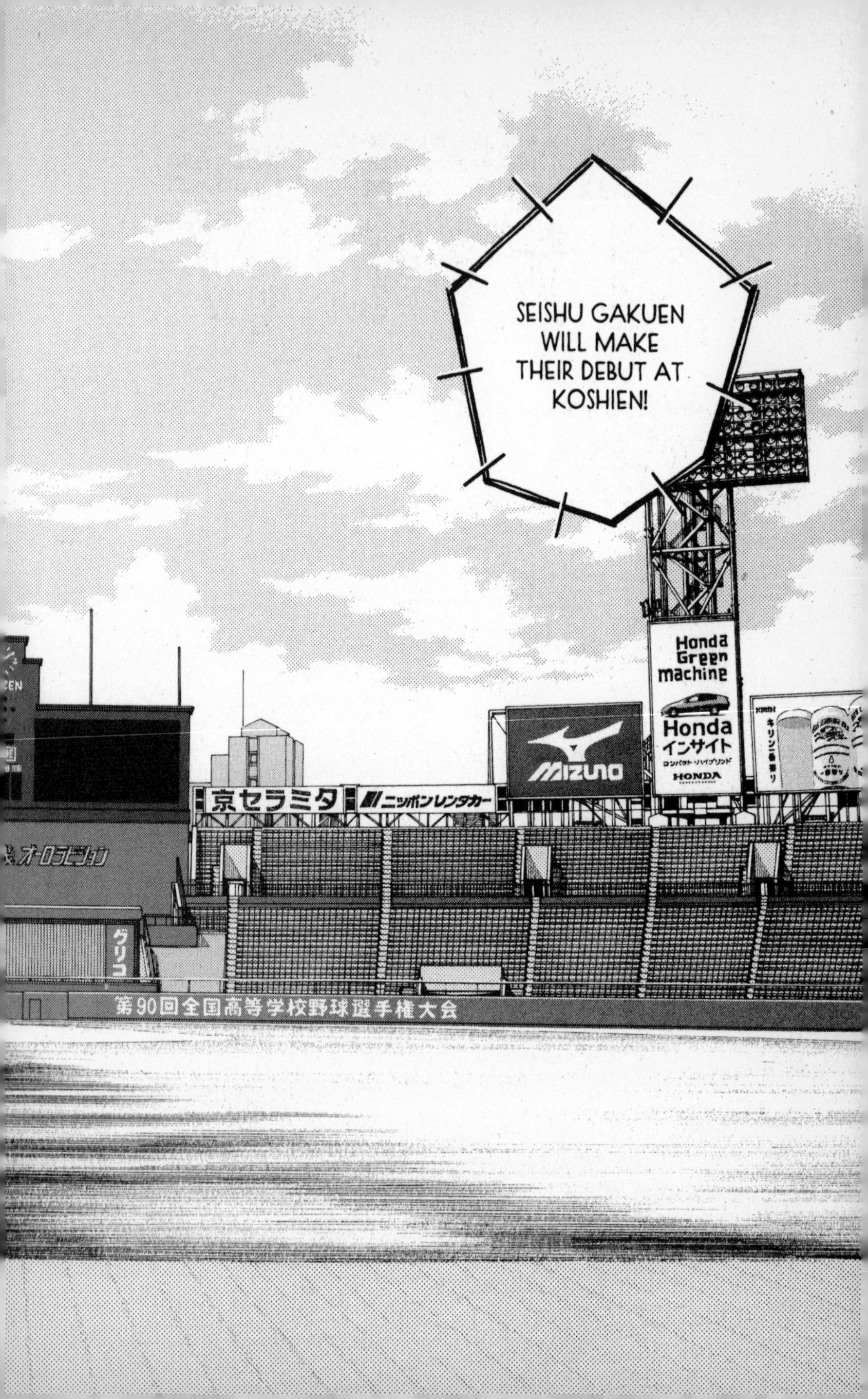
SEISHU GAKUEN WILL MAKE THEIR DEBUT AT KOSHIEN!
Honda Green machine
Honda インサイト
HONDA
MIZUNO
京セラミタ
ニッポンレンタカー
グリコ
第90回全国高等学校野球選手権大会

CHAPTER 159
I KNOW

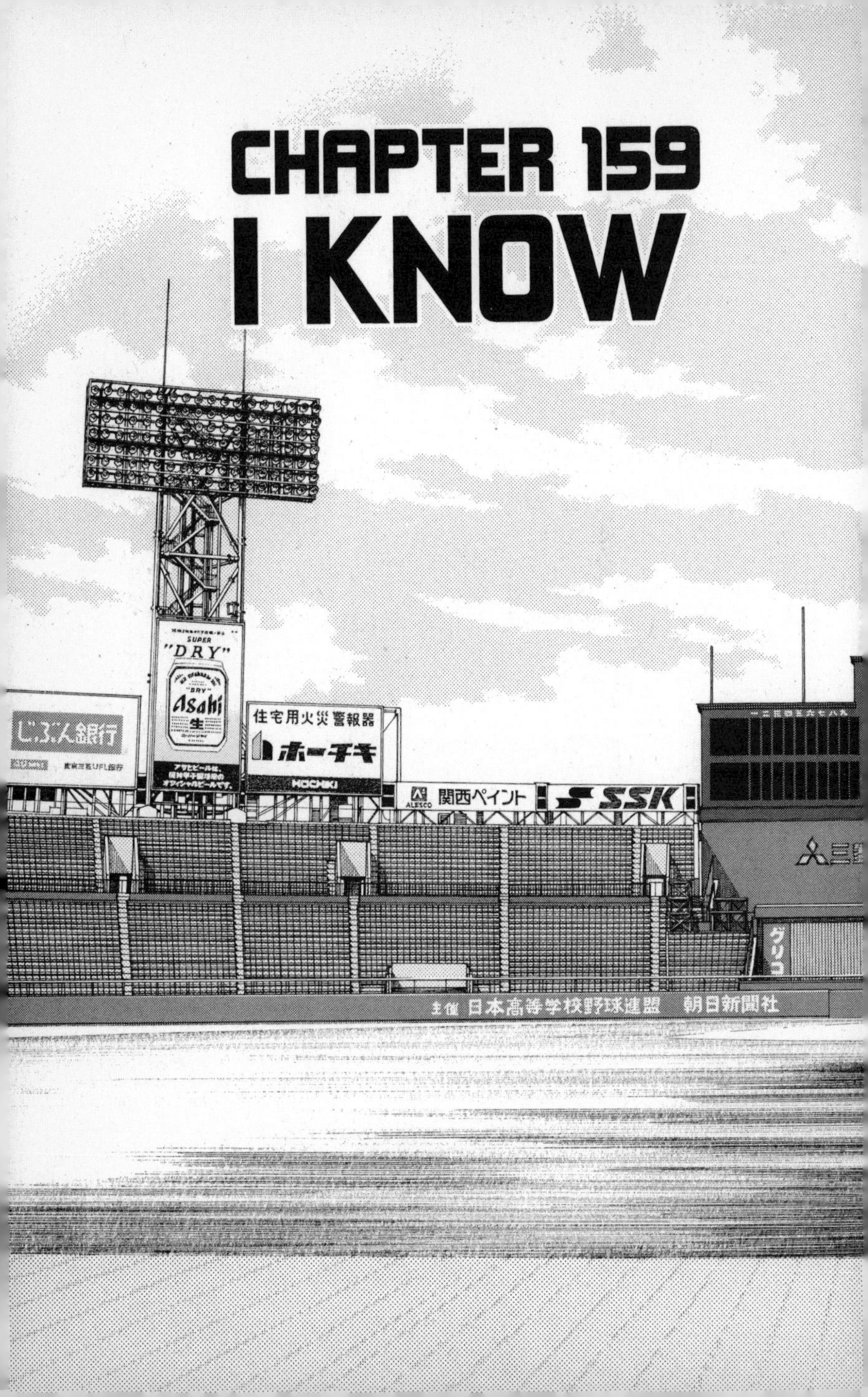
SUPER
"DRY"
Asahi
生
じぶん銀行
住宅用火災警報器
ホーチキ
HOCHIKI
ALESCO
関西ペイント
SSK
主催 日本高等学校野球連盟 朝日新聞社

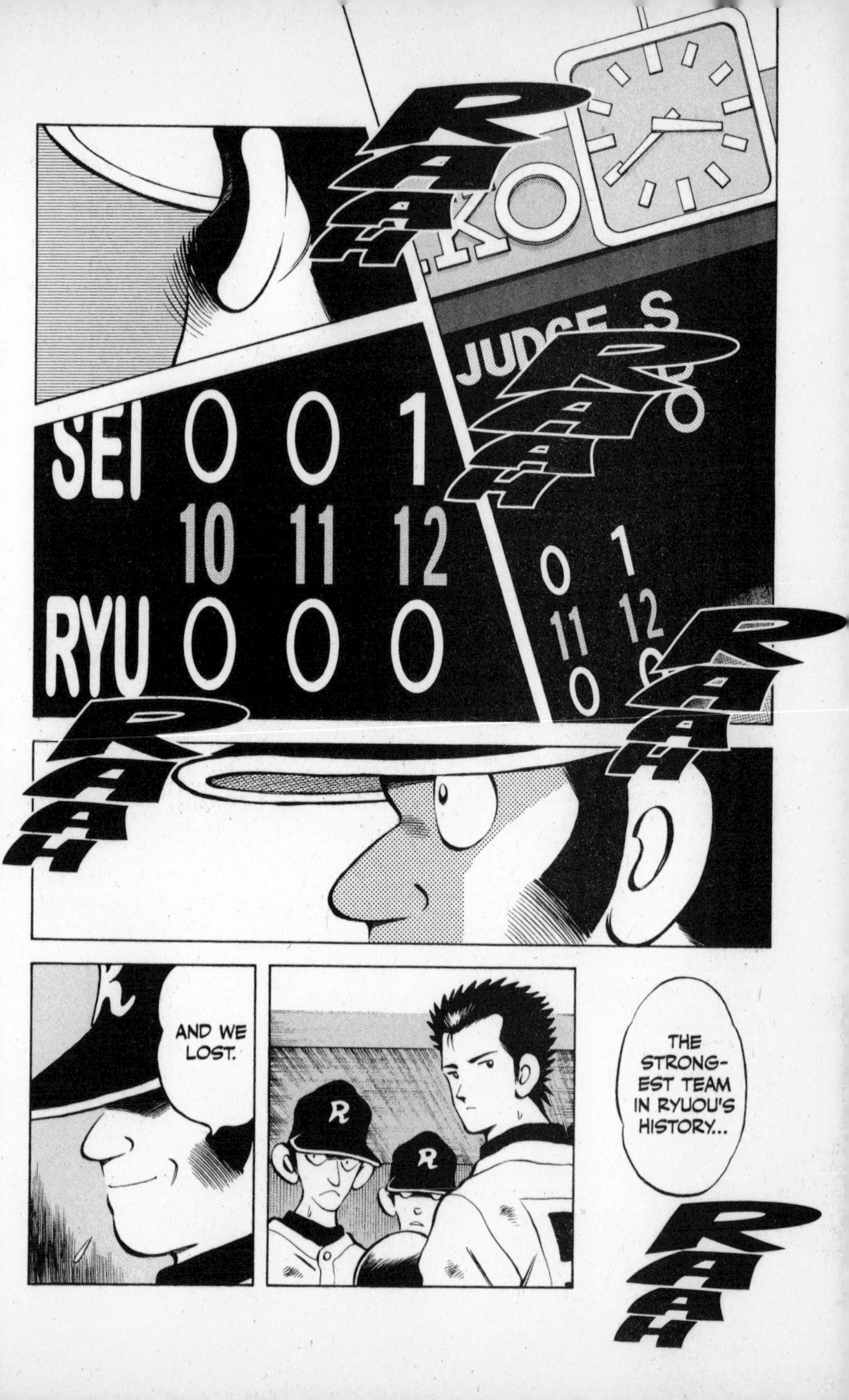
RAAH
JUDGE S
RAAH
SEI 0 0 1
10 11 12
RYU 0 0 0
RAAH
RAAH
THE STRONG-EST TEAM IN RYUOU'S HISTORY...
RAAH
AND WE LOST.

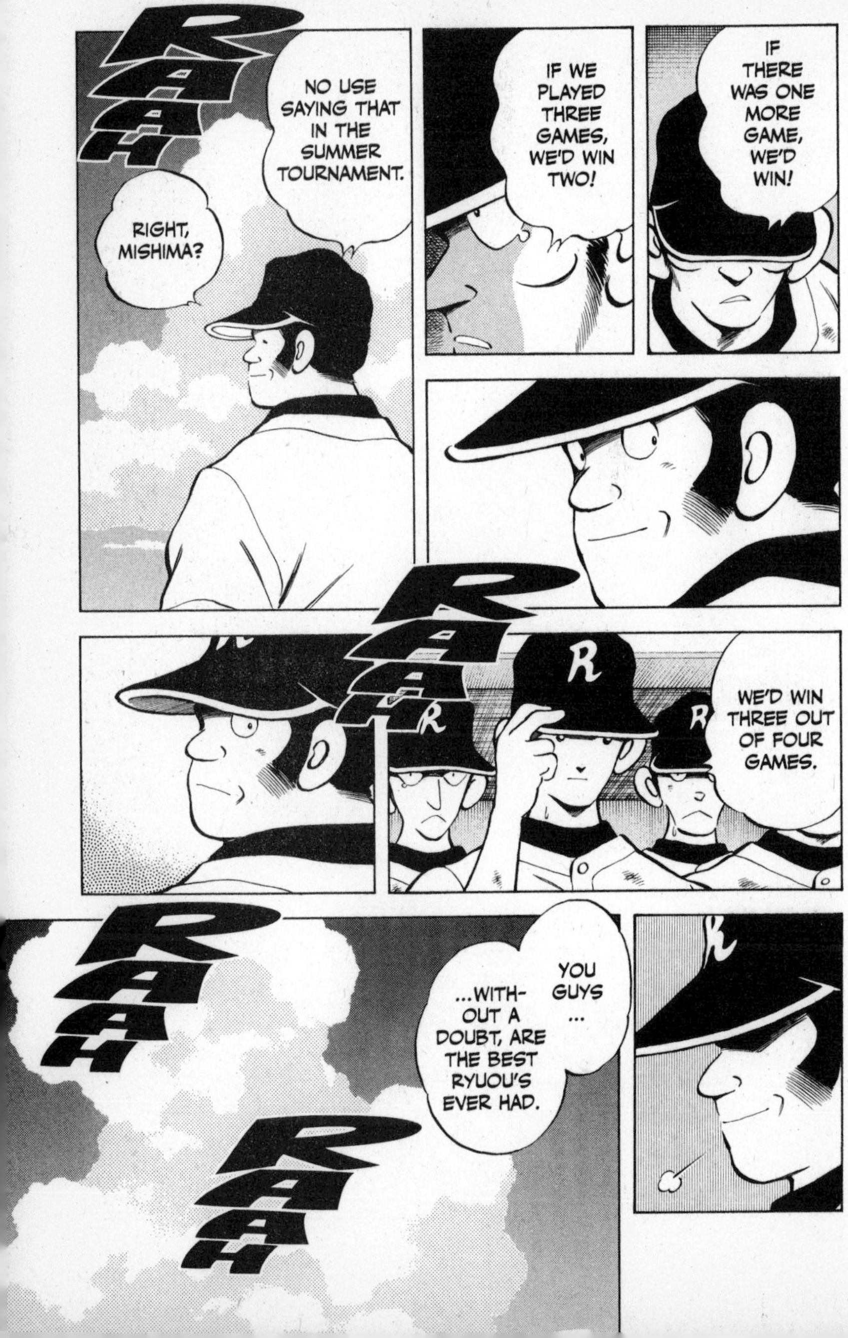
IF THERE WAS ONE MORE GAME, WE'D WIN!
IF WE PLAYED THREE GAMES, WE'D WIN TWO!
RAAAH
NO USE SAYING THAT IN THE SUMMER TOURNAMENT.
RIGHT, MISHIMA?
RAAAH
WE'D WIN THREE OUT OF FOUR GAMES.
YOU GUYS ...
...WITH-OUT A DOUBT, ARE THE BEST RYUOU'S EVER HAD.
RAAAH
RAAAH

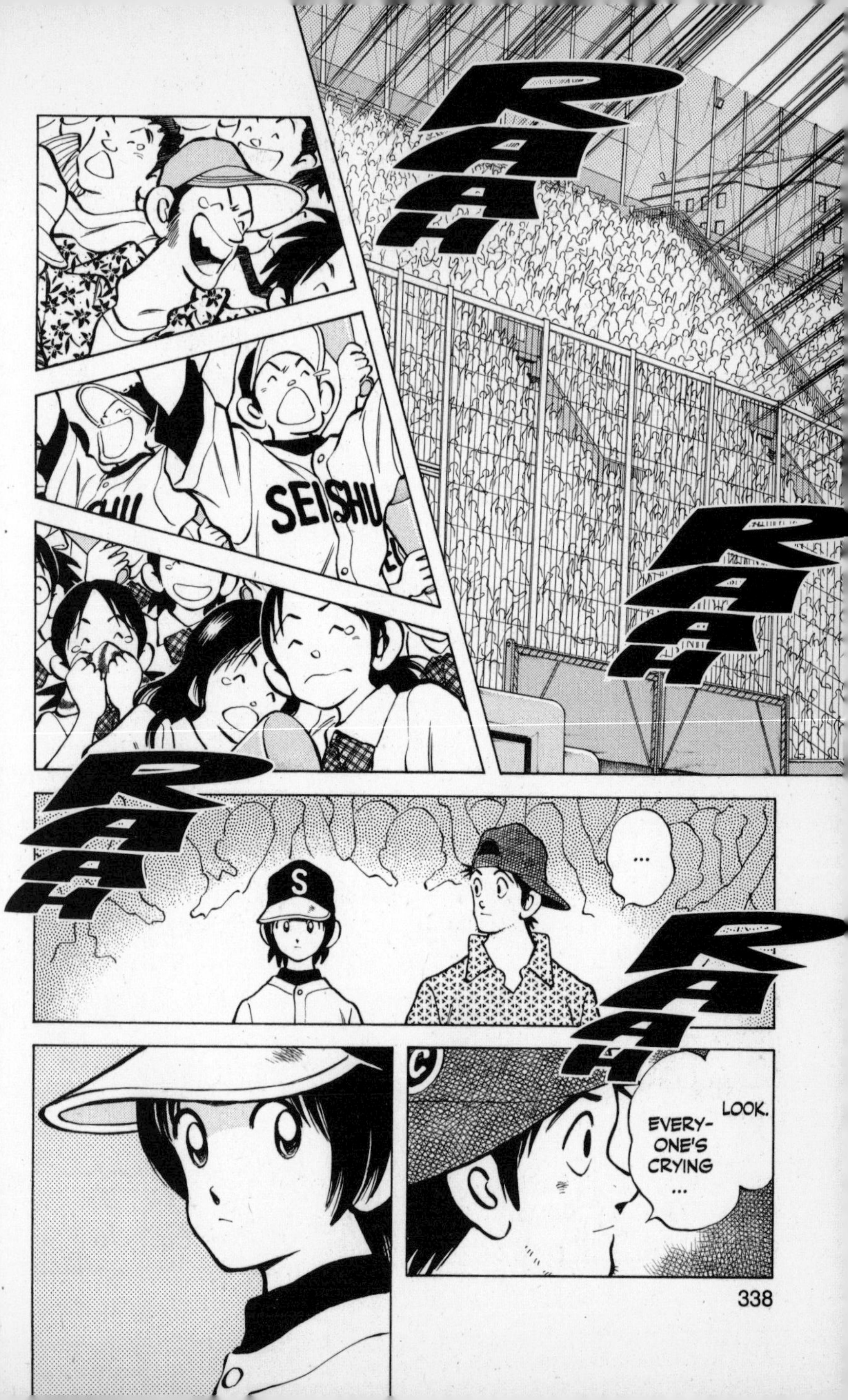
RAAH
SEISHU
RAAH
RAAH
...
RAAH
LOOK.
EVERY-ONE'S CRYING ...

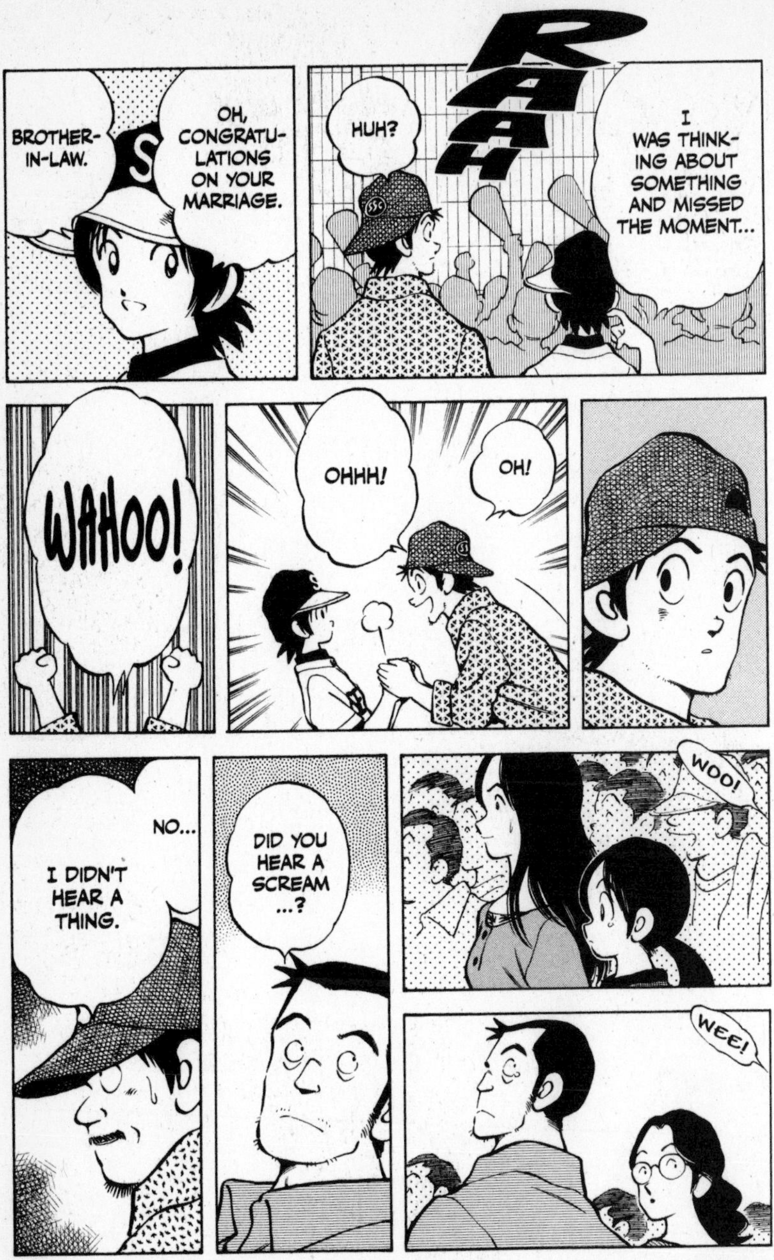
RAAH
I WAS THINKING ABOUT SOMETHING AND MISSED THE MOMENT...
HUH?
OH, CONGRATULATIONS ON YOUR MARRIAGE.
BROTHER-IN-LAW.
OH!
OHHH!
WAHOO!
WOO!
WEE!
DID YOU HEAR A SCREAM ...?
NO...
I DIDN'T HEAR A THING.

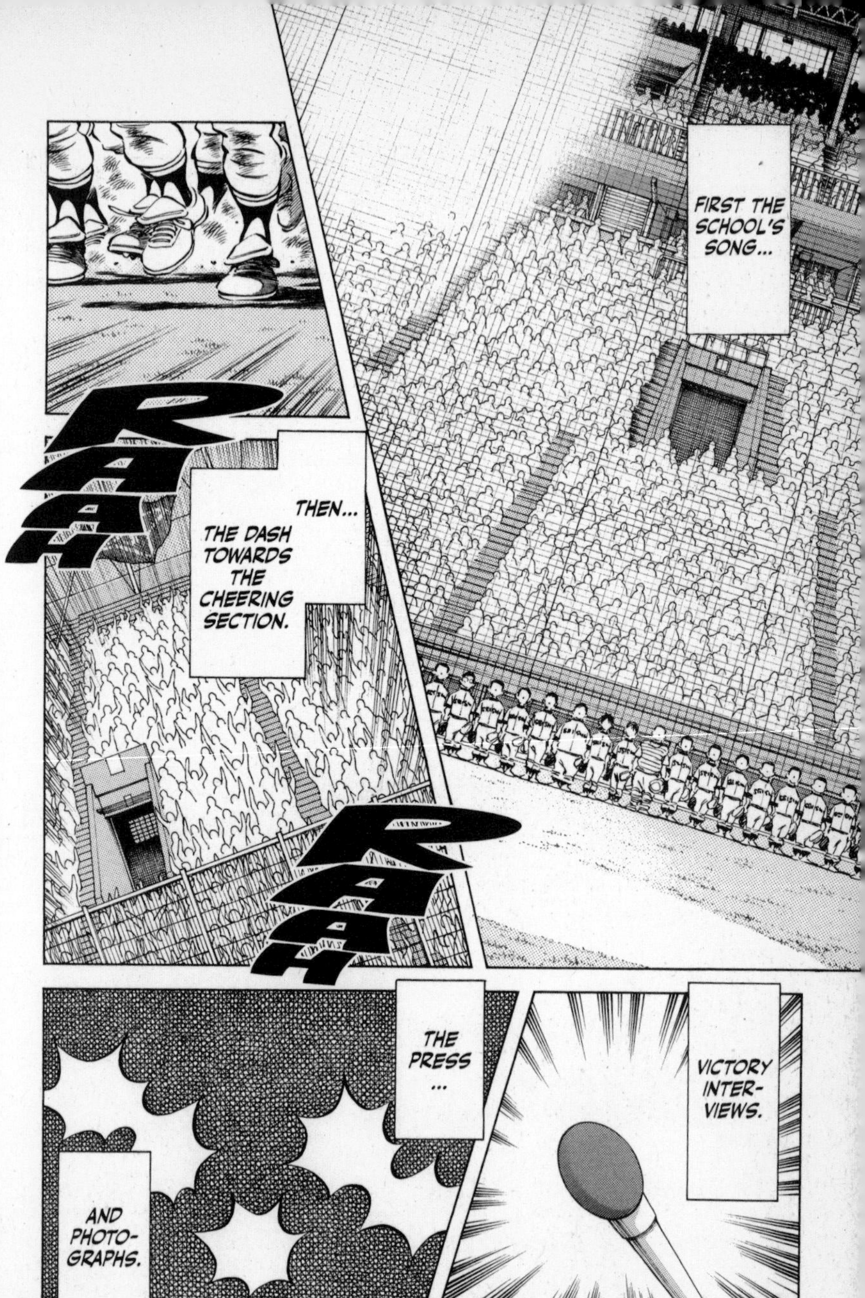
FIRST THE SCHOOL'S SONG...
RAAAH
THEN... THE DASH TOWARDS THE CHEERING SECTION.
RAAAH
VICTORY INTER-VIEWS.
THE PRESS ...
AND PHOTO-GRAPHS.

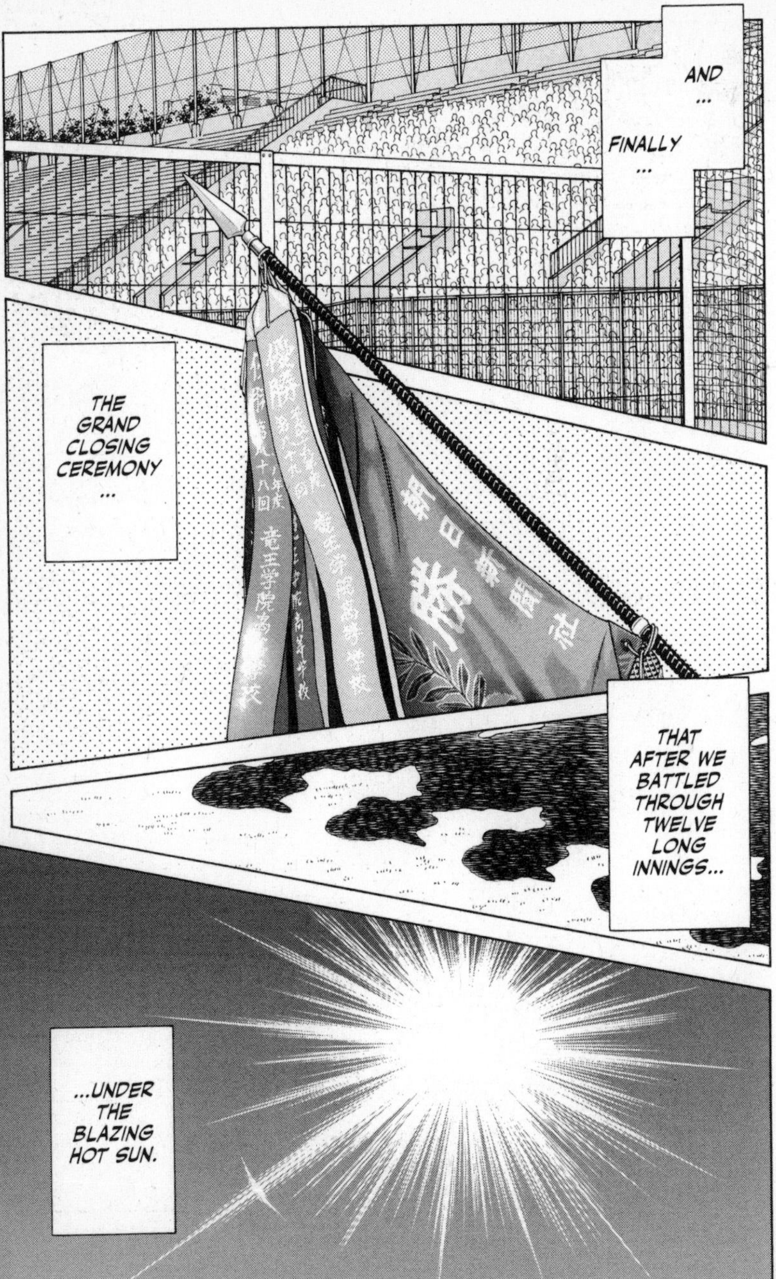
AND ... FINALLY ...
THE GRAND CLOSING CEREMONY ...
THAT AFTER WE BATTLED THROUGH TWELVE LONG INNINGS...
...UNDER THE BLAZING HOT SUN.

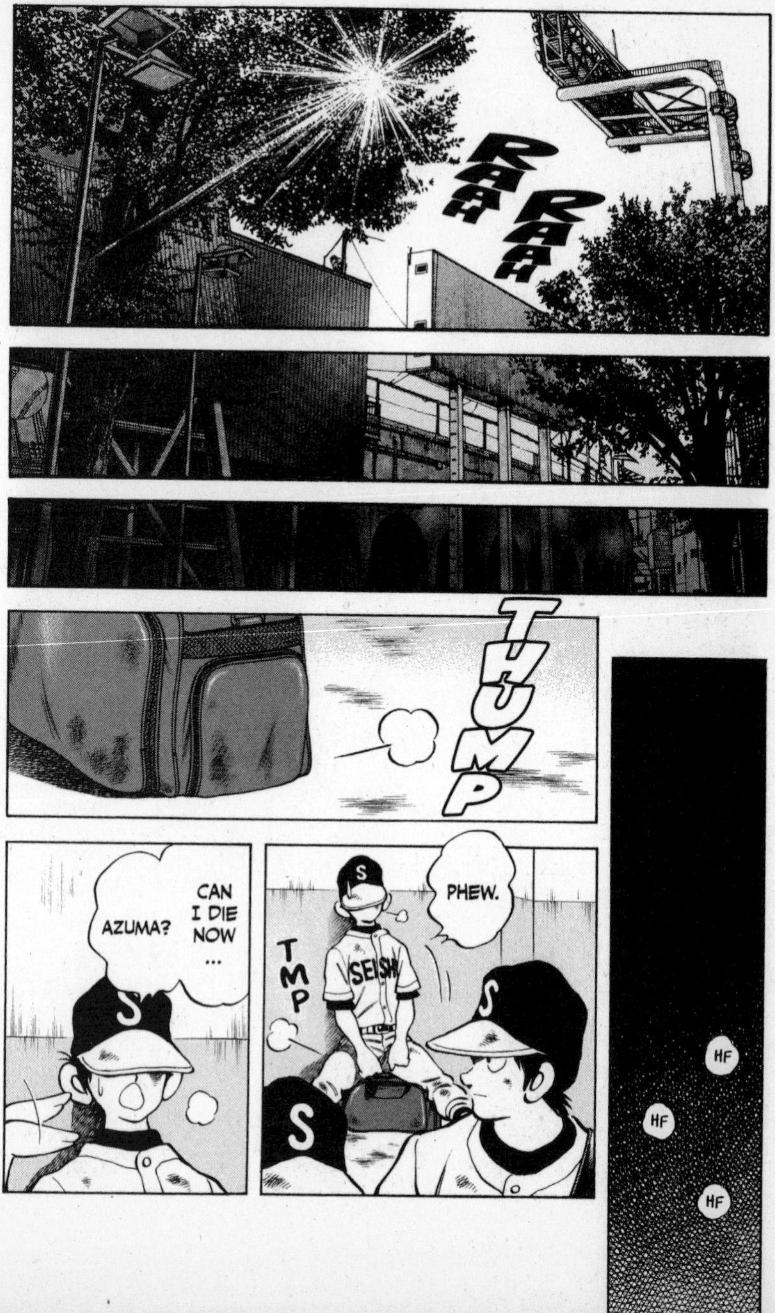
RAAH RAAH
HF
HF
HF
THUMP
PHEW.
TMP
CAN I DIE NOW...
AZUMA?

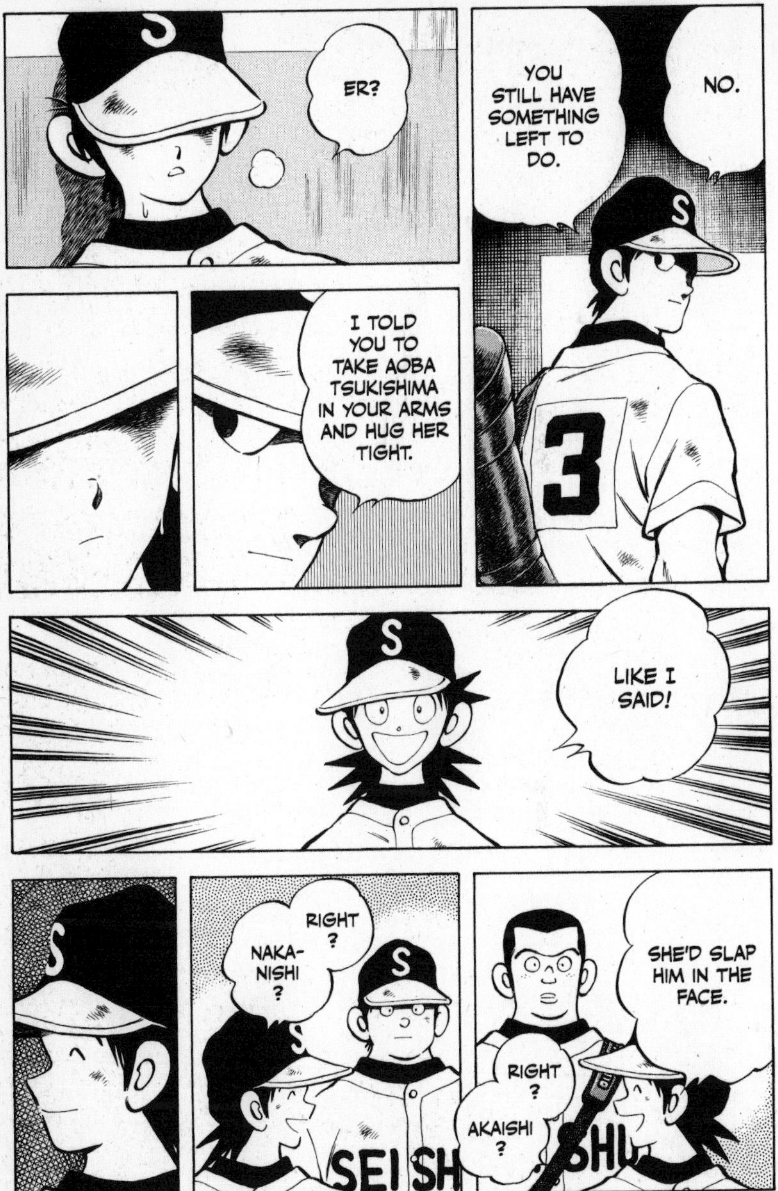
NO.
YOU STILL HAVE SOMETHING LEFT TO DO.
ER?
I TOLD YOU TO TAKE AOBA TSUKISHIMA IN YOUR ARMS AND HUG HER TIGHT.
LIKE I SAID!
SHE'D SLAP HIM IN THE FACE.
RIGHT?
AKAISHI?
RIGHT?
NAKA-NISHI?

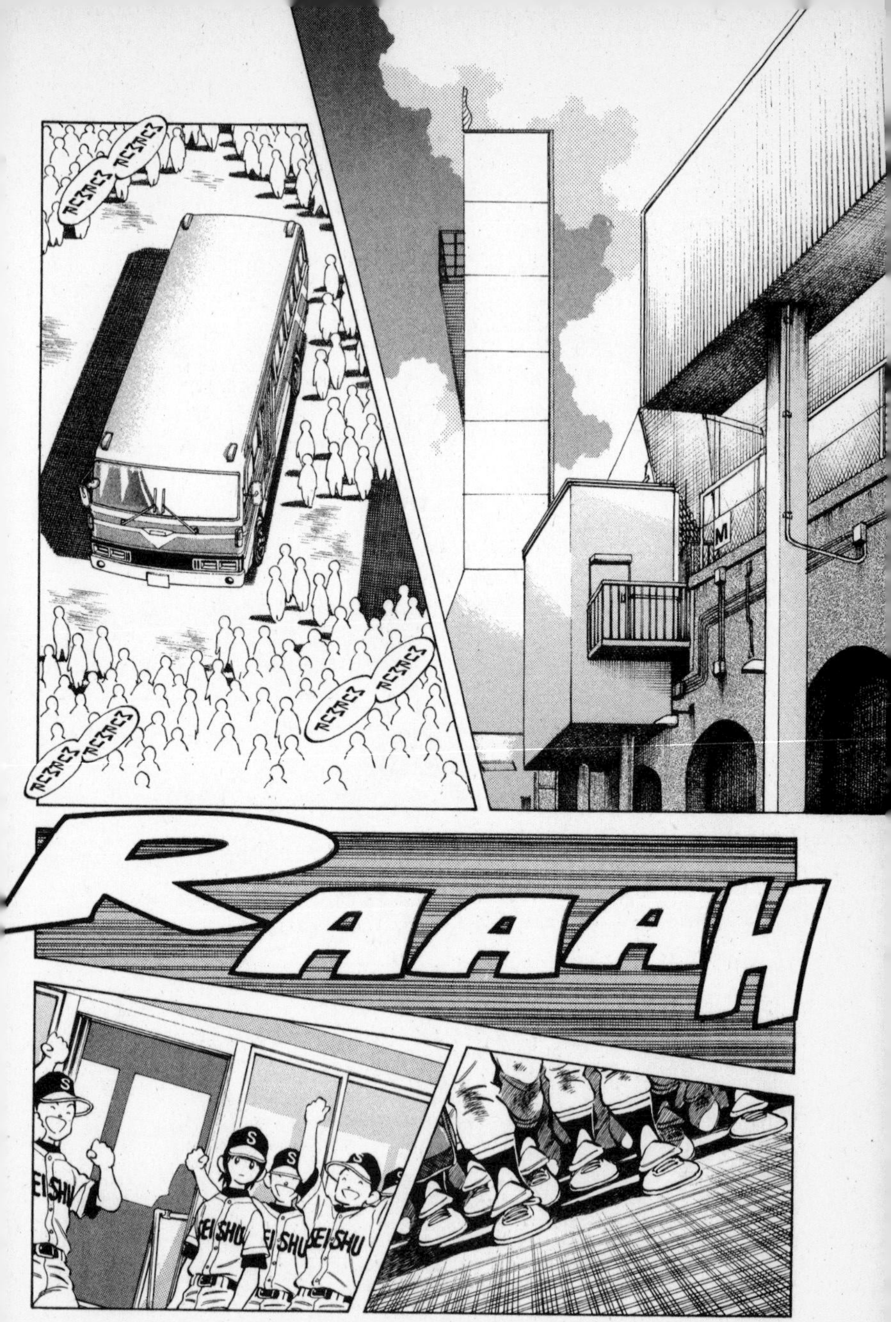
RAAAH

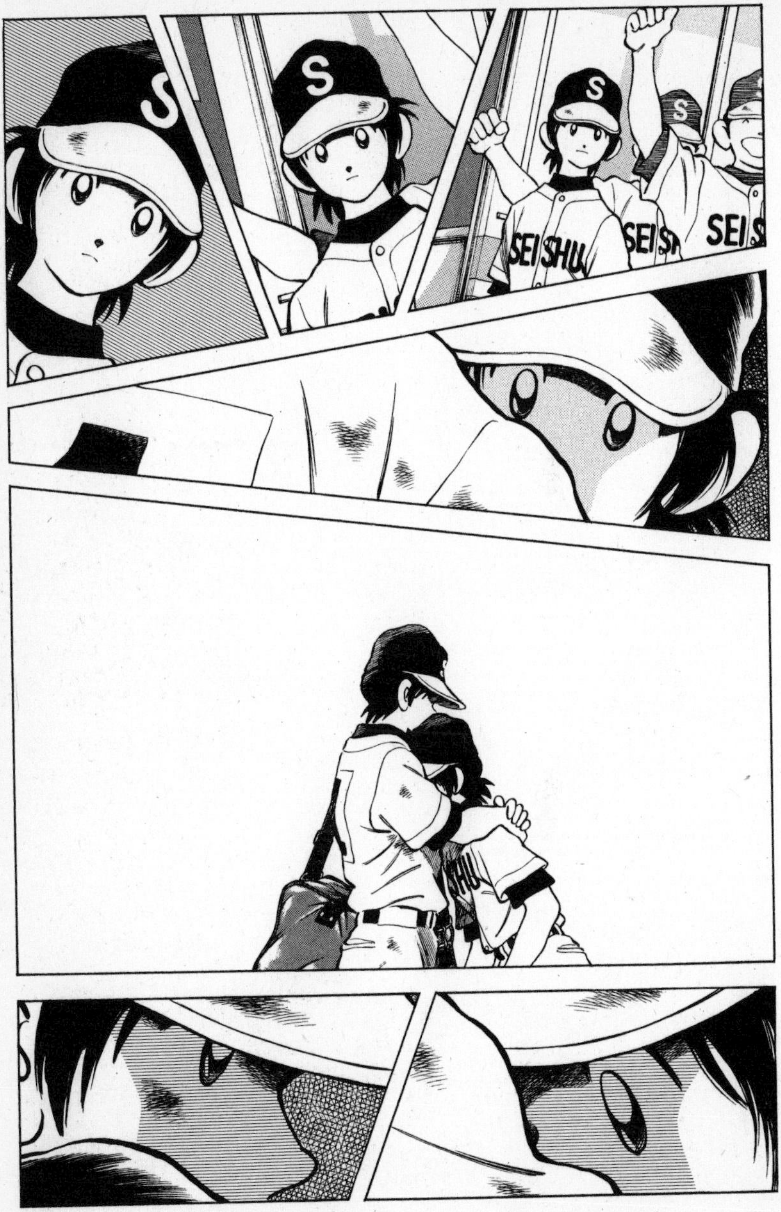
SEISHU

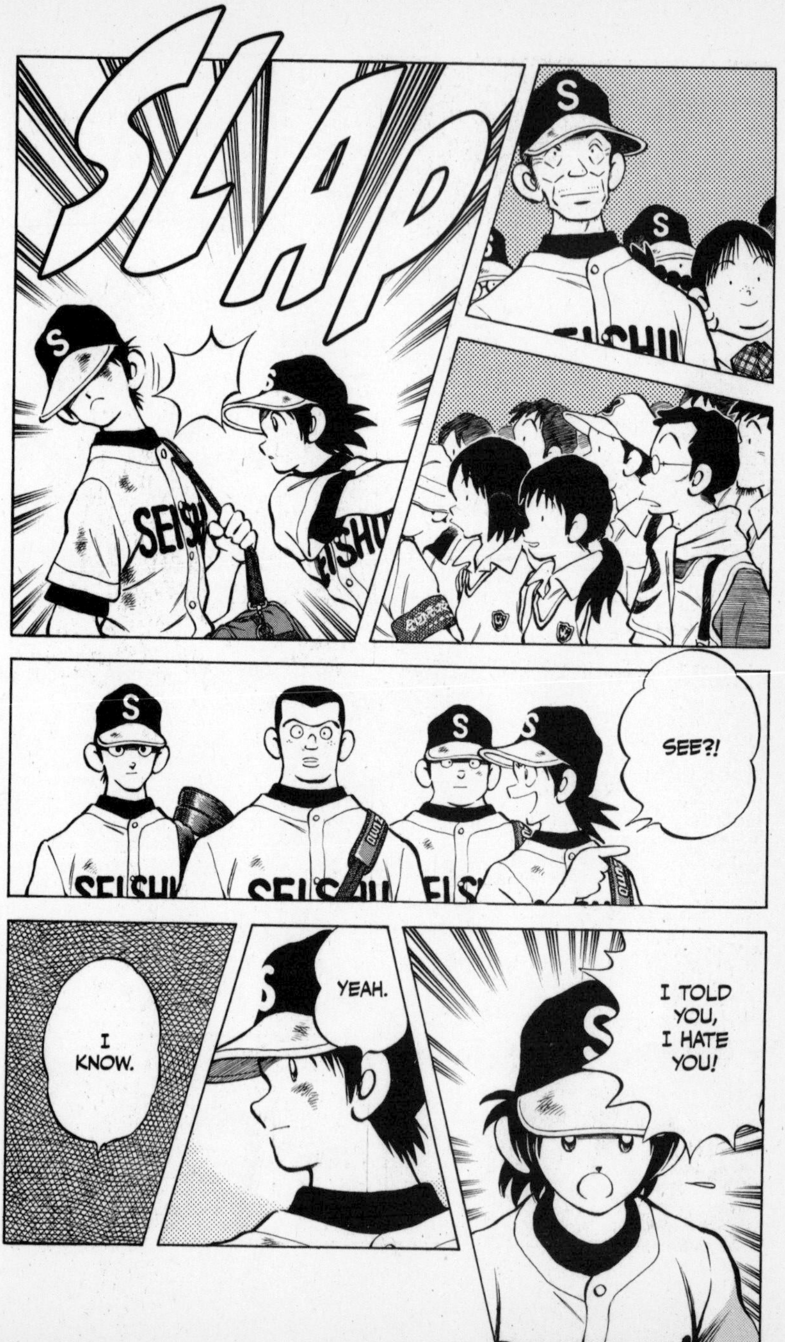
SLAP
SEE?!
I TOLD YOU, I HATE YOU!
YEAH.
I KNOW.

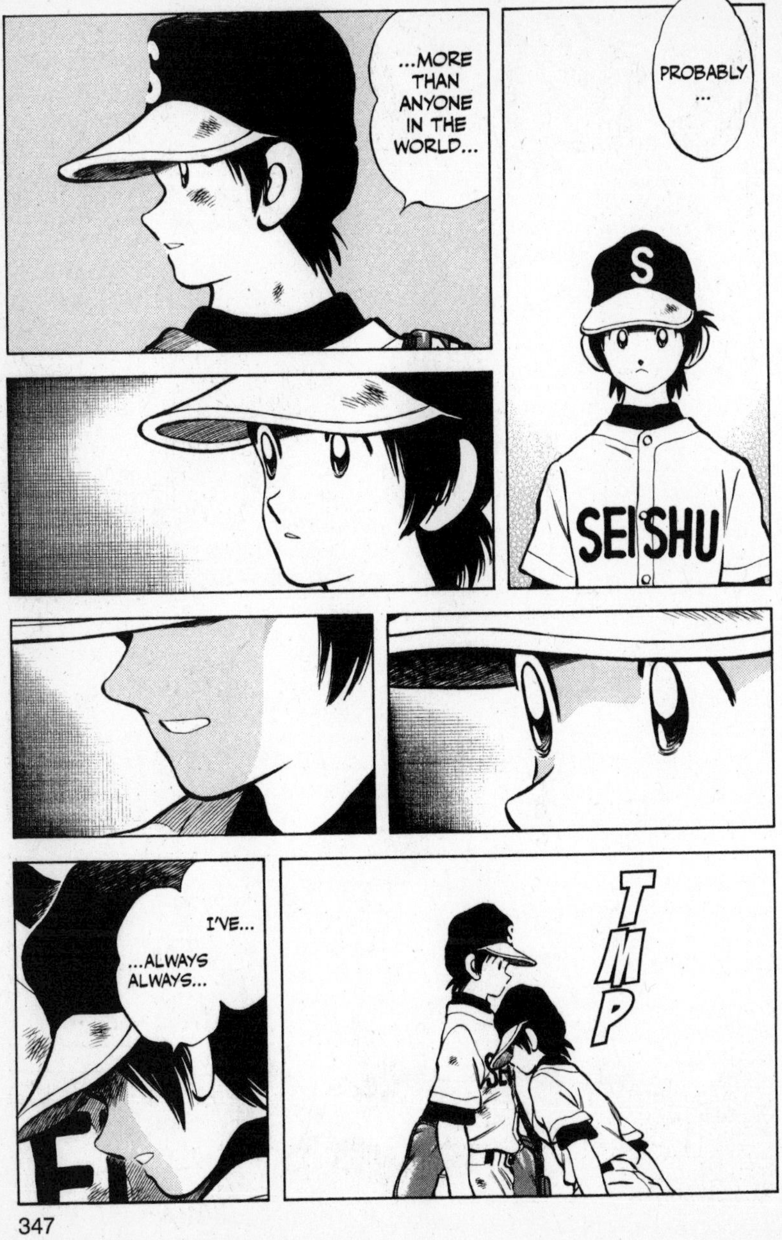
PROBABLY ...
...MORE THAN ANYONE IN THE WORLD...
TMP
I'VE...
...ALWAYS ALWAYS...

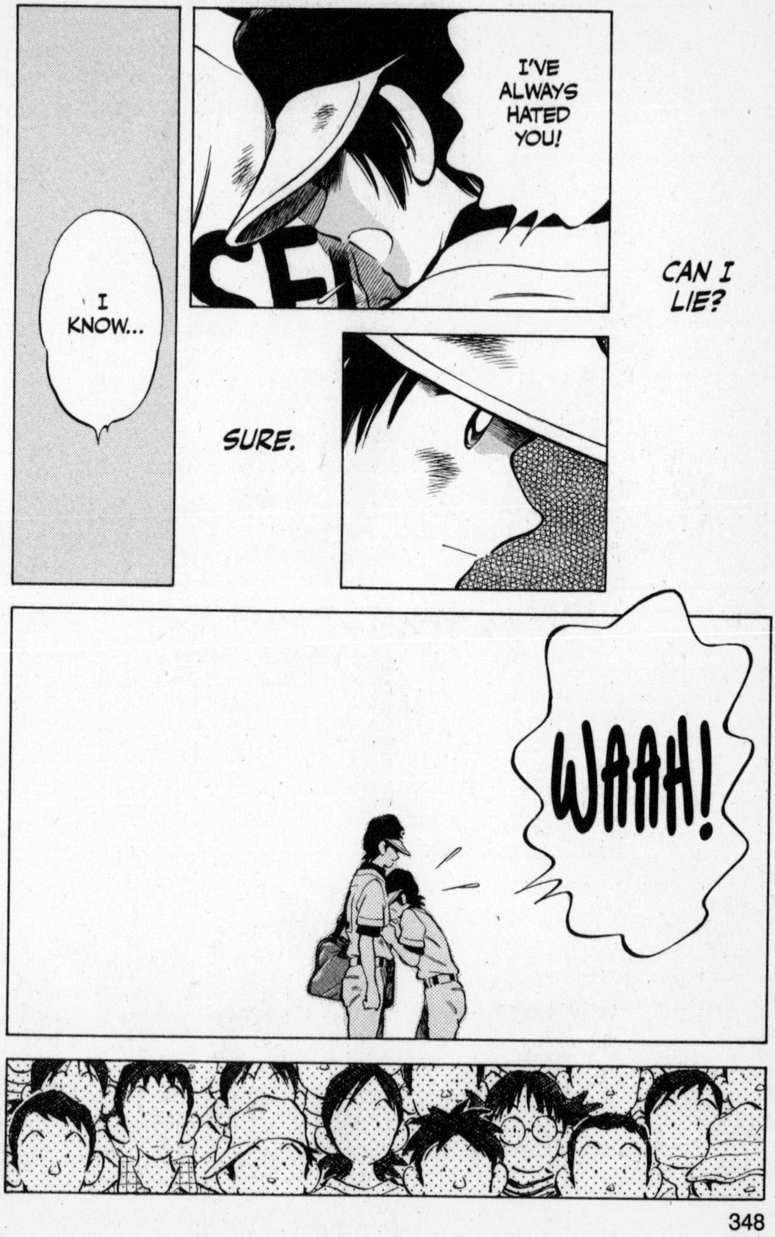
I'VE ALWAYS HATED YOU!
CAN I LIE?
SURE.
I KNOW...
WAAH!

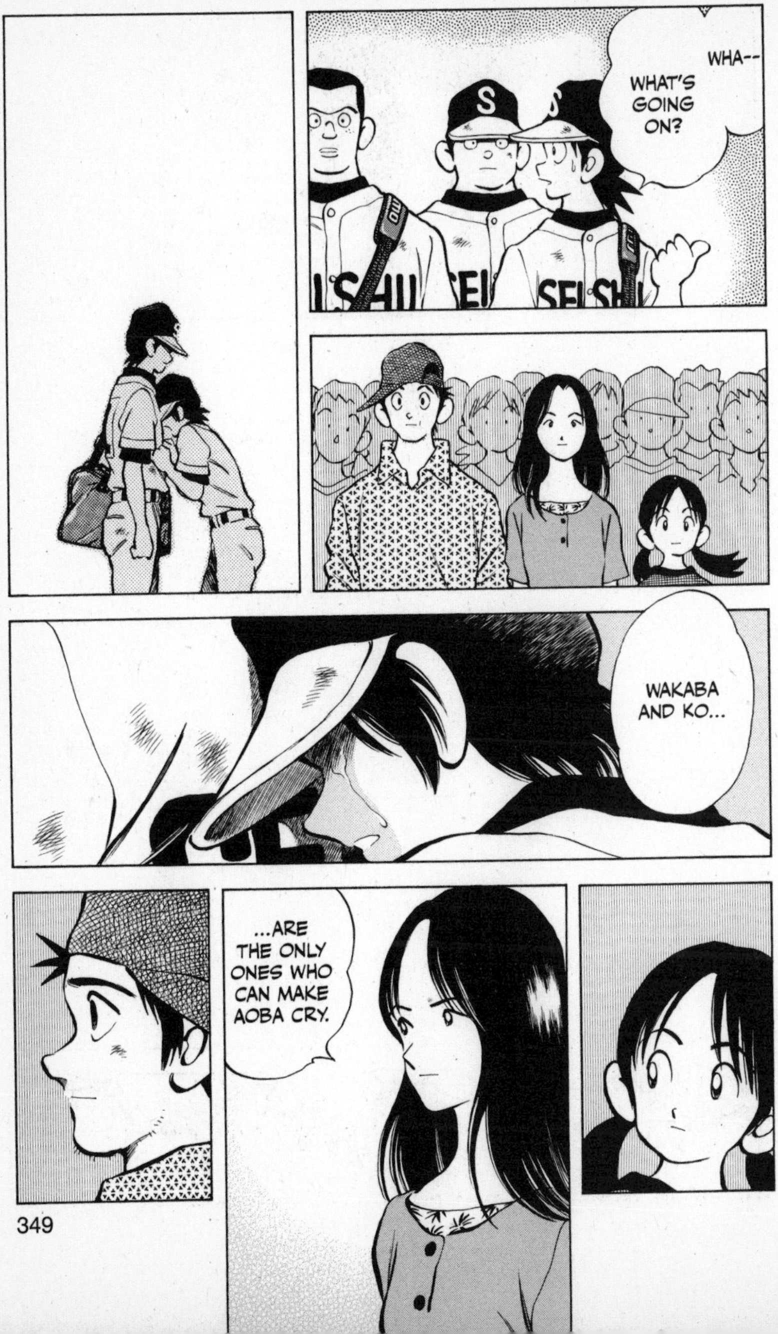
WHA--
WHAT'S GOING ON?
WAKABA AND KO...
...ARE THE ONLY ONES WHO CAN MAKE AOBA CRY.

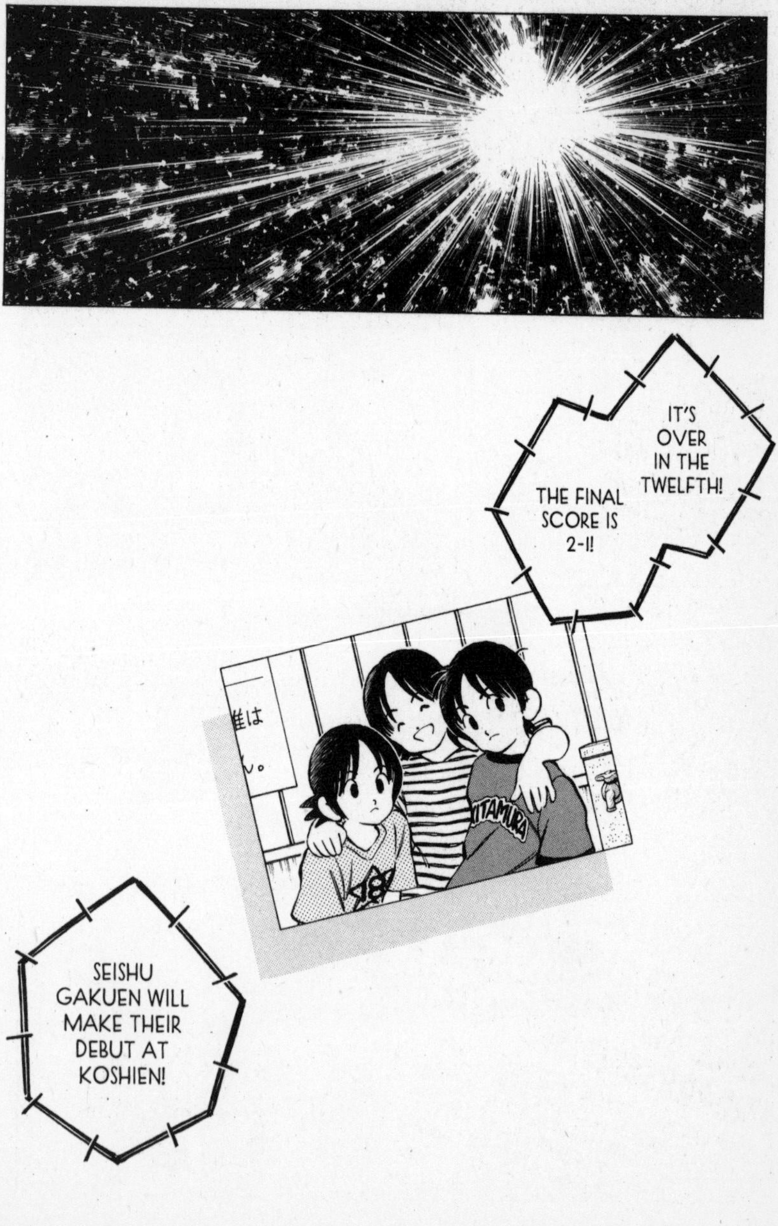
IT'S OVER IN THE TWELFTH!
THE FINAL SCORE IS 2-1!
SEISHU GAKUEN WILL MAKE THEIR DEBUT AT KOSHIEN!

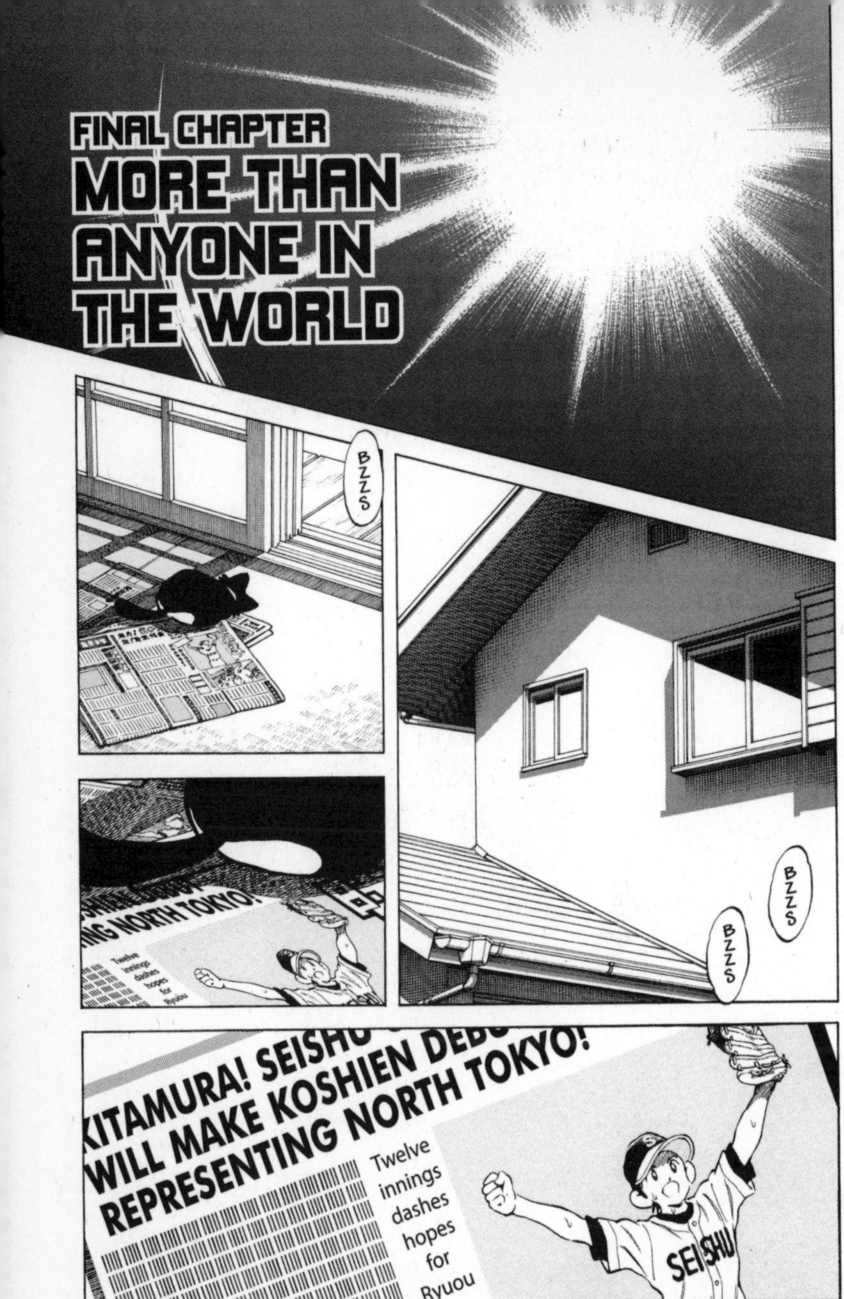
FINAL CHAPTER
MORE THAN ANYONE IN THE WORLD
BZZS
BZZS
BZZS
Twelve innings dashes hopes for Ryuou
KITAMURA! SEISHU
WILL MAKE KOSHIEN DEBU
REPRESENTING NORTH TOKYO!
Twelve innings dashes hopes for Ryuou
SEISHU

FINAL CHAPTER
MORE THAN ANYONE IN THE WORLD

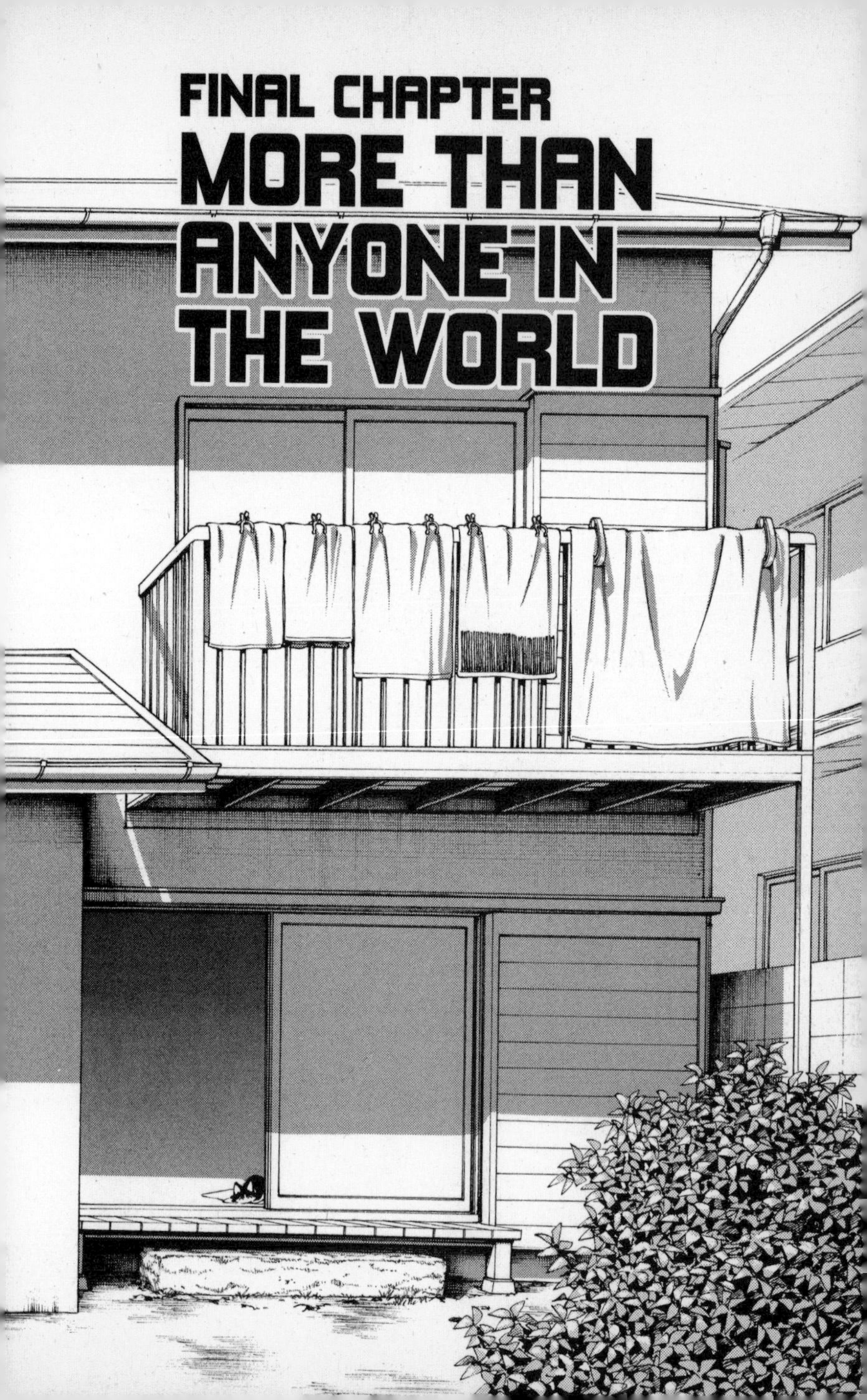

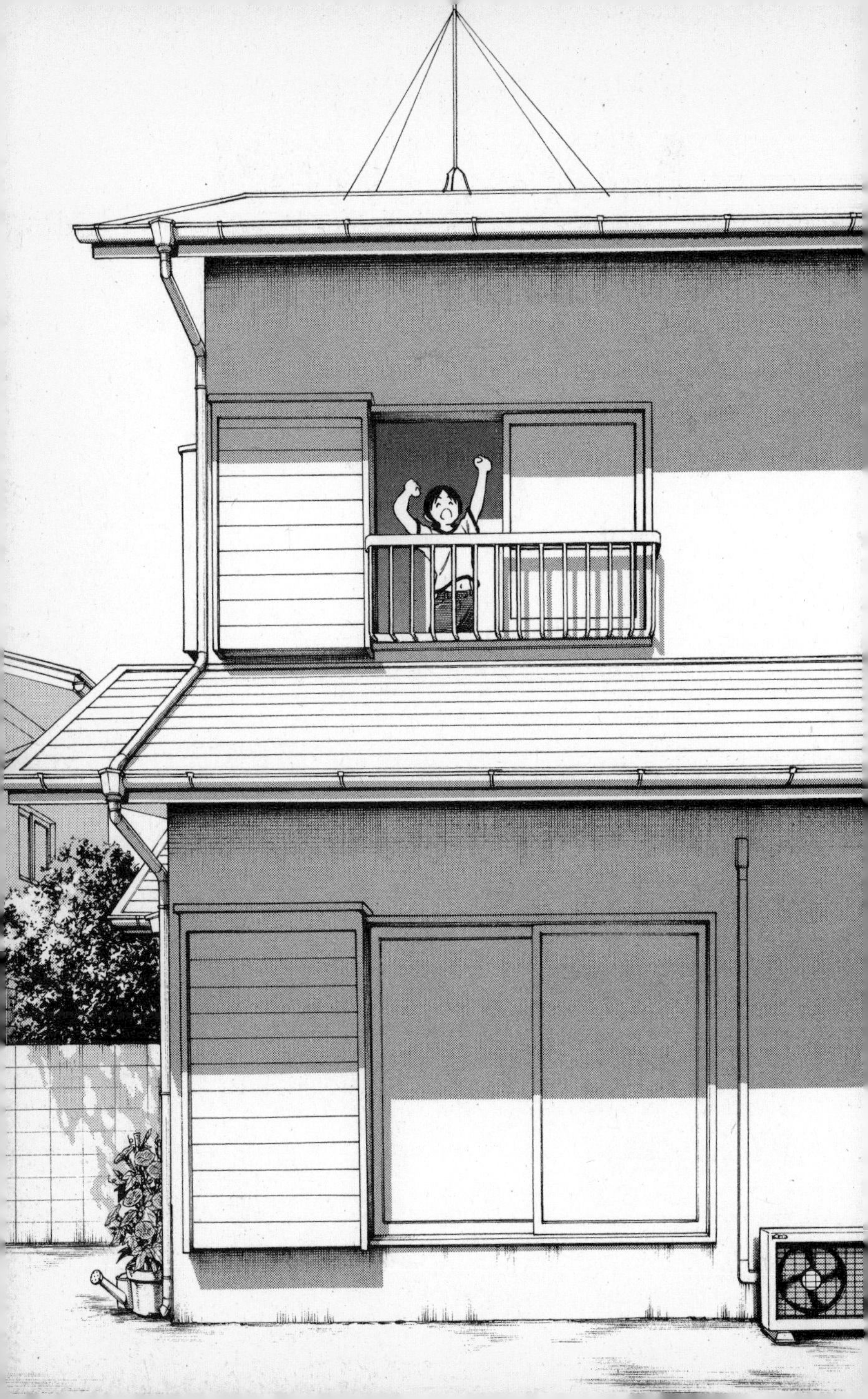

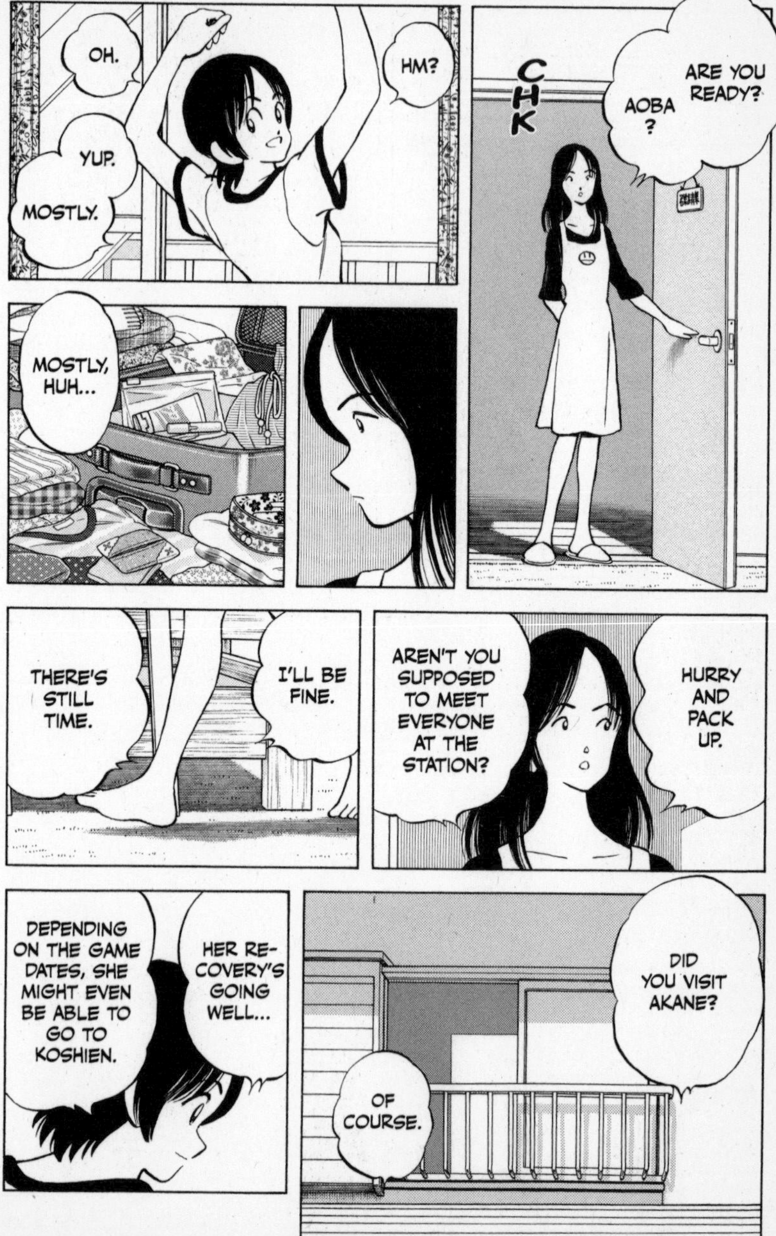
CHK
AOBA? ARE YOU READY?
HM?
OH.
YUP.
MOSTLY.
MOSTLY, HUH...
HURRY AND PACK UP.
AREN'T YOU SUPPOSED TO MEET EVERYONE AT THE STATION?
I'LL BE FINE.
THERE'S STILL TIME.
DID YOU VISIT AKANE?
OF COURSE.
HER RE-COVERY'S GOING WELL...
DEPENDING ON THE GAME DATES, SHE MIGHT EVEN BE ABLE TO GO TO KOSHIEN.

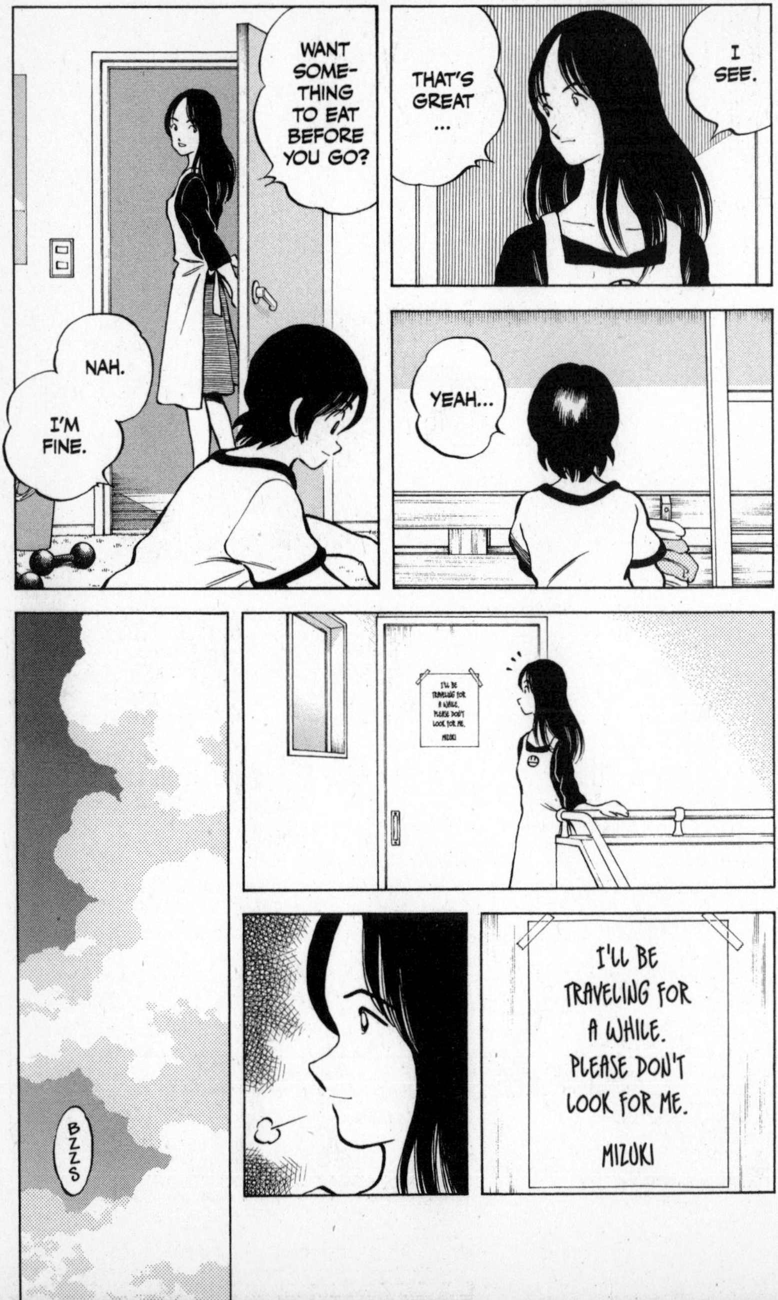
I SEE.
THAT'S GREAT ...
YEAH...
WANT SOME-THING TO EAT BEFORE YOU GO?
NAH.
I'M FINE.
I'LL BE TRAVELING FOR A WHILE. PLEASE DON'T LOOK FOR ME.
MIZUKI
I'LL BE TRAVELING FOR A WHILE. PLEASE DON'T LOOK FOR ME.
MIZUKI
BZZS

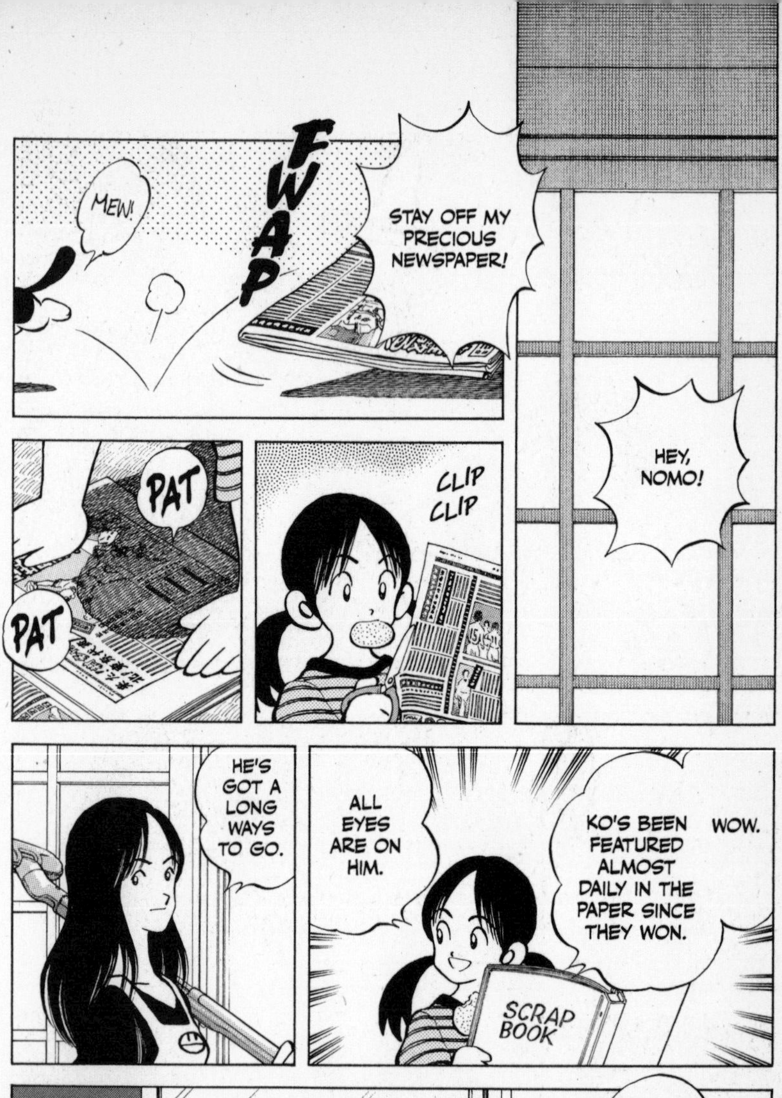
HEY, NOMO!
STAY OFF MY PRECIOUS NEWSPAPER!
FWAP
MEW!
CLIP CLIP
PAT
PAT
WOW.
KO'S BEEN FEATURED ALMOST DAILY IN THE PAPER SINCE THEY WON.
ALL EYES ARE ON HIM.
SCRAP BOOK
HE'S GOT A LONG WAYS TO GO.
THE REAL THING HAS YET TO BEGIN.

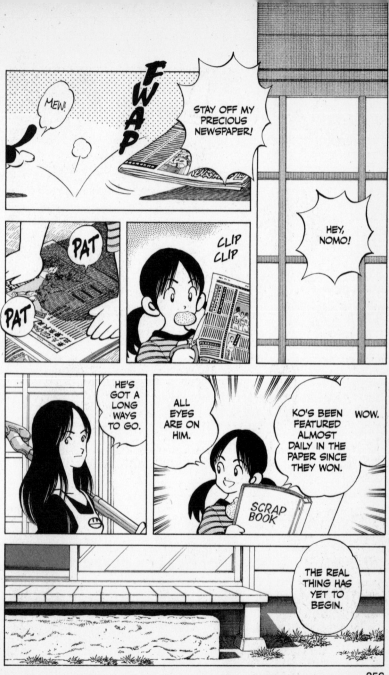

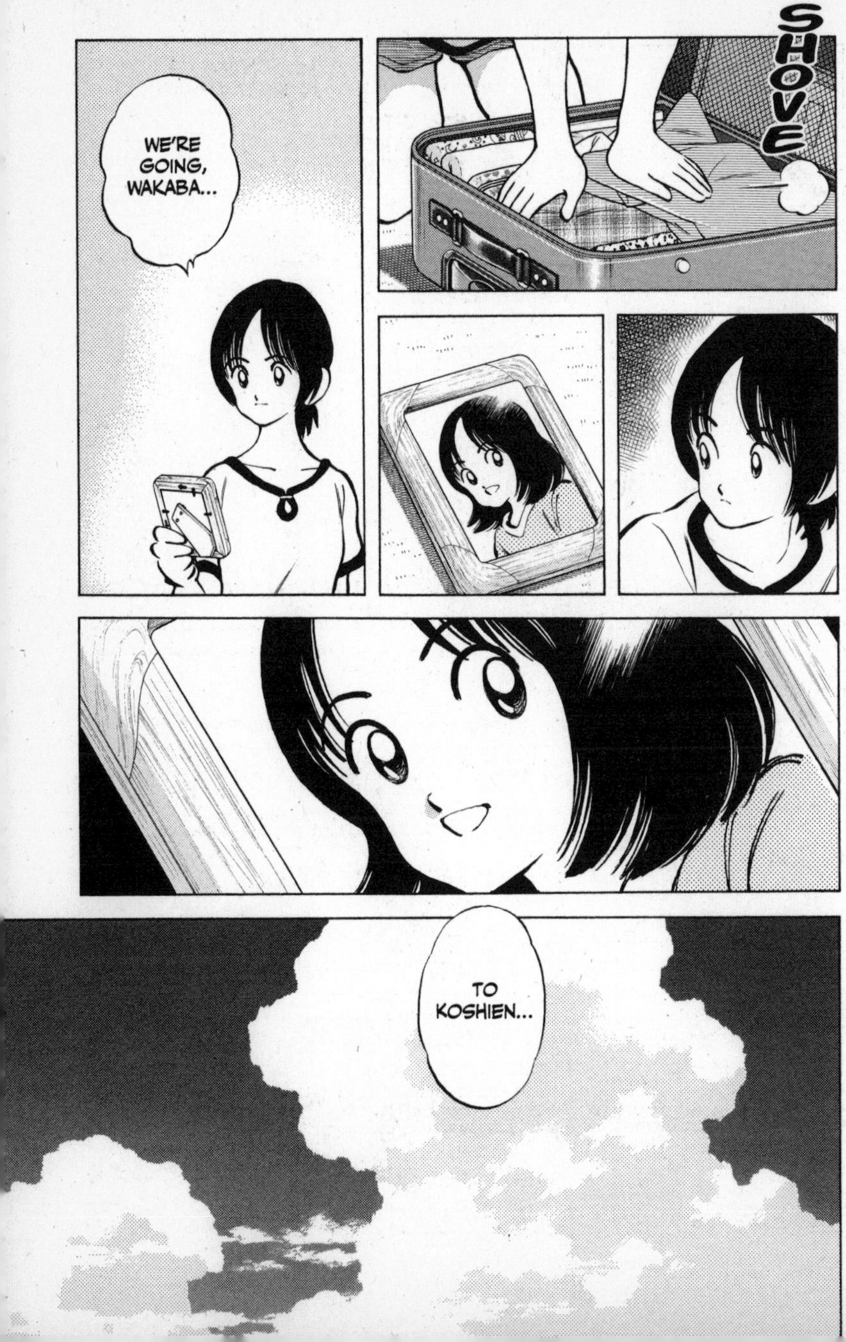
SHOVE
WE'RE GOING, WAKABA...
TO KOSHIEN...

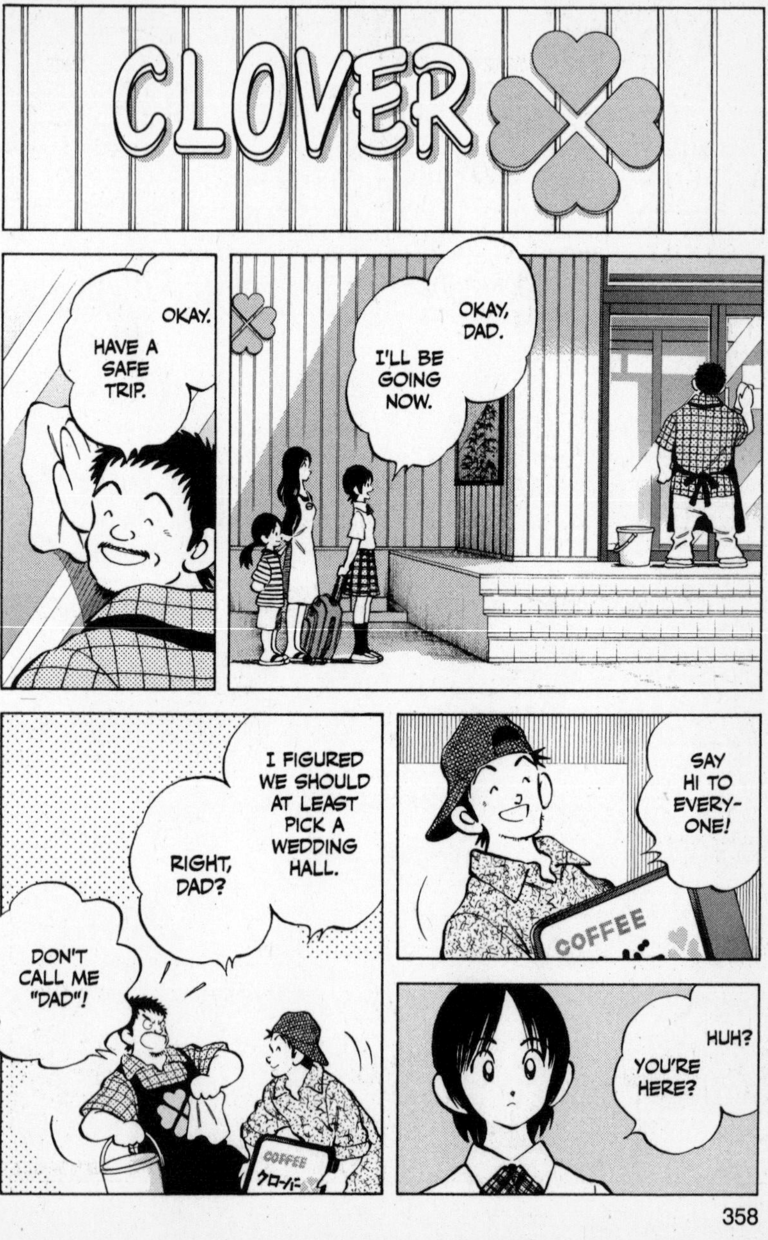
CLOVER
OKAY, DAD. I'LL BE GOING NOW.
OKAY. HAVE A SAFE TRIP.
SAY HI TO EVERY-ONE!
COFFEE
HUH? YOU'RE HERE?
I FIGURED WE SHOULD AT LEAST PICK A WEDDING HALL. RIGHT, DAD?
DON'T CALL ME "DAD"!
COFFEE
クローバー

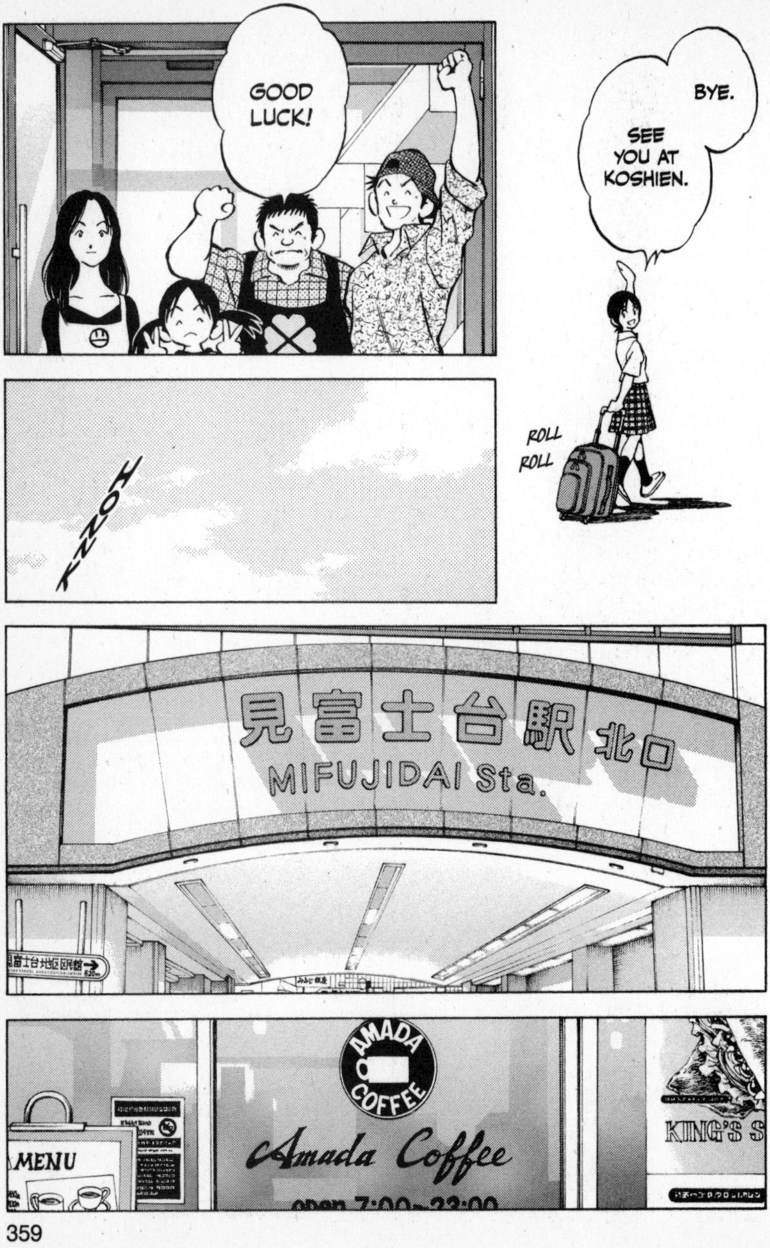
BYE.
SEE YOU AT KOSHIEN.
ROLL ROLL
GOOD LUCK!
HONK
見富士台駅 北口
MIFUJIDAI Sta.
AMADA COFFEE
Amada Coffee
MENU
KING'S S

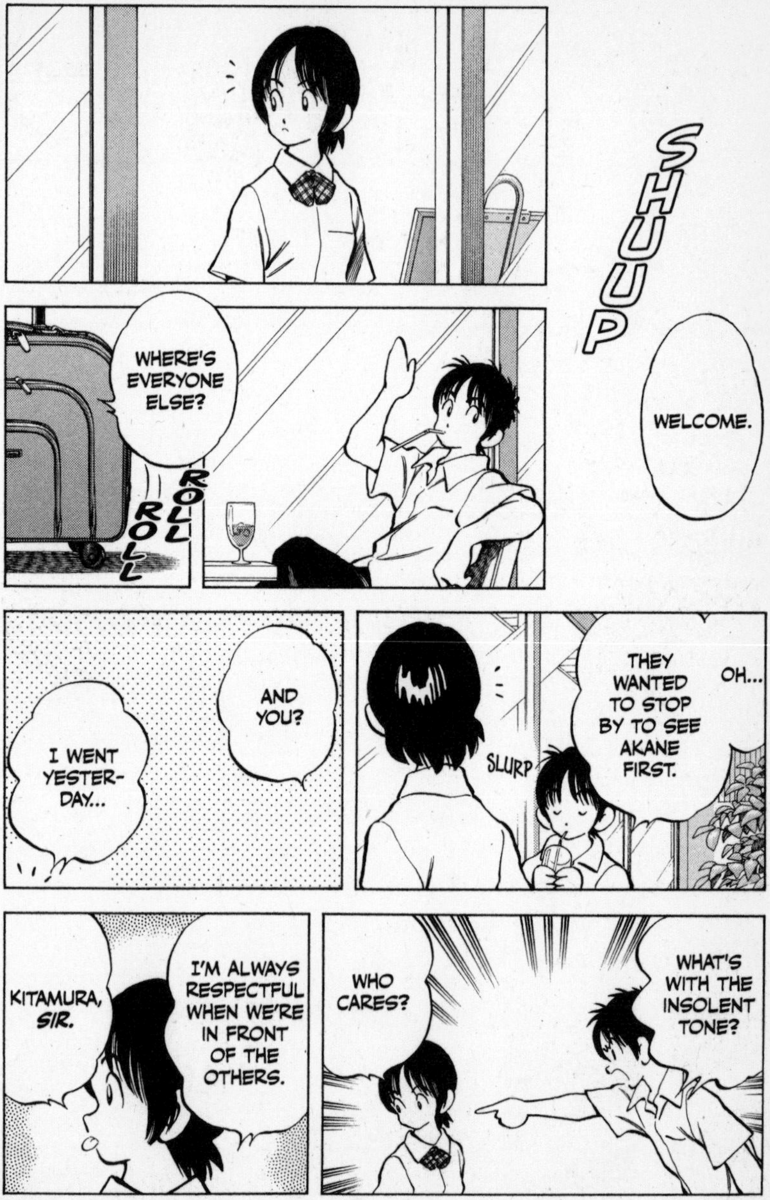
SHUUP
WELCOME.
WHERE'S EVERYONE ELSE?
ROLL ROLL
OH...
THEY WANTED TO STOP BY TO SEE AKANE FIRST.
SLURP
AND YOU?
I WENT YESTER-DAY...
WHAT'S WITH THE INSOLENT TONE?
WHO CARES?
I'M ALWAYS RESPECTFUL WHEN WE'RE IN FRONT OF THE OTHERS.
KITAMURA, *SIR.*

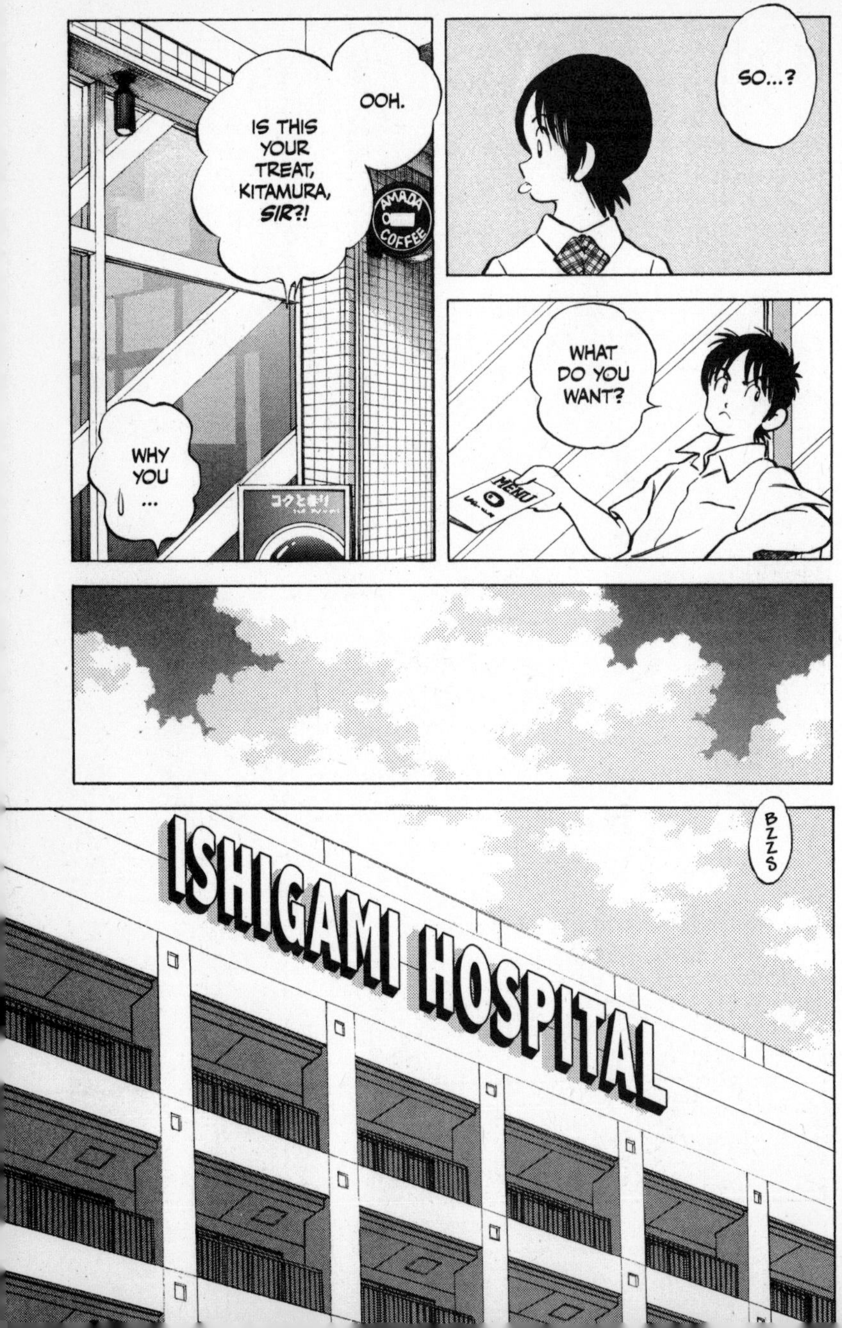
SO...?
WHAT DO YOU WANT?
MENU
OOH. IS THIS YOUR TREAT, KITAMURA, SIR?!
AMADA COFFEE
WHY YOU ...
BZZS
ISHIGAMI HOSPITAL

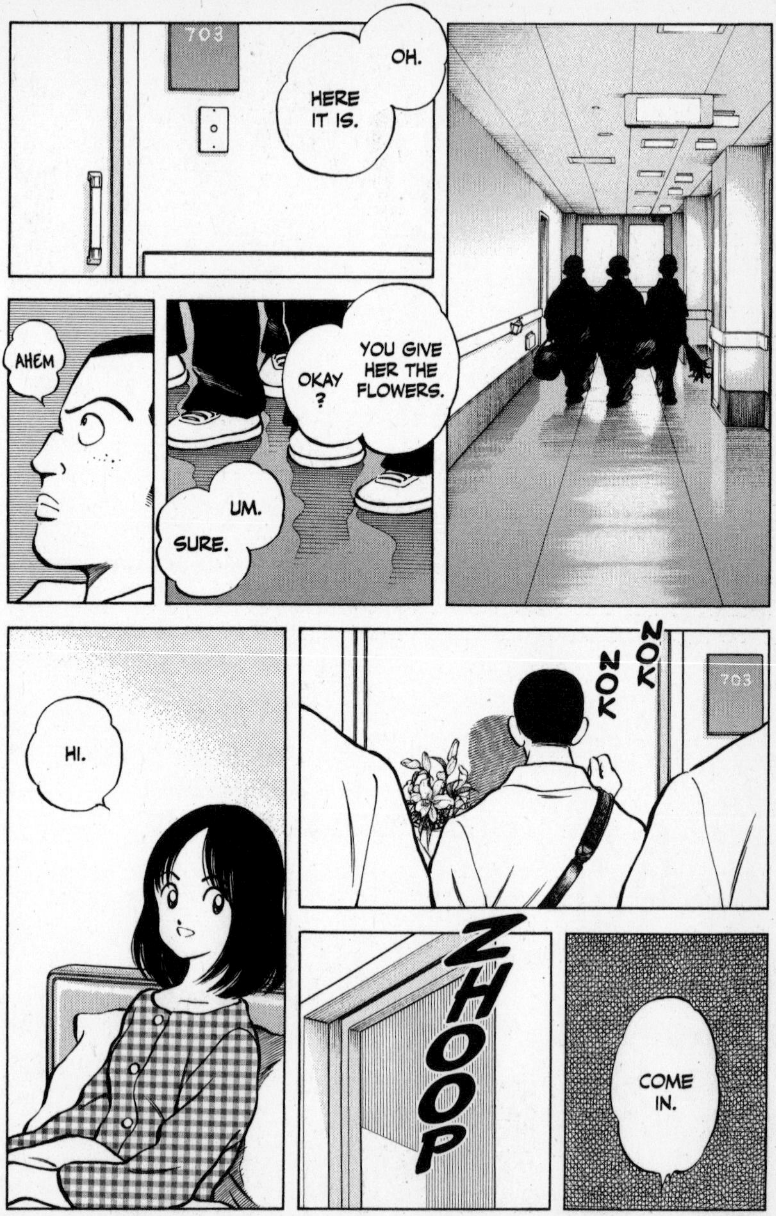

OH.
HERE IT IS.
YOU GIVE HER THE FLOWERS.
OKAY?
UM.
SURE.
AHEM
NOK NOK
COME IN.
ZHOOP
HI.

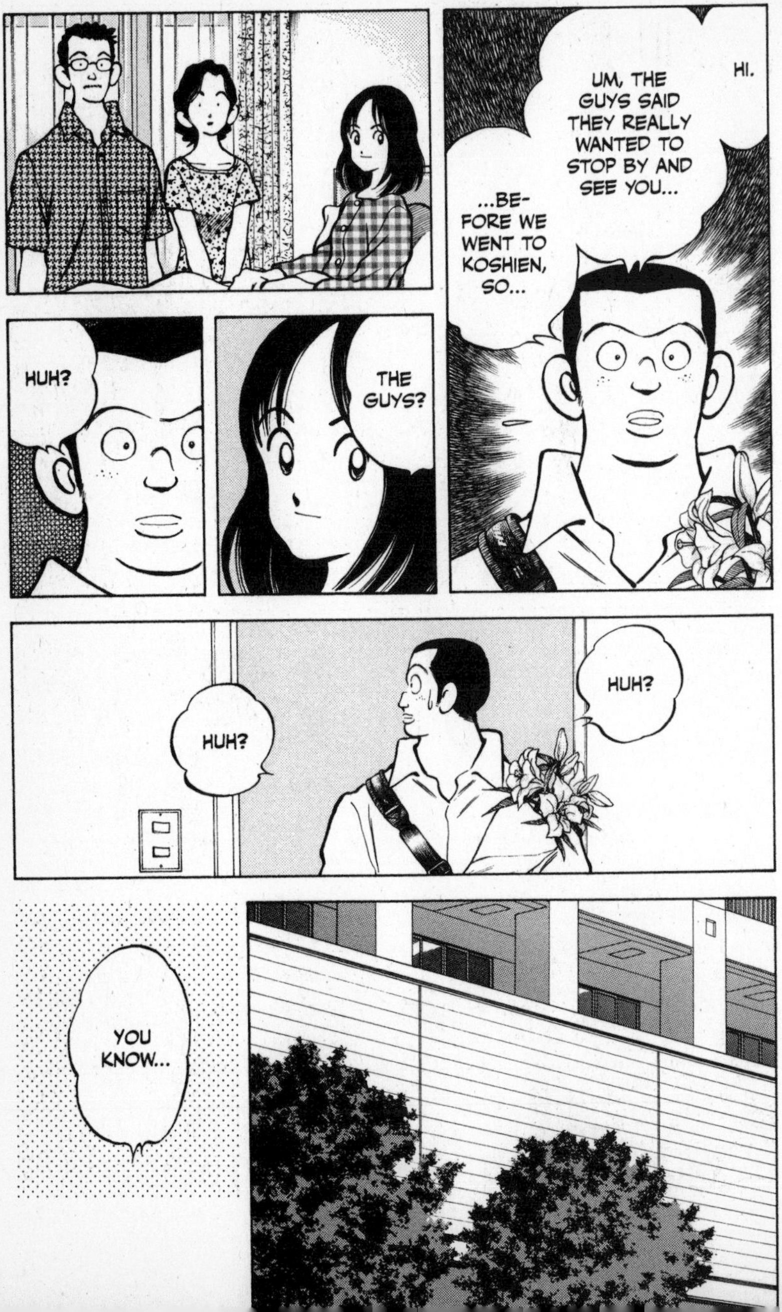
HI.
UM, THE GUYS SAID THEY REALLY WANTED TO STOP BY AND SEE YOU...
...BE-FORE WE WENT TO KOSHIEN, SO...
THE GUYS?
HUH?
HUH?
HUH?
YOU KNOW...

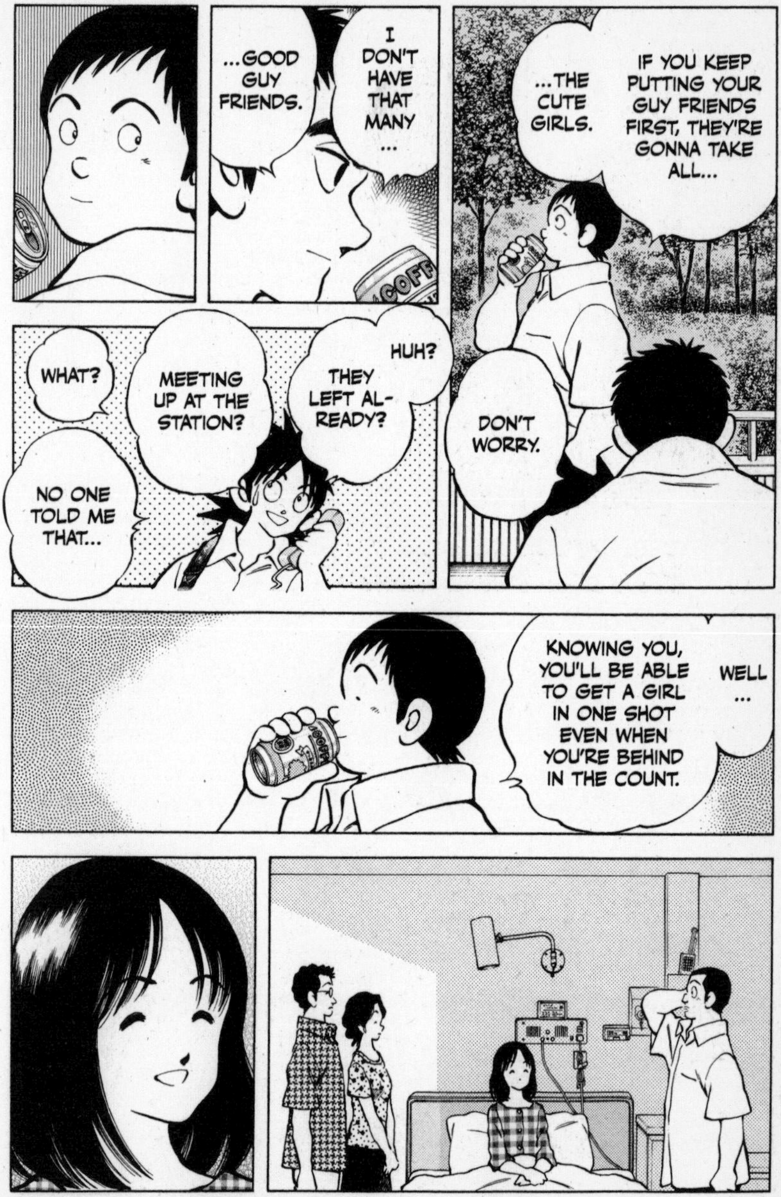
IF YOU KEEP PUTTING YOUR GUY FRIENDS FIRST, THEY'RE GONNA TAKE ALL...
...THE CUTE GIRLS.
DON'T WORRY.
I DON'T HAVE THAT MANY...
...GOOD GUY FRIENDS.
HUH?
THEY LEFT AL-READY?
MEETING UP AT THE STATION?
WHAT?
NO ONE TOLD ME THAT...
WELL...
KNOWING YOU, YOU'LL BE ABLE TO GET A GIRL IN ONE SHOT EVEN WHEN YOU'RE BEHIND IN THE COUNT.

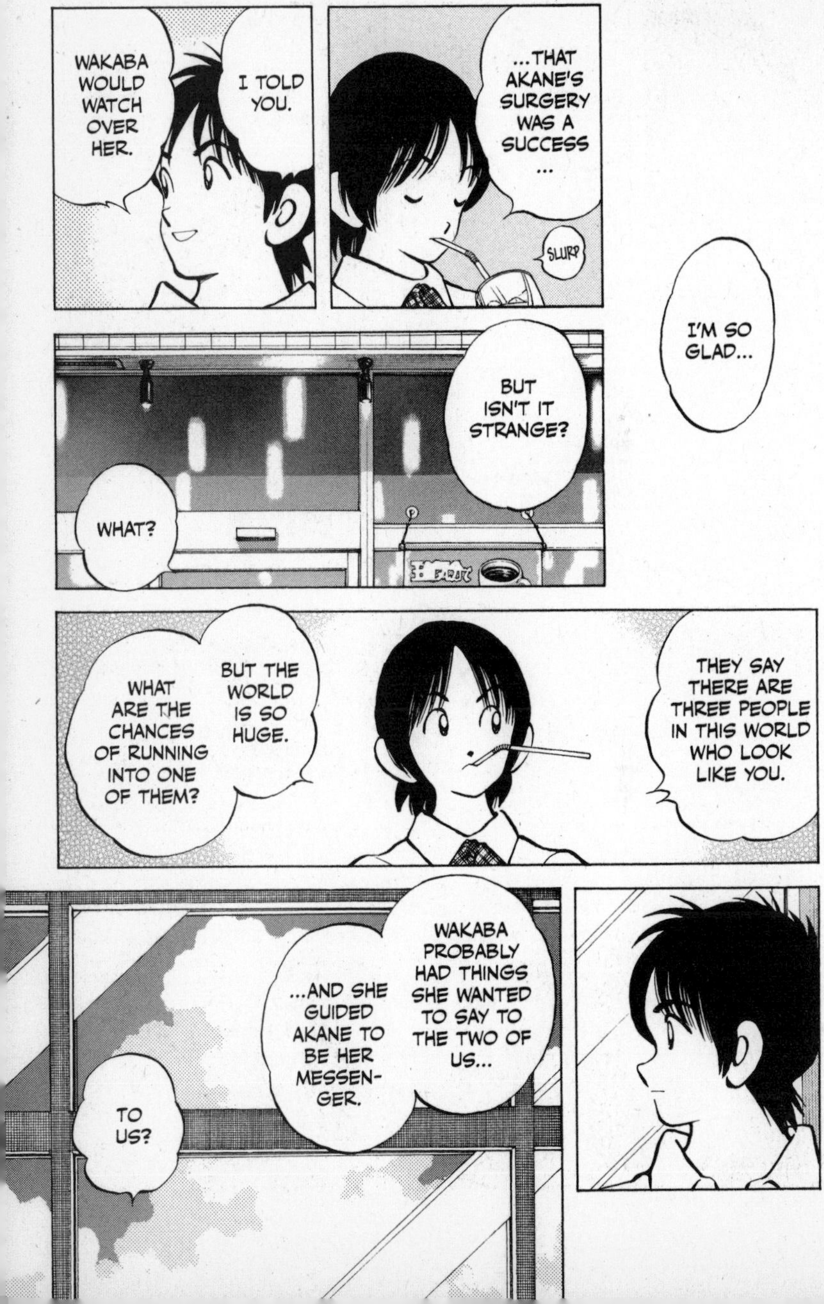
I'M SO GLAD...
...THAT AKANE'S SURGERY WAS A SUCCESS ...
SLURP
I TOLD YOU.
WAKABA WOULD WATCH OVER HER.
BUT ISN'T IT STRANGE?
WHAT?
THEY SAY THERE ARE THREE PEOPLE IN THIS WORLD WHO LOOK LIKE YOU.
BUT THE WORLD IS SO HUGE.
WHAT ARE THE CHANCES OF RUNNING INTO ONE OF THEM?
WAKABA PROBABLY HAD THINGS SHE WANTED TO SAY TO THE TWO OF US...
...AND SHE GUIDED AKANE TO BE HER MESSENGER.
TO US?

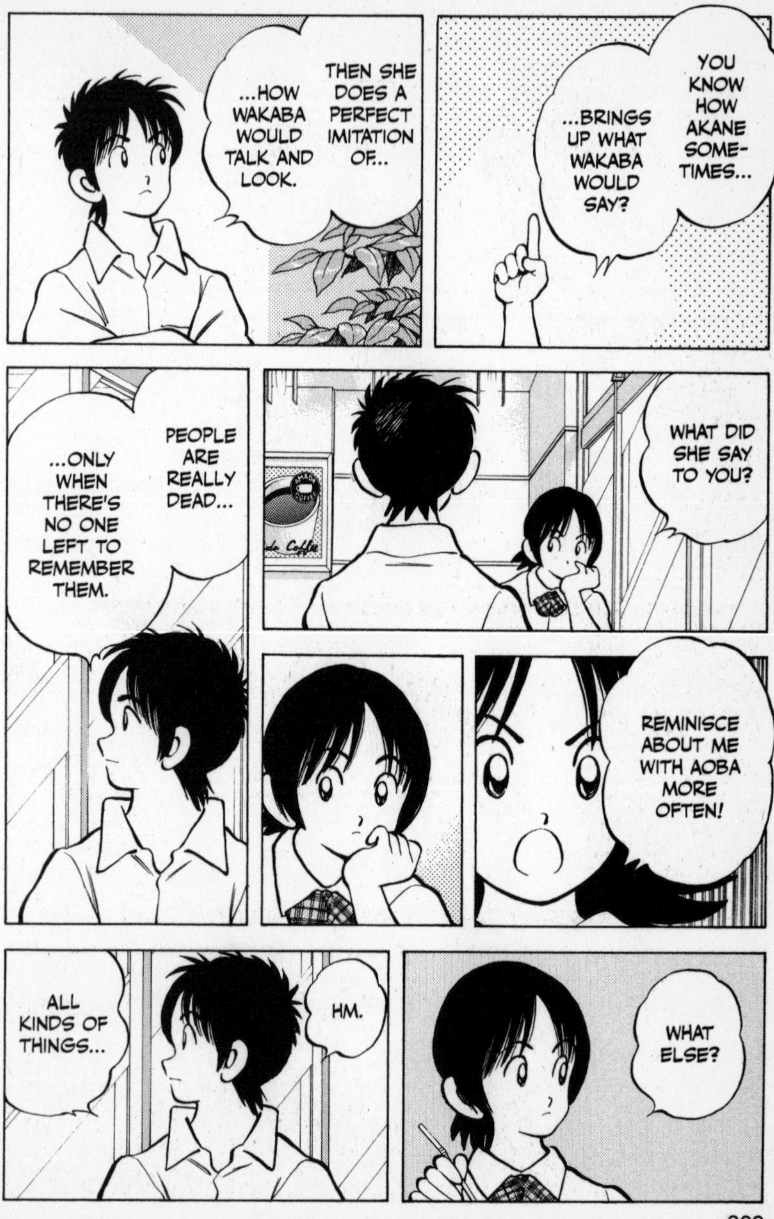
YOU KNOW HOW AKANE SOMETIMES...
...BRINGS UP WHAT WAKABA WOULD SAY?
THEN SHE DOES A PERFECT IMITATION OF...
...HOW WAKABA WOULD TALK AND LOOK.
WHAT DID SHE SAY TO YOU?
REMINISCE ABOUT ME WITH AOBA MORE OFTEN!
PEOPLE ARE REALLY DEAD...
...ONLY WHEN THERE'S NO ONE LEFT TO REMEMBER THEM.
WHAT ELSE?
HM.
ALL KINDS OF THINGS...

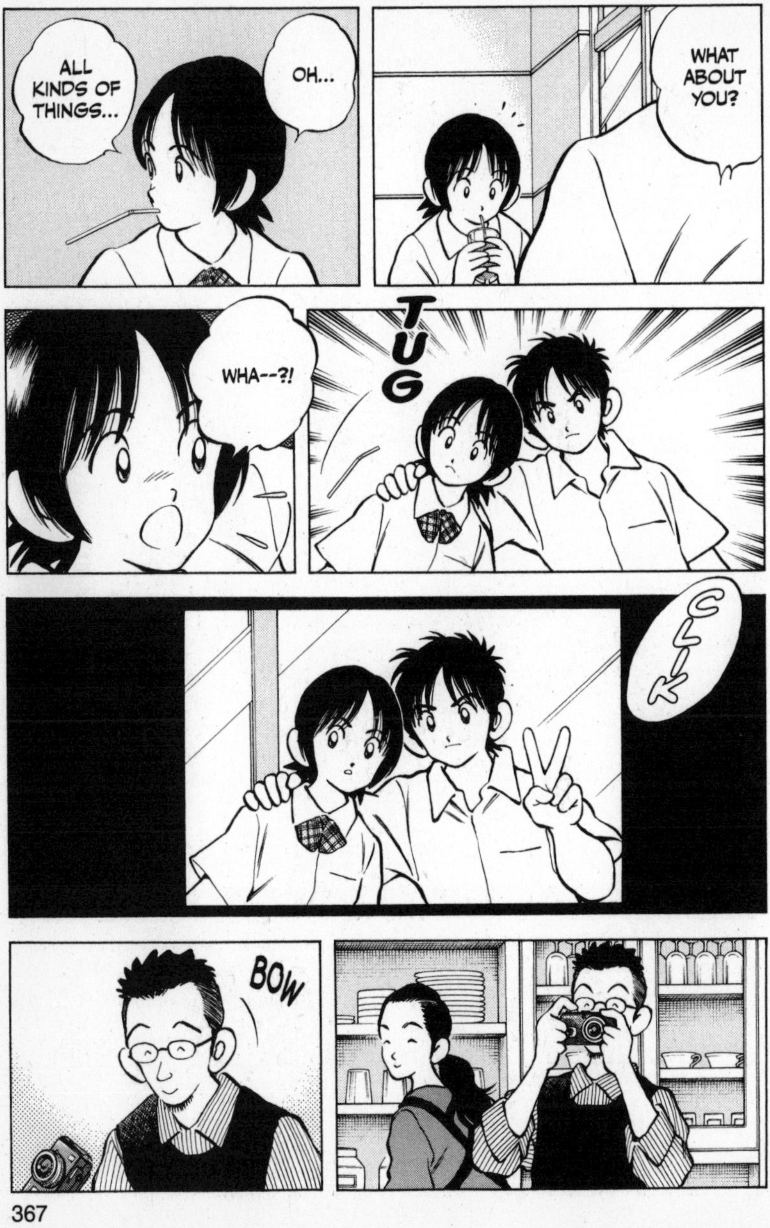
WHAT ABOUT YOU?
OH...
ALL KINDS OF THINGS...
TUG
WHA--?!
CLIK
BOW

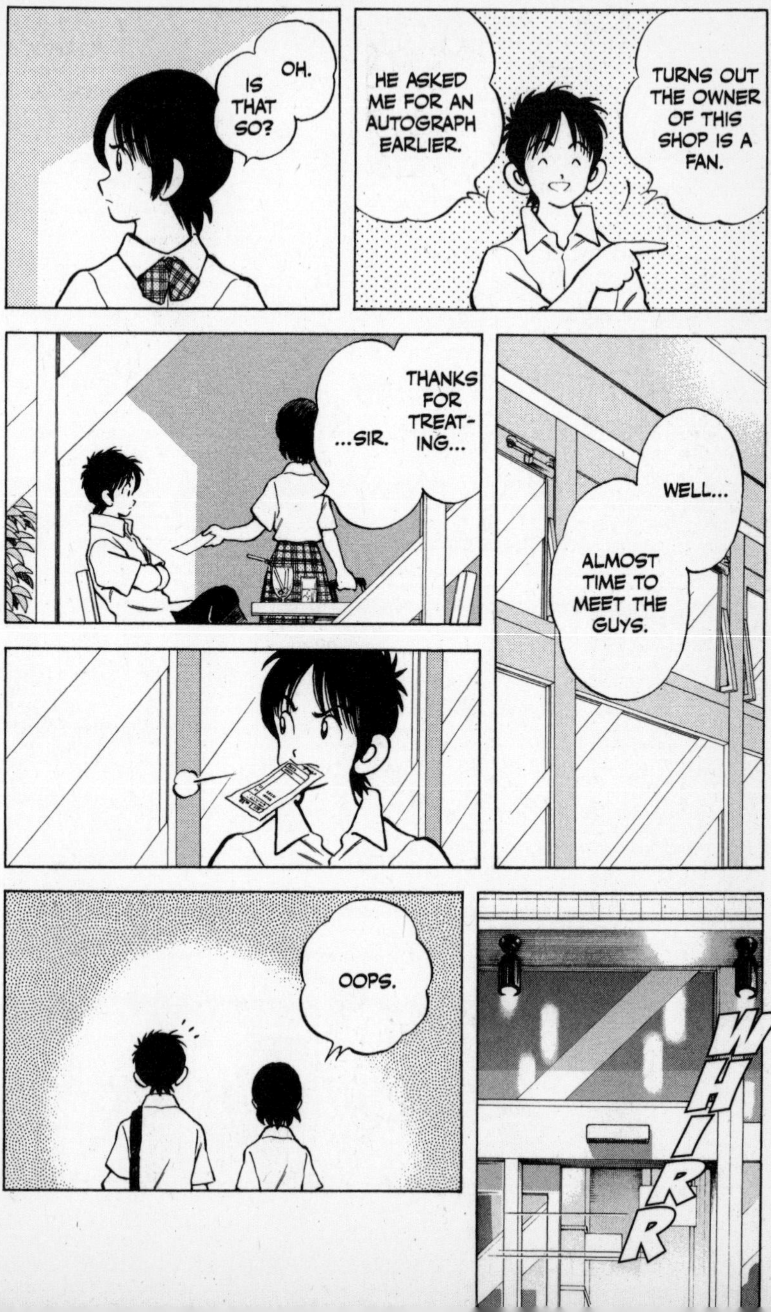
TURNS OUT THE OWNER OF THIS SHOP IS A FAN.
HE ASKED ME FOR AN AUTOGRAPH EARLIER.
OH.
IS THAT SO?
WELL...
ALMOST TIME TO MEET THE GUYS.
THANKS FOR TREAT-ING...
...SIR.
WHIRR
OOPS.

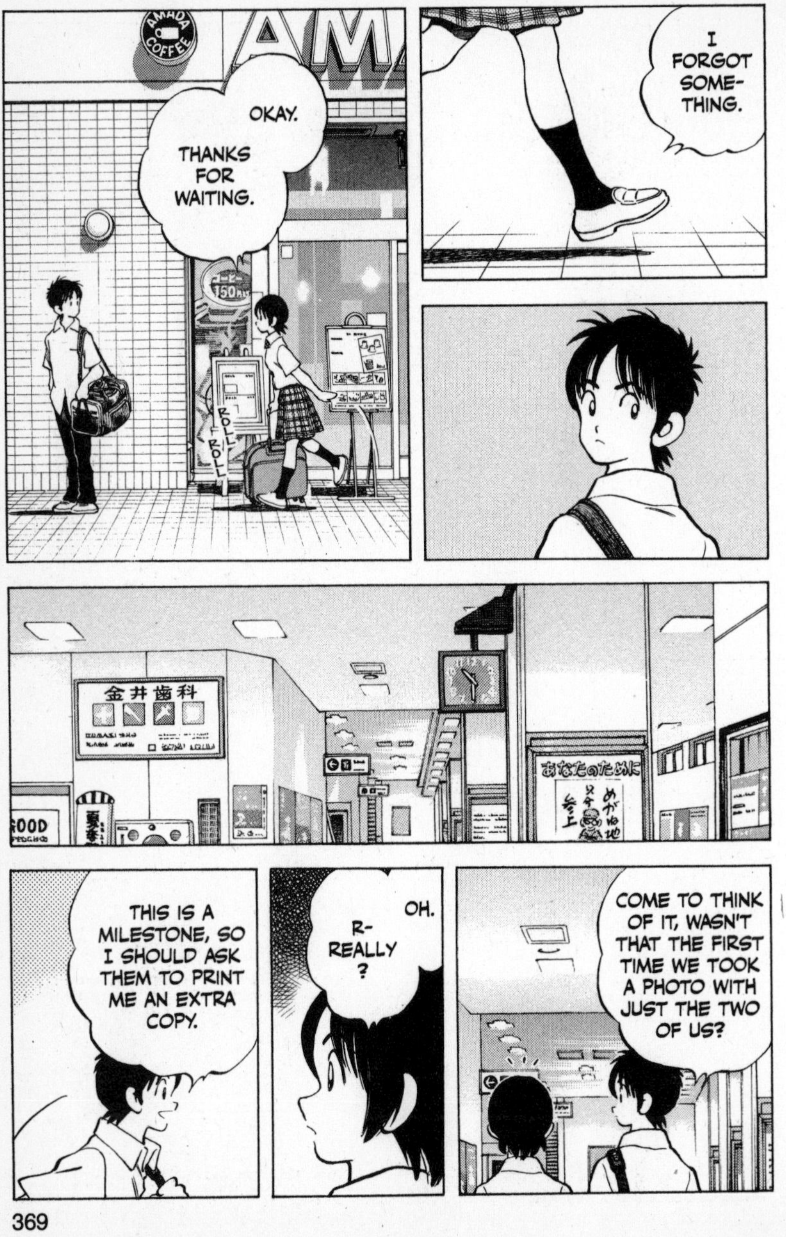
I FORGOT SOME-THING.
OKAY.
THANKS FOR WAITING.
AMHADA COFFEE
コーヒー 150円
ROLL
ROLL
金井歯科
あなたのために
COME TO THINK OF IT, WASN'T THAT THE FIRST TIME WE TOOK A PHOTO WITH JUST THE TWO OF US?
OH.
R-REALLY?
THIS IS A MILESTONE, SO I SHOULD ASK THEM TO PRINT ME AN EXTRA COPY.

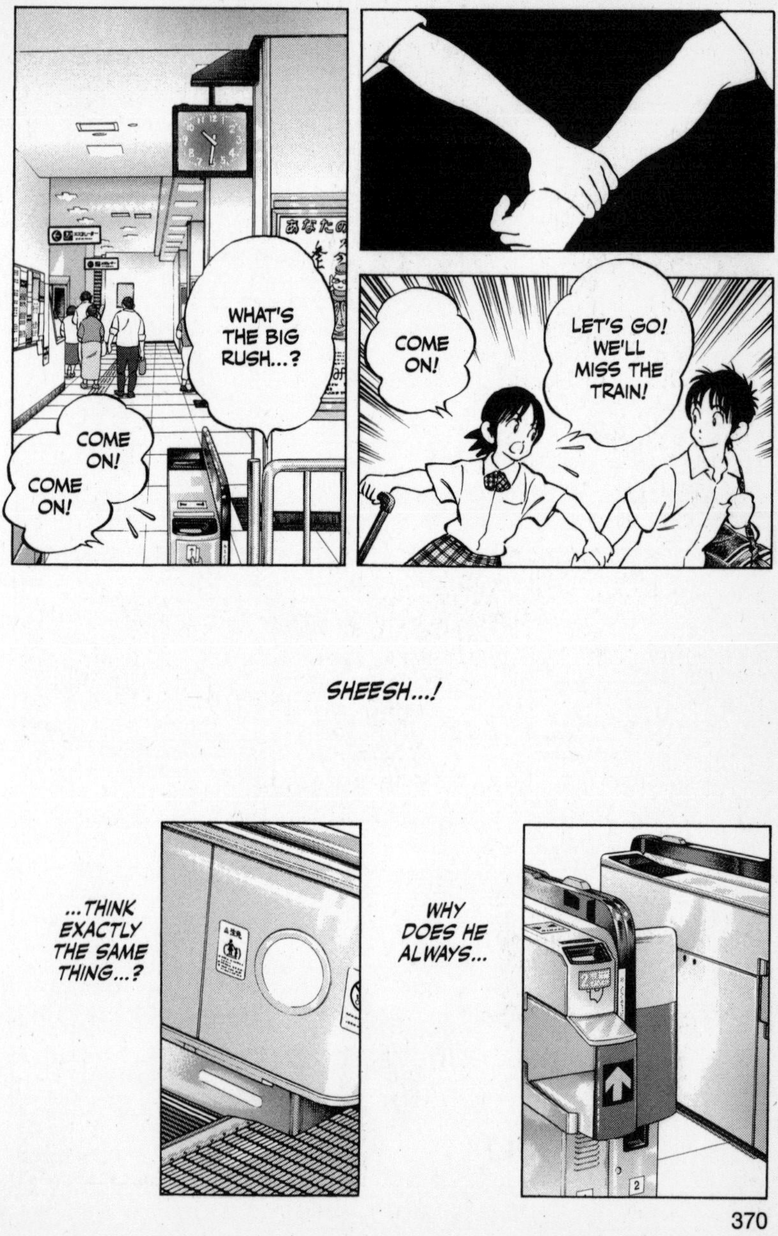
LET'S GO! WE'LL MISS THE TRAIN!
COME ON!
WHAT'S THE BIG RUSH...?
COME ON!
COME ON!
SHEESH...!
WHY DOES HE ALWAYS...
...THINK EXACTLY THE SAME THING...?

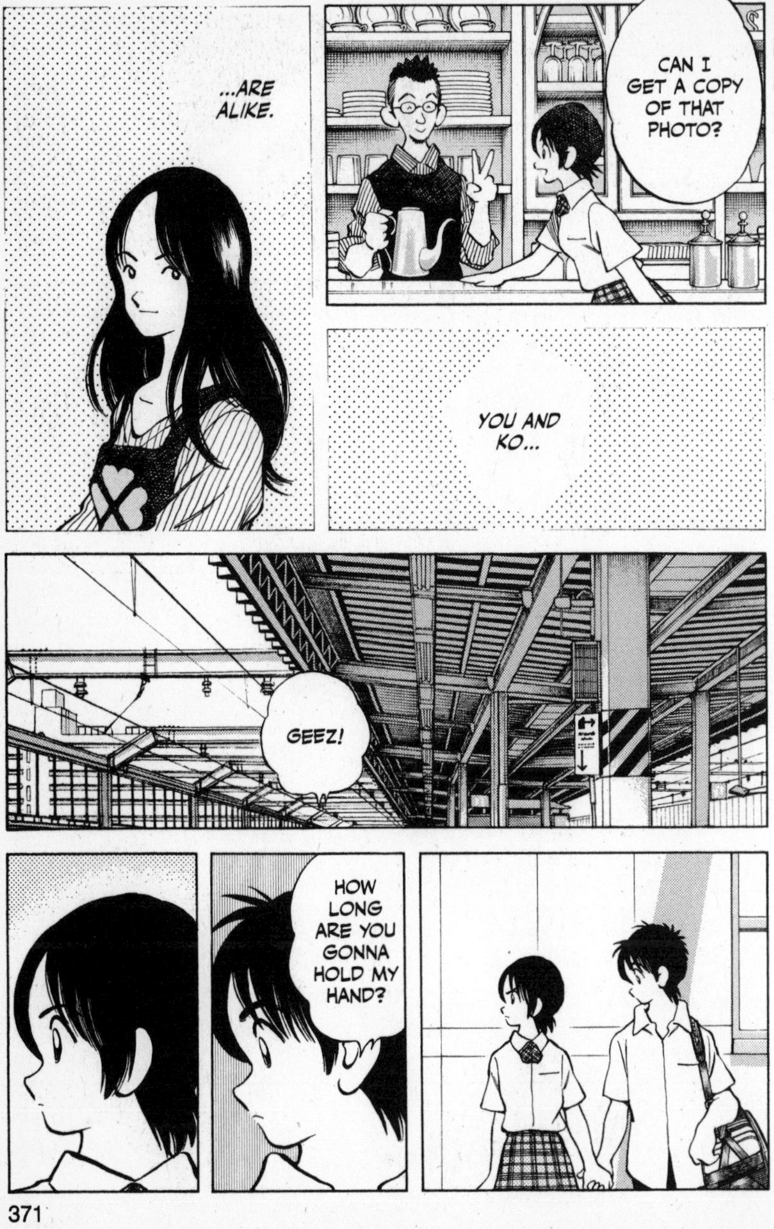
CAN I GET A COPY OF THAT PHOTO?
YOU AND KO...
...ARE ALIKE.
GEEZ!
HOW LONG ARE YOU GONNA HOLD MY HAND?

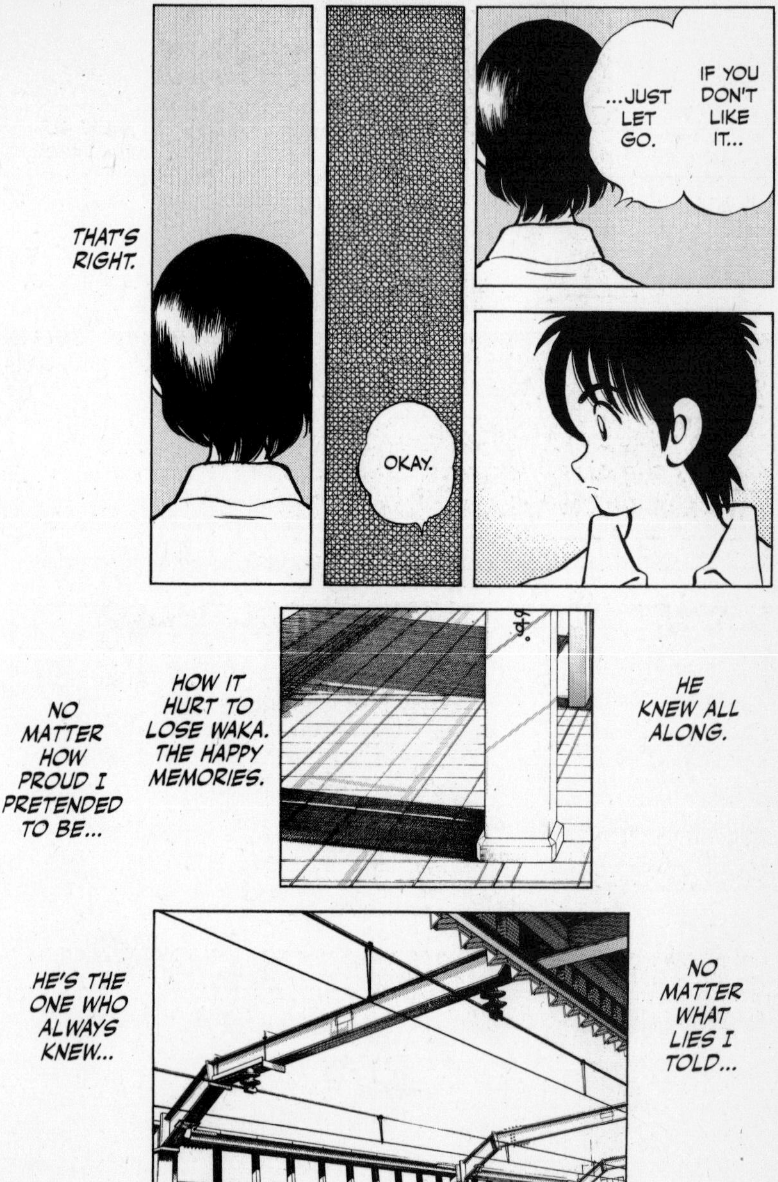
IF YOU DON'T LIKE IT...
...JUST LET GO.
OKAY.
THAT'S RIGHT.
HE KNEW ALL ALONG.
HOW IT HURT TO LOSE WAKA. THE HAPPY MEMORIES.
NO MATTER HOW PROUD I PRETENDED TO BE...
NO MATTER WHAT LIES I TOLD...
HE'S THE ONE WHO ALWAYS KNEW...

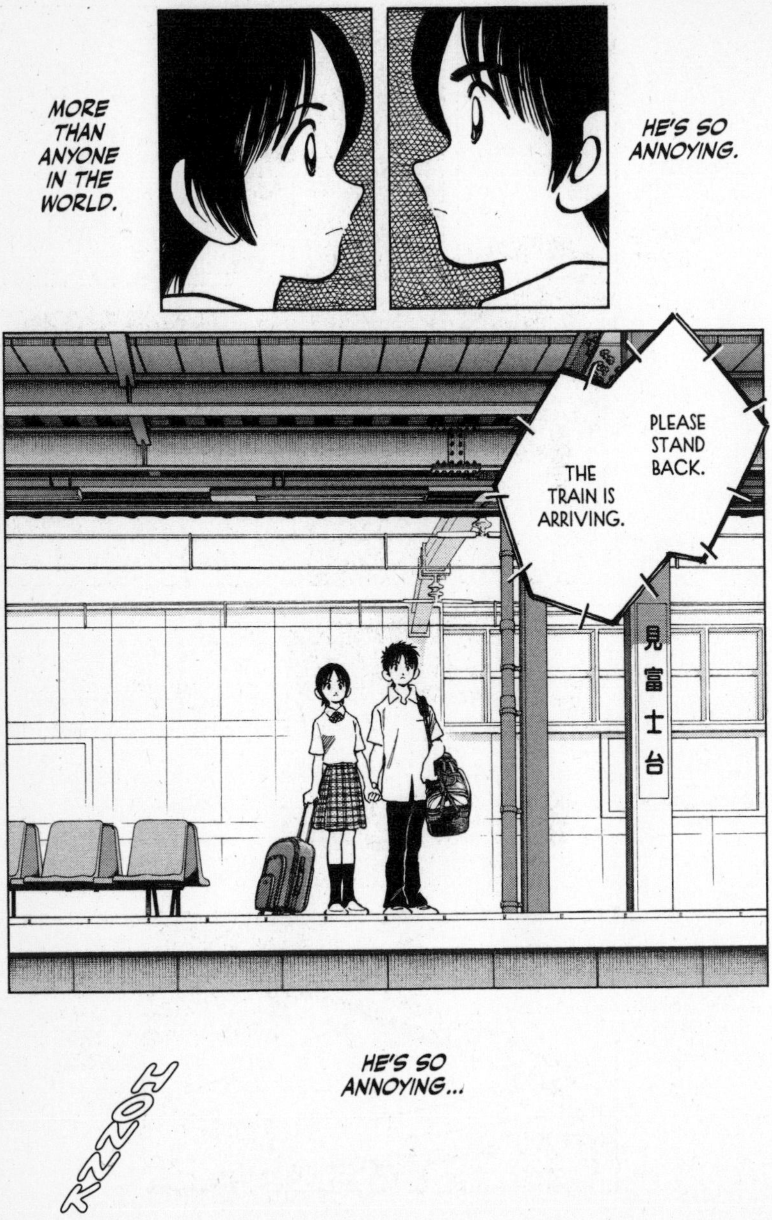
HE'S SO ANNOYING.
MORE THAN ANYONE IN THE WORLD.
PLEASE STAND BACK.
THE TRAIN IS ARRIVING.
見富士台
HE'S SO ANNOYING...
HONNK

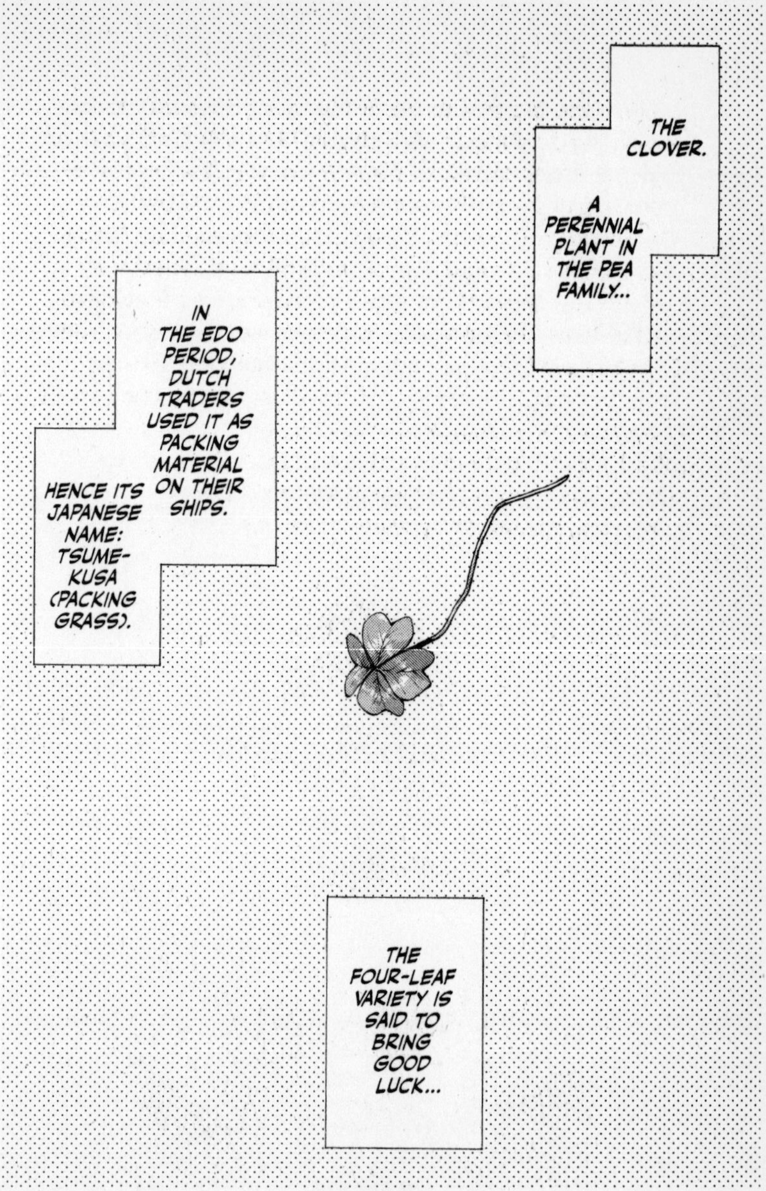
THE CLOVER.
A PERENNIAL PLANT IN THE PEA FAMILY...
IN THE EDO PERIOD, DUTCH TRADERS USED IT AS PACKING MATERIAL ON THEIR SHIPS.
HENCE ITS JAPANESE NAME: TSUME-KUSA (PACKING GRASS).
THE FOUR-LEAF VARIETY IS SAID TO BRING GOOD LUCK...

—THE END—

One of the biggest names in the manga industry today, Mitsuru Adachi made his debut in 1970 with *Kieta Bakuon* in the pages of *Deluxe Shonen Sunday*. The creator of numerous mega-hits such as *Touch*, *Miyuki* and *Cross Game*, Adachi Sensei received the Shogakukan Manga Award for all three of the aforementioned series. Truly in the top echelon of the manga industry, his cumulative works have seen over 200 million copies sold, and many of his series have been adapted into anime, live-action TV series and film. A master of his medium, Adachi has come to be known for his genious handling of dramatic elements skillfully combined with romance, comedy and sports. He, along with Rumiko Takahashi, has become synonymous with the phenomenal success of *Shonen Sunday* in Japan.

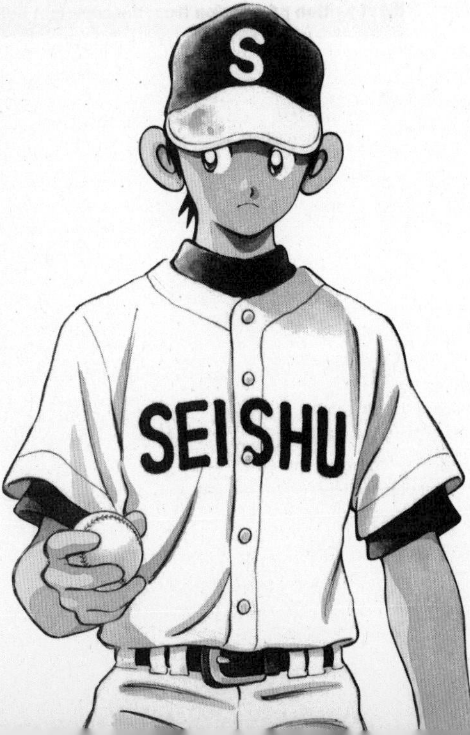
S
SEISHU

CROSS GAME
VOLUME 8
Shonen Sunday Edition

STORY AND ART BY
MITSURU ADACHI

© 2005 Mitsuru ADACHI/Shogakukan
All rights reserved.
Original Japanese edition "CROSS GAME" published by SHOGAKUKAN Inc.

Translation/Lillian Olsen
Touch-up Art & Lettering/Mark McMurray
Cover Design/John Kim, Yukiko Whitley
Interior Desig
Editor/Andy N

The stories, ch   re
entirely fiction

No portion of   m or by
any means wit

Printed in the U.S.A.

Published by VIZ Media, LLC
P.O. Box 77010
San Francisco, CA 94107

10 9 8 7 6 5 4 3 2 1
First printing, November 2012

www.viz.com   WWW.SHONENSUNDAY.COM

PARENTAL ADVISORY
CROSS GAME is rated T for
Teen and is recommended for
ages 13 and up.
ratings.viz.com